LAWYER'S
DESK BOOK

FOURTH EDITION

**The Lawyer's Everyday
Instant Answer Book**

by
William J. Casey

Revised by
IBP Research and Editorial Staff

Institute for Business Planning, Inc.

IBP Plaza, Englewood Cliffs, New Jersey 07632

Fourth Edition

Second Printing, September 1975

© Copyright, 1975, by
Institute for Business Planning, Inc.
IBP Plaza, Englewood Cliffs, New Jersey 07632

Library of Congress Catalog Card Number: 66-28535

HOW TO USE THIS DESK BOOK

Keep it on or near your desk. Its purpose is not to give you all the law. It is designed to give you a quick and practical check on *what* is *involved* in 75% of the kinds of matter that cross your desk most frequently. It will give you a quick refresher on the law that pertains to each problem. It will give you a checklist on the facts that are important. It will increase the chances that your first interview will be productive by helping you elicit necessary information from the client. It will help you use the first phone call to tell the client what to bring to the office.

In addition, this desk book will serve as a concise adviser which can be of immediate assistance, even while the client is in the reception room or at your desk, when you need that preliminary "feel" of a client's general legal position. From this point, deeper research will be required and this desk book suggests sources of further help.

All of us learn things as we work through various matters and struggle to remember them the next time the same kind of thing comes along. This book contains the highlights that you won't want to overlook yourself and will also provide benchmarks for the younger lawyers in your office.

The IBP Research and Editorial Staff

TABLE OF CONTENTS

v

TABLE OF CONTENTS

APPENDIX

vi

ACQUIRING, MERGING, SELLING A BUSINESS

[¶101] The lawyer's first task in this kind of transaction is to assist in negotiating and shaping the deal. Is the transaction to be for stock or cash? Is the consideration to be absolute, contingent, payable in fixed installments? Is the buyer going to acquire stock or assets? Should the acquisition take the form of a merger or merely an exchange of stock or stock for assets?

Then the lawyer will examine the other business, the one his client is acquiring or the one whose stock or obligations are being received by his client for his business. He will measure existing liabilities, search for hidden liabilities and legal pitfalls. What antitrust, SEC, Blue Sky, corporate law, stock exchange, tax problems and requirements does he see? He will formulate methods of protecting his client against undisclosed liabilities and securing him for full payment of the purchase price. He will scrutinize existing contracts, accounting methods, pension and stock-option plans in his evaluation of assets and liabilities and his formulation of the techniques to be used in taking over the assets and protecting against liabilities not bargained for. If all these problems can be handled, if there is a meeting of minds between the principals, then he will get down to preparing a contract, getting necessary approvals, making necessary filings, and closing the transaction. Here is a checklist of the things he should think about. For forms of contracts, see IBP FORMS OF BUSINESS AGREEMENTS.

[¶101.1] Broker or Finder's Fee

Lawyers for both parties should determine whether a broker or finder may have been employed by buyer or seller, which party may become legally responsible to pay him, the extent of the liability and how it is to be divided. If the claim is not explicit, it is desirable to reduce it to a definite understanding before the contract to close the deal is signed, and the contract should represent either that there were no obligations to brokers or finders, or provide who is to pay any admitted obligations.

Remember that an implied contract may exist if the broker acts with the consent of the principal, whether given in writing, orally, or by implication from the conduct of the parties. A conversation about a possible sale and an introduction furnished by the broker to the ultimate buyer may be enough to entitle the broker to a commission on the theory that an implied contract of employment existed between the seller and the broker. If this kind of a cloud hangs over the negotiations, try to eliminate it by a written understanding.

1

[¶101.2] Assets or Stock

The seller will normally prefer to sell stock to avoid the trouble, cost and risk of liquidation and depreciation recapture. Double tax in selling assets can generally be avoided by liquidating within one year under §337 but depreciation recapture still applies (IRC §1245, 1250). The buyer will usually want assets to get a high basis and to avoid seller's liabilities including recapture potential. Investment credit recapture and its availability on used property may also be a factor. Where there is a tax advantage in the corporation stemming from operating losses or high basis assets, a buyer might still prefer stock. However, a corporate buyer can get the basis step-up by liquidating within two years under §334.

[¶101.3] Stock or Cash

A cash sale will produce capital gain tax liability while a disposition for stock can be set up as a tax-free exchange. More fundamental considerations are whether the acquirer wants to increase its capitalization and whether the sellers are willing to take and hold shares of the acquirers. They will probably have to give investment letters and face SEC restrictions on subsequent sales of the acquirer's shares.

[¶101.4] What Kind of Tax-Free Acquisition?

Here are the possibilities: (1) merger, under IRC §368(a)(1)(A); (2) stock for stock, under §368(a)(1)(B); (3) stock for assets, under §368(a)(1)(C). Stock for stock may be ruled out because registration would be necessary if the shares of the acquired business are widely held. A merger may be indicated because the consideration is not limited to voting stock of the acquirer. A merger or stock for assets deal may be indicated by the uncertainty of getting enough shares in a stock for stock deal. In a merger or stock for assets deal, if the vote of the requisite percentage of shareholders is obtained, dissenters are forced to come along unless they want cash from the exercise of their appraisal rights. A stock for assets deal permits the acquirer to offer something besides voting stock, namely (1) assumption of liabilities, or (2) money or other property which together with assumed liabilities does not exceed 20% of the fair value of the assets acquired. In a stock for assets deal it is necessary to get substantially all of the assets of the acquired business and getting a ruling is advisable if any substantial amount of receivables, inventory or plant is to be left behind. If unwanted assets exceed 10% of the assets, a favorable ruling may not be forthcoming. In looking for a tax-free exchange watch the following pitfalls:

(a) Application of the so-called step transaction theory which may result in IRS contending that all of acquired corporation assets were not acquired if it is a recently created subsidiary to which some of the parent's assets were transferred.

(b) The contention that employment commitments to the seller, his commitment to pay out additional stock in the future, his commitment to pay registration costs of shares received by seller constitute consideration other than voting stock.

[¶101.5] Purchase of Some Stock and Redemption of Balance

This will enable use of the corporation's own funds for part of the purchase price. The seller will get his money as capital gain, and there will be no unfavorable tax results to the buyer if in acquiring the initial shares he did not personally obligate himself to redeem the balance of the stock and then have the corporation take over the obligation. (*Zenz v. Quinlivan,* 213 F.2d 914). If the buyer obligates himself to buy all the shares and has the purchased corporation provide some of the money, he will be charged with a taxable dividend (*Woodworth v. Comm.,* 218 F.2d 719; *Wall v. U.S.,* 164 F.2d 462).

[¶101.6] Where the Seller Has More Than One Business

Here we have these alternatives:

(a) Incorporate one of the businesses, and spin it off and sell the stock. The spin-off will be tax free, and the subsequent sale effected at capital gain rates if the sale was not prearranged, the two businesses have been conducted for 5 years, and the other requirements of IRC §355 are met.

(b) Effect a partial liquidation of the corporation by distributing the assets of the business to stockholders to be sold. If the partial liquidation meets the requirements of §346(b), the sale can be worked out at a single capital gains tax.

(c) A corporate sale of assets. This leaves the proceeds in the corporation with the result that there will be a second tax cost in distributing the proceeds to stockholders.

A ruling that the transaction is tax free is needed to clear up these questions.

[¶101.7] Other Tax Objectives and Pitfalls

(a) If the deal is to be a taxable one, can seller's gain be taxed as ordinary income because his corporation is collapsible (IRC §341)? (IRS has ruled that in a "C" reorganization there is no ordinary income on the exchange of collapsible corporate stock for non-collapsible stock although the stock was sold after the exchange (*Rev. Rul. 73-378* CB 1973-2, 113).)

(b) Does seller want to spread out tax on gain by qualifying the deal as an installment sale or making the price contingent? If a sale is made for deferred payments, watch out for imputed interest (§483).

3

(c) Watch out for minimum tax on tax preference income, including capital gains, under §56-58.

(d) If merger involves $5 million or more of debt, watch for loss of interest deduction (§279).

(e) Under §1245, any excess of the amount paid by the buyer for certain types of depreciable property (such as machinery, equipment, and patents) over its book value is taxed as ordinary income to the seller to the extent of post-1961 depreciation. Depreciation on real estate is also subject to recapture under §1250 measured by the lower of "additional depreciation" (generally, depreciation in excess of straight-line) after 1969 or the gain on disposition. If the gain is greater than additional depreciation, then there is also recapturable the applicable percentage of the lower of additional depreciation before 1970 or the excess of gain on disposition over additional depreciation after 1969.

(f) Investment credit is also recapturable if there is a premature disposition of the property.

(g) Is salary paid part of the purchase price? Where an asset is sold to a corporation and the seller is subsequently paid a salary, the payments will be scrutinized to determine whether they are for the property or for services rendered.

(h) The preservation of tax attributes of the selling corporation, subject to restrictions in §269, 381 and 382 on use of losses and credits, can be accomplished by keeping the selling corporation alive.

[¶101.8] Allocation of Purchase Price Among Assets

If business assets are sold as a unit for a lump sum consideration, the sales proceeds must be allocated among the individual assets of the business and the gain or loss computed accordingly. The owner is not permitted to treat the sale of his business as the sale of a single capital asset. (*Williams v. McGowan,* 152 F.2d 570). Moreover, the burden of proving that any portion of the sale proceeds are attributable to the good will and other capital assets of the business is upon the vendor. The problem may be eased by drafting the contract of sale or bill of sale to provide for specific prices for each individual asset in the business (*Wilson Athletic Goods v. Comm.,* 222 F.2d 926).

The buyer will want to allocate as much of the purchase price as possible to depreciable assets. He may prefer to rely on an appraisal if he can't get a favorable allocation agreed to in the contract.

The following chart shows the conflicting desires of Buyer and Seller.

4

Asset	Price Benefiting Buyer	Price Benefiting Seller
(1) *Capital* (Good will, trade name, covenant not to compete ancillary to sale of good will)	Low (not depreciable)	High (capital gain)
(2) *Property used in the trade or business:*		
(a) Machinery, fixtures, etc.	Medium (recoup cost via depreciation). High (up to $50,000 for investment credit)	High (capital gain or ordinary loss under §1231)
(b) Land	Low (not depreciable)	High (capital gain or ordinary loss under §1231)
(c) Copyrights (for use in business)	Medium (recoup cost via amortization)	High (capital gain or ordinary loss under §1231)
(d) Patents	Medium (amortization)	High (capital gain §1235)
(3) *Non-Capital:*		
(a) Inventory and stock in trade	High (recoup via cost of goods sold)	Low (ordinary income)
(b) Accounts Receivable	High (recoverable as collected)	Low (ordinary income)
(c) Copyrights and intellectual property sold by the creator	Medium (recoup cost via amortization)	Low (ordinary income)
(d) Covenant not to compete	Medium (usually recoup cost via amortization)	Low (ordinary income)
(e) Interest on Deferred Payment of Purchase Price	Medium (deduct as ordinary business expense)	Low (ordinary income)

[¶101.9] SEC Problems

Where stock is used to make an acqusition, the transaction can be handled in one of these ways for SEC purposes:

(a) File a registration statement and pay the seller in registered shares. This involves expense, but the serious detriment is delay in completing the acquisition.

(b) Make a determination that the distribution of the buyer's stock to the selling corporation or its stockholders does not involve a "public offering" so that registration is not necessary. When there is any question as to the fact of

5

a private offering or a public offering, an opinion or a no-action letter should be sought from the SEC.

You should be aware of the fact that under Rule 145, the SEC requires registration of securities arising from a business combination where the transaction is one which has required a vote of the seller's outstanding shares of stock.

[¶101.10] Antitrust Problems

The seller's contracts and pricing arrangements should be studied to see whether the buyer will be inheriting any antitrust problems. Distribution contracts, the pricing of sales to large customers, and other arrangements which may be basic to the profitability of the business being acquired and to the value being placed upon it should be studied from the antitrust standpoint to determine whether there is a possibility that the value of the business may be undermined if any of these arrangements are found to be in violation of the antitrust laws. Then, it is necessary to appraise the chances that the acquisition itself may be blocked as a violation of §7 of the Clayton Act. This can happen where in any line of commerce or in any section of the country, the effect of the acquisition may be substantially to lessen competition or to tend to create a monopoly. To make an initial determination of whether there is a possible §7 violation, check the share of the market enjoyed by the buyer and seller and see whether the acquisition results in a substantial increase in the share of the market held by the buyer or makes the buyer significantly more dominant in the market. Then, evaluate the impact of the acquisition in terms of whether it seeks to substantially lessen competition and make a judgment as to whether there is likely to be any complaint from competitors, suppliers, customers, or any companies who fear the acquisition would result in the loss of an important market for their products or that it will result in their loss of a source of supplies. There is an advance clearance procedure in the Justice Department under which on submission of full information about the economic impact of the proposed acquisition, an informal but not necessarily binding opinion can be obtained as to whether or not the acquisition would violate §7 of the Clayton Act.

[¶101.11] Stock Exchange Requirements

Where the acquiring corporation issued additional shares, an application must usually be filed with the appropriate stock exchange to approve the listing of these additional shares. Sometimes this will require stockholder approval where it would not be necessary under state law. For example, the New York Stock Exchange rules require stockholder approval of the acquisition of a company if the amount of stock to be issued for it represents an increase in outstanding shares of 20% or more or where the combined value of stock and all other considerations approximates 20% or more of the market value of the outstanding common stock. New York Stock Exchange rules also require extreme care in keeping negotiations and studies concerning possible acquisitions on a confidential basis in order to avoid predisclosure. Timely disclosure of an acquisition or of the termination of negotiations is required where knowledge of a possible acquisition had gotten around.

[¶101.12] State "Blue Sky" Laws

It may be necessary to register stock issued by the buyer with the state securities commission or to notify the state's securities commission. Failure to take this step may make it possible for stockholders of the seller to avoid the transaction.

[¶101.13] Sale of Control

The courts have generally held that a sale of a controlling block of stock at a price above the market will not by itself subject the sellers to any liability to minority stockholders. However, where the buyers intend to loot the company and the sellers should have anticipated this possibility on the basis of the past performance of the buyers, the sellers may have incurred a liability to minority stockholders. Also, if the selling stockholders participate in a change of control, giving up their offices, resigning from the board of directors, and designating representatives of the buyers to succeed them, the courts may hold that any premium received by the sellers over and above the prevailing market price of the shares constitutes a trust fund in which minority shareholders may participate. The safest way to avoid this risk is to insist that a similar offer be made to all shareholders. If this is not practicable, then it is incumbent upon the selling shareholders to investigate carefully the reputation and the purpose of the buyers and to accept no obligation which might be deemed to constitute a sale of control and an active participation in a change of control over and above the simple sale of their shares.

[¶101.14] Obligation of Insiders to Minority Shareholders

Where the officers and directors are selling their stock, what obligation do they have to disclose the price and the transaction to minority stockholders? In some states the courts held that insiders had an obligation to disclose all information to minority shareholders. Other states restricted the directors' fiduciary duty to the corporation and required no disclosure to other shareholders. Today, it is generally considered that Rule 10b-5 under the Securities and Exchange Act of 1934 requires full disclosure to minority stockholders. In one important case under the common law, the president of a company who had a deal to sell his stock at a high figure and went out and bought up shares from other shareholders at a lower figure so that he could profit on the difference was obligated to turn the difference over to the shareholders whose stock he had bought up.

[¶101.15] Binding the Deal

Frequently, as soon as buyer and seller have gotten together on a price, they want the lawyer to draw up a binding agreement right away. Normally, that is neither possible nor desirable. A short-form agreement will leave so many aspects of the transaction undetermined and subject to dispute that it is likely to cause only trouble and misunderstanding. Sometimes, the buyer will want a period of time in which to investigate. He can get this in two forms: an option to buy or a letter of commitment from the seller that for a period of time he will not deal with anybody else. The only thing that gives the buyer any certainty is an option, and an option cannot be very meaningful unless there is appended to it a fully detailed contract covering all the terms and provisions of the acquisition. For such an option, a price is usually required. Sometimes, the buyer will want to commit himself to a contract but will be concerned about his ability to get the financing necessary to consummate it. In this situation, paying a limited amount for an option until financing methods can be determined or entering into a binding contract with a provision that the down payment constitutes liquidated damage in the event of the buyer's default will permit the buyer to limit his risk if he is unable to work out the financing. In many instances, the best procedure is for the investigation of the business to proceed simultaneously with the development of a detailed contract, the provisions and conditions of the contract being worked out as problems and circumstances are revealed by the investigation. Where this procedure is followed, it is sometimes possible to complete the contract and close almost simultaneously, or even to close without the formality of an executed contract. However, the more normal course is to develop a fully detailed contract, give the buyer a period of time within which to check the representations made in the contract, and provide for a closing date after that period of time has elapsed.

For forms on option agreements, see IBP FORMS OF BUSINESS AGREEMENTS.

[¶101.16] Representations of the Seller

The seller should be required to represent the basic condition of the business, balance sheet, obligations, contracts, and commitments. These representations normally relate to three periods of time: (1) the date as of the latest certified balance sheet, (2) the date of the signing of the contract as to which the seller represents that the business has not been adversely affected by any event since the balance sheet date, and (3) as a condition precedent to the closing, the seller should be required to represent that, as of the time of the closing, no significant adverse events and no changes in the financial condition of the business except those occurring in the normal course of business operations had occurred.

[¶101.17] Tax Liabilities

It is well to have the seller represent the status of the company with respect to tax audits and important to have the seller assume responsibility for tax liabilities other than those represented on the balance sheet submitted.

[¶101.18] Conditions of the Closing

Either seller or buyer may not want to be obligated to the contract unless tax rulings, SEC rulings, antitrust rulings, and similar approvals have been obtained. Other conditions precedent may be the obtaining of an SEC approval for treating the acquisition as a pooling of interests for accounting purposes and the exercise of appraisal rights by no more than a percentage of shareholders.

[¶101.19] Covenant Not to Compete

It may be critically important to get assurance that the sellers will not compete with the business which they are selling. If there is any payment for this covenant, it will be deductible by the buyer and have the effect of converting that portion of the proceeds received by the sellers from capital gains to ordinary income. To accomplish this, it is important to specify the amount being paid for the covenant not to compete. If this result is not desired and there is a covenant not to compete in the agreement of sale, to protect the sellers from possible ordinary income it is well to provide that the covenant is incidental to the sale of the stock and has not been separately bargained or paid for.

Forms of covenants not to compete will be found in IBP FORMS OF BUSINESS AGREEMENTS.

[¶101.20] Unintentional Assumption of Liabilities — Purchase of Stock

Where a business is acquired by the stock of the corporation which operates it, the liabilities automatically follow the business into the hands of the buyer. In this situation, the only way to protect the buyer is to require the seller to warrant that the liabilities of the corporation do not exceed those reflected in its latest financial statement and the contractual obligations specified in the purchase contract. The only way to enforce this warranty is to require the selling stockholders (who will not always be willing or, particularly where

9

there are many of them, find it practical) to assume this kind of an obligation. This will always be a matter of negotiation, and sometimes the trading power of the buyer is strong enough to get selling stockholders to agree that part of the purchase price be set aside in escrow to meet corporate liabilities or to assume such liabilities to a limited and specified extent.

[¶101.21]   Unintended Assumption of Seller's Liabilities — Acquisition of Assets for Cash

When assets are purchased for cash in an arm's length transaction, only those liabilities which are explicitly assumed should follow the buyer, unless:

(a) The buyer makes the mistake of paying the cash directly to the stockholders of the selling corporation rather than to the corporation itself. This may result in the buyer finding himself liable to undisclosed creditors of the seller.

(b) If the requirements of the state bulk sales law are not complied with, undisclosed creditors may be able to enforce their claims against the assets purchased by the buyer. This risk can be handled by requiring strict compliance or, in the event of waiver, getting a warranty and providing for deposit, or escrowing of the purchase price.

[¶101.22]   Unintended Assumption of Seller's Liabilities — Purchase of Assets for Stock

A buyer of assets for stock may find himself liable to satisfy undisclosed liabilities of the seller, even though the purchase contract specifically provides that the buyer is not assuming any of the seller's liabilities. Sometimes this result is achieved on the basis that the assets acquired constitute a trust fund for the creditors, sometimes on the basis that in effect the acquisition constituted a merger in which the acquirer is the continuing company and thus remains liable for all the obligations of both parties to the merger. If the state law can result in this kind of unintended assumption of liabilities, the only way the lawyer for the buyer can protect his client is to get an indemnification from the seller and require that enough of the purchase price be held in escrow to protect the buyer against any such unassumed liabilities.

[¶101.23]   Transferability of Contracts

In an assets deal or in a stock acquisition where subsequent liquidation is contemplated, it is necessary to review all important contracts to see whether they contain a prohibition of assignment or a requirement that the other party's consent be obtained in order to make the assignment effective. Counsel for the acquiree should make the selling corporation undertake to obtain any consents that are necessary.

〔¶101.24〕 Labor Problems

In this area possible trouble can come from three directions. They are: (a) The duties and obligations imposed upon the employer by the Labor Management Relations Act, as amended, and applicable decisions of the National Labor Relations Board and the courts; (b) Civil actions which may be brought against the employer by employees of labor organizations affected by a change in business operations; and (c) Court decisions compelling or confirming arbitration proceedings which may arise from grievances concerning a change in business operations, initiated pursuant to arbitration provisions of collective bargaining agreements between an employer and a labor organization.

Check union contracts to see whether they contain a provision that they are binding on successors or a nonassignability clause. This is particularly important where the plant of the acquired company is to be consolidated or moved. Where a consolidation or move of location or a large reduction in force is contemplated, the acquirer must give careful study to the possibility that he will face an action on behalf of union employees to protect rights under a pension, health, and welfare plan. Another vital labor question is whether a surviving corporation is guilty of an unfair labor practice if it refuses to bargain with a union certified as collective bargaining agent with the absorbed corporation. The courts have held that the successor-employer must deal with the union during the period, usually the balance of the existing year, since certification. Where the successor corporation already has a contract with another union, the Labor Relations Board has held that the certification of the union to the acquired corporation was no longer in effect where the employees of that union fell into a minority status in relationship to the employees of the combined corporation certified to the conflicting union. Where the work force is being shrunk, how do you determine who will work and who will be displaced? This is something to examine carefully and work out with the management of the selling business. An allocation between the two work forces or a determination on the basis of length of service affords protection from a union charge that an arbitrary selection was made. Where a union is not involved, merit will usually be the basis of selection. Where a union is involved, the matter may have to be negotiated, at least to some extent; and, in that event, seniority will probably be reflected.

〔¶101.25〕 Employee Benefit Plans

What shall be done with the employee benefit plan of the absorbed corporation? If the corporation is maintained as a subsidiary, the simplest thing is to permit it to carry on existing employee benefit plans. If subsidiary operation is deemed impractical, so that the employees have to be integrated, it is probable that the rights employees have acquired under the absorbed corporation's plan cannot be transferred to the surviving corporation's plan, because such plans rarely mesh satisfactorily. The choice then is between terminating the old plan and paying out all vested amounts or freezing the old plan and holding the amount accumulated in trust for the benefit of employees of the absorbed company until they retire or their service is terminated.

[¶101.26] **Executive Arrangements**

The surviving corporation usually assures the management of the absorbed corporation that their services will be needed and that their rights under executive compensation plans will be respected. It is appropriate to cover this in a clause in the contract, which obligates the buyer to continue employment of the principal officers of the seller for a specified minimum period at not less than their existing salaries. If stock options have not been exercised prior to an acquisition, they may become valueless because a merged corporation will no longer be able to issue stock or because the stock of an acquired corporation may no longer have any market. Therefore, the acquisition agreement may provide that these stock-option rights be converted into stock options of the surviving corporation. Where the acquisition price per share is greater than the option price, the executives can protect their interests by exercising their options prior to the merger.

[¶101.27] **Unemployment Insurance**

Check the conditions of the appropriate state law or regulations under which a merit rating record for unemployment insurance tax purposes can be transferred from a predecessor to a successor company after a merger. The appropriate state agency should be notified of an impending merger, and it will supply the necessary information as to the procedure to be followed to effect a proper transfer of the merit rating account.

[¶101.28] **Demands for Appraisal by Minority Stockholders**

Too many demands for appraisal and payment of cash instead of stock to dissenting stockholders may put too great a financial strain on the surviving corporation. These demands can usually be presented right up to the time of the stockholders' vote on the measure, and it may be possible that appraisal demands delivered through the mail can still be effective even though received a few days subsequent to the date of stockholder approval. Where there is a limited number of stockholders and state law permits, uncertainty in this respect can be eliminated by obtaining written consent from all stockholders, so that it will be unnecessary to hold a stockholders' meeting to approve a merger. Where this uncertainty cannot be avoided, the merger agreement should include a clause giving both companies the right to abandon the merger if stockholders' demands for appraisal are excessive (that is, if they exceed a specified percentage).

[¶101.29]   Bank Loan Agreements

The seller's outstanding bank loan agreements may contain restrictions which a buyer doesn't want to assume. Also, the buyer's bank loan agreements may not permit the seller's loans to remain outstanding. The seller's bank loan agreements may even prohibit the acquisition. Where any of these situations exist, the bank's consent or a refinancing of the bank debt will become necessary.

Forms of financing agreements will be found in IBP FORMS OF BUSINESS AGREEMENTS looseleaf Service.

[¶101.30]   Sales and Use Tax

Check to see whether sales and use taxes apply to the sale of changeable assets in connection with an acquisition of a business. In most sales and use tax laws, there is an exemption for an isolated transaction or transfers in connection with the change in ownership of an entire business. Where a great deal of money is involved in the acquisition, this consideration can influence the transaction towards an acquisition of stock rather than assets to avoid imposition of tax. In some jurisdictions, the practice is to close the transaction outside of the state; but where tangible assets transferred are physically located in the taxing jurisdiction, the transaction may still be subject to use tax. It is important to get the opinion of local counsel on the possible applicability of sales and use taxes.

[¶101.31]   Examination of Books

To check capitalization get a copy of the charter and all amendments, the bylaws, and all minutes to date and verify that all shares have been legally authorized and issued, paid for by adequate consideration and reflected in the financial statements. This should be verified by a certified statement of the company's accountants.

In examining the records of a corporation to be acquired, examine all indentures, loan agreements, leases and other documents which might contain covenants of a burdensome nature. Examine any labor contracts, employment contracts, stock option, pension and profit-sharing plans of the company and report the terms of each. Look for stockholder agreements and other similar contracts affecting the control of a company and the transferability of its securities.

【¶101.32】 Stamp Taxes

We need no longer be concerned with federal stamp taxes on the issuance or transfer of stock or debt securities or on conveyances of real estate. However, a number of states have filled the federal void on conveyances of real estate. In some states, a merger may avoid the sales taxes or license fees to which acquisitions of assets are subject. Only New York and Florida have stock transfer taxes. Check the state law on these various taxes.

【¶101.33】 Inventory Problems

Valuation of the seller's inventory to be purchased normally presents special problems. How far should the parties be bound by the seller's past practice in valuing inventory? Should any values be assigned to obsolete items or items not normally physically inventoried by the seller? How do you value "slow-moving" products? The rules for valuing inventory are normally determined jointly by the accountants of the seller and the buyer. It is desirable to secure a warranty of salability with respect to the inventory, but usually the seller will balk at this. The seller ought to be willing to warrant that the inventory is of "merchantable" quality and adequate for the conduct of the business as previously conducted. However, this is not a common provision.

【¶101.34】 Accounts Receivable Problems

Here the buyer may not wish to assume the risk that the seller's reserve for bad debts is adequate. The contract may provide for an adjustment in price to reflect any difference between the accounts receivable shown on the seller's books and the amount actually collected at the end of a specified period of time. Where this is the deal, the seller is usually given an opportunity to take the uncollected accounts and see what he can do with them. There are usually advantages in having the accounts receivable collected by the continuing business.

【¶101.35】 Title Searches

A real estate title search should be made early; and if there are any clouds on the title which would hurt the operation of the business, they should be brought to the buyer's attention promptly and before the purchase agreement is signed if possible. The buyer could agree to bear the cost of such a search if the deal did not go through.

【¶101.36】 Public Announcements

The acquirer may want to control any releases. The matter of informing customers and suppliers of the seller may have commercial significance. In some cases the new affiliation should be emphasized; in others it should not be. The question is primarily one of keeping the seller's customers happy.

[¶101.37] Use of a Tender Offer

The tender offer is a favored way of acquiring a company whose stock is publicly traded. Compared with an acquisition via a merger, the tender offer has these advantages:

(1) Stockholder approval is not required and consequently there's no need for proxy solicitation.

(2) A tender offer does not involve any additional securities registration problems.

(3) Dilution of ownership and control is not present.

(4) Acquisition of shares via a tender offer is not a taxable event so far as the offeror is concerned. An exchange of securities in a merger may be.

(5) A tender offer can be cloaked in secrecy until you're ready to go and think you have a fair chance of succeeding, but with a merger you are required to tip your hand in the initial stages.

However, the Securities Exchange Act of 1934 regulates the use of tender offers and requires disclosure of certain facts.

[¶101.38] Checklist of Post-Closing Steps

Here's a rundown of the steps to be taken following the closing of a merger or acquisition:

☐ 1. *Publicity:* Comply with the requirements of public announcement, if any, contained in the agreement. Furnish wire services with immediate accurate release. Place advertisements if required.

☐ 2. *SEC Reports:* File 8K Reports reporting stockholders' meeting and acquisition.

☐ 3. *Tax Returns:* Prepare tax returns for acquired corporation for part of fiscal year before closing.

☐ 4. *Changeovers:* Change bank accounts, insurance policies, unemployment compensation filings, workmen's compensation filings, and similar items.

☐ 5. *Corporate Name:* Protect corporate name of acquired corporation. (One way is to form a dummy corporation.)

☐ 6. *Pending Litigation:* Effect substitutions of parties.

☐ 7. *Registration Statements:* Check to make sure of compliance with SEC requirements including filing of past-effective amendments to registration statements and prospectuses.

☐ 8. *Withdrawal of Acquired Corporation:* See that acquired corporation is withdrawn from states where it may be registered.

☐ 9. *Stock-Option Agreements:* If new stock-option agreements are to be substituted, see that they are executed.

●

For Further Reference . . .

Choka, *Buying, Selling and Merging Businesses,* American Law Institute, Philadelphia, Pa.

Scharf, C., *Techniques for Buying, Selling and Merging Businesses,* Prentice-Hall, Englewood Cliffs, N. J.

The Five Corners of a Corporation: Organization, Acquisition, Reorganization, Liquidation and Sales, New York University Institute on Federal Taxation 73:255, 1973.

AGENTS OR INDEPENDENT CONTRACTORS

[¶301]   Whether an agent or independent contractor relationship has been created can be important in determining the liabilities of the principal, the powers of the agent, the ability of the agent to bind his principal, liability for the agent's torts, etc. Similarly, the precise nature of the relationship may be important in determining whether the employee or agent comes within the definition of employee for purposes of withholding under the Internal Revenue Code, for purposes of workmen's compensation, for purposes of social security, unemployment compensation, etc. The parties will not necessarily be able to establish the nature of the relationship merely by a recital in their agreement. The recital will probably be binding in relationships between the principal and the agent, employee-employer, etc., but will not be binding upon third parties. Where the facts are unclear, a recital may be important in eliminating ambiguity. The following table, however, shows factors which are often used by courts in determining the relationship which exists.

Factors which tend to show independent contractor relationship	Factors which tend to show employee-employer relationship
Basis of Compensation	
Where the person employed agrees to do particular work for a specific sum.	Where remuneration will be determined in accordance with the length of the employment.
Where the compensation will be based on the amount of work done by the person doing the work.	In some jurisdictions where there is a cost plus arrangement, it will lean in favor of principal agent rather than an independent contractor relationship.
Where the remuneration is to be based on the amount of money the agent is to disburse.	
Control	
Where the contractor exercises complete control over the work and his only obligation is to get the work done, i.e., one who is engaged in the trucking business, uses his own truck, loads it himself and comes and goes as he pleases (*Elickbenger v. Industrial Accident Commission,* 181 Cal. 425, 19 ALR 115).	Where the employer has the absolute control over the work—however, the employee may exercise some control over the work without effecting a change.
Where employed to exterminate an apartment house (*Medley v. Trenton Investment Co.,* 205 Wisc. 30, 76 ALR 1250).	

17

Factors which tend to show independent contractor relationship	Factors which tend to show employer-employee relationship
Contracts to paint smokestacks for a fee–and furnish his own tools (*Litts v. Risley Lumber Co.*, 224 NY 321, 19 ALR 1147).	Where a tractor owner spent his entire time in the employ of one trucker operating his own tractor he was held to be an employee where the trucking company designated routes, times, etc. (See *Western Express v. Smeltzer,* 88 F.2d 94).
Contracts to drill the holes and place the dynamite at a specific sum per foot, where he furnishes his own assistants.	
Where the contractor has the complete control over and pays the other workmen on the job.	
Where the person has the right to discharge workmen on the job.	

Materials and Tools

Where the contractor furnishes the materials and tools it will be an indication of his independence.	Merely furnishing the tools in a trade like carpenters, machinists, etc., will not mean that there is no employee relationship.

Nature of the Calling

Persons operating certain vessels, architects, painters, physicians, nurses, plumbers, window washers, etc., are generally considered independent contractors where they are in business for themselves.	Domestic servants, chauffeurs, gardeners, are generally not considered independent contractors although they have their own callings.

Justice Miller in the famous New York case of *Hexamer v. Webb* (101 NY 377) said, "As a general rule, where a person is employed to perform a certain kind of work, in the nature of repairs or improvements to a building by the owner thereof which requires the exercise of skill and judgment as mechanic, the execution of which is left entirely to this person with no restriction as to his exercise and no limitation of his authority conferred in respect to the same, and no provision is especially made as to the time in which the work is to be done, or the payment for the services rendered; and the compensation is dependent upon the value thereof, such person does not occupy in relation of a servant under control of the master, but he is an independent contractor, and the owner is not liable for his acts or the acts of his workmen who are negligent and the cause of the injury to another."

[¶301.1] Lack of Employer-Employee Relationship

In the following cases, the court held that no employee-employer relationship existed:

Life Insurance Agent: The relationship between a life insurance company and its agents is not that of employee-employer within the meaning of the unemployment insurance (*Northwestern Mutual Life Insurance v. Tone,* 125 Conn. 183; 121 ALR 993).

Motor Truck Operator: A motor truck owner-operator who furnishes his own truck, fuel and maintenance and is paid by the mile or ton is not an employee within the meaning of the unemployment insurance law. (See *Commercial Motor Freight, Inc., v. Bright,* 143 Ohio 127, 151 ALR 1321. See also *Mutual Trucking Co. v. United States* 51 F.Supp. 114.)

Subscription Solicitor: For purposes of workmen's compensation, a person who solicted newspaper circulation was not an employee but an independent contractor even though the newspapers supplied him with papers, etc. and he was required to turn in subscription lists and money at the end of each day (less, of course, his percentage commission). (See *Heubner v. Industrial Comm.* 290 NW 145, 126 ALR 1113.)

A book subscription solicitor was held to be an independent contractor — the publisher was not liable for the independent contractor's torts. In this case, it appeared that the solicitor sold books for the publisher and other publishers — was paid on a commission basis, had no limited territory, but was furnished with samples and order books by the publisher. (See *P. F. Collier & Sons Co. v. Hartfeil,* 72 F.2d 625.)

Garageman: A garageman called to repair a car is not an employee of the owner for the purpose of holding the owner liable for the garageman's torts. The garageman may be a bailee. However — some states have statutes which hold a bailor liable for the torts of his bailee while operating the bailor's motor vehicle. (See *Nawrockie v. Cole,* 41 Wash. 2d 474, 35 ALR 2d 799.)

Auto Race Mechanics: The owners, drivers and mechanics involved in a commercial auto race are not the employees of the promoter of the series of races for labor law purposes. (See *Outdoor Sports Corp. v. AFL Local 23-132,* 6 NJ 217, 29 ALR 2d 313.)

Repairman: Where the contract was to repair the water tower and the city had no control over how the repairman was to make the repairs, the court held that no employee-employer relationship existed in that case. (See *Hammond v. Eldorado Springs* 262 Mo. 530, 31 ALR 2d 1367.)

Where the hotel hired a man engaged in the roofing and cornice business to repair the roof so that pigeons would not nest in the cornice, the court held that the repairman was an independent contractor rather than an employee of the hotel. (See *Hexamer v. Webb supra.*)

For forms relating to sales agency agreements, see IBP FORMS OF BUSINESS AGREEMENTS.

[¶302] HOW TO SET UP DESIRED AGENT-PRINCIPAL RELATIONSHIP

Generally, the circumstances of a particular situation will dictate the relationship which the parties want to create. The following checklist of basic principles of agency should be helpful in determining what relationship is most appropriate for a particular situation.

[¶302.1] Control

Where the principal wants to exercise absolute control over the agent, he will want to make the agent an employee. However, where the employer really wants to have the agent accomplish a particular goal, and does not care how the goal is accomplished, he may appoint the employee an independent contractor. The degree of control will be extremely important in determining whether the representative is an agent, an independent contractor or an employee.

[¶302.2] Liability

Where the representative is an employee, the principal will have a vicarious liability for the employee's torts—and other wrongs arising out of the employment. A principal may be relieved of liability for his employee's torts where the torts occur outside of the scope of the employment. The employer is generally not liable for the torts of an independent contractor or the employees of the independent contractor. (See *Robbins v. Chicago,* 18 Lawyers Edition 427.) If the employer maintains control of the work or interferes with the contractor's performance of the work, the employer will be responsible for any tortious injuries which occur as a result of his interference or control over the work. An exception may also be made to the rule where the work performed is inherently dangerous.

The employee's liability will generally be concurrent with that of his employer. In many situations the employer will be entitled to indemnification from the employee where the employer was required to answer for the employee's torts. Generally contribution between joint tort-feasors will not be available where one joint tort-feasor was an active joint tort-feasor and the other joint tort-feasor was passive.

[¶302.3] Ability to Bind Principal

The agent will be in a position to bind his principal where the agency is disclosed. However, the ability to bind the principal will be governed by the nature of the agency and the authority which has been expressly vested in the agent. Where an agent has been expressly denied particular authority but the principal has made it appear that the agent has the authority, or has placed the agent in a position where it would be customary for the agent to have the indicated authority, the principal will be estopped from denying the agent's authority. Generally, however, where the agent acts beyond his authority and the doctrine of apparent authority is not applicable, the third party dealing with the agent will not have a cause of action against the principal. In some jurisdictions, however, the third party will have a cause of action against the agent for breach of the agent's implied warranty of authority.

[¶302.4] Implied Authority

An agent will generally have whatever authority necessary to carry out the purpose of the agency — subject to extension or limitation by the agreement between the parties. Secret instructions from the principal reducing the authority which the agent would appear to have will not be binding against third persons who are unaware of any secret limitations.

[¶302.5] Authority to Delegate

The agent will have the special authority or implied power to delegate or employ sub-agents unless the agreement between the parties indicates to the contrary. Where the agent himself is an employee, his right to delegate to some agents or employ some agents will depend on the nature of his employment. If the employee has been employed to manage a business, he will generally be deemed to have wide authority to bind his principal and will be authorized to employ sub-agents or employees of his principal. In this instance, the employees would be employees of the principal rather than of the agent. Where the relationship is one of independent contractor, the independent contractor will be authorized to employ sub-contractors and agents. The relationship between the independent contractor and the agent will be distinct from that between the independent contractor and the person who initially contracted with the independent contractor. Where an agent, be he an employee or independent contractor, is employed to manage a business, he will be deemed to have wide authority to bind his principal in contracts for the operation and repair of business property including the hiring of sub-agents and independent contractors.

[¶302.6] Authority to Make Purchases

The agent's authority to make purchases of personal property will depend on the nature of the position in which the principal has placed the agent. Where it appears that the agent is a manager of a retail shop, it will appear that he has the authority to purchase goods so long as it is customary for an agent in his position to have the authority to make such purchases. Where an agent has the authority to make purchases, he will generally have the implied authority to set the price. However, if the price which he set is so unreasonable as to put a prudent man on his guard, the price set by the agent will not be binding on the principal. (See *Leavens v. Finkham and McKevitt,* 164 Cal. 242.) Where a principal authorizes his agent to make purchases for cash and supplies him with the necessary cash, the agent will have no implied authority to make purchases for credit in an ordinary case.

[¶302.7] Duty of Loyalty

An agent will have absolute duty of loyalty to his principal unless this absolute duty has been altered by the agreement between the agent and principal. Generally, absent a specific agreement to the contrary, an employee will be required to devote his full time to the principal's business—and not work against the principal. Where it appears that a salesman several months prior to the expiration of his principal's lease aided in leasing the property to a third person, the salesman was said to have breached his obligation of loyalty to his principal. However, where the contract calls for full-time employment, the employee will be permitted to use some time for the conduct of his personal affairs without breaching the employment contract.

The obligation of an employee to assign inventions to his employer are dealt with at ¶2311.

[¶302.8] Undisclosed Principal

Often an agent will have the authority to enter into a transaction but will not disclose the identity of his principal. Regardless of whether the agent indicates that he is representing a principal and fails to identify the principal, or whether he conceals the fact that he is representing a principal, the agent will remain liable on the contract. After the principal's existence has been disclosed, however, the principal will also become liable on the contract.

Who can act as an agent? Any person may act as an agent provided he is not incompetent. A principal cannot avoid a contract made by his agent merely because the agent is an infant. However, an infant principal could avoid a contract made by his agent unless the contract was for necessities or some other contract which the infant could not avoid if he were the principal and contracted for himself.

[¶302.9] Ratification

Where an agent acts without authority, his principal may ratify the act and the result will be the same as if the agent was acting with full authority. For a principal to ratify, he must have full knowledge of the material facts, the act must have been done for the principal initially and the principal must have the intention to ratify.

[¶302.10] Tort Liability

Generally, the principal or owner will be relieved of tort liability for the acts of an independent contractor or agents of the independent contractor although he would be vicariously liable for similar acts by his employees or agents. However, this will not relieve the principal of responsibility for his own negligence. Similarly, the owner-principal will also risk liability where the work to be done by the independent contractor is inherently or intrinsically dangerous. In addition, the owner may not suffer a nuisance on his property. For example, if the employer should hire an independent contractor who uses a scaffolding which is improperly set up, the owner may be responsible for injuries to a third person because he permitted a nuisance on his property.

[¶302.11] Sales Agents

Special rules will be applicable to sales agents. The greatest flexibility in setting up a transaction in advance generally surrounds how to handle the sales agents or other sales people. A sales agent will generally have the authority to do whatever is necessary to make the sale. This is true without regard to what specific category he may fit into (agent, independent contractor, employee, etc.). A commercial traveler who has been given a catalog, and possibly samples, will generally be authorized only to solicit orders for acceptance by his home office. A salesman who has been entrusted with the goods will generally have the apparent authority to accept the money and deliver the goods. Where the sales agent is a merchant dealing in the type of goods involved, he will have the authority to sell any goods which have been entrusted to his possession. Section 2–403 of the Uniform Commercial Code provides that any entrusted possession of goods to a merchant who deals in goods of that kind gives him power to transfer all rights of the person entrusting him with possession to a buyer in the ordinary course of business.

As a general rule, an agent who is authorized to sell is authorized to sell only for cash unless he is specifically authorized to sell on credit. (See *Woodward v. Jewell,* 140 US 247.)

An agent may have the express authority to give a warranty. Absent express authority, the agent will have implied authority to warrant the goods if it would be normal for an agent in his position to have such authority. The agent will also have the authority to bind his principal to a warranty which would, in the absence of an express warranty, be implied. Thus the agent would have the authority under the Uniform Commercial Code to bind his principal to the warranty of merchantability and the warranty of fitness for purpose. Similarly, where a sales agent makes a sale by sample, there is a warranty that the bulk of the goods will conform to the sample.

In some states an agent will require express authority of his principal to sell real property. In some states, this express authority must be in a writing sufficient to satisfy the requirements of the statute of frauds.

[¶303]   WITHHOLDING PROBLEMS

Where wages are paid to an "employee" they will be subject to withholding. The Regulations provide that the relationship of employer-employee generally exists when the person for whom services are performed has the right to control and direct the individual who performs the services, not only as to the result to be accomplished by the work but also as to the details and means by which that result is accomplished. It is not necessary that the employer actually direct or control the manner in which the services are performed to bring the employee within the definition for withholding tax purposes. As is the case in state law, the right to discharge is also an important factor indicating that the person possessing that right is an employer. (See Reg. §31.3401(c)-1.)

The following table indicates situations where withholding tax must be paid.

Employee	Nonemployee
Accountant keeping the books of a concern under the direction of the person engaging him.	Accountant offering his services to the public.
Attorney engaged by a law firm as an associate.	Attorney retained by a person or firm, paid a retainer on a yearly basis. (S.S. T.86; CB 1937-1, 462).
Auctioneer where the employer controls and directs his professional services (S.S.T. 149, CB 1937-1, 380).	Auctioneer.
	Corporate Directors (unless also an employee of the corporation).
Nurses aides, nurses on the staff of a hospital.	Registered Nurse and licensed practical nurses engaged in private duty nursing.
Physician who works under the supervision of the head physician for a company, is required to be present for a set number of hours each day and receives all the benefits of an employee.	Physician engaged in private practice and also treats the employees of a company on a part-time basis.
Persons engaged in performing services for a trust or estate are employees of the trust or estate.	Real estate salesmen, who do not receive a guaranteed amount of compensation.
Bakery goods "dealers" who were required to furnish their own trucks where it appeared they were employees.	Fiduciary or trustee for a trust, a bankrupt, etc., within the scope of his official duties.

Employee	Nonemployee
Newspaper correspondents compensated on a monthly basis although not required to furnish a minimum amount of work.	Cab drivers who rent the cabs and are not accountable for the fees collected (*Martin v. Wichita Cab Co.*, 161 Kan. 510).
A professor engaged by a university to carry out a research contract will be subject to withholding.	Individual who operates a laundry business on a commission basis where the operator pays rent, heat, etc., of the store out of the commission (Rev. Rul. 56-15, CB 1956-1,451).
	Owner-driver of a truck where he is not given any rules to follow, his route cannot be changed without his consent and he is responsible for seeing that his route is covered at all times.

Generally, similar rules will be applicable in determining whether unemployment compensation, workmen's compensation and disability taxes must be paid. These rules will vary from state to state.

●

For Further Reference . . .
American Jurisprudence, Agency.
American Jurisprudence, Independent Contractors.
Kempin, F. G., Corporate Officer and the Law of Agency, 44 *Virginia Law Review* 1273.
Meecham on Agency, Callaghan & Co., Chicago, Ill.
Restatement of Agency, American Law Institute, Philadelphia, Pa.
Seavey, W. A., Agency, Highlight and Sidelight, 2 *Practical Lawyer* 15.
Seavey on Agency.
Tiffany's Text on Agency, West Publishing Co., St. Paul, Minn.
Witney, *The Law of Modern Commercial Practices,* Baker, Voorhis.

ARBITRATION

⟦¶501⟧ Commercial arbitration may offer an attractive alternative to litigation in many instances. Proponents of arbitration claim it's more economical and speedier than litigation, offers more privacy and less acrimony, and is more effective, particularly in its use of expert decision makers. A closer look at the claimed advantages, however, produces a number of qualifications.

Looking at costs: It's true that if the parties cooperate they can save expenses, but if they're going to litigate the right to arbitrate, pull out all the stops before the arbitrators, and then seek judicial review of the award, there is likely to be no saving in time or money.

The arbitration proceeding itself will be in privacy and this may be commercially desirable, but privacy will be lost if the parties resort to the courts before or after arbitration.

There's apt to be less acrimony in arbitration but this is usually a by-product of a willingness to submit to arbitration and cooperate in seeking a solution of a dispute rather than any inherent ingredient of the arbitration proceeding itself.

For forms of agreements to arbitrate contained in various forms of contracts, including building agreements, corporate organization agreements, employment contracts and sales, see IBP FORMS OF BUSINESS AGREEMENTS.

⟦¶502⟧ EFFECTIVENESS OF ARBITRATION

When we come to examine the effectiveness of arbitration we must consider four elements: (1) predictability of result; (2) fairness of the hearing; (3) adequacy of the relief; and (4) adequacy of judicial review. Arbitration doesn't offer the same predictability as litigation because arbitrators aren't bound to follow rules of law or rules of evidence unless, of course, the parties by their agreement make it clear that they must. But even if the agreement does so provide, you have a problem of judicial enforcement if they don't follow the rules. One of the factors tending to make for fairness in judicial proceedings is the requirement that the court make findings of fact and give reasons for its decision. These elements are missing in arbitration proceedings unless the parties themselves call for them. When it comes to relief, the final relief awarded will usually be adequate to the necessities of the case, but it must be borne in mind that the arbitrators may grant either legal or equitable relief, that is, either a money judgment or injunctive relief or recision and other kinds of equitable relief, and they won't be bound by the judicial rule which bars equitable relief unless the legal remedy is inadequate. The arbitrator's power to grant interim relief, that is, relief pending the proceedings, will depend on statutory provision and is apt to be less than adequate and may require application to a court. The same is true of pre-trial procedure.

[¶503]   WHEN TO ARBITRATE

Despite these limitations a resort to arbitration may be called for in cases:
(1) Where the issues of fact are simple and the law is clear.
(2) Where pre-trial procedures aren't vital and the risk of an unfair hearing by arbitrators not required to follow the law is small.
(3) Where technical matters are involved and the rule of law is clear.
(4) Where privacy is essential.
(5) Where court calendars are crowded and speed is important.
(6) Where a jury trial isn't wanted.
Of course, you can't go to arbitration in any case unless both parties agree. The agreement may be in advance of any dispute or may be entered into after a dispute has arisen.

[¶504]   ARBITRATION STATUTES

Most states have statutes governing arbitration. Some of these apply only to submission of existing disputes, others only to agreements to arbitrate future disputes, and still others to both. So, you will have to check out the statutes in your state.
A submission of an existing dispute must cover these points:
(1) The names of the parties.
(2) The subject matter of the dispute, clearly stated.
(3) Names of arbitrators (required by statute in some states).
(4) The court by which judgment is to be entered (required by statute in some states).
(5) Other provisions required by statute.
Permissible provisions, in most jurisdictions, include the following:
(1) Method of appointing arbitrators and filling vacancies in appointments.
(2) Time and place of hearing.
(3) Rules governing hearing.
(4) Time for making award.
(5) Discontinuance of pending suit.
(6) Revocation of submission.
(7) Binding effect of award.
(8) Submission of questions of law to court.

27

(9) Rendition of judgment on award.

(10) Costs and expenses of arbitrator and of proceedings.

The U. S. Arbitration Act makes written provision for arbitration valid, irrevocable, and enforceable in maritime transactions and in contracts involving interstate commerce (9 USC 1).

In most states which have adopted arbitration statutes the agreement must be in writing to be enforceable. Generally, a clause in a contract which provides for the settlement of all disputes for arbitration will be enforceable. In states which have adopted the Uniform Arbitration Act there must be consent of both parties to evoke an arbitration agreement. The death of a party may revoke the arbitration agreement where the state arbitration statute does not provide for irrevocability.

[¶505]   ARBITRABLE ISSUES

In some states the subject matter of arbitration is limited by statute. Generally, a contract which provides that any controversy arising out of the contract will be subject to arbitration will be enforced. In most states property rights in personal or real property may be determined by arbitration. In some states real property issues are expressly excluded by statute. Probate matters will be subject to arbitration where all parties agree to the arbitration in most states. However, in some states the courts take the position that probate proceedings are in rem and therefore are not subject to arbitration. A tort case may be submitted to arbitration. However, arbitration will not be available in criminal matters or in other matters having a public interest. Arbitration will not be available to determine custody, visitation rights and support proceedings in most jurisdictions.

[¶506]   ENFORCEMENT OF ARBITRATION
                              AGREEMENTS

In many states statutes provide machinery for the enforcement of arbitration agreements on a summary basis.

The Uniform Arbitration Act and the Federal Arbitration Act provide for summary remedy in case one of the parties refuses to arbitrate or denies the existence of a valid arbitration agreement.

Where the agreement is revocable, the courts will generally refuse to specifically decree performance of agreements to arbitrate because the parties have a right to revoke. (See *Red Cross Line v. Atlantic Fruit Co.,* 264 US 109.)

Where the arbitration agreement is irrevocable, the statutes in many states provide for a proceeding to enforce the arbitration clause in which case it will be treated as an action for specific performance. Under the Federal Arbitration statute a proceeding for enforcement of an arbitration agreement is treated as an action for specific performance. (See *Standard Magnesium Corp. v. Fuchs,* 251 F.2d 455.)

[¶507]   SELECTING THE ARBITRATOR

Where a contract calls for settlement of disputes by arbitration, the arbitrator will be determined either prior to the dispute or subsequent to the disputes. Where a particular arbitrator is appointed prior to the time the dispute arises, the party should appoint an alternate in the event the original arbitrator is unable to serve. The parties may also provide that the arbitrator is to be determined in accordance with the rules prescribed by the American Arbitration Association. Under those rules the American Arbitration Association will send each party to a dispute a copy of a list of proposed arbitrators, technically qualified to resolve the controversies involved. In preparing this list, the Association is guided by the nature of the dispute. Each party is then given 10 days to cross off any names objected to and number the arbitrators according to their preference.

The Association will appoint an arbitrator who is acceptable to both parties. If no arbitrator is acceptable to both parties, a new list will be provided. If the parties are unable to select an arbitrator mutually acceptable, the Association will administratively appoint an arbitrator but the appointed arbitrator will not be one of those crossed off previously by the parties.

An alternative method for selecting arbitrators is to provide that each party to the controversy will appoint an arbitrator and the arbitrators will appoint a third arbitrator. If the arbitrators are unable to agree upon a third arbitrator, the court may be called upon to do so.

[¶507.1] Qualifications of an Arbitrator

Any competent disinterested person can be an arbitrator irrespective of legal status. However, in some cases, the parties will want to designate an attorney or one familiar with the applicable legal principles. Where the arbitrator is biased or interested in the transaction or dispute, he may be removed. An arbitrator will not necessarily be disqualified where he has previously served as counsel to one of the parties in different litigation, is friendly with one of the parties or has previously served as an arbitrator in similar cases. Trade associations frequently employ a panel of arbitrators to settle disputes between their members.

[¶508] **PROCEDURE**

As already noted, the strict rules of procedure known to the courts are greatly relaxed in arbitration proceedings. However, certain basic requirements must be fulfilled. For example, the parties to the arbitration must be given notice and an opportunity to be heard. The strict requirements of service applicable to obtain jurisdiction in a conventional civil action prosecuted in the courts will not be applicable.

The Federal Arbitration Act and the Uniform Arbitration Act authorize the issuance of subpoenas for the attendance of witnesses and the administration of oaths for arbitrators. (See Federal Arbitration Act §7, 9 USC 7 and Uniform Arbitration Act §7(a).)

Under the American Arbitration rules service is made by supplying the adversary with a "demand for arbitration." The demand should include a statement of the dispute, full text of the arbitration clause and agreement giving rise to the arbitration, identification of the parties and must be signed by an authorized person. The respondent may mail an answering statement to those statements. Both statements should be filed with the American Arbitration Association where the parties intend to be governed by and utilize the facilities of the American Arbitration Association.

Although it is customary for the complaining party to proceed with his oral argument initially, the arbitrator may alter this procedure. In an arbitration proceeding, there are no formal rules for the determination of the burden of proof. ". . . Each party must try to convince the arbitrator of the correctness of his position and no hearing is closed until both have had an opportunity to do so." The award of an arbitrator will not be set aside merely because he permitted the introduction of evidence which would not be admissible in court but his award will be set aside where he fails to permit the introduction of pertinent evidence. The arbitrator may decide to inspect or undertake further investigation either at the request of a party or on his own initiative.

[¶509] **VACATING AN ARBITRATION AWARD**

The Uniform Arbitration Act provides for vacating an arbitration award in the following instances:
(a) Procurement by corruption, fraud, or other undue means.
(b) Partiality on the part of an arbitrator appointed as a neutral.
(c) Misconduct or corruption of the arbitrators.
(d) Refusal of the arbitrators to hear material evidence.
(e) Refusal of the arbitrators to give a postponement when there was sufficient cause.
(f) Prejudicial misconduct of the hearing.

(g) Lack of a valid arbitration agreement.

Some cases have held that an arbitration agreement may be attacked where there has been perjured testimony before the arbitration—especially where the perjury was by or procured by the successful party. (See *Fire Association of Philadelphia v. Allesina,* 49 Or. 316.) If the award has been reduced to a judgment, perjury will not be sufficient grounds to attack the award unless an ordinary judgment could be attacked in the same manner (*Chambers v. Crook,* 42 Ala 171).

[¶510] ENFORCEMENT OF THE ARBITRATION AWARD

The arbitration award is not self executing. However, either party is entitled to bring an action on the award and have it enforced as a contract. The Federal Arbitration Act provides a summary for confirmation of an arbitration award within one year but the parties will not be precluded from maintaining an action on the award after the one year statute of limitations for the summary remedy of confirmation has elapsed. (See *Kentucky River Mills v. Jackson,* 206 F.2d 111, 9 USC §9.)

The Uniform Arbitration Act (§11) also provides for the confirmation of an award unless grounds are urged for vacating or modifying or correcting the award. The Uniform Act also provides for the entry of the award as a judgment enforceable as any other judgment. (See Uniform Arbitration Act §14, 15.)

Once an award is reduced to judgment in one state, it is entitled to full faith and credit in other states. Other states cannot question the judgment unless it could be questioned in the state rendering it.

●

For Further Reference . . .

American Arbitration Association, *Rules,* New York, N.Y.

American Jurisprudence, Arbitration.

Commercial Arbitration, 17 *Law and Contemporary Problems* (Nos. 3 and 4) (entire issues devoted to commercial arbitration).

Commercial Arbitration, Practising Law Institute, New York, N.Y.

Horowitz, Guides for Resorting to Commercial Arbitration, 8 *Practical Lawyer* 67.

BANKRUPTCY

[¶601] In law practice, the lawyer will have contact with the Bankruptcy Act when:

(1) He wants to secure a creditor's debt in anticipation of the possible bankruptcy of the debtor. See ¶4901 on how to secure a debt.

(2) He wants to protect a creditor by putting the debtor in bankruptcy.

(3) He wants to press a claim against or recover an asset from a bankrupt estate.

(4) He represents a harassed debtor who wants to be discharged of his debts.

(5) He wants the protection of the court to rehabilitate a financially embarrassed business. See ¶4601.

[¶602] PUTTING A DEBTOR IN INVOLUNTARY BANKRUPTCY

Three creditors with claims aggregating over $500 in amount are necessary, except in those cases where the bankrupt has less than twelve creditors, in which event one petitioning creditor will suffice. The creditors will have to show one of the six acts of bankruptcy defined in §3 of the Bankruptcy Act. The more important ones are a fraudulent transfer, a preferential payment during insolvency, failure of an insolvent debtor to discharge a judgment within 30 days or five days before the sale of property to which the lien attaches. Insolvency here means that the debtor's liabilities exceed his assets taken at fair value.

Why does the creditor want to force involuntary bankruptcy? There are several reasons:

(1) There is a sequestration of assets immediately without the risk of having the bankrupt dissipate or conceal the property available to pay his debts.

(2) There is an orderly administration of his estate and a procedure under which claims against him can be established expeditiously.

(3) If the bankrupt has made any substantial preferences, that is to say, if he has favored any relatives or friends, these favored creditors can be required to return the property to the estate for ratable distribution among all claims.

(4) There is provision in the Bankruptcy Act for the examination of the bankrupt and witnesses to determine the nature of the acts, conduct and property of the bankrupt whose estate is in the process of administration.

32

[¶603]   STEPS IN BANKRUPTCY PROCEEDINGS

The steps in a bankruptcy proceeding are these:

(1) Filing of petition—a voluntary petition constitutes an adjudication, an involuntary petition may be contested.

(2) To contest a petition, an answer has to be filed. Usually, it will deny the act of bankruptcy or deny the insolvency, which is necessary for a preferential payment or permitting a judgment lien to constitute an act of bankruptcy.

(3) The bankrupt must file an inventory of all his property and a list of all his creditors, secured and unsecured, showing the amount owed each. He must also file a "statement of affairs" giving information as to his financial history, the volume of business, his income and other pertinent information. The schedules are prepared in triplicate and filed with the clerk of the court and must be sworn to. The schedule must claim any exemptions the debtor believes he's entitled to, otherwise the exemption may be lost.

(4) When adjudication takes place the referee fixes a date for the first meeting of creditors not less than 10 days nor more than 30 days after adjudication and gives the creditors written notice of the meeting. The meeting is presided over by the referee and the bankrupt is required to attend and to submit to a broad examination covering every phase of his operations. If it turns out to be a "no asset" case the applicant for examination may wind up having to pay the stenographer's fee. This suggests the wisdom of having an agreement with other creditors before assuming the initiative. It's worth noting that the creditors don't have to wait until their first meeting to examine the debtor but can do so even before adjudication.

(5) The trustee in bankruptcy is elected at the first meeting of creditors by a majority of the unsecured creditors both as to number and amount of claims. Claims of secured or priority creditors aren't counted except to the extent they exceed the value of their security or priority. This, of course, can lead to a contest and the referee will have to decide which claims he'll allow to vote.

(6) The trustee has the key role in bankruptcy proceedings. He must take over and gather together all the bankrupt's assets. To this end he has the job of uncovering fraud and concealment and recovering preferences and fraudulent transfers. In this job he will be assisted, of course, by the attorney he selects.

[¶603.1]   Executory Contracts

Contracts to which the bankrupt is a party which haven't been fully performed, in other words his executory contracts, such as contracts to manufacture or sell goods, perform services, and leases, must be assumed or rejected by the trustee within sixty days of adjudication. Actually, if he doesn't assume, there's an automatic rejection, but it will be best to get the rejection on record anyhow. The trustee will naturally assume if he thinks it's going to help the estate but he won't be able to if the contract in question contains a provision for automatic termination on bankruptcy. Such a provision is, of course, quite common in leases.

【¶603.2】　Strongarm Provisions — Sections 70(c) and 67(a)

Here is the heart of the bankruptcy proceeding. First, §70(a) of the Bankruptcy Act spells out the property of the debtor which passes to the trustee. Section 70(c) puts the trustee in the position of a lien creditor whose interest vests in all the bankrupt's property at the moment of adjudication, regardless of whether or not such a lien creditor actually exists. This puts title in the trustee ahead of all unsecured creditors and all secured creditors who have failed to perfect their lien.

【¶603.3】　Transfers Voidable as to Any Creditor

Section 67(d) of the Bankruptcy Act in effect picks up most of the provisions of the Uniform Fraudulent Conveyance Act and the trustee may avoid fraudulent transfers made within one year before the bankruptcy petition. This covers transfers made without a fair consideration while insolvent or which render the debtor insolvent or without reasonable capital to conduct his business, or by a debtor who expects to incur obligations beyond his ability to pay, as well as transfers made with intent to hinder, delay or defraud creditors. Unlike the situation under the strongarm provision, here the trustee will have to show that there actually is a creditor against whom the transfer was fraudulent when made. If it turns out that the property has been passed along to a good faith purchaser, a lienor or someone else who paid fair value for the property, the trustee won't be able to get back the property itself.

Section 70(e) gives the trustee still another weapon. Under this section he can avoid any transfer which is fraudulent or voidable as to any creditor having a provable claim under the Act. Again the trustee has to show that there actually is such a creditor who could have avoided the transfer.

Section 67(a) voids liens obtained by legal or equitable proceedings within four months of bankruptcy while the debtor is insolvent.

Here's how §67(a) and 70(e) might work together in a case where the strongarm provision, §70(c), wouldn't help. The debtor executes a mortgage, say 15 months prior to bankruptcy, which is recorded 3 months before bankruptcy, a week after a creditor obtained a lien by legal proceedings on the property covered by the mortgage. As previously stated §70(c) won't help because the security interest was perfected before bankruptcy. But §67(a) will help because subdivision (3) of §67(a) preserves liens voidable under the section for the benefit of the bankrupt's estate. As a result the trustee can preserve the creditor's lien and using §70(e) he can beat the mortgage which wasn't recorded until after the creditor obtained his and hence was voidable as to him. Then he can avoid the creditor's lien under §67(a).

[¶603.4] Avoidance of Preferences

Section 60 gives the trustee power to avoid preferences. The elements of a preference are: (1) A transfer of the debtor's property (voluntary or involuntary with the latter taking in liens by legal proceedings); (2) while insolvent; (3) for or on account of an antecedent debt; (4) within four months of the filing of the petition in bankruptcy; (5) enabling the creditor to get a greater percentage of his debt than other creditors of the same class; and (6) the creditor must know or have reasonable cause to believe that the debtor was insolvent at the time of the transfer.

The fourth element, simple enough on its face, can give rise to many problems once you go beyond the type of transaction where the transfer is perfected for all purposes by delivery of the property or cash payment. But not every transfer will be so perfected by delivery. Section 60 spells out the rules governing in determining when transfers will be deemed perfected for the purposes of applying the four months provision. A transfer of any property *other than real estate* will be deemed perfected when no subsequent lien obtainable by legal or equitable proceedings on a simple contract could be superior to the rights of the transferee. As to real estate, the transfer is deemed perfected when no subsequent bona fide purchaser from the debtor could get superior rights. In both cases you have to look to state law to determine when perfection occurs. More specifically, in most cases you have to look to state statutory recording and filing requirements and who's protected against unrecorded or unfiled transfers.

[¶604] MAKING CLAIMS AGAINST A BANKRUPT

There are two special sections in the Bankruptcy Act which deal with the matter of filing proofs of claim. One of these is §57 which is headed "Proof and Allowance of Claims," and the other is §63 and is entitled "Debts Which May Be Proved."

So far as the proof and allowance of claims is concerned a creditor establishes a claim in bankruptcy by filing what is known as a proof of claim. The Supreme Court of the United States, pursuant to provisions of the Bankruptcy Act, was authorized to promulgate rules and forms. Pursuant to this power, the Supreme Court has fixed the form of a proof of claim in bankruptcy. You can go into practically any legal stationery store and buy appropriate forms.

For practicable purposes, almost all claims are provable—with two important exceptions. (1) An action for negligence where litigation has *not* been instituted prior to the filing of the bankruptcy petition. (2) Landlords' claims which, although provable, are limited in amount under the provisions of §63a(9) of the Act.

Extending credit to a bankrupt after the filing of a petition docs not automatically give the supplier an administration expense claim that would be entitled to payment in full. The Bankruptcy Act (§63b) says that credit extended after the filing of the petition and before the appointment of a Receiver or the adjudication, whichever first occurs, gets no better treatment than if it had been extended before the petition was filed.

Don't jump in to file a small claim against a small bankrupt estate in a distant locale. When you file a claim you submit to the jurisdiction of the Bankruptcy Court. This exposes you to the possibility of having to defend against a claim made by the trustee a long way from home.

Staking Out Claims: The person entitled to property believed to be in the hands of the trustee should act diligently to notify the trustee of his claim as soon as he learns of the bankruptcy and make sure that the property is identified as his.

Secured Claims: Although strictly speaking a secured claim isn't provable if the collateral is to be sold in bankruptcy and the creditor relegated to the proceeds of the sale, he should follow the customary practice of filing proof of his secured debt. Another thing to bear in mind is that to the extent that the security is worth less than the claim the creditor is considered an unsecured creditor and as such has a provable claim. Generally, the value of the security must be determined under the control and supervision of the court.

Priority Claims: Certain claims are entitled to priority of payment under §64(a) of the Act and these should be filed as priority claims and if only part of the claim is entitled to priority the amount of priority should be indicated. In such case the balance will be provable as an ordinary unsecured claim.

[¶604.1] Reclamation Proceedings

Reclamation proceedings are the reverse of turnover proceedings. That is, they're a quick way for a third party to get hold of property which belongs to him which is in possession of the trustee. Of course, in many situations where it is clear that the third party is entitled to property in possession of the trustee he's not going to have to start a reclamation proceeding to get it, but if there's any doubt about the matter, chances are he'll resort to reclamation proceedings. He won't necessarily have to if he's the absolute owner of the property because he'll win out as against a purchaser from the trustee if it comes to that unless, of course, the property in question is an intangible and is negotiable. If the claimant holds a security interest only, the trustee won't hand it over if the property is worth more than the claim it secures. In that case he'll either ask the court to permit the secured creditor to sell the property outside of bankruptcy and pay over the excess or to permit sale by the trustee, free and clear, and give the creditor an interest in the proceeds. The first course is only apt to be followed where the property in question is at some distant point and can't be sold conveniently with the other assets.

Typical Uses of Proceedings: Typical situations where reclamation proceedings are apt to be used are in cases where the reclaimant holds a security interest and is entitled to possession as under a chattel mortgage, conditional sale or pledge, or claims the property as bailor or as one from whom the bankrupt got the property by fraud.

[¶604.2] How Claims Are Proved

All claims provable under the Act must be filed within six months of the first meeting of creditors. If a claim is timely filed, it can usually be amended after the six-month period so long as the amendment doesn't amount to an entirely new claim.

Claims should be submitted on the official forms. While the claim itself need not be verified, if a power of attorney is filed with it, the power should be acknowledged before a notary. If the claim is based on a written instrument, the instrument should be attached to the proof.

[¶604.3] Allowance of Claims

At the first meeting of creditors, a provisional allowance of claims will be made for voting purposes but this isn't an allowance for purposes of dividend participation. However, as a general rule, claims filed at or before the first meeting will be allowed at that time if no objection is raised. If an objection is raised, either by the trustee or one or more creditors, the referee will fix a date to hear and determine the points raised. There's no time limit on filing objections, but the referee may in his discretion refuse to entertain objections filed too late. Secured and priority claims will be allowed only to the extent they're unsecured. If a creditor has received a transfer, lien or preference which is voidable, his claim won't be allowed until he surrenders it to the trustee.

[¶605] HOW THE ASSETS OF THE BANKRUPT ARE DISTRIBUTED

The Act sets up five classes of claims entitled to priority on distribution. Claimants in a lower order of priority get nothing until everyone in the classes ahead have been paid in full. If there's not enough to pay every one within the same class, then whatever there is will be split up among the members of the class on a pro rata or proportional basis. Here are the five priority classes:

(1) Administrative costs (this takes in almost every expense in connection with the proceeding including fees for the attorney of the bankrupt, the trustee, the petitioning creditors, and the receiver, and commissions for the trustee and receiver);

(2) Wage claims up to the amount of $600 earned within three months (vacation and severance pay may present problems);

(3) Costs and expenses incurred by *creditors* in successfully opposing a discharge or getting it set aside or in getting evidence resulting in conviction of a bankruptcy offense;

(4) Tax claims — federal, state and local — all stand on an equal footing within the class (taxes accruing during bankruptcy will normally be within the first class);

(5) Debts having priority under federal law and rent claims entitled to priority under state law.

The Federal government and its sureties seem to be the only ones entitled to priority under federal law; it's still an open question whether federal agencies such as FHA or VA come within the law and the decisional law in this area must be checked for further developments. Rent claim priority is limited to three months' rent due and owing for actual use and occupancy, thus knocking out claims based on an acceleration clause in the lease.

[¶606]　　　　　　　　LIENS AND PRIORITIES

It must be understood that before you get to any question of priorities, as a general rule all claims based on valid liens or other types of security interests in the bankrupt's property will have been satisfied out of the property or the proceeds of the property subject to the lien or security interest. All liens and interests in property of the bankrupt, except those struck down under the rules discussed above under ¶603.3 "*Transfers Voidable as to Any Creditor*," and ¶603.4 "*Avoidance of Preferences*," that is, fraudulent conveyances, preferences and transfers void or voidable under federal or state law, will be upheld as valid. Here again we would draw attention to the discussion of statutory liens in connection with the discussion of "*Avoidance of Preferences*." Specifically, it should be borne in mind that §67(h) upholds statutory liens in favor of employees, contractors, mechanics and landlords, and federal and state liens for taxes or debts even though they might otherwise fall within the proscription of §60, the preference section. But at the same time you have to bear in mind that under §67(c) these statutory liens, if asserted against personal property and not accompanied by possession of the property before bankruptcy, will be subordinated to priority claims for administrative expenses and wages. Also, remember liens for wages and rent are limited in amount by §64.

[¶607]   GETTING DEBTS DISCHARGED

From the bankrupt's viewpoint, the discharge of his debts is the most important feature of the entire proceedings. He's entitled to a discharge as a matter of right unless proper objections are made and sustained. For everyone but a corporation, adjudication operates as an automatic application for a discharge. A corporation has to file an application within six months of adjudication otherwise it will lose its right to a discharge, but this isn't too important in the case of a corporation because it usually goes out of business anyway, and in practice corporations rarely apply for discharges.

[¶607.1]   Grounds for Objecting to or Denying Discharge

There are seven grounds for objecting to and denying a discharge:

(1) Commission of criminal bankruptcy offense at any time in any bankruptcy proceeding;

(2) Failure to keep or preserve books or records showing financial condition and business transactions;

(3) Obtaining money or property on credit by false financial statement (applies only to those in business as sole proprietor, partner or corporate executive);

(4) Fraudulent conveyance or concealment of property in year before filing of petition;

(5) Discharge in bankruptcy or confirmation of an arrangement or wage earner plan during six-year period before filing petition;

(6) Refusal to obey a lawful order of the court or to answer a material question approved by the court; and

(7) Failure to satisfactorily explain any loss or deficiency of assets.

We can sum up these seven grounds by saying that a discharge in bankruptcy is available only to an honest debtor who has kept adequate records, cooperated in the bankruptcy proceedings, and hasn't been through bankruptcy proceedings for more than six years. Therefore, the debtor who looks to bankruptcy as a way out of his financial problems, as a way to get a fresh start free from his present debt burdens, had better make sure that he qualifies for a discharge, and will continue to qualify by cooperation in the proceedings, before he decides to file a voluntary petition. Otherwise, he'll only wind up with more debts than when he started, fewer assets and an even worse credit rating.

〔¶607.2〕 What Debts and Liabilities Continue After Discharge?

A discharge won't relieve a bankrupt of all prior obligations. Here's a list of those that survive:

(1) Claims not provable, such as certain tort claims, fines and penalties;

(2) Taxes—generally, federal, state or local, owing within three years preceding bankruptcy;

(3) Liability for obtaining money or property by false pretenses or representations;

(4) Liability for willful and malicious injuries to the person or property of another;

(5) Alimony and support payments;

(6) Liability for seduction;

(7) Debts not scheduled;

(8) Fraud or embezzlement by the bankrupt while acting as a fiduciary;

(9) Wages earned within three months prior to bankruptcy;

(10) Sums due employee by bankrupt employer under contract authorizing retention of sums to secure faithful performance of employment contract.

It should be pointed out in connection with item (7), debts not scheduled, that a creditor who is aware of the bankruptcy proceeding can't just sit back and be sure his claim is not going to be wiped out by bankruptcy simply because he's not listed in the schedules. Proof that he knew of the proceeding and did nothing may operate to make the discharge effective against him. In connection with item (9), bear in mind that wages earned within three months have priority to a limited amount, and what we are talking about here is survival of the obligation to pay the balance.

If the claim was one which was based on the extension of a credit induced by a false financial statement in writing, the unsecured creditor would have a non-dischargeable claim. The Act also says that, in certain cases where a false financial statement in writing has been given by one engaged in business, that is a basis for opposing the discharge in bankruptcy. However, your creditor-client must file a timely application with the bankruptcy court (which now has exclusive jurisdiction). Otherwise, the debt will be discharged.

•

For Further Reference . . .
American Jurisprudence, Bankruptcy.
Collier, *Bankruptcy* (9 vol.).
Herzog, *Bankruptcy,* Matthew Bender, New York, N.Y.
Hirsch and Krause, *Bankruptcy and Arrangements Under Chapter XI of the Bankruptcy Act,* Practising Law Institute, New York, N.Y.
Mulder, John E., *Bankruptcy and Arrangement Proceedings,* Joint Committee on Legal Education.

BROKERAGE

[¶701] The broker's right to a commission will depend upon the type of contract that he has made with the seller (who ordinarily would be his principal). The general type of an arrangement can vary from an open listing to an exclusive agency or an exclusive right to sell. Somewhere in between is the conditional agency, where the owner of the property conditions his liability for commission on some specific event or perhaps on the ultimate closing of the deal.

For forms in this area, see IBP FORMS OF BUSINESS AGREEMENTS.

[¶701.1] **When is the Commission Earned?**

Unless the owner has set some additional condition in hiring him, the broker is entitled to his commission when he can show the following:

(1) The broker's services were performed during the specified time of the agency.

(2) The deal was consummated (if that was a condition of the broker's rights to a commission).

(3) The broker produced a buyer ready, able, and willing to buy.

(4) There was a meeting of minds between the two parties.

(5) The broker was the procuring cause.

Ready, Able, and Willing: In order to be ready, able, and willing, the purchaser must be, "ready, able and willing" to satisfy the conditions which have been specified by the owner. But if the broker has brought the parties together and they make a different contract from the one which the broker was employed to obtain, the broker will still be entitled to compensation. "Ready" means that the buyer will execute a contract of sale. "Able" means that the buyer will be able to get up the necessary funds to close the deal within the time required. He must have the money to meet the cash payment and be able financially to meet later installments. "Willingness" is the voluntary act of the purchaser without any compulsion or coercion. Under these definitions, the purchaser who is insolvent and who has failed to deposit a required security is not ready, able, and willing.

Meeting of the Minds: The parties have to agree on all the terms of the transaction of sale. This will include, among other things, the purchase price, the amount of the purchase money mortgage, the date, time and place of taking title, form of deed, adjustments, cancellation provisions on default, and the physical condition of the property and subject clauses as to liens, encroachments, assessments, covenants, leases, etc. But an agreement between the parties on terms which are different from those which were originally given to the broker will not prevent the broker from obtaining his commission if he was

41

the procuring cause of the buyer and if negotiations which he began ended in an executed contract. But if the parties negotiate on different terms than those given to the broker and do not reach agreement the broker has no rights. (Of course, if the broker has produced a buyer willing to meet all of the seller's terms, and the agency is an exclusive one or the broker beats out other brokers under an open listing arrangement, the broker is entitled to his commission even if the deal does not go through because the seller does not want to sell.)

Consummation of the Transaction: This will be important where the broker's right to a commission has been conditioned upon the final conclusion of the transaction. Here, again, if the deal goes through the broker is entitled to his commission even if the parties have changed the terms from those which were originally given to the broker. Or, if the deal does not go through because of default on the part of the owner, in bad faith, the broker is entitled to his commission. In an exclusive agency or an open listing, where the broker's right to a commission has not been conditioned upon the final conclusion of the transaction, the broker will get his commission even if the purchaser fails to carry out the deal after having made a valid contract.

Procuring Cause: The broker has to show that his efforts were the primary and direct cause of the consummation of the transaction. For example, if someone finds out that the property is for sale and purchases it without ever meeting, talking to, or having any business with the broker, the broker is not the procuring cause of the sale. But if the broker had an exclusive right to sell, procuring cause would not enter into the brokerage situation and he would be entitled to his commission regardless of how the sale took place. Or in the case of an exclusive agency, the broker gets his commission even if the employer hired another broker who actually sold the property, since here the owner broke a contract he made to sell only through this broker.

To establish that he was the procuring cause the broker can show: that he advertised the property; that he introduced the parties; that he was the first to call the purchaser's attention to the property; that he was continuously engaged in the transaction by correspondence or conversations.

If several brokers were involved, if there was a disagreement between the parties after the first broker brought them together and later a second broker came in and got the parties to agree, the second broker is the procuring cause. However, the first broker is a procuring cause if he brought about a substantial agreement and the second broker worked out details.

●

For Further Reference . . .

American Jurisprudence, Brokers.

Forms of Business Agreements looseleaf Service. Institute for Business Planning, Englewood Cliffs, N.J.

Real Estate Desk Book, Institute for Business Planning, Englewood Cliffs, N.J.

Van Buren, Dewitt, *Real Estate Brokerage and Commissions.*

BUSINESS CONTROL

[¶801] Those associating themselves to invest in or manage a business will look to the lawyer for advice on how they can best protect the association from intrusion or unwarranted participation by additional unknown parties and how each individual participant can be protected from oppression by some combination of the others. This gets down to how the enterprise will be governed, what limitations can and reasonably should be placed on the majority, what limitations will be placed upon the participants in the transfer of their interest to others, what opportunity or what right each participant will have if things should take a turn where a participant wants to get out of the venture and recover his investment, what assurance the participants can properly obtain as to the opportunity they will have to serve the business and the benefits they will obtain.

These questions are likely to be raised in either a partnership or a corporate venture. In a partnership venture, they will be determined primarily by the partnership agreement. In a corporate venture, they will be determined by a combination of provisions of the corporate charter, the corporate bylaws, a supplementary agreement between the stockholders and, possibly, by loan agreements, employment contracts and other agreements running from the corporation to a particular stockholder. The lawyer will be expected to put together a package of agreements, charter and bylaw provisions which carries out the mutual intent of the participants as to their rights and obligations.

More important than drafting the necessary instruments is the process of pointing out to the participants the various kinds of relationships, assurances and undertakings which might be appropriate to the venture they contemplate and leading them to the necessary decisions.

One decision which the lawyer will have to make primarily will be, once the objectives have been hammered out, whether to place the necessary protective provisions in the charter, in the bylaws, in a shareholders' agreement or in some combination of those instruments. This will depend on the kind of provisions which the state corporation law allows to be inserted in the charter, the attitude of the local courts toward restrictive and management charter provisions, the importance of keeping such provisions confidential, which would be possible in a supplementary agreement or a bylaw but not in a corporate charter which becomes a public instrument open to public inspection. He will also consider that it is easier to amend or repeal a bylaw provision than a charter provision. Of paramount importance is the fact that it is usually possible for less than all of the stockholders to amend or revoke a charter or bylaw provision whereas an agreement between stockholders can protect each stockholder individually and, unless otherwise provided in the agreement, the consent of each individual will be necessary to alter or amend the rights and obligations created by the agreement. It has sometimes been successfully contended that a by-law provision amounted to a contract between the parties so that repeal or modification by a simple majority, or whatever percentage is permitted by either charter or state law, could not be accomplished. But this is dubious, and a contract is much less vulnerable to change without unanimous agreement. For forms in this general area, see IBP FORMS OF BUSINESS AGREEMENTS.

[¶801.1] Checklist of Business Control Provisions

Here is a checklist of the provisions which should be considered in developing a scheme for control of a business and the protection of individual participants:

1. Obligation to Commit Additional Capital: This can be accomplished in a shareholders' agreement or partnership agreement or an enforceable subscription agreement which is in writing and otherwise complies with the requirements of the appropriate local law.

2. Restrictions on Transfer of Interest: An absolute restriction may be defeated by the prohibition against unreasonable restraint on alienation of property interests. However, an obligation to give others an option or the right of first refusal is both common and enforceable. This will most usually be accomplished by an appropriate clause in the agreement and a marking of the stock certificates so that anyone who acquires in violation of the restriction will be on notice.

Forms of restrictions on transferability can be found in IBP FORMS OF BUSINESS AGREEMENTS.

3. Employment and Salary Commitments: Any commitments with respect to employment and salaries are usually provided for in an agreement between the parties. This can be specified in a shareholders' agreement or partnership agreement or in a separate contract between the affected individual and the particular entity. Care must be exercised to avoid making commitments of this character so rigid that they will impair the conduct of the business operation, or so specific that they impinge on the authority of the directors in the election of officers, etc.

Forms of salary provisions can be found in IBP FORMS OF BUSINESS AGREEMENTS.

4. Voting Provisions: Sometimes the participants in a venture are so distrustful of each other that they want assurance that things will go the way it is originally contemplated, and that a mere majority will not have the right to make alternative decisions. There are these mechanisms to accomplish this kind of an objective:

(a) Fixing of voting rights — providing for voting and nonvoting stock, providing that a nonvoting stock will acquire voting rights if certain contingencies occur, providing for cumulative voting in order to assure minority representation, staggering the election of directors so that there cannot be a complete turnover of control in any one election—these are methods of setting up voting rights in the charter and the fixing of the characteristics of the stock in order to influence control.

(b) Contractual obligations—the shareholders' agreements can require participants to vote their stock in a specified manner on a specified issue. For example, all the parties can be required to vote their stock for the election of each of the parties as a director.

(c) Voting trust—the parties can be entered into a voting trust under which some of them are designated as voting trustees and there can be an agreement among them as to the exercise of their voting rights.

(d) Irrevocable proxies—some state corporation laws explicitly recognize the validity of an irrevocable proxy issued to a person designated in an agreement. Other state laws permit the granting of an irrevocable proxy as long as it is "coupled with an interest." State law has to be carefully checked before approving the use of an irrevocable proxy.

(e) Charter provisions — depending on state corporation law, it may be possible to provide quorum requirements or a requirement that all or a specified majority of the shareholders vote in order to approve specified corporate acts. To insure the continued effectiveness of such a requirement in a corporate charter, be sure that amendment of the corporate charter is similarly restricted.

For forms in this area, see IBP FORMS OF BUSINESS AGREEMENTS.

5. Deadlock Provisions: Either the agreement or the corporate charter can provide for arbitration, dissolution or a rejectable offer technique in the event of disagreement which impedes the operation of the corporation. The rejectable offer technique provides that a party who is dissatisfied can offer his stock to the other party at a price, and if the other party doesn't buy then the party making the offer has the right to buy the stock of the party rejecting the offer at the price specified in his offer.

[¶802]   CORPORATE BUY-SELL AGREEMENTS

Participants in a new venture will usually want an agreement which will require that on the death or departure of one of them, the survivors will have an opportunity to buy his interest.

There are these basic kinds of buy-sell agreements:

(1) The corporation (if it cannot, then the surviving shareholders) must buy and the estate of a deceased shareholder is obligated to sell.

(2) First the corporation, then the surviving shareholders, have an option to buy the stock of a deceased stockholder and, if this option is exercised, the estate is obligated to sell.

(3) The estate of a deceased stockholder has the right to offer the stock to the survivors or to the corporation and if it does, either the survivors or the corporation are obligated to buy.

(4) There is no obligation either to buy or sell, but if a stockholder or his estate wants to sell, the stock must first be offered to the other stockholders or to the corporation before it can be sold to an outside party.

Forms of buy-sell agreements can be found in IBP FORMS OF BUSINESS AGREEMENTS.

[¶802.1] Stock Retirement or Cross Purchase

Should the corporation purchase the stock of a deceased stockholder or should the purchase be made by the survivors? In making this critical decision we must consider these aspects:

(1) Source of Funds—The stock retirement plan permits the use of corporate funds. The cross purchase plan requires the use of funds which the stockholders have presumably taken out of the business and on which an individual income tax is payable.

(2) Enforceability—A cross purchase agreement is clearly valid and enforceable while a stock retirement plan may not be enforceable if the corporation has or may have insufficient surplus to make the purchase and state law requires that stock may be redeemed only out of surplus. This potential deficiency in the stock retirement plan can be met by having the agreement provide that the survivors will either purchase or contribute sufficient surplus to the corporation, in the event that the corporation is prevented from retiring the stock of a deceased stockholder by state laws requiring that such purchases be made only out of surplus. In drafting the stock retirement agreement, the corporation should first be required to increase its available surplus by reducing its required capital or by increasing its capital to reflect a value for unrealized appreciation in assets. If this is insufficient and the survivors cannot either purchase or contribute additional funds to permit the corporation to meet the surplus requirement, the decedent's legal representative can be given the right to demand that the corporation be liquidated. These supplementary steps will make the stock retirement plan sufficiently valid and enforceable.

(3) Complication in Ownership of Insurance Policies—If the plan is to be funded by insurance, the stock retirement plan requires only one policy on each stockholder and permits the corporation to have continuous ownership of that policy. In the cross purchase plan each stockholder has to carry insurance on

the lives of the others. Transfer of the policy from the estate of a deceased stockholder to the surviving stockholders will result in the loss of the income-tax exemption when these policies mature by death—unless the policies are transferred to those who are insured by the policies or to the corporation in which the insured is a shareholder or officer (IRC §101(a)(2)).

(4) Cost Basis of Stock—In the stock retirement plan, the value of the stock of the survivors is generally increased when the corporation retires the stock of a deceased shareholder. However, the cost basis of the stock of the survivors remains the same. Thus a latent capital gains tax liability is built up. On the other hand, in the cross purchase plan, when the survivors purchase the stock of a deceased shareholder they step up the basis of the stock to the price at which they buy.

(5) Shift of Control—In the stock retirement plan, the proportionate interest of the survivors automatically remains the same when the corporation buys in the stock of a deceased shareholder. For tax problems in retiring stock, see ¶901.5.

[¶802.2] How to Make the Purchase Price Binding for Estate Tax Purposes

The price set in a mandatory buy and sell agreement will be controlling for federal estate tax purposes if these requirements are met:

(1) The agreement is bona fide and entered into at arm's length.

(2) The price has to be reasonable at the time the agreement is executed. The test is not whether the price is fair and reasonable at the time the agreement becomes operative. It is recognized that both parties have carried the risk that they will be bought out by the other at the price at which they have agreed.

(3) Disposal of the stock during the lifetime of the parties must be either prohibited during life or restricted so that a stockholder cannot sell during life without first offering the stock to the other party at no more than the price established in the agreement to apply at death. If the option is in the estate of the deceased stockholder or if the estate is merely obligated to make a first offer to the survivors, the price in the agreement has no effect for estate tax purposes. The regulations provide that the price must be bona fide (Reg. §20.2031-2(h); 20.2031-3(c)).

[¶802.3] How to Set the Price

Actually, the valuation formula of close corporation stock is usually the most controversial factor in drafting any buy and sell agreement. A proper valuation is essential:

(1) Fixed Price Method—This is the most common method. The stockholders set a fixed price per share in the buy and sell agreement, and leave room for revising this price, with the controlling price to be the last price stated prior to the death of the first stockholder. For example, the agreement may provide for a new price to be set annually at the close of the year. However, experience has shown that often the annual revaluation is never made. This raises the danger of an unfair depressed or inflated price being used. A possible solution is to use this method in conjunction with the appraisal method, and to provide in the contract that if no revaluation was made within fourteen or more months prior to the death of a stockholder, the price of the stock will be determined by appraisal. Another way is to provide that the last agreed price is to be automatically adjusted by increases or decreases in earned surplus.

(2) Appraisal Method—Price is left open for future appraisal. The buy and sell agreement provides that value be determined at the death of the first stockholder by a disinterested appraiser.

(3) Net Worth or Book Value Method—Valuation is based on the corporation's last balance sheet prepared prior to the death of the first stockholder, and the net worth is adjusted to the date of death. Or the company's accountants may be required to determine book value as of the date of death. Neither way is adequate, since neither reflects the true value of the business as a going concern, including the earning power of intangible assets like good will. The use of a stated formula, based on net worth, usually corrects this shortcoming. When this method is used the following items should be considered:

(a) *Inventory.* Will it be figured at cost or its real worth?

(b) *Accounts Receivable.* Will there be uncollectible accounts and what percentage of these does not show up in the book figures?

(c) *Machinery and Equipment.* Does the present book figure fairly reflect the present worth? Has it become obsolete?

(d) *Buildings.* Does book figure reflect current market value? Real estate is sometimes carried on books at cost and then depreciated substantially.

(e) *Insurance Proceeds.* If the company is to buy up the interest of the deceased associate and if there is insurance payable to the company, are the proceeds to be considered in determining book value?

(4) Straight Capitalization Method—The corporation's average net profits are capitalized at a specific rate, say 10%, and the result reflects the total value of the business including good will. The buy and sell agreement usually calls for averaging the net profits for the last five years immediately preceding the death of the first stockholder, after which they are capitalized at the 10% rate. The resulting total value is then divided by the number of outstanding shares to determine the value per share. Adjustment must be made to reflect the absorption of profits in the form of stockholders' salaries, or the average net

profits will be distorted. The multiple at which the profits are capitalized will depend upon the nature of the business and the history of the particular corporation involved.

(5) Years' Purchase Method —This also relies on average net profits. The book value is averaged over a stated number of years, usually allowing a fair return of 6%. This is then subtracted from the average net profits, and the remainder which represents excess earnings is multiplied by the stated number of years' purchase to arrive at the value of good will. This good will is then added to the book value to determine the total value of the business, and the corresponding value per share of stock.

(6) Combination of Methods—A combination of different valuation methods is sometimes used to overcome the shortcomings of one or the other method.

[¶802.4] Payment of Purchase Price

The agreement must specify how and when the price is to be paid. The plan must provide for the source of the funds. Life insurance on the stockholders will produce the necessary funds when they are needed. The excess of the total price over the insurance proceeds and other free cash available can be made payable on an installment basis. This obligation should be evidenced by notes and secured by the interest being purchased. Additional security can be provided in the form of mortgages on assets or additional insurance policies. Provide the right to prepay the obligations and for acceleration of the full obligation in the event of default of payment, bankruptcy or sale of the business and other specified contingencies.

[¶803]   HOW TO WORK OUT A PARTNERSHIP
BUY-SELL AGREEMENT

(1) Spell out the obligation of the survivors to buy the deceased's interest and the obligation of the estate of the deceased to offer the interest for sale on the agreed terms. You may want to set up an option on the part of either the survivors or the estate; but in most cases, you'll probably want a binding obligation to go through with the sale.

(2) The partners individually, the partnership (where it is going to make the purchase), the partners' wives (in some cases; and definitely, in community property states), and the trustee (if one is used) should all be parties to the agreement. The buy-sell agreement can be part of the partnership agreement or it can be incorporated into a separate agreement.

(3) As to how to fix prices for the partnership interest, see ¶4101 et seq. Also keep in mind the problems of valuing good will and the significance of putting

a value on it in the agreement. And spell out how the purchase price is to be paid. Keep in mind here that payments can be made, in effect, deductible by the partnership (and ordinary income to deceased's beneficiaries) or nondeductible to the partnership (and capital gain or nontaxable to the beneficiaries). See IRC §736.

(4) Spell out what life insurance is to be acquired, who is to hold it (entity or cross purchase), the kind of policies to be acquired, how the premium burden is to be shared (where entity insurance is used), how the policies on the survivors held by the deceased are to be transferred.

(5) Provide for releasing estate of deceased of obligations of partnership after the partnership interest of deceased is bought.

(6) Where insurance is used, agree on who should hold the individual policies —an escrow agent, keep in safe deposit box? Require notice to other partners before any partner can exercise any rights under the policies he holds. Consider use of trustee to hold the policies and carry out the terms of agreement. For tax problems see ¶901.6.

Forms of buy-sell agreements between sole proprietor and employee can be found in IBP FORMS OF BUSINESS AGREEMENTS looseleaf Service.

●

For Further Reference . . .
Corporate Planning, Vol. 3, Closely-Held Corporations, Institute for Business Planning, Englewood Cliffs, N.J.
Hornstein, *Corporation Law and Practice,* West Publishing, St. Paul, Minn.
O'Neal, H., *Close Corporations.*
Willis, *On Partnership Taxation,* McGraw-Hill Book Company, New York, N.Y.

BUSINESS INSURANCE

[¶901] Whether a corporation is redeeming some stock or the surviving stockholders are buying a deceased stockholder's interest (or surviving partners are buying the deceased partner's partnership interest), cash is needed. The difficulty of accumulating the cash needed to buy a business at an adequate price, or to finance retention of a business, has become so great that it may be necessary to use more than one method. Here is a checklist of possibilities:

(1) Life insurance is the fastest and least costly method of introducing new cash into the picture. For relatively small annual payments we can get a guarantee that additional cash will become available on a tax-free basis at the maturing of the death tax liability and the family cushion requirement.

(2) Co-owners or employees can commit to buy all or some of the deceased's interest at his death. Their ability to pay can be assured by their carrying insurance on the owner's life.

(3) The corporation can redeem some of the deceased's interest. Here, again, the corporation might carry insurance on the owner's life so that the cash will be available.

(4) It may pay to transfer personally owned insurance to a corporate business and have the corporation pay future premiums so that the owner's family can use the premium money to build a family cushion. When the insurance proceeds mature to the corporation, they can be used to redeem stock passing to the estate.

For help in working out the type of arrangements which may be funded by life insurance, see ¶801 et seq.

Forms for business insurance are to be found in IBP FORMS OF BUSINESS AGREEMENTS.

[¶901.1] **How to Handle Policies and Premiums**

The lawyer will have to decide whether policies should be applied for, owned, and paid for by:

(1) Partners and stockholders on the lives of fellow partners and stockholders, or

(2) The partnership or corporation on the lives of partners or stockholders.

In either case, the owner will be named in the policy as a beneficiary. This decision will depend on the design of the plan for the retirement of stock or partnership interests. See ¶4101 et seq.

It is important for the lawyer to bear in mind that premiums paid for life insurance are not deductible, and that insurance proceeds are not taxable income unless they have been transferred for value so as to run afoul of IRC §101(a)(2). If the corporation should pay premiums on policies owned by

52

stockholders, this will constitute taxable income to the stockholders and may be deductible by the corporation if the effect of the payment is that of additional compensation.

Insurance proceeds may pass into the hands of a beneficiary free of estate tax if the insured has no attributes of ownership in the policy. See ¶3209.1.

[¶901.2] Trusteed Buy-Sell Agreement

Legal ownership of the insurance policies is in an impartial trustee, who distributes the proceeds and the deceased's stock. The policies may be taken out by the corporation, by the stockholders on their own lives, or by the stockholders on the lives of each other in criss-cross fashion. The procedure is not unlike that described above, except that the trustee is designated the beneficiary for the purpose of effectuating the agreement.

In general, the trusteed agreement will be advisable where there is a relatively large group of owners or where there may be valuation or distribution problems. The trustee may be given the right to fix valuation of the interests under a formula provided in the agreement. With a trustee there is no problem of reassigning or transferring policies after the death of one owner. And there is no problem of including the value of the proceeds of the decedent's policy in corporate assets in order to value decedent's interest.

A variation under this type of agreement is to permit the trustee to hold the policies and the stock and to distribute both to the appropriate persons at the death of one of the owners. The trustee is not the designated beneficiary of the policy and the proceeds may or may not be paid to the estate of the deceased. The heirs or other persons designated as beneficiaries may elect one of the settlement options. Though this plan does provide for the transfer of stock to the survivors, it may not provide the estate with cash. So if liquidity is one of the considerations in setting up the buy-sell agreement, this type of arrangement isn't feasible.

Forms for trusteed buy-sell agreements are to be found in IBP FORMS OF BUSINESS AGREEMENTS looseleaf Service.

[¶901.3] Burden of Insurance Premiums

In the stock retirement plan, with the corporation buying the insurance, the cost of the premiums is pooled and allocated to the stockholders in the ratio of their stock interests. The older stockholders with the larger interests pay most of the premiums while the younger stockholders with the smaller interests, who stand to benefit most, pay a smaller proportion. This inequity can be evened out by including a portion of the proceeds of the policy on the deceased stockholder's life in the purchase price formula. In the cross-purchase plan, the younger stockholders pay a larger proportion of the premium because they have to carry enough insurance to buy out the largest stockholder and carry enough insurance to buy out the largest stockholder and they have to pay rates based on the ages of the older stockholders. Sometimes this burden is so great as to make the financing of any cross purchase plan impractical.

[¶901.4]   How Should Insurance Proceeds Be Reflected in the Price?

If the commitment of the corporation is funded with insurance on the stockholders' lives, the question will arise whether the policies must be included in the computation of corporate values in determining the price to be paid for the stock. To make this concrete — suppose we have a corporation owned in equal shares by four stockholders. The corporation had previously acquired $75,000 insurance upon the life of each owner. Upon the death of shareholder A, the worth of the corporation (not taking into consideration the proceeds of the insurance policy on A or any cash values built up in the other policies) is $300,000. But the corporation has now received an additional $75,000 in each. It also has the present values of the policies on the lives of shareholders B, C and D, which have not been included in fixing the price. If the estate of the decedent receives only $75,000, he is not getting any benefit out of the premium money paid by the corporation. But his corporate share bore one-quarter of the burden. He has made as heavy a contribution as any of the other parties. If he receives no benefit, the three survivors have acquired a corporation worth $300,000 plus the cash values of the policies on B, C and D. It would seem fairer that the decedent's estate should receive the same proportionate benefit as each of the others. Nevertheless, the parties must consider what the corporation has lost by the death of A. Its future earning capacity may be substantially decreased. The benefit of the insurance flowing only to the survivors may be justified on the theory that this may be necessary to offset the expected loss of corporate earnings for one or two or more years. The decision as to what to do will have to be made in the light of the particular circumstances in each case and it should be made only after a thorough exploration of the facts to arrive at a fair and equitable result.

Forms discussing insurance proceeds and price can be found in IBP FORMS OF BUSINESS AGREEMENTS.

[¶901.5]   How Corporate Insurance Proceeds Can Be Applied

Two types of arrangements are used: (1) the corporation redeems part or all of the deceased stockholder's stock; (2) the surviving stockholders buy up the deceased's stock. In either case, insurance can be used to provide part or all of the funds needed to make the purchase. Here are the special tax considerations to keep in mind:

(a) Insurance can be carried by the corporation on the lives of its stockholders. Or each stockholder can carry insurance on the lives of the others. In either case premiums are not deductible. In each case the proceeds will be received by the beneficiaries free of income tax. Where the corporation carries the insurance, the insured stockholders can name the beneficiaries if receipt of the proceeds is conditioned on the transfer of the deceased stockholder's stock to the corporation. In most cases, the corporation will receive the proceeds and then proceed to buy up the deceased's stock. Where each stockholder owns insurance on the other, the individual stockholders will receive the proceeds and use them to buy the stock.

(b) When the corporation buys up the deceased's stock, there is usually no dividend to the surviving stockholders (*Holsey,* 258 F.2d 865; *Rev. Rul. 59-286,* C.B. 1959-2, 103).

(c) If the corporation assumes the stockholders' liabilities to buy up the stock of the deceased (as where there was an original agreement calling for the surviving stockholders to purchase but they then had the corporation make the purchase), the stockholders whose liabilities are being taken over by the corporation can have a dividend (*Wall,* 164 F.2d 462). However, where there is a good business reason for the corporation to redeem the deceased's interests which the survivors were supposed to buy (e.g., to keep the stock from falling into outsiders' hands) and the remaining stockholders' proportionate interests are not changed by the redemption, some courts have said the redemption does not result in a dividend to the survivors (*Decker,* 6th Cir., aff'g 32 TC 326). It's also possible to avoid a dividend to the survivors — where the survivors are obligated to buy the deceased's stock and the corporation buys the stock instead — if the agreement permits the survivors to cause the corporation to be liquidated as an alternative to buying out the deceased's interest. See *Rev. Rul. 59-286, CB 1959-2, 103.*

(d) When a stockholder dies, his estate or heirs take as their basis for the stock its market value at date of death. So, normally, a complete redemption at that value does not involve a taxable gain or loss. In any event, however, a complete redemption would not constitute a dividend. IRC §302(b)(3).

(e) Since less than a complete redemption can result in a dividend, you have to watch out for the attribution rules — rules which attribute ownership of stock held by another to the one whose stock is being redeemed. For example, an estate is deemed to own the stock of its beneficiaries. So, if the estate's entire stock holding is redeemed but some of the beneficiaries of the estate also own stock in the corporation, the estate is deemed to own the beneficiaries' stock, and so there is no complete redemption. See *Lewis,* 35 TC 71. It may be necessary to get the stock into the individual beneficiaries' hands before the redemption to avoid the attribution rules. The individuals, however, can still be deemed to own stock held by partnerships, trusts, estates, and corporations in which they have an interest, or by partners, beneficiaries, and stockholders of those partnerships, trusts, estates and corporations. So, you must check the attribution rules of §318(a) very carefully.

(f) Even where there is a partial redemption, a dividend can be avoided. The usual method is to qualify under IRC §303. Under this section there is no dividend if the stock redeemed makes up more than 50% of the taxable estate or more than 35% of the gross estate *and* if the amount received does not exceed the total of the death taxes (state and federal) and funeral and administration expenses.

(g) Another form of partial redemption that escapes dividend treatment is the so-called disproportionate redemption. This occurs when after the redemption, the stockholder's total percentage of holdings in the corporation is less than 80% of what it was before the redemption. For example, if before the redemption the stockholder owned 50% of the corporation's stock, after the redemption he has to have less than 40% of the corporation's outstanding stock (80% of 50% is 40%). IRC §302(b)(2). Here, too, the attribution rules apply to determine how much stock a stockholder held both before and after redemption. And here, the attribution rules are broader than where there is a complete redemption. In addition to the attributions described above you also count stock held by family members—spouse, children, grandchildren and parents.

(h) Corporate accumulations beyond reasonable needs of the business may cause the corporation to pay a penalty tax. IRC §531. Accumulation to provide funds for corporate buy-outs have been approved as reasonable. See *Mountain State Steel Foundries,* CA-4 284 F.2d 737.

[¶901.6] How Partnership Insurance Can Be Applied

Just as with corporation buy-outs, two methods are used here, too: (1) the partnership itself redeems the partnership interest of the deceased; (2) the surviving partners buy out the deceased's interest. In either case, life insurance is usually used to supply part or all of the funds necessary to make the purchase. Here are the tax considerations involved in partnership buy-outs:

(a) Premiums on life insurance paid by the partnership or by the individual partners to underwrite a buy-out agreement are not deductible. But the insurance proceeds when received are not subject to income tax.

(b) When a partner dies, the value at date of death of his interest in the partnership (other than accrued income) becomes the basis to his estate or heirs. (This value of the income is also included in his estate; but when the income for the taxable year is paid out to his heirs, they are taxed on it and get an appropriate credit for the estate tax paid on that value.) So, the heirs are not taxed to the extent they get paid for the partnership interest in fixed assets and good will (provided the partnership agreement calls for a payment for good will), and the surviving partners get no deductions for these payments. See IRC §736.

for good will), and the surviving partners get no deductions for these payments. See IRC §736.

(c) In addition to a payment for the partnership interest, the agreement may call for a payment of a percentage of profits or guaranteed payments for a period of time to the deceased's estate or heirs. These payments are taxable to the recipient as ordinary income and are excluded from the survivors' income. Where the partnership has unrealized receivables or substantially appreciated inventory, payments allocable to these items are taxable to the recipient as ordinary income items rather than in payment for the partnership interest. See IRC §736. For other legal problems see ¶803.

•

For Further Reference . . .

Life Insurance Desk Book, Institute for Business Planning, Englewood Cliffs, N.J.

Life Insurance Planning (looseleaf service), Institute for Business Planning, Englewood Cliffs, N.J.

Mehr and Hedges, *Risk Management in the Business Enterprise.*

Rough Notes, *Policy Form and Manual,* Indianapolis, Ind.

Willis, *On Partnership Taxation,* McGraw-Hill Book Company, New York, N.Y.

BUSINESS ORGANIZATION

[¶1001] When a client wants advice on setting up a business, he will usually want to know the tax costs, the liability exposure and the practical convenience of the various forms in which the business might be conducted —partnership, corporation, corporation electing to be taxed as a partnership, etc.

As the risk of potential liability increases, whether from the nature of the business to be undertaken or from the extent of your client's possessions, the value of eliminating personal liability increases and the advantage of the corporate form increases correspondingly. The expense of the corporate form is not usually a matter of real significance.

Simplicity: If the venture is likely to be a stable one with little prospect of growth, there is a lot to be said for the sole proprietorship or, where there are several working together, the partnership form. Orders are easy to give. Formalities are easy to forget. And dissolution is available at the will of any partner at any time, so that he may freely make a new start in a new direction if he wishes, in the absence of any contract to the contrary. The very large number of firms that remain as partnerships is a sufficient demonstration of the workability and practicality of this simple method of doing business.

Organizational Flexibility: The corporate form permits great variation in operation and development. Greater or lesser powers may be conferred, for example, on a governing board of directors, with a larger or smaller number of members. Smaller working committees, with specified powers, may be established for particular purposes, whether overall management on an interim basis, like an executive committee, or special fields on a continuing basis, like a finance committee or a retirement committee. Departments may be created and branches established and offices created at various levels with supervisory personnel below them in any number of levels that the needs of the business may require. The modern corporate form has, in short, developed an almost unlimited flexibility of managerial organization. Its advantages increase in direct proportion to the size of the business involved.

Financing: In the early stages, financing will probably depend on the personal credit of the principals. They will have to endorse corporate paper. But if the business accumulates assets and shows earning power, it should be able to get credit without involving the principals. Further on in this development, the availability of corporate shares will be important in providing additional capacity to attract financing and liquidity for the interest of the owner.

Continuity: Continuity is assured through the corporate form better than through any other. An individual dies and a partnership terminates upon the death of a member. In each case a final accounting must be had with a determination of the current value of assets. As the size and complexity of the business increase, the burden of these steps becomes all the more oppressive. But a corporation continues no matter how many of its directors or officers or stockholders die. Its title to property remains unaffected and likewise its contracts. Stock transfers can be accomplished speedily and new elections can be held as needed. The corporation is the vehicle ideally suited for continuing a business beyond a single generation and this advantage grows in importance with the size of the business.

Transferability of Shares: If a business prospers, its owners will normally desire to distribute interests in it to their children over a period of years. This is not feasible in a sole proprietorship or in a partnership. It is, however, readily feasible through the corporate form by transfers of stock.

Good Will: If good will is likely to develop into an asset of substantial value, the corporate form is likely to be advantageous in accumulating good will and maintaining public identification.

Compensation Arrangements: The corporate form makes it possible to attract and reward talent with stock options, stock purchases, deferred compensation arrangements, participation of the owners in pension and profit-sharing plans, etc.

Estate Liquidity: The possible future sale of corporate shares and the possible creation of a public market hold the promise of easing estate liquidity problems. Even when this is not likely to occur, the corporate form may make the way easier to accumulate earnings and pay for insurance to facilitate the redemption of shares owned by a deceased stockholder.

Participation of Inactive Investors: The corporate form is the best medium for capital appreciation. On the other hand, a limited partnership may offer an investor a better route to participation in earnings because his share in earnings would not be burdened by a tax at the corporate level as in the case of dividends on common and preferred stock.

Splitting Income Among the Family: A family partnership may be the best way of splitting both income and capital values to both children and other members of the family.

[¶1002]   TAX FACTORS

The choice of the form for doing business will play an important and continuing role in determining the tax cost of doing business. Different forms will be indicated at different times. The basic strategic considerations are these:

(a) A new and risky business or one in which losses are sustained to build capital value should be operated in unincorporated form or in a going corporation so that any losses may be applied against income and offset with tax savings;

(b) A very small business may best be operated in unincorporated form to avoid double tax on corporate and dividend income;

(c) After we reach the 22% and 48% corporate rates in the individual brackets, the corporation is at least a temporary tax shelter;

(d) But unless we can continue to use earnings to expand the business, we will reach the point of double taxation as it becomes necessary to distribute dividends;

(e) In the corporate form we have a latent capital gains tax to pay when we cash in on accumulated earnings by liquidation or sale of stock. If stock is held until death and then sold by the family we avoid capital gains tax on the accumulation of earnings;

(f) Income can be brought into lower tax brackets by splitting it through a family partnership or by dividing operations between several entities, unrelated corporations or a combination of corporate and unincorporated entities;

(g) The division of income among more than one corporation (unless they are affiliated) can bring $25,000 into the 22% tax bracket and save $6,500 a year for each additional corporation;

(h) If the business is closely held (fewer than five stockholders at the last half of the taxable year) and close to 60% of the income will come from investment sources, care must be exercised to avoid the personal holding company penalty tax.

[¶1003]　　　PARTNERSHIP V. CORPORATION

The choice isn't limited to either incorporating or remaining a proprietorship. For instance, there is the alternative of operating as a partnership. Following is a comparison between the two forms—corporation and partnership —with respect to the factors that will be most important. The checklist covers first general considerations, then tax considerations.

[¶1003.1]　General Considerations

Partnership	Corporation
Life	
For the term specified in the partnership agreement; death of a partner may dissolve it earlier.	Continues until dissolved by law (unless statute limits the time).

Partnership	Corporation
Entity	
Has no separate entity from the partners.	Has entity separate from its stockholders. Can sue and be sued, hold and deal in property.
Liability	
General partners are individually liable for all partnership obligations; special partners usually liable only up to the amount of their capital contributions.	Stockholder has no individual liability; only his capital contribution is involved (exception: some state laws subject bank stockholders to double liability).
Changing Ownership	
Change in interests creates a new partnership. Other partners must consent. Arrangements necessary to end liability of ex-members.	Stock can ordinarily be sold or otherwise transferred at will.
Raising Capital	
Only by loan, by new membership or contributions of present members, or by remaking the firm.	By sale of new stock or bonds or other securities.
Making Policy	
Unanimous agreement of partners usually required involves problems of personality.	Authority centered in Board of Directors, acting by majority agreement.
Credit	
Depends on standing of individual partners; partnership interests usually can't be pledged.	As separate entity, has credit possibility apart from stockholders; in close corporation, stock is available as collateral.
Management	
By partners; they are responsible (except silent partners).	Stockholders not responsible; managers are employed.
Flexibility	
Partners have leeway in their actions except to the extent limited by the partnership agreement (occasionally by law).	Limited to the powers (express and implied) in its charter from the state; may be subjected to judicial construction.

61

[¶1003.2] Tax Considerations

Partnership	Corporation

Income Tax

Partners taxed on proportionate shares of partnership income whether or not distributed. Partnership return is merely an information return.

Income taxed to corporation; stockholders taxed only on dividends distributed to them, reduced by dividend credit.

Accumulation

Partners taxed on accumulated as well as distributed earnings.

Stockholders not taxed on accumulations. However, penalty tax applies if purpose is to avoid the tax on dividends distributions and accumulation exceeds certain amount.

Capital Gains and Losses

Partners taxed on their proportionate shares of gain and loss. They apply the limitations and the alternative method of computing just as if they had only individual gains and losses.

Uses the alternative computation too; but, unlike individuals, there is no deduction of 50% of the excess of long-term gain over short-term loss.

Exempt Interest

Partners not taxed on exempt interest received from the firm; however, credit for partially exempt interest received cannot exceed proportionate shares of partnership income.

Exempt interest distributed by a corporation would be fully taxable income to the stockholders.

Sick Pay

Partner isn't entitled to the limited tax-free treatment for accident and sickness pay from an employee's Accident and Health Plan under I.R.C. §105.

Regular employee gets limited tax-free treatment for his accident and sickness pay.

Charitable Contributions

The partners add their proportionate shares of the partnership's contributions to their own personal contributions in computing their incomes.

Corporations take their own deduction for charitable contributions; but the limitation is only 5% as against the individual limitation of 30% (20% for private charities).

Pension Planning

Partners are not proper beneficiaries of an exempt pension trust. Firm can't deduct payments for partners, except under Keogh plans.

Officer and employee stockholders can be beneficiaries of a pension trust. Corporation can deduct its payments to the extent allowed by law.

Partnership	Corporation
Social Security	
Partners don't pay Social Security tax on compensation from the firm, but must pay self-employment tax.	Compensation to officer and employee stockholders is subject to Social Security tax.
Assignment of Income	
Partner's interest can't be assigned except with the consent of all partners; new partnership may result.	Stockholder has freedom to assign his stock without consulting anyone; but earnings can't be assigned separately of the stock.
Death Benefits	
No exemption for payments to partner's beneficiaries.	Benefits up to $5,000 can be received tax free by stockholder employee's beneficiaries (§101).
State Taxes	
In most states, partnership not subject to state income and purchase taxes.	Corporations subject to these taxes, although deductibility on Federal return lessens cost.

[¶1004] OTHER ORGANIZATIONAL POSSIBILITIES

In addition to the usual choice of corporation or partnership, we have these possibilities:

(1) Limited Partnerships: These have all the legal and tax features of partnerships except that the liability of limited partners can be limited to the capital that they commit to the venture.

(2) Combination of Partnership and Corporation: A corporation can be set up to manufacture or perform some other function, for which limitation of liability or some other objective makes the corporation particularly suitable, and a partnership can sell or perform some other associated function. Here it is necessary to keep the price or commission rates charged on transactions between the corporation and the partnership on arm's length terms, supported by comparison with the terms of similar transactions between unrelated entities.

(3) Multiple Corporations: Tax savings can no longer be achieved through the use of multiple corporations. The Tax Reform Act of 1969 gradually eliminated the tax advantages of multiple corporations considered part of a controlled group. The result is that for taxable years beginning after December 31, 1974, a controlled group of corporations is to be limited to one $25,000 surtax exemption and one $150,000 accumulated earnings credit. But you may consider the possibility of escaping from the "controlled group" concept (two

or more corporations which are owned 80% or more [by voting power or value] by five or fewer persons provided these five or fewer persons identically owned more than 50% of each corporation).

Also, of course, there may be valid nontax reasons for using multiple corporations.

(4) Incorporate but Keep Certain Assets Out of the Corporation: Frequently it is desirable to keep a patent or piece of real estate out of the corporation and have the corporation make rental or royalty payments to the individual owner for that property. Here again caution is necessary to justify the rates of rent and royalty, particularly to stockholders. This arrangement offers an opportunity to take income out of the corporation on a deductible basis.

(5) Corporation Electing Not to Pay Corporate Tax: If there are to be ten or less stockholders and very little investment type income, the corporation may qualify under Subchapter S of the Internal Revenue Code, with the result that the corporation will retain all the legal advantages of limited liability, etc. Income tax at the corporate level will be avoided. The corporation must be domestic, all stockholders must be individuals or estates, none of whom is a nonresident alien. There can be only one class of stock outstanding. The corporation must not be a member of an affiliated group of corporations connected to a common parent, and all stockholders must agree to the Subchapter S election.

●

For Further Reference . . .

Tax Planning looseleaf Service. Institute for Business Planning, Englewood Cliffs, N.J.

Israels, *Corporate Practice,* Practising Law Institute, New York, N.Y.

Knapp and Semmel, *Forms of Business Organization and the Federal Tax Laws,* Practising Law Institute, New York, N.Y.

Rohrlich, C., *Organizing Corporate and Other Business Enterprises,* 3rd Ed., Matthew Bender, New York, N.Y.

Sarner, Leonard, and Shinehouse, George F., Jr., *Organizational Problems of Small Businesses,* Joint Committee on Legal Education.

COMMERCIAL PAPER

[¶1201] Notes and checks are governed by Article 3 of the Uniform Commercial Code and by Article 4 covering bank deposits and collections in all states but Louisiana. This chapter deals with all phases of the subject except the rights and liabilities of guarantors of commercial paper which is dealt with in ¶2906.

[¶1202] THE IMPORTANCE OF NEGOTIABILITY

Although negotiable instruments are not money, they often serve as convenient substitutes for money in our credit-system economy. They are contracts to pay money. But they have one important difference from a non-negotiable contract to pay money. Once they are negotiated in due course (i.e., passed on to a third party) they are not subject to the defenses for non-payment to which an ordinary contract may be subject.

[¶1203] TYPES OF PAPER

A promissory note is simply a written promise to pay a sum certain (i.e., generally a stated or determinable amount) at a future determinable time or on demand. It can take various forms—installment notes, collateral notes and mortgage notes are some examples.

A promissory note differs from a bill of exchange (i.e., a check or a draft). In a note, the maker — the person issuing it — promises to pay; in a bill of exchange, the maker or drawer orders the drawee or acceptor to pay (e.g., when a check is issued, the drawer orders his bank to pay).

Various forms of notes, including simple time and demand notes with interest, installment notes, judgment notes, and secured notes, are set out in IBP FORMS OF BUSINESS AGREEMENTS.

[¶1204] HOW TO MAKE A NOTE NEGOTIABLE

The following requirements must be met to make a promissory note negotiable (bear in mind that just about the same requirements must be met for all negotiable instruments):

(1) It must be in writing.

(2) It must be signed by the maker.

(3) It must contain an unconditional promise.

(4) It must promise to pay a sum certain in money.

(5) It must be payable on demand or at a certain fixed time.

65

(6) It must be payable to order or bearer.

[¶1204.1]   How to Make Sure You Have a Promise and That It's Unconditional

To be negotiable, a note must contain a promise. The mere acknowledgement of a debt won't do (*UCC §3-102(1)(c)*). That's why an "I.O.U." is not negotiable. However, an "I.O.U." which also contains a promise to pay can be negotiable.

What makes a promise conditional? UCC §3-105 makes it clear that the condition must be expressed in the note itself; an implied or constructive condition will not make a note conditional. The Negotiable Instrument Law (NIL) was not clear on that point; decisions under that law have held that implied or constructive conditions make the note conditional.

The following table indicates what the rule appears to be as to a number of possible recitals or statements that might be expressed in a note. The rule is given under the UCC.

Type of Provision in Note	Rule under U C C
Statement in note that it was given in exchange for an executory promise (i.e., one still to be carried out).	Not conditional; note is negotiable.
Promise to pay is expressly conditioned on carrying out executory promise.	Conditional; not negotiable.
Informational references—e.g., nature of the consideration given for the note; the transaction which gave rise to the note; promise to pay matures in *accordance with* or *as per* some transaction.	Not conditional; references to a separate agreement or that note arises out of the agreement are okay; similarly references to letter of credit under which notes are drawn are okay.
Statement that the note is *subject to* or *governed by* another instrument.	Conditional; not negotiable.
Recital of the security given in so-called title security notes.	Not conditional; negotiable.
Statement that note is to be paid from a particular fund.	Conditional; not negotiable.

TAX REDUCTION ACT OF 1975
Summary of Temporary and Permanent Provisions

This Desk Book contains all the latest permanent tax law changes up to and including the Tax Reduction Act of 1975 that are pertinent to the subject matter of the text. However, many of the provisions of this 1975 tax legislation are temporary in nature, intended only to provide an economic "shot in the arm" for one or two years at the most.

Some of these temporary changes will last no longer than a single taxable year beginning with calendar year 1975. A few others will expire at the end of taxable years beginning with calendar year 1976.

These temporary provisions will have no effect on the tax discussions in this Desk Book after their expiration. Therefore, the IBP Research and Editorial Staff has summarized the non-permanent provisions of the Tax Reduction Act of 1975 in this handy special supplement. It is suggested that this special supplement be retained even after the expiration of the described provisions: It will make a useful and concise historical reference.

In addition to the more complete coverage in the Desk Book, the permanent provisions of the Tax Reduction Act of 1975 have been summarized in Part II of this special supplement to provide a concise introduction to the permanent tax changes wrought by the 1975 Act.

I. Temporary Changes

The temporary alterations of the Tax Reduction Act of 1975, intended as short-term stimulants, are as follows:

Rebate of 1975 Individual Income Taxes

In 1975, taxpayers received a refund of 10% of their 1974 tax liability. However, because of several limiting qualifications, the rebates fell in four general categories:

(1) 1974 Tax Liability of Less Than $100: The amount of the rebate was the amount of the tax liability.

(2) 1974 Tax Liability of More Than $100 but Less Than $1,000: The amount of the rebate was $100.

(3) 1974 Tax Liability of More Than $1,000: The amount of the rebate was 10% of the tax liability, up to a maximum of $200. (Note, however, the additional limitation of paragraph (4), below.)

(4) Limitation for Adjusted Gross Income Over $20,000: Taxpayers who had a 1974 adjusted gross income (AGI) in excess of $20,000 had the amount of their rebates reduced as follows: The amount of rebate in excess of $100 they otherwise would have been entitled to was reduced by the ratio of the difference between their AGI and $20,000 over $10,000.

Tax Credit for 1975 Personal Exemptions

A $30 tax credit was provided for each personal exemption a taxpayer was entitled to claim for himself, his spouse, and his other dependents on his 1975 return. Exemptions for age or blindness did not result in a credit. The personal exemption tax credit offset 1975 tax liability dollar for dollar up to a maximum of a taxpayer's aggregate allowable credit.

Low-Income Allowance and Standard Deduction

The percentage standard deduction for 1974 was 15% of adjusted gross income (AGI), subject to an overall ceiling of $2,000 ($1,000 for married taxpayers who filed separate returns). For 1975 only, the Act increased the percentage standard deduction to 16% of AGI, subject to new ceilings of $2,300 for single taxpayers, $2,600 for married taxpayers filing jointly and surviving spouses, and $1,300 for married taxpayers who file separate returns.

The low-income allowance for 1974 was $1,300 ($650 for married taxpayers who filed separate returns). (The appropriate allowance figure is taken as a personal deduction regardless of how low income was.) For 1975 only, the Act increased the low-income allowance to $1,600 for single taxpayers, $1,900 for married taxpayers who file jointly and surviving spouses, and $950 for married taxpayers who file separate returns.

Special Filing Requirements for 1975: In order to reflect the standard deduction changes, the Act increased, in the following instances, the minimum income levels at which taxpayers had to file tax returns for 1975 income:

Taxpayer Class	Income Level Requiring Filing of Return	
	1974	1975
Married, separate return	$ 750	$ 750
Single	2,050	2,350
Surviving spouse	2,050	2,650
Single, age 65 or over	2,800	3,100
Married, joint return	2,800	3,400
Married, joint return, one spouse age 65 or over	3,550	4,150
Married, joint return, both spouses age 65 or over	4,300	4,900

Optional Tax Tables Revised: For 1974 and earlier years, IRS has prepared optional tax tables for taxpayers with $10,000 or less in income who claimed the percentage standard deduction or low-income allowance. In order to reflect the combination of changes in the Tax Reduction Act, the new law authorized IRS to issue new tables for use in computing 1975 taxes. Taxpayers who do not itemize their personal deductions and who have adjusted gross incomes of $15,000 or less must use the "optional" tables.

Earned Income Tax Credit

Low-income workers with dependent children who maintained a household in 1975 qualified for a tax credit of up to $400 on their 1975 income tax returns. The basic credit was set at 10% of earned income, up to $4,000. To the extent that adjusted gross income exceeded $4,000, however, the amount of the credit has to be reduced by 10% of the excess.

The credit was made available for either calendar year 1975 or fiscal years that began in 1975. Note, however, that the credit would not have been available to taxpayers who filed for a taxable year of less than 12 months.

The earned income tax was made refundable. That means that where the credit exceeds the amount of the taxpayer's tax liability, a refund will be made. Thus, taxpayers who otherwise would not be required to file a return for taxable year 1975 have to do so in order to receive a refund of this credit.

The following definitions are necessary to determine qualification for and computation of the earned income tax credit:

(1) Earned Income: Earned income for purposes of the credit includes wages, salaries, tips, other employee compensation, and self-employment net earnings. Community property income, pension and annuity distributions, and the earnings of nonresident aliens are disregarded.

(2) Maintaining a Household: This is defined as the taxpayer's providing a domestic, principal place of abode for himself and his child for whom he can claim a dependency exemption under Code §151(e)(1)(B).

Tax Credit for New Housing Purchases

Taxpayers who buy as a principal residence a single-family or mobile home, condominium, or cooperative were made eligible for a tax credit of 5% of the home's purchase price, up to $2,000, subject to the following operative dates:

Homes Built by Taxpayer: If a taxpayer started to construct his own home, the construction must have begun prior to March 26, 1975. In addition, the home must have been acquired and occupied after March 12, 1975, and before January 1, 1977. No work performed prior to March 13, 1975, can count for credit purposes.

Homes Not Built by Taxpayer: For all other homes, construction must have begun prior to March 26, 1975. In addition, title must have passed after March 12, 1975, and before January 1, 1977.

The following rules also apply to the credit:

● To qualify the home for the credit, the seller must have certified that the purchase price the buyer paid was the lowest price at which the home was ever offered for sale. An individual who gave a false certificate can be found liable for criminal and treble damage civil penalties.

● The basis for the credit is not always to be computed upon what was paid for the house. If the taxpayer had escaped recognition of gain on the sale of a previous residence, the amount of gain not recognized had to be excluded from the purchase price of the new home.

● The taxpayer can't get credit if the new home was purchased from certain specified relatives, or business entities and tax-exempt organizations in which the taxpayer is directly or indirectly related, or a trust in which the taxpayer has a beneficial or certain other interests.

● A taxpayer who sells his new house within three years from the purchase date (or, for taxpayers who built their own homes, the occupation date), will trigger recapture. This means he'll owe a tax equal to the amount of his credit. He'll escape recapture, though, if he purchases or constructs a new principal residence within the time period specified in amended Code §1034 and the combined holding period for both homes is at least three years. However, to the extent that the replacement residence costs less than the amount received for the sale of the home the credit was given on, recapture will occur as computed under the following formula:

$$\frac{\text{Adjusted sale price of old residence less purchase cost of new residence}}{\text{Adjusted sale price of old residence}} \times \text{tax credit allowed} = \text{recapture amount}$$

Increase in Investment Credit

Taxpayers were granted a 10% investment tax credit for qualified business property ("§38 property") acquired and placed in service between January 22, 1975, and December 31, 1976. This new rate is an increase in the regular credit of 4% for public utilities and 7% for all other taxpayers and provides benefits for eligible purchases for nearly a two-year period. Here are some additional rules applying to the investment credit changes:

☐ **Self-Constructed Property:** Property constructed by the taxpayer beginning prior to January 22, 1975, but completed thereafter qualifies for the higher credit to the extent that expenditures were incurred after that date.

☐ **Dollar Limitation Doubled:** During roughly the same period (i.e., for calendar years 1975/1976 and 1976/1977), the dollar limit for used investment credit property was doubled to $100,000 ($50,000 for a married taxpayer filing separately). For public utilities, the maximum limit was removed altogether for the same two years. Thereafter, the previous limit of $25,000 plus 50% of the tax liability in excess thereof is phased back in until it is in full effect in 1981.

☐ **Employee Stock Ownership Plan:** A corporation will have an additional 1% investment credit (for a total of 11%) if it contributes the extra percentage to an employee stock ownership plan (ESOP). Corporations that would use the extra 1% and elected to set up such a plan would in effect be funding a significant fringe benefit with the tax savings provided by the Treasury.

☐ **Recapture Impact:** Property qualifying for the special 10% or 11% credit in 1975 or 1976 is subject to recapture at the same rates.

Changes in Corporate Surtax

The table below shows the regular tax rates for corporations and what they will pay in 1975:

	Marginal Tax Rate	
Corporate Income	*Regular*	*1975*
0 - $25,000	22%	20%
$25,000 - $50,000	48%	22%
$50,000 and over	48%	48%

For large corporations, overall savings will be modest. Small businesses will have reaped a more significant savings.

Federal Welfare Recipient Employee Incentive Credit

A tax credit was made available to an employer of an individual who was:
(1) Hired after March 29, 1975;

(2) Hired after he had been receiving aid to families with dependent children (AFDC) for at least 90 consecutive days;

(3) Not replacing a person already employed;

(4) Not a migrant worker; and

(5) Not a close relative of his employer.

Such an employer is entitled to a credit amounting to 20% of the employee's full-time salary (to be calculated from his first day on the job but only deductible after 30 consecutive days of full-time work) until July 1, 1976, or twelve months, whichever comes first. The credit was made applicable for use against 100% of the first $25,000 of the employee's tax liability and 50% of the liability over $25,000. If the employee's work did not involve the employer's trade or business (example, full-time housemaid), the employer could use the 20% credit up to a maximum of $1,000 annually.

II. Permanent Changes

The following is a brief description of the principal permanent changes in both the personal and corporate tax provisions of the Tax Reduction Act of 1975:

Deduction for Child and Dependent Care

Effective with their 1972 returns, taxpayers had been able to take as an itemized deduction up to $400 per month spent for the care of children or disabled dependents that enabled the taxpayer to be gainfully employed. Principally, this measure has aided working mothers, married or not. One restriction, however, has greatly limited the deduction: It must be adjusted downward on a 50% basis as a taxpayer's adjusted gross income exceeds $18,000. Thus, for AGIs in excess of $27,600, the deduction was entirely eliminated.

The new law nearly doubles the adjusted gross income level at which the phaseout of the maximum deduction begins. Now the figure is $35,000. Thus, some deduction will be available for taxpayers whose adjusted gross incomes range as high as $44,600. The provision is effective with tax years beginning March 30, 1975, and thereafter.

Increase in Tax-Free Replacement Period on Sale of Principal Residence

Code §1034 allows the postponement of recognition of gain on a taxpayer's sale of his principal residence provided that he meets certain reinvestment conditions. This provision has been liberalized to allow nonrecognition of gain where and to the extent that a taxpayer uses the amount of the gain to acquire and occupy a new principal residence within 18 months before or after the sale.

Easing in Accumulated Earnings Rules

A corporation that accumulates its earnings unreasonably (in excess of its actual business needs) may face a penalty of 27-1/2% of the first $100,000 and 38-1/2% of the remainder. One advantage has been the "accumulated earnings credit," which reduces the amount so taxed, in effect establishing a minimum tax-free accumulation. This credit has been increased from $100,000 to $150,000.

Phaseout of Oil and Gas Percentage Depletion

The Act repeals the depletion allowance (actually an income exclusion computed as a percentage of gross income from oil or gas production) for oil and gas produced after December 31, 1974. There are two exclusions:

☐ **Certain Natural Gas:** The 22% rate was made to apply to (1) gas sold under a fixed contract in effect on February 1, 1975, but only if the contract provided for no adjustment in price based on the possible repeal of depletion or (2) regulated natural gas produced and sold before July 1, 1976, and without price adjustment after February 1, 1975.

☐ **Independent Producers:** Small, independent producers are exempted from the repeal. The definition depends on the average daily oil or gas production, measured in barrels per day or cubic feet of natural gas per day. Even for those who qualify for this exclusion, the percentage depletion is lowered to 15% over the period between 1981 and 1984. Where a taxpayer holds a partial interest (including a partnership or joint venture interest) in oil or gas property, his production equals the total production of such property multiplied by his percentage participation in the revenues from such property.

An Exception: The exemption for independent producers is not available to any producer who owns or controls a retail outlet for the sale of oil or gas products or who engages in certain refining activities.

A producer of any size will be affected by the phaseout of the allowance. Limited partners in many oil drilling ventures will not be affected, however, depending on the size of their interest.

Availability of Investment Credit for Progress Payments

Taxpayers may now utilize the investment credit as §38 property is paid for, even though the §38 asset is not actually placed in use, if the property takes two or more years to construct and has a useful life of at least seven years in the taxpayer's hands. The progress payment rules are phased in over a five-year period.

Type of Provision in Note	Rule under UCC
Same as above, but note is issued by a government, government agency, or government unit; or note is issued by a partnership, unincorporated association, trust or estate payable out of the entire assets of the issuer.	Not conditional; negotiable.

The following example summarizes the above rules:

S and B enter into a contract of sale for furniture. B issues a note payable to S in which he promises to pay S the purchase price of the furniture and the note recites that "this note is given in the purchase of furniture." It is negotiable under the UCC. If it has additional language to the effect that "the furniture is to be delivered three weeks from date," it would still be negotiable under the UCC. A statement that this note is "in accordance or as per the contract entered this date" would not affect negotiability. However if the note states that "this note is subject to or governed by the contract entered into this date," it would be non-negotiable under the UCC.

[¶1204.2] Promise to Pay a Sum Certain in Money

The fourth element of negotiability which we mentioned at the outset is that there must be a promise to pay a sum certain in money. The money part isn't apt to be of concern in commercial transactions, but the "sum certain" element can give rise to doubts if the note also calls for interest payments and, perhaps, has one rate before maturity and another after, or if it calls for a discount, if paid before a certain date, or an additional amount, if not paid before a certain date. Doubts may also arise where there's a provision for payment of costs and attorneys' fees. There may also be doubts where a note is payable in the United States in foreign currency, on the theory that no one knows what the exchange rate will be at the time of payment.

Basically, the rule for a sum certain is that a holder must be able to determine from the instrument itself—including any necessary computation—the sum payable. ·

The following checklists indicate what you can and cannot include in a ngeotiable note concerning the sum payable.

What You Can Include

(1) Payments to be made with stated interest or stated installments.

(2) Payments to be made with stated different rates of interest before or after default of a specific date.

(3) Payment to be reduced by a stated discount for early payment.

(4) Additional payment required if paid after maturity.

(5) Payment to be with exchange or less exchange, whether at a fixed rate or at current rate.

(6) Provision for acceleration of payment *(UCC §3-106)*.

(7) Provision for payment with costs of collection or attorneys' fees or both upon default *(UCC §3-106)*. But consult local law as to validity and enforceability of this type of provision. In any event, only reasonable fees will be allowed.

(8) Provision for payment in foreign money is okay under UCC §3-107. The UCC provides that *unless otherwise agreed,* an instrument payable in foreign currency "may be satisfied by payment of that number of dollars which the stated foreign currency will purchase at the buying sight rate for that currency on the day which the instrument is payable or, if payable on demand, on the day of demand."

What You Cannot Include

(1) A provision that interest be paid at the current rate. Since that is not known, the sum payable is not certain.

(2) A provision to pay, in addition to principal and interest, taxes levied on the paper. Decisions render a note with this type of provision non-negotiable. The UCC is silent.

[¶1204.3] When the Note Is Payable

One of the requirements for negotiability is that the note be payable on demand or at a fixed time.

Demand: A demand instrument is one payable at sight or on presentation or one in which no time is stated for payment. *(UCC §3-108.)* If you want a note to be payable on demand, make sure that dates which appear in the form don't make it payable at some definite date. Inclusion of the phrase "payable on demand" or "on demand promise to pay . . ." also removes ambiguity. Note that demand operates two ways: (1) It gives the holder the option to call for payment at any time. (2) It gives the maker the option to pay at any time.

Fixed Time: The UCC says "definite time." Under the UCC *(§3-109)* the time of payment is definite only if it can be determined from the face of the instrument. For example, under the UCC, a promissory note payable at a fixed period of time after the death of the maker or of some other person is not negotiable.

Acceleration: A provision for acceleration does not upset the requirement for payment at a definite time *(UCC §3-109(1)(c)).* Under the Code you can include acceleration clauses if you, as a holder of a note, feel insecure about its payment. When payment will become due, you can cause the note to become due right away. Under the NIL this could have made the note non-negotiable because, it was argued, the acceleration depended on the holder's whim or caprice; so the note could not be said to be payable at a fixed or determinable time. (See *Puget Sound State Bank v. Washington Paving Co.,* 94 Wash. 504, 162 Pac. 870 (1917).)

[¶1204.4] You Must Use Words of Negotiability

If you want a note to be negotiable, you must use so-called words of negotiability, that is, either "order words" or "bearer words." A note is payable to order when it is payable to the order or assigns of a named person or to him or his order. The Code expressly includes "assigns" (as equivalent to order) *(UCC §3-110).*

Which Form Should You Use? While both order and bearer instruments are negotiable, there's a legal difference between the two which dictates the use of an order instrument in most situations. The difference is that if a bearer instrument is lost or stolen and winds up in the hands of a bona fide purchaser for value, he can collect on it, whereas if it had been an order instrument, he couldn't collect, even though the endorsement of the payee had been forged.

On the other hand, a creditor who wants to dispose of commercial paper before maturity and is concerned about liability as an endorser might want to have the note payable to bearer so that he could dispose of it by delivery without endorsement. But as a practical matter he could do so only where the maker was of unquestioned financial worth.

When Do You Have a "Bearer" Note and When Is It "Order"? If your note meets the basic requirement of order paper, it may be payable to the maker, a payee not the maker, or two or more payees together or in the alternative. If you're going to make it payable to two or more payees, you should give thought to whether they're to be joint tenants with a right of survivorship or simply tenants in common, and use clear enough language to accomplish your intention.

The UCC provides that an order instrument may be payable to an estate, trust or fund *(UCC §3-110),* in which case it is payable to the representative or to his successor. The Code also provides that an order instrument may be payable (1) to an office or an officer by his title in which case it is payable to the principal, but the incumbent or his successors may act as the holder or (2) to a partnership or unincorporated association, in which case it is payable to the partnership or association and may be transferred by any person authorized by it. UCC §3-117 further provides that an instrument made payable to a named person with the addition of words describing him as an agent, an officer or fiduciary is payable to the principal.

It's clear that a note will be considered bearer paper if it's payable to: (1) Bearer; (2) A named person or bearer; or (3) Cash or the order of cash. Occasionally you'll see a note payable to "order of bearer." This usually happens where a printed form of order note is used and the word "bearer" is filled in where the name of the payee is intended to go. In such case some authorities had taken the view that you had an order note. The Code, however, rejects this view and makes it a bearer instrument.

Under the UCC in the case of a note payable "to the order of " the Code makes clear that it is to be treated as an incomplete instrument.

[¶1205]   NOTE PROVISIONS YOU MAY WANT TO INCLUDE OR AVOID

Although you meet all the requirements to make a note negotiable, as listed above, there are other provisions in a note that can give you special advantages you require or give you trouble if not handled properly.

Interest Rates — Usury: All but a few states have some kind of usury law which prohibits charging interest that's higher than the legal rate. In many situations, additional fees and other charges can be included, in addition to interest, without running afoul of the usury laws. And a number of states prevent corporations from pleading usury as a defense — so as to corporate makers in those states, there is no effective legal bar on the interest they can be charged.

In most states if more than the legal rate is charged, the note is void and the maker has a complete defense as to both principal and interest. In some states, just the usurious interest is forfeited. Under either type of state law, usury may be a criminal offense, and thus care should be taken in drafting notes to see that they comply with the usury laws. If you're dealing with a businessman from another state, and you send him a note for execution, check the usury laws in his state. The legal interest rate in his state may be higher or lower than the rate in yours.

Sale of Collateral: You can incorporate in a note a provision which will authorize sale of collateral by the holder of the note, without destroying negotiability of the note. Such a provision might be desirable if the maker of the note doesn't have an especially good credit rating—and so you require him to give collateral which you have authority to sell pursuant to the provision. Under the Code it may be made operative upon any default, including default in the payment of interest *(UCC §3-112(b))*. The Code also permits a clause containing a promise or a power to maintain or protect collateral, or to give additional collateral, whether on demand or on some other condition, which will not affect negotiability. See also *UCC §9-504.*

For forms of collateral notes see IBP FORMS OF BUSINESS AGREEMENTS.

Confession of Judgment: A provision for confession of judgment, if the amount owing is not paid when due, won't affect the negotiability of a note under the Code *(UCC §3-112(i)(d))*. However, in some states it's a misdemeanor to make or transfer a note with such a provision, and in many states the provision will be ineffective. Therefore, you have to check the applicable law—either the law of the state of the holder or that of the maker—to make sure you're not getting involved in a criminal offense or jeopardizing the validity of the entire note.

Waiver of Benefit of Any Law: A provision under which the obligor waives the benefit of any law intended for his benefit will not destroy negotiability under the UCC, although it might be invalid under local law. A waiver of the benefits of the Statute of Limitations, for example, is invalid under the law of many states. On the other hand, a waiver of presentment and notice of dishonor will universally be recognized as valid, and will be included in most notes as a matter of course.

Note Payable At a Bank: Often a note will be made payable at a named bank. When it is, does that mean that the named bank is ordered or authorized to pay it? The initial version of the NIL (§87) said "Yes," but the states adopting the NIL in many cases amended §87, and in a good many parts of the country where it wasn't amended the banks and the business community disregarded it in practice. In the Southern and Western states, when a note came in which was payable at the bank, the bank would ask for instructions from the maker. If the maker said "No, don't pay," the bank wouldn't pay. It treated the "No" as a revocation, equivalent to a direction to stop payment. In the Northeastern states, however, many banks followed the rule of §87 and treated the note as the equivalent of a draft drawn on the bank. Faced with this situation, the drafters of the Code thought it best to preserve the status quo, especially since notes are the main instruments involved (the Code section also takes in acceptances) and they rarely cross state lines. Hence, in §3-121, the Code sets forth alternative provisions. The first of these says that the note or acceptance is the equivalent of a draft drawn on the bank, payable when it falls due out of any funds of the maker or acceptor available for payment. The second says that the note or acceptance is not of itself an order or an authorization to the bank to pay it.

The essential counselling point is that if you're going to make or take a note payable at a named bank in another state, don't assume that it's going to mean the same thing in that state as it does in your own state, even though now both are UCC states.

[¶1206] **TRADE ACCEPTANCES AND BANK ACCEPTANCES**

Trade acceptances have already been defined as drafts drawn on the purchaser of goods and accepted by him. If instead of drawing the draft on the purchaser, it's drawn on the purchaser's bank which has agreed with the purchaser to accept on his behalf, then on acceptance by the bank you have what is known as a bank acceptance.

Here's how you might use a bank acceptance in foreign commerce: Let's say you're in San Francisco and want to sell $5,000 worth of widgets to a merchant in Yokohama, Japan, with whom you've never done business and whom you don't know. What you might do would be to have him make arrangements with his bank in Yokohama to accept drafts drawn on it up to the amount of $5,000 on presentation of specified documents (bill of lading, insurance papers, etc.). The bank on presentation of the draft and documents will accept as agreed on and the seller will have a piece of paper, assuming that the Yokohama bank is sound and well-known, which will be readily convertible into cash. A trade acceptance in that situation would obviously not be so readily convertible.

[¶1206.1] **Discounting Trade Acceptances**

A good part of the commercial utility of trade acceptances lies in the fact that the Federal Reserve Act provides for the rediscounting of trade acceptances and for their purchase in the open market by Federal Reserve Banks. This, plus the fact that a trade acceptance serves as greater assurance of payment because it carries with it proof of the transaction and in some instances the purchaser's approval of the goods, should make for greater marketability for trade acceptances than ordinary drafts.

If you plan to have a trade acceptance rediscounted under the Federal Reserve Rules, the acceptance should have a maturity not more than 90 days from its date (nine months may be OK for agricultural or livestock acceptances). If a draft is payable at sight or on demand, on indorsement by any member bank, any Federal Reserve bank may purchase or discount it if the draft arose in connection with a domestic shipment or a foreign shipment of non-perishable, readily marketable, agricultural or other staples secured by bills of lading and other shipping documents securing title to the staples. Here are some other Federal Reserve rules that you must keep in mind:

(1) The acceptance must bear on its face the statement that it arises out of the purchase and sale of goods.

(2) The acceptance must be a clear, definite order to pay without any qualifying conditions.

(3) The acceptance must be written across the face of the draft.

(4) The draft must be conspicuously labelled "Trade Acceptance."

The Code provides that "a promise or order otherwise unconditional is not made conditional by the fact that the instrument . . . states . . . the transaction which gave rise to the instrument." See *UCC §3-105*. Therefore, you may and should write on an acceptance this phrase:

"The transaction which gives rise to this instrument is the purchase of goods by the acceptor from the drawer."

Any variance from this form may involve the risk of having the instrument declared non-negotiable. For example, the addition of words such as "per invoice of" or "as per contract" have been held to affect negotiability. A title retention clause has also been held to render it non-negotiable. However, the Code contains provisions in §3-105 which may alter the result of these decisions and permit references such as "as per" and to reservation of title.

In any case you may put in the following clauses without affecting negotiability:

(1) Waiver of exemption and attorneys' fees.

(2) Provision for costs of collection.

(3) Provision for payment of interest after maturity.

[¶1206.2] Checklist for Trade Acceptances

Here are the major additional points which must be kept in mind in dealing with trade acceptances. Because these rules aren't limited to trade and bank acceptances but apply to all drafts they are discussed below under a separate heading at ¶1206.3 et seq.

(1) A trade acceptance should never be used where you wouldn't grant an open account credit.

(2) A trade acceptance shouldn't be used to cover a past due account.

(3) If the seller indorses an acceptance, he guarantees that it will be met at maturity. The seller must, therefore, be sure that the paper is good.

(4) An acceptance form authorizing discount if paid before a certain date may render the instrument non-negotiable according to some authorities. Make this arrangement outside the draft, i.e., 2%, ten days, net 30, would give purchaser option of discounting in ten days.

(5) Make sure that the acceptance form matches the terms of the sale.

(6) If a trade acceptance is made payable at a bank, as a general rule, it will be treated as a check drawn on a bank.

(7) The acceptor of a trade acceptance has the same right to stop payment as the maker of a check would have.

(8) If the drawer of a trade acceptance would otherwise have a mechanic's lien for the goods, he won't as a general rule lose his lien merely by taking the trade acceptance. However, watch out if the time of payment of the trade acceptance runs beyond the time for enforcing the mechanic's lien. Some courts have held that this amounts to waiver of the lien.

[¶1206.3] UCC Rules As to Trade Acceptance

A drawee isn't liable on a draft or check until he assents in writing to the order of the drawer. This assent is called acceptance in the case of a draft and certification in the case of a check.

Under the UCC, acceptance may be simply by signature. It is perfectly clear that the acceptance must be written on the draft (§3-410). The drawee's failure to accept before the close of business the day after presentment does not operate as a constructive acceptance *(UCC §3-506).* It should be noted that the Code's rejection of the doctrine of constructive acceptance in case of refusal of the drawee to accept or return the draft doesn't mean that the drawee can't be held liable for conversion or breach of a contractual obligation. On the contrary, UCC §3-419 recognizes the possibility of liability for conversion and UCC §3-409 recognizes the possibility of contractual liability.

The UCC provides that where the holder of an instrument assents to an acceptance varying the terms of the draft, each drawer and indorser who does not affirmatively assent to the variance is discharged *(UCC §3-412(3)).*

The UCC contemplates that the drawee named in the bill is the person to be looked to in the first instance for acceptance, but states that you may designate another person to whom resort may be had in case of dishonor by the named drawee. This secondary party is known as a "referee in case of need." The usual form followed is to write below the drawee's name: "In case of need apply to John Doe." This will give the holder the option to resort to the person secondarily named. He may, however, ignore this and treat the instrument as dishonored if the drawee refuses to accept *(UCC §4-503).*

[¶1206.4] Certification of Checks

The Code says flatly that certification of a check is acceptance *(UCC §3-411(1)).* This same section then continues the rule of *NIL (§188)* to the effect that a certification procured by the holder discharges the drawer and all prior indorsers but a certification procured by the drawer will leave him liable. In any event, unless otherwise agreed, a bank has no obligation to certify *(UCC §3-411(2)).*

Under the Code, a certification must be in writing and signed by the drawee *(UCC §3-410 and §3-411).*

The UCC says certification must be on the check itself. The UCC rejects all forms of extrinsic acceptances or certifications.

Certification by the bank creates a new contract independent of the check itself, so that even though there might be a defense to the check itself, as for example that it was void as given in payment of a gambling debt, the bank may not be able to raise the defense.

Even if the drawer's signature is forged, the certifying bank will be liable to a holder in due course — on the theory that it knows the drawer's signature and by certifying warrants its genuineness.

Under Code §3-413, the certification relates to the check as it is at the time of certification and not as it was originally. So even though the amount of the check has been hiked or the name of the payee changed, the bank will be fully liable. This means that if you take a certified check, you don't have to worry about its having been hiked — provided that the bank's form of certification doesn't undertake to pay the check only as originally drawn. In the past, many banks have adopted this form of limited certification.

Certification makes the bank primarily liable on the check. As a matter of practice, as soon as the bank certifies a check, it will charge the drawer's account with the amount. This protects the bank on the primary liability it has assumed. It does not mean, however, that the funds of the depositor have been set aside as a sort of trust fund for the benefit of the holder of the check, so that if the bank is or becomes insolvent the holder will be assured payment of the full amount. The fact is that on insolvency of the bank the holder of a certified check will be in the same class as holders of uncertified checks. And if certification was procured by the holder there can be no recourse against the drawer or prior indorsers.

[¶1206.5]   Postdating and Antedating Checks

You can postdate or antedate a check without worrying about its negotiability *(UCC §3-114).* Where a check is antedated or postdated, and it is payable either on demand or after a fixed time after date, the stated date controls. One of the underlying motivations of a drawer in using a postdated check may be to avoid liability and prosecution under "bad check laws." But he will have to check this out against the law of his particular state.

[¶1206.6]   Stopping Payment on Checks

There may be occasions when you will find it desirable to stop payment on checks which you've issued — for instance, when you discover your check was made out for too large an amount, the goods or services it was intended to pay for proved defective, or the check was lost in transmittal to the payee or by him.

A payment made in violation of an effective stop order is an improper payment, even though it's made by mistake, and the bank will be liable to its customer for the damages suffered. However, the customer has the burden of proving the amount of his loss. See UCC §4-403(3). If the customer would have been liable to the holder of the check if payment had been refused, as where the holder had the status of a holder in due course, or if not a holder in due course, held the check in payment of an enforceable debt of the drawer, the drawer hasn't suffered any loss. The bank will not be liable to him for paying over his order. In other words, an effective stop payment order doesn't necessarily mean that you can't be held liable on the check, or that you can always recover from the bank if it pays over your order.

You can stop payment of a check at any time before actual payment, acceptance or certification. The Code makes it clear that you can't do so after acceptance or certification *(UCC §4-303)*. This is a change from pre-Code rulings, which took the view that if certification was procured by the drawer he would still have the right to stop payment after certification, on the theory that he was still liable on the check.

Under the Code oral as well as written stop orders are recognized, but an oral order is good for only 14 days while a written one will stand for only six months unless renewed in writing *(UCC §4-403(2))*. In Louisiana you will have to look to the statutes of the state to determine whether an oral or written order is permissible, and how long the order will stand.

Even though an oral order is valid, it will be a good idea to follow it up with a written order to the branch where you have your account. The order must be positive and unqualified and describe the check—its date, number, amount, name of payee and anything else pertinent should be included. Make sure that the date given is accurate — substantial inaccuracies will make the order ineffective.

Under the Code, a bank can't relieve itself of the duty of exercising ordinary care in complying with stop payment orders by a special agreement with the depositor *(UCC §4-103(1))*.

A payee or indorser can't stop payment.

[¶1206.7]   Bad Check Laws

All states have so-called "bad check laws." While these laws may be cast in different forms, basically they make it a crime for a maker to issue or a holder to negotiate a check knowing that it will bounce. In most states the offense is a misdemeanor—in some it's a misdemeanor or a felony, depending on the amount involved.

Most of the statutes do not require subjective intent, but rather the issuance of the check and its dishonor because of lack of funds establishes a prima facie case of intent to defraud and of knowledge of insufficient funds. Most statutes provide for a presumption of intent to defraud and of knowledge of insufficient funds. These presumptions are rebuttable. It cannot be emphasized too strongly that these bad check laws with the presumptions involved are in many instances pitfalls for the unwary.

You should be extremely careful in making out checks to insure that your funds are sufficient or at least have some arrangement with your bank that where, because of inadvertence, there are insufficient funds, they will honor the check or give you prompt notice so that you can offset the deficiency. In many states the statute specifies a period of time after notice of dishonor in which you can make good for the amount. You should be aware of the local statutory framework so that you know what you can do when faced with the problem.

[¶1207]   HOW AN INSTRUMENT IS NEGOTIATED

You can negotiate an instrument either by delivery or by indorsement and delivery. If it's "bearer" paper, delivery will be enough. For "order" paper, it will take indorsement plus delivery.

Set forth below in checklist form are the matters to be considered in making or dealing with indorsements:

(1) Who must make— An indorsement must be made by the holder or someone authorized by him.

(2) Where made—Usually on the instrument and on the back side. The use of an allonge, a writing attached to the instrument, is all right only when necessary, as where the instrument is covered with indorsements and there's no more room.

(3) Ambiguous signature—Unless the instrument clearly indicates a signature is made in some other capacity, it will be considered an indorsement *(UCC §3-402).*

(4) Two or more indorsees—Indorsement in favor of two or more indorsees, e.g., "Pay A and B," will be effective negotiation. Indorsees will normally take as tenants in common, rather than joint tenants. Spell out the desired result in order to make sure.

(5) Partial assignments— An indorsement which purports to transfer less than the entire instrument or the unpaid balance under it is a partial assignment and will be ineffective as a negotiation. Examples of partial assignments: "Pay A one-half"; "Pay A two-thirds and B one-third."

(6) Words accompanying indorsement— Words of assignment, condition, waiver, limitation or disclaimer of liability, or guaranty will not, under Code §3-202(4), prevent an indorsement from being effective as a transfer of the

indorser's interest, but they may affect the rights and liabilities of the indorser, the indorsee or subsequent holders.

(7) Misspelling or wrong name—Under the Code, if an instrument is payable to someone under a misspelled name or a name other than his own, he may indorse in either name or both and a person paying value for the instrument can require indorsement in both *(UCC §3-203).* As a transferee, you should insist on both names.

(8) Maiden name of married woman—If the paper uses the maiden name of a woman and she tries to negotiate by her married name, have her use both names in her indorsement.

(9) Rights if order paper transferred without indorsement—In such case transferee gets whatever rights his transferor had, and if transferee paid value, he can insist on indorsement, but gets status of holder in due course only from time of indorsement and not from time of transfer *(UCC §3-201).*

(10) Blank, special, qualified, restrictive or conditional indorsements—These are the various types of indorsements which may be used. Set forth below, following this checklist, is a table listing these various types of indorsements, giving specimen forms of each type, and showing their meanings and effect.

(11) Effect of indorsement—An unrestricted, unqualified and unconditional indorsement passes title to the paper and makes the indorser secondarily liable to subsequent holders—that is, the indorser impliedly contracts to pay if the party primary liable, the maker, drawer or acceptor, fails to. The effect of various types of indorsement under the UCC is shown in the table following this checklist.

[¶1207.1] Table of Indorsements—Their Meaning and Effect

Type and Wording	Meaning and Effect Code
Blank:	
(1) Joe Roe	Specifies no indorsee of person to whom paper payable;
(2) Pay to bearer Joe Roe	payable to bearer and negotiable by delivery until specially indorsed (§ *3-204(2)*). Blank indorsement may be converted into special indorsement by holder (§ *3-204(3)*).
Special:	
(1) Pay to John Doe or order Joe Roe	Specifies the person to whom or to whose order instrument
(2) Pay to order of John Doe Joe Roe	is payable and it may be negotiated only by special indorsee's indorsement (§ *3-204(1)*).

78

Type and Wording	Meaning and Effect Code
Qualified:	
(1) Without recourse Joe Roe	Code doesn't use term but § 3-414 makes clear that ordinary contract of indorser can be disclaimed or qualified.
Restrictive:	
(1) Pay to order of X Bank for Deposit Joe Roe	Makes bank agent of depositor for collection and credit to depositor's account. Any transferee other than intermediary bank must act consistently with purpose of collection. Does not prevent further negotiation. See § 3-205, 3-206.
(2) For collection Joe Roe	Makes indorsee agent of indorser for collection. Comments in re paragraph (1) above apply. Relatively rare.
(3) Pay any bank all prior indorsements guaranteed National Bank	Indicates purpose of deposit or collection. Except for intermediary bank must act consistently with purpose. Does not prevent further negotiation. See § 4-205, 4-206. "Prior indorsements guaranteed" is implied (§ 4-207(3)).
(4) Pay any bank, banker or trust company National Bank	Common form used by banks but not expressly mentioned in Code. See comments re paragraph (3) above.
(5) Pay to John Doe only Joe Roe	Same as unrestricted indorsement. Further transfer or negotiation not prevented. See §*3-205, 3-206.* Same is true of any other indorsement purporting to bar further transfer.

Type and Wording	Meaning and Effect Code
(6) Pay to John Doe as trustee for Jack Smith Joe Roe	Rule is the same as for restrictive indorsements for deposit or collection except here the duty to act consistently with indorsement is limited to first taker. See § 3-206(4).
(7) Pay John Doe as agent for Jack Smith Joe Roe	See comments re (6).
(8) Pay John Doe for Jack Smith Joe Roe	See comments re (6).
Conditional:	
(1) Pay the within sum if and only if the SS Roe arrives in N.Y. by Sept. 30, 1963. John Doe	Rarely used. Treated as restrictive indorsement. Payor *must* disregard condition. Collecting bank not affected by. Other indorsees must see to application of proceeds and to extent they do become holders in due course and further negotiation not prevented (§ 3-205, 3-206).

[¶1207.2]   Changing Bearer Paper to Order Paper and Vice Versa

Under the Code, if a note is initially order paper, the last indorsement will control the next negotiation. If the last indorsement is in blank, it will be bearer paper negotiable by delivery, but if it's special, it will be order paper which may be further negotiated only by the special indorsee's indorsement.

The Code says that if bearer paper is specially indorsed it becomes payable to the order of the special indorsee and may be further negotiated only by his indorsement *(UCC §3-204)*. It leaves untouched the order paper rule.

Under the Code, the holder can convert a blank indorsement into a special indorsement by writing over the blank indorsee's signature the words "Pay to the order of [specified person]." In this way, you as the holder can protect yourself against the possibility of loss or theft of the paper and its acquisition by a good faith purchaser.

[¶1208]   PRESENTMENT, NOTICE OF DISHONOR AND PROTEST

Presentment is a demand for payment or acceptance made on the maker, acceptor, drawee or other payor by or on behalf of the holder. It is part of the process necessary to charge parties secondarily liable with liability if the party primarily liable fails to pay an instrument.

Notice of dishonor is notice of non-payment or non-acceptance of an item by the party primarily liable, and this too is part of the process generally necessary to charge parties secondarily liable.

In the case of indorsers, under the Code presentment and notice of dishonor are both necessary to charge them with liability *(UCC §3-501(1)(b), (2)(a)).*

[¶1209]   RIGHTS OF THE HOLDER IN DUE COURSE

One of the most important features of a negotiable instrument is that a holder in due course takes it free from any defenses which would be available against any other holder (e.g., an assignee of a claim). So, it becomes important to pin down the definition of a holder in due course—if you pay for a negotiable instrument, for example, you want to be sure you are a holder in due course.

The Code defines a holder in due course as one who takes the instrument for value, in good faith and without notice that it is overdue or has been dishonored or of any defense against or claim to it on the part of any person *(UCC §3-302(1)).* The Code expressly provides that a payee may be a holder in due course if he meets the requirements. Here's how this might work: "A" defrauds "M" and gets him to make a note payable to you as payee. You pay A for the note, acting in good faith and without notice, and the maker delivers it directly to you. In that case, you'd be a holder in due course under the Code.

To be a holder in due course you don't have to buy the whole interest in the paper.

Under the Code a purchaser of a limited interest can qualify to the extent of the interest purchased *(UCC §3-302(4)).*

[¶1209.1]   "Personal" Defenses and Real Defenses Against a Holder in Due Course

The defenses we've mentioned as not being available against a holder in due course are the so-called "personal" defenses; there are other defenses, so-called "real" defenses, that can be asserted against even one qualifying as a holder in due course. Generally, the basic distinction between these two types of defenses is that personal defenses don't deny the existence of a contract between the prior parties, but claim the contract has become voidable, in whole or in part, for some reason, whereas real defenses go to legal efficacy of the instrument from its inception; that is, they assert the instrument was void from the beginning. Failure of consideration, mistake and breach of warranty are examples of personal defenses; forgery and fraud in the execution are examples of real defenses.

81

This basic distinction doesn't stand up in all cases, however. The Code makes infancy a real defense to the extent that it is a defense to a simple contract *(§3-305(2)(a))* and follows decisions under the NIL to the effect that infancy may be asserted against a holder in due course even though the effect of infancy is to make the instrument voidable, not void. Other forms of incapacity, or duress, or illegality may be asserted against a holder in due course only if they render the obligation of the party a nullity *(UCC §3-305(2)(b))*. Local law determines whether the effect is to render the obligation voidable only or void.

The Code also makes misrepresentation inducing a party to sign an instrument without knowledge or a reasonable opportunity to obtain knowledge of its essential terms a real defense *(§3-305(2)(c))* and in so doing follows the majority rule under the NIL. Further, the Code makes it clear that any discharge in bankruptcy or insolvency proceedings can be set up against a holder in due course.

[¶1209.2]   Rights and Liabilities of a Holder Not in Due Course

Under the Code, if you are a holder but not in due course, you can enforce payment in your own name. *(UCC §3-301.)*

Under the Code if you are not a holder in due course you take the instrument subject: (1) to all valid claims to it on the part of any person; (2) to all defenses of any party which would be available in an action on a simple contract; and (3) to the defenses of want or failure of consideration, non-performance of any condition precedent, non-delivery for a special purpose; and (4) to the defense that you or a person through whom you hold the instrument acquired it by theft or that payment or satisfaction to such holder would be inconsistent with the terms of a restrictive indorsement.

[¶1209.3]   Discharge of Underlying Obligation When You Take Third Party's Paper

If you sell goods to A and take someone else's note or check in payment, you may have trouble collecting from A if the paper is dishonored. That's because, under pre-Code law, when the instrument of a third party is given concurrently with the creation of a debt, it is generally presumed that the parties have given and received the instrument in payment of the underlying debt, in this instance, the obligation of a buyer to pay for goods purchased. This is an exception to the general rule that the basic debt is not discharged by taking a negotiable instrument unless and until the instrument itself is paid.

The Code changes this exception. In the first place it makes no distinction in terms of the time of giving the instrument to the creditor. Secondly, the rule applies only when a bank's paper is taken, that is, a bank is drawer, maker or acceptor of the instrument and then only if it's not otherwise agreed *(UCC §3-802(1))*. In other words you don't have to worry about discharging the person liable on the underlying obligation by taking a third party's paper, either at the time the underlying obligation is entered into or at some later time, so long as a bank's not on the paper. But if a bank is on the paper, as where a bank cashier's check or a certified check is given, the underlying obligation will be discharged unless it's otherwise agreed. If a bank is on the paper about the only reasons you might have for wanting to keep the underlying obligation alive would be if you were engaged in an international transaction and a foreign bank was on the paper or in a domestic transaction where the bank was unknown or of uncertain solvency or was out of town and you had some reason to believe that payment of the obligation might be resisted and you might have to sue the bank to collect. In any such case you'd want to keep the underlying obligation alive and you can do so by agreement.

•

For Further Reference . . .
Bailey, Brady on Bank Checks, 3rd Ed., *Banking Law Journal.*
Clark, John J.; Bailey, Henry J., III; and Young, Robert, Jr., *Bank Deposits and Collections.*
Forms of Business Agreement looseleaf Service, Institute for Business Planning, Englewood Cliffs, N.J.
Penney, Norman, Uniform Commercial Code—A Summary of Articles 3 & 4, *The Banking Law Journal,* American Law Institute, Philadelphia, Pa.
Willier and Hart, *Forms and Procedures Under the U.C.C.,* Matthew Bender, New York, N.Y.

COMPENSATION METHODS

[¶1301] The lawyer may be called upon to help develop special compensation methods to attract and hold key personnel, to protect executives from the impact of high personal tax rates, to create incentives and tie their interests to the company. The art is to judge if any of these plans fit and if so, to select the most appropriate one. Two quick tests are:

1. Is the company's credit good enough so that the executive will be willing to have his pay deferred and left at the risk of the business?

2. Is the market for its stock good enough to make stock plans interesting?

Here are the available techniques and the problems to watch in setting up a compensation arrangement. (See also Employment, ¶2301.)

[¶1301.1] Reasonable Compensation

All payments to compensate an employee for services rendered are deductible—provided they are "reasonable." Generally, this question of reasonableness is directed at payments to stockholder-employees of a closely held corporation. Where the payment to a stockholder-employee is compensation, the company gets a deduction; where the payment is a dividend, the company gets no deduction. Thus it's more advantageous for the stockholder-employees to draw as much of the company's earnings as they can in the form of compensation rather than as a dividend, especially if their earnings are high enough to benefit from the maximum tax on earnings.

The question of reasonable compensation is one of fact. Generally, it is the amount that would "ordinarily be paid for like services by like enterprises under like circumstances" (Regs §1.162-7). Among the factors most often considered by the courts are: (1) The employee's special qualifications; (2) the nature, extent and scope of his work; (3) the size and complexities of the business; (4) the prevailing general economic conditions; (5) comparison of salaries to dividends; (6) rates of compensation for comparable positions in comparable concerns; (7) the "arm's length" element in the compensation deal; (8) consideration for past services and compensation in prior years; (9) comparison of salaries paid with employees' stock ownership.

[¶1301.2] Accrual of Bonuses

An employer is entitled to deduct bonuses (as well as other forms of compensation) in the year paid or accrued, depending on his accounting method. Briefly, an expense accrues when "all events" have occured within the taxable year which fix the amount and the fact of the liability. Thus an employer can deduct a bonus in one taxable year, so long as the liability is said to have accrued—even though it is paid in another year.

84

However, this is not true where the parties are considered "related taxpayers" (e.g., a stockholder and a closely held corporation). In that case, the employer can deduct the accrued bonus provided it is paid (or "constructively received") within two and one-half months after the close of the employer's taxable year in which the bonus accrued. If payment is made later, the employer loses the deduction (IRS §267).

[¶1301.3] Constructive Receipt of Accrued Bonus

An employee on a cash basis is normally not taxed until he actually or "constructively" receives the bonus. An employee "constructively" receives a bonus when it is unconditionally made available to him. Employee-stockholders of closely held corporations have to be careful of the application of this rule. The Commissioner has argued that since an employee-stockholder has the *power* to effect the payment by his control over the payer-corporation, he, in effect, is in constructive receipt of the bonus when the bonus is unconditionally voted by the company. However, the Tax Court has rejected this theory, holding that the employee-stockholder must have an unrestricted right to payment (*Basila*, 36 TC 111).

In these "related taxpayer" cases, however, the "constructive receipt" doctrine may be helpful to the taxpayer—rather than the government. As noted above, where a closely held corporation does not pay an accrued bonus within two and one-half months after the end of its taxable year of accrual, it loses the deduction for the bonus. However, where it can be shown that the employee was in "constructive receipt" of the bonus within this time, the company will be allowed the deduction. IRS has held that "constructive receipt" by an employee within two and one-half months after the corporation's taxable year is sufficient to qualify for the deduction (Regs §1.267(a)-1(b)).

[¶1301.4] Qualified Pension and Profit-Sharing Plans

This is one of the most attractive methods of paying both rank and file employees and executives. Basically, it is an arrangement whereby the employer makes a current payment (contribution) for the employee's services, but the pay is not enjoyed by the employee until a later period: at retirement in the case of pension plans; upon retirement or earlier termination in the case of profit-sharing plans. See ¶4201 et seq.

[¶1301.5] Deferred Pay Contracts

This type of arrangement is used where the employer wants to defer payment of compensation to a future period but does not want to adopt a qualified compensation plan. Under a nonqualified plan, the employer can pick and choose who will benefit; he is not committed to a class of employees. Moreover, this arrangement is normally less ambitious and therefore more attractive to employers with smaller organizations.

Generally, it is used to defer the pay of an executive. The plan is to have the company accumulate funds for the benefit of the executive and pay them out to him in later years (post-retirement years) when he is in a lower tax bracket. This technique helps to minimize the executive's income tax liability.

In the normal deferred compensation arrangement, the employee has no right to collect the deferred compensation until a future time. Nor does the employer set aside the deferred funds in a trust or in any other way "fund" the deferred compensation. It is, however, permissible for the employee to have a vested right to the deferred compensation — that is to say that the only condition to his collection of the deferred amount can be the passing of time (although other conditions can be put into the contract as well).

In this type of arrangement, IRS has agreed that the employee is not taxable on the deferred compensation until he receives it. The employer, however, is not entitled to a deduction for the payment until he makes the payment — regardless of the accounting method he may follow (*Rev. Rul. 60-31,* CB 1960-1, 174).

For forms of deferred compensation agreements see IBP FORMS OF BUSINESS AGREEMENTS looseleaf Service.

[¶1301.6]   Cash Bonus Plan

This plan is used to assure the employee of an immediate share of the company's profits over and above his regular compensation. In a noncontractual cash bonus plan, the amount of the bonus, who is to get it, and in what proportions are usually determined on a year-by-year basis.

Under a formal contractual basis, these features are determined beforehand. Under this arrangment the employees know exactly what to expect as a bonus. If a certain profit is reached, they will get their share. This contractual cash bonus plan usually generates direct incentives because the employees know exactly what they are going to get when the employer makes a profit.

[¶1301.7]   Stock Bonus Plan

This is like the cash bonus plan, except that payments are made in company stock. The basic advantage of paying an employee a bonus in stock rather than cash is that the employer retains the cash he would ordinarily have to pay as compensation for needs of the business operations. On the incentive side, the employee shares in the company's profits through his stock ownership, and becomes a "partner" in the business.

A stock bonus plan may be geared to current distributions of company stock, or distribution after a short period of deferral, or even to retirement years.

[¶1301.8] Qualified Stock Bonus Plan

What was said concerning qualified pension and profit-sharing plans applies equally to qualified stock bonus plans. Briefly, the difference is that under these plans the contributions are made or invested in company stock. Furthermore, the distributions from the plan are also made in company stock.

But there is one added tax advantage in a distribution under this type of plan. Where the employee receives company stock as a distribution from the plan he is not required to pay tax on the appreciated portion of the stock until he actually sells it. He only pays tax (computed under special favorable provisions) on the amount which was paid at the time the stock was purchased.

[¶1301.9] Stock Purchase Plan

This plan usually provides for a systematic purchase by the employee of the company's stock. This type of plan works as a good incentive where the employees themselves are interested in acquiring ownership in the company. What the company does is to make company stock available to the employees under favorable terms not offered to outsiders.

Generally, employees purchase stock on an installment basis, directly or through a trustee either with their own money or with the funds which have been accumulated by a saving plan. The employer is willing to make the stock available since ownership of stock is a decided employee incentive.

[¶1301.10] Stock Option Plan

Essentially, a stock option gives the employee the opportunity to purchase the company's stock at some future date at a price (or a formula) which will result in a profit to the employee in the event the market price of the stock has risen.

One of the big advantages of a stock option plan is that it reduces the employee's risk in investing in company stock to practically nothing. The employee, in effect, gets a "free ride" on the appreciation of his company's stock. If the company's stock goes up, he buys; if it goes down he doesn't buy, but he doesn't lose any money.

Where the option is a "qualified stock option" under the tax law, there are also significant tax advantages.

[¶1301.11]   Qualified Stock Option Plans

No regular income tax is imposed on the employee either at the time the option is granted or at the time the option is exercised. In order to qualify for this favored tax treatment, however, the option price must be not less than the market value of the stock at the time the option is granted. When you eventually sell the stock, you have capital gains on the entire gain, provided the stock was held for three years from the date of exercise.

The spread between option price and the value of the stock at the time of exercise is tax preference income subject to the minimum tax.

The option must be granted pursuant to a plan which sets forth the eligibility requirements and otherwise complies with many technical rules. And the employee who receives the option cannot own, immediately after receiving it, 5% of the total combined voting power or value of all classes of stock except in certain cases involving small businesses with equity capital below $2,000,000 where the allowable amount can go as high as 10%. See IRC §422. For forms, see IBP FORMS OF BUSINESS AGREEMENTS looseleaf Service.

[¶1301.12]   Employee Stock Purchase Plans

Where the intention is to benefit all employees rather than just the highly compensated ones, the option price can be as low as 85% of the market value of the stock at the time of grant. On eventual disposition, the portion of the gain equal to the spread between actual option price and value at grant is taxed as ordinary income; the balance as capital gain.

[¶1301.13]   Phantom (Shadow) Stock Plans

Under this plan the selected employee is given the benefits of stock ownership in the company without actually receiving any company stock. The way it's done is to credit the employee's account with a number of participating units (phantom stock) *as if* these units were actually company stock. When the company declares a dividend on its stock, the employee's account is credited with an amount equal to the dividends to the extent of his participating units. When he retires or terminates, he receives all the accumulated dividends plus an amount equal to the appreciated value of the stock units which were credited to his account. This approach differs from stock options in that there the optionees are given a right to purchase actual shares of the company; also, in profit-sharing plans compensation is measured in terms of company profits —rather than distributions as here.

[¶1301.14] **Contingent Allotment Plans**

Basically, this is a contingent bonus plan. At the end of each year, a committee determines which employees will be awarded a bonus and how much. The bonus is then paid (or credited to an employee account) from a reserve fund to which the employer annually contributes. These contributions can be made in cash, stock, or other property which can be passed on to the employee. The advantage of such a plan is that it rewards employees for their actual performance during the year. The device of the committee gives the employees assurance that the bonus program of the employer is on a fair and impartial basis, and thereby provides good incentive.

[¶1301.15] **Insurance Plans**

Insurance is recognized as a significant vehicle for funding compensation arrangements, and also for providing employees with a fringe benefit. There are very few "compensation packages" which do not include some element of insurance and indeed, there are some compensatory plans which are made up entirely by insurance.

[¶1301.16] **Key Man Insurance**

In this type of arrangement, the employer takes out an insurance policy on the life of its valuable employees. The employer pays the premiums and collects the proceeds of the policy. He can use the proceeds, among other things, to pay death benefits to the employee's family for a period of time as a continuation of the employee's salary after death; or he can buy the deceased employee's stock in the company at his death; or use it as benefits under a pension or profit-sharing plan if the employee dies prematurely and before he is able to accumulate a large fund.

The employer gets a tax deduction when the employee receives the benefits —not when the premiums are paid on the insurance. When the premiums are paid all the employer is doing is building up an asset—the life insurance policy. But when he pays the benefits of the policy over to the widow (or beneficiary) of the deceased employee, he is paying compensation and is therefore entitled to a deduction.

[¶1301.17] **Death Benefits**

On the employee's side, $5,000 can be paid to the family of the deceased employee income tax free (IRC §101(b). Where an employee's family receives $5,000 from two or more employers, the excludible amount is still limited to only $5,000. The rule applies to distributions under a qualified plan, but does not apply to amounts to which the employee had a nonforfeitable right.

[¶1301.18] Split Dollar Plans

Under a typical setup, the employee pays that part of the premium on an ordinary life insurance policy which is attributable to life insurance protection; the employer pays the balance which is attributable to the cash surrender value. The cash surrender value is owned by the employer. On the employee's death, the employer receives an amount equal to the cash surrender value. The employee's beneficiary receives what's left of the proceeds. The advantage of such an arrangement is that after the first few years, the employee is able to obtain high insurance protection at a very low cost, since the employer is, in effect, paying for part of this protection through earnings on funds which belong to the employer. The "economic benefit" received by the employee under this plan is taxable (*Rev. Rul. 64-328,* CB 1964-2; *Rev. Rul. 66-110,* CB 1966-1, 12).

[¶1301.19] Group Life Insurance Plans

This is a valuable fringe benefit whereby the employees are offered an opportunity to purchase life insurance by the "group" rather than individually, and thereby obtain life insurance protection at low cost—or at no cost where the employer pays the premiums. There are three types of group insurance in general use:

(1) Group-Term Life Insurance: This simply provides insurance protection for the insured for a short period of time. It has no paid up or cash surrender value. An employer can provide an employee with up to $50,000 of this type of insurance tax free, provided it is "group-term" as defined in IRS Regs. This is the only type of life insurance coverage which an employer can provide for an employee tax free. All other forms of life insurance protection are taxable to the employee.

(2) Group Paid-Up Life Insurance: This offers permanent protection by having a single premium buy for a specific employee a stated unit of life insurance that remains in force during the lifetime of the employee, without payment of further premium.

(3) Group Level Premium Insurance: This is a "group permanent contract." The premium on each employee's life is the same every year based upon his age when issued. This type of coverage offers paid-up insurance at retirement age and also makes cash or annuity values available either at retirement or upon termination.

[¶1301.20] Group Health Insurance Plans

This is another very valuable fringe benefit. It provides for the reimbursement of medical and hospitalization expenses incurred by an employee and his family. Premiums are tax deductible by the employer and not taxable to the employee—even though the plan provides for the protection of the employee's family. This plan is widely used by many employers to provide their employees with at least the basic health and accident protection. Some employers extend their plan to include reimbursement of major medical expenses. This coverage supplements the basic plan and provides some shelter to the employee in the event of a serious or prolonged illness.

[¶1301.21] **Salary Continuation Plan**

Another widely used fringe benefit is to provide for the continuation of an employee's salary while he is absent from work because of sickness or an accident. This is often used with high-paid executives because it is not required, for tax purposes, that the plan include a special class of employees. The company can, therefore, provide this coverage for anyone it pleases, but the payments must be made pursuant to a definite plan.

The employer gets a tax deduction for his payments under a salary continuation plan, but the employee's tax consequences are much different.

Under prior law, sick pay was excludable up to $100 per week. Under the 1964 tax law, only the sick pay received after the first 30 days is excludable up to $100 per week. For the first 30 days of absence you can exclude only up to $75 per week provided, however, that this $75 constitutes 75% or less of your regular weekly wage rate. If it constitutes more than 75% of your regular weekly wage rate, you will not be entitled to any sick pay exclusion for the first 30 days of sickness. Finally, the benefits received for the first seven days are not excludable unless you are hospitalized.

[¶1301.22] **How Tax Reform Affects Compensation Plans**

The Tax Reform Act of 1969 and the Employee Retirement Income Security Act of 1974 affect compensation arrangements in these ways: (1) The maximum tax on earned income, effective since 1972, is 50%; (2) Employer contributions to qualified pension and profit-sharing plans when distributed in the form of a lump sum distribution are taxed partly as capital gains and partly as ordinary income under a special ten-year forward averaging provision; (3) The amount that a Subchapter S corporation can contribute tax free to a qualified plan for an over-5% stockholder is limited to 15% of compensation or $7,500, whichever is smaller, and the over-5% stockholder is barred from participating in forfeitures; (4) Restricted stock is taxable to the employee on receipt as though it were unrestricted, unless it is subject to a substantial condition of forfeiture in which case it is taxable to him only when the stock becomes nonforfeitable; (5) The difference between the option price of stock and its market value at the time of exercise is tax preference income subject to an additional tax of 10% on the amount of tax preference income in excess of $30,000 plus regular income taxes payable; (6) Tax preferences over $30,000 reduce dollar-for-dollar the earned income eligible for the 50% ceiling rate; (7) Income averaging is available for income in excess of 20% of the base period. Long-term capital gains, wagering income and income from gifts and bequests are included within the averaging provisions but if you use averaging, you can't use the alternative capital gains rate nor can you use the maximum tax on earned income.

●

For Further Reference . . .

Cohn, Allan, Stock Purchase Plans and Stock Bonus Plans, *21st NYU Institute on Federal Taxation 545.*

Pay Planning (2 vol. looseleaf service), Institute for Business Planning, Englewood Cliffs, N.J.

Sellin, Henry (Ed.), *Taxation of Deferred Employee and Executive Compensation,* Prentice-Hall, Englewood Cliffs, N.J.

Washington, G. T., and Rothchild, V. H., *Compensating the Corporate Executive,* Ronald.

CONTRACTS

[¶1601] All that can be attempted here is an indication of when the practicing lawyer should reach for Williston or Corbin. His contact with the law of contracts will be explicit and formal when he is called upon to wrap up an understanding by drafting a contract. Here he can get help from the thinking reflected in dozens of good form books and hundreds of contracts which have drifted into or been produced by his office. He is likely to have more trouble with the contract problems which drift into his practice unannounced as such. For example, the handling and qualification of discussions and correspondence so that a contractual commitment is either avoided or created, what should be done to protect contractual rights in carrying out a contract and in accepting tenders of performance, how a client may be relieved of possible onerous obligations in a contract which is not working out.

In sales and purchase transactions, the Uniform Commercial Code now effective in all the states but Louisiana has substantially changed the law of contracts. Here we deal primarily with contracts which are not governed by the UCC; i.e., those not involving the present or future transfer of goods (movable things other than securities). On sales transactions check also ¶4801 et seq.

[¶1602] IS THERE A BINDING CONTRACT?

In considering a conversation, a letter, or a course of dealing to determine whether it may or can be converted into a contract by mere acceptance, what we must determine is whether there is an offer, a definite promise to be bound, which can be converted into a contract.

To avoid this exposure, make such a statement indefinite or make it clear that it is merely intended to be part of preliminary negotiations. Fortunately, advertisements, price quotations, trade circulars, catalogues, and the like ordinarily are not sufficiently definite as to quantities, terms and prices to indicate an intention to make an offer. It is generally accepted that it is the customer responding to such information who makes the offer, so that the seller's acceptance is necessary to bind the parties to a contract. At auction sales it is the bidder who is making the offer and it is the auctioneer who makes the acceptance when he slams his hammer on the table. This is why the seller can reject a bid and withdraw the property from sale unless the auction is announced to be without reserve.

Offer: Apart from the Uniform Commercial Code, an offer can be revoked at any time before acceptance and to keep an offer open it is necessary to give consideration and that constitutes an option. An offer will lapse at the end of

93

the period specified in the offer for acceptance or, where no time limit is set, if an unreasonable time elapses without acceptance. What is an unreasonable time depends on the circumstances, particularly in the way in which the offer was made. But in a sale of goods under the Code a merchant's written offer not limited in duration by its terms remains open for a reasonable time not exceeding three months without any consideration. Rejection of an offer terminates it automatically, and a counteroffer operates as such a rejection. Apart from the Code, an acceptance attempting to introduce new terms is really a counteroffer which will constitute a rejection of the offer. On the other hand, a mere inquiry as to whether a variation in terms would be acceptable may not constitute a rejection of the original offer. In practice, this sort of distinction tends to be very fine indeed; and it is important for the practicing lawyer considering answers to correspondence and the like to make their contractual import explicit by characterizing them accurately; i.e., stating that this is a mere inquiry and the offer is still being considered.

Acceptance: Where a valid offer can be spelled out of conversation or correspondence, what constitutes a valid acceptance which will convert it into a binding contract? To constitute an acceptance, a response must not only *not* introduce new terms but must also be unconditional. Under the Uniform Commercial Code, an acceptance can add new terms which can become part of the contract if not rejected and if they don't materially alter the offer. For guides to controlling the addition of new terms, see ¶4803.1. "An acceptance subject to contract" means that there is no enforceable agreement unless and until a formal contract has been drawn up, agreed upon, and exchanged. Similar qualifying phrases such as "subject to approval by the board of directors" will similarly prevent a valid acceptance. Here again there is a very fine distinction to be carefully watched. A statement saying "I accept the terms of your offer and will ask my lawyer to prepare a formal contract" constitutes a valid acceptance. It is assumed that the formal contract will merely reflect the terms of the offer and acceptance and spell out conditions and obligations which would be implied by the law in any event. In New York and some other states, a written offer is irrevocable if it so states within the time specified and if no time is specified, within a reasonable time.

Indefinite Terms: For an exchange to constitute a contract, there must be certainty of terms. However, a person making or accepting an offer can be bound by terms he should reasonably have expected. The courts are able to supply any missing terms on the basis of the usage of the trade or of the previous course of dealing between the parties or merely to give business effect to the contract. Terms can be implied into a contract by statute—for example, as to the fitness or quality of goods sold. If there is an offer and acceptance but the offer is so indefinite that a court would not be able to reasonably infer

94

to what the parties have agreed, there is no valid contract. Where the agreement explicitly leaves important terms to future agreement, there is only an agreement to agree which is no agreement at all. Thus, if the correspondence states that the parties will agree on the price or the completion date or any condition which is not immaterial, then no obligation at all is created. Note that if an essential term is not mentioned at all, it can be implied that a reasonable price or a reasonable time was intended; but if it is specified that this term will be agreed upon later, there is no agreement. However, if the UCC applies, the price can be left open without violating the agreement.

Consideration: Unless otherwise provided by statute, a promise not supported by consideration is unenforceable. However, the courts are quick to find the existence of consideration in an act, a forbearance, a mutual promise. Consideration is deemed to exist whether or not it is adequate. Generally, past consideration is no consideration, but there may be, as there is in New York, a statutory provision that a subsequent promise supported by a past consideration is enforceable if in writing and signed by the promisor. Promises which are enforceable despite the absence of consideration include charitable subscriptions, a promise to pay a debt barred by the statute of limitations, or discharge in bankruptcy.

Statute of Frauds: The Statute of Frauds will require specified types of contracts, notably those not to be performed within a year and those involving real property, to be in writing. Compliance with the Statute of Frauds can be found in letters and other signed, written memoranda. A showing that the contract can be performed within a year in the manner contemplated by the parties will make certain oral agreements enforceable. In this connection, don't forget the parol evidence rule under which the writings making up an agreement cannot be varied or supplemented by prior agreements, oral or written, or by contemporaneous oral agreements. Parol evidence can be admitted only to show meaning, to prove facts which would make the agreement void or voidable for fraud, duress, mistake, or lack of consideration, or to prove the falsity of recitals of any fact in the written agreement, or to show the existence of a condition precedent. The Uniform Commercial Code has significantly relaxed the Statute of Frauds on Sales. See ¶4805.

[¶1603] VOID, VOIDABLE AND UNENFORCEABLE CONTRACTS

If a client comes in with a signed agreement, some correspondence, or the report of some conversations which add up to a contract which he doesn't want or which has become burdensome or inoperable, what advice can be given?

First, what circumstances can make the apparent contract invalid, void, voidable, or unenforceable?

The distinction between invalidity and unenforceability is important. To illustrate, an oral agreement for the sale of land is not enforceable; but if the buyer happens to have paid a deposit, the contract is valid to the extent of permitting the seller to retain the deposit if the buyer defaults.

[¶1603.1]   Can the Contract Be Set Aside?

The things to look for in trying to set aside a contract are:

(1) Lack of legal capacity: Examples are infancy or insanity.

(2) A mistake: This could affect the validity of the contract. This has to be a mutual mistake, putting the parties at cross purposes, using ambiguous language, or creating a meaningless or unenforceable agreement.

(3) Misrepresentation: It takes an untrue statement of fact by one of the parties which the other party was intended to act upon and which did, in fact, induce him to enter into the agreement to his detriment to make the contract voidable by the party who has been misled. Silence is ordinarily not a representation and therefore not fraudulent, unless there is a fiduciary relation involved or unless there is a failure to inform a buyer of a defect known to the seller and not apparent on ordinary inspection.

(4) Duress or undue influence: These can nullify the contract.

(5) Illegality: This means being contrary to public policy. The important instances of illegality arising in general commercial practice are violation of antitrust laws and violation of usury statutes.

[¶1603.2]   Can the Contract Obligations be Considered Terminated?

Now suppose that the client's statements and documents reveal an enforceable agreement and fail to reveal any defense. Or suppose the client has a perfectly proper, fully executed, written agreement which has become unworkable or burdensome. Can you find a basis for considering him discharged from his agreement? If he has substantially performed all his obligations, he may be discharged. If he has offered performance at a reasonable time and place and the other party rejected it, he can be considered discharged and he can sue the other party for breach of contract. He can also be considered discharged and be in a position to recover payment for whatever he has done where the other party has in fact accepted partial performance or has himself prevented complete performance. Your client can be considered discharged if the contract was frustrated by some unexpected event which makes it impossible to perform. For example, the death of an actor would frustrate any future engagements.

However, events which merely make the contractual obligations more burdensome without changing them fundamentally will not constitute an out under the theory of discharge by frustration. Whether a change is fundamental enough to let a party out of a contract is a question of fact. When the Suez Canal was seized and ships had to go around the Cape of Good Hope, some courts held that the shipping contracts were frustrated, and others held that they merely became more burdensome but nevertheless had to be performed.

Another possible method of getting a client out of an agreement is to find a subsequent agreement rescinding or agreeing not to enforce the original contract. This new agreement must have the same necessary elements as the original contract; the mutual release of the parties from obligation under the first contract is sufficient consideration for the contract of recision.

Finally, you may be able to get your client out of a contract if the other party has committed a breach. To get this effect, this breach must be of a term or condition which goes to the very root of the agreement. It is not enough if a term which is merely collateral or incidental to the main purpose of the agreement is breached. In that case, your client is still obligated, although he has a claim for damages against the other party. A breach may be found by express repudiation or by conduct totally inconsistent with performance under the contract. It may simply be failure to perform the contract when the due time arrived.

[¶1603.3] If Your Client Is Dissatisfied

When a client comes in to complain about not getting what he is entitled to from the other party, there is a different set of problems. Where the other party has partially performed, it is important to explicitly negate this as adequate performance under the contract if you want to preserve your client's rights to sue or demand full performance.

[¶1604] DAMAGES

In the case of a breach of a contract, compensatory damages are generally available to the injured party. His damages will usually be limited to the amount of actual loss rather than the purchase or contract price. However, the contract price will be the measure of damages in certain instances where title has already passed to the buyer or in some cases where the merchandise was manufactured specifically for the buyer. A party who is in breach of an agreement, however, will not be responsible for loss which he could not have contemplated. For example, if a seller breaches his agreement to sell 100 widgets at $1.00 each, and because of the seller's failure to deliver the buyer loses a sale to a third party at ten dollars each, the original seller will not be liable for the entire loss if he could not have contemplated a loss of that type. Loss of profits may be an important element of damages in contract situations where they can be measured with reasonable accuracy. For example, if an automobile agency agrees to sell an automobile which it purchased from the factory for $3,000 for $3,500, and the buyer fails to accept delivery, the automobile agency may recover damages from the buyer even though they resell the same car to another buyer. Recovery in this instance would be for loss of the sale and would be based on the assumption that they would have sold another car to the second buyer if the party who breached the agreement had performed as required by the agreement. However, it may be difficult to establish the appropriate measure of damages in this situation.

[¶1604.1] Liquidated Damages

Often parties will want to fix the amount of damages in advance of an agreement where it appears that measuring damages would be costly in terms of expert witnesses, etc., or incapable of being ascertained with any certainty. Liquidated damage provisions will be enforceable where it appears that they are compensation for damages actually sustained rather than a penalty. The reasonableness of the amount in the light of the circumstances will generally determine whether a liquidated damage provision will be enforceable.

[¶1605]   ANTICIPATORY BREACH

In some states, the courts have held that a party to an agreement is justified in withholding his performance under an agreement where it is apparent that the other party to the agreement will be unable to or refuses to perform as required by the agreement. In situations where the Uniform Commercial Code is applicable and where a party to an agreement for the sale of goods has reasonable grounds for insecurity as to the other party's ability to perform as required, he can demand adequate assurance of performance. Where assurance is not forthcoming, he may treat the agreement as breached.

[¶1606]   SPECIFIC PERFORMANCE

Generally, a court will specifically enforce an agreement where damages would not afford complete relief to the injured party. Specific performance is most readily available where there is an agreement to convey real property and the owner of the property refuses to perform according to the terms of the agreement. However, specific performance may also be available in agreements involving unique chattels, etc.

Specific performance is not generally available to require a person to perform services or exercise discretion. Similarly, specific performance is not available where the job to be done requires supervision—as a court of equity will not undertake to supervise a project. Specific performance is not generally available to affirmatively enforce an employment agreement, although it may be available in the form of an injunction to restrain an employee from taking on other employment.

Specific performance is generally available only in courts with equity jurisdiction—it is a matter totally discretionary with the court. A court of equity may refuse to specifically enforce an agreement although it would be enforceable at law—as where there is consideration for an agreement but the court finds that the consideration is sufficient. Although an action to specifically enforce an agreement is brought on within the statute of limitations prescribed for contract actions, a court of equity may rely upon the doctrine of laches and refuse to enforce it. Similarly a court of equity may refuse to enforce a contract because the plaintiff has not come into court with "clean hands."

Where a court of equity refuses to give specific performance, the procedure in some states provides for the alternative relief of damages in the same action. However, it may be necessary to have a new trial or impanel a jury to determine damages to preserve the parties' right to trial by jury.

[¶1607] CHECKLIST FOR DRAFTING A CONTRACT

A lawyer can find himself drafting a contract when he helps his client write or answer a letter, even when he tells him what to say orally, as well as when he is drafting a formal agreement either in letter or in formal contract style and when he is preparing a sales or purchase order form. Here is a checklist to run down when you are performing one of these functions:

(1) What restrictions are necessary to keep the other party from adding an unwanted term or condition?

(2) Do you want to merge all prior communications into the written agreement?

(3) Do you want to exclude the possibility of future oral modifications?

(4) Do you want to make sure that some future act will not be deemed to constitute a waiver of a contractual right?

(5) If you are relying on the other party's representations, get them stated as an express warranty, rather than a mere "whereas" recital. If it is merely a recital you will have to prove fraud to get relief if the facts are different, whereas even if the misrepresentation is innocent you will be able to void the contract if it's set up as a warranty.

(6) Make sure that the party who signs the agreement has the necessary authority.

(7) When your client's obligation is dependent on the other party doing something, make the condition express and explicit. Otherwise your client may be subject to a claim for damages even in the event the other party fails to perform.

(8) Stipulate whether representations are to survive the transaction or not.

(9) If your client is selling something "as is," expressly exclude any implied representations. If you want to protect your client from any warranties of title, state that the assignment is without recourse.

(10) Provide for duration and right to terminate. If it appears that the parties are likely to continue on in a business relationship beyond the express term, consider providing for automatic renewals for a year or some other appropriate period of time, always preserving your client's right to terminate on appropriate notice.

(11) Spell out exactly what constitutes performance (use quantities, descriptions, time, drawings, specifications, acceptance tests, etc.). Specify who is responsible for taking all steps necessary for getting permits and meeting all other necessary requirements of performance.

(12) Unless you provide that time is of the essence, your client is apt to find himself unable to get his requirements without risk of duplication, if the other party fails to make timely performance. If you want your client to be able to cancel if the other party fails to perform on time, expressly reserve this right.

(13) Make sure your client does not incur liability from unforeseeable contingencies by inserting a force majeure clause.

(14) In the absence of a contrary provision, delivery and payment are concurrent provisions. If the intention is otherwise, express provision is needed. If payment is to be made in installments, consider acceleration and prepayment provisions.

(15) If collateral security is to be furnished, see ¶4901 et seq. on Secured Transactions.

(16) If the other party's performance is to be guaranteed or your client is to be indemnified or held harmless, see ¶2901 on Guarantees and Indemnities.

(17) If your client's sale or use of what the other party delivers might infringe a third party's patent, have a patent indemnity clause. See ¶4802.

(18) If your client is making a deposit, consider getting that accepted as liquidated damages. If you provide for liquidated damages in the event of the other party's default, make sure they are not so heavy as to be held to be a penalty.

(19) Protect your client against inadvertent default by providing for notice and a subsequent time period within which any default may be cured. Provide whether notice becomes effective upon mailing or upon receipt and whether it has to be given by registered or certified mail.

(20) If you can specify the governing law, you will avoid perplexing conflict of laws problems.

(21) Provide explicitly whether the contract is to be assignable or not, and whether or not the original party is released from liability upon assignment. Consider providing that the assignment is not effective until the assignee assumes the assignor's obligations in writing.

(22) Use special care in drafting conditions. If one party is excused from performance on the happening of a condition, say so clearly. If the condition is concurrent, as, for example, delivery of merchandise on payment of the price, make this clear. If the condition is subsequent, as where the agreement is continued until either party exercises his option to cancel it, make it clear that only upon compliance with the termination procedure may the agreement be cancelled. If the condition is precedent, as where one party must complete his part of the agreement before the other party is obligated to render his performance, make it clear that substantial or full completion is necessary before the other party is obligated to act. The use of conditions will also determine whether the parties intend the agreement to be entire or severable. Provide for concurrent or conditional performance, if you don't want the agreement divided into separate, self-contained units each independent of the next unit and standing alone as a separately enforceable agreement.

(23) Whenever money or goods have to be advanced before completion of the other party's performance, find out whether protection against insolvency is needed. If it is, have money placed in escrow and see that either title to or a lien on property is held by your client.

(24) Do you want to provide that the other party has made his own investigation and has not relied on any statement or preliminary representation made by your client?

(25) If you are considering arbitration, see ¶501 et seq.

(26) It is always safest to specify the consideration which makes the contract binding even though in some states the law makes a written instrument of agreement binding without consideration. Where consideration is necessary it will make later proof easier if it is specified.

(27) In preliminary negotiations, to avoid the risk that oral and letter negotiations may create an agreement before you're ready for one, make it clear that there is no agreement until a final document is signed.

(28) If a party is to have the right to cancel the agreement if it is breached by the other party it is advisable to include a clause to that effect. Otherwise, it may be necessary to establish that the breach is serious enough to defeat the purpose of the contract in order to be relieved of its obligations.

(29) Exclude the authority of any salesman or agent of one of the parties to change the conditions of sale and shipment specified in the agreement.

(30) Are the parties to have any right to inspect the books and records of another party?

(31) Specify who is to carry risk of property loss during contract period. What insurance is to be carried? By whom?

(32) If concurrent performance is a condition say so. If complete and exact performance is a condition say so. If a party is to be relieved of a performance upon the happening of some event, say so. If you want exact performance, expressly exclude the doctrine of substantial performance.

(33) Shall a provision be included requiring any change and modification of the contract to be in writing and signed by both parties?

(34) Is the illegality of any provision to invalidate the contract as a whole?

(35) An all-purpose modification clause should spell out the "how" of changing the agreement, especially where there is maximum daily contact on all levels between both parties. This will protect you against unauthorized amendments agreed upon by subordinates without your approval. Limit modifications to formal contacts between the highest levels, or name the authorized personnel.

(36) If your agreement leaves certain items (price, delivery dates, etc.) to be revised later, as conditions change, make sure you provide an "out" clause if mutual agreement cannot be reached. An arbitration, liquidated damage, or cancellation clause will cover the loophole.

(37) Do you need an escape clause? Usually, escape clauses are two-way streets—each party has the same option to end the agreement. But the one-way escape clause is not uncommon and serves usefully to end an agreement where the other party has defaulted or has breached or when some basic consideration (obtaining favorable tax rulings, zoning clearance, export license, steel quota, franchise renewal, etc.) has backfired. A good escape clause should fix a period and method of notice, leaving no doubt about items which have accrued prior to the termination date.

For forms illustrating the various points made above, including price terms, risk of loss, storage of goods, passage of title, manner of shipping, default provisions, and warranties, see IBP FORMS OF BUSINESS AGREEMENTS.

●

For Further Reference . . .

American Jurisprudence, Contracts.

Corbin on Contracts, West Publishing Co., St. Paul, Minn.

Mandel, *Preparation of Commercial Agreements,* Practising Law Institute, New York, N.Y.

Restatement on Contracts, American Law Institute (state annotations are available for some states), Philadelphia, Pa.

Whitney, *The Law of Modern Commercial Practices*, Baker, Voorhis.
Williston on Contracts, Baker, Voorhis.

CORPORATE FORMATION

[¶1701] There are these main phases in forming a corporation:
(1) Determine the basic business objectives and the basic business bargain of the principals.

(2) Develop the concept of a corporate form, capital structure, financing arrangements and supplementary agreements which fit these objectives and carry out the bargain.

(3) Check the organizational plan in the light of tax considerations and make the necessary modifications.

(4) Make the fundamental decisions prerequisite to drafting corporate papers, where to incorporate, how many shares and what kind (par or no par, preferences or not), preemptive rights, any organizational controls, and put them in the charter or separate agreement, etc.

(5) Draft the corporation charter, by-laws, stock certificates, and organizational minutes.

(6) Make the filings, pay the taxes, and take the other procedural steps necessary to bring the corporation into being.

(7) Hold the organizational meeting, have directors accept subscriptions, accept transfers of property, etc.

(8) Where are voting and other controls to rest?

In this chapter we will outline the essential considerations and the steps to be taken in each of these phases.

[¶1702]   BUSINESS OBJECTIVES AND BARGAIN

Where the clients are persons of considerable business experience and sophistication, they may sometimes come to the lawyer with their business objectives and their basic agreement well articulated and worked out and counsel will not be called upon to assist in developing the basic agreement. But normally the parties will not be so well prepared and it will be found that important points haven't been covered in their agreement. This will be either because they haven't considered them or because having considered them they haven't been able to resolve the issues posed. In either case counsel must call attention to the omissions and will very likely be called on to suggest or work out solutions.

[¶1702.1]   Basic Elements of Business Bargain

The basic elements of the business bargain are covered in the following checklist designed for use at the first interview with the clients:

(1) What are the corporate purposes and business activities to be?

(2) Proposed corporate name, and the importance, if any, of the name to the business?

(3) Names of participants, and personal details as to age and outside income?

(4) Functions of participants and compensation proposed to be paid, if any?

(5) Capital investments? Who is to contribute cash or property and what is value of contribution?

(6) Estimate the corporate profits projected for a period of years.

(7) How do the parties contemplate dividing the profits—in relationship to contributions, services, etc.?

(8) Where are voting and other controls to rest?

[¶1702.2] The Decisions Needed

In the light of a full exploration and formulation of objectives and discussion of the legal mechanics available, decisions have to be made on these broad questions:

(1) The state of incorporation and the corporate name. The corporate name must be cleared and the right to use it obtained.

(2) The type of capital structure to be used. This involves these questions:

(a) Shall common shares be par or no par?

(b) How many shares shall be authorized and issued?

(c) Shall preferred shares be used or shall debt securities be issued?

(3) If preferred shares are to be used, it is necessary to answer additional questions:

(a) Their face value—how much of a preferential claim will they be entitled to in dissolution?

(b) Shall they be redeemable and at what price may they be redeemed?

(c) Shall they be convertible into common?

(d) What rate of dividend shall they bear and when shall dividends be payable?

(e) Shall dividends be cumulative?

(f) Shall there be a sinking fund provision and, if so, what terms are desired?

(g) Shall the preferred shares have voting rights?

(h) What rights shall holders of preferred shares have if dividend obligations are not met; i.e., conditional voting rights.

(4) For what consideration shall the shares be issued?

(5) Should shareholders have preemptive rights?

(6) What kind of voting rights are desired? Is cumulative voting desirable to give minority interests certain representation? Can representation be provided by quorum provisions, special meeting provisions, agreements between the parties, etc.?

(7) What organizational provisions should be written into the charter and by-laws?

(8) In what state should the corporation be incorporated? In what states will it do business and in which of those states should it or need it be qualified to do business as a foreign corporation?

[¶1703]   FIXING THE CAPITAL STRUCTURE

The capital structure of the business must be tailored to fit the bargaining position, needs and interests of the participants in the enterprise. The structure can be as simple or complex as the considerations mentioned require.

Normally, if all the participants have essentially the same economic interests in the enterprise, as where they are all investing cash and they are all on a more or less even keel as to services or other contributions to the business, the capital structure will consist of a single class of stock distributed pro rata in proportion to investments. But even in this type of situation, the income tax situation of particular investors or the projected tax situation of the enterprise as such might call for a certain amount of debt in addition to the single class of stock. The use of debt and the problems of thin incorporation that it may pose are discussed below under an appopriate heading.

Assuming, however, that the various participants are not on an equal footing and that their disparate economic interests are to be reflected in the capital structure, how is this to be done?

The basic elements that may be used to build a capital structure that will reflect these economic interests are earnings, assets and voting or management power. Here we consider separately the use of each of these elements.

[¶1703.1]   Earnings

One investor or class of investors may be given a preference in or disproportionate share of earnings by using preferred stock or by using two classes of stock. The use of preferred stock is perhaps the commonest way of giving one class of investors a priority in earnings. If the investors are in a position to demand a share in earnings in addition to their preferred dividend this may be done either (1) by making the preferred participating as to further dividends or (2) by giving them common in addition to their preferred. The first route presents problems, however, if the preferred is to be callable as it normally should be, because then it should also be made convertible if the holders are to share in the growth of the company (as they bargained for), and if it's convertible for an extended period there will be serious problems in working out fair conversion rates. Hence, the second route is apt to be favored.

Where the situation calls for one class of investor receiving a disproportionate share of earnings, as distinguished from priority in the earnings, a two class

106

stock setup will usually be called for. For example, a two class stock arrangement might be used where investor A is willing to put in $55,000 and is willing to settle for 45% of the earnings provided he is given 55% of the voting control of the business and B is willing to put in $45,000 provided he gets 55% of the earnings and is willing to wield only 45% of the vote.

Where you use two classes of stock, care must be exercised to make sure they are properly labelled. Where the two classes share dividends on a percentage basis, for example, it might be incorrect to designate the class getting the larger percentage as "common." You might have to call them Class A shares. The other class could be designated common.

[¶1703.2] Assets

Some investors may demand priority or preferential participation in the distribution of assets on premature liquidation. For example, suppose one group of investors makes two-thirds of the cash or tangible investment for one-third of the shares, and the so-called talent gets two-thirds of the shares for only one-third of the tangible investment, and let's say the respective investments are $100,000 and $50,000. If the corporation were to liquidate at a time when the assets were worth $150,000, the "talent" would come out with $50,000 more than they went in, this at the expense of the "money" investors. The "money" investors would come out even only if liquidation occurred at a time when the asset value had doubled. Two classes of shares bearing different participation rights in the distribution of assets, as distinguished from a preference in distribution, might be used to assure an equitable result. Thus, Class A might be given $2 for every $1 to be distributed to Class B until the original investments were repaid, with provision for equal distribution of assets thereafter.

[¶1703.3] Voting

Here we consider the distribution of voting power by the use of securities with different voting rights, as distinguished from the use of agreements enlarging, restricting or otherwise affecting voting rights.

Minority investors may want representation on the board of directors. One way of assuring such representation is by establishing two or more classes of shares and providing for the election of a certain number of directors or a certain percentage of the total number of directors by each class. The latter will, of course, prevent changes in representation by changes in the number of directors, and will, therefore, normally, be preferred.

Participation in voting for directors may be made absolute or it may be contingent, or conditional, as on passing preferred dividends for a fixed time. Where both common and preferred are used, the voting rights of the preferred are usually made contingent or conditional on preferred dividends being in arrears (normally for a year or more). When that occurs the preferred shareholders become entitled to elect board members (usually a majority) until the default is cured.

So far the discussion has been limited to voting for directors and on this level it is quite clear that you may create securities without the right to vote for directors. But voting may, of course, concern other matters, and it is equally clear that you cannot create a class of securities that is barred from voting on all matters including those affecting the interests of the class. The statutes of the state of incorporation must be checked to determine the issues on which class voting is required. The issues may include certain types of charter amendments, and mergers and consolidations adversely affecting the class.

On the other hand, the voting rights of particular securities may go beyond those matters as to which shareholder votes or consents are required by law. Voting rights may be conferred as to specific matters when required by the terms of the business bargain. The participation may be on the basis of class voting (requiring a certain percentage of the class) or pooling all the classes and requiring a certain percentage of the votes of all those entitled to vote on the particular issue.

[¶1703.4] Provisions for Redemption and Conversion

Debt securities and preferred stock are used to give the investors some protection for their capital investment and some assurance of income. When the corporation has established itself these senior securities may no longer be necessary or the capital which they represent may be had on better terms. This is what makes it desirable to make the senior securities redeemable or callable at the option of the corporation or provision may be made for compulsory retirement. Where the latter is the case, the security should provide for a sinking fund.

The law of incorporation must be checked as to permissible provisions for redemption, and their application to particular securities, i.e., debt, preferred, common.

Making senior securities convertible may be tied in with the idea of redemption. As the corporation grows and prospers the holder of a convertible senior security may be induced to give up whatever priorities he may have as to earnings or assets or both in favor of a full share in the equity.

[¶1703.5] Rights, Options, Warrants

Many corporate statutes permit rights and options to purchase shares, sometimes called "warrants." Use of these may be considered but normally their use will be limited to later stages in the development of the business.

〔¶1703.6〕 Use of Debt

Debt securities are usually issued to represent borrowed money and may take various forms, the most common being bonds, debentures and notes. Bonds are usually secured and when secured by a mortgage may be referred to as "mortgage bonds." Those secured by a pledge of personal property may be called "collateral trust bonds." "Debentures" or "notes" are generally unsecured. Local law must be checked for provisions authorizing the holders of debt securities to vote for directors or other matters, as well as for requirements as to the consideration for their issuance. The use of debt securities in the capital structure must be with an eye to the tax consequences of "thin incorporation," discussed in point 8 of the Checklist of Tax Considerations which follows ¶1704, and with due regard to possible non-tax consequences. In case of insolvency, for example, the debt to shareholders may be subordinated to other claims and shareholders may be held personally liable for the debts. Attention must also be focused on the effect of debt on the balance sheet. It may lead to an investigation by persons transacting business with the corporation of the relationship between the holders of the debt securities and the shareholders of the corporation. If such a relationship is discovered, the next step may be to ask for a contractual subordination of the debt. This will, of course, result in the debt holder being placed in essentially the position of a shareholder.

〔¶1703.7〕 Par or No Par

If par or stated value shares are provided for it will be necessary to see that the consideration for which shares may be issued under the state corporation law—usually money, property (tangible or intangible) and services—has value equal to the stated value of the shares. Otherwise, the shares are not "fully paid and nonassessable," and their issuance will be fraudulent as against the corporation, existing stockholders and creditors, and directors approving their issuance, and purchasers of the shares may be personally liable at least to the extent of the "watering." There will usually be no dollar floor on the consideration which may be accepted for no par shares, but there is the general requirement that the directors fix a fair value for the shares and make a determination that the corporation has received suitable consideration of that value for shares issued. Statute and case law determines for each state whether speculative patents and secrets, promoters' services, promissory notes, obligations to render future services or to make future payments constitute suitable consideration for the issuance of shares.

To protect organizers from liability, counsel must see that the terms of the bargain between those forming the corporation do not overvalue services and assets contributed by the organizers as against third parties. The tax collector has an interest in this, too, because the value of shares given to organizers not supported by the value of assets contributed by them may be treated as taxable compensation for services. This "watering" tax and balance sheet problem can usually be handled by getting supporting appraisals for assets or creating a debt or preferred stock leverage in the capital structure. Stamp tax considerations may also play a role in the decision to use par or no par stock.

[¶1703.8] **Preemptive Rights**

Preemptive rights may seem desirable from the standpoint of protecting the beginning shareholders. But as the corporation grows, the number of shareholders increases and additional funds are needed, preemptive rights can become very cumbersome, force unnecessary registrations and increase underwriting problems and costs so that it will become desirable or necessary to eliminate them. In most states, it is necessary to specifically negate or specifically provide for preemptive rights at the outset.

[¶1703.9] **Subscriptions**

Check statutory requirements for the enforceability of subscriptions, the requirement for writing, signature, the need to specify duration, time of payment, any limitations on notes or installment obligations, requirements as to uniformity of calls, procedure on default, propriety or forfeiture of sums paid on account, etc.

[¶1704]   TAX CONSIDERATIONS

The usual disadvantage of the corporate form lies in the variety of federal, state and local taxes which are levied against the corporate entity, and the double tax burden which is normally imposed against the corporate earnings which are distributed as dividends to shareholders. However, this disadvantage may well be turned to the advantage of the organizers if the effective corporate tax rate lies in a lower tax bracket than that of the organizers. Moreover, this double tax bite may be avoided by a small business corporation electing to be taxed as a partnership — the so-called Subchapter S election.

Tax considerations also play a vital part in the form of capital structure to be adopted.

The checklist set out below covers the main tax considerations.

1. Subchapter S Corporation: Will it be desirable to avoid the corporate tax by having the corporation elect under Subchapter S to be taxed as a partnership (IRC §1371-1377)? What about limitation on retirement plan contributions for over-5% stockholders of Subchapter S corporations?

2. Tax-Free Incorporation: Property can be transferred on incorporation tax free, if the transferors wind up owning stock possessing at least 80% of the total combined voting power of all classes of stock entitled to vote and at least 80% of the total number of shares of all other classes of stock of the corporation (IRC §351; 368(c)).

3. Disproportionate Stock Interests: Giving an edge to a promoter or a member of the family may result in taxable compensation to the promoter. There may be a taxable gift for a party who contributes more to the corporation than he receives in order to benefit a member of his family.

4. Step-Up in Basis of Transferred Property: If the property being transferred to the corporation has increased in value and if it is desirable to pay a capital gains tax to step up its value in order to get higher depreciation allowances, it may be desirable to make the incorporation a taxable transaction (IRC §362(a)).

5. Transfer of Liabilities: If you transfer encumbered property to the corporation and it assumes the debt, the excess of the liabilities assumed plus liabilities to which the property is subject will be taxed to the transferors to the extent that they exceed the cost or other tax basis of the property (IRC §357(c)).

6. Leasing Instead of Transferring Property: Are there tax savings in leasing property to the corporation and having it pay deductible rent while the lessor deducts depreciation rather than transferring the property to the corporation?

7. Avoiding Tax to Promoters: Consider saving the promoters from having stock received by them taxed as compensation by having them buy cheap stock prior to the full financing of the corporation or by having them transfer patents, plans or models in exchange for stock in the incorporation transaction. The earlier the promoters acquire their stock the safer they are.

8. Use of Debt Plus Equity: Having those transferring property or cash to the corporation take back debentures or other corporate debt instead of stock will permit them to get deductible interest from the corporation and to have their debt paid off out of corporate earnings without having those earnings taxed to them as dividends. This is true as long as the capitalization is not so thin that the debt is held to constitute equity. You get protection against this by keeping the debt to equity ratio down around 2 or 3 to 1, by keeping the debt to an amount which banks would lend, by having the corporation meet its financial needs by borrowing from a bank even if the incorporators have to endorse, and by having the proportion of debt to stock vary as between individual stockholders. See *Ruspyn Corp.,* 18 TC 769; *Gilbert,* 262 F.2d 512.

111

9. Making Debt Obligations Stand Up: Make sure the debt obligations obtained from the corporation constitute genuine debt — i.e., have a real and definite maturity date, call for interest payments at a fixed rate, give the holders a security status over stockholders. Making stockholder debts subordinate to regular corporate creditors is frequently necessary but it increases the risk that the debt will be considered equity. See *Wetterau Grocer Co.,* 179 F.2d 158; *Gooding Amusement Co.,* 236 F.2d 159. See IRC §385 and regs thereunder.

10. Using Preferred Stock: Consider creating a preferred stock as part of the original capitalization. Subsequent creation of preferred stock after the corporation has earnings and profits will result in the preferred stock becoming §306 stock so that gains on selling it will be taxed as ordinary income.

11. Assuring Ordinary Loss Deductions if Business Goes Bad: Consider qualifying the stock under §1244, making it small business stock by an appropriate resolution, so that any loss on the investment will be deductible against ordinary income to the extent of $25,000 a year or $50,000 on a joint return.

12. Avoiding Collapsible Corporations: Don't overlook the collapsible corporation rules. These provisions convert the capital gains available on liquidations and the sale of corporate stock into ordinary income. If more than 70% of the gain is attributable to appreciated corporate property which has been held for less than three years, these rules may apply (IRC §341).

13. Deducting Organization Expenses: Code §248 permits a corporation to treat organization expenditures as "deferred expenses," and to write them off as tax deductions. The length of the "writeoff" period may be selected by the corporation provided it is not less than sixty months; and it starts when the corporation begins business.

14. Employee-Stockholder Benefits: Employee-stockholders of the corporation may secure the benefits of a pension or profit-sharing trust. And the corporation's contributions (within certain limitations) are deductible by the corporation. See IRC §401-404, 1379. In addition other fringe benefits, such as group term insurance (up to $50,000 coverage), reimbursement of medical expenses, tax-free wage continuation payments, are also available. See IRC §79, 104-106.

15. Avoiding Personal Holding Company Penalties: A corporation in which five or fewer individuals own more than half the stock during the last half of the taxable year may be a personal holding company if 60% or more of its income comes from dividends, royalties, interest and rents. Rents equal to at least 50% of adjusted ordinary gross income are not personal holding company income if other personal holding company income does not exceed 10% of ordinary gross income. A personal holding company is subject to a 70% penalty tax (IRC §541-543).

16. Accumulation of Surplus: A corporation may accumulate up to $150,000 before it becomes liable for the accumulated earnings penalty tax. After that, there is an additional tax liability (27½% on the first $100,000 of accumulated taxable income and 38½% on the balance of that income) if there are unreasonable surplus accumulations. However, a corporation may retain earnings for such business purposes as the redemption of stock to pay death taxes (IRC §537).

17. Cushioning Loss: ¶5603.1 has a discussion of How to Cushion Loss, which contains a number of ideas useful in doing business in the corporate form.

[¶1705]   WHERE TO INCORPORATE

Ordinarily the state of principal business activity will be the state favored for incorporation. Selection of any other state will usually add to organizational and recurring operational costs, including tax costs, and will involve further disadvantages such as the possibility of suit against the corporation in what will likely be an inconvenient, if not hostile, "foreign" forum. If the suit is in the state of its actual operations, it will be treated there as a "foreign" corporation and as such, for example, it may be subject to attachment proceedings. The chances are that the "better" laws of another state will not be enough to offset these disadvantages. One reason for this will be the fact that many of the states once considered not so favorable have in recent years, in the process of competing for business, improved their statutes. There is today even greater uniformity in corporate statutes with the result that in most cases foreign corporate pastures are not apt to be greener.

Nevertheless the fact is that some states are more favorable than other states. The favorable climate may reside not only in statutory enactments but also in a state's courts and executive departments. Delaware is generally considered to offer a most favorable climate. Other preferred states include Illinois, Indiana, Maryland, Massachusetts, New Jersey, New York, Pennsylvania and Tennessee. Additions to the list are constantly emerging as states vie for new business.

[¶1705.1]   Corporate Factors in Selecting State

Here are some of the corporate features which may determine a decision in favor of one state or another:

1. There may be restrictions on the use of a corporate name in some states. These restrictions may come from statute or because the name has been pre-empted. It may be possible to qualify a name in one state and not in another. Where a pre-existing unincorporated name or trade name has such value that

it should be reflected in the corporate name, this may be a controlling factor.

2. Most modern corporation laws permit broad purposes, but onerous restrictions as to purpose may still crop up in some state corporation laws.

3. Some states do not authorize shares without par value. Others don't permit par-value shares of less than one dollar. Also, in some states the right to vote cannot be denied to a class of stock; for example, it may not be possible to have a nonvoting preferred stock.

4. Some states require cumulative voting in electing directors.

5. Are restrictions on the redemption of shares onerous? Can capital be used for that purpose? Can capital be restated by way of reduction or increase through appraisal in order to facilitate the purchase of shares out of surplus?

6. Does the state corporation law unduly restrict corporate indebtedness or the right to mortgage property?

7. Are there undesirable restrictions as to the sources from which dividends may be declared and paid? This phase is particularly important for a corporation selling oil or timber or any other wasting asset. If dividends are restricted to earnings without either provision or clarity as to the treatment of depletion, it may be better to go to another state which expressly authorizes directors to determine the net profits from the exploitation of wasting assets without provision or discretion as to the provision to be made for consumption of wasting assets which constitute part of the capital.

8. The place where the stockholders' meeting is required to be held, and the discretion to hold it out of the state, may be an important operational factor.

9. What percentage of the vote is required to amend the charter, sell assets? To assure control for a 51% stockholder may be important; it may be important that the percentage of the vote required for this step should be less than two-thirds, for example. Also, a requirement of two-thirds or more may become difficult to meet if the shares become widely dispersed.

10. What liability may be inflicted on stockholders under the corporate law? There are differences, for example, as to whether or not stockholders may be liable for wages due employees for services rendered prior to insolvency.

11. There may be differences in the liability which may be inflicted upon directors for improper declaration of dividends or for acts or omissions which result in loss to the corporation, the stockholders, or its creditors. This difference may be as to the exposure to liability or the measure of damages.

12. There may be restrictions on or lack of a clear provision for the indemnity by the corporation of directors for alleged misconduct.

13. Some lawyers think that having the corporation form outside of the main locale of its business may produce an advantage in creating the likelihood of diversity of citizenship, which will give the corporation an option to take suits between the corporation and its customers or suppliers into the Federal Courts.

14. Some states have publication requirements or approvals by state officials which cause delay. Where one wants to have a corporation right away, this may dictate the choice of a state where it is sufficient merely to file the corporate charter.

〔¶1705.2〕 Tax Factors in Selecting State

Property Tax: This will usually be levied by the state in which the property is located, which will be controlled by business considerations.

Intangibles: If the corporation will own securities, or maintain large bank balances and accounts receivable, it will become necessary to consider whether the state of incorporation as well as the state in which the principal business office is maintained may try to tax intangibles.

Capital Stock Tax: Check to see whether the state or domicile imposes a tax on the going value of the corporation itself.

Income Taxes: Most states imposing income taxes do not distinguish between domestic and qualified foreign corporations in allocating income attributable to the state and subjecting it to income tax. In most cases the amount so allocated would usually be taxed at the same rate. Thus, the income tax factor does not particularly influence the choice of a state of incorporation. There are still a few states which levy tax upon the entire net income of domestic corporations, while permitting foreign corporations to allocate their income in accordance with an established apportionment formula. This may be mitigated by allowing credit for income taxes paid to other states, or a deduction of that income for business or investment in another state. Other things to check in determining the impact of a state income tax law are whether the deduction of Federal income taxes is permitted and whether operating loss carryovers are allowed.

Franchise Taxes: Some states impose an annual franchise tax on domestic corporations but not upon foreign corporations. In most states there is substantial uniformity of treatment of domestic and qualified foreign corporations as far as the rate and base of the annual franchise tax are concerned. In a few states, there is a difference between either the rate or the base of the tax as applied to domestic and qualified foreign corporations. Also, a few states base their franchise taxes upon the entire authorized capital stock of a domestic corporation. In most states, the base is the proportion of issue capital or capital and surplus represented by property located and business transacted within the state. There are wide variations in rates.

[¶1706]   **PROCEDURAL STEPS IN CORPORATE
                        ORGANIZATION**

The steps required to carry through incorporation will vary. Here is a comprehensive checklist of such steps, all of which will not be required in any one jurisdiction:

1. Check availability of name and reserve.
2. Complete and execute preincorporation agreements.
3. Draft and file articles of incorporation (sometimes publication of notice and filing a proof of publication are required—in other instances approval of a court or state official may be required).
4. Pay filing fees and organization tax.
5. Hold organizational meeting.
6. Get subscriptions to the stock.
7. File any other papers required — designation of agent for service of process, statement of paid-in capital, officers' oaths are some of the things that may be required.
8. Check to see whether there is any local filing requirement in city or county.
9. Draft by-laws.
10. Check to see whether any special authorization is required to issue securities.
11. Get corporation outfit — seal, stock register, minute book, and stock certificate book.
12. Hold meeting at which incorporators elect permanent directors and take other organizational steps.
13. Hold organizational meeting of board of directors.
14. Authorize issuance of stock, accept stock subscriptions.
15. Get payment or transfer of property for stock and issue certificates. See that directors get appraisals of property or otherwise make a determination of value.
16. Pay applicable state stock-issue tax, affixing and cancelling tax stamps.
17. File whatever papers are required subsequent to organization; i.e., list of shareholders, directors, officers, statement of location of office, designation of agent, etc.
18. Qualify in other states where business is to be conducted.

[¶1706.1]   **Drafting Articles of Incorporation**

Preparation of "articles of incorporation" or "the corporate charter" or "a certificate of incorporation," the governing document required by the law of the state in which it has been decided to incorporate, is the first step in the actual incorporation process. Many states have statutory forms of certificates of incorporation. Sometimes these are required, sometimes optional. Where there are no such forms, as is the case in New York or Delaware, it is necessary to draft a charter which specifies the essentials of the corporate arrangements as permitted and required by applicable law. The governing statute should be checked to determine the necessary contents of the articles of incorporation. The following articles are usually required:

1. Corporate name.

2. The purposes for which the corporation is formed.

3. The location of its office.

4. The duration of the corporation if it is to be other than perpetual.

5. Its powers if it is to be endowed with powers other than those prescribed by the governing law.

6. The designation of the Secretary of State as an agent for the service of process and an address to which he is to mail process.

7. The number and classification of shares and whether they are with or without par value; if more than one class of shares is authorized, the designations, the relative rights, preferences, and limitations of each class are to be specified with respect to voting, priority in liquidation, income, etc.

Items which *may* be required are these:

1. A minimum capital, if required by law, with which the corporation will commence business.

2. Extension or elimination of preemptive rights.

3. Whether the private property of the shareholders will be liable for corporate debts and if so to what extent.

4. The name and address of each incorporator.

5. The number of directors constituting the initial board of directors.

A broad range of regulatory provisions may be incorporated in the charter. Among them are these:

1. Provisions restricting the transfer of shares.

2. Provisions for amending, repealing or adopting bylaws.

3. Reserving the shareholder's right to fix consideration for no-par shares.

4. Quorum requirements for shareholders' meetings (either providing for more or less than a majority).

5. Cumulative voting.

6. Restrictions on the powers of the board.

7. Classifying directors so as to provide for a staggered board.

8. Quorum requirements for directors' meetings (more or less than a majority).

9. Voting requirements for directors' meetings (specifying matters on which unanimity or more than a majority is required).

10. Provision for executive or other committees.

11. Reservation to shareholders of the power to elect officers.
12. Provision for dissolution at demand of minority stockholders.
13. Removal of directors by shareholders.
14. Provision for special meetings.

[¶1706.2] The Corporate Name

There are several requirements with respect to the corporate name:

1. It must be the same name filed with the state office which keeps corporate records. This means that it must not be the same or so similar to the name of other corporations that it will either confuse or deceive.

2. The name must include corporation, incorporated, company, or limited, or an abbreviation of one of these names. Sometimes, as in New York, the name "company" is considered as not to indicate clearly that the entity is incorporated and is therefore not permissible.

3. The name must not include a word or words which would indicate an activity or implied powers that a corporation may not have, such as the practice of a profession which would require incorporation under a special statute (investment, bank, insurance, etc.).

The name selected, backed up by one or more alternatives, should be submitted to the proper officials for preliminary clearance at an early stage in the organizational proceedings before expense is incurred for corporate stationery, record books, share certificates, seal, etc. Many states permit reservation of a corporate name, but the reservation may not amount to final clearance, and if it doesn't, you can't bank on it. When alternate names are submitted, the submission should be in the order of preference, since the state officials will usually stop checking when they've found one name that is OK.

In some cases you might want to check out the assumed names filed in the locale where the business is to be carried on. The fact that the corporate authorities clear a name doesn't give you immunity from claims of unfair competition if in fact the name approved duplicates or is confusingly similar to another's name.

It should be borne in mind that a corporate name may also serve as a trade name and may be registered as such so that it may be desirable to check the name in the state or federal register of trade names.

[¶1706.3] Bylaws

Bylaws aren't necessary unless they are made so by statute or by the certificate or articles of incorporation. Some statutes state the law unless otherwise provided in the articles or certificate of incorporation, while others state the law unless otherwise provided in the articles or bylaws and some unless otherwise provided in the bylaws. Where you have statutes of the first or last type, it is clear that there is no choice as to whether a particular matter within the ambit of the statute is to be dealt with in the articles of incorporation or the bylaws. The choice exists only in the intermediate type of statute.

There is no fixed rule for making the choice. Generally speaking, the regulation of business methods is an appropriate matter for the bylaws. One thing to bear in mind is that the articles or certificate of incorporation become a matter of public record, whereas the bylaws are private and not open to examination by members of the public.

Apart from changing statutory provisions, some look on bylaws as something to be used by the officers and directors of the corporation as a sort of administrative checklist and so include in the bylaws matters clearly covered by statute. Others follow the practice of excluding from the bylaws provisions covered by statute and rely on a separate memo to guide the officers and directors.

A reasonably concise document is apt to be more effective in most cases than a long, involved one. This is especially true in the case of small corporations where formal niceties tend to be disregarded.

If you're in a state which has adopted the Model Business Corporation Act, there is an official form of bylaws for use under the Act.

The important thing for the draftsman to keep in mind is that a good set of bylaws is one geared to the needs of the specific corporation and which anticipates, so far as possible, future developments.

Look to your local statutes to see if there's a provision as to amendment of bylaws. If you're not restricted by statute, consider writing in a provision giving the directors power to amend, except maybe provisions fixing their own qualifications, classifications or terms of office, subject to stockholder veto. Giving the Board the right to amend bylaws is likely to result in more flexible and effective administration.

●

For Further Reference . . .

Corporate Planning (looseleaf service), Institute for Business Planning, Englewood Cliffs, N.J.

Israels, *Corporate Practice,* Practising Law Institute, New York, N.Y.

Knapp and Semmel, *Forms of Business Organization and the Federal Tax Laws,* Practising Law Institute, New York, N.Y.

McDonald, *Corporations and Corporate Distributions,* Practising Law Institute, New York, N.Y.

Oleck, Howard, *Modern Corporation Law.*

CORPORATE LEGAL EXPOSURE AND PROTECTION

[¶1901] The practicing lawyer is expected to be aware of the legal liabilities to which a corporation may be exposed, to advise the management as to the steps to be taken to protect the corporation from these liabilities and to review the operation of the corporation from time to time to see that unnecessary liability is not being incurred and that necessary protective measures are being kept in force. The unexpected difficulties which plagued corporations recently in exposure to antitrust and conflict of interest liability sharply pointed up the need for regular review and systematic education of officers, salesmen, engineering executives and others to the risk that may unwittingly or innocently inflict legal liability on the corporation and educate them as to the protective steps that should be taken.

A checklist which can be used to review the legal posture of a business client follows.

1. Accident, Liability and Property Damage: This is an area which should be regularly analyzed and reviewed to determine the type and amounts of risk exposure that may exist and the adequacy of insurance protection. See ¶3101 et seq.

2. Antitrust Risks: This involves pricing policy, distribution and licensing agreements, sales procedures and competitive practices in general.

In this area, it is highly desirable to prepare a statement of company policy on compliance with the antitrust laws, disseminate this to all employees coming into contact with policy or with the public, and require them to submit written reports with respect to any conversation or other occurrences which raise any possibility of an allegation of antitrust violation.

3. Inventions and Proprietary Data: Corporate funds may be expended on product development and design, either carried out by employees of the corporation or by outside contractors. To protect this investment, it is important to place employees and outside contractors under written obligation to assign to the corporation any inventions developed with company money and time and to hold research information confidential. Employees having access to customers should be placed under confidential disclosure and possibly non-competition agreements. See Chapter on Employment (¶2301).

4. Submitted Ideas: In the course of a year many people may send unsolicited letters containing ideas and suggestions which relate to a company's business and its products. Some of the ideas are technical and others relate to business proposals, advertising techniques or corporate procedures. Many of the ideas submitted will be known to the corporate officers or will merely contain information which would have been normally developed in the course of the research preparatory to considering any new line of activity. The company will be exposed to a claim for compensation if it unconditionally accepts an idea or proposal and later engages in any activity resembling the proposal. To protect the company against this kind of a claim, it is important to respond quickly to all submissions and not entertain them unless the submitter has signed a written agreement with respect to the understanding under which his idea is submitted. See Chapter on Ideas and Secrets (¶3001).

5. Conflicts of Interest: To avoid conflicts of interest it is desirable to write out a company policy with respect to the kind of investment interest which will be considered permissible and require employees to disclose their interests in any supplier, customer or other organization with which the company does any business.

6. Corporate Opportunity: It is advisable to adopt a rule requiring directors and officers who may be offered business opportunities which may conflict with the interests of the company or which may be of value to the company to present such matters to the Board of Directors for review and determination as to whether or not the acceptance of such a business opportunity would be in any way objectionable.

7. Securities Sales: The improper sale by the company of unregistered securities or a failure to make full disclosure in a registration statement can make the company liable for the return of the money for which the securities were sold. See Chapter on Securities, Their Ownership and Transfer (¶5101).

8. Records Retention: Management is interested in saving the labor and storage costs involved in preserving records and counsel is interested in seeing that all records which may preserve the company's legal interest are kept. The scope of the problem can be realized by noting the great number of records a corporation is required to keep by statute. In the first place every corporation subject to tax is required to keep such permanent books of account or records, including inventories, as are sufficient to establish the amount of gross income and deductions, credits and other matters called for by any tax return. Wage-hour and unemployment insurance programs require detailed payroll records. Miscellaneous regulatory agencies require that particular records be kept. For its own protection a corporation must keep certain records for periods covered by statutes of limitation.

In general, permanent records consist of real estate deeds, copyright and trademark papers, retirement and pension plans, corporate organization papers, tax returns and receipts, payroll records, cancelled checks and bank records.

Tax records must generally be kept for as long as necessary to establish tax claims. Papers relating to government contracts must be kept for periods varying from three to six years. Statutes of limitation vary in terms of one year to twenty years, depending on the particular matter involved.

State law requires that stock books containing the names and addresses of each stockholder be maintained.

Counsel should advise on a program of record retention and record disposal.

9. Dividend Policy: Where corporate earnings are accumulated rather than distributed to a significant degree, see that a record is kept of the purpose for which the funds are being accumulated in order to protect the corporation against the imposition of a penalty tax under §531 for unreasonable accumulation of earnings. Of course it is important to check all dividend action against State law with respect to source of payment to avoid possible liabilities to creditors.

10. Labor Relations: Impress upon corporate officers the importance of talking to counsel whenever there are demands for union representation, the threat of strikes or boycotts, demands for arbitration of disagreements. Check State minimum wage laws and Federal Fair Labor Standards Act (the latter if interstate operations are involved) against actual wage policies. Check wages and working conditions, not only with statutory requirements, but with the prevailing local standards. Make sure that corporate management faced with union organizational activity understands that it is not permitted to use threats, coercion or promises to combat such activity and cannot fire employees because of their organizational efforts. At the same time management should be advised that it otherwise retains freedom of speech and communication with its employees, and has a right to demand and ordinarily should demand an NLRB or equivalent State Board election when a union claims to be the bargaining representative of the employees, even if the demand is backed with signed cards of a majority of employees, since their signatures may have been given not out of conviction but to avoid argument. Check union contract, if any, and make a note of expiration date so that timely notice can be given to proper Federal and State authorities as well as to the union with respect to desired changes in the contract. If the union sends such notice and the employer doesn't, the subjects open to negotiation will be restricted. A blanket termination notice is often a good idea as it may assure reconsideration of all matters covered by the contract.

11. Libel and Slander Exposure: Labor disputes, proxy contests, employee discharges, collection letters, sales letters and ordinary business letters—all these can result in the corporation being sued for libel and slander. Misrepresenting or disparaging a competitor's product can result in a defamation suit or a cease and desist order from the Federal Trade Commission. The corporation can be liable for statements of its agents or employees. To minimize the risk of this exposure, see that employees follow a set of rules somewhat like the following:

(a) Use temperate and dignified language when you communicate with employees, with other companies, or with the general public. Venomous or insulting language, besides inviting lawsuits, may cause loss of the defense of truth by making the statements appear malicious.

(b) If you must make a statement which might be defamatory, remember that the statement should say no more than the situation demands. For instance, if you want it a matter of record that a particular employee was dismissed for dishonesty, say just that; don't include a secondary charge that he was drunk on occasion as well.

(c) Investigate the accuracy of any proposed statement that might be defamatory. Be sure it's the truth.

(d) Don't communicate the statement to those with no interest in its subject matter.

(e) Above all, avoid unnecessarily defaming anyone. Do this by deleting references to rumors, opinions or personalities in company communications.

12. Discrimination in Employment: Discrimination in hiring practices because of race, creed, color or national origin is now prohibited by most states; many include age, and a few, sex. Federal law bars discrimination based on race, color, religion, sex, age, or national origin.

Violators may be subjected to civil suit, cease and desist orders, fines or imprisonment. Additional costs are:

(a) Constant inquiry and intervention by the govenment agency in charge.

(b) Costly and time-consuming litigation.

(c) Complaints from employees or employee prospects with loss of good will.

(d) Characterization of the company in many quarters as un-American

Here are some things that your employment interviewer should avoid:

(a) Don't ask an applicant for his original name if his name has been changed by court order.

(b) Ask for proof of age in the form of working papers issued by school authorities and not for a birth or baptismal certificate.

(c) Don't ask questions which would indicate or attempt to determine religious identification or customs.

(d) Don't ask an applicant to attach a photograph to his application form.

(e) Don't ask an applicant for his nationality or that of his parents or his wife. You can ask if he can read, speak or write a foreign language.

Where work on classified government contracts is involved, it is permissible to go a little further in inquiring into background, national origins, etc.

13. Inducing Breach of Contract: In hiring an employee or in taking business away from a competitor, be careful that the corporation has not committed the tort of inducing another party to breach or terminate its contract. Officers and directors of the corporation, as well as the corporation, can be sued for wrongly interfering with the contract relationships of another party.

14. Product Liability: Consumers of a company's product are increasingly being awarded damage verdicts against manufacturers, whether there was an express warranty or not, and even whether there was any privity of contract between the injured person and the manufacturer. This risk can be covered by product liability insurance, which may be expensive. Even if it is, suits of this character create bad publicity. Here is a list of steps to have your clients take to minimize exposure to this kind of liability:

(a) Get products pretested by an independent laboratory.

(b) Set up a quality control program.

(c) Make instructions crystal clear and display them prominently on labels.

(d) Make warranty definite—stating exactly what is being warranted and what is not. If the component parts or accessories are being warranted by others, see that these warranties are passed on.

(e) Check product advertising and promotion to see that the claims being made do not unnecessarily attract product liability lawsuits.

(f) Carry product liability insurance. A policy with proper coverage can protect you against claims against defective products, mislabeled ones, products sold for improper use or under improper circumstances, negligence and breach of implied warranty.

●

For Further Reference . . .

Corporate Planning (looseleaf service), Institute for Business Planning, Englewood Cliffs, N.J.

Feuer, M., *Personal Liabilities of Corporate Officers and Directors,* Prentice-Hall, Englewood Cliffs, N.J.

Israels, *Corporate Practice,* Practising Law Institute, New York, N.Y.

Oleck, *Modern Corporation Law.*

Seward, *Basic Corporate Practice,* American Law Institute, Philadelphia, Pa.

CORPORATE OFFICERS' AND DIRECTORS' LIABILITY

[¶2001]   Neither insiders nor outsiders are insurers of the corporation. So long as there is a reasonable basis for making a certain decision, and the board acts in good faith, courts are reluctant to impose liability for mistakes in business judgment. The degree of care required is that of an ordinarily prudent man in managing his own affairs. This involves diligence: the director must pay attention to corporate affairs. (Note: a suing stockholder has the burden of proving that neglect led to the loss of which he is complaining.)

[¶2001.1]   Duty to Attend Directors' Meetings

It must be assumed that stockholders are relying upon a director's services to the corporation as a member of the board. If they are mistaken, and poor health or other factors require absence regularly from meetings, a resignation is in order. But there are other ways in which a director can familiarize himself with what's going on. He can confer with fellow directors at other times, examine the minutes and corporate records. He can let his views be known, preferably in writing. Continued inattention, while co-directors are committing breaches of trust, renders an innocent liable as well for losses sustained to the corporation.

[¶2001.2]   Responsibility of Directors to Examine Financial Statements

A director is supposed to spot the chief executive who may be treating the business as his own, misapplying funds in good or bad faith for his personal benefit. It's his job to supervise the acts of officers. He should get financial reports directly from the responsible financial officer, not second hand. He should know the terms of underlying corporate obligations, as well as the provisions of the company's charter and bylaws. If management is pursuing improper policies and practices, a director cannot avoid responsibility on grounds of ignorance.

[¶2002]   CONSEQUENCES OF NEGLECT

Directors or officers guilty of neglect may leave themselves open to:

(1) Stockholder Suits: Any holder of a substantial number of shares or one who puts up a bond to cover all estimated expenses may bring suit in behalf of the corporation against any or all directors or officers to recover money lost to the corporation by reason of breach of duty. If defendants are adjudged liable, the corporation will pay the counsel fees and expenses of the complain-

125

ing stockholder, subject to approval by the court of the reasonableness of the fees. Similarly, if the named defendants are vindicated, the corporation will practically always reimburse such defendants for their costs of the litigation. But a losing party cannot look to be indemnified.

(2) Criminal Charges: The federal government is increasingly using its most potent weapons against the individuals who make the corporation tick — the threat of imprisonment and heavy fines. Antitrust suits are the best-known instance of this. Failure to see that tax returns are filed can be another ground for criminal prosecution. The securities laws and regulations have criminal sanctions. *Note:* Misrepresentations in a registration statement are actionable not only against the signing officers but against every person who was a director at the time. Indemnification against fines and expenses may or may not be forthcoming; but no amount of money can make up the hurt of serving a term in prison.

[¶2003] DISCLOSURE OF CONFLICTING INTERESTS

In recent years the existence of conflict has been a major basis of stockholder suits. Secret profits can be recovered by the corporation. The key to avoiding trouble here is full disclosure—if you don't keep it a secret, you can't be liable. Indeed, as long as such information is divulged, it is very often considered desirable to have directors (as distinguished from officers) who have familiarity as counselors with similar businesses.

Examples of Conflict: Acquiring interest in a corporation, supplier or customer, whether it's a financial or management interest, is clearly in point; so is buying, selling or leasing property to or from the corporation. But less obvious, and hence more likely to be a pitfall, is the case of a director or substantial stockholder who comes into the corporation—perhaps through a pooling of interests—and omits to mention that he has been engaged also in another business of a similar interest which he continues to operate.

[¶2003.1] Procedures for Disclosure

Here are some steps to be taken in connection with disclosure:

(1) Policy Statement: Have the corporation adopt a statement of policy. Such a statement should be disseminated tactfully, preferably through the public relations department, and should be accompanied by an explanatory letter over the signature of the chief executive officer. If all officials, employees, customers and suppliers are so advised of the company's stand with respect to situations of political conflict, problems of this kind will probably never arise.

126

(2) Questionnaires: Self-disclosure is the best means of advising management of those affiliations and activities which may be susceptible to outside influences. Questionnaires for this purpose should be circulated at the time of preparation of the policy statement and periodically thereafter, perhaps annually when directors and key employees are furnishing information needed for the proxy statement.

The mere existence of outside interests is not sufficient disclosure, because the corporation should be advised of the size of holdings in the other firm, and the value of such holdings in relation to total wealth, whether a policy-making position is occupied there, and the extent to which the individual votes shares with or against the corporation, as well as the amount of personal profit anticipated from the other firm, and gifts or favors expected. Remember that members of the immediate family of directors and key employees are included.

(3) Divulge Activity in Stock of Outside Firms: Owning securities (but not a substantial quantity, such as 10%) of a publicly owned corporation which are regularly traded on the open market is O.K., even though the company is a competitor. Or maybe through a real estate firm a director or officer is landlord of the enterprise which he is bringing into the corporation. In either of these cases, he had better divulge and divest: offer the other business, or the real estate, first to the corporation, then to disinterested parties.

[¶2004]   CORPORATE OPPORTUNITIES

A director or officer may not acquire property in which the Company has an interest or which it requires as essential to its business, and he may not in his individual capacity seize business opportunities in conflict with the Company's interests.

Directors and officers must remember that they are not free to disregard the interests of the Company and, while acting for it, they cannot divert to themselves business opportunities which properly belong to the Company. However, there is a vast field for individual activity which lies outside the duty of a director or officer yet within the scope of the Company's business. The test is whether as a matter of fact there is a specific duty on the part of the director or officer to act in regard to any particular situation as the representative of the Company. If there is no specific duty, the director or officer may act on his own and acquire outside interests even though the Company may be in some way interested in the matter. For example, if the Company is unable to avail itself of a business opportunity or if the opportunity is not essential to its business and is not competitive with it, then an officer or director, acting in good faith, may accept the opportunity for himself. A business matter ceases to be a corporate opportunity if the Company is unable to avail itself of it because of financial reasons or legal restrictions or business policy decisions.

The Company's operations may involve such matters as patents, real property, corporations in allied fields which may be acquired as subsidiaries and others. The conflicts of interest in each case may arise in various circumstances: (1) cases in which directors undertake to negotiate for the corporation and then close the transaction for themselves; (2) business opportunities needed by the corporation to the knowledge of the directors accepted by the directors for themselves; (3) the purchase of patents necessary or useful to the corporation by directors in their individual capacities (a subsequent license to the corporation to the profit of such directors would certainly be colorable); or (4) the purchase of land known to be needed by the corporation (the resale of such land to the corporation at a profit would certainly come within the doctrine of corporate opportunity which would require the offending directors to repay such profit to the corporation).

The extreme case to which the doctrine would be applied (and has been in decided cases) is the situation where a business opportunity is developed for the individual benefit of directors or officers at the expense and with the facilities of the corporation. It should be noted that the situations in which liability is imposed on officers and directors have had special qualities of value to the particular corporation: unique real estate, important patents or formulas, a competing business or one required for the corporation's expansion. In all cases, however, the question to be resolved is whether or not the directors or officers have profited at the expense of the corporation because of disloyalty to its interests and welfare.

[¶2005] COMPETITION WITH THE CORPORATION

The standards to which a director and an officer are held in connection with competition with the corporation are somewhat different.

Director: It's expected that an outside director will have other business interests—these may even be competition. There's no harm so long as information gained from the relationship with the corporation is not used to its disadvantage. If an outside director goes too far, he must expect, if a stockholder prevails in his derivative suit, to account to the corporation for profits derived from the competing business.

Officer or Key Employee: Chances are that the employment contract specifically prohibits competition—unless certain exceptions are expressly enumerated. An officer or other employee is required to use his full working time and best efforts in behalf of the corporation. Failure to do so is a breach even if the other activity is not competition. Your client is then accountable to the corporation for profits from the other venture.

[¶2005.1] Examples of Improper Activities

If your client serves the other firm as a consultant, even though he is not active in its management, he is deemed to be competing. Soliciting the corporation's customers for the rival business is wrong. So is causing cancellation of a contract of the corporation, then having the rival take over; or using power and influence to prevent the corporation from seeking business in competition with the rival. What about after resignation? The answer is that your client still can't disclose to others confidential information acquired in the course of his association with the corporation. Nor can he take customer lists. Such information and lists are in the nature of trade secrets, and the foregoing restrictions are applicable to a director, officer or any employee both during employment and after termination of the employment.

[¶2006] TRANSACTIONS WITH THE CORPORATION

Your client is exposed to danger when the contract is between the corporation, himself, his family, associates, related corporations. Trouble lurks also when it's a deal between companies with interlocking directors. In a stockholder suit the court might force a price revision or rescision of the contract. Here's how to head off trouble.

(1) Get Independent Corporate Representation: This means having a majority of disinterested investors vote to approve the transaction. The difficulty is that the interested director might have to be counted in order to determine whether a quorum exists, even apart from counting his vote on the transaction itself. Or the interested director may so dominate the board that it's impossible to get a majority that's truly disinterested.

(2) Helpful Charter and By-Law Provisions: The trend is to eliminate the requirement of an independent quorum. Check whether your charter or by-law provisions go further and provide that the vote of the interested director may be counted. If so, remember that the test of fairness must still be met, and the burden is on the interested director, to prove the transaction is fair to the corporation.

(3) Resort to Consent of Stockholders: It may be impossible to get approval by disinterested directors. Maybe the interested director dominates or controls the board; or it's a case of reciprocal voting where each director in turn abstains on the matter in which he has an interest. To play safe in such cases, call a stockholders' meeting and seek approval by a disinterested majority of stockholders. (Or see if the charter or bylaws let interested stockholders vote also.) Then nobody can question the fairness of the transaction.

Unless stockholder approval is unanimous, a claim can yet be made that the self-dealing constitutes a gift of corporate assets, or that the compensation is so excessive as to constitute waste. *Note:* The burden of proof here is on the objecting minority stockholder.

[¶2006.1] Ultra Vires — Not Lawful Corporate Purpose

Ultra vires has been an old standby of suing stockholders; but as laws and charters broaden the scope of permissible activities, its use has been limited, except, perhaps, when it comes to corporate loans or gifts.

[¶2006.2] Consequences of Self-Dealing

A complaining stockholder may prevail upon the court to rescind the transaction by invalidating the corporate resolution which authorized it or impressing a constructive trust, which means profits must be held for the benefit of the corporation. If compensation is excessive, restitution may be required, with a credit for a fair amount.

[¶2007]   DEALINGS IN CORPORATE STOCK

Whenever company stock is about to be bought or sold, either on a personal or company level, check to see whether there is any duty or liability under state or federal securities laws, especially SEC Rul 10b-5 (the anti-fraud rule) and §16(b) of the Exchange Act of 1934 (the short-swing profits recapture provision).

[¶2007.1] State Laws

State securities laws vary greatly. Some require merely partial or full disclosure along the lines of the federal securities laws. Others impose substantive criteria which must be satisfied before the securities can be publicly sold.

The Uniform Securities Act adopted in many states contains provisions modelled on the federal laws and SEC rules, notably, Rule 10b-5.

In addition, a common-law doctrine makes any profits made by an insider trading on inside information recoverable by the corporation in a suit by a stockholder. See *Diamond v. Oreamuno,* 29 App. Div. 2d 285, N.Y. Supp. 2d 300 (1968).

[¶2007.2] Double Liability

Diamond v. Oreamuno upheld on appeal a shareholder's derivative suit which was instituted in state court against insiders for an accounting of profits realized by them when they sold shares of the corporation's stock, in anticipation of a market decrease, after learning that earnings would be sharply reduced, a fact undisclosed to the public. The court held that the insiders must account to the corporation for any profits made, since the use of the inside information was in effect a conversion of corporate property. The court recognized the possibility that the insiders might also be sued under 10b-5 by purchasers of their stock for failure to disclose material information, thus incurring double liability to the corporation and to the purchasers.

[¶2007.3] Federal Securities Laws

Section 10(b)(5) of the Securities Exchange Act of 1934 and SEC Rule 10b-5, as in the *Texas Gulf Sulphur* case (401 F.2d 833) and hundreds of other cases, prevent officers, directors and others with inside information about company affairs from utilizing their information to make profits in buying or selling company stock before the information is made public or made known to people buying or selling from or to the insider, i.e., in a fraudulent manner. The rule is applicable whether or not the security being traded is registered, listed, sold over the counter or privately, just as long as the transaction takes place in "interstate" commerce. The rule may be enforced by administrative proceedings or by private action to recover damages or rescind the transaction.

[¶2007.4] Disclosure of Inside Information to Selected Customers

The registered broker-dealer and its employees who, in connection with underwriting, received information regarding issuer's earnings, disclosed that information to some of its customers. The customers bought and sold short before the inside information was publicly disclosed. The underwriters were held to have violated the antifraud provision of the Securities Act of 1933 and the Exchange Act of 1934. *In re Merrill Lynch, Pierce, Fenner & Smith, Inc.,* Exch. Act Release No. 8459, 11/25/68.

[¶2007.5] Moral of Merrill Lynch Case

The *Merrill Lynch* case is important not only because it extends 10b-5 liability to tippees, but also because it emphasizes the inherent danger open to persons who function in a dual capacity. *Merrill Lynch* got into trouble because in functioning as investment advisor and broker it disclosed information which it had received as an underwriter to some of its big institutional investors. Underwriters who are also brokers are going to have to isolate the two functions. The same would apply to anyone else in a potential conflict-of-interest situation, e.g., a lawyer or accountant who comes across inside information in the course of his work for a corporation had better not pass it on to others in his capacity as a trustee or agent.

Tippees: Information is deemed material if it would be meaningful to a reasonable speculator, not merely a conservative investor.

Insiders who purchased on the basis of undisclosed material information had to give up their profits in the *Texas Gulf Sulphur* case. (the profit was the mean average price of Texas Gulf stock the day the strike news hit the investing public, less the price the insiders paid).

What's more, insiders who recommended the purchase of Texas Gulf when they had material information were liable for the profits made by their tippees.

Precautions: Obviously, if you're an insider who knows something the investing public doesn't and you buy your company's stock, you run afoul of the antifraud rule. But if you don't know and then the news of a big deal is revealed, and your stock skyrockets, find out what's going on before you do any trading of your company's stock.

[¶2007.6] Rule 10b-5

Rule 10b-5 doesn't say anything about civil liability. Numerous court decisions quite early in the history of the Rule sustained a right of private action for violation of 10b-5. Court-inferred civil liability has helped to catapult the rule into its now prominent position.

The rule declares that it is unlawful for any person, directly or indirectly, by the use of the mails or any means of interstate commerce in connection with the purchase or sale of any security:

(1) to use any device, scheme, or artifice to defraud;

(2) to make any untrue statement of a material fact or to omit a material fact which makes the statement made misleading; or

(3) to engage in any act, practice or course of business which operates as a fraud or deceit on any person.

[¶2007.7] Illustrations of Material Facts

Here are some illustrations, taken from actual cases, of material facts calling for disclosure under the rule:

(1) The improved financial condition of the firm.

(2) A dividend cut.

(3) A contract for the sale of corporate assets.

(4) A contemplated liquidation of a subsidiary for the purpose of capturing inventory appreciation of the subsidiary.

(5) A new ore discovery.

(6) The fraudulent trading in company's stock by a third party.

Under Rule 10b-5: Experts usually include the following in any list of potential insiders:

(1) Directors, officers, and majority security holders.
(2) Lower echelon employees.
(3) Outside professional advisers: lawyers, accountants, engineers, management counselors, public relations consultants, financial advisors, and testing labs.
(4) Business connections: lenders, underwriters, proposed merger partners, customers, and suppliers.
(5) Analysts and institutional investors; their firms, associates, and families; and their brokers.
(6) The press until it disseminates.

Add to this the liability of "tippees" under the *Texas Gulf Sulphur* ruling and the liability ramifications of disseminating inside information multiply even further.

〔¶2007.8〕 Insiders

Texas Gulf Sulphur imposes a duty on every corporation whose securities may be traded to disclose any and all material facts that would affect investors' trading *whether or not* the corporation or insiders have traded a single share.

〔¶2007.9〕 Applicability of 10b-5 to Small Corporations

Small companies may be more vulnerable to 10b-5 attacks than larger outfits. Often, they may fall into 10b-5 traps because of their lack of counsel and inability to keep up with developments.

What's more, small corporations and closely held corporations are apt to have a particularly heavy burden regarding disclosure because many more things will be material to them than to large firms. For instance, almost any acquisition by a small company is a material fact whereas an acquisition involving millions might not be material to an outfit like General Motors.

〔2007.10〕 "Reasonable Waiting Period" Construed

It's not the actual time the item appears on the ticker, but the time when it could *reasonably have been expected to appear.* There is dictum in *TGS* to the effect that insiders would be advised to refrain from trading for a "reasonable waiting period," to give the news a chance to filter down and be evaluated by the investing public. A longer time might be required for news of developments affecting a closely held corporation. The New York Stock Exchange recommends a suspension in trading until 15 minutes after tape appearance, unless there is an unusual influx of orders.

[¶2007.11]   Indemnification and Insurance Protection

Corporation indemnification is probably the most widely used technique for protecting the officer or director from personal liability. However, indemnification statutes contain their own limitations regarding the class of persons covered, the requirement of good faith, etc. In *Globus et al. v. Law Research Service, Inc. and Blair & Co.*, U.S.D.C., S.D.N.Y., 7/2/68, the court prohibited the underwriter from enforcing an indemnification agreement against the company, as a way of motivating the underwriter to faithfully perform his duties under §11 of the Securities Act of 1933.

Another possible avenue of protection is insurance coverage. The last 20 years have seen the growth of the directors' and officers' liability policy (D&O). It generally covers SEC liability (excluding §16(b) liability) and is usually written with a larger deductible provision plus a co-insurance clause. However, newly formed corporations and closely held companies may find it difficult to get D&O coverage. Specific SEC coverage is also available but this covers only federal securities law and rules violations with public offering.

[¶2007.12]   Short-Swing Profits

If an officer, director or 10% stockholder, within a six-month period, buys and sells, or sells and buys (whether pursuant to an option or otherwise) registered securities of the corporation, any profit he makes in so doing is recoverable by the corporation under §16(b) of the 1934 Act.

The basic purpose of §16(b) is to prevent insiders from speculating in the stock on the basis of information not available to others but the rule is so framed as to apply whether or not in a particular case the insider has any "inside" information, and irrespective of any intention he may have as to holding a security bought or repurchasing a security sold. The only thing with which §16(b) is concerned is that the insider bought and sold within six months and made a profit. It gives a maximum degree of predictability and a minimum degree of equity, contrasted with Rule 10b-5, which has been said to give a maximum degree of equity with a minimum degree of predictability.

Section 16(b) applies only when there's a "purchase" or "sale." The Act says that the terms "buy" and "purchase" both include any contract to buy, purchase or otherwise acquire, and the terms "sale" and "sell" both include any contract to sell or otherwise dispose of securities. Bona fide gifts will not be considered "sales" by the donor nor "purchases" by the donee.

Who's an "Officer"? The president, vice president, treasurer, secretary and comptroller are subject to the insider trading requirements. The SEC has said that anyone performing functions corresponding to those usually performed by the officers named is within the reach of the section. Assistant vice presidents, treasurers, secretaries, or comptrollers won't normally be subject to the section but they may be if the principal officer is so inactive that the assistant performs the chief's functions. Functions rather than the title control.

[¶2007.13] Timing of Short Swings

A director is liable for short-swing profits even though he was not a director at the time he bought the stock. See *Adler v. Klawans,* 267 F.2d 840 (1959). Purchases and sales before or after your tenure of office are to be matched against sales or purchases made after you took office in figuring your short-swing profits liability. Transactions after you are no longer an officer or director are exempt, at least if they occur in the month after your retirement or resignation. You are, however, required to report transactions occurring in the month after your severance. The date on which you become an officer or director can be very important. Check to see that the corporate records accurately reflect your status.

[¶2007.14] Short Swing Extended and Limited

The common-law liability recognized in *Diamond* (supra) may catch those situations which escape §16(b) liability as, for example, where transactions in company stock occur outside the six-month, short-swing limitation. However, common-law liability requires proof and use of the insider's knowledge, whereas §16(b) is applicable whether or not the insider has or uses any confidential information. If the particular deal fits into the time limitation, the insider again could be faced with double liability to the corporation.

The SEC has contended that a single or package plan for a two-step stock sale comes within the purview of §16(b). Thus, it maintained that if a corporation makes an initial purchase of over 10% of a target corporation's stock it becomes a 10% owner at the time of purchase and is subject to the short-swing profit rule; it cannot avoid liability by selling, within six months, sufficient shares to reduce its holdings to 10%, and sell the remainder subsequently. However, while the SEC position was upheld in the federal district court, it was rejected by the United States Supreme Court in *Emerson Electric Company v. Reliance Electric Company,* 438 F.2d 918.

If you're an officer or director and you paid a premium to gain control of a corporation, the proper measure of damages will be fair market value of the stock *PLUS* any premium over market if you trade or convert within the statutory six-month limit.

135

A suit to recover short-swing profits can be brought by the corporation or any security holder if the corporation fails or refuses to do so within 60 days of request. The federal District Courts have exclusive jurisdiction of these suits. Suit must be brought within two years from the time the profits are realized.

Counsel is entitled to a generous percentage of the profits recovered as a fee. A fee may also be earned by serving a request on the corporation to institute suit where the corporation does so and recovers.

[¶2007.16]   Risks and Pitfalls Under §16(b) and Rule 10b-5

	§ 16(b)	Rule 10b–5
Transactions covered	Short-swing purchase *and* sale or sale *and* purchase	Purchase *or* sale
Subject matter of transaction	Equity security, registered or not	Any security, registered or not
Must firm have other registered securities?	Yes, equity securities	No
Who is subject to liability?	Officers, directors and 10% stockholders	Officers, directors and controlling stockholders, plus corporation, and persons with "inside" information
Is misrepresentation, omission or scheme necessary to impose liability?	No	Yes
Exempt transactions?	Yes, a variety of exemptions exist	No
Is direct dealing with party necessary?	No	No
Who has right of action?	Corporation	Person buying from or selling to insider or SEC
Remedies available?	Action for damages	Action for damages, rescision, disciplinary proceedings, criminal proceedings
Measure of damages?	Lowest price in, highest out, or vice versa, during short-swing period	Compensatory

【¶2007.17】 Liability to Individual Buyer or Seller of Stock

You may be liable to an individual buyer or seller of stock under SEC Rule 10b-5 (¶2007.2 above) even though the transaction is effected through a broker and the individual concerned is faceless and unknown. But, of course, the individual concerned may never become aware of the fact that he has a claim under the insider rules and if he does, there will be serious problems of proof. Nevertheless, the requirements of the Rule cannot be ignored by insiders for, in addition to civil liabilities, there are criminal sanctions and possible SEC action to be reckoned with.

【¶2007.18】 Sale of Controlling Interest

Buyers may recover damages if they are defrauded. There is also a duty to the remaining stockholders not to turn over the corporation to a purchasing group which may have intentions of looting the company. If a premium is being offered, the remaining stockholders may have some claim on the premium. But if the premium's not excessive there should be no legal problem.

【¶2008】 ANTITRUST LITIGATION

In connection with antitrust litigation, we have to consider both possible criminal and civil liability of officers and directors.

【¶2008.1】 Criminal Liability

There are criminal sections against price fixing, division of markets, allocation of customers, boycotts, blacklists, price discrimination, allowances, rebates, etc. The government has its choice whether to try to fix criminal or civil liability. It favors criminal proceedings because of the deterrent value of stiff fines, imprisonment, or both. You can be guilty even though acting in what you believe to be the best interests of the corporation. If you knowingly participated in or authorized or ordered the illegal practices, or failed to take action to stop such practices when they came to your attention and which you had authority to prevent or stop — then you are vulnerable.

【¶2008.2】 Civil Liability

The government can elect to proceed on the civil side. A finding in a criminal action that you have violated the antitrust laws is admissible as prima facie evidence against you in a civil suit brought by a stockholder for treble damages. *Note:* It is not so admissible if the criminal action resulted in a consent decree or where there was a plea of nolo contendere — which explains the popularity of such steps on the part of defendants. If the corporation is subjected to a fine in criminal antitrust litigation, there is some question as to whether a stockholder can then prevail against the corporation's directors for having got the company into such a jam.

[¶2009]   PROTECTING OFFICERS AND DIRECTORS AGAINST LIABILITY

Here is a checklist of actions to be taken to protect against liability or mitigate damages.

(a) Rely on Professional Advice: Outside independent opinion can minimize liability in some cases but the specialist can't help you if it turns out that you fed him inaccurate data or withheld some pertinent facts. And there are situations where you must make a personal check.

(b) File Dissent: But this is not enough, you must continue to exert influence wherever possible to deter the corporation from embarking on the course which you believe is wrong and improper.

(c) Resign: This drastic step is prescribed by federal securities laws where you find that a registration statement is misleading or defective. As soon as you become aware thereof, you must protest to the corporation, advise the SEC and (if it's after the effective date of the statement) give reasonable public notice. All this, in addition to severing your connection with the corporation. It's no wonder great care is given to the preparation of registration statements.

(d) Policies of Insurance Against Liability: Available to officers, directors and others covering general liabilities while acting on corporate business or, more specifically, SEC liabilities in connection with securities registrations and offerings.

(e) Exculpatory Clauses: Look in the company's bylaws or charter for a section to the effect that a transaction shall not be invalid or an individual liable by reason of the fact that he has a personal interest in such transaction. Nowadays such blanket clauses are very common. But by far, the best protection to you lies in a specific mention of the situation in a board resolution authorizing the matter. If the deal is a fair one to the corporation, without secret profits to yourself, and you have made known all the pertinent facts, based upon which a disinterested majority of the board has indicated its approval in writing — you should have nothing to fear from a complaining stockholder.

(f) Indemnification by the Corporation: Sources of undertakings to hold you harmless in event of suit may be state laws, the company's charter or bylaws, or your own employment contract—if all so provide, so much the better. There are exceptions, however: You will not be made whole if you are adjudged liable

for negligence, or for misconduct or breach of duty, or if you are found guilty in criminal proceedings. What about the effect of settlement? In a stockholder suit the individual defendants can usually look to the corporation for reimbursement of expenses. But the plea of nolo contendere, resulting in a consent judgment in criminal litigation, leaves open the question of indemnification. Some courts hold that the defendant having been convicted, public policy forbids indemnity; others make it turn upon whether the crime was a conscious and deliberate act of wrongdoing. Such a plea is a shield as to subsequent stockholder suits, but may expose the defendant to footing his own bills in the criminal proceeding.

●

For Further Reference . . .

Corporate Planning Vol. 2, *Regulation of Securities,* looseleaf Service, Institute for Business Planning, Englewood Cliffs, N.J.

Feuer, M., *Personal Liabilities of Corporate Officers and Directors,* Prentice-Hall, Englewood Cliffs, N.J.

Israels, *Corporate Practice,* Practising Law Institute, New York, N.Y.

Jackson, Percival, *Liabilities of Corporate Director.*

Washington, G. T., and Bishop, W., *Indemnifying the Corporate Executive,* Ronald.

CREDIT AND COLLECTIONS

⟦¶2101⟧ The lawyer must be concerned with all the legal aspects of the extension of credit and should ordinarily be able to eliminate completely any risks affecting the validity of the creditor's claim against the debtor or those jointly or secondarily liable with him. Here we want to review the legal and practical considerations that the practitioner should bring to bear when he is called on to lay the legal groundwork for an extension of credit.

⟦¶2102⟧   USE OF FORMS

The use of a carefully selected form will go a long way toward eliminating legal uncertainties in the transaction. There is some diversity of opinion, however, as to whether a long or a short form should be used. The proponents of the short form say that it's safer to use a simple form that sets forth clearly the basic relationship between the parties, and to rely on general principles of law, custom and usage to take care of unusual conditions or events that may arise. Besides, they say, it is not possible to provide against every possible contingency, and if the creditor attempts to do so, he may lose out under the legal maxim "expressio unius est exclusio alterius" which freely translated carries the idea that the expression of one implies the exclusion of all not expressed.

Nevertheless, most practitioners prefer to use longer forms which undertake to spell out the rights of the parties under all of the contingencies that may possibly occur during the lifetime of the instrument. Even if a provision does nothing more than make express what would otherwise be implied it will at least serve to eliminate possible doubt as to what will in fact be implied.

⟦¶2102.1⟧ Execution of Forms

The rules applicable to the execution of other contracts apply to the execution of instruments used in credit transactions. If a person signs a credit instrument, he won't ordinarily be permitted to show that he didn't know its contents or didn't read it. Of course, if he was prevented by fraud or artifice from reading or learning the contents, he may avoid the contract. Hence, it is generally a good idea to have any instrument which is to be used plainly labelled for what it is, i.e., note, guaranty, pledge or the like.

⟦¶2103⟧   BINDING A CORPORATION

The doctrine of ultra vires is one that is in the process of change and the current status of the doctrine in your jurisdiction should be checked before your client enters any substantial transaction involving the extension of credit if there is any possible room for doubt as to its application. More than half of the states now have statutes limiting the use of the doctrine and, apart from statute, a majority of states follow the rule that a corporation accepting benefits under a contract is estopped from relying on the doctrine as a defense, but this still leaves a minority of states in which the defense may bar a creditor's claim based on contract, subject to a possible quasi contractual recovery against the corporation. Moreover, the rule of estoppel based on receipt of benefits won't help in those situations where the corporation hasn't received any direct benefits. Thus, it must be borne in mind that corporations generally have no power to guarantee the obligations of, or lend credit to, another person or corporation. Attempted validation of the contract by a majority of the stockholders won't even save it. If the act of guaranteeing is found to be actually in furtherance of the business of the corporation or was reasonably calculated to promote the business, the corporation may be bound. The general rule is that a corporation may guarantee the obligations of a subsidiary, but the converse is not true. The rules as to corporate power to guarantee must be borne in mind not only in connection with transactions which on their face are guarantees but also as to transactions which although not in form guarantees partake of their nature such as subordination agreements and consents to pledge executed by corporations.

Every transaction involving the extension of credit to a corporation does not, of course, require a corporate resolution or the sanction of a bylaw to sustain its validity. In practice, however, if the transaction is a substantial one, the creditor will want to satisfy himself that the corporation has power to enter into the transaction and that the officers executing the papers evidencing the transaction on behalf of the corporation are actually duly authorized to do so, and for this purpose will require a certified copy of a resolution of the board of directors authorizing the officers in question to act on behalf of the corporation in connection with the transaction. The certificate should also recite that the resolution adopted is in accordance with the bylaws of the corporation, since in the event of conflict between the resolution and the bylaws, the latter would be controlling.

[¶2104]   BINDING A PARTNERSHIP

A person extending credit to a partnership will want to know that the person he's dealing with has authority to bind the partnership. The authority of a partner to act as agent for the partnership is limited to transactions within the scope of the partnership business. As to such transactions each partner is personally liable. Persons dealing with a firm have a right to assume that the authority of the partner is coextensive with the business transacted by his firm, but this presumption can be rebutted by evidence that credit was given to the individual partner alone or by proof that it was known that the partner acted without the authority and consent of his copartners. An unauthorized act of a partner may, of course, become binding on the partnership by subsequent ratification and acceptance of benefits with knowledge of the facts may operate as ratification. If there is doubt as to the authority of the partner, the creditor will want the consent of the other partners, or if they are not available, he will at least want to check out the articles of partnership.

[¶2105]   LIABILITY OF HUSBAND, WIFE, FATHER AND MINOR CHILDREN

When the prospective debtor is a married woman or a minor and she or the child refuses to pay, what's the legal situation? When can you hold the husband of the woman liable for her debt or the father liable for his child's debt?

Generally, a man is not liable for his wife's debts except those she runs up for necessaries. These consist of food, clothing, housing and medical care. The extent of the liability is measured by so-called station in life or what she has been accustomed to. The husband can escape from this type of liability by showing that he provided her with sufficient funds to pay for the necessaries.

Essentially the same rule applies so far as a father's liability for the debts of his children is concerned, except that in the case of a child some courts have held expenses of education to be necessaries in addition to the other items.

A minor is himself liable for debts incurred in buying necessaries, and this liability may include money borrowed for the purpose of buying necessaries and actually used for that purpose. Beyond this the minor is generally not liable for debts incurred. However, there are exceptions. In some states such as New York and Virginia you can hold a minor to an agreement made by him in the course of business, although in Virginia the minor has an "out" if the fact of his minority is posted and advertised. Also a minor may lose his contractual disability if he is "emancipated," as by marriage, or the rarer cases of consent of parents or decree of court. Further, a minor's misrepresentation of his age in entering a transaction will in a few states bar him from relying on infancy to get out of the deal.

Limited Liability: Both the father's liability for his child's necessaries and the child's own liability for them is limited to the reasonable value of the goods or services and is not measured by what the minor agreed to pay.

Age Limits: The age of minority may vary from state to state but generally it's either under twenty-one or under eighteen. On this you'll have to check your local statutes.

These rules, both those affecting a father's liability for his child and a husband's liability for his wife, must be borne in mind whenever the question involves extension of credit to a married woman or minor.

[¶2106] HOW TO HANDLE COLLECTION CLAIMS

As soon as a claim is received, a numbered file should be opened for it and the client furnished with an acknowledgment of receipt showing the file number. The acknowledgment should also refer to any special fee arrangement applying and should call for additional details that may be necessary to process the claim.

[¶2106.1] Information to be Obtained

The following is a rundown of questions you may want your client to answer before proceeding with collection steps:

(1) Identity and character of debtor? If individual, infant or married woman (where material)? Partnership? Corporation? Has debtor been known by any other name?

(2) Nature of claim? Alimony? Installment contract? Goods sold? Money lent or had and received? Services (nature, professional, etc.)? Evidence?

(3) Other persons liable or security? Nature of liability of others, joint or several, surety or guarantor? Evidence?

(4) Has client sent one or more bills which debtor has accepted without protest as to liability or amount, and, if so, when?

(5) Defenses or disputes as to claim, client's evaluation thereof, evidence relating thereto, correspondence, record of conversations, names of witnesses and expected testimony.

(6) Evaluation of business relationship and possibilities of continuance thereof.

(7) Financial condition of debtor. Did debtor at any time furnish financial statement? If danger of insolvency, client's knowledge as to assets, bank accounts, real estate, cars, securities, etc. Current credit report, if available.

[¶2106.2] Legal and Factual Analysis of Information

When the information gathering process has ended, the lawyer must then make a legal and factual analysis of the claim taking into consideration the applicable law, the nature of the claim, the character of the debtor and all other pertinent data. If others are liable he must decide whether their liability is joint or several, primary or secondary, whether they are guarantors or sureties, and if there is a guaranty whether it is one of collection or payment. If the obligation is on an installment contract, he must consider the default and acceleration provisions, and the avoidance of splitting causes of action. If the claim is against a partnership or an individual partner, consideration must be given to the method of service on the partnership and the method of reaching the partner's interest in the firm. If it's against a corporation, consideration must be given to the method of service, the possibility of the appointment of a receiver, or of asserting personal liability against officers, directors or stockholders, as on wage claims.

Claimant's attorney must also consider the defenses available, such as statute of frauds and statute of limitations and meeting them; whether complaint can be framed so as to make it one that will survive discharge in bankruptcy, for example, fraud or uttering materially false financial statement; and the advisability and availability of provisional remedies, such as attachment or arrest.

[¶2106.3] Legal Pitfalls in Collecting

Watch out for means of collection that may subject the user, attorney, client or agent, to possible civil liability as for extortion, libel or slander, or invasion of the right of privacy, or criminal liability.

Mental anguish on the part of a debtor resulting from threats to expose him as a delinquent to his employer or a credit group, or from fear engendered by the use of simulated legal process may afford a basis for both civil and criminal liability.

The mailing of publicly exposed matter tending to reflect on the character of the addressee may offend the postal laws and at the same time give rise to a cause of action for libel.

Libel is perhaps the most frequent basis for liability flowing from collection operations especially since no showing of special damages is required where the publication involved may be considered libelous per se, as where it imputes a crime or moral turpitude, or has a direct tendency to injure in business, and the requirement of publication may be satisfied by showing the matter was communicated to a stenographer or other agent of the creditor.

While truth may be offered as a defense to an action sounding in libel, it is no defense in those jurisdictions where invasion of the right of privacy based on publication of the fact of indebtedness affords a basis of action (*Brents v. Morgan,* 221 Ky. 765, 299 S. W. 967, 55 A. L. R. 964). See also 138 ALR p. 91 et seq.

The interchange of credit information between those legitimately concerned therewith may be privileged and not give rise to civil liability for publication of delinquency.

Agreements between creditors for the adjustment of debts or providing a method for the orderly payment of debts to different creditors on an equitable basis are ordinarily unobjectionable, but there have been evils in connection with such arrangements, such as excessive charges, failure to make payments to creditors, and the offering of legal advice by unauthorized practitioners, which has led to legislative intervention in a number of states. Such intervention has taken various forms, including regulation of rates, bonding requirements, licensing and in some instances outright prohibition of "budget planning" as defined by statute. California, Georgia, Illinois, Maine, Massachusetts, New York, Ohio, Oklahoma, Pennsylvania, Virginia and Wyoming are numbered among the states which have adopted legislation touching the subject. Due regard for applicable statutes must, therefore, be had in drafting agreements calling for debt pooling, budget planning, adjustment or the like.

[¶2106.4] Contact and Settlement

Depending on all the factors involved, including the amount of the claim, past efforts at collection, the relationship of the client with the debtor and similar factors, and the factors discussed in ¶2106.3 above, you will then determine whether to make the initial contact by mail, phone or a personal visit, the latter being often effective by way of impressing on the debtor your earnestness and the imminence of suit.

Usually the most feasible and often the best approach will be to send the debtor a letter showing you mean business and want payment within a certain period and if you don't get it, other steps will be taken. Of course, it should be pointed out that the debtor will be liable for the costs of a legal action and will incur other expenses as well. There may also be a suggestion that his credit rating will be further impaired by the institution of legal proceedings.

In any case, whatever the form of the contact or communication with the debtor, insist on an early response. His response may point up why he hasn't paid and whether he intends to or not. It may also apprise you of possible defenses which he feels are available to him, and may possibly serve to pin him down to those set forth.

On the expiration of the period given for response you must be prepared to proceed with the next step. If you have written or phoned and decide to make a personal visit, it is usually desirable to make the visit prepared to serve a summons, if efforts to dispose of the matter without suit should fall through.

But normally it will be best all around to settle without suit. The settlement should be evidenced by agreement covering:

(1) Acknowledgment by debtor of amount claimed and, if feasible, acknowledgment of absence of defense, counterclaim or set-off.

(2) Recital of the amount of the settlement agreed on and the terms of payment, specifying the place of payment and time and whether or not any period of grace is permitted.

(3) Default clause, providing that on nonpayment of any installment when due or within period of grace, if any, entire amount owing shall become

immediately due and payable and creditor may enter judgment by confession. The provision for confession of judgment must be drawn with due regard for common law and statutory requisites as well as statutory limitations on their effectiveness. The statutory requisites may include the filing of a statement explanatory of the facts and circumstances under which the indebtedness arose, which statement may be required to be verified or acknowledged in a particular manner and form, as by attesting to the truth of the statement, rather than the execution thereof. Where the confession is by a corporation, a certified copy of an appropriate corporate resolution should be demanded, and in the case of a partnership, execution by all the partners is a desirable safeguard.

(4) When the settlement is drawn after an action has been commenced and an answer served there should be a provision for withdrawal of the answer or discontinuance of the action without costs, and you, as attorney, should be authorized to enter judgment, without notice to the debtor or his attorney, for the amount demanded in the complaint or agreed on, together with interest, costs and disbursements.

As part of the settlement, try to get notes or post-dated checks to cover the installment payments promised, and an indorsement of them by a financially responsible person with an appropriate waiver clause (waiver of protest, demand, presentment and notice of dishonor and consent to modification or release of any party liable or of any collateral). Provision should also be made for acceleration of the entire unpaid balance on default in installment without notice or demand.

If possible you should get collateral security for payment. Mention of the collateral should be made in the settlement and the security interest must be created with an eye to the rules governing secured transactions.

On fulfillment of the terms of settlement, whether before or after suit, a general release may be granted, if demanded. You must make sure that it evidences the exact transaction and is not delivered until final payment, either in cash or by certified check, has been made. If payment is to be made by an uncertified check, the release should be held in escrow until the check has cleared.

[¶2107]   COLLECTION BY SUIT

Normally, collection by suit is a last resort when other methods of collection and settlement have failed, but sometimes you will want to start suit immediately on receipt of the claim. The facts furnished by the client and such additional information as you have been able to garner from other sources will control your decision. If, for example, you know that a petition in bankruptcy is about to be filed by or against the debtor, you have nothing to lose by immediate suit. But if the debtor is a long-time, good customer of your client and the relationship may be expected to continue following an amicable settlement, you wouldn't be helping your client by starting suit.

In ¶2106.2, we have already mentioned some of the matters that must be considered by the attorney in deciding how to proceed to realize on a claim. Here we want to deal with some other requisites of success in litigation or collecting by suit.

If you have a choice of courts within the same venue, it is generally desirable to choose the inferior court because of the likelihood of greater speed and economy of effort. Use a verified complaint where such complaint calls for a verified answer, and motions calculated to smoke out the defense, if any, and to bring you into contact with your adversary for a chance to talk settlement. In this category are motions for examination before trial, bill of particulars, or summary judgment, if available. Settlement with counsel should be accompanied by settlement agreement as discussed above. If settlement fails, you should normally try to go to trial as soon as possible consistent with the requirements of careful and skillful preparation.

[¶2107.1] Remedies After Obtaining Judgment

Once judgment is obtained, the remedies available vary quite widely from state to state but the treatment that follows should serve as a general guide.

Getting and Preserving the Lien of Judgment: A judgment does not by itself operate to create a lien on the judgment debtor's property. The creation, validity and duration of a judgment lien depends on compliance with statutory conditions and requirements and these may vary. But generally, some record or notation of the judgment must be made before it can operate as an effective lien. Some statutes require recording of the judgment, entry on the judgment docket, or on the judgment index, or some combination of these requirements. Usually the place where this is done is in the county where the property sought to be subjected to the judgment is located. It will normally cover all real property or so-called chattels real owned or subsequently acquired by the debtor and will remain effective for a statutory period, usually ten years, unless it is sooner satisfied.

Execution: This is generally, if not universally, available as a remedy for the enforcement of judgment, but will reach only property, real or tangible personalty, as to which debtor's title is undisputed, and which is not exempt (statutes in varying terms provide exemption for specific kinds and amounts of personal and real property, such as homesteads, household goods, wearing apparel, insurance and wages). Ordinarily, if a debtor has sufficient property subject to execution to satisfy the judgment, payment will be forthcoming. Collection problems arise, of course, where he lacks such property, but they may also arise when he attempts concealment, or succeeds in obtaining a stay of execution. The inadequacy of execution in certain cases has resulted in the adoption of statutory proceedings supplementary to execution which commonly provide for a full and searching examination of the debtor and of third persons having possession of property of the debtor or indebted to him, and other remedies.

Examination of the Debtor: This is most valuable and calls for the marshalling of every bit of information you have about him. There are generally available good printed forms of examination covering as many as 100 questions concerning the debtor, his residence, occupation, employment, salary, social security number, bank accounts, insurance policies, interests in real estate and various forms of property, liabilities, judicial proceedings against, books and records, transfers, expenses, income tax returns, willingness to be adjudged a bankrupt, and other matters. Too heavy reliance should not be placed on such forms, however, and the attorney should be alert to develop lines of inquiry suggested by the answers given. Use of a stenographer is desirable where the promise of the examination seems likely to justify the expense. In examining as to bank accounts bear in mind the possibility of different types of accounts: commercial, special checking, special interest, Christmas Clubs, savings bank, postal savings, savings and loan accounts, and accounts of others where debtor's signature is authorized. Use trade reports or financial statements by debtor as basis for full examination. If possible, adjourn the examination at least once to permit review and consideration of lines of inquiry. Consider aspects of substantive law bearing on the matter, such as possible liability of directors or stockholders of corporation for unpaid stock subscriptions, personal liability of stockholders for wage claims, voidability of transfers by debtor, such as under bulk sales law, transfers voidable under the Bankruptcy Act or provisions of state law as intended to hinder, delay or defraud creditors or to prefer one creditor over another, or as constructively fraudulent, as where under state law, a transfer is made while insolvent without fair consideration. Fruitful examination of debtors in supplementary proceedings requires a basic familiarity with the Bankruptcy Act, especially those provisions defining acts of bankruptcy and those dealing with voidable transfers and preferences, liens obtained by legal proceedings within four months, what debts are not discharged, and the grounds for opposing discharge. It requires also familiarity with state laws designed to protect creditors.

Examination of Third Persons: Third persons alleged to have possession of property belonging to the debtor or to be indebted to him, and witnesses who may be expected to have knowledge of the debtor's assets and other pertinent matters may also, as a general rule, be examined in supplementary proceedings. The principles governing the examination of debtor are likewise ordinarily applicable to their examination.

Garnishment, Trustee Process and the Like: Where as a result of the examination of the debtor or another or by other means it appears that a third person holds property of the debtor or is indebted to him, or debtor is entitled to receive wages or salary, trust funds, profits, insurance disability payments or the like from a third person, procedure exists in practically all states in one form or another, usually, but not always, called "garnishment" by which a creditor may reach such property, debts or claims.

The substantive and adjective provisions of "garnishment" statutes vary from state to state to an extent barring broad generalization. Variations exist as to whether the remedy is available before or after judgment or before the return of execution unsatisfied, and as to the types of debts and claims subject to garnishment. Usually, unliquidated or uncertain claims may not be reached.

Appointment of a Receiver: This approach may properly be used in aid of execution or in aid of a creditor's bill. The statutes providing for proceedings supplemental to execution generally authorize such appointment. Usually, but not always, the exhaustion of legal remedies is a prerequisite and it must be shown that the creditor has reasonable ground to believe that the debtor has property applicable to the judgment. In general, the title with which the receiver is vested and his authority, rights and duties are those of receivers generally.

If administration of property owned by the debtor is involved, especially real property, the appointment of a receiver is generally desirable. In any case where a receiver is appointed, the attorney for the creditor should not assume that he will take care of everything but should continue proceedings to discover assets for the benefit of the receiver.

Creditors' Bills and Discovery: These are additional weapons in a creditor's arsenal. A bill of discovery is a means of compelling a debtor to make a general disclosure of his assets and the names of his debtors. A creditor's bill may be used to reach property or interests of a debtor which cannot be reached by legal process. Both remedies may, therefore, be viewed as concerned with matters generally within the ambit of supplementary proceedings or garnishment proceedings, as discussed above. To the extent that the latter proceedings are available and offer an adequate remedy, the practitioner need not, and indeed, ordinarily may not, undertake to use these equitable remedies. However, where statutory remedies are nonexistent or not available under the facts presented, recourse may be had to these equitable remedies, as where one seeks to reach equitable interests which are not within the reach of the statutory remedies.

Executions Against the Person: In a number of jurisdictions, executions against the person may be used as a means of enforcing certain types of claims, usually those involving elements of fraud. Return of execution against property either wholly or partially unsatisfied is an essential prerequisite to an execution

149

against the person. The remedy may not be available against women. In any case extreme caution should be exercised in the use of this remedy because of the risk that arrest of the debtor may operate as a satisfaction of the judgment or at least create a presumption of satisfaction, and also because of the further risk that its use may give rise to civil liability for wrongful arrest if it should turn out that the remedy was improperly invoked.

[¶2108]   ACTIONS TO SET ASIDE TRANSFERS

Steps should be taken to bar transfers by the debtor while collection proceedings are under way. Some statutes providing for supplementary proceedings or other proceedings in aid of execution expressly forbid or enjoin transfers by the debtor or third persons as soon as proceedings in aid of execution are initiated. Others may authorize such injunctive relief on application. Where a creditor resorts to equitable process to collect, as by a creditor's suit, it is clear that the court may grant an injunction against transfers on a showing that it is necessary to make the equitable remedy effective. The creditor's attorney should attempt to enjoin transfers of property which he believes belongs to the debtor even though the property may not be held in the debtor's name and it may be necessary to establish the debtor's title by suit.

An action to set aside a transfer made by the debtor which is void or voidable as to the creditor either as fraudulent or for other reasons may offer a means of collecting on a judgment. Where a transfer is wholly ineffectual as to the creditor, the rule in most states is that the property may be levied on and sold under an execution against the debtor-transferor and this is the rule under the Uniform Fraudulent Conveyance Act. Generally, where this rule prevails, there is no need for an action to set aside the transfer. Also, since exhaustion of legal remedies is ordinarily essential to the maintenance of such action, it is doubtful whether the action can be maintained at all unless and until execution has been issued and has been returned unsatisfied. Where the action may properly be maintained, if real property is involved, a lis pendens should be filed. Where pre-trial examinations may be had in the action to set aside the transfer, it is desirable to examine both the debtor-transferor and his transferee, even though both may have been previously examined in supplementary or other proceedings. If this is not done, there is a possibility of not being able to use the examination against both during the trial.

[¶2108.1]   Elements of a Fraudulent Transfer

The basic elements of a fraudulent conveyance are: (1) A transfer of property to which the debtor had title when the creditor acquired the right to have his claim satisfied; (2) This transfer was made with intent, either actual or constructive, to hinder, delay or defraud one or more of his creditors by putting

150

the property beyond the creditor's reach in the hands of a third person. Transfer includes every payment of money, assignment, release, mortgage or pledge of tangible or intangible property and also the creation of a lien or encumbrance. Exempt property, however, can't be the subject matter of a fraudulent transfer.

The statutes aren't limited to transfers taking place after judgment has been rendered but enable the creditor to set aside transfers made at any time after he became such. The Uniform Fraudulent Conveyance Act (§1), for example, defines a creditor as "a person having any claim, whether matured or unmatured, liquidated or unliquidated, absolute, fixed or contingent." Actually, this definition would take in tort claimants whom we don't ordinarily think of as creditors at all.

[¶2108.2] Evidence of Fraud

As already noted, a fraudulent intent, either actual or constructive, must be shown in order to set aside a transfer. There's a lot of law on this question of fraudulent intent which we can't go into here. However, you should know that you will be aided in your proof of fraudulent intent by a variety of presumptions or statutory equivalents of proof of intent. The presumptions or equivalents and their strength, whether conclusive, prima facie evidence or something else, may vary depending on decisional and statutory law, but here are some common badges of fraud:

(1) Transfers which render the transferor insolvent.

(2) Transfers made without fair consideration by a person in business leaving the transferor with unreasonably small capital.

(3) Transfers made without fair consideration if the transferor intends or believes he'll incur debts beyond his ability to pay.

(4) Transfers by a partnership when insolvent if to a partner or if to a non-partner without fair consideration.

(5) Transfers made in anticipation of or pending litigation.

(6) Transfers with secret reservations of beneficial interests.

(7) Transfers which leave the transferor in possession on some fictitious ground.

The Bankruptcy Act invalidates conveyances which are invalid under state law and at the same time has its own provisions governing fraudulent conveyances in violation of the terms of the Bankruptcy Act.

[¶2109]   HANDLING REMITTANCES

On receipt of payment on a collection item you normally have a choice of sending the client the full amount collected, together with your bill, or sending him the net amount after deducting your fee. The former, of course, carries with it a vote of confidence in the client, but if this is in fact lacking, the latter method will be used and the client will be given a full explanation of the deductions made for fees and expenses.

〔¶2109.1〕   Checks Marked "Payment in Full"

Watch out for checks for less than the full amount owing which are marked "payment in full." Theoretically, of course, if a debt is liquidated and undisputed, you won't be prejudiced by accepting such a check. You'll still be able to collect the balance. But the theory won't help much because in most cases where the debtor sends such a check the debt is either unliquidated or disputed. In such case, provided the dispute, if any, is an honest one, the creditor will be stuck if he accepts the check. The creditor won't help himself either by crossing out the endorsement or advising the debtor that payment is being credited "on account." One court has said that the creditor must immediately reject the offer and return the check. While this might be an extreme position and other courts might not go along with it, there's no reason why you shouldn't follow a practice of playing it safe by sending back such checks the day they're received. Before sending it back, however, you'll first have to decide whether in the light of the nature of the dispute, the amount offered in terms of the amount of the debt, the possibilities of further customer relationships, and other matters, you might not be better off accepting the check as "payment in full." If you decide to send it back, two cautions: (1) Make a photostatic copy for your files; and (2) Return it by registered or certified mail. The latter will give you undisputable proof of the fact and time of return and forestall a claim that you impliedly accepted the check.

〔¶2110〕   FORWARDING COLLECTION ITEMS

It is clear of course that an attorney can have a hand in collecting items all over the country and in other countries for that matter and is not limited to his own particular bailiwick, and this fact should be brought home to the client.

The normal way of handling out-of-town collections will be by forwarding them to another attorney. Barring an established contact or a solid reference the attorney to whom the matter is to be forwarded should be selected from one of the established law lists certified as complying with the American Bar Association standards. The publisher of the list will also have certain standards for listing which he will disclose on inquiry.

The forwarding letter to a new contact should indicate the basis of selection —law list or reference—and should discuss the fee. If, for example, you should decide to use the Commercial Law League schedule of fees (see ¶2111 on Fees) the letter should make this clear. These fees will not, of course, include the fees of the forwarding attorney who must add on his own fee when he bills his client.

A number of law lists use bonded attorneys and where this is the case you should notify the publisher of the list as soon as you forward a matter to an attorney on his list. If you fail to do so, the bond may not be available to you if and when you might need it.

The forwarding attorney can't just forget about a matter once it has been forwarded. He must check periodically with the out-of-town attorney and keep the client informed as to the status of the collection process.

[¶2111]   FEES

There is, of course, no precise formula for determining fees for handling items for collection. The fee must of necessity vary depending on the amount collected, the nature of the item and the nature of the services called for. Nevertheless, the schedule of rates charged by mercantile agencies may offer some worthwhile guideposts to the attorney in working out a fee arrangement. The schedule of the Commercial Collection Division of Dun & Bradstreet may be considered fairly representative, and as such useful for illustrative purposes.

Their arrangement calls for a one-year subscription contract for $49.00 as a minimum annual service charge, plus charges based on the rates set forth below, as well as disbursements and any other extraordinary expense which may be incurred at the request of the subscriber:

1. Reminder Service. Two courteous and effective Reminders for Claimant's use on letters and statements before accounts are placed for collection. No additional charge for results.

2. Free Direct Demand Service. A demand written on the stationery of Dun & Bradstreet, Inc. and mailed direct by it for payment of undisputed commercial accounts. No additional charge for any payments received during Free Direct Demand period, the number of days for which is designated by Claimant but not to exceed 10 days from date of demand. No accounts accepted for Free Direct Demand Service only.

3. Supplementary Service. Additional efforts consisting of various types of demands for payments appropriate to the individual account. Customary charges, contingent upon collection, on commercial accounts are: 23% of first $1,000 collected; 19% of next $3,000 collected; 16% of next $2,500 collected, and 15% of sums collected in excess of $6,500; minimum charges: $31.50 on collections of $63 to $137 and 50% of collections less than $63.

4. Personal Collection Service. Tactful presentations of accounts by trained representatives throughout the United States and Canada. Customary charges, contingent upon collection, on commercial accounts are the same as stated in paragraph 3.

153

5. Forwarding Service. Forwarding accounts to attorneys or others, in Claimant's behalf, and conducting, as a convenience to Claimant, the necessary correspondence with those to whom accounts are forwarded, in accordance with instructions from Claimant. The charges, contingent on collection, of most attorneys on commercial accounts are the recommended minimum charges of The Commercial Law League of America, as follows: 20% on collections of $125 to $300; 18% of next $1,700 collected, and 13% in excess of $2,000; minimum charges: $25 on collections of $75 to $125 and 33⅓% of collections less than $75. *There are additional charges by attorneys when suits or other legal proceedings are authorized by Claimant, consisting of a suit fee, advance costs and, in some instances, a retainer.*

In addition to the charges of attorneys or others to whom commercial accounts are forwarded in Claimant's behalf, customary charges for the separate services rendered by Dun & Bradstreet, Inc. in Forwarding Service are: 6% on collections of $167 to $2,000 and 5% of collections in excess of $2,000; minimum charges: $10 on collections of $60 to $167 and 16⅔% of collections less than $60. *The charges of Dun & Bradstreet, Inc. are not dependent upon any services rendered by attorneys or others in Claimant's behalf but are for services rendered and expenses incurred by it.*

Bear in mind that these are rates for commercial accounts, that is, claims against corporations, partnerships or individuals engaged in business; that agencies usually reserve the right to accept or reject accounts offered for collection, including commercial accounts, and may accept them only if higher rates are agreed to; and that additional charges may be imposed if installment payments are involved.

The League's schedule spells out details as to suit fees. Here's what it says:

6. Suit Fees. Minimum suit fees to the receiving attorney $7.50. A suit fee is not contingent. It is payable in addition to commissions. It belongs exclusively to the receiving attorney unless there is a division of service or responsibility between the attorney forwarder and the receiving attorney. Where a division is recognized between the attorney forwarder and the receiving attorney, each shall receive such portion of the suit fee as is commensurate with his service or responsibility, but in no event shall the suit fee to the receiving attorney be less than $7.50. Before starting suit, the attorney should always endeavor to arrange for a suit fee commensurate with the services to be rendered, the amount involved, and the results to be accomplished.

For Further Reference . . .
Denonn and Stoll, *Collecting Claims and Enforcing Judgments,* Practising Law
  Institute, New York, N.Y.
Moore and Countryman, *Debtor's and Creditor's Rights.*

EMPLOYMENT

[¶2301] The practicing lawyer will be called on to participate in the framing of an employment arrangement and the subsequent drafting of an agreement primarily in these situations:

1. He is acting for an executive or for a corporation which is hiring an executive.

2. He is acting for a corporation which wants to set up a more or less standardized employment arrangement for sales or technical personnel.

3. He is called in to help develop a special compensation arrangement.

The terms of an employment agreement are more or less standardized except for the critical compensation, disability, retirement, and death provisions and provisions designed to retain for the employer the benefits of what has been created or developed through the employee's services. In the latter category are provisions dealing with inventions, confidential disclosures, restrictions against competing upon termination of employment. Sometimes the lawyer will have to handle an agreement involving an employee who is subject to an existing collective bargaining agreement, in which case the provisions of the employment agreement will have to be coordinated with those of the collective bargaining agreement. This is likely to occur in the entertainment field where the development of satisfactory employment arrangements for actors and writers has many challenging aspects.

It is difficult to enforce an employment agreement because an unwilling employee is not worth the compensation paid him. But the agreement is essential to protect the employer's rights in information necessarily obtained during employment.

Forms of employment agreements to implement the ideas discussed in this chapter will be found in IBP FORMS OF BUSINESS AGREEMENTS under the tab heading "Employment Agreements."

[¶2302] EXISTING EMPLOYMENT AGREEMENT MAY CREATE LIABILITY FOR EMPLOYER

One of the first things to question in developing an employment arrangement is whether the employee is under contract to another employer. If he is, the prospective new employer may be incurring a liability for damages to the present employer for intentionally inducing an employee to leave his employment.

[¶2303] DIRECTOR AND STOCKHOLDER APPROVAL

Where the employee is a director, it is important to make sure that the contract is authorized by a majority of the directors without the participation of the director-employee in the vote. If his vote is necessary to carry the resolution, the contract may be void or voidable. Where the vote of a disinterested majority cannot be obtained, the contract should be approved or ratified by the stockholders.

[¶2304] EMPLOYEE'S DUTIES AND OBLIGATIONS

The agreement should define the employee's duties as broadly as possible or require him to perform such duties as the president or board of directors may direct. The employee should agree that he will perform his duties under the supervision and subject to general direction of the employer or its president or, if the agreement concerns the president, the board of directors. Since the board of directors has the right to appoint the officers, the employment contract should not undertake to employ a person in that capacity but should provide for employment in an executive capacity. It may also be provided that if the employee is to be elected as an officer or to a specified office, the employee will have an out if the board of directors fails to so elect him. If the job is too specifically defined and the employer is not given the specific right to change the employee's duties and title, the employer may be forced to choose between continuing an assignment that is uneconomic and breaching or "buying out" the contract.

The contract should provide that the employee will devote his entire time to the employer's business or expressly reserve to the employee the right to do whatever outside work may be contemplated. Consider inserting a clause restricting the employee's authority to incur obligations or to make representation or other commitments on behalf of the employer. If the employee has apparent authority, the employer may nevertheless be held liable to a third party; but there will be recourse against the employee for having exceeded his authority.

In these days of nation-wide and world-wide business, the employer may want the express right to change territories and to assign the employee to other offices, whereas the employee may want to limit such a right. This gets to be a matter of relative bargaining power.

[¶2305] TERMINATION OF THE AGREEMENT

Unless a definite term is specified in the agreement, the employment can be terminated by either party at any time. Where the employment agreement expresses a term and continues beyond the initial term, there may be an implied

157

renewal for another term unless this is negated by specific provision or by the conduct of the parties. There is a conflict of authority whether an automatic renewal is for one year or for the same term as the initial term. To avoid questions like this, the contract should provide that the contract will continue from year to year if employment continues without change beyond the original term.

[¶2306]   COMPENSATION

Compensation of officers must usually be authorized by directors and for lower level employees either fixed by the directors or delegated by them under their general power to manage the corporation. The reasonableness of compensation can be challenged by the Internal Revenue Service in disallowing deductions. This usually occurs only with respect to employee-stockholders where the contention is made that salary is in excess of reasonable compensation, so that a portion of it can be said to be a disguised dividend which is not deductible by the employer. A stockholder who feels that an officer's compensation is excessive can sue the officer on behalf of the corporation to recover the excess. An employment contract under which most of the compensation is for past services can be found to be an illegal gift of corporate assets and voided. It has been held by a Delaware court that stockholder ratification does not validate such a contract. The important things are to frame the type of compensation and define the way it is to be calculated and the conditions under which it is to be paid. Where provision is made for a bonus, specify when it is to be paid and whether the payment is conditioned upon the employee's being in service at the end of the year or at the time of payment or whether a prior termination will require an apportionment. Where the bonus is based on profits, the definition of profits is vital. Do they include capital gains and investment income? Are there any exclusions for a fair return to stockholders before profits are determined for bonus purposes? Is the bonus based on profits before or after taxes? Is definiteness obtained and the posssibility of dispute minimized by a provision that the auditor's figures shall be conclusive and binding on both parties?

[¶2307]   COMMISSIONS AND DRAWINGS

In an agreement for employing a salesman on a commission basis, special care is needed in defining the sales amounts to which the commission rate applies. Usually, it applies to the net selling price; and this should be defined to exclude discounts, returns and allowances, freight charges, taxes, and other necessary expenses. When is a commission earned? Is it when the order is obtained and accepted, or is it when payment is made? Is the salesman penalized for bad debts? Must he wait for payment to receive commission, or is it enough for commissions on sales for which payment is not received to be charged back against future commissions? Should there be a restriction on the employer's right to reject orders on which the salesman would otherwise get commissions? The contract should specify the salesman's right to commissions on orders received after termination. Usually, he is entitled to commissions obtained before termination but not shipped until afterwards. Sometimes, as a reward for building up a territory, a salesman can bargain for a continuation of commissions, perhaps at a lower rate, for a limited period of time after retirement or other termination. The employer should be required to furnish statements so that the salesman can follow shipments made to his customers and the commissions to which he is entitled. One value of such statements is obtained if the contract requires the employee to make any complaint about the calculation of his commission within a specified period of time after receipt of the statement.

Where a salesman is paid a draw, there can be confusion as to whether or not this is an advance which he is obligated to return if he doesn't earn commissions to cover it or whether it is a minimum salary which he need not return. In some states the absence of an unequivocal agreement to repay the excess of a draw over commissions earned will be held to indicate that a minimum salary was intended, so that the employee has no obligation to return the excess upon termination of employment.

[¶2308]　　　　　　　　EXPENSES

The contract should specify the degree to which the employer is assuming responsibility for the employee's expenses, any limitation on or approval required for the incurring of expenses, the supporting data to be submitted in order to justify expense reimbursement, etc.

The nature of the understanding between an employee and an employer about expenses may prevent a loss of a valid business expense deduction, reimburse the employee for expenses which he could not deduct himself, permit the employee to take his own deductions and still elect the optional standard deduction. To insure the deduction for expenses, it is essential that proper records be kept. The records must show cost, dates, place, business purpose, business relationship. Where the deduction is for goodwill entertainment directly preceding or following a substantial and bona fide business discussion, it is necessary to be able to prove the time and date and location of the business discussion, the nature of the business discussed and the name and business relationship of each participant.

[¶2309]   NONCOMPETITION

If an employee is going to learn a great deal which would be valuable to a competitor or establish contacts which would make it possible for him to take business to a competitor, and the employer wants to protect himself against this eventuality, it is necessary to include a specific provision in the contract which commits the employee not to compete against the employer. However, if this restrictive covenant is too broad in scope, or time, or territory, it may be unenforceable. Even where it is limited, courts may be willing to enforce it only to the extent they consider it necessary for the employer's protection. Courts are inclined to strike down or strictly limit covenants which prevent or unreasonably restrict an employee from applying the experience he has gained in prior employment. A covenant on the part of a salesman not to solicit business from the employer's customers for a reasonable period of time after termination of employment is generally enforceable. Also a covenant on the part of a scientist or engineer not to engage in the same line of research and development work for a reasonable period of time after he has left the employer's employment should be accepted as reasonable. Restrictions on the employee going into business are frowned upon, even though limited as to time and geographic area. See *Murray v. Cooper,* 294 N.Y. 658, where the New York Court of Appeals refused to enjoin a dancing instructor from opening his own business, although the covenant he violated was limited to one year and to a radius of 25 miles.

Employers sometimes worry lest a lump-sum distribution from a profit-sharing plan will give an employee the money to go into competition. This risk is frequently minimized by a provision that severance payments will be made only over a period of time.

[¶2310]   CONFIDENTIAL DISCLOSURE

Where the employee will have access to confidential research information, mailing lists, customer lists, other trade secrets, it may be desirable to have an explicit provision obligating the employee not to disclose this information either during or after employment. Here the obligation is of a somewhat longer duration, and should be permissible. The test is whatever is reasonable in the circumstances. An employer may want to keep a trade secret forever. He may want confidential research information to remain undisclosed until a patent is issued or his product is on the market. A practice of having employees expressly acknowledge in their employment contracts that their employment involves a disclosure of employer's trade secrets, and have the employee expressly agree that he will not divulge or otherwise disclose these trade secrets after the duration of his employment, except with the written consent of his employer, will not only protect the employer from unfair competition by the

160

employee but will also afford protection to the employer against piracy of his trade secrets against others.

[¶2311]   **INVENTIONS**

If an employee makes an invention during the course of his employment, the employer automatically has a shop right which is an unexclusive license to practice the invention, and if the employee is especially hired to develop a particular article, the invention automatically becomes the property of the employer. However, it is highly desirable to have a specific provision in the employment contract rather than to rely on these general principles of law. The employee can be expressly obligated by contract to assign inventions and patents developed while on the job to his employer. To implement this obligation, the contract should provide that the employee will make prompt disclosure in writing of any inventions or discoveries he makes during the period of his employment, and that he will file such patent applications as the employer may request and, at the employer's request, execute assignments of such applications or any patents issued to him.

[¶2312]   **UNIQUE SERVICES**

It may be desirable to have an employee of unique and particular talent acknowledge that his services are unique and not readily replaceable. This will put the employer in a better position to get an injunction or otherwise enforce the contract if the employee breaches it. It will also help in establishing damages if the employer should want to sue a pirating employer for inducing breach of contract.

[¶2313]   **INDEMNITY**

The employee may want indemnity against any liability which he may incur as an employee. Where the employee is a corporate officer, the extent of indemnity may be governed by state corporate laws. Public policy may prohibit indemnity from criminal prosecution. Possible civil or criminal antitrust violations may be an important area for indemnity. Generally, a corporate officer cannot be indemnified against shareholders' derivative actions except for expenses of defense if it's determined that he acted properly.

●

For Further Reference . . .
American Jurisprudence, Corporations, §864-866, 879-888.

Application and Effect of "Shop Right Rule" or License Giving Employer Limited Rights in Employees' Inventions and Discoveries, 61 *ALR* 356.

Blake, H. M., Employee Agreements Not to Compete, 73 *Harvard Law Review* 625.

Mandel, *The Preparation of Commercial Agreements,* Practising Law Institute, New York, N.Y.

Power of Corporate President to Hire Employees for Life, 28 *ALR 2d* 940.

Prosser on Torts, West Publishing Co., St. Paul, Minn.

Rezac, W. J., Validity of Contracts Assigning Employee Inventions to Employers, 42 *Journal of the Patent Office Society* 177.

Washington, G. T., and Bishop, W., *Indemnifying the Corporate Executive,* Ronald.

Washington, G. T., and Rothchild, V. H., *Compensating the Corporate Executive,* Ronald.

ESTATE ADMINISTRATION

[¶2401] Set out below is a list of the steps, in their approximate order of occurrence, which will usually be necessary in probating a typical estate. In all cases, of course, it will be necessary to check local law and practice to determine the precise steps to be taken in will probate and the various time limits and statutory waiting periods which are imposed in the different jurisdictions.

(1) Notify banks where decedent had accounts, obtaining data on same.

(2) Arrange for the collection and custody of decedent's personal property.

(3) Check insurance coverages on all of decedent's property.

(4) Investigate all of decedent's brokerage accounts.

(5) Make a preliminary estimate of the decedent's estate to determine what form the probate and the administration of the estate will take.

(6) Have additional copies of the will made for beneficiaries, taxing authorities, personal representatives, etc.

(7) List contents of decedent's safe deposit box, if any, in presence of member of decedent's family and taxing authorities.

(8) Hold preliminary conference with family members and others named in will for the purpose of reading the will and determining whether there will be any objections or renunciations.

(9) Hold conference with decedent's personal representative(s) for purpose of getting all the details needed for the preparation of the petition for probate.

(10) Make arrangements with Post Office for custody of decedent's mail.

(11) File will and petition with probate court.

(12) Make copies of petition available to executor and taxing authorities, accompanied by affidavit as to the total property affected by the will, and the amounts going to the beneficiaries together with their relationships to the decedent.

(13) Obtain copies of death certificate (as many as possible).

(14) Assist beneficiaries in collection of life insurance proceeds, obtaining necessary IRS forms from insurance companies.

(15) Collect unpaid wages, salary or commissions owing to decedent.

(16) Inquire as to exact benefits due from company pension and/or profit-sharing plans and other company programs, and from union or association benefit programs.

(17) Change automobile registration, if in decedent's name.

(18) If decedent was a businessman, check for business continuation agreements, etc.

(19) Arrange for continued collection of loans, rents, interest, dividends, royalties, etc., and attempt to collect delinquent obligations.

163

(20) Mail notice of hearing on petition together with order limiting time to file claims (all in accordance with local law requirements).

(21) Arrange for publication of order for hearing (in accordance with local law).

(22) File affidavit of mailing of notice of hearing (in accordance with local law requirements).

(23) Send copies of will and preliminary estimate of estate to appropriate heirs.

(24) Arrange for ancillary administration, if necessary.

(25) Collect all pertinent information for income tax returns.

(26) If decedent was sole proprietor of a business, determine if there is an outstanding obligation for employers' tax.

(27) Collect all amounts due from retirement plans, etc.

(28) File social security claims.

(29) File VA claims, if any.

(30) Arrange for witnesses to appear at hearing, obtaining written depositions, if necessary.

(31) Send copy of will to widow and minor children, if not already done, and notify them as to their rights (and advise them as to tax considerations).

(32) File affidavit of mailing of notice of widow's and children's rights (as required by local law).

(33) Assemble data on all non-probate property (joint tenancy property, life insurance, living trusts, property subject to a power in the decedent, etc.).

(34) Inquire into all substantial gifts made by decedent within 3 years of his death, and all transfers made in trust at any time.

(35) Make inquiry as to requirements for fiduciary bond, discussing same with named executor, and prepare application therefor, if necessary.

(36) Prepare executor's form of acceptance.

(37) Attend formal court hearing on petition for probate with witnesses and any required written testimony.

(38) File acceptance by executor.

(39) File fiduciary bond, if required.

(40) Obtain certified copies of letters testamentary.

(41) To limit appeal time, serve copy of order on petition to interested parties.

(42) Have appraisers appointed, unless estate consists entirely of cash.

(43) Executor should notify post office, banks, and others of his appointment.

[¶2402]   **DUTIES OF FIDUCIARIES**

An executor's duties are more circumscribed than those of a trustee, and usually of much shorter duration.

[¶2402.1]   Executor's Duties

From the point at which the Probate Checklist above leaves off (right after the probate of the will) until the final distribution of the estate, we can, depending upon the nature of the estate, comprise a checklist of as many as 100 or more additional detailed steps to be taken by the executor (aided by the attorney for the estate).

Reaching back into the probate and pre-probate period, as well as the post-probate period, the executor's overall duties generally encompass the following:

(1) The collection and conservation of the personal property of the estate. (Real property usually vests immediately in the devisees, with the executor only being able to sell such property in the event that personal property is inadequate to meet claims, etc.)

(2) The payment of all valid debts, including fees and expenses incurred in administration, death taxes, income and other taxes owed by the decedent, etc.

(3) The distribution of whatever property remains in accordance with the testator's wishes.

Intermeshed within these three overall duties may be any number of detailed duties which must be performed if these major functions are to be accomplished.

Such duties as the executor has are to be ascertained not only from the terms of the will, but also, except to the extent that the testator can and does decree otherwise, by reference to the statutes and case law of the state whose law governs the operation of the will. (This, of course, is also true of an administrator of intestate property, except that all of his duties arise from local law.) An example of a duty sometimes imposed upon an executor by operation of law is the duty to make unproductive assets productive when there is to be a relatively lengthy delay before distribution can be made.

[¶2402.2]   Trustee's Duties

The duties outlined below are the usual duties of a testamentary trustee, although they might just as well apply to a trustee under a living trust. A testamentary trustee's duties begin at the point where the executor's duties leave off. Although state law may impose certain duties and restrictions upon a trustee, particularly a testamentary trustee, most of his duties are derived from provisions in the testator's will. To a great extent, they overlap what is known as the "trustee's powers." The trustee's duties include:

(1) Taking possession and control of the trust property.

(2) Investing and reinvesting such property prudently for the production of income.

(3) Paying all necessary taxes and other reasonable expenses of trust administration.

(4) Exercising all mandatory directions recited in the governing instrument, except those which are impossible of fulfillment.

(5) Exercising any discretionary duties with "discretion" and with impartiality.

(6) Keeping records and rendering accounts when required to do so.

(7) Paying over income (and principal, maybe) to those entitled to receive it.

(8) Refraining from dealing with the trust property personally, and from commingling such property with its own.

(9) Refraining from delegating any of the above duties to others except to the extent permitted by the governing instrument or by local law.

[¶2403]   TAX DUTIES OF FIDUCIARIES

Death of a decedent or the setting up of a trust creates a new taxpayer. The responsibility for filing the returns, paying the taxes, and carrying out the other tax duties falls on the executor or trustee, as the case may be. The executor or trustee is more than just an agent in the carrying out of these duties; he acts in his capacity as a fiduciary taxpayer.

The duty to discharge the tax liability may be particularly onerous. For although normally the fiduciary is responsible for paying out only the funds entrusted to him as a fiduciary, in some cases he can become personally liable for the taxes.

[¶2403.1]   Tax Returns

The fiduciary must prepare and file not only the federal tax returns, but also those required by state and local authorities. Timely filing is important; valuable elections, such as the choice of the optional valuation date for the federal estate tax return, can be lost through failing to file on time (IRC §2032). Failure to file properly, where penalties are provided, may result in the fiduciary being personally surcharged.

[¶2403.2]   Estate Tax Return

An estate tax return (Form 706) must be filed by the executor or administrator for any decedent whose gross estate exceeds $60,000 as of the date of death.

This is true even if the estate goes below $60,000 by the alternate valuation date.

If the gross estate of a nonresident alien situated in the United States exceeds $30,000 in value at death (Reg. §20.6018-1(a)), Form 706NA is used. The return is due nine months after the date of decedent's death (Reg. §20.6075-1). Extension to file a return (generally, up to six months) can be granted (Reg. §20.6081-1(b)(3)). The return must be filed with the service center for the state in which the decedent had his domicile at the time of his death. For a nonresident citizen the return must be filed with the Internal Revenue Service Center, 11601 Roosevelt Boulevard, Philadelphia, Pennsylvania 19155.

[¶2403.3] Income Tax Return of Estate

If the estate has $600 or more of gross income, it must file a return on Form 1041 (IRC §6012(a)(3)). If there is a nonresident beneficiary, the return is required regardless of the amount of gross income. For purposes of filing, a taxable year for the estate must be selected, which need not be a calendar year, and need not coincide with the date of death. It may be advantageous to use a short taxable year for the estate's initial return. Bearing in mind that the tax interests of the beneficiaries must be considered, the choice of a fiscal year may help split the income and thus reduce the tax.

The return must be filed by the middle of the fourth month following the end of the tax year (§6072); estates and trusts can pay the tax quarterly (IRC §6152(a)(2)). It may be advisable to complete the return early in order to be able to give advance notification to the distributees of the amounts they must include in their own returns.

[¶2403.4] Decedent's Income Tax Returns

The executor must also file the decedent's final income tax return on Form 1040 and, if necessary, delinquent returns for prior years. If death occurred between Jan. 1 and April 15, there will generally be two returns to file, assuming decedent was on a calendar year basis.

The decedent's return is a tougher proposition for the executor than the estate's return. He has the information for the latter; but unless decedent was the unusual taxpayer who kept detailed records of such things as deductions, the executor may have to resort to making an estimate under the *Cohan* (39 F.2d 540) rule.

A joint return may be filed for a married decedent for the year of death, unless the surviving spouse should remarry before the close of the tax year, or the decedent or the surviving spouse had a short tax year caused by a change of accounting period (IRC §6013(a)). The liability for the full tax in such cases is joint and several (§6013(d)). Where the decedent's income was less than that

167

of the surviving spouse and the latter isn't the sole beneficiary, the executor's consent to a joint return, without limiting the estate's liability, may expose him to surcharge.

The surviving spouse may file a joint return if no executor has been appointed by the time the return is due. If the executor qualifies within a year after the due date (including any extensions for filing), he may disaffirm the joint return by filing a separate return within the one-year period (IRC §6013(a)). This rule protects the estate in the event the surviving spouse files a return that is detrimental to the estate; it will be up to the executor to disaffirm unless the estate is fully indemnified.

[¶2403.5]   Gift Tax Return Filed by Executor

The executor should review the decedent's entire lifetime giving; a gift tax return may have been required (Form 709), even though no gift tax was payable. If there is doubt about the necessity to file, the executor probably should file anyway in order to start the Statute of Limitations running. The executor should always seek the surviving spouse's consent to have half the decedent's gifts attributed to her under IRC §1000(f), so as to reduce any gift tax payable by the estate. Where it is the spouse who made the gifts, some thought would be required before giving consent to have half attributed to the decedent.

[¶2403.6]   Income Tax Return of Trust

The trustee (whether the trust is testamentary or inter vivos) must file an income tax return (Form 1041) for any year where the trust has any taxable income, or has gross income of $600 or more (IRC §6012(a)(4)). The principles governing the determination of an individual's income tax apply also to estates and trusts.

As with estates, the choice of fiscal year and method of accounting may be significant in determining the total tax impact on the ultimate beneficiaries. Remember too that there is a relationship between the amount of income taxed to the beneficiary and the amount taxed to the trust. To the extent the income is distributed and taxed to the beneficiary, the trust has a deduction; this provides a good opportunity to cut the total tax by some prior planning.

[¶2403.7]   Information Returns

Executors and trustees are required to file information returns (Forms 1096 and 1099) when paying $600 or more of income in any calendar year (IRC §6041). The fiduciary must report payments by both the decedent and the estate. This doesn't mean payments to distributees, for which the fiduciary tax return serves also as an information return.

[¶2404]   TAX LIABILITIES OF FIDUCIARIES

An executor or administrator who pays a debt due by the person or estate for whom he acts, before he pays the federal tax liabilities, becomes personally liable for any such taxes that remain unpaid (§3467 US Rev. Stat.). For purposes of applying this rule to estate taxes, the distribution of any portion of the estate to the beneficiaries is deemed payment of a debt. The rule making the executor personally liable applies only where the Treasury has a priority as a creditor against the estate's assets (§3466 US Rev. Stat.). Thus, funeral expenses and widow's allowances, to cite examples, could be paid with impunity by the executor or administrator of even an insolvent estate, since these items have priority over all debts, including that owing to the United States.

Whether or not the executor is personally liable with respect to income tax liability, he is responsible for paying these taxes in his representative capacity. There is no doubt that he would be personally liable if the income taxes in question were those owed by the decedent and not those of the estate, and he used up the estate's assets to satisfy other obligations. To protect himself, the executor would be wise to check not only the decedent's prior returns, but also all of the decedent's transactions that might have produced income which wasn't reported on his returns. The check should go back beyond the period of the Statute of Limitations, since it is always possible the decedent committed fraud, and for this there is no limiting period.

In addition to his representative and personal responsibilities, the fiduciary is also subject to transferee liability the same as any other taxpayer (IRC §6901(h); 7701(b)).

[¶2404.1]   **What Protection Has the Fiduciary Against Personal Tax Liability?**

Although the possibility of personal liability is a serious problem for the fiduciary, he is not without protection. For example, unpaid gift taxes aren't likely to be charged against him, since the tax follows the gift and can be satisfied out of the gift property. Even if the donee has parted with the property, the fiduciary is still safe, since the gift tax then becomes a lien against the donee's other property. The fiduciary may be in some danger when the gift is in trust; because of the difficulty in reaching the beneficiaries, the Treasury may contend the trustee is to be treated as the donee.

With respect to the estate tax, the executor can ascertain the amount of estate tax due by making written request to the Commissioner. The latter must notify the executor of the amount within nine months. If the executor pays this amount, he is entitled to a written discharge from personal liability (IRC §2204). Discharge from personal liability for decedent's gift and income taxes is also available (IRC §6905).

There is also a time limit on the personal tax liability threat to the fiduciary. Any assessment against the fiduciary personally must be made not later than one year after the liability arises or not later than the expiration of the period for collection of the tax in respect of which the liability arises, whichever is later (§6901(c)(3)). This is in addition to the Commissioner's 6-year period within which he is permitted to collect a validly assessed tax.

Enforcement of personal liability against the fiduciary is made by the same processes (jeopardy assessment, distraint, etc.) and is subject to the same restrictions (90-day letter, etc.) as with any other tax collection.

[¶2405] POST-MORTEM TAX PLANNING

The draftsman of the will, the executor, and the beneficiaries can collaborate to achieve important tax savings after the testator's death. The time to think of these is when or before drafting the will. But some opportunities will remain open to the executors or present themselves for the first time even after the testator's death. The tax savings available here fall into these categories —

(a) Estate tax savings by altering the testamentary dispositions.

(b) Income tax savings for the estate in administration.

(c) Income tax savings for the beneficiaries.

[¶2405.1] Checklist of Post-Mortem Tax Planning Steps

Here is a checklist of some post-mortem maneuvers which can be employed by executors or estate beneficiaries to achieve certain tax advantages. For more detail, see IBP ESTATE PLANNING DESK BOOK.

1. Election Against the Will: A failure to qualify for the marital deduction can be remedied by a spouse who (pursuant to local law) exercises his or her right to take against the will.

2. Will Contests and Family Settlements: Where a will contest or settlement results in property passing to the surviving spouse, the property qualifies for the marital deduction provided the surrender or assignment is a bona fide recognition of enforceable rights in the decedent's estate.

3. Renunciation or Disclaimer: Property which passes to a surviving spouse by disclaimer increases the marital deduction provided the interest itself qualifies for the deduction (Code §2056(d)(2)). However, the disclaimer must be made before acceptance of the property and before the due date of the estate tax return. Disclaimer by the spouse as to property in excess of the marital deduction can avoid an estate tax on the spouse's death.

4. Picking a Fiscal Year for the Estate: By selecting a fiscal year which will produce a short year at the beginning of the estate administration and a short year at the end, income which will be taxed to the estate can be spread out to maximum advantage. Since an estate beneficiary must report the income during his taxable year within which the tax year of the estate ends, the selection of a taxable year for the estate also has a direct bearing on the beneficiary's tax picture.

5. *Timing of Distributions:* Where the executor has discretionary powers in connection with distribution, he is in a position to make substantial savings in taxes by proper timing of the distributions from the estate. In years when the estate is in a lower bracket than the beneficiaries of the estate, the executor might want to accumulate the income of the estate in order to have it taxed in its lower bracket. If the reverse, the beneficiaries are in lower brackets than the estate, the executor might want to accelerate the distribution of the income of the estate in order to have it taxed as the income of the beneficiaries.

6. *Valuation of Estate:* The valuation placed on estate assets for estate tax purposes will affect (a) the amount of the estate tax; (b) the amount of the marital deduction, and of the wife's and other beneficiaries' shares; and on the income tax side, (c) the taxable gain or loss on a subsequent sale of the assets by the estate or by the beneficiaries; and (d) the basis for future depreciation deductions. The relationship of the applicable estate tax rates and the future income tax rates will point up possible tax economies here.

7. *Deduction of Administration Expenses:* The executor must elect whether to deduct administration expenses on the estate tax return or on the estate's income tax return. Or he can split them in both returns. It's not enough just to look at the respective rate tables. The executor must think in terms of effective rates—i.e., where the full marital deduction is claimed, the effective rate of tax saving from an estate tax deduction of an administration expense is roughly one-half of the nominal estate tax rate. And the executor also has to look at the effect of his election on the beneficial interests as well as on taxes. An election based strictly on effective tax rates may warp the interest of competing beneficiaries—for example, where the income and residuary interests are not the same.

8. *Termination of Administration:* Termination of the estate closes its taxable year. While the termination cannot be unduly delayed, wherever possible, the executor should avoid having more than twelve months' distributions taxed to the beneficiaries in one year. Ideally, the estate should be closed at such time as will bring the final distribution of income into another tax year of the beneficiary. On the other hand, if the final year of the estate is one of excess distributions which can be claimed by the beneficiaries, it might be preferable to close the estate at a time when the beneficiaries can realize the maximum benefit from those excess deductions.

9. Income in Respect of a Decedent: The type of income which comes to an estate as a result of its having been earned by the testator during his life will not be taxed in the last return of the decedent. Instead it will be taxed in the year received as it is received by the estate, or to a person named by contract as having the right to receive that income or to a person who has the right to receive the distribution by the estate *before* the cash is actually paid (IRC §691). Income in respect of a decedent is included in the decedent's estate tax return. But the estate tax paid on this income can be taken by the recipient as an income tax deduction (IRC §691(c)). While most of the planning for income in respect of a decedent should be taken care of before death (via contractual provisions or will provisions), there is still much that can be done by the executor—especially if the will gives him discretionary powers in this regard. If he has the power to distribute these income rights before they are collected, he can spread them over a number of beneficiaries rather than have them come into an estate which is taxed as a single taxpayer and doesn't get any benefit of income splitting. If we just transfer the income from the estate to a married beneficiary before the income is realized, this would produce an important income tax saving right there.

10. Decedent's Final Income Tax Return: If the decedent was married at the time of his death, the executor and the surviving spouse can file a joint return for the decedent and the surviving spouse. This will, as a rule, bring about a lower tax than separate returns. But local law will have to be checked if the will itself does not contain explicit authorization to the executor to join in a joint return. This is because the joint return may subject the estate to liability for the income tax upon the surviving spouse's income. But, once again, if the will authorizes it, the executor's okay.

11. Deferring Tax Attributable to Business Interest: An executor can pay the estate tax in ten equal installments rather than within nine months after the decedent's death provided a major estate asset is a closely held business. The value of the business interest must exceed 35% of the gross estate or 50% of the taxable estate. Making the election doesn't prohibit the executor from obtaining early discharge from personal liability for any future estate tax deficiency. As a result of the election, the estate, in effect, gets a loan of the amount of the installments at a low interest rate of 9%. By so electing, an executor can meet the estate tax liability without affecting the business interest which otherwise might have to be sold or liquidated to meet the tax obligation.

●

For Further Reference . . .
Estate Practice and Procedure, Institute for Business Planning, Englewood Cliffs, N.J.
Harris, *Estate Practice Guide,* Baker, Voorhis, Mt. Kisco, N.Y.

Nossaman, *Trust Administration and Taxation* (looseleaf), Matthew Bender, New York, N.Y.

Wormser, Casey, Thornberg, *The Planning and Administration of Estates,* Practising Law Institute, New York, N.Y.

ESTATE PLANNING

[¶2501] An estate is planned by assembling all pertinent information and data about an individual and his family, analyzing the assets and income and the offsetting liabilities, estimating what will be left after death has cut off his earning power and the maturing liabilities have been discharged, and programming a distribution and investment for the remainder that will best meet the family's needs for income and capital.

In the estate planning process, it is necessary to (1) consider how income and assets may be shifted so as to minimize future liabilities, (2) accumulate additional liquid assets so that future liabilities can more readily be met, (3) augment capital (by life insurance or income accumulation, or some other means) so that investment income will more adequately meet family needs in the future, and (4) provide for the orderly consumption of capital to meet family needs where it appears that future income will not do the job.

[¶2501.1] Steps in Estate Planning

The series of steps with which the estate planner approaches the planning of an estate will run something like this—

Step 1: Get a complete inventory of the assets, current income, and any increments in assets and/or income anticipated by way of inheritance or otherwise. List each asset, setting out its cost, its current value and its probable date-of-death value. In the case of insurance, set down cash value as current value and face value as date-of-death value. In sizable estates which show indications of growing rapidly, estimate future values at, let's say, five-year intervals. The valuation of business interests is very intricate and the estate planner should look behind the owner's estimate to determine whether he is undervaluing or overvaluing a business interest to any substantial degree. The list of assets should embrace those owned by each member of the family and indicate the form of ownership. Make a similar listing of income and its sources.

Step 2: Classify assets into three categories—those that represent cash, those that are to be converted into cash and those that are to be retained if possible. The amount of cash which can be raised with each asset and the problem of converting assets into cash should be analyzed and discussed with the owner. After determining the cash requirements of the estate, it may be necessary to go back and reconsider the classification of assets, decide what additional assets should be retained because of their income-producing power, or what assets previously classified for retention would have to be sold to meet cash needs or given away to reduce cash requirements.

Step 3: Estimate the amount of debts and claims which will have to be met out of assets of the estate. This estimate should include current income tax liabilities, debts, funeral and last illness expenses and administration costs.

Step 4: After deducting from the total value of assets at death the estimate of all debts and claims, calculate the estate tax liability which will probably be due. It will be necessary to make some assumptions and to make more than one calculation. You will want to determine the total tax liability which will fall due at the death of the husband and the death of his wife. This is necessary to determine what will be left for the children if both parents should die within a relatively short period of time. Where estate tax liability is to be minimized by use of the marital deduction, it is necessary to determine how much greater the liability will be if the earlier death of the wife makes the marital deduction no longer available. By adding the total estate taxes and expenses and debts in both estates the estate owner can be shown a close approximation of the total transfer cost to his children or other ultimate beneficiaries under the current estate asset arrangement.

Step 5: Schedule the liquidation of estate liabilities. Apply cash amounts from the list of cash assets and assets convertible into cash (as determined in step number 2) against the schedules of debts, claims, administration costs (step number 3) and estate tax liability (step number 4). Then see whether there is enough cash left to meet the cash needs of the family during the administration of the estate. This comparison of cash available to the estate with liabilities which the estate will have to meet will point up whether there is a surplus of liquid assets or a deficit and permit the estate owner and the estate planner to determine whether it is necessary to arrange for the conversion of additional assets into cash or to add additional liquid resources to the estate picture.

Step 6: Assign the remaining assets to individuals or trusts according to the estate owner's will. This will indicate how much is available to satisfy the testamentary wishes of the estate owner and will provide a basis for his re-evaluation of the dispositions he wishes to make in the light of what is likely to be available.

Step 7: Prepare a schedule showing the assets that will be in the hands of each beneficiary after distribution and show how much annual income these assets will produce. Include the separately owned property of each beneficiary. The annual income available from these sources should be compared with the amount of annual income which the estate owner thinks should be available for the beneficiary.

Step 8: Suggest methods of reducing liabilities. For example, show how lifetime gifts can reduce estate tax liability and increase assets and income available to family beneficiaries.

175

Step 9: Show how assets can be increased. For example, inadequacy of liquid assets to meet cash liabilities or of net assets to produce family income may call for additional insurance or additional annual savings to lay out and complete an investment program.

Step 10: Show how income can be reorganized to increase liquidity or add to family assets. Show how the shifting of income-producing properties to other members of the family will save income tax as well as estate tax. Show how charitable deductions can add to liquidity. Show how the transfer of income-producing assets to a trust can carry additional insurance, how the shifting of dividend-producing assets to a family corporation can build up liquid assets within the corporation, etc.

Step 11: Make a new and final projection of assets, liabilities, liquid assets available to meet liabilities, net assets available for distribution and annual income produced by these assets — after reflecting the steps which have been recommended to increase assets, improve liquidity and reduce estate liabilities.

Step 12: Project the increase and accumulation of estate assets until the owner's retirement age. Take annual savings, assume a conservative rate of investment return, apply a compound interest table to determine what should be accumulated at the age which the owner specifies for his own retirement. Take the cash value of insurance policies at that time and convert that into annual income. Add to this any Social Security and any pension income or profit-sharing assets which may become available at that age. Tabulate total assets and anticipated income for the owner at retirement age. Determine whether or not additional saving or other steps are indicated to provide for the owner's retirement security.

More details on wills will be found beginning at ¶6001. Forms showing how all the detailed information required may be organized by the will drafter or estate planner will be found in IBP ESTATE PLANNING, VOL. II looseleaf Service.

[¶2502]   HOW TO MAKE LIFETIME
TRANSFERS OF PROPERTY

(1) Gifts—can be made tax free up to $3,000 a year to each donee, plus an additional $30,000 lifetime exemption (double this if a spouse joins in the gift); beyond that the gift tax rates are only three-quarters of the estate tax rates, gift property is taken from the top estate tax brackets to start at the bottom of the gift tax brackets and the gift tax is based on the net value of the gift (not including gift tax liability) while estate tax is based on the gross estate including the estate tax liability.

176

(2) Private Annuities—by which property is transferred in exchange for the promise of the transferee to make annual payments over the balance of the transferor's life. There is no estate tax on this transfer and no gift tax if the annual payments are in line with the commercial annuity which can be purchased with the value of the property transferred. There is no capital gain tax until the annual payments received by the transferor exceed the cost of the property. The transferee gets no deduction for the annual payments made to the transferor.

(3) Family Partnership—in which an interest can be acquired by another member of the family either by gift or by purchase so that future income and increments of value will accrue to his benefit.

(4) Family Investment Company—in which preferred and common stock can be distributed to family members either by gift or by purchase so that accumulation of income and appreciation in property value will accrue to the common stockholders.

(5) Life Income Charitable Gift—in which property is transferred to a charity or a trustee for a charity with income reserved for the life of the transferor and the specified members of his family, after which the property goes to charity. This is a method of transferring future income to other members of the family at an actuarially reduced gift tax cost, which is offset by the income tax deduction for the actuarial value of the remainder of the interest. It can make it possible to shift investments without capital gain tax. The life interest passing to the others will be subject to estate tax on the transferor's death, but at actuarially reduced values. This will increase the amount of other property which can go to a spouse tax free under the marital deduction to offset estate tax on the additional life interest.

The Revenue Act of 1969 eliminated the deduction for charitable remainders unless they qualify as a so-called charitable remainder "annuity trust" or a "unitrust."

An annuity trust is one from which a certain or a specified amount (which must be not less than 5% of the net fair market value of the property placed in the trust) must be paid to the income beneficiary, not less frequently than annually.

A unitrust is a trust from which a fixed percentage (which is not less than 5%) of the net fair market value of its assets as determined each year must be paid at least annually. As an alternative, provision can be made for distribution of 5% of the said value or the amount of the trust income (excluding capital gains), whichever is lower.

(6) Installment Sale—selling property to members of the family for a small down payment plus installment obligations shifts income and future apprecia-

tion to the buyer. Set the terms of the transactions realistically to avoid possible imposition of gift tax on any bargain element of the deal.

(7) Sale-Leaseback—between members of the family can shift rental income and future appreciation. Again set realistic figures for the price and rent to avoid possible gift tax.

(8) Funded Life Insurance Trust—in which income-producing property is placed in trust to carry life insurance on somebody other than the grantor. This shifts income and assures its future accumulation into capital which will accrue to the beneficiaries named in the trust.

(9) Salary Continuation Agreements—in which an employer is committed to make continued payments to the widow of the employee. These payments, if kept in reasonable line with the value of the employee's services during his life, can shift substantial value to his wife or children; these values will be supported by payments which the employer can deduct and the estate tax will be based on the actuarially reduced value of the future payments at the time of the employee's death.

(10) Split-Dollar Insurance—in which an employer can advance part of the money needed to carry insurance policies for an employee, or any member of a family can advance part of money needed to carry an insurance policy for another member of the family, with the result that the windfall profit of the insurance would accrue to the benefit of the beneficiary named in the policy.

[¶2503] HOW TO USE INCOME TO BUILD THE ESTATE

Very often a person will enjoy high income but have little capital. A similar problem is presented when a very wealthy person has big income, a large estate but inadequate liquidity. In both cases the problem is to convert highly taxed income into additional liquid capital. Here are possible methods which should be canvassed:

(1) A funded life insurance trust, in which income is shifted to the lower tax bracket of the trust and used to buy life insurance and guarantee additional liquid capital on the death of somebody other than the person creating the trust.

(2) An accumulation trust with income shifted to the lower tax bracket of the trust and accumulated for designated family beneficiaries. See IRC §665, 669 on tax treatment of distributions.

(3) A short-term trust to which income-producing capital is transferred for a limited period of time with the income distributed to or accumulated for the

benefit of some member of the family and the income-producing capital reverting to the grantor when the trust ends.

(4) Give illiquid assets to a family foundation or other charity to save income-tax cash which can then be used to carry life insurance or otherwise build liquid assets.

(5) Transfer dividend-paying stock (or other income-producing assets) *into a corporation* where income can be accumulated at lower tax rates.

(6) Instead of increases in compensation get your employer to continue salary payments or other *death benefits to your widow.*

(7) Get your employer to finance additional life insurance on a split-dollar basis.

(8) Retain earnings in a corporation for redemption of stock to pay death taxes and other death costs. See IRC §531, 537.

[¶2504] HOW TO TRANSFER THE MOST BY WILL

An individual may draw his will in any one of a number of different ways to accomplish his stated objective. Three of the most widely used methods are as follows:

(1) The "Outright" Method—He may leave his estate in its entirety outright to his wife with the expectation that she, in turn, will leave it to the children at her death.

(2) The "Strict Trust" Method—He may direct that all his estate be placed in a trust at his death with the income to go to his wife for life; the property itself to be distributed to his children at her death or some other future date.

(3) The "Marital Deduction Trust" Method—He may direct that his property be placed in two equal trusts at his death with the income of both to go to his wife for life. The wife must be given the minimal right to direct to whom and how the property in one of the two trusts shall be distributed at her death. (This appointive power is designed to qualify such trust for the "marital estate tax deduction.")

The three methods will produce entirely different death costs. These are outlined below. The totals given in each case assume:

(1) That the husband's estate will have a value at his death of $250,000.

(2) That his wife has no separate property of her own.

(3) That the estate administration expenses will equal 5%

(4) That he will predecease his wife.

(5) That she will survive him by ten years.

179

(6) That his estate will eventually pass to his children.

In computing the totals shown, no effect was given to state estate, inheritance, or succession taxes beyond estimating the federal estate tax on a "gross" basis without reduction by the credit for state death taxes.

(1) Under the "Outright" Method—leaving all his property outright to his wife—the approximate death costs will be as follows:

i. At the husband's death	$21,688
ii. At the wife's death	49,185
iii. Total charges over both deaths	$70,873

(2) Under the "Strict Trust" Method—putting his estate in an irrevocable trust at his death—the approximate death costs will be as follows:

i. At the husband's death	$56,450
ii. At the wife's death	None
iii. Total charges over both deaths	$56,450

(3) Under the "Marital Deduction Trust" Method—utilizing the marital estate tax deduction in conjunction with trusts—the approximate death costs will be as follows:

i. At the husband's death	$21,688
ii. At the wife's death	9,188
iii. Total charges over both deaths	$30,876

Forms of wills to accomplish a variety of objectives appear in IBP Estate Planning, Vol. ii—Checklists/Forms.

[¶2504.1]　The Marital Deduction Trust

The outline of one widely used form of the "marital deduction trust" method of property distribution is as follows:

(1) The husband would first direct in his will that the estate which he leaves at his death should be divided into two equal parts.

(2) He would secondly direct that the first half be placed in a trust at his death for the benefit of his wife. The income from the property in the trust would be paid to his wife for life. She would be given the right to direct in her will how and to whom the property should be distributed at her death. He would finally direct in respect of this trust that the trust property would pass to his children at his wife's death (or a further delayed date) in the event that

she failed to exercise the privilege of directing to whom it should go at her death.

(3) He would thirdly direct that all the taxes, charges and expenses against his estate be paid out of the second part of his estate.

(4) He would finally direct that the balance remaining of the second part of his estate be transferred to a second trust. The income of this second trust would likewise be paid to his wife for life. The property itself would be distributed to his children at his wife's death or some other selected date.

The above four-step outline sets forth the bare mechanics of one form of the "marital deduction trust" method. Many additional precautions must be taken in its actual formulation to satisfy the requirements of §2056 of the Internal Revenue Code of 1954. And provisions can be inserted to add to the trust's flexibility.

Forms to implement this outline and other marital deduction trust methods will be found in IBP ESTATE PLANNING, VOL. II — CHECKLISTS/FORMS.

[¶2504.2]   The Use of Tax Formula Clauses for Achieving the Maximum Marital Deduction

Since the federal estate tax is imposed at progressively higher rates, the idea in planning for maximum overall estate tax savings is to come as close as possible to equalizing the taxable estates of the property owner and his wife. The objective is to give the wife enough of the husband's property (both testate and non-testate) so that (1) the husband's estate qualifies for the maximum marital deduction, and (2) the wife's estate immediately following her husband's death is roughly equal in amount to one-half of her husband's adjusted gross estate. (Of course, where the wife has substantial property of her own, maximum overall estate tax savings will usually obtain where something less than the maximum marital deduction is qualified in the husband's estate.)

The only sure way of accomplishing the maximum marital deduction is by use of a formula marital deduction clause in the will. Without such a clause, the property owner can only estimate whether he is giving his wife an amount equal to the maximum marital deduction. This is because a subsequent increase or decrease in his estate can cause either an underqualification or an overqualification. On the other hand, a tax formula clause, being based upon the value of the estate at the time of death (or alternative valuation date), assures that the wife will receive an amount exactly equal to the maximum marital deduction.

One objection to formula clauses is that they might bring about a conflict of interest between the widow and other beneficiaries which could cause the executor quite a bit of embarrassment. For example, the marital gift via a tax formula may be larger or smaller depending on whether the executor elects to take certain administration expenses as estate tax or income tax deductions,

181

or on whether the estate is valued as at the date of death or at a date one year later. The answer to this objection is that a testator will usually indicate to his executor by a provision in his will just who it is who is to be preferred when a problem arises involving the use of the executor's discretion. Within this framework, the executor should not have too much difficulty in working with a tax formula clause.

[¶2504.3]   Pecuniary Bequest or "Fraction of the Residue" Formula

Although there are variations, the two main types of formula clauses are the pecuniary bequest and the fraction of the residue formula. The first provides for an amount equal to 50% of the adjusted gross estate to go to the wife; the second gives the wife that fraction of the residue which will equal the maximum marital deduction. In substance, they both aim at and achieve the same thing — the exact maximum marital deduction. But they may result in important differences.

Since the pecuniary bequest is in the nature of a general legacy, it has the effect of creating a dollar legacy. Unless there is a provision to the contrary in the will, assets used to satisfy a legacy of any kind must be valued at the date of distribution values. Paying such a dollar legacy (of say $200,000) with assets which were worth $150,000 at date of death but have appreciated between the date of death and the date of distribution will subject the executor to capital gains tax on the appreciation. However, the gain may be minimized by an adroit selection of assets.

On the other hand, where the fraction of the residue formula is used, since the wife is a residuary legatee, there is no capital gain to the executor on the delivery of appreciated assets to her. She takes the assets at the executor's basis.

An even more serious problem which may result from the use of a pecuniary formula is the possible distortion of the testamentary plan if there is any substantial appreciation or depreciation in the estate assets between the date of death and the date of distribution. For example, whether an estate increases in value from $200,000 to $300,000, or decreases to $100,000, the pecuniary marital deduction gift remains $100,000. Thus, the possibility of gain and the risk of loss are shifted to the residuary beneficiaries. A fraction of the residue formula avoids this result with both the marital and non-marital shares dividing pro rata any appreciation or depreciation.

To avoid the problem of distortion a pecuniary marital deduction gift may give the executor the option or require him to satisfy the bequest with assets taken at estate tax values. But if this is done care must be exercised because a wrong step here can knock out the marital deduction.

Under *Rev. Proc. 64-19*, CB 1964-1, (Part 1) 681, IRS will not allow the marital deduction in cases where the executor (or trustee) is either required to or has the option to satisfy a pecuniary bequest — either of the formula type or the simple non-formula type—with assets taken at estate tax values *unless* applicable state law or the provisions of the will or of the trust instrument require the executor or trustee to distribute to the surviving spouse either (1) assets, including cash, having an aggregate fair market value at the date or dates of distribution amounting to no less than the amount of the pecuniary bequest or transfer in trust, as finally determined for federal estate tax purposes; or (2) assets, including cash, fairly representative of appreciation or depreciation in value of all property available for distribution in satisfaction of the pecuniary bequest or transfer in trust. See Article IV (5) of the will at ¶25,111-1, Article III(B) of the will at ¶25,108-1, and the alternative clause at ¶25,281-3—all in IBP ESTATE PLANNING, VOL. II—CHECKLISTS/FORMS—for pecuniary formula clauses which meet one or the other of these requirements. The clause at ¶25,281-3 makes use of the precise language of *Rev. Proc. 64-19.*

If neither of these two conditions is met, there's no marital deduction. IRS takes the position that it will not be able to ascertain at the time of decedent's death just what property interest has been transferred to the surviving spouse whenever the property available for distribution includes fluctuating type assets such as stocks, real estate and the like, a condition likely to obtain in most estates.

However, if a pecuniary bequest to a spouse does not meet the requirements of (1) or (2) above, but the will or trust instrument was executed prior to October 1, 1964, IRS, to prevent unnecessary hardship, will still allow the marital deduction if it receives appropriate agreements from both the fiduciary and the surviving spouse—the wording of the agreements being set forth in *Rev. Proc. 64-19* itself.

[¶2504.4]   Allocating the Death Tax Burden

Since the adjusted gross estate is arrived at without reduction for death taxes (federal and state), apportioning any part of such taxes to the marital share, whether under the will or under state law, may result in the reduction of the marital deduction to the extent of the tax charged against the bequest which qualifies for the marital deduction. For this reason, any marital deduction wills should contain a provision charging all death taxes to the non-marital portion. This is equitable since it results in having the tax charged against the property on which the tax is based.

[¶2504.5]   Common Disaster and the Marital Deduction

In the great majority of states, the Uniform Simultaneous Death Act or similar statutes provide a presumption, where the order of death of two or more persons cannot be established by proof, that neither survived the other or others. This has the effect of preventing the property of each from unnecessarily passing through the estate of the other or others. To save the marital deduction, this presumption can be reversed by a provision in the will. However, the presumption that the wife survived should only be used where the husband's estate is substantially larger than the wife's. This is basically a matter of arithmetic — figure the taxes in each estate both ways. One other situation in which the presumption that the wife survived might be used is where the husband wants to leave his entire estate to his wife and she has a relatively small estate. In this case the bequest to the wife should be limited to the maximum marital deduction in the event that the order of deaths cannot be established by proof.

On the other side of the coin, the legacy to the wife can be conditioned upon her survival for a period of not more than six months without losing the marital deduction (provided she actually survives for such period). This time survivorship provision may be used to advantage when both estates are substantial and the wife has a long life expectancy. In such cases it offers a small safety valve to diminish the danger of using the marital deduction.

[¶2505] THE NON-MARITAL DEDUCTION TRUST

The non-marital deduction property, if left outright, will be taxed both in the decedent's estate and again in his spouse's estate upon her subsequent death unless consumed or given away in the period between the two deaths. This means that there is a good possibility that by the time the property reaches the children it will have been depleted by estate taxes in the husband's and wife's estates.

By placing the property which qualifies for the deduction in a marital deduction trust and the remaining property in a second trust, the maximum marital deduction can be assured and a double estate tax on the non-marital deduction property avoided.

The second trust, in a typical two-trust arrangement will, will be set up primarily for the protection of the wife during her life, but without giving her such control over the trust as to make its principal taxable on the wife's subsequent death.

Here are some objectives and possibilities for this kind of trust:

(1) Income tax savings may be made available by setting up a separate trust for each child beneficiary so that each trust will be considered a separate taxpayer. This accomplishes a division of the total income among several taxable entities, bringing lower annual income tax brackets into play.

(2) Provision may be made that the wife shall receive the annual income from the trust property.

(3) It may not be desirable to direct the income to the wife if it will put her into an excessively high income tax bracket at a time when she will no longer

enjoy the benefit of split income. In this case, provision may be made for the accumulation of trust income, state law permitting, or the distribution of trust income to the children, and protect the wife by giving the trustee discretion to apply the principal for the support and maintenance of the wife and children if necessary.

(4) The trustee may be directed to "sprinkle" so much of the income of the non-marital trust among the wife, children and grandchildren of the testator as their maintenance and educational requirements dictate.

(5) The ultimate distribution of the corpus of the second trust must be specified. Provision may be made for the distribution of the corpus of each of the separate trusts when the child beneficiary attains a specified age, or portions of the corpus at various ages, or further savings of estate tax may be realized by deferring distribution of the trust property until the death of the child beneficiary, passing it to grandchildren or surviving sisters and brothers or their descendants if that beneficiary has no children.

●

For Further Reference . . .

Bowe and Parker, *Page on the Law of Wills,* Wolf, Anderson Co., Cincinnati, Ohio.

Casner, *Estate Planning* (2 vol.), Little Brown & Co., Boston, Mass.

Estate Planning Desk Book, Institute for Business Planning, Englewood Cliffs, N.J.

Estate Planning looseleaf Service, Institute for Business Planning, Englewood Cliffs, N.J.

Estate Practice and Procedure, Institute for Business Planning, Englewood Cliffs, N.J.

Prentice-Hall Estate Planning (looseleaf), Prentice-Hall, Englewood Cliffs, N.J.

Scott, *Scott on Trusts,* Little Brown & Co., Boston, Mass.

Trachtman, Joseph, *Estate Planning,* Practising Law Institute, New York, N.Y.

Wormser, Renee, *Guide to Estate Planning,* Prentice-Hall, Englewood Cliffs, N.J.

EXPERTS, PROFESSIONAL SERVICES, AND OTHER INFORMATION SOURCES

[¶2601]   There are many kinds of service, information, and opinion which a lawyer requires in his work. He needs facts, records, proof, analysis, measurements, calculations, opinions of all kinds — value, conclusions to be drawn from scientific facts, probability, etc. This list is certainly not complete nor exhaustive, but it is fairly substantial and certainly indicative of the kind of services which a lawyer may find himself in need of and sources to which he can turn.

Sources of public information will vary from state to state, depending upon the local and state governmental structure. There is a fairly common pattern running through the various states; and although the nomenclature will frequently be different, the following checklist will serve some function as a lead to lawyers looking for public information in any state.

[¶2602]   EXPERTS

Accountants: Expert opinion on good accounting practices, analysis of financial statements, going concern value, estate accounting, drafting and interpretation of valuation, pricing and valuation formula, and similar portions of business contracts.

Actuaries: Assistance in development and operation of pension and welfare plans, the determination of present worth, determination of life and remainder interests, and tabulation of various probabilities.

Aerial Photographs: Useful in helping witnesses explain accidents, damage to and value of land, etc.

Aerodynamics Engineers: Expert opinion as to reasons for aviation accidents and losses.

Appraisers: Expert opinion on value for condemnation, contesting real estate tax assessment, estate tax proceedings, corporate proceedings in which value is an issue, insurance claims.

Architects: Acceptance of responsibility under building contracts, arbitration of building matters; expert opinion on accepted building practice, on replacement cost, on useful life and depreciation allowances.

Ballistics Experts: To relate wounds, bullets, and guns.

Chemists: Testimony on contents of containers, intoxication, analysis of stains.

186

Civil and Construction Engineers: Testimony as to construction practices, cost of delay, damages for unanticipated conditions, damages for failure to make site available.

Electricians: Strength and impact of shock, safety requirements and adherence thereto.

Fingerprints: Interpretation and identification can be established by public officials and investigators experienced and trained in police work.

Fire Experts: Usually on the payroll with insurance companies, can submit expert testimony as to the cause of fire damage.

Handwriting Experts: To tie up or disassociate a person through his handwriting with signatures and documents.

Investment Bankers, Brokers, and Counsellors: Expert opinion on valuation of securities, on prudent investment policy, on effect of business policies, and securing liquidations on markets, quoted prices, and realizable values; valuation and estate tax proceedings; on propriety of terms of transactions between stockholders and corporations and other non-arm's-length dealings.

Medical Doctors: Testimony as to standard practice, malpractice actions, extent of injury, probable future capacity.

Nurses: Opinion as to standards of hospital care, observation of health, and degree of damage in pain and suffering inflicted on accident victim.

Paper Experts: To submit expert testimony as to whether age of paper supports dating.

Photographers: To get valid photographs of accidents, sites, other scenes; to testify as to reliability of photograph, source and character of distortion; newspaper photographers at the scene of an accident may be an important source of information and testimony.

Psychiatrists: Particularly on plea of insanity, can testify as to deficiency of intellectual functioning, memory defects, degree of depression, and other mental factors concerning the person's capacity; also used in incompetency proceedings.

Statisticians: Expert opinion on statistical relationships, probabilities, analyses, evaluation of market and other surveys, etc.

Surveyors: Aid in fixing boundaries of properties, describing land acquired or to be conveyed, measuring, and drawing to scale diagrams of intersections where accidents occurred, other locational and topographical matters—used in real property matters, trespass, accident litigation.

Toxicologists: Poison, alcohol intake, other medical matters.

Traffic Consultants: Expert opinion as to conditions at crossing, whether conditions were so hazardous as to require owner, in the exercise of due care, to take extra precautions to warn pedestrians, motorists, etc. May give opinion as to speed of vehicle based upon length of skid marks, type of road surface, weight of vehicle, tread of tires.

Typewriter Experts: To identify forgery by typewriter; to verify typewriter as source of disputed document.

[¶2603]   PROFESSIONAL SERVICES

Abstract and Title Insurance Companies: These companies gather and interpret information as to the condition of title to real property and guarantee the accuracy of the information, usually in the form of a title insurance policy, the coverage of which may vary. They will usually offer attorneys assistance in the preparation and prosecution of actions to clear title (probate proceedings, action to quiet title, partition, action for declaratory judgment, etc.) including in addition to such matters as furnishing a title report or litigation guarantee, consultation on procedural and pleading points, and examination of the form of judgment in the action. They may offer services aiding in concluding a sale, as by serving as escrow agents, or giving the buyer a title policy which omits a particular defect and taking from the seller a hold harmless agreement backed up by a cash deposit or bond conditioned on removal of the defect. In addition to general title searches and reports these companies will aid in getting a correct legal description of property, and will issue reports limited to one or more specific matters affecting title, such as judgment liens, mechanics' liens, covenants, restrictions and easements, taxes, record ownership, homestead declarations. They will also run searches for judgments against named individuals, whether or not liens, covering any period of time requested or any designated court, and will issue chattel reports showing recorded or filed security interests or involuntary transfers. They will also furnish without charge a variety of real estate forms.

Bank Services: Most commercial banks offer the following commercial services:

(a) *Deposit services* including commercial and special checking accounts, savings accounts except for corporations and other organizations excluded by law, time deposits and certificates of deposit for entities barred from regular savings accounts permitting withdrawal on special notice, and time and demand deposits of public funds.

(b) *General services* including bank drafts (checks drawn on banks in another part of the country usually used for large payments out of state), money orders and cashier's checks, certification of checks, traveler's checks, collections on notes and other credit instruments, domestic credit information supplied to persons seeking information on depositors giving the bank as a credit reference and consenting to disclosure, advisory services in special areas such as industrial and community development and small business, and safe deposit boxes.

(c) *Loan Services* including personal loans, business purpose loans, farm loans (crops, farm equipment and livestock), and real estate loans.

(d) *International banking services* including issuance of letters of credit and the passing and making of loans against documents of title, placing orders on foreign stock exchanges, furnishing credit information on foreign firms and current economic and financial information in specific fields, recommendation of foreign counsel, and maintenance of liaison with international banking organizations, such as Export-Import Bank, International Bank for Reconstruction and Development and the International Cooperation Administration.

(e) *Guardianship services* which banks and trust companies may perform include services as the guardian or conservator of the estate of a minor or incompetent, usually under court supervision.

(f) *Escrow services* in some parts of the country where trust companies and banks may act as escrow holders in connection with sales, purchases and exchanges of real estate and real estate loans, or as the holder of documents and funds in connection with bulk sales escrows, or as the holders of stock certificate escrows.

(g) *Trustee and agency services for corporations* where trust companies and banks may: serve as the trustees of pension and profit-sharing trusts; assist attorneys in setting up such trusts and plans; serve as trustees under corporate bonds or indentures; act as transfer agents for securities transfers or registrars of stock, paying agents for bonds and coupons, fiscal agents with varied duties (such as depositary of special funds), agents for the purchase and redemption of stock, payroll agents; handle proxies; serve as agents for transfer, consolidation and payment of script certificates, and as custodians of funds or securities for underwriters, mutual funds, investment trusts, etc.

Banks' and Trust Companies' Trust Services: The following suggests the scope of services offered by trust companies and banks offering trust services:

(a) *Bailment services,* including storage of suitably packaged personal property, safe deposit boxes, and services as depositary of securities or other assets of a fiduciary, enabling the fiduciary to have amount of bond adjusted to cover value of property remaining under his control;

(b) *Agency services,* including agencies relating to securities involving full management (bank has full discretion to take any action necessary to protect principal's interest), limited supervision accounts (bank regularly reviews portfolio and makes recommendations), and custodianship (bank has physical possession of securities, clips coupons, collects interest and dividends, etc.) and agencies relating to real property, such as management (collection of rents, payment of taxes, making repairs, etc.) and management or servicing of loans secured by real estate mortgages and deeds of trust;

(c) *Estate and estate planning services,* including services as executor or administrator, furnishing information to attorney to aid in estate planning, and performance of accounting and administrative details resting on individual personal representative (fee may be same as if bank were named personal representative and functioned as such rather than as agent);

(d) *Trust administration services,* including services as trustee or co-trustee of living trusts (especially short-term trusts) and testamentary trusts, life insurance and charitable trusts, and trusts for specific purposes, such as the liquidation of a business and "pour-over" trusts (i.e., property in decedent's estate to be "poured over" into and administered in accordance with the terms of a living trust).

Blood Grouping Tests: Used in paternity, filiation, and bastardy proceedings; also for identification purposes in criminal cases. Blood grouping tests are based on the principle that certain properties of the blood tend to perpetuate themselves in offspring, and results of blood grouping tests are thus relevant in determining whether a given adult is the mother or father of a particular child. Note that the results are usually negative and only positive in the sense of indicating a possibility.

Corporation Companies: There are a number of organizations which provide assistance in incorporation, qualification, dissolution, reorganization and operation of corporations, such as the Prentice-Hall Corporation System, Corporation Trust Company, and the U. S. Corporation Company. Incorporation services include the providing of information giving basis for review of relative advantages of incorporation in one state or another, the handling of such matters as reserving name, preparation of certificate, articles or by-laws, filing documents, paying fees, recording, publishing, supplying accommodation incorporators and temporary directors.

Corporate qualification services involve the same basic type of service for qualifying a corporation to do business in another state as is provided in connection with incorporating.

Dissolution and reorganization services are in the form of assistance in carrying out corporate dissolution, merger, consolidation, amendment, or other reorganization.

Corporate operations services include such items as providing agents for the service of process or receipt and forwarding of official communications, providing tax information (notices of tax deadlines, information and form for filing tax returns), assistance in preparation for meetings (advance notice of due dates, forms and information required to prepare, receipt of proxies, furnishing inspectors of election, counting and tabulating votes).

Credit Association Services: Credit associations provide facilities for meetings between business debtors and creditors and assistance in arranging out-of-court settlements, having personnel to compile inventories, analyze accounts receivable and business operations, prepare minutes of meetings, and get signed consents to agreements.

Credit Information Publishers: There are a number of organizations which publish information of value to credit people and which may be of value to attorneys in evaluating steps to be taken against debtors. The information covered may include records of suits or judgments, bankruptcies, assignments for the benefit of creditors, ancillary receiverships, secured transactions, wage assignments, lis pendens and mechanics' liens. They may also publish information as to federal tax liens filed, both present and past.

Credit Reporting Services: Some firms offer general reporting services but many organizations, especially trade associations, limit themselves to a particular trade or industry. Most services are limited to persons granting credit and are not directly open to attorneys. Subscribers can get reports on the financial condition of debtor and experience of creditors in collecting, and changes affecting credit (changes in ownership, deaths, fires, liens, litigation, liabilities).

Intoxication Test: Based on the amount of alcohol recovered from the blood or urine: less than .05% alcohol in the blood means that a person is not drunk as far as driving a car is concerned, but .15% or more alcohol in the blood or equivalent amounts in the urine or breath puts the person under the influence of alcohol as far as driving a car is concerned. In between leaves the matter in dispute. Another set of measurements is that one milligram makes a patient decently drunk, while two milligrams make him thoroughly drunk, and three milligrams is likely to make him disorderly, while one more milligram will put him out. There are drunkometers and alcohometers to give blood tests in addition to the blood and urine tests.

Law Lists: Law lists are legal directories of attorneys available for professional employment. The American Bar Association reviews law lists and approves those meeting the requirements of the Canons of Ethics. There are a variety of general law lists, and a number of commercial law lists, as well as insurance and probate law lists. There are also foreign law lists and state legal directories.

Lawyers' Service Organizations: Many communities have organizations which undertake to perform for the attorney various routine matters connected with everyday practice, including the service of process, subpoenas, and other papers and documents, the filing of papers and documents, answering motion

191

and trial calendars, searching records for information, obtaining copies of papers and documents, and various other services of a clerical nature or such as might be performed by a law clerk.

Legal Notices: Newspapers publishing legal notices will assist an attorney drafting proposed legal notice to assure compliance with statutory requirements as to contents, time and manner of publication, etc.

Lie Detectors: Most investigative agencies now have the capacity to use equipment which registers the pulse rate, the blood pressure, and the galvanic reflex or electrodermo. These rely on the principle that an attempt to deceive will increase the blood pressure, change the pulse rate, suppress or otherwise alter breathing, and stimulate the sweat glands. Although results of a lie detector test are generally inadmissible as evidence, they are used in evaluating testimony, excluding or verifying lines of investigation, breaking down witnesses, etc.

Model and Cast Makers: To prepare charts to illustrate testimony on complicated procedures and relationships.

Private Investigators: Private investigators may be used to gather evidence (get pictures, statements from witnesses or parties, police reports, and other evidence), to find missing persons (parties, witnesses, heirs, debtors, etc.) or locate assets available to satisfy a claim or judgment.

Process Servers: There are usually available official process servers (those holding public office such as sheriffs), private individuals and agencies. The attorney will not be liable for acts committed by an official, nor for acts committed by a process server employed by an agency as an independent contractor, but may be liable for acts of an individual. The latter may, nevertheless, be used for other reasons, such as possibly greater persistence. Some process serving agencies work with skip tracers without additional charge.

Property Management Services: Many real estate firms furnish property management services including collection of rents, control and payment of repairs, payment of taxes and the like.

Sound Recordings: To provide the basis for cross examination and to prepare testimony. Bear in mind the necessity to show capacity of the recording device, competency of the operator, both authenticity and correctness of the recording, absence of changes or deletions, the manner in which the recording was preserved, identification of the speakers, absence of duress. Laws against wire tapping and avoiding privileges may make this kind of information inadmissible, but it may still be of value in preparation of cases.

Stenographic Reporters: Reporters are available to take depositions, statements, affidavits and record conferences and corporate meetings.

Sureties and Bonding Companies: Bonds may be required of fiduciaries (executors, administrators, guardians, conservators, trustees, etc.), and to guarantee performance of contracts, or legal duties (appearance or bail bonds), protect the adverse party in litigation against steps taken (attachment, execution, injunction), and various other purposes (admiralty, public official, license and permit bonds, etc.) and may be obtained from bonding companies, bail bond agents (brokers) and individual sureties.

Trade Association Management Services: There are organizations that provide full services for trade associations including membership, providing official representation before government bodies, offering advice or taking steps to promote intra-industry relations, labor relations, quality standards, product specifications, publicity and public relations, running exhibits and shows, providing management for meetings and guidance on budgets and financing.

Translators: There are a number of agencies which offer services in legal and commercial translation, both into and from the foreign.

Visual Presentation Experts: To prepare charts to illustrate testimony on complicated procedures and relationships.

[¶2604] PUBLIC RECORDS

Bankruptcy Records: Records of petitions, decrees and judgments under the Federal Bankruptcy Act are on file in the Federal District Courts sitting in bankruptcy and some states make provision for filing copies of such records in local state offices.

Birth, Death and Marriage Records: An official record should be on file where the event occurs. Request for record should include full name of person involved, sex and race (in some instances), parents' names, including maiden name of mother, month, day and year of event, place of event. If birth certificate is not on file, consider hospital or physician's record of birth, baptismal or church record, school records, insurance, selective service records, census records (Personal Census Service Branch, U. S. Bureau of Census, Pittsburg, Kansas will search decennial records on "Application for Search of Census Records" made on Form 10–611), driver's licenses and permits, and marriage certificates and licenses. Almost all states have central vital statistics offices where copies of birth, death or marriage records may be obtained. In the remaining states an official in the city, county or other local political subdivision in which the event occurs keeps the records and issues copies.

Blue Sky Law Applications and Permits: Applications and exhibits filed by the corporation and copies of all permits issued by the state under its Blue Sky laws in connection with the issuance of corporate securities are usually a matter of public record. The records will usually furnish information as to the names, addresses and occupations of the officers and directors of the corporation at the time of filing the application, the certificate of incorporation and corporate by-laws, the provisions of any document defining or limiting the rights of the corporation's security holders, the business address and nature of the business of the corporation, the names of the persons to whom permission was granted to issue shares under a "closed" permit, the amount and nature of the consideration for which the corporation was authorized to issue shares, any conditions imposed on the issuance of securities and provision, if any, for holding the securities in escrow.

Corporate Documents: Corporate documents, such as the certificate of incorporation and amendments thereof, required to be filed centrally (usually with the Secretary of State), may also be required to be filed locally (usually with the County Clerk) where the corporation has its principal place of business or in some cases in any county where the corporation maintains an office or owns real estate.

Court Records: Courts of record maintain records of every matter before the court and of the proceedings in each matter. Usually the records are chronological and the date of commencement of the action or proceeding or its filing number is needed to make use of the records. Courts also maintain calendars showing the cases assigned for trial on a particular day, the scheduling of pre-trial conferences, and the dates for hearings on demurrers, motions, etc.

Dissolution of Partnership: Some states make provision for filing affidavits of publication of notices of dissolution.

Divorce Records: Most states file divorce and annulment records in a central office of vital statistics. In the remaining states these records may be on file in a local office, usually in the office of the clerk in the court where the divorce or annulment was granted. In many states details concerning the divorce or annulment proceedings will be sealed on the application of the parties.

Fictitious Names: Statutes substantially similar in substance, although varying as to the penalty imposed for noncompliance, usually require any person doing business under a fictitious or assumed name or a designation not showing the names of the persons interested as partners in the business to file with the county or town clerk a certificate showing the name under which the business is to be conducted and the names of the persons conducting the business with their addresses. Provision is also made for filing certificates of abandonment of the use of such names and affidavits of publication.

Limited Partnership: Certificates of limited partnership and amendments of such certificates are usually filed with the county or town clerk of the place where the business is conducted.

Military Service Records: Many states make provision for recording or filing discharges, certificates of service, reports of separation, or notice of separation of military personnel and for issuing certified copies of these papers.

Motor Vehicle Records: Records on file with state motor vehicle departments offer a source of information on various matters: (1) The license application will usually give the applicant's name, mailing address, residence, his place of business, age and date of birth, marital status, height, weight, etc., and show suspension and revocation of prior licenses, defects and illnesses affecting driving; (2) The registration application will usually give the name and address of the owner, his place of business or employment; (3) Title certificate will show liens and encumbrances; (4) Some states have special registration forms which may show type of vehicle, origin, circumstances of acquisition (lien sale, bankruptcy sale, etc.) and ownership; (5) Accident reports (these may be confidential except as to certain matters such as names and addresses of persons involved and registration numbers and description of vehicles, date and time of accident and names and addresses of witnesses) filed by the parties themselves and filed by the police.

Recordable Documents: State statutes govern the kinds of documents which may be recorded or filed and the effect of their recording or filing. Following is a list of some kinds of documents usually subject to recording or filing:

(1) Instruments transferring interests in real estate (deeds and the like, mortgages, contracts for sale or transfer, powers of attorney to convey, leases, and assignments of such instruments, satisfaction or release of mortgage; (2) Notices of mechanics' liens; (3) Notices of attachments on real estate; (4) Notices of pendency of actions affecting title to or possession of real estate; (5) Copies of decrees or judgments of courts of record or records of judgments constituting liens on real estate; (6) Instruments creating security interests in personal property, assigning or releasing such interests (chattel mortgages, conditional sales, factors' liens, trust receipt financing statements, leases of personal property intended as security, and Uniform Commercial Code form of security agreement or financing statement); (7) Instruments describing or relating to the separate property of married women; (8) Marriage contracts (in some states); (9) Official bonds; (10) Wills.

Securities Exchange Commission Registration Statements: All registration statements filed with the Securities Exchange Commission are available for public inspection in Washington, D. C., except for contracts or material portions thereof accorded confidential treatment under Rule 485 (SEC determines disclosure would impair value of contract and is not necessary for protection of investors).

195

Tax Records: Tax assessors must maintain records of all property subject to assessment (real and personal, tangible and intangible depending on state or local law) within the governmental unit (state, county, municipal). The records will show the name and address of the owner of the particular property subject to assessment, the nature of the interest owned, such as mineral rights, leasehold, building and improvements, and the assessed valuation. Records indicating whether or not a corporation has filed required returns and paid all taxes assessed against it.

Voting Records: Local officials—voting registrars, the county clerk, the town clerk, etc.—maintain records based on information furnished by the registrant which may be of value in identifying a person, establishing his residence or other facts about him. The contents of the records may vary but will usually cover the following: The full name of the registrant and any change of name; current address and for how long, and in many cases the last prior address; citizenship and how acquired; occupation; marital status and in many cases the name of spouse and date and place of marriage; name of parents; signature of registrant; certain criminal records affecting qualification to vote; certain physical characteristics may also be noted; and the registrant's death or adjudication of incompetency may also be noted.

In many states voters' political enrollment is a public record.

•

For Further Reference . . .
Richardson, *Modern Scientific Evidence.*

FORECLOSURE OF REAL ESTATE AND OTHER COLLATERAL FOR DEFAULTED LOANS

⟦¶2701⟧ The foreclosure of real estate and chattel mortgages and similar security interests in personal property is largely statutory and subject to local variances. Hence, it will always be necessary to check out specific statutory provisions. Nevertheless, the Uniform Commercial Code marks out a common pattern for the foreclosure of security interests in personal property, and a common pattern is also discernible in the case of real estate mortgages, although there is no "uniform" law as such in this area.

⟦¶2702⟧　　　FORECLOSING AND REDEEMING A
　　　　　　　REAL ESTATE MORTGAGE

The attorney in general practice will on occasion be faced with the problem of representing either the mortgagor or the mortgagee in a foreclosure proceeding. Financial institutions in many cases are reluctant to foreclose because legal expenses, loss of interest and commissions often exceed 20% of the value of the property. This frequently will exceed a home owner's equity and thus result in loss to the lending institution. So, the attorney representing a client faced with foreclosure should always make the attempt to obtain a period of forbearance by the lender or an extension agreement which will reduce monthly payments without scaling down the total debt. To make an extension stick it must normally be supported by consideration. If no satisfactory agreement can be made, the following points should be borne in mind:

(1) Notice Required by Mortgage: Many mortgage instruments prevent the lender from commencing foreclosure proceedings until notice of the default has been given to the borrower, and he has not cured the default within the period specified. Frequently, this will be 30 days, although in certain circumstances, it may be less, as where the borrower abandons the property or otherwise exposes it to immediate risk.

(2) Process of Foreclosure: A mortgage is often in form an absolute conveyance of property which will become void upon the mortgagor's compliance with stated conditions (payment of the debt and compliance with other conditions such as payment of taxes, etc.). Some authorities say a breach of any condition by the mortgagor immediately vests absolute title in the mortgagee. Others minimize or deny that a mortgage operates as a conveyance and regard it as a security or lien for the performance of an obligation. In fact, all jurisdictions require the mortgagee *either* to initiate a judicial proceeding *or* to make a public sale of the property. The purpose of these requirements is to give the mortgagor an opportunity to redeem his interest or to insure that if

the value of the property exceeds the mortgage debt, the excess will be returned to the mortgagor. There are four variations of the foreclosure process followed in the various American jurisdictions.

(3) Strict Foreclosure: This requires the mortgagee to maintain an action for foreclosure. Once a decree of foreclosure is issued, the mortgagor is given a relatively short period (up to six months) during which he may regain the property by payment of the mortgage debt plus litigation expenses incurred by the mortgagee. At the end of the period of redemption, the property belongs to the mortgagee without any requirement of a public sale. This proceeding is used extensively only in Connecticut and Vermont, although it is permissible in a number of other states.

(4) Judicial Foreclosure Followed by Sale: This is the most common method used. It varies from strict foreclosure in that after the period of redemption has expired, a public sale of the property is required. In theory, this will result in the mortgagor receiving the difference between the value of the property and the mortgage debt. However, since these sales often take place during depressed markets or the property has undesirable features, the mortgagee is often the only bidder. In some states, a period of redemption also follows the sale which further reduces the probability that the property's true value will be realized.

(5) Non-Judicial Foreclosure Followed by Sale: Although barred in some states, a frequently used method of foreclosure is by the exercise of a power of sale which is given to the mortgagee in the mortgage instrument. This eliminates any need for a judicial proceeding which is not only time consuming but expensive. The sale must be a public one, preceded by proper public notice and advertisement. There may or may not be a period of redemption following the sale.

(6) Judicial Foreclosure by Entry and Possession: In several of the New England states, the mortgagee obtains a decree of foreclosure after a judicial proceeding, and after a period of redemption, may enter and take possession of the property. A period of redemption also follows the repossession. This method may be used without a judicial proceeding provided repossession can be made without force. In effect, this type of proceeding is similar to strict foreclosure.

(7) Additions to the Mortgage Indebtedness: The mortgagee is entitled to add to the unpaid debt the expenses of foreclosure as well as taxes and other obligations of the property which are paid by the mortgagee. Generally, the mortgage instrument will provide for interest to be paid even after default and this will usually be allowed by the court. Attorneys' fees will be allowed if provided for in the instrument; otherwise they may not. However, any specified

amount must be reasonable. Similarly, insurance premiums on the property may be added to the unpaid debt in some jurisdictions provided the mortgage instrument so provides.

(8) Personal Judgment for Deficiency: If the proceeds from the sale of the property following the foreclosure are insufficient to satisfy the mortgage debt, the mortgagee in most states may obtain a personal judgment against the mortgagor for the deficiency. As a practical matter, this is not often done since the mortgagor presumably is without assets. However, where the mortgagor is a business concern which remains in operation, a deficiency judgment may well be sought. As a result of the experience of the 1930's, when foreclosed properties were often bid in far below their value, many states now give the mortgagor a defense of "fair market value" in a proceeding for a deficiency judgment. The effect of this is to limit the judgment to the difference between the unpaid mortgage debt and the fair market value of the property. The bid price at the foreclosure sale is irrelevant. Since these laws have never been tested in a period of severe recession, it is impossible to say how well they would protect mortgagors under such circumstances.

(9) Deeds in Lieu of Foreclosure: If foreclosure seems imminent and the mortgagor has no hopes of redeeming the property or realizing an excess on foreclosure, the parties should consider a voluntary conveyance to the mortgagee to avoid the expense and delay of a judicial proceeding. The consideration for the transfer of the property is the cancellation of the mortgage debt.

(10) Moratorium Laws: During the depression, many states passed laws imposing a moratorium on the institution of foreclosure proceedings. Although these have expired, one moratorium law now in existence is the Soldiers' and Sailors' Civil Relief Act. This is a Federal statute intended to benefit members of the armed services who can show that by reason of their induction, they have been unable to pay their debts. The statute requires that in the case of foreclosure proceedings, the military defendant be granted a stay during the period of military service. The court may impose such conditions including payments on a reduced scale as it deems fair and equitable.

[¶2703]   LIQUIDATION OF PERSONAL PROPERTY POSTED AS COLLATERAL

If the personal property given as collateral is not in the lender's possession at the time of default, the first step, of course, is to go out and get it or "repossess it."

The next steps are apt to rest largely on the terms of the security agreement covering the collateral and applicable statutory provisions. Many states have special provisions designed to protect the defaulting purchaser of consumer goods, automobiles, home appliances, etc., which must be looked to whenever applicable.

In the absence of any contrary provision, statutory or contractual, the holder of a promise to pay money secured by collateral may, upon default in the payment of the debt according to the terms of the instrument, either bring an action on the promise to pay or sell the collateral without judicial process, upon such notice, if any, as may be required, or bring suit to foreclose and obtain a judicial sale thereof. This is essentially the situation that prevails when property is pledged and possession delivered to the pledgee.

A contrary agreement may be express or it may be found in the surrounding circumstances or in the course of the parties' dealings.

[¶2703.1]   Can the Sale of a Pledge Be Private?

Pledge agreement provisions specifying a private sale, and the terms and conditions thereof, including a private sale upon such terms and conditions as deemed proper by pledgee, are generally upheld. Usually such provisions are upheld even though a sale without notice, demand or advertisement is expressly designated thereby. Even where the pledge instrument provides for sale without notice, demand or advertisement, the pledgee is held to a requirement of good faith toward the pledgor with respect to such sale. In most jurisdictions, where the terms and conditions of private sales are not specified in the pledge instrument, they are circumscribed in scope by general requirements of fairness and openness, requiring some sort of notice to third persons and some sort of competitive bidding for validity.

The law is clear that the creditor may not get good title to the collateral unless he acquires it in accordance with the law of pledgor and pledgee. The almost universally accepted rule is that the pledgee, absent contractual or statutory authorization, cannot purchase pledged property at a non-judicial sale.

[¶2703.2]   How Can a Proper Judicial Sale of Pledge be Accomplished?

By notifying a fair number of persons known or believed to be interested in the purchase of the collateral to submit written bids within a certain time, or to make oral bids at a specified time and place, to have the pledgee submit its own bid, and then to permit the highest bidder, no matter who he may be, to become the purchaser and to reject all other bids. This method is not exclusive. Any equitable method, that is, one which permits competition and which exhausts the possibility of obtaining a price better than the one officially accepted, would not be objectionable. The power to sell, whether a private or public sale, should not be construed in a manner which permits the pledgee to sell secretly or to one not the highest bidder, for to do so would be contrary to the general rule that the sale must be fair and open. Even where the collateral note permits sale without notice, the debtor should be given notice, particularly if the creditor may buy in the collateral.

[¶2703.3] Liquidation Under the Code

Under §9–501 of the Uniform Commercial Code the parties to a security agreement may as heretofore provide for sale on default but the following duties imposed by the named sections may not be waived or varied: (1) the requirement for an accounting for surplus proceeds of collateral (§9–502(a)); (2) the disposition of collateral (§9–504(3)) and (§9–505(1)), except as provided in (§9–505(1)); (3) the acceptance of collateral as discharge of the obligation (§9–505(2)); (4) the redemption of collateral, except as permitted under §9–506; and (5) the secured party's liability for failure to comply with the provisions of Part 5 (§9–507(1)).

It is well to consider including in the security agreement as permitted by §9–503 an obligation upon the debtor to assemble the collateral at a place designated, which place must be reasonably convenient. Likewise under this Section and the following Section, the secured party may leave the collateral on the debtor's premises, render it unusable in preparation for sale and sell it on such premises.

The secured party may sell, lease or otherwise dispose of any or all of the collateral (§9–504). This Section should be noted carefully to follow the basis for application of the proceeds of sale and particularly to be aware of the right of a junior lienee on notice to the secured party to obtain part or all of the excess proceeds. The secured party may require proof of the claim and indemnity before paying to the subordinate secured party.

Unless otherwise provided in the security agreement, the debtor is liable for any deficiency, but, in the case of accounts, contract rights or chattel paper, the debtor is liable for a deficiency only if the security agreement so provides (§9–504). The sale must be on a commercially reasonable basis. Unless the collateral is perishable, or its value threatens to decline speedily or it is customarily sold on a recognized market, reasonable notice of sale must be given to the debtor and also, except in the case of consumer goods, to any person who has a security interest and who has filed and indexed in the name of the debtor (§9–504).

•

For Further Reference . . .
American Jurisprudence, Chattel Mortgages, Mortgages, Pledge and Collateral
  Security.
Kratovil, Robert, *Real Estate Law.*

Real Estate Desk Book, Institute for Business Planning, Inc., Englewood Cliffs, N.J.

Real Estate Tax Shelter Desk Book, Institute for Business Planning, Inc., Englewood Cliffs, N.J.

GUARANTEES AND INDEMNIFICATION

[¶2901] Businessmen use various devices to assure that obligations owed to them will be fulfilled. In the Secured Transactions chapter (beginning at ¶4901), you can see how security interests in all kinds of personal property may be used to secure a credit sale or a loan. Here, we examine another common method of getting protection — the surety and the guarantor.

[¶2902]   GUARANTORS AND SURETIES

The law governing sureties and guarantors is somewhat specialized. Basically, it deals with the relationship of three individuals:
(1) An *obligee* (the person to be protected),
(2) The *principal obligor* (the buyer, borrower or contractor), and
(3) The *surety or guarantor* (the person giving the added protection).
Sureties and guarantors can be used in many areas where the obligee demands security because of the obligor's weak financial position. They can be used to secure an installment sale, for example, even though the seller retains a security interest in the property sold. Similarly, they may be used to back up a secured loan.

There are certain areas where the functions of the surety and guarantor have special uses. One important area is in dealing with a newly formed corporation with thin capitalization. In such cases the stockholders will ordinarily be called on to act as sureties or guarantors for the corporation. In so doing they will aid both the creditor and the corporation. The creditor gets the personal liability of the stockholders; the corporation benefits to the degree that the stockholders, realizing their personal liability, will be less disposed to weaken the corporation's financial condition by making large withdrawals.

Sureties and guarantors are frequently required in building and construction contracts in order to guarantee performance. As a matter of fact, statutes may require the posting of surety bonds, especially when public contracts are involved, and in some instances, where private contracts are involved. Such surety contracts take on the appearance of insurance contracts and some states do look on them as such.

A third area of general use is familiar to all. Often a financially successful person will guarantee a loan for a close relative, who is starting a new venture. This arrangement might even be made without the principal obligor's knowledge, in order to place him on his own responsibility.

Businesses which have successfully operated for a period but have begun to falter may also be called on to furnish a surety or guarantor.

Forms of guaranty and indemnity agreements appear in IBP FORMS OF BUSINESS AGREEMENTS looseleaf Service.

[¶2902.1]   What to Look For in a Surety or Guarantor

If you're dealing with a paid surety, one who is in the business of being a surety, you will not ordinarily have to worry about the surety being able to make good on the principal's obligations. This is because paid sureties are subject to state regulation, which normally gives some assurance of their financial condition. Private sureties and guarantors are something else. Their obligation is no better than their financial standing.

If you are going to rely on a non-professional guarantor or surety to backstop the principal's obligation, you will normally want to run a credit check through an established agency, get character references and financial statements. The relationship of the surety or guarantor to the principal obligor is often an important consideration. The chances are that a surety acting for his son, for example, will be more apt to fulfill his obligations than if a stranger is involved.

[¶2902.2]   Differences and Similarities Between Sureties and Guarantors

If you are looking to the additional protection of a surety or guarantor in a transaction, it's important that you spell out exactly what you expect from this surety or guarantor and that the surety or guarantor undertake the obligation you expect. *Reason:* There are some fine-spun legal distinctions in some states, and no distinctions in others, between sureties and guarantors.

Generally, both sureties and guarantors perform essentially the same commercial function. Both lend their names and credit standing to the principal obligor and agree to make good his shortcomings in the performance of his obligations to the obligee. But, according to many courts, there are differences between the two —

—A surety is a co-promissor with the principal obligor and is equally liable with him on his obligation.

—A guarantor, on the other hand, is said to be a collateral promissor whose liability arises only after all attempts to make the principal obligor perform have failed.

On this basis, the guarantor must receive notice of the principal obligor's default before there can be any obligation on his part. However, the differences begin to break down when some of the same courts pronouncing these distinctions talk about sureties being guarantors of payment—a true guarantor, they say, is merely a guarantor of collection.

Other courts have used the terms surety and guarantor interchangeably, and the Uniform Commercial Code says the term surety includes guarantor *(UCC §1–201(40))*.

In view of these distinctions some states spell out specifically the obligation or liability of the third party to the deal. Generally, if you want him to guarantee payment, it will not be enough to have him simply sign the instrument or contract to be guaranteed as a guarantor—you'll want him to endorse "payment guaranteed." On the other hand if you are being asked to give a guarantee and all you want to give is a guarantee of collection, spell that out —"Collection guaranteed." This is especially important if you're dealing with an "instrument" within the reach of the Commercial Paper Article of the UCC, which says that use of words of guaranty, without more, operates to guarantee payment (UCC §3–416(3)). See ¶2906 for a discussion of guarantors of commercial paper.

[¶2902.3] Capacity or Authority to Become a Surety or Guarantor

The contract of a surety or guarantor will not, of course, be worth anything unless he has legal capacity to enter into the contract. Age and mental capacity usually present no problems.

However, when a partnership or corporation is going to act as surety or guarantor, you may have problems or, at least, some questions to check out. Ordinarily, a partner has no implied authority to make contracts of surety or guaranty in the firm name. True, in the case of certain types of partnership business, the required authority may be implied from the common course of business of the firm. A partner in a firm engaged in selling puts and calls, for example, may be deemed to have implied authority to guaranty performance of the obligations under a put or call which it has sold. Also, authority may be implied from a previous course of dealing with the partnership. That is, if you've had a series of dealings in which a particular partner has acted on behalf of the firm, committing it to a suretyship obligation, and the firm has fulfilled its obligations without questioning the partner's authority, it's pretty clear that he has implied authority or that the firm is barred from questioning it.

Make sure, therefore, that the partner or partners acting on the firm's behalf have either express or implied authority to bind the firm—if they do not, you may get only the *individual* obligations of those purporting to act for the firm. And further, partners acting on the firm's behalf will want to be sure that they have full authority, so that the firm and all the partners are bound by the agreement and those signing the agreement won't have to bear the obligation alone. Because of this factor, you can normally expect full cooperation from individual partners in settling the questions of partnership liability.

When you plan to deal with an uncompensated corporate surety or guarantor, remember that the corporation's authority or capacity to act as surety or guarantor is severely limited. A number of rules have been developed which must be borne in mind.

The first rule is that a corporation cannot become a surety or guarantor *solely* for the principal obligor's benefit, unless it is given such power by its charter or statute—as where it is in the business of being a surety. Within the prohibition are guarantees of loans to directors, officers or stockholders. So far as the rule operates to protect stockholders, you can get around it by getting the consent of all of the stockholders. But creditors of the corporation may claim that the obligation assumed was beyond the corporation's authority. Usually, such a claim would be made only in situations where the corporation is not meeting its obligations to its creditors, and shouldn't present a grave problem if the corporation has a very good credit rating.

The second rule to bear in mind is that a corporation does not need *express* power to act as a surety or guarantor but has *implied* power to do so when such action will "directly" promote its business purpose. The problem here is what kind of activity promotes business purpose. The following acts have been held to benefit corporate business purpose directly:

(1) Guaranteeing a customer's loan where there is a potential benefit from increased sales.

(2) Protecting the corporation's own interest by guaranteeing a loan to a subsidiary.

(3) Guaranteeing a debt of one of the corporation's own debtors in order to keep him going and so increase its chances of being paid.

If you're going to rely on the corporation's obligation, you will want a corporate resolution which directly relates the guarantee to the promotion of a business purpose. If a resolution cannot be legitimately formulated in these terms, the obligee should not rely on the corporate obligation and the corporate directors should not give it. Two courses are then open: (1) unanimous stockholder consent, or (2) a guarantee by the stockholders or directors or some of them as individuals.

[¶2903] THE SURETY OR GUARANTEE AGREEMENT

The surety or guarantor's contract should be put in writing, for two reasons. First, because these contracts are generally regarded as contracts to answer for the debt or default of another and, under the Statute of Frauds, must be in writing. You can argue that a straight suretyship contract or guarantee of payment makes the surety or guarantor jointly liable with the obligor, so that there is no contract to answer for the debt of another, but don't count on winning this argument — play safe and put the contract in writing.

Second, a writing helps avoid disputes as to the rights and obligations of the parties. What finally goes into the contract will depend on the skill and judgment of the parties and their relative bargaining position.

Here is a checklist of the main negotiating and drafting considerations in a suretyship or guarantee agreement:

(1) The obligation(s) secured — present, past, future.

(2) The nature of the guarantee or the suretyship.
  (a) Primary or secondary, payment or collection.
  (b) Conditions of liability.
  (c) Amount of liability.
    1. Costs and expenses.
    2. Attorney's fee.
    3. Interest.
    4. Limitation of liability to a specified maximum.
    5. Where there are two or more guarantors or sureties.
  (d) Duration of liability.
    1. Revocation — when and how agreement can be revoked.
    2. Effect of death, insolvency, etc. of co-sureties or co-guarantors.
  (e) Exceptions to liability — for example, acts of God as excusing performance.
  (f) Persons protected and persons bound by the agreement.
(3) Notice to the guarantor or surety.
  (a) Principal's default.
  (b) Creation or amount of indebtedness.
  (c) Alterations or changes in contract.
  (d) Claims or liens against principal.
(4) The effect of alterations or changes in the principal's obligation.
  (a) Generally.
  (b) Compromise or settlement with principal debtor.
  (c) Time extensions to principal debtor.
(5) Indemnification of the surety or the guarantor.
(6) Subrogation to the rights of the principal or obligee.
(7) Waivers — necessity of having these in writing.

As stated above, these are the main points to watch for. Special situations may call for special provisions not suggested in this list.

Various forms of guaranty will be found in IBP FORMS OF BUSINESS AGREEMENTS.

[¶2903.1] The Continuing and Restricted Guarantee

A guarantee need not be restricted to a specific transaction. It can be a continuing one—that is, one contemplating future uses or a series of transactions.

Courts have had difficulties interpreting whether a continuing or restricted guarantee was intended. Thus, the guarantor will want clearly to spell out what type is intended. The continuing guarantee can be a very dangerous and expensive instrument from the guarantor's point of view. So it is wise to set forth in detail the conditions of the guarantee. The most important thing is, of course, to limit the amount guaranteed and the period over which it will be effective. Also, limit the guarantee as to the type of transaction for which it can be used—if this is not done, you may find yourself guaranteeing some of the principal obligor's personal obligations.

[¶2903.2]   Getting the Principal's Signature on the Contract

The question of whether or not you have to have the principal obligor's signature on the contract of the surety or guarantor is one that has given the courts considerable difficulty. While there are numerous decisions to the effect that his signature isn't necessary, it will ordinarily be best to play safe and get it. In the rare case where you don't want the principal to know that his obligation is being guaranteed, check the applicable law in your state before entering into the contract.

[¶2903.3]   Acceptance, Approval and Filing

A contract of suretyship, like any other contract, requires acceptance. When the obligation runs to a governmental body or agency, certain persons or officers will usually be entrusted with the duty of accepting and approving the bond or contract; and there may be special provisions for filing or recording the instrument after its approval.

[¶2903.4]   Indemnity, Exoneration, Subrogation and Contribution

Indemnity, exoneration, subrogation and contribution are terms commonly used to describe certain phases of the suretyship or guaranty and we should know what they mean and how they are used.

Indemnity: The principle of indemnity is that once a surety or guarantor has paid the principal obligor's debt *or* performed his contract, he has a right to be reimbursed—indemnified—by the principal for the amount it cost him. Note that there is no right of indemnity until the surety or guarantor has paid out money and then he has a right to collect the amount he paid out. So if he is able to work out a compromise and settlement with the obligee for less than the full amount owing, he can enforce his right to indemnity only up to the compromised amount. You don't have to spell out a right of indemnity in the contract — it will be implied. Nevertheless, it is best to put it in writing, specifying just how far indemnification goes (court costs, counsel fees, etc.) and how the surety or guarantor is to prove his payment before he has the right to indemnification.

Exoneration: This is an important aid to the surety and guarantor. Here's how it works. Assume that the principal obligor's debt or performance has become due, and the obligee fails to take action. Statutes in many states give the surety a right to bring a suit and compel the creditor to sue the principal obligor and thus collect the debt. Some states even allow the surety to sue the principal and compel him to pay. What exoneration boils down to is that the surety need not pay the obligee and then try to get reimbursed from the principal obligor — he can take the initiative in forcing the obligor to pay.

Subrogation: What this means is that the surety or guarantor can step into the obligee's shoes after he has paid off on his obligation. He receives all the remedies which the obligee has against the principal and he can also have any collateral securities which the obligor pledged with the obligee. When you couple the right of subrogation with indemnity, the surety may, in certain instances, acquire the preferred status of the obligee and thus be surer of receiving reimbursement. For example, suppose a person becomes a surety on a government contract, and the principal obligor fails to perform. After the surety pays or performs for the government, he will be subrogated to the rights of the principal obligor and he will then have the government's preferred status over other creditors.

Contribution: It only arises when there are two or more sureties or guarantors. Contribution means that a surety who pays the obligee can compel the other sureties to pay their shares in order to make all the shares equal. The only requisite for this right is that all concerned be sureties for the same principal and the same obligation. They may be bound on separate instruments and they may not even be aware of one another.

[¶2904]   DISCHARGE OF THE SURETY OR GUARANTOR

An obligee has to be careful in dealing with the principal obligation, or with the security received to secure the obligation. Some actions may discharge the surety or guarantor, unless consented to in advance or after the event by the surety or guarantor.

Here are the main causes of discharge:

(1) Material alteration of the principal obligor's contract.

(2) Extension of time for payment of the principal debt.

(3) Failure of obligee to comply with request or notice to sue the principal obligor where a statute gives the surety or guarantor that right.

(4) Release or loss of the security.

(5) Payment or performance by the principal obligor.

(6) Release or discharge of the principal obligor.

(7) Change of principals or obligees.

Here are some of the things to watch out for in connection with these causes: a material alteration, *even though it may be to the advantage of the principal,*

209

as in case of a reduction of the interest rate on a loan, may work a discharge in some states. Both with regard to alterations and extensions, a compensated surety—one in the business—will be less readily discharged than an unpaid surety. The compensated surety will have to show damage before he can be relieved.

Mere failure to pursue the principal when the debt falls due does not operate as an extension. The extension has to be the result of a positive act. Most states have an exception to the rule of discharge by extension, and that is that there is no discharge if the obligee, in granting an extension, reserves his rights against the surety.

Release of the security held by the obligee will operate to release the surety *to the extent that the remaining security is not enough to cover the debt.* Similarly, negligence on the part of the obligee in dealing with security in his hands, resulting in its loss, may release the surety. And failure to perfect or to record the security can result in discharge. (As to perfecting and recording security, see ¶4902.)

A surety may be discharged in some states if the Statute of Limitations runs out on the principal debt. In other states this won't work a discharge. If you are an obligee, don't let yourself get in a position where the rule can be applied against you—go after the principal obligor as soon as he is in default.

Bankruptcy of the principal obligor, although it results in his discharge, won't discharge the surety. The surety in this situation can only claim reimbursement from the bankrupt's estate.

Changes in the personnel of a partnership, even though the partnership keeps the same name, can result in discharge, but a mere change in name of the principal obligor, whether a partnership or a corporation, will not have that effect.

What you have to do when you set up the surety or guarantor relationship, is to try to anticipate the various causes for discharge and get consent to them at that time. Where necessary, insert in the agreement any limitations which give the surety or guarantor the protection he demands. If you fail to get the requisite consent initially, try to get it before you do anything that can result in discharge. Consent to an extension of time, for example, may not be too hard to obtain if the surety can see himself as benefiting also. If you do get the consent you're looking for, get it in writing.

In addition to "discharge" of the surety in the various ways suggested there are other points for the obligee to remember if he is to hold the surety or guarantor to his contract. These things may not operate to "discharge," but the effect will be the same. Included in this category are some matters already discussed such as the capacity or authority of the surety or guarantor, and the necessity of a written agreement to hold someone responsible for the debt of another. Certain defects in the principal obligor's contract may discharge the surety's obligation, such as lack of consideration, illegality, usury or impossibility of performance. The defect must be one that *voids* the contract and not one that makes it *voidable*. For example, if a principal has not reached the age at which he can enter into a legally binding contract, this fact will ordinarily operate to make his contract *voidable,* and will not automatically relieve the surety of his obligation.

[¶2905]   PROTECTING THE SURETY'S INTEREST IN COLLATERAL GIVEN BY OBLIGOR

Sureties often require some type of security from the principal obligor. Usually it will be quite obvious that the security interest granted, if it's to be good against third persons, will have to be perfected in one of the ways we've discussed in our chapter on secured transactions. But sometimes this won't be quite so obvious. For example, the surety on a contractor's bond demands and gets an assignment of the payments which become due under the contract in order to secure his rights against the principal. The surety will have to follow UCC procedures to perfect his interest and make it stand up against other creditors of the principal obligor or others claiming an interest in the payments through him.

If the assignment of payments under a contract covers payments due at the time of the assignment, a somewhat different approach may be required. A surety who requires tangible or intangible security from the obligor in order to protect himself must be alert to the possibility that he has a security interest which is not perfected against third persons unless he takes positive steps to this end.

[¶2906]   SURETIES AND GUARANTORS ON COMMERCIAL PAPER

You can create a relationship of suretyship or guarantee without using a separate contract and without using words of suretyship or guarantee. Actually, accommodation parties on commercial paper, whether their names appear as makers, drawers, acceptors or endorsers, will be, in effect, sureties or guarantors.

Under *UCC §3–415(2)* an accommodation party incurs contract liability on the instrument *in the capacity in which he signs.* So if he signs a note as a maker, he will have the liability of a maker. If he signs as an endorser, he will have the liability of an endorser. Payment by the accommodating party to the holder creates a cause of action in favor of the accommodating party based on the accommodated party's implied obligation to indemnify the accommodating party. Accommodation endorsers should include a waiver of suretyship defenses if that is the parties' intent. These various liabilities are discussed in detail beginning at ¶1207. Here it is sufficient to point out that the obligee will be in a better position if the accommodation party can be induced to sign as maker. As maker, his liability will be primary and not conditioned on presentment of the note as might be the case if he signs as endorser.

Under the Code, the liability of an accommodation party will run to a holder for value, even though the holder knows of his accommodation nature. Under *Code §3–415(2)*, this is true only if the holder takes the instrument before it is due. And under this section of the Code, liability is imposed on an accommodation endorser even though the endorsement takes place after delivery to the holder.

Under the UCC, as against anyone taking the paper with knowledge of the accommodation character, or a holder who is not a holder in due course, the accommodation party can set up any of the defenses that an ordinary surety might set up to relieve himself of liability. For example, he can get off the hook by showing an extension of time for payment made without his consent, and without an effective reservation of rights against him. (See *UCC §3–606*.) He will also be discharged by a release of collateral. If the accommodation party consents to any action which might discharge him, he will not be discharged. Therefore, consent in advance to certain actions, such as extension of time, is commonly incorporated in the instrument over the accommodation party's signature. If such consent is not obtained in advance, it can be given afterwards, and it will be binding even without consideration.

Normally, a holder in due course without actual notice of the accommodation need not be concerned about the defense of the accommodation party. However, an endorsement which is not in the chain of title—the irregular or anomalous endorsement — will be notice of the accommodation character. *(UCC §3–415(4).)* Here's an example of such an endorsement: a note payable to Able or his order and made by Baker is endorsed by Charlie (the accommodation party) before Baker negotiates the note to a holder in due course.

The UCC makes it clear that both paid and gratuitous sureties may be accommodation parties.

[¶2906.1] **Difference Between Guaranteeing Payment and Collection**

There is a big difference between guaranteeing payment and guaranteeing collection: He who guarantees payment says in effect he will pay the instrument when it becomes due, regardless of whether the holder has tried to collect from the party primarily liable. He waives presentment and any necessary notice of dishonor and protest and any demand the holder has against the maker or drawer. In short, he becomes a co-maker or co-drawer, jointly and separately liable. On the other hand, the man who guarantees collection says in effect that if the instrument is not paid when it becomes due, he will pay it, *if and only if* the holder first goes against the maker, drawer or acceptor by suit and execution or shows that such action would be useless. However, he, in effect, also waives presentment and any necessary notice of dishonor or protest.

UCC §3–416 codifies these different meanings in accordance with commercial understanding and the accepted meaning of these terms under prior law.

When using these forms of guarantee consider:

(1) Limitation on the amount of the guarantee. It doesn't necessarily have to be of the full amount of the instrument.

(2) Consent to extension of time of payment or release of collateral.

(3) Payment of collection expenses, including attorneys' fees.

[¶2907]   INDEMNITY AND HOLD HARMLESS AGREEMENTS

Every business involves certain risks which become part of the cost of doing business. The businessman who can reduce these risks or shift some of them to others is going to be able to reduce his costs and improve his competitive position. Various forms of indemnity and hold harmless agreements are used to shift the risk of loss in commercial transactions from one party to another.

Both are agreements under which one party to the agreement promises to make good the loss which the other party will sustain on the occurrence of a certain event or contingency. The two types of agreements — indemnity and hold harmless — are closely related and often considered identical. Sometimes a distinction is drawn on the basis that a true indemnity agreement merely provides indemnity against an actual loss suffered, while a hold harmless agreement may, and often does, provide for the defense of claims made against the indemnitee or the party to be held harmless. On the other hand, this distinction isn't always followed and indemnity agreements, as such, fall into two main types: (1) indemnity against loss and (2) indemnity against liability.

Whatever fine-spun distinctions there may be, the two forms of agreement can, for the most part, be considered identical and we will use the terms interchangeably and refer to the parties in both types of agreements as indemnitor and indemnitee. These agreements may be used to:

(1) Assume the legal liability of others.

(2) Create an entirely new liability for the indemnitor.

(3) Create a contractual liability for the indemnitor in cases where he is already liable in tort for the same risk.

We give you examples of these different uses in paragraphs which follow. But first let us make clear, in connection with (3) above, why anyone would want to add contractual liability to tort liability. Let's say you buy a heating plant and the seller agrees to install it. The seller will be liable in any case for negligence in installing it but you are in a better position if you have not only his tort liability (negligence) but his contractual liability to hold you harmless as well. There are a number of reasons for this but the main ones are:

(1) In a contract action all you will have to prove is the contract and the damages. You won't have to show negligence on the part of the seller and you won't have to worry about the defenses of contributory negligence or assumption of risk.

(2) You can spell out the measure of damages in a contract action, and even without doing so your damages may be greater in a contract than in a tort action.

(3) The time to sue is usually longer for contract actions than for tort actions.

Various forms of indemnity agreements and clauses appear in IBP FORMS OF BUSINESS AGREEMENTS looseleaf Service.

The indemnification of corporate directors, officers and other employees is discussed in the chapter of Corporate Officers' and Directors' Liability ¶2001 et seq.

[¶2907.1] Legality of a Hold Harmless Agreement

It is quite clear that an indemnity agreement will not offer the indemnitee positive protection against his own wrongful or illegal acts if they are willful, grossly negligent, or contrary to strong public policy. The Restatement of Contracts §572 states that a bargain to indemnify another against the consequences of committing a tortious act is illegal, unless the performance of the tortious act is only an undesired possibility in the performance of the bargain and the bargain does not tend to induce the act. This leaves the door open for indemnification against acts of ordinary negligence and in this respect is in line with the law in most states. But check state law on the subject.

Bear in mind that even though you plan to insure the hold harmless agreement via contractual liability insurance, as discussed at ¶2908, the insurance can't be any better than the agreement. And if the agreement is void, the insurance will be useless.

[¶2907.2] Commercial Transactions Where Hold Harmless Agreements May Be Used

These agreements are used in many situations or settings. They are used in construction contracts, where today they have become the rule rather than the exception, in real estate leases, easements, side track agreements, concessionaire contracts and various forms of operating and maintenance agreements. Our concern here is limited to their use in commercial transactions falling within the scope of this book. Here are a number of such commercial transactions where indemnity or hold harmless agreements may be used:

(1) Protection of retailer or wholesaler against products liability.

(2) Protection of purchaser against claims, losses or expenses growing out of delivery, installation or use of equipment or merchandise.

(3) Protection of lessor of equipment against claims, losses or expenses growing out of lessee's use of the equipment or failure to insure against liability or loss of the property leased.

(4) Protection of a secured creditor against failure of a debtor to insure his collateral.

(5) Protection of a guarantor.

(6) Protection of the endorser of commercial paper.

When we take a closer look at some of these situations we see that they may offer guides to other situations where hold harmless agreements may be called for.

In a situation under (1) above, suppose a retailer has sold a packaged food to someone who eats it and gets sick because it contained a foreign substance. The consumer sues the retailer, basing his suit on an implied warranty of fitness or merchantability. The retailer is called on to investigate and defend the claim and to pay any judgment recovered. He can then turn around and get reimbursement from the wholesaler who sold him the food and the wholesaler can in turn get reimbursement from the processor, packager or manufacturer. Here you have a situation where parties may be held liable to persons injured even though they have no real control over the product, its packaging, processing or manufacture. Because of their potential liability, they are each called on to investigate and defend claims seeking to impose liability on them, whether meritorious or not. Through the use of hold harmless agreements, responsibility for investigating and defending claims may be focused on the party ultimately liable. The elimination of duplicate investigations and defenses can make possible cost savings which will improve the competitive position of all concerned.

This analysis suggests that whenever you have a situation where there is potential legal liability on the part of one party who can get reimbursement from someone else, you have a situation which may call for a hold harmless agreement. Of course, each of the parties could have his own insurance to protect himself against the risks involved. But this solution would also involve duplicate investigations and defenses — in this case on the part of different insurance companies — and would be more expensive in the aggregate than a hold harmless agreement, even a hold harmless agreement backed by insurance procured by the indemnitor.

In situation (2) above, let's say you buy fuel oil from an oil company that also services your oil burner installation, including the tank. The truck driver in making the delivery fails to check the oil in the tank and relies on the whistle in the tank to tell him when it's full. The whistle doesn't work. The oil overflows into the street. A pedestrian crossing the street slips, a car trying to avoid him skids and overturns, and gasoline from the overturned car combines with the oil and a spark to cause a fire causing damage to several cars parked on the street. In this situation you and the oil company might be regarded as jointly and severally liable to the persons injured. You might be sued alone. Or they might sue both of you but only be able to serve you with a summons. In about half of the states, if this happened you could get contribution from the oil company. But in the other half of the states you could not even get contribution, except perhaps on the basis of the oil company's contract to service your oil burner installation, on the theory that failure to maintain the whistle was responsible for the loss.

Here you have a situation where the oil company is really in control of the situation and in the best position to prevent the accident. But you, by reason of your ownership of the premises or by reason of the fact that title to the oil had passed to you on delivery, or for some other legal reason, come under liability to the persons injured. Through the use of a hold harmless agreement ultimate responsibility may be placed on the oil company where it equitably belongs.

We can conclude from this second example that whenever you have a situation where two parties can be held liable in tort, although only one is really in control of the situation, a hold harmless agreement may be called for, especially if there is uncertainty as to the right of the party least responsible to get reimbursement or contribution from the other.

Situation (3) above is one where the owner of property leased or otherwise placed in the custody of and use of another can be held liable to third persons injured by the lessee or bailee even though the owner has no real control over the situation. Let's assume that the accident occurs solely by reason of negligence in the use of the property, and not by reason of any defects in the property or because of the owner's failure to maintain it. Again placing the risk on the party able to control the situation via a hold harmless agreement seems to be a fair and business-like solution.

Situation (4) involves protection of a party against another party's failure to perform a duty owed to him. In the illustration used, the secured creditor would be better off by seeing to it himself that adequate insurance was obtained, but this is not always feasible.

The illustrations in (5) and (6) are cases where, usually, the party to be indemnified has not received any real benefit from the transaction—or at least, no benefit commensurate with his liability exposure, and can, therefore, reasonably expect to be held harmless.

[¶2908]   THE INDEMNITOR AS AN INSURER

A hold harmless agreement in effect puts the indemnitor in the insurance business. But the usual indemnitor is not in the same class as a seasoned insurance carrier. And a hold harmless agreement is not going to be as good for the indemnitee as an insurance policy. Here are the important points where they differ:

(1) If the hold harmless agreement is merely against loss, the indemnitee must pay the loss before seeking reimbursement. An insurer, of course, pays the loss.

(2) The defense clause in an insurance policy is usually more favorable to the insured than such a clause is apt to be in a hold harmless agreement.

(3) Insurance carriers are likely to do a better job than the usual indemnitor in investigating and defending claims and suits.

(4) The financial worth of an insurance carrier and ability to make good on its obligation to the policyholder is apt to be better than that of the usual indemnitor.

[¶2908.1]   **Insuring the Hold Harmless Agreement**

Because the average indemnitor will probably not have the qualifications of an insurance carrier, many indemnitees will not be satisfied with a simple hold harmless agreement but will want it backed up with insurance. Viewed from the indemnitor's side of the coin, because he doesn't have the ability to spread the risk he's assumed the way an insurance carrier can, he may want to insure his hold harmless agreement in any case, regardless of whether the indemnitee requires it.

Having reached the conclusion that one or the other parties wants to insure the hold harmless agreement, what kind of insurance should be obtained? There's a special form of coverage known as contractual liability insurance. This coverage will usually be obtained by way of a special endorsement on the indemnitor's liability policy. The usual liability policy won't cover assumed or contractual liability without a special endorsement because the standard form of exclusion in almost all forms of liability policies reads:

"This policy does not apply to liability assumed by the insured under any contract or agreement."

Contractual liability coverage obviously won't automatically cover all contracts which the insured has undertaken or which he may undertake during the policy period. It will be tailored to the insured's particular situation and will cover only specific contracts or types of contracts, and will be subject to the exclusions set out below. The policy limits, that is in terms of amount, will normally be the same as those used in manufacturers' and contractors' liability policies. Rates will normally be fixed after submission of the specific contracts or types of contracts for rating.

Exclusions: The standard contractual liability endorsement has a number of exclusions some of which may be deleted for an additional premium. Here's a list of the exclusions:

(a) Liability for any warranty of goods or products. Products liability coverage is needed for this.

(b) Damages awarded in arbitration proceedings in which the insurer is not permitted to participate. Make sure, therefore, in drafting your hold harmless agreement, if it provides for arbitration, that the insurer is permitted to participate.

(c) Any obligation for which the insured may be held liable by a third-party beneficiary of a contract. This can be deleted for an additional premium.

(d) Defects in maps, plans, designs or specifications of the insured. This can be deleted for an additional premium.

(e) War.

(f) Dram shop. Many states impose absolute liability on those selling or giving drinks to one already drunk, for the damage the drunken person may do. This may be deleted for an additional premium.

(g) Workmen's compensation, unemployment compensation or disability benefits laws. Contractual claims brought by an employee are not, however, excluded.

(h) Property owned, occupied, rented or in the care, custody or control of the insured. The idea here is that if the hold harmless agreement includes claims for property owned, rented or in the care, custody or control of the indemnitor-insured, he should get property damage insurance—inland marine or other.

(i) Goods, products or work completed out of which the accident arises. This is the same exclusion found in products insurance and is used in contractual liability insurance for the same reason — to bar covering the insured's own business risk of replacing defective products or work out of which the accident arises.

(j) Water damage. This can be deleted for an additional premium.

(k) Nuclear energy. This hazard is covered by the nuclear energy pools.

A form to be used for insuring the hold harmless agreement appears in IBP FORMS OF BUSINESS AGREEMENTS.

[¶2909] DRAFTING AND NEGOTIATING CHECKLIST FOR HOLD HARMLESS AGREEMENTS

Here are the main points to be covered in negotiating and drafting a hold harmless agreement:

(1) Names and addresses of indemnitors and indemnitees.

(2) Consideration for the agreement—if it is part of a sale or of a lease, a separate statement of consideration will not be necessary.

(3) Scope of the indemnity:

    (a) Is the indemnity to be against *liability* or against *loss?* If against liability, the indemnitee's legal rights arise as soon as his liability becomes fixed. If against loss, his rights arise only after he has made payment or suffered an actual loss.

    (b) Does it cover the costs and expenses of investigating or defending against liability or loss, including attorney's fees?

    (c) Does it obligate the indemnitor to investigate and defend claims against the indemnitee?

    (d) Is the indemnity agreement in limited, intermediate or broad form? The limited form gives indemnification where the indemnitor is guilty of active negligence and the indemnitee's negligence, if any, is at most passive. The intermediate form indemnifies even though the indemnitee may be guilty of active negligence. The broad form gives third parties rights against the indemnitor irrespective of his or anyone else's fault. These forms correspond to the classes used for normal rating purposes when contractual liability insurance coverage is to be used. Insurance rates will vary considerably, depending on which form is adopted.

    (e) Is interest to be included? If the parties intend indemnification for damages and interest, interest should be expressly mentioned because there have been decisions excluding interest unless it is expressly included.

    (f) Maximum amount of liability of the indemnitor.

(4) Duration of the indemnity.

(5) Notice to the indemnitor:

    (a) When necessary.

    (b) Time, mode of service.

    (c) Contents.

(6) Rule of strict construction against the indemnitee. Bear in mind that courts often manage to cut the heart out of indemnity agreements by adopting a rule of strict construction against the indemnitee — especially in the case of agreements in intermediate or broad form. If indemnification against the indemnitee's own acts of negligence is intended, say so expressly.

(7) Compromise of claims by the indemnitee.

(8) Evidence of liability or loss.

(9) Security for the performance of the indemnitor's obligations under the agreement:
(a) Insurance.
(b) Bond.
(c) Deposit.

This is not intended as an exhaustive listing of all points to be covered. Other matters to be considered will be suggested by the circumstances of your particular situation.

Various forms of hold harmless agreements and clauses appear in IBP FORMS OF BUSINESS AGREEMENTS.

[¶2910] TAX ASPECTS OF GUARANTEES AND INDEMNIFICATIONS

The different and not wholly consistent tax treatment given bad debts and losses under the tax law gives rise to the need for precision in the drafting of guarantee, surety and indemnity agreements. If the deal goes sour, the party ultimately making good may have (1) the status of a creditor of the defaulting obligor (as in the case of a guarantor) and suffer a bad debt if he cannot collect, or (2) the legal status of an independent obligor himself (as in the case of an indemnitor) and simply be considered to have suffered a loss.

[¶2910.1] Bad Debts v. Losses

The tax treatment of bad debts and losses as allowable deductions from taxable income revolves around four variables: Transactions (1) by individuals or (2) by corporations and which are (3) business or (4) nonbusiness. Corporations are generally deemed to be business entities so their bad debts or losses are fully deductible. An individual is allowed a full deduction in a business transaction whether the obligation arises by way of bad debt or loss. Thus in the case of corporations and individuals becoming obligated in *business* transactions, the distinction need not be so sharply drawn for tax purposes, unless the business nature of the transaction is itself in question. However, IRC §166(d) provides an individual with a limited deduction, equivalent to a short-term capital loss, for a nonbusiness bad debt, but allows no deduction at all for a loss sustained in a transaction not entered into for profit.

[¶2910.2] Business v. Nonbusiness Bad Debts

The development of judicial distinctions between transactions deemed to be business and those deemed nonbusiness has resulted in a confusing case law. The distinction between business bad debt and nonbusiness bad debt rests on whether the debt was incurred in connection with the trade or business of the taxpayer (covering debts becoming worthless after the taxpayer has gone out of business) or incurred in the taxpayer's business. If it was, it is a business bad debt. Section 166(f) extends business bad debt treatment to a transaction not involving the taxpayer's business when the payment is made by a taxpayer who is a noncorporate indemnitor (or endorser or guarantor) and (i) the person whose obligation is covered is also not a corporation; (ii) the borrower's obligation to the original creditors was worthless at the time of payment; and (iii) the proceeds of the debt were used in the borrower's trade or business. Similarly, unless §166(f) applies, an individual's loss (as distinguished from bad debt) will be deemed a business one and deductible if it was incurred in trade or business or incurred in a transaction entered into for "profit" (even though not connected with trade or business). Of course, the IRC also makes provision for nonbusiness casualty losses. §165(c).

[¶2910.3]   **Stockholder's Guarantee of Corporate Debt**

A stockholder's guarantee of his corporation's obligations is considered to be a nonbusiness transaction. If the stockholder is an individual and he has to make good, he is entitled to a short-term capital loss on a nonbusiness bad debt (*Putnam*, 352 US 82). It is clear that this is the tax treatment even if the corporation is insolvent at the time of payment and it could be argued that a claim to reimbursement by subrogation to creditor's rights is worthless. Ordinary loss treatment is available to an officer or employee who had to make loans to hold onto his job (*Generes*, 405 US 93).

[¶2910.4]   **Guarantee by a Parent Corporation of Subsidiary's Expenses and Dividends**

Generally a parent corporation must capitalize payments made to pay a subsidiary's business expenses and dividends (when called upon to honor its guarantee) by adding the same to its basis for the stock of the subsidiary, unless a direct benefit to the parent can be shown—for example, where the subsidiary performs vital services for the parent. A bona fide loan by a parent to its subsidiary might be better, since at best a full business bad debt deduction could be taken and at worst it would be treated as a capital expenditure.

[¶2910.5]   **Payments Under Certain Guarantees Not Deductible**

Bad debt deductions are not allowed in the following situations:
(1) When the guarantee is given as a part of purchase price of a capital asset, as distinguished from guaranteeing a loan, the guarantor's payment to the creditor is treated as a capital expenditure when the debtor doesn't pay up.
(2) Where a corporate guarantor pays off obligations of its stockholders—such payments are considered as dividends and are not deductible.

221

(3) Guarantee of the obligation of family member—this is closely scrutinized to determine whether there is a valid business purpose before the business bad debt deduction is allowed. If the guarantor never expected repayment from the debtor-relative, the transaction might be considered a gift.

(4) Where debtor is not liable to guarantor at law or, at the time of making the guarantee, there was no reasonable expectation of repayment. Before the guarantor can get a bad debt deduction he must be able to show that (1) originally he had reason to expect repayment and (2) after he honors his guarantee, the debtor's obligation to him is worthless.

[¶2910.6]   Timing of Loss by Cash Basis Taxpayer

To a large extent, given business justification, a cash basis guarantor or indemnitor can choose the year in which his loss will occur, since the loss is sustained only when (1) the guarantor's claim against the original debtor is worthless due to the latter's insolvency, and (2) the guarantor actually makes out of pocket cash disbursements in satisfaction of his liability under the guarantee. If the guarantor gives the creditor a new note covering his liability under the guarantee such a note does not constitute a cash disbursement until payments are made on it. But the deduction can be lost if the guarantor simply sleeps on his legal rights — e.g., the Statute of Limitation runs against him.

[¶2910.7]   Capital Loss by Indemnitor

Payment made under an indemnity agreement will be treated as a capital loss if the indemnity was given as a part of the consideration for the sale of a capital asset.

[¶2910.8]   Timing of Loss by Accrual Basis Taxpayer

If an accrual basis taxpayer is an indemnitor, he may be able to deduct an indemnity loss in advance of the actual payment, but if he is a guarantor, he will have to wait until the year of payment, since the debt between the guarantor and the debtor doesn't arise until then (which becomes bad if the debtor can't pay off guarantor).

●

For Further Reference . . .
American Jurisprudence, Guaranty.
Forms of Business Agreements, Institute for Business Planning, Englewood Cliffs, N.J.
Indemnification of Directors: The Problems Posed by Federal Securities and Antitrust Legislation, 76 *Harvard Law Review* 1403.

Sterns, *Law of Suretyship.*

Washington, G. T., and Bishop, W., *Indemnifying the Corporate Executive,* Ronald.

IDEAS AND SECRETS

[¶3001] The protection of ideas and secrets and protection against false claims for appropriation of ideas and disclosure of secrets is an important part of commercial practice, notably in entertainment, advertising, and technological fields. The practicing lawyer may be called upon to protect an idea or an accumulation of information which is not patentable. He may be called upon to advise on placing a protective net around trade secrets or other confidential information. He may be called upon to protect a client who is asked to consider a proposal against a possible subsequent lawsuit for use of the information being disclosed to him in negotiations and contracts; on licenses, sales of business, and employment, he will be called upon to draft appropriate provisions concerning the disclosure of confidential information and the maintenance of confidentiality.

[¶3002]   HOW TO PROTECT AN IDEA

Inventions can be protected by patent applications. Forms of expression, literary, musical, artistic, and even photographic, can be protected by copyright. The really difficult thing is to protect the pure idea, the concept, which cannot be reduced to practice, which can have any number of modes of expression.

The lawyer may be called upon to protect the commercial value of an idea and, also, to protect one to whom an idea is submitted from having to pay through the nose for the exaggerated notion of value which the creator of the idea may have.

There are many possible ways of creating and protecting value for an intellectual idea: It may be patentable. It may be expressed so that the expression can be copyrighted. It can be identified with a trademark or tied to a personal identity which is protected by the right of privacy. A contractual obligation to compensate its use may be created. The person to whom it is submitted may be placed under a confidential or fiduciary obligation. He may be brought into this status willingly or unwillingly.

The person to whom an idea is submitted must be protected against contractual or fiduciary obligation which he does not want. He must be shown how to put the submitter of an idea in the position where he must rely on his patent right, copyright, or trademark for protection.

These are all problems which the practicing lawyer will be called upon to handle at one time or another in the course of an ordinary commercial practice. Here are some guide posts:

1. A title or a concept cannot be copyrighted.

2. Copyright—statutory or common law—protects only methods of expression —word or symbol used. Sometimes an idea can be reduced to a set of words or symbols which will have value. But this occurs only if somebody else cannot easily conjure up a set of words or symbols which will as effectively or equally project and utilize the idea.

3. Pure ideas are free for all. The lawyer's task is to convert the pure idea into a property right. To even start in this direction, two things must be accomplished:

a. The idea must be original or established as such. There are no really original ideas. But the idea must be established as different. It may be enough that the idea is original to the actual or potential user, even though others have known about it and even used it.

b. The idea must be reduced to concrete form. This means putting it down on paper or some other concrete form like a model or a projection. The more detail in the concrete form, the better. If it is an advertising idea, it should be developed into a campaign. If it is an entertainment idea, it should be developed into a script.

4. Establish the date of formulation. Spelling it out and transmitting it in a sealed, registered letter or in acknowledged correspondence to an attorney or agent, or an affidavit with a witness will accomplish this. The purpose is to make it difficult for the one who appropriates the idea to claim that he has had it before.

5. Submit it to a potential user. The desirable ways to do this are these:

a. Disclose it and get a letter acknowledging receipt and promising compensation if it is used.

b. Disclose it to the potential user or his representative in a place or circumstances which indicate that he is accepting it on a confidential basis.

c. Submit the idea under a disclosure agreement in which the potential user will agree that he is accepting it on a confidential basis, will not disclose it to others, and will compensate for its use.

Forms of agreement and release concerning submitted ideas, trade secrets and secret formulae appear in IBP FORMS OF BUSINESS AGREEMENTS.

⟦¶3002.1⟧ Theories Under Which One Can Get Paid for an Idea

Of course, one can get whatever the person to whom an idea is submitted will pay if it is used. In addition, however, the law has developed two broad theories under which it is possible to create a property right and collect value for an idea.

In the first of these—the relational aspect—the common law regulates the use of creative property by persons having a contractual or confidential relation with the owner. The applicable rules arise either from contract law or the principles of equity.

In the second of these—the "unfairness" aspect—the common law bars use of creative property when such use violates minimal standards of fairness. That the latter are highly subjective is obvious; their limits are conjectural and vary from judge to judge and from courtroom to courtroom. Such "unfairness" rules are at the margin separating law and morality; the extension and elucidation of the precise elements of "unfairness" represent the continuing absorption of moral precepts into legal rules. The common term for these rules is "unfair competition"—which we shall use hereafter—but since the competitive element is at times nonexistent, the initial emphasis has been on the "unfair" aspect.

The three areas — the statutory, the relational, the "unfair" — overlap. A story may be capable of copyright and (whether or not copyrighted) still may be protectable under a relational or unfairness doctrine. On the other hand, certain kinds of creative property are protectable under one doctrine and not another, as will be seen as we discuss each one.

As might be expected, the broadest protection granted creative property is that arising from an express contract between the "creator" and the proposed user. In the typical case, the latter promises to pay a fixed or variable fee for an idea (to be revealed after the execution of the contract) which is represented as one which will be profitable to the user. If the promise to pay is made after disclosure of an idea, the disclosure is past consideration and hence insufficient to support a contract. (Certain states, e.g., New York, have changed this by statute.) Assuming the other requirements of contract are satisfied, the sole issue is whether the contract is unenforceable for lack of consideration on the ground that the "creator" has given nothing of value.

Two elements will determine value of an idea: (1) concreteness (how much additional work is necessary to make the idea usable); (2) originality (did the creator actually develop it or is it merely new to this user). Three possible alternatives will exist:

(a) The creator has a concrete idea developed by himself. He will recover.

(b) He has an abstract idea developed by himself. The public interest in favor of the free exchange and development of abstract ideas makes recovery difficult. If he can show that the final concrete "expression" by the user arose from his idea, he may recover, but such proof is difficult.

(c) He has a concrete idea, not developed by himself but new to the user; e.g., a way to save taxes. Recovery here will depend so much on the particular circumstances that no general statement can be made. The obviousness of the idea is important; the suggestion to raise prices as a way to increase profits is hardly a "creative" idea even though it would be successful if done at that time and in fact had not occurred to the proposed user. Formerly, recovery was rare in this situation but the courts today will judge each case on its merits.

[¶3002.2] Implied-In-Fact Contracts

An implied-in-fact contract exists when, although no express oral or written promise was made, the circumstances are pregnant with such promise. The contract is tested by the same concreteness and originality as express contracts, but their presence must be shown more strongly to permit the inference of a promise to pay. Trade custom and usage are relevant evidence to show the likelihood of such a promise. Other elements tending to imply a promise to pay are solicitation of the idea by the user, and submission accompanied by an express warning that there is to be no use without compensation.

[¶3002.3] Implied-In-Law or Quasi Contracts

The doctrine of equity of implied-in-law or quasi contracts is closely related to the concept of "unfairness." On occasion, a court will expand the traditional equity concept beyond its usual bounds to include the rules of "unfair competition." The strict doctrine of quasi contract, however, requires the following elements:

(a) no express or implied-in-fact promise to pay;

(b) the receipt of benefits which are normally not given without compensation;

(c) circumstances showing an expectation of payment by the giver; i.e., no gift was intended.

The typical example of quasi contract is the granting of benefits under the mistaken belief that a contract exists, and the receipt of such benefits with knowledge of the misunderstanding. When your house is painted instead of your neighbor's while you watch, you must pay.

Quasi contract will permit recovery for the use of creative property only where the elements of concreteness and novelty are clearly present.

[¶3003] UNSOLICITED IDEAS FROM OUTSIDERS

Listening to an idea submitted by an outsider may place the business under an obligation to compensate the outsider if the idea is subsequently used. This may be even though the idea is one which the listener has already been working on for some time. In any event, unless the submitter expressly waives his rights it is always possible that he will make a claim and institute a lawsuit, the outcome of which has to be considered unpredictable. To collect, the idea has to be novel. This is an unpredictable question of fact. Where a man submitted the idea of selling advertising space in railroad cars and stations, he sued and lost because the Court found that advertising space has been sold since the time of the Romans and was not a new idea. A man who submitted an idea as simple as using a contest to stimulate employees was able to collect on a showing that it was agreed that financial arrangements would be made after it was seen how the plan would work out. The plan was put into effect and resulted in over 2500 new accounts. The store refused to pay because there was no written contract, but the Court found an oral agreement and awarded $10,000 as the reasonable value of this plan (*Brunner v. Stix, Baer & Fuller Co.*, Mo. S. Ct. 1944, 181 S.W. 643).

In the case of inventions and technical improvements, the most satisfactory way for both the inventor and the corporation to be protected from litigation and misunderstanding is for the inventor to obtain a patent on his invention. This will clearly establish his rights in the invention and will give him a firm basis on which to negotiate with companies that may wish to use or develop his invention. But the inventor may not be able to or may not wish to patent his invention for a variety of reasons: (1) He may be the owner of the trade secret but not the actual inventor of it; (2) He may not be able to show the novelty, utility and invention which are necessary to obtain a patent; or (3) He may wish to keep the invention secret.

Where an inventor offers to disclose his invention to the company with a view to selling it, and the company then invites the disclosure, it receives the invention in confidence. This means the corporation cannot use the idea without buying it, and if it does use it without first entering into a contract with the inventor, it will be liable on the basis of the profits it made from the invention (*Hoeltke v. C. M. Kemp Mfg. Co.*, 80 F.2d 912, cert. den. 298 U.S. 673).

To protect against claims of this kind, two steps are desirable:

(1) A form letter responding to volunteers. When an offer to disclose an idea or invention is received by the company, a properly worded letter to the suggester will help prevent liability. The courts have held that where the company makes certain stipulations or lays down certain conditions subject to which it will accept the disclosure, the inventor is bound by these conditions if he then submits his idea.

(2) Requiring the person submitting the idea to sign a statement indicating that he agrees to stipulated conditions along these lines:

(a) In taking any suggestion or idea under consideration we assume no obligation of any kind.

(b) We will not receive any submitted material in confidence, we will not establish a confidential relationship with anyone in respect to such material and we make no guarantee of secrecy. You agree that in consideration of our examining your idea, we may freely use and communicate it to others without any liability to you. You agree to release us from responsibility or connection with your suggestion or liability because of use of any part thereof except such liability as may arise under valid patents now or hereafter issued to you.

(c) We will not consider ideas submitted from outside the United States unless a United States patent application has been filed.

(d) If the idea you have submitted is found to be of no interest to us, we will so inform you. However, we assume no obligation to inform you of the reasons for our action.

(e) If the idea appears to be of interest to us, we may enter into negotiations to explore the possibility of acquiring rights. No obligation is assumed by the Company unless or until a formal written contract has been entered into and the obligation shall be only such as is expressed in the formal written contract.

(f) It is necessary for us to retain a complete record of the matter submitted and, therefore, it must be submitted in writing. Since material may become lost or mislaid in transit between the submitter and the Company or between various departments of the Company, no obligation can be assumed by us for the safekeeping of submitted matter.

A form of letter agreement concerning submitted ideas appears in IBP FORMS OF BUSINESS AGREEMENTS.

[¶3004]   TRADE SECRETS

The Restatement of Torts defines a trade secret this way: "A trade secret may consist of any formula, pattern, device or compilation of information which is used in one's business, and which gives him an opportunity to obtain an advantage over competitors who do not know or use it." (Restatement, Torts, §757, Comment *b* (1939)). Whether we have a trade secret which can be protected depends in large measure upon the conduct of its owner, and this is developed in §757 of the Restatement of Torts:

"The subject matter of a trade secret must be secret. Matters of public knowledge or of general knowledge in an industry cannot be appropriated by one as his secret. Matters which are completely disclosed by the goods which one markets cannot be his secret. Substantially, a trade secret is known only in the particular business in which it is used. It is not requisite that only the proprietor of the business know it. He may, without losing his protection, communicate it to employees involved in its use. He may likewise communicate it to others pledged to secrecy. Others may also know of it independently, as, for example, when they have discovered the process or formula by independent invention and are keeping it secret. Nevertheless, a substantial element of secrecy must exist, so that, except by the use of improper means, there would be difficulty in acquiring the information. An exact definition of a trade secret is not possible. Some factors to be considered in determining whether given information is one's trade secret are: (1) the extent to which the information is known outside of his business; (2) the extent to which it is known by employees and others involved in his business; (3) the extent of measures taken by him to guard the secrecy of the information; (4) the value of the information to him and to his competitors; (5) the amount of effort or money expended by him in developing the information; (6) the ease or difficulty with which the information could be properly acquired or duplicated by others."

Where these requirements are met, the unauthorized disclosure of a trade secret creates a liability which is also spelled out in §757 in the Restatement of Torts:

"One who discloses or uses another's trade secret, without a privilege to do so, is liable to the other if

"(a) he discovered the secret by improper means, or

"(b) his disclosure or use constitutes a breach of confidence reposed in him by the other in disclosing the secret to him, or

"(c) he learned the secret from a third person with notice of the facts that it was a secret and that the third person discovered it by improper means or that the third person's disclosure of it was otherwise a breach of his duty to the other, or

"(d) he learned the secret with notice of the facts that it was a secret and that its disclosure was made to him by mistake."

Courts are generally reluctant to restrain employees from revealing alleged secrets both because of the difficulty of distinguishing a secret from the skill and experience that result from diligent labor, and because such restraints may prevent the employee from finding another job. However, restraints will be imposed where:

(i) the employee, or other party, has learned a secret

(ii) in the course of his employ

(iii) and as the result of a confidential relationship; i.e., a relationship which he knew or should have known gave him access to information his employer, or the other party, regarded as secret.

Frequently, an employee enters into an express negative covenant against revealing secret information or entering into competition with his employer. However, where proper grounds are present, an injunction may be issued even without such a covenant. And regardless of an express promise, the restraints imposed will be strictly limited to those necessary to protect the employer, since from the employee's point of view, the restraint is on his right to work. The restraint against the dissemination of secrets may be permanent; but insofar as it applies to competing employment, it must be limited in time and place.

Where appropriate, equity will declare a constructive trust with the duty to account for all profits arising from improper use of secret material.

Section 758 of the Restatement of Torts provides as follows:

"One who learns another's trade secret from a third person without notice that it is secret and that the third person's disclosure is a breach of his duty to the other, or who learns the secret through a mistake without notice of the secrecy and the mistake,

"(a) is not liable to the other for a disclosure or use of the secret prior to receipt of such notice, and

"(b) is liable to the other for a disclosure or use of the secret after the receipt of such notice, unless prior thereto he has in good faith paid value for the secret or has so changed his position that to subject him to liability would be inequitable."

It is important to place employees working with confidential information under a contractual inhibition from disclosing confidential information, both during and after their employment. Other protective measures are to stamp all reports and other papers containing confidential information as "Confidential," or "Secret"; to control distribution of confidential papers; to limit access and record visits to restricted areas.

Forms of contracts for technical employees with clauses relating to disclosures, secrecy and competition appear in IBP FORMS OF BUSINESSS AGREEMENTS.

●

For Further Reference . . .

Ernst & Schwartz, *Privacy,* Macmillan.

Forms of Business Agreements looseleaf Service. Institute for Business Planning, Englewood Cliffs, N.J.

Hollander, *International Law of Art,* Bowes and Bowes.

Spring, *Risks and Rights,* Norton.

Turner, *Law of Trade Secrets,* Sweet & Maxwell.

INSURANCE AGAINST LOSS AND LIABILITY

[¶3101] The practicing lawyer will be expected to spot liabilities and risk of loss in business and be able to advise on appropriate insurance coverage. He can get information and recommendations from insurance agents and brokers. But to do his job, he will want independent information on everything in his client's situation related to these two questions:

(1) What possible events can cause him loss of property or impose liability — that is to say, what is his *loss exposure?*

(2) How much can be lost from a single event — that is to say, what is his *loss potential?*

Loss Exposure: This requires the identification of all possible risks that are involved in the particular business or activity in question. One way to approach the problem of loss to the insured is to study any available financial statements. The balance sheet will indicate all the assets subject to loss or damage. The profit and loss statement will reveal sources of income which may be shut off or interrupted. Another approach, for uncovering possible liability, is to analyze the property and operations of the client to determine what can happen to whom.

Loss Potential: This involves an estimate of the maximum loss which may be incurred. The fact that a loss is unlikely is not usually the relevant consideration, since the purpose of insurance is to guard against the unlikely. In addition to this, the more likely the loss, the less is the economic justification for insurance, since the premium must be large enough to compensate for the loss and permit payment of the insurer's expenses and profit. Small losses, even though unlikely (and hence subject only to a small premium for insurance) may call for self-insurance by the client, since his own resources may be sufficient for this purpose. In brief, it is the *maximum* and *unlikely* loss that must be guarded against.

[¶3101.1] Types of Risks and Types of Insurance

Generally speaking, risks fall into two classes:

(1) Liability risks (the insured may be liable to others because of his own actions or those of his employees and agents).

(2) Property loss, including credit and income loss (the insured may suffer personal loss or injury due to his own actions or the actions of others).

The tables at ¶3109 list the most common types of risks for business transactions generally, for particular types of business transactions, and for the owners or lessees of real estate. The usual insurance policy to cover each risk is also indicated. In the following checklist, the most common types of policies are briefly described.

232

[¶3102]   **LIABILITY INSURANCE**

Those engaged in commercial transactions are exposed to the hazard of lawsuits not only for their own negligence, but also the negligence of their employees, agents and other representatives. Particularly exposed are sole proprietors and partners who do not have the limited liability furnished by the corporate umbrella.

The liability policy generally provides coverage only for sums which the insured becomes *legally obligated to pay resulting from accident.* The basic policy provides no coverage against liabilities for which the insured is not obligated under negligence law, or liabilities assumed by the insured voluntarily. Nor does it provide coverage for occurrences which are not considered accidents, i.e., illnesses caused by repeated exposure to unhealthy or unsanitary conditions over long periods of time. Broader coverage on policies can often be obtained for an additional premium, such as deleting the words "caused by accident" and substituting "occurrence." Some policies, such as the Comprehensive General Liability, offer broader coverage in the basic policy.

Most liability policies are divided into two separate sections—Coverage A for bodily injury liability, and Coverage B for property damage liability. Different limits of liability may be provided for each coverage, or the policy may be written under Coverage A only.

[¶3102.1] **Basic Liability Coverages**

The following are the basic liability coverages:

(1) Owners', Landlords' and Tenants' Liability Policy (OLT): The basic policy insures against claims resulting from the ownership (or lease) and operation of the covered premises. Office buildings, retail stores, wholesale stores, hotels, theatres, etc., are insured under this form of policy. The policy is usually a scheduled policy, that is it names the particular properties and risks insured against. Another type of policy, the Comprehensive General Liability Policy offers similar coverage on a non-scheduled basis. A manufacturer or contractor can obtain parallel coverage under a Manufacturers' and Contractors' Liability Policy (M & C).

(2) Products Liability Policy: This policy covers liability arising out of the handling or use of goods or products which are manufactured, sold, handled or distributed by the insured. The liability depends upon the existence of a defect or unsafe condition in the goods. Products liability also covers a service business or a contractor who installs equipment against claims arising from a defect in the installation or the equipment.

(3) Contracts Liability: This policy covers liability arising out of a contract or agreement. Manufacturers, distributors, retailers and service men some-

233

times assume liability under easement agreements, railroad sidetrack agreements, purchase orders or sales and service contracts. The contractor may enter into an agreement with his principal in which he undertakes to hold the principal harmless and indemnify him for any accidents arising out of the work being done. A lessee frequently agrees to protect his lessor from any consequences arising out of the leased property.

(4) Owner's and Contractor's Protective Liability Policy: This covers an owner or contractor against any liability arising out of work done by another, such as an independent contractor or a subcontractor.

[¶3102.2] Supplementary Benefits Under Liability Insurance

In addition to satisfying money claims, liability insurance provides a number of valuable services and additional benefits.

(1) Defense of Suits: The insurance company will defend, in the insured's name, all suits brought against him even if false and groundless (but the suit must be one which if successful would constitute a claim under the policy). The policy pays all costs including investigating the claim, procuring witnesses, and legal defense.

(2) Court Costs and Interest on Judgment: These are paid by the insurer.

(3) Premiums for Bonds: The policy also pays for bonds required in the appeal of any suit and bonds to release attachments.

(4) Reimbursement of Insured's Expenses: Reasonable expenses incurred by the insured at the company's request, other than his loss of earnings, are reimbursed. Examples of such expenses are travel, obtaining witnesses, getting affidavits, etc.

(5) Immediate Medical and Surgical First Aid: If furnished by the insured at the time of the accident will be paid for by the policy.

(6) Inspection Service: It is standard practice for insurance companies to inspect risks to minimize hazards.

The above benefits are payable, regardless of their amounts, *over and above* the limits of the policy.

(7) Medical Payments Coverage: This can be added to a liability policy for an additional premium. It covers all reasonable medical, surgical, funeral, etc., expenses, incurred within one year of the accident, to each person who sustains bodily injury, sickness or disease caused by an accident regardless of whether the insured is legally liable or not. Medical payments do not usually cover the insured, any partner, tenant or any person regularly residing on premises, or any employee of the insured or tenant.

Medical payments coverage is generally written with two limits. The first limit is the limit per person; the second is the limit payable to all persons injured in a single accident.

[¶3103]   PROPERTY INSURANCE

Property insurance covers direct loss to tangible property, and usually also covers loss of use of the property actually damaged. Consequential loss, such as loss of use or lessening in value of property that is not itself physically damaged, can sometimes be added for an additional premium.

There is a certain amount of overlapping among various property coverages, and it is often possible to provide coverage in several different ways. There has been a trend to combine separate coverages into one package, loosely termed "multiple-peril coverages," or to provide all-risk coverage under a "floater" policy. Following is a rundown of the more important property coverages.

1. Fire Insurance: Covers the perils of direct loss by fire and lightning. It also covers certain types of damage by smoke — for example, smoke damage caused by a hostile fire whether involving the insured property or uninsured property, such as a neighboring building. Other types of smoke damage, for instance, that caused by a defective heating apparatus on the premises, are not covered by the basic fire policy.

2. Extended Coverage: Coverage for other perils can be added by endorsement to the fire policy. The *extended coverage* endorsement insures against windstorm, hail, explosion, riot, civil commotion, aircraft, smoke, explosion and vehicles. The *additional extended coverage* endorsement insures against collapse, explosion of steam or hot water systems, fall of trees, glass breakage, vandalism, and malicious mischief, vehicles owned or operated by insured or tenant, water damage, and ice, snow and freezing.

Some of these coverages may be written separately, such as the vandalism and malicious mischief endorsement. The extended coverages must be written for the same amount as the fire policy itself and they do not increase the face amount of the policy — they merely extend the coverage to include the added perils.

3. Allied Lines: Coverages by endorsement to a fire policy or as a separate contract — earthquake insurance, sprinkler leakage, hail on growing crops, etc.

4. Physical Damage to Motor Vehicles: Physical damage to autos, trucks, tractors, etc., can be insured under collision, comprehensive, fire and theft, and other policies. Type of coverage and rates will vary with the construction and use of the vehicle, the principal city in which the vehicle is garaged and radius of miles in which the vehicle is used. Larger risks can get reductions through fleet rates and experience rating.

Similar physical damage coverage is available to company-owned airplanes, yachts, etc.

5. Burglary and Theft: The open *stock burglary* policy insures against loss by burglary to merchandise, furniture, fixtures and equipment (not money, securities, records and accounts) and damage to the premises.

The *mercantile safe burglary* policy covers loss of money, securities and other property and other damage resulting from burglarly of a safe.

The *mercantile robbery* policy covers various robbery hazards both inside and outside.

The *paymaster robbery* policy is designed for businesses whose principal exposure to robbery is its payroll funds.

The *storekeeper's burglary and robbery* policy is a package policy for smaller mercantile risks.

The *office burglary and robbery* policy is a package policy for professional offices and service businesses.

The *money and securities broad form* policy is comprehensive coverage for most mercantile risks, providing coverage against virtually all risk of loss of money and securities.

6. Fidelity Bonds: This type of bond covers an employer against the loss of any kind of property—money, securities, raw materials, merchandise, equipment, real property — resulting from dishonest actions of employees. Some bonds insure only named individuals, others cover all occupants of named positions, and others cover all employees of a firm. If the insured is a partnership, the fidelity bond will not cover actions of partners, since they are not employees. In a corporation, all officers are covered since they are employees. Directors of a corporation are excluded unless they are also officers or employees.

7. Floaters: Floater insurance generally provides *all-risk* coverage to personal property with certain exclusions, such as gradual deterioration, wear and tear, moths and vermin, confiscation by government or public authority, contraband or illegal trade, war. Sometimes coverage is on a *specified perils* basis. Under many floaters, the insured is required to schedule the insured articles, with a description and a valuation proved by appraisal or bill of sale; others cover categories of property customary to the risk insured. There are many types of floaters designed for various commercial risks.

8. Multiple Peril Coverages: There has been a tremendous growth of multiple peril, or package, policies which combine in one policy many different coverages. The advantage to the insured is broader coverage, elimination of overlapping coverages and claims, and lower cost. Some policies provide all-risk coverage while the others insure specified perils.

Manufacturers output policy insures merchandise and other personal property of manufacturers while the property is away from the premises of the manufacturer. It is intended for large stocks of goods in dispersed locations.

Industrial property policy covers all the personal property held by a manufacturing concern, including property of others, on his own premises, usually in diversified locations. It may also insure buildings.

Commercial property policy insures all kinds of personal property of retailers and wholesalers, including limited off-premises coverage. It is not available to businesses that can buy the "block" policy, such as a jeweler or furrier.

Office contents policy covers all forms of personal property located in an office. It may be purchased by someone who occupies an office and also owns the building, as well as by tenants. An *office package policy* is designed for the owner of an office building.

Jeweler's block policy insures a jeweler for loss or damage to goods in his possession—his own property and property of others. Other lines of business have followed suit—for example, the furrier's block policy.

[¶3104]   CREDIT INSURANCE

Credit insurance indemnifies a wholesaler, manufacturer, or jobber for unusual losses incurred by him through the failure of his customers to pay what is owed. This coverage is generally not available to retailers, since credit rating and information are usually lacking on their customers. Most prudent firms have a reserve for bad debts, usually the amount ascertained by experience to be the average annual loss. This may be satisfactory in a normal year, but unexpected losses, such as the bankruptcy of one large customer, might wipe out profits—this is where credit insurance comes in.

Coverage is provided under *specific* and *general policies.* Specific policies are used by businesses that have occasional, high class accounts to whom considerable credit is extended for short terms. Coverage of these accounts is usually afforded after investigation of each specific risk by the insurance company. General policies cover the accounts of the insured described in the policy. These usually are all customers who have the credit rating required by the policy, and there is no need for investigation and approval of individual accounts.

A valuable collateral benefit of credit insurance is the collection services offered to policyholders. Specific policies usually provide for compulsory collection of accounts due—the insured must file a claim for collection within two months after due. Other types of policies provide severe penalties if claims for collection are not filed within 90 days. A few policies make filing for collection optional with the insured.

The insurance company can afford to devote more time and expense to collection, and can do this more effectively than the insured. Since the insurance company is in effect a partner with the insured in credit losses, it is as interested in preventing and reducing credit losses as is the insured.

[¶3105]   SURETY BONDS

Many commercial transactions are guaranteed by suretyship—an individual, corporation or partnership lends its name or credit to obligations of another. A typical example is where a stockholder in a close corporation is co-signer of a loan to the corporation. In many types of business transactions, corporate suretyship provided by bonding companies or insurance companies is required. Following is a checklist of typical bonds:

1. Contract Bonds: Contract bonds are used and required in many cases to guarantee the satisfactory completion or performance of a contract. Contract bonds are written for the *term of the contract* and cannot be cancelled during this term. The initial premium usually covers a period of two years, and the renewal premium charged after that is based on an estimate of time needed to complete work still remaining.

2. Bid Bonds: These bonds are generally required to accompany bids of contractors for public work jobs. They are sometimes required by private builders too. The bond guarantees that the bidder, if awarded the contract, will enter into the contract and furnish the prescribed performance bond (and payment bond if required). If the bidding contractor defaults, the surety becomes liable for the difference between the bid of its principal and the next lowest bid. The Bid Bond may be written with a *fixed penalty* or *an open penalty.*

3. Performance Bonds: The various types of performance bonds include the following:

Construction contract bond—guarantees faithful performance of the contractor for construction of a building. It may run to the lender of construction monies and may be called a *completion bond.*

Labor and material payment bond—guarantees that the contractor will pay all bills for labor and materials. This is written either as a separate policy or as part of the Construction Contract Bond.

Maintenance bond—guarantees that work done by the contractor will be free of defective workmanship or materials. This is written either as a separate policy or as part of the Construction Contract Bond.

Supply contract bond—guarantees a contract to supply goods or materials.

[¶3106]   CONSEQUENTIAL LOSS COVERAGES

A fire or other peril may cause a financial loss other than that resulting from the direct destruction of the property. Such losses are called "consequential losses" and include those resulting from the loss of use of the property destroyed, such as interruption of business, and property loss from indirect connection with the hazard rather than from direct destruction. The main types of insurance against consequential losses are these:

(1) Business interruption insurance.

(2) Contingent business interruption insurance which covers losses resulting from the interruption, not of the insured's business, but of a supplier or some other activity on which the continued conduct of the business is dependent.

(3) Extra expense insurance which covers the cost of emergency operation by newspapers, banks and other types of operations which cannot afford to have their operations interrupted.

(4) Rent insurance and rental value insurance which covers the loss of rents during the time when a building has become unusable because of fire or other insured peril.

(5) Delayed profits insurance, which covers loss of profits that might result from a delay in the completion of a project.

(6) Profits and commission insurance, which covers profits on finished goods when sales will be lost as a result of the destruction of goods. This is appropriate for seasonal goods, specially built machinery, etc.

(7) Leasehold insurance is designed to cover a tenant's financial loss if he has a lease more financially advantageous to him than he could secure at the time of the loss and the lease is cancelled because of the loss.

(8) Excess rental value insurance which covers the difference between the current rental value of the property and what the landlord is receiving from the tenant under the lease where the tenant or the landlord may cancel the lease following a specific percentage of damage to the property. It is the reverse of the leasehold interest insurance.

[¶3107]   RENT INSURANCE

This policy protects the owner of a building for loss of rental income after a fire or other peril.

The insured is entitled to indemnity for rent income lost to him whether the property is rented or vacant at time of loss, beginning on the date of loss and ending on the day on which the building could, with the exercise of due diligence, be restored to the same tenantable condition as before loss. Expenses which do not continue after the loss, e.g., elevator service, maintenance, are not covered.

[¶3108] HOW MUCH INSURANCE

In fire resistant buildings and in areas having fire protection, most fires do not result in total destruction. In order to distribute equitably the cost of insurance in proportion to the total existent hazard as between individual property owners, insurance companies have attached to their policies a Co-insurance or Contribution clause.

An owner who has a policy with a Contribution clause and who carries an amount of insurance less than the required percentage will find himself under-insured at the time of loss and will suffer a penalty whether his loss is only partial or total. One of the most misunderstood provisions of an insurance policy is the Co-insurance or Contribution clause, but the following illustration may clarify its operation. An insurance company will pay the owner only its pro rata share of a loss on the basis of the ratio of the amount of actual coverage to the required coverage. In the case of underinsurance the owner is a "co-insurer" or contributor with the insurance company. For example, a building having an insurable value of $100,000 is insured against fire under a policy bearing the 80% Contribution clause. The owner should, therefore, carry at least $80,000 insurance. If he does carry $80,000, he meets the requirement of the Contribution clause and any fire loss he sustains will be paid in full up to the limit of his policy.

On the other hand, if the same owner carries only $40,000 insurance, he is carrying only half the required amount. Under these circumstances, if he sustains a loss, he will be paid only half of the loss, but the insurance company will not pay more than the limit of its policy, namely $40,000. In this example if he sustains a loss of $1,000, he will collect only $500 and will have to contribute or absorb the other $500.

Similarly, if the owner carries $60,000 insurance under the same circumstances, he will be able to collect 60/80ths of any loss or 75%. A loss of $1,000 will entitle him to collect $750, etc.

Since the Contribution clause can inflict severe penalties for underinsurance, many prudent owners carry more insurance than is required by the Contribution clause. For example, their policies may contain the 80% clause, yet they may carry 85% insurance to insurable value. This is relatively inexpensive and leaves a margin for error or for a future increase in value.

The existence of a Contribution clause makes it especially important that the insurable value of the property be accurately determined and that it include all property insured by the policy.

Whatever the insurance policy covers should be taken into account as respects valuation and amount of insurance, since at the time of loss the insurance company will include all values when ascertaining that the Contribution clause has been complied with.

Whatever the insurance policy covers should be taken into account as respects valuation and amount of insurance, since at the time of loss the insurance company will include all values when ascertaining that the Contribution clause has been complied with.

[¶3108.1] What Amounts of Liability Insurance?

The limits or amounts of liability insurance to be carried are always determined on the basis of judgment on the part of the owner. The size of a building and the number of tenants is not necessarily the determining factor. Serious accidents can occur in small buildings as well as large. The extent of injuries need bear no relationship whatever to the size or value of the building nor to the financial responsibility of the owner. In all cases, the owner has to decide upon limits which he feels will adequately cover him under any circumstances. Although the limit of recovery of damages for accidental death is determined by law in many states, no limit is placed on recovery for temporary or permanent disability, and since juries are inclined to give extremely liberal awards in personal injury suits, most owners in recent years have increased their limits of insurance substantially. The added premium cost of the higher limits is reasonable enough to warrant the placement of higher amounts than may be normally considered necessary.

Limits are generally expressed as "$50/100" or "$50,000/100,000", each illustration meaning the same thing, namely, up to $50,000 available for the payment of a claim for injuries to one person hurt in one accident and if more than one person is injured, up to $100,000 limited to $50,000 for any one person. As indicated, a series of accidents is fully covered with the limits applying separately to each, and no reduction in the amount of coverage occurs by reason of payment of claims.

Until a few years ago, limits on Owners', Landlords' and Tenants' Liability policies of $50,000/100,000 were fairly standard and considered adequate. In recent years many owners have increased these limits to $100,000/300,000 and higher.

[¶3109] TABLES OF RISKS AND COVERAGE

The following tables summarize the various risks arising in business, the potential losses, and the available insurance coverages to protect against those risks.

[¶3109.1] Risks Arising out of the Operation of a Business Generally

Risk	Liability to Others	Loss to Insured	Maximum Loss	Policy
Boiler or machinery explosion	√	P.D. & P.I.	?	Boiler & Machinery Policy

241

Risk	Liability to Others	Loss to Insured	Maximum Loss	Policy
Same		Consequential damage through loss of use	?	Consequential damage endorsement
Tort (false arrest, libel, etc.)	√		?	Personal injury liability coverage
Tort by advertisement (defamation, etc.)	√		?	Advertiser's liability
Employee accident or disease	√ (Workmen's Compensation or common-law liability)		?	Workmen's Compensation & Employer's Liability
Liability assumed by contract	√		?	Comprehensive general liability
Accident on premises	√		?	Comprehensive general liability
Accident on elevators	√		?	Comprehensive general liability
Accident due to operation of independent contractors	√		?	Comprehensive general liability
Defective or unsafe product	√		?	Products liability
Patent infringement	√		?	Patent Infringement
Airplane accidents		P.I.	?	Aviation Accident
Broken Glass		P.D.	Replacement Cost	Comprehensive Glass

Risk	Liability to Others	Loss to Insured	Maximum Loss	Policy
Burglary		Loss of inventory or equip.	Replacement Cost	Mercantile open stock
Robbery (on & off premises)		Loss of property	?	Mercantile robbery
Employee fraud or dishonesty		Loss of property	?	Blanket position bond or individual fidelity bond
Damage to suppliers or purchasers		Loss of earnings	?	Contingent business interruption
Damge to business		Loss of earnings	?	Business interruption
Fire or lightning		P.D. (building & contents)	?	Fire
Windstorm & Hail		P.D. (building & contents)		Windstorm & Hail
Earthquake		P.D. (building & contents)		Earthquake
Water Leakage or Overflow		P.D.	?	Water damage
Loss of cargo at sea		Property loss	Value of cargo	Ocean Marine Cargo
Loss of books & records		Non-collection of accounts receivable	Value of accounts receivable	Accounts Receivable
Loss or damage to personal property (on or off premises)		P.D. or property loss	?	Inland Transit Floater

243

Risk	Liability to Others	Loss to Insured	Maximum Loss	Policy
Non-payment by customers		Loss of income	Loss experience	Commercial Credit

〔¶3109.2〕 Risks Peculiar to a Particular Business

Business and Risk	Liability to Others	Loss to Insured	Maximum Loss	Policy
Banking— Criminal Acts & Disappearance		Property Loss	Depends on deposits	Bankers' Blanket Bond
Garages— Accidents to Person & Property	√		?	Garage Liability
Druggists— Error in Prescription	√		?	Druggists' Liability
Innkeeper— Loss or Damage to Guests' Property	√		?	Innkeepers' Liability
Manufacturers & Contractors —Accidents from Operations	√		?	Manufacturers' & Contractors' Liability
Stockbrokers— Criminal Acts & Disappearance	√		?	Brokers' Blanket Bond
Vending Machines— Damage or Loss		P.D. & Loss of Income	?	Vending Machine Floater
Warehousemen— Loss or Damge to Customer's Property	√		?	Warehousemen's Liability
Malpractice by Accountants, Attorneys, Doctors, Dentists, Real Estate Agents, Architects & Engineers, Insurance Agents	√		?	Professional Liability

Business and Risk	Liability to Others	Loss to Insured	Maximum Loss	Policy
Automobile Accident (Insured's Automobile)	√	P.D. & P.I.	?	Automobile Comprehensive
Aircraft Accident (Insured's Aircraft)	√		?	Aircraft Liability
Decrease in Corporate Net Worth due to Its Liability		Value of Stock	?	Stockholder's Protective Insurance
Loss of Securities or other Instruments		Property Loss	?	Lost Securities Bond

【¶3109.3】 Risks to Owner or Lessee of Real Estate

Risk	Liability to Others	Loss to Insured	Maximum Loss	Policy
Physical Damage During Construction		P.D.	Cost of Completed Building	Builders' Risk
Time Losses due to Delay in Construction		Loss of Rent or Use	?	Rent Insurance
Physical Damage to Completed Building		P.D.	Replacement Cost	Fire & Extended Coverage
Same		Loss of Rent or Use	?	Rent Insurance
Injuries to Persons or Property on Premises	√		?	Landlords' Protective Liability
Injuries to Lessees or Their Property	√		?	General Liability
Loss of Leasehold due to Damage to Building		Leasehold Interest	Market Value of Lease Minus Rent	Leasehold Interest

245

Risk	Liability to Others	Loss to Insured	Maximum Loss	Policy
Loss of Lease-hold due to Damage to Building		Continued Obligation to Pay Rent	Remaining Rent under Lease	Rent Insurance
Damage to Lessees' Improvements		P.D.	Replacement Cost	Improve-ments & Betterments
Damage to Building by Lessees' Negligence	√		Replacement Cost of Building	General Liability
Injury to Person or Property on Premises	√		?	General Liability

[¶3110]   PROTECTING CREDITORS' INTERESTS IN INSURANCE

There are a number of methods of providing insurance protection to creditors:

(1) *Separate policy for a creditor:* The creditor takes out, or is furnished, a separate policy covering his own interest. The owner may have a separate policy covering his ownership interest.

(2) *Assignment of owner's policy:* The owner assigns his policy to the creditor. Whether the consent of the insurance company is required and the rights of the respective parties may depend upon the type of insurance and the jurisdiction.

(3) *Loss payable clause:* This is an endorsement upon the owner's policy of a "loss payable clause" which stipulates "loss, if any, payable to _____, as his interest may appear." The effect of this varies in different jurisdictions —some put the creditor in the same shoes as the owner, while others give him broader rights. The creditor normally is given possession of the policy and the owner gets a certificate or memorandum of insurance.

(4) *As interest may appear clause:* This may be found in a policy such as one covering a bailee, which covers "for the benefit of whom it may concern" or "for others as their interests may appear."

Make sure that the matter of the procurement of insurance and the payment of premiums is covered by the agreement between the debtor and creditor. The agreement should spell out the kind and amount of coverage, the character of the carrier, who is to get the coverage and keep the policy, who is to pay the premium, what happens if one party or the other fails in his duties with respect to insurance or payment, and any other matters that are important in the particular transaction.

●

For Further Reference . . .

Mehr, Robert I., and Hedges, Bob A., *Risk Management in the Business Enterprise.*

Rodda, William H., *Fire and Property Insurance.*

INSURANCE — LIFE

[¶3201] The life insurance policy is frequently a vital element in a plan for family security, an estate plan, a program to retire corporate stock or partnership interests, a plan to provide business continuity, an employee pension and profit-sharing plan and many other family and business arrangements in which a lawyer will be asked for advice. It is important that he understand the elements of the life insurance contract, the alternatives available to the insured, the status of life insurance as property, how life insurance is taxed, etc.

[¶3202] **TYPICAL STANDARD PROVISIONS**
IN A LIFE INSURANCE POLICY

The following provisions are customarily included in life insurance policies. A number of them are required by law in the various states.

Grace Period: If you don't pay your premium on the due date, the company will accept payment within 31 days after the date specified in your policy and premium notice.

Extended Insurance Coverage: If you don't pay the premium within the 31-day grace period, your policy (if it is a permanent type insurance) does not automatically expire. Your insurance will usually be continued as term insurance for a period of time measured by the amount of cash value standing to the credit of your policy. You can request, however, that loans be made automatically for the specific purpose of paying the delinquent premiums from the cash values in your policy. You can select this automatic premium loan provision when you first make your application for the policy. Many policies contain automatic premium loan clauses without the necessity of special selection by the policyholder.

Reinstatement: If you fail to pay premiums and your policy later lapses when your cash values expire, you can later have the policy reinstated by paying the unpaid premiums with interest. Here you will have to show satisfactory evidence of good health; you will usually have several years within which to apply for reinstatement of your policy.

Premium Adjustment: Most policies provide today that in addition to the death benefit itself, your beneficiary will receive a refund of that portion of the current premium which covers a period beyond the month of death.

Incontestability Clause: Once the policy has been in force for two years (one year in some cases), upon your death your beneficiary will receive the proceeds without a contest by the company. This is so even where misstatements were made in the original application. However, if the misstatement pertains to the insured's age, then an adjustment will be made. For example, if you are actually older than is stated in the application and the policy, while death benefits will be paid, the payments will be less than the face amount of the policy. Conversely, if it turns out that you are actually younger than the application states, your beneficiary will receive more.

Suicide: If death results from suicide within two years after the policy is issued (1 year in some policies), the beneficiary will recover only the actual premiums advanced; after two years, the full death benefit will be paid.

Cash Values: Your policy contains a table of values which spells out the amount of cash you can pick up at any given time, should you desire to surrender the policy. If you would rather receive the cash under one of the income options, you can select one of several guaranteed arrangements spelled out in the policy. Here, too, there are tables which show just what you can expect in dollars and cents.

Loan Values: Permanent-type insurance permits you to borrow generally up to 95% of cash value at guaranteed interest rates.

Paid-up Insurance: The policy also contains a table showing amount of paid-up life insurance that can be taken instead of cash when policy is surrendered. The paid-up policy will contain cash values.

Payment of Dividend and Dividend Options: Participating policies provide for payment of a dividend, and describe the various dividend options — such as cash, reduced premium, paid-up additions, interest, additional one-year term.

Ownership Clause: The person who owns the policy is named. He is usually the insured, but may be the beneficiary or someone else. For example, in order to remove proceeds from insured's estate, his wife or a trust may be owner of the policy.

Beneficiary Provision: Insured can name first, second, third or more beneficiaries, and arrange payment of proceeds through settlement options. Some policies, such as group insurance, may restrict the number of beneficiaries that can be named, and the variety of settlement arrangements that can be chosen.

Policy Change: The policy sets forth what plans of insurance the existing policy can be converted to and the procedure for such conversion. Policies can generally be converted without medical to higher premium plans; with medical to lower premium plans; generally conversion to term is not permitted.

Assignment: The policy spells out procedure for making an assignment. Usually the company states that it is not bound until written notice of assignment is received; that the assignment shall be subject to any loan to the company; and that the company accepts no responsibility for the validity of the assignment.

Deferment Clause: This gives the company the right to defer payment of cash value or giving loan up to six months. This often applies also to withdrawal of proceeds retained at interest or commutation of proceeds under settlement options. This clause is similar to one on bank savings accounts, and is practically never invoked by the insurance companies.

Basis of Policy Reserve: This sets forth the method of computing the reserve that the company uses, such as the 1958 CSO mortality table.

[¶3203] LEGAL ASPECTS OF LIFE INSURANCE

Although the life insurance policy is a legal contract, usual contract law has been modified by state law in many respects. These changes protect the policyholder, and cause the contract to be interpreted strictly against the insurance company in the event of a dispute between the company and an insured.

Following is a rundown of the most important legal aspects of life insurance.

(1) Offer: If the application is accompanied by payment of first premium, the offer is made by the applicant and the company generally agrees by issuing a conditional receipt to insure the applicant if he meets the insurability requirements of the company. If a policy other than that applied for is issued, then the new policy becomes a counter-offer by the company. An application without premium is merely an invitation for the company to make an offer, which it does by issuing the policy and delivering it.

(2) Acceptance: An offer may be accepted by the company delivering the policy or the insured paying the first premium. Unreasonable delay by the company in processing an application accompanied by the first premium is considered in most states to be a rejection of the applicant's offer; in some states, it constitutes an acceptance.

There are various forms of conditional receipts used by companies, and on the wording of the particular receipt depends whether the issuance of the receipt constitutes an acceptance or the actual delivery of the policy is required.

(3) Consideration: The consideration given by the insurance company is its promises as defined in the contract. The consideration given by the insured is his statements made in the application and payment of the first premium.

(4) Legal Capacity: The insured must be of legal age and of sound mind. The usual legal age has been modified in many states for life insurance contracts. For example, in New York the legal age for a minor making a contract for insurance on his own life is over 14½ (insurance age 15).

(5) Insurable Interest: The applicant must have an insurable interest in the life of the insured. This has been defined as a reasonable expectation of financial benefit from the continued life of the insured or financial loss if insured dies. A general rule is that even though an insurable interest exists, you may not insure the life of another without his consent. Insurable interest need exist only when the policy is purchased; it need not exist when the policy becomes a claim. The insured has the right to name anyone as his beneficiary without regard to insurable interest.

(6) Utmost Good Faith: Neither "buyer beware" nor "seller beware" applies to a life insurance contract. Each party has the right to rely on the utmost good faith of the other.

(7) Representation: Most states provide that, in the absence of fraud, all warranties in life insurance contracts (statements in the application and medical exam) are to be interpreted as representations. The policy is voidable by the company if there is a misrepresentation of a material fact — one which would have led the company to deny the insurance or charge a higher premium. However, a misrepresentation of an immaterial fact is not sufficient to rescind the contract.

(8) Concealment: The company may also rescind contract if there has been concealment — the applicant remaining silent when he had a duty to speak. However, the concealment must be both material and intentional.

(9) Creditors' Rights: The rights of creditors of the insured (and sometimes creditors of the beneficiary) have been modified in most states by statute to give special protection to life insurance.

(10) Authority of Agents: There is generally a presumption of agency if the company has supplied a person with forms, rate books, applications, etc., which make it logical for one to assume that he is an agent of the company. The company would be bound by acts of this person as though he had been given express authority to act as agent.

The insurance agent's authority is outlined in his agency contract. His authority usually includes soliciting and taking applications for new business, arranging medical exams, collecting the first year's premium or a partial premium. Rights usually excluded are to make, alter, or discharge any contract; to waive any forfeiture; to waive payment in cash; to extend the time of payment for a premium; to accept payment of a past due premium; to approve evidence of good health.

In addition to express authority granted in his agency contract, the agent is held in common law to have certain implied authority—any authority which the public may reasonably assume an agent to have. Limitations of the agent's authority are communicated to the public in application forms, conditional receipts, and in the policy. Policies contain a provision that only certain designated officers of the company have the power to make or modify the contract, or extend time for paying a premium.

The knowledge of the agent is assumed to be the knowledge of the company. Thus, if the agent knows a material fact about the applicant, it is presumed that the information has been given to the company whether or not in fact it has been. Should the company discover the information after the policy is issued, it cannot then rescind the contract because of concealment or misrepresentation.

The responsibility of the company, when an agent interprets a policy provision incorrectly to an insured, generally depends on whether the wording in policy is clear or ambiguous—if ambiguous, the agent's interpretation is held valid.

Most states make a distinction between a broker and an agent—the broker is the agent of the insured, not the company. However, other states make the broker the agent of the company, and some make him the agent of the company only for delivering the policy and collecting the premium.

[¶3204]　　　　　　　　　DIVIDEND OPTIONS

Following is a rundown of typical dividend options available to a policyholder.

(1) Cash: The policyholder can receive his dividend in cash. The most frequent use of this option is for paid-up policies. Another situation where this option is attractive is if insured is disabled and premiums are being waived. In most other cases, the advantages of the other options should be considered.

(2) Reduce Premiums: Insured can apply dividends as part payment of premiums. This dividend is used when insured needs this money to help meet premium obligations, or if a low net expenditure for insurance is desired. It is used on minimum deposit plans when reducing instead of level coverage is wanted.

(3) Accumulating at Interest: This election permits the insurance company to retain dividends on deposit and have it build up at a guaranteed rate of interest. If the company's earnings are less than the rate it guarantees, the policyholder will still be credited with the specified interest rate; should the earnings be greater he often will receive the higher interest.

Dividend accumulations are often used when insured wants to increase the guaranteed retirement income provided under policy's retirement options.

(4) Paid-up Additions: Dividends are applied to buy additional paid-up insurance. The increased protection acquired via dividend additions requires

no medical examination and serves as a valuable tool when health impairment otherwise prevents other additional insurance.

(5) The "Fifth" Dividend Option: This is a relatively new choice which provides for the purchase of one-year term insurance usually equal to the cash value. The balance of the dividend may be left on deposit to accumulate future cash value purchases or may be applied under one of the other dividend options.

What the option accomplishes is to increase the face value of the policy by the amount of the cash value. The net result here is to eliminate the policy owner from becoming a co-insurer on the policy.

In non-participating policies, where dividends are not paid, there is usually available a rider that permits the purchase of the same amount of term insurance as would be provided in a "fifth dividend" case in a participating policy. The cost of this additional rider is relatively low.

[¶3205] LIFE INSURANCE RIDERS

There are many extras you can add to your basic life insurance policy. Some of these "riders" cost from a few cents to a few dollars per year for each $1,000 of death benefit provided in the policy itself; the cost of others is based on the amount of benefit provided in the rider itself; and other valuable endorsements may be added to the policy free of charge. Whether the insured needs some of these "extras" depends on the purpose of the insurance policy — family protection, business insurance, retirement fund—and, in other cases, his own personal preferences.

[¶3205.1] Waiver of Premium Benefit

This provides that if the policyholder becomes totally and permanently disabled, his insurance will remain in force without any further premium payments. The disability generally must occur before age 60 for the clause to apply, and it does not take effect until the disability has continued for a specified waiting period, usually six months. Disabilities typically excluded from coverage are those resulting from war and those which are intentionally self-inflicted.

In addition to the premiums being waived if you are disabled, if the policies are of the cash-value type—ordinary life, limited-pay life, endowment—then the cash values will grow just as if you were continuing to pay the premiums yourself. For example—a 40-year-old person purchases a $100,000 ordinary life policy with waiver of premium benefit at annual premium of approximately $2,350. He becomes disabled in the first year. Not only is the premium of $2,350 waived thereafter, but the cash values in the policy accumulate so that at age 65 he has a cash fund of about $49,000 available. If the need arises during the period of disability he can borrow against the cash values in the policy.

The premium for waiver of premium benefit is very little for the protection offered. The premium will vary with the age and sex of the insured and the amount and type of the insurance plan. On an ordinary life policy, the premium will run less than $1 per $1,000 for a man in his thirties, gradually increasing to about $3 for a fifty-five year old.

Some companies do not charge separately for waiver of premium benefit. They incorporate it in the basic policy and include the cost in the basic premium.

The waiver of premium benefit is included in G. I. insurance, and is often also found in group, association, and credit insurance plans.

For almost all types of policies and purposes, this extra is usually looked upon as a necessity. In a family protection policy, it guarantees maintenance of your life insurance at a vital time when your ability to earn enough to pay the premium would be gone. In a retirement plan, it guarantees the accumulation of the retirement fund. In a partnership agreement, it might provide part of the funds for a pay-out of a disabled partner.

Payor Benefit: This is a waiver of premium benefit in connection with juvenile insurance. It covers the risk of death or disability of the applicant (i.e., usually the child's father) before the insured child reaches age 21 or 25, by providing for waiver to age 21 or 25 of the regular premiums under the juvenile policy. There are two types of waivers available at an extra premium:

(1) Waiver in event of death of applicant.

(2) Waiver in event of death or disability of applicant. For example, a typical additional premium on a $1,000 ordinary life policy for a child of 10 and father age 35 for the first waiver is about $1.50 and for the second waiver about $1.80.

[¶3205.2] Accidental Death Benefits

This rider stipulates that if the policyholder dies by "accidental death," the company will pay the beneficiary a multiple of the face amount of the policy (as much as four times in some cases).

Some typical exclusions on the rider are deaths due to war, certain kinds of flying accidents, and accidents that stem from illness or infirmity such as a man who has a heart attack while driving a car. Death generally must take place within 90 days of the accident and before the insured reaches a specified age, usually 65, at which point the extra coverage expires.

Premiums for accidental death are at a flat rate of about $1.00 per $1,000 for a young person and gradually increase to about $2.00 for an older person.

Although the premium is low, whether you should add the accidental death rider is often a matter of personal preference. Note that it only covers accidental death, which is no more likely to create extra financial burdens than death from any other cause. The theory that the family needs extra money when death strikes suddenly, without warning, is debatable since sufficient life insurance protection would avoid this.

However, even though accidental death benefits may not be necessary for a sound life insurance program, the average insurance buyer is often attracted by the small amount of premium required to increase his estate materially should he die accidentally.

In some cases this rider can serve a useful purpose. For example, it may be used by a business to protect against the loss of key personnel. For an executive who travels extensively by airplane, it provides less costly, year-round coverage for accidental death than airplane policies.

[¶3205.3] Accidental Death and Dismemberment

Some policies, typically group and association plans, provide, in addition to accidental death, benefits for dismemberment—loss of a limb, blindness, etc.

Some policies provide a *disability payout provision* under which the face amount of the policy is paid out in installments in the event of total disability.

[¶3205.4] Guaranteed Insurability Rider

This rider guarantees that a specified amount of insurance may be purchased by the insured on certain future "option dates" at standard rates and without evidence of insurability. A typical rider permits the purchase of up to an additional $10,000 at ages 25, 28, 31, 34, 37 and 40. For example, a 28-year-old man buys a $10,000 ordinary life policy and adds this rider. He has the option to pick up an additional $10,000 at ages 31, 34, 37 and 40 for a total of $50,000 regardless of his health during the intervening years.

The guaranteed insurability rider can be a valuable extra for a young man as it gives him the guarantee of an increasing insurance program. It is also a good addition to children's life insurance policies.

By adding the guaranteed insurability rider on to a $5,000 "jumping juvenile" policy (a special policy for children whose face value increases five times at age 21), a father or grandfather can guarantee to a child an eventual insurance estate of $85,000 whether insurable later or not. The $5,000 policy increases automatically to $25,000 at age 21; then $60,000 additional can be obtained by exercising the options.

Premiums for a guaranteed insurability rider in the amount of $10,000 range from about $10 a year for a fifteen-year-old boy to about $20 a year for a man in his thirties.

Premiums are payable to the insured's age 40 or to the end of the premium-paying period of the basic policy, whichever is earlier. Generally, the new insurance must be applied for on or within 60 days prior to an option date. There is no carryover of the right to buy from one designated period to another. Failure to exercise the right to buy on a particular date, however, will not affect the right to purchase on a subsequent date.

[¶3205.5] Additional Term Riders

There are a variety of term riders that can be added to a basic policy to provide additional low-cost life insurance coverage. The following paragraphs examine them in detail.

[¶3205.6] Disability Income Rider

Some life insurance companies offer a disability income rider that provides a monthly income to the insured if he becomes totally disabled. Many limit the maximum amount of disability income from the rider from $300 to $500 a month. A typical rider provides a monthly disability income of 1% of the face amount of the policy—a $50,000 policy could provide $500 per month disability income protection; monthly payments continue until age 65 and then the policy endows for its face value and all obligations under the contract cease. Thus, a man who becomes totally disabled at age 45, who has a $50,000 life insurance policy with a 1% disability rider, would receive payment of $500 a month until age 65 and then would receive $50,000 in cash. Most riders require a six-month waiting period before disability payments begin, although a policy with a four-month waiting period is available.

[¶3205.7] Free Riders

There are a number of free extras that can be included in insurance policies:

Automatic Premium Loan Clause: This is a provision that makes your policy "lapse-proof." The company is authorized to borrow from the cash value to pay a premium if you fail to do so. This valuable clause may keep your protection from lapsing if due to an oversight or illness you neglect to pay your premium on time.

Settlement Agreement: Payment of policy proceeds under various options and different beneficiary designations can be combined in one agreement attached to the policy in order to effectuate your estate plan. For example: part of the proceeds can be paid in cash to pay off debts, estate taxes and final expenses; the balance, in the form of a monthly income to your wife, if she survives you; otherwise by monthly payments to a trustee for the children, and so on.

Retirement Options: You may plan to use the cash values and accumulated dividends in your policies to provide you with a monthly annuity when you retire. You can receive a lifetime income, installments for a period of time, or you and your wife can get a joint and survivor annuity. If these options are not already included, they generally can be added to your policies.

Change of Policy Ownership: You may want to make a gift of a policy to your wife or to a trust in order to remove the proceeds from your estate. Or you may want to use a policy as collateral for a loan. The insurance company will make the proper endorsements on your policy.

Spendthrift Trust Clause: Some states have laws that automatically exempt proceeds of life insurance from the claims of creditors of the beneficiary. Many states also allow the insured to add a "spendthrift trust" provision to his policy protecting the proceeds. These clauses are usually worded to the effect that proceeds shall not be assignable and are to be exempt from claims of creditors.

Common Disaster Clause: In states that do not have the Uniform Simultaneous Death Law, a common disaster clause might be added to the policy to achieve the same result. This clause states that if the insured and the beneficiary (husband and wife, for example) die in a common accident, the presumption will be that the beneficiary died first. The proceeds would then be paid to the secondary beneficiary or, in the absence of any, to the estate of the insured. This will save the cost and delay of the proceeds passing through the wife's estate instead of going directly to the children.

Deferment Clause: This clause will defer payment of policy proceeds for a 30-day or 60-day period. Upon death of the insured, the proceeds are held at interest for a specified period and then paid to the primary beneficiary at the end of that period, if surviving, otherwise to the secondary beneficiary. This clause, like the common disaster clause, will keep proceeds out of a wife's estate where the wife dies shortly after the husband — proceeds will go directly to children.

[¶3206]   SETTLEMENT OPTIONS

Insurance proceeds payable on the death of the insured, or cash value (when a policy is cashed in) can, of course, be received in a lump sum. But that is not the only way the proceeds can be received. There are four other so-called settlement options:

The Interest Only Option
The Installment Time Option
The Installment Amount Option

The Life Income Option — which may be further subdivided as follows:
(a) Life Income with definite number of payments guaranteed.
(b) Life Annuity Income — no definite number of payments guaranteed.
(c) Cash Refund Life Annuity Income.
(d) Refund Life Annuity Income.
(e) Joint and Survivorship Annuity Income.

[¶3207]   PRINCIPAL OWNERSHIP AND BENEFICIARY ARRANGEMENTS

(A) Insured purchaser and owner — executor named as beneficiary.

(B) Insured purchaser and owner — designated individual as beneficiary.

(C) Insured purchaser — another individual, corporation or other entity as owner and beneficiary.

(D) Insured purchaser — trustee as owner and beneficiary.

(E) Person other than the insured as purchaser, owner and beneficiary.

[¶3208]   LEGAL ASPECTS OF BENEFICIARY DESIGNATIONS

The selection of a beneficiary and wording of the beneficiary designation often have important legal consequences. Following is a checklist of some of these.

(1) Naming the estate of the insured as beneficiary will make policy proceeds subject to creditors of insured; naming specific beneficiaries will give protection of state law.

(2) Naming the estate beneficiary will make proceeds subject to estate tax. If there is a named beneficiary, it may escape estate tax—for example—where wife is owner and beneficiary; where named beneficiary receives insurance proceeds of pension and profit-sharing plans, etc.

(3) If no beneficiary is named in the policy, or if none survives the insured, the proceeds, unless otherwise provided, are paid to the insured's estate. Distribution becomes a matter of his will or, if he has no will, the laws of descent.

(4) Failing to name sufficient contingent beneficiaries may cause proceeds to pass to persons not intended. For example—insured names wife as primary beneficiary and children as secondary but fails to name third beneficiary; entire family is killed in an automobile accident, but the wife is last survivor; then all proceeds might go to wife's relatives unless she left a will making a different disposition.

(5) A "revocable" designation is one in which insured reserves the right to change the beneficiary. He may then at any time make a change without the beneficiary's permission.

[¶3208.1] **Contingent Beneficiary**

In arranging beneficiary designations, provision should always be made for a contingent or final beneficiary to receive the policy proceeds in the event the first named beneficiary is dead. This is especially important when payment is made through long-term settlement options where it is entirely possible that there will remain a balance either of installment payments or of principal, after the death of the primary beneficiary.

Particularly under long-term income options, difficulties can arise if the insured's estate is named final beneficiary. Suppose the primary and contingent beneficiary live a reasonably long time and upon the latter's death there is a balance to be paid out. By that time the insured's estate will have been settled; it would be troublesome to attempt to reopen the estate, especially since the balance of principal would probably be meager.

An insured might consider naming a favorite charity as contingent or final beneficiary. This would not only avoid tax questions, but would assure all concerned that there would be an institution in being which would be a worthy recipient of the benefits. Here again, care should be exercised in properly identifying the organization by exact legal corporate name.

[¶3209]   **LIFE INSURANCE AND ESTATE TAXES**

Life insurance proceeds are taxable for estate tax purposes in the decedent's estate—unless measures are taken during lifetime to put the insurance beyond the reach of the estate tax law or to soften the impact of that law.

[¶3209.1] **How to Transfer Ownership to Escape Estate Tax**

A popular estate planning device is the transfer of ownership of life insurance policies to intended beneficiaries. Code §2042 says that death benefits paid to persons other than the estate are taxable only if the insured at his death possesses "incidents of ownership" in the policy. This means that if the insured makes a complete transfer of the policy and at the time of his death does not possess any rights of ownership, then, Code §2042 does not apply.

All that must be done is to assign the policy to a wife or child or to a trust.

To achieve this there must be an absolute assignment together with the surrender of any power over the policy and its benefits. This means the insured forfeits his right to surrender, pledge, or cancel the policy; to further assign the policy or revoke the assignment; to borrow on the policy; or to change the beneficiary. There should be no more than one chance in twenty that the proceeds can revert to the insured's estate because the beneficiaries died before him.

Once the policy is transferred, the insured can continue to pay premiums and the proceeds will still be protected from the impact of the estate tax provided there is no gift "in contemplation of death" problem. If the policy is transferred within three years of death, the proceeds will usually be included in the insured's estate. If the policy is transferred more than three years before death any premiums paid by the insured within the last three years would be included in his estate.

[¶3209.2] How Life Insurance Proceeds Qualify for the Marital Deduction

In computing the Federal estate tax we have what is known as the marital deduction which permits up to one half of the adjusted gross estate to be eliminated from estate tax. There are two conditions: The property must be left to the surviving wife either outright or for life with the general power of appointment.

Life insurance proceeds may qualify for the marital deduction. However, the policyholder should make sure that the proceeds become vested in his wife upon his death. Some policies state that, in order to become vested with the policy proceeds, it is mandatory for the widow to file proof of his death within her lifetime. This provision would prevent the proceeds from qualifying for the marital deduction (*Rev. Rul. 54-121,* CB 1954-1, 196).

It is therefore wise in such situations to endorse the policy so that the widow has an immediate right to the policy proceeds upon the insured's death if she survives him irrespective of when the proof was actually filed. Sometimes, a common disaster clause, which presumes that the widow survived the insured, has the same effect *(Reg. §20.2056(b)-3).*

Generally there are three ways by which life insurance proceeds will qualify for the marital deduction:

(1) By making the proceeds payable to the widow in a lump sum.

(2) By making the proceeds payable to a trust which itself qualifies.

(3) By making the proceeds payable under any one of the installment options if:

(a) the principal or any remaining unpaid installments are payable to the wife's estate on her death or,

(b) the surviving wife is given a general power to designate the beneficiary of the principal remaining at her death.

Where an option is selected by the insured with a fixed number of installments, the widow's estate should be named as a beneficiary to take the balance of the installments. If a contingent beneficiary is named, the insured runs the risk that the proceeds will not qualify *(Reg. §20.2056(b)-1(g) example (3)).*

If the proceeds of a life insurance policy are payable to the widow and then to contingent beneficiaries, and she has the power to appoint all the proceeds to herself or her estate, the proceeds qualify for the marital deduction if the power of appointment satisfies these requirements:

(1) All proceeds are payable to the widow solely during her lifetime.

(2) Payments must be payable annually or more frequently and must commence within 13 months after the insured's death.

(3) The widow has the sole power to appoint all the proceeds or a portion of them to herself or her estate.

(4) The power is exercisable in all events.

(5) The widow's power is not subject to a power in any other person to appoint any part of the proceeds or a portion of them to anyone other than the wife *(Reg. §20.2056(b)-(6))*.

It is not necessary that the widow actually exercise her power of appointment. Neither is it necessary that the phrase "power of appointment" be used in the policy. The widow's right to withdraw the principal sum in installments is, in itself, the equivalent to a power of appointment and so qualifies for the marital deduction, provided this right exists from the time of the insured's death *(Reg. §20.2056(e))*.

[¶3210]   PROTECTION OF LIFE INSURANCE FROM CREDITORS

Following is a checklist of the rules affecting creditors' claims:

(1) Creditors of Insured—Cash Values: In most states, the wording of laws exempting insurance from creditors' claims is broad enough to exempt cash values of policies from creditors of insured. Court decisions have been divided where the statute is not clear. In some cases, where the statute uses the term "proceeds" without adding "cash values" or "avails," cases have restricted the protection to death proceeds only.

(2) Creditors of the Insured—Death Proceeds: Most state statutes restrict the rights of creditors of the insured in proceeds of life insurance. Some states exempt the entire proceeds; others limit it to a certain amount. Some limit the protection to proceeds payable to the insured's wife or children; others to any dependent relative; and some to any beneficiary other than one who is himself the insured.

Proceeds paid to a trust for the benefit of a specific beneficiary normally have the same protection from creditors as if paid directly to the beneficiary.

(3) Creditors of the Beneficiary — Cash Values: Usually creditors of the beneficiary have no claims against cash values. The beneficiary has no vested right to cash values unless named irrevocably, and even then cannot usually cash in the policy without the insured's consent. Thus the beneficiary's creditors would have no rights without the consent of the insured.

(4) Creditors of the Beneficiary — Death Proceeds: Most statutes exempt proceeds from the claims of insured's creditors only. In a few states the exemption applies to creditors of the beneficiary also.

If law does not exempt the proceeds from the beneficiary's creditors, the insured can extend this protection by adding to the settlement agreement in the policy a *spendthrift trust clause.* This states that proceeds payable to beneficiary may not be assigned, transferred, commuted or encumbered by the beneficiary, nor subject to legal process, execution, garnishment or attachment. Policy proceeds have to be made payable to the beneficiary under an installment or life income option. This arrangement usually has to be set up by the insured. The spendthrift trust clause only protects the money held by the company—when the beneficiary receives a payment, the money is available to creditors.

(5) Annuities: Creditors' rights in annuities are not usually limited by exemption laws applying to life insurance — an annuity may be reached by creditors of the annuitant. A few states give a limited exemption to annuity income. One case held that a trustee in bankruptcy could reach the annuity income payable to an insured from the cash values of the life insurance policy *(Schaeffer, 189 Fed. 187).* Where a person purchases an annuity for another person, a few states exempt these from creditors.

(6) Common Law: Where there are no specific state laws, common law may apply. Under common law, creditors' rights to life insurance cash values and proceeds usually depend on how the beneficiary is named in the policy. If the insured or his estate is the beneficiary, creditors can reach the proceeds as part of the general assets of insured's estate. The general rule is that cash values can be reached, but some cases make this depend on the policy provisions.

If other than insured or his estate is named beneficiary, the proceeds of the policy belong to the beneficiary and may not be claimed by creditors of the insured. The proceeds are subject to the claims of the beneficiary's creditors, unless the spendthrift trust arrangement has been set up.

●

For Further Reference . . .

Forms of Business Agreements looseleaf Service, Institute for Business Planning, Englewood Cliffs, N.J.

Life Insurance Planning (looseleaf service), Institute for Business Planning, Englewood Cliffs, N.J.

Mehr, Robert I., and Oster, Robert W., *Modern Life Insurance* (3rd Edition).

White, E. H., *Business Insurance* (3rd Edition).

LANDLORD AND TENANT

[¶3501] The provisions in a lease, and the manner in which its various clauses are worded, will affect the lessor and the lessee in two different ways: (1) They will first determine the legal rights and duties of the one to the other; and (2) They will secondly affect the tax obligations and liabilities of the two in many important respects. At the bargaining stages, both parties will normally try to conform the various provisions in the lease to the form which will yield them the maximum economic and tax advantages. The reconciliation of the two possibly conflicting viewpoints places a premium upon proper planning and drafting at the initiatory stages of any lease arrangement.

In leases which are characterized by long terms, the tax advantages which are obtainable by either the lessor or the lessee may not only be substantial —they may, in fact, be the motivating force behind the whole transaction. This is especially true where the lessee is required to erect new buildings on the property or to make substantial improvements or alterations to the property. Since the lessor and the lessee usually have equal bargaining power in the long-term situation, the final lease is ordinarily preceded by extensive negotiations at both the economic and the tax levels. The number of detailed provisions in the lease will ordinarily reflect this bargaining process.

[¶3502] NEGOTIATING AND DRAFTING LEASES

The three important types of leases are those for (1) office space; (2) commercial space; and (3) an entire building where the lessee intends to sublease to others. (The third type frequently is in the form of a ground lease calling for construction of the improvement by the lessee.) The following paragraphs highlight the significant points to be kept in mind in negotiating and drafting these leases.

[¶3502.1] Rental Payments

The most important question about rent is the amount to be paid. There are a number of alternative ways of fixing rent:

(1) Flat Rental: This calls for a uniform rate throughout the term and is most common in the short-term office lease. Its defect to the landlord is its failure to protect him against unreimbursed increases in taxes and operating expenses.

(2) Step-up Lease: This provides for a gradually increasing amount of rent, to step up at specified intervals. It may be used to compensate the landlord for increased expenses but more commonly, it may be an inducement for a tenant newly started in business who initially can only afford a small rental.

263

(3) Expense Participating Lease, or Escalator Lease: Long-term office leases usually are of this type. Under it, the tenant pays a basic fixed rent plus a specified portion of the real estate taxes, insurance, and repairs other than structural ones. The expense participating lease requires the tenant to pay an immediate share of these costs, while under the escalator lease, the tenant pays only a portion of any increases in costs during the lease term.

(4) Cost of Living Lease: Here, the tenant's rental obligation is increased or decreased at specified intervals depending on the fluctuation of the dollar as revealed by price indices or other agreed measures of the degree of inflation or deflation which has occurred.

(5) Re-evaluation Lease: This calls for an appraisal of the property and a fixing of the rent as a percentage of the appraised value at specified intervals. The new rental value may be fixed on the basis of the value of the land and building, or on the rental value of the premises occupied by the tenant. The latter method may result in a higher figure because the appraisers may take into consideration the business success of the tenant.

In addition to the amount of rent, the lease should set forth the method of paying it. Many leases state the rental obligation in terms of a yearly figure and in theory the landlord may require it to be paid one year in advance, even though monthly payments are customary. Sometimes, where the tenant's income is seasonal, monthly payments may be of unequal amounts.

The date for the initial rental payment should be set forth specifically. The tenant will want the lease to postpone the payment of rent if occupancy is unavailable at the date agreed on. If the landlord has granted rent concessions, the lease should indicate the months which are to be rent free. Part of the concession may come at the beginning of the lease and the remainder at the end.

[¶3502.2] Percentage Rentals

A percentage lease is one that fixes the rental on the basis of a percentage of the tenant's gross income. There are at least four possible types of percentage rentals:

1. Fixed minimum rent with percentage of gross added to minimum.

2. Fixed minimum rent with additional rent based on percentage of gross being payable only after the applicable percentage applying to the gross has earned the minimum.

3. Percentage lease with no minimum.

4. Minimum rent plus the percentage with a maximum rent which the percentage may produce.

Where the percentage is the most important part of the deal, it is usual to have a clause giving the landlord the right to cancel after a specified period of time if the tenant's business fails to attain an agreed upon minimum volume of sales. This minimum volume may be stepped up periodically. The tenant may be given the right to keep the lease in force by paying the rental which would have been produced by the stipulated minimum volume. The tenant also is sometimes given the right to cancel if his volume fails to attain a stated minimum.

The following matters should be covered in the lease:

(a) Definition of "gross receipts." For example, do they include sales taxes collected by the tenant, or sales made by a subtenant or concessionaire of the tenant?

(b) Record of gross receipts. The landlord may want the tenant to record all transactions on a cash register or similar device, and submit a sworn statement weekly or monthly. The landlord may also want the right to examine the register at any time.

(c) Diligent operation. The landlord may want a covenant by the tenant that he will give full time to the operation of the business and not attempt to divert business to a different location.

(d) No partnership. Sharing of profits may be construed to make the landlord a partner of the tenant unless a contrary intention is clearly spelled out in the lease. The landlord, of course, wants to avoid creating a partnership since this would make him liable for any losses of the tenant.

For a form calling for additional rental based on tenant's gross sales see IBP FORMS OF BUSINESS AGREEMENTS.

[¶3502.3] Security Deposits and Advanced Rentals

Here are the main security devices which landlords use to obtain protection against tenant's abandonment of the property or his non-payment of rent or other default.

1. The tenant is required to deposit money or securities with the landlord. Interest may have to be paid to the tenant on this deposit. If the tenant abandons the property or is evicted for a default in rent the lease provision authorizes the landlord to relet the premises and to collect any damages out of this security deposit.

2. The tenant makes a security deposit and the lease provides that the amount so deposited is to be retained by the landlord as liquidated damages if the tenant abandons or defaults.

3. The tenant is required to pay a bonus for obtaining a lease and the landlord is entitled to this money whether or not the tenant fulfills his obligation under the lease. Sometimes the tenant is given credit for this bonus by reduced rentals at the end of the lease term.

4. The lease requires the tenant to pay the last several months' rent in advance. If the tenant abandons the premises or is evicted for default in rent the lease permits the landlord to retain the advance rents.

[¶3502.4] Term of the Lease; Space and Term Options

The tenant's willingness to sign a long-term lease will depend in part on his privilege to increase or decrease the amount of space he must pay for, so that the space and time provisions of the lease should be treated as interrelated obligations.

Usually basic terms of a lease are 5, 10, 15 and 21 or more years. New buildings usually require ten or more. The lessor normally wants as long a lease as he can get; among other things, his ability to obtain financing depends in part on the stability of his rent roll. The tenant may prefer a shorter term, on the theory that as newer buildings are put up, his bargaining position will become stronger. However, if the tenant expects to make expensive alterations, he will want a term long enough to amortize them.

If the tenant is in a position to demand it, he will want a renewal option at the same or a slightly higher rental. At the very least, however, the lessor will demand that the renewal rental cover any increase in real estate taxes and operating costs. For this purpose, an escalator clause may be used.

Cancellation and Additional Space Options — Two common problems for tenants who sign long-term leases are (a) what happens if expected growth fails to occur, and (b) what happens if growth is far greater than anticipated? Both of these can be solved by options, if the lessor will grant them. Under a cancellation option, the tenant has the right at designated periods and upon adequate notice to drop a specified amount of space. Usually a penalty will be payable to the lessor. The additional space option works in a similar manner. At designated periods, the tenant is given the right to lease additional space at a fixed rental.

The landlord should not overlook the benefits to him of these types of options. By means of a cancellation option, he may be able to fill up the building more quickly and with a fewer number of tenants, which simplifies his financing and bookkeeping problems. In many cases, the "normal" 3% growth in white-collar workers will insure that cancellation options are not used. The additional space option is even more beneficial to the landlord. According to some experts, 80% of the tenants who leave well-maintained office buildings do so because they can't obtain additional space in the building. In some cases, a landlord will go so far as to make short-term leases for space adjoining that of his major tenants so that space will be available when and if required by them.

〔¶3502.5〕 The Right to Sublease Space

A provision giving the tenant the right to sublease space (or requiring the lessor to have reasonable cause for refusing his consent) not only will protect the tenant against unexpected developments but is one way to solve the problems of changing space requirements. If the tenant believes he will need less space in the future, a sublease clause can substitute for a cancellation option. If more space will be needed, the tenant can lease it immediately and sublet it during the interval when it isn't required. Sometimes, the lessor himself will agree to be the subtenant; then he has the responsibility of finding someone to occupy the space.

Apart from local variations, there are two basic types of sublease clauses. One is a standard clause contained in the printed form of many commercial leases. This states that the tenant may sublease with the written consent of the landlord. The other modified version of this clause adds that the landlord will not unreasonably withhold his consent.

In leases where the standard form is used, there are few alternatives open to the tenant if the landlord is unwilling to give his consent. Consequently, a tenant signing such a lease should be prepared to remain at the location for the full term; in the event he does wish to move, the landlord is in a position to demand a substantial consideration even though he may already have another tenant ready to move in.

When Is Landlord's Refusal Reasonable? However, even when the modified clause prohibits an unreasonable withholding of consent by the landlord, he may refuse to approve a sublease for a number of reasons not immediately apparent at the time of the original lease. These reasons include:

1. The fact that he is carrying other vacant space in the building and is trying to consolidate both spaces into a single unit to be offered to a single tenant who requires large office area.

2. He believes that the space in his building is worth more than the original tenant is paying under his lease and since the owner is not carrying it vacant he decides that he will rent it only at a higher rental rather than permit a sublease at the same rental.

3. The proposed subtenant may not be as desirable from the point of view of prestige of the building as the original tenant.

4. If the original tenant has not yet signed his lease for new space, the landlord may believe that he can prevent him from doing this by advising him that he will not give him his written consent for subletting.

267

〔¶3502.6〕   Taking Over an Existing Lease; the "Back-to-Back" Lease

In some cities, the competition for tenants will force the lessor to offer to take over the unexpired term of an existing lease in order to rent space. If such a concession has been offered, the lessor's obligations should be spelled out in the new lease. If the lessor already has found a subtenant for the old space, the lease should specify any obligation on his part if the subtenant defaults on the sublease.

Parties who enter into such a "back-to-back" lease should be aware of the problems involved. One is that the landlord under the existing lease will very often have no incentive to make alterations when he already has a signed lease for the space. So this will deter a prospective new subtenant. Sometimes the lessee may be persuaded to make a contribution towards alterations of its present space to conform to the requirements of its prospective subtenant. If not, the lessor must make a careful analysis of the space so that he can show a prospective subtenant that a move would require little or no alterations.

Another problem presented by "back-to-back" leasing is the reluctance of prospective subtenants to negotiate for space occupied by a tenant who has not signed a lease for other quarters in another building. It is not infrequent to find both the sub-landlord (the original tenant) and the subtenant in agreement and ready to execute a sublease only to discover that the new space for the proposed sub-landlord has already been leased to someone else during the time that the sub-landlord was seeking to obtain a subtenant.

Try to avoid this situation by keeping the owner of the new building informed of what is going on. The full leasing negotiations can be simultaneously planned and executed. There also can be a simultaneous closing arranged involving the two tenants and the owners of both the new and the old buildings.

〔¶3502.7〕   Appurtenances

In a commercial lease, the tenant frequently is given rights in addition to the right to the demised premises. For example, he may have the right to use parking space, railroad sidings, unloading and storage facilities. These should be detailed in the lease. Any right to place signs on the property or put advertising on building walls also should be stated. These rights are particularly important in shopping centers because of the large amount of common space.

〔¶3502.8〕   Restrictive Covenant by Lessor

A commercial tenant will want the landlord's covenant that he will not rent other space on the premises to a competitive business. The landlord's agreement will depend on the relative bargaining strength of the parties, whether the landlord is receiving a percentage rental, and how restrictively the covenant is drawn. For example, the landlord may grant the tenant an exclusive right only as to goods of a certain price range.

[¶3502.9] **Restrictive Covenant by Lessee**

The landlord may insist that the tenant restrict his business to specified areas. This may be done by either a "purpose and use" clause or by an "exclusion" clause. The first of these limits the tenant to the uses spelled out in the lease. The second one lists certain areas which are prohibited to the tenant.

[¶3502.10] **Who Is to Make Alterations?**

The alteration clause is very important and should cover a number of points. If the lessor is to make alterations for the tenant, these should be spelled out in detail and quality specifications should be included where relevant. The obligation to pay rent should be conditioned on these alterations, so that the tenant need not move in until they are made.

Alterations made by the tenant are usually subject to the lessor's consent. Potential disputes can be reduced if a list of approved alterations is included in the lease. Denial of consent for future alterations should require reasonable cause for the lessor's objections. In addition, the lessor may agree that certain minor types of alterations can be made at any time without consent.

Finally, the lease should provide for disposition of any fixtures attached or affixed to the premises by the tenant. The standard lease provides that all alterations shall be the property of the lessor unless he elects otherwise, and if he does elect otherwise, the tenant is responsible for removing them (and restoring the space to its original condition). The tenant may seek to modify this clause to provide (a) that the tenant may take specified fixtures when he vacates or (b) that the tenant need not remove specified alterations when he vacates because of the expense involved.

[¶3502.11] **Repairs**

Another area where the tenant may be taking on unexpectedly burdensome obligations is in the area of repairs. Naturally, the tenant should be responsible for its own neglect, or that of its employees, etc., and tenant should be covered by insurance. But the repair clause in most standard leases makes the tenant responsible for damage from air conditioning unit or system (without distinguishing whether the air conditioning was the landlord's or the tenant's), short circuits, flow or leakage of water, steam, illuminating gas, sewer gas, sewerage or odors, frost, bursting or leaking of pipes or plumbing works or gas, or from any other cause of any kind or nature whatsoever due to its carelessness, neglect, etc. This may be all well and good where the tenant is in possession of the entire building, but a tenant might properly consider the clause too broad where it merely occupies a part of a building which is under the control of the landlord.

The tenant might well hold out for a clause providing that the tenant is only obligated to make repairs where damage results from a misuse of the property by it. All other repairs should be made by the landlord.

[¶3502.12] Subordination of Lease to Mortgage

Subordination clauses usually provide a blanket subordination of the lease to any future underlying mortgage or any future underlying lease. This may be all right if the future mortgage is placed with a lending institution. But a private individual may toss out all of the tenants if he forecloses. Therefore, a tenant might try to have his clause provide that the lease will be subordinated only if the holder of any future lease or mortgage shall agree that the lease will not be terminated or otherwise affected by an enforcement of such mortgage or lease as long as the tenant is not in default. If he can't get that type of clause, the tenant might try to limit subordination to mortgages placed with lending institutions.

Before signing the lease, the tenant should try to get a non-disturbance agreement from the holder of any existing mortgages or underlying leases.

[¶3502.13] Destruction or Condemnation of Premises

If the premises are completely destroyed, landlord has the option of rebuilding but, in the usual standard lease form, within 90 days of the casualty he may notify the tenant that he will not rebuild. At this point the lease will come to an end. But tenant is given no option to cancel his lease even though the remaining period may be short and it would be more practical for the tenant to permanently relocate elsewhere. Nor does the clause usually spell out tenant's rent obligation adequately during the period between the destruction of the premises and its restoration.

Several things can be done to improve this clause from the tenant's point of view. For one thing, you can provide that the landlord's insurance policies cover all possible causes of destruction and that the landlord will look to his insurer in the event of destruction of the premises. The tenant will want no distinction to be made as to whose neglect may have caused the destruction. And in the event of a total destruction of the premises, the tenant will want an option to cancel the lease if the destruction occurs during the last few years of the term. The tenant may also try to keep the period during which the landlord has the option to cancel relatively short, about 30 days rather than the usual 90.

As far as condemnation is concerned, the landlord will ordinarily want a clause entitling him to the full condemnation award. A tenant who plans to make substantial improvements and who is in a strong bargaining position may be able to modify this so as to give him some reimbursement for his investment. Otherwise, a tenant can only try to ascertain if there is any risk of condemnation during the term of the lease.

[¶3502.14] Other Items in Office Leases

In addition to the foregoing, the following items should be considered for inclusion in an office lease:

(1) What is the amount of usable space? The rent will be based upon a square foot rate; the rate may be quoted on a rentable or a usable area. Rentable space means the actual office area, plus a share proportionate to this space of facilities and corridors which service the floor on which the office is located. This concept is used in most new buildings. Usable space is the actual space located within the walls of the office and excludes any part of the service facilities. It is important to keep this distinction in mind when comparing the rents for different buildings.

(2) Who pays the broker's commission? Although the broker has been working for the tenant, his fee is ordinarily paid by the lessor. One exception to this is where the broker has rendered special services to the tenant, and in this event, the tenant will normally have agreed to payment in advance. The lease should reflect these obligations.

(3) Has the lessor's insurance carrier waived its subrogation right? This is one clause which could end up saving the tenant a lot of money. If a fire occurs in the building which is due in some manner to the negligence of the tenant or its employees, the lessor's insurance carrier will have the right to sue the tenant (which it may not choose to exercise). However, by this clause the carrier agrees in advance that it will not seek reimbursement from the tenant if such event occurs. While not a standard clause, it normally will be included if the tenant asks for it.

(4) On what basis is electric current to be paid? The tenant will pay for his electric current. However, the cost of it can be computed in two different ways. Sometimes, a flat rate is added to the monthly rental, and sometimes each office is provided with its own meter and charged only for electric current consumed there. The tenant should be aware of the system used.

(5) What building services will be provided? In an office building, the landlord normally provides all maintenance services, including elevator service, air conditioning, restroom maintenance, etc. If the tenant expects to use the office

at odd hours, he should be sure an elevator will be in operation at those times. Air conditioning should be provided on specified days and during specified hours; the landlord may require the tenant to pay for overtime use. Many new buildings now have parking space available underneath or on top of the building; the tenant's right to use this space and the cost of it should be spelled out.

(6) Is there a "most-favored tenant" clause? If a tenant moves into a new building that is only partially filled, he may demand a clause in the lease that will give him the benefits of any rental concessions that the landlord may subsequently make in order to obtain tenants.

[¶3503]   LEGAL CONSEQUENCES OF THE
                LANDLORD-TENANT RELATIONSHIP IN THE
                        ABSENCE OF AGREEMENT

A lease is a contract and the parties to it can insert any provisions they wish (with some exceptions) to govern their relationship. But sometimes a tenant will occupy property without entering into any formal agreement with the landlord. And even a comprehensive lease may leave certain matters to be governed by statutory and common-law rules. While these rules may differ considerably in detail in the various jurisdictions, there is general similarity in the legal principles applied. Among the important areas are the following:

1. Periodic Tenancies: If a tenant occupies property without any agreement as to term, he will be deemed to be a periodic tenant for a period measured by the rental payments. Thus if rent is paid weekly, the tenancy is week-to-week; if monthly, month-to-month. The important distinction between a periodic tenancy and one for a fixed term relates to their termination. A tenancy for a fixed term ends automatically at the end of the term without the necessity for notice by either party. A periodic tenancy continues until one party gives notice of termination. The amount of notice varies between jurisdictions but it may range from seven to 30 days. In addition, the date of termination must coincide exactly with the end of the period which measures the tenancy. A notice ending a month-to-month tenancy must specify the final day of the month.

A written lease which for some reason is void may convert the tenancy into a periodic one. Since many leases make the payment of rent an annual obligation (payable in monthly installments for the benefit of the tenant), the period will become year-to-year. As a result, if neither party gives the required notice prior to the end of the term stated in the lease, either party may hold the other to a further one-year term.

2. Holdovers: In states which have not changed the common-law rule by statute, a tenant who holds over (remains in possession) after the expiration of the lease term may be held by the landlord for a further term of one year (the tenant has no reciprocal right to hold the landlord). The landlord, of course, also may evict the tenant. The hold-over rule is a harsh one and the courts will often refuse to apply it if they find the tenant was unable to move for compelling reasons (such as illness) or if the landlord impliedly consented to the holding over for a shorter period of time. For example, if the parties are actively negotiating a new lease when the old lease expires, the tenant will usually be considered as a month-to-month tenant. In addition, the parties may agree in the original lease that holding over will not convert the tenancy into one year-to-year.

3. Actual Possession: A lease frequently is silent about the landlord's duty to deliver actual (as opposed to legal) possession of the premises at the commencement of the lease. In such case, the states are divided as to whether the landlord or the new tenant has the duty of evicting the holdover tenant.

4. Defective Premises: Generally, a tenant takes the premises as is in the absence of any representations or covenants by the landlord in the lease. (Two exceptions to this are concealed defects and rental of a furnished residence for a short period.) This places the burden of examining the premises on the tenant. Once the tenant takes possession, the duty to repair various portions of the premises depends on which party is in control of them. In a multi-tenant structure, the landlord usually is responsible for all the common areas, such as stairways, halls, yards, etc., while the tenant is responsible for the area under his direct control. This rule is frequently changed by statutes which impose a greater duty on the landlord, particularly in apartment buildings.

5. Consequences of Failure to Repair: Frequently a lease will specify which party has the duty to repair the premises but will not indicate what the other party may do if the duty is breached. In most jurisdictions, if the landlord fails in his duty to repair, the tenant has several alternatives. He may make the repairs himself and deduct the cost from the rent; he may pay the rent and sue the landlord for the decrease in rental value; or he may pay a lesser rental due to the decreased value of the premises. If the tenant is injured by the landlord's failure to repair, there is a split as to whether the landlord is liable for the injuries. The states that hold no liability do so on the theory that the tenant had the duty to make the repairs and then seek to recover the cost from the landlord.

Where a defective condition exists in an area over which the landlord does not retain control, the landlord's duty to repair (if it exists) depends on prior notice of the defective condition. Since this is invariably a matter of dispute between the parties, such notice should always be in writing.

6. Constructive Eviction: An eviction by the landlord or one having rights superior to the landlord's terminates the tenant's obligation to pay rent. But most disputes about eviction deal with constructive rather than actual eviction. A constructive eviction takes place when the premises become uninhabitable due to the landlord's failure to repair or otherwise maintain the premises. However, the condition must be more than a merely inconvenient one. Cutting off heat in the winter would be a constructive eviction whereas a noisy plumbing system normally would not be. The tenant must actually move out of the premises if he claims a constructive eviction. However, he may remain a reasonable time in order to find new quarters or in reliance on the landlord's promise to remedy the condition.

[¶3504]   INCOME TAX CHECKLIST FOR LESSORS AND LESSEES

Type of Payment	Effect on Landlord	Effect on Tenant
Advance Rent and Bonus Payments by Tenant		
Advance rent to be applied to a later period	Taxable when received	Deductions prorated over term of lease
Bonus to secure lease	Taxable when received	Deductions prorated over term of lease
Security Deposit	Taxable when obligation to repay tenant is terminated and it is applied as rent	Deduction when landlord may apply it as rent
Payment by Tenant of Various Landlord's Costs		
Real estate taxes, interest, mortgage amortization payments, insurance and operating costs	Treated as rent; taxable when received	Deductible as rent
Payment of Costs of Capital Improvements		
By Landlord		
If construction is not called for in lease	Depreciation deductible over life of property	No depreciation allowed
If tenant agrees to restore property to original condition at end of lease	No depreciation allowed during period tenant is in possession	No depreciation allowed

Type of Payment	Effect on Landlord	Effect on Tenant
Payment of Costs of Capital Improvements		
By Tenant		
With title to pass to the landlord at end of lease	No depreciation allowed —increased value not taxed as income at end of lease	Depreciation deducted over life of improvement or term of original lease, whichever is shorter.
If payments are considered part of rent	Treated as rent; taxable when received	Deductible as rent
If he keeps title to improvements and may remove them at end of lease	No depreciation	Depreciation deducted over life of improvement
If he must restore leased property to original condition at end of lease	No effect	Cost of restoration deductible in year it is paid or incurred
Alterations by Landlord for Particular Tenant		
Made to obtain tenant and have no value at end of lease	Deductible over lease term	No effect
Building demolished to secure tenant	Cost of building deductible over lease term	No effect
Commissions and Fees		
By Landlord		
To brokers and attorneys on making the lease	Deductible over term of lease	No effect
Unamortized amount of commissions and fees when lease is cancelled	Deductible in year of cancellation	No effect
Commissions for rent collection and management	Deductible in year paid	No effect
By Tenant		
To broker to obtain lease	No effect	Deductible over term of lease
Payments to Cancel Lease		
By Landlord		
If he needs lease to sell property	Add to cost of property	Taxable in year received
In order to erect new building	Add to cost of new building	Taxable in year received
To get property for own use or for rental to another party	Spread over remaining period of old lease	Taxable in year received

275

Type of Payment	Effect on Landlord	Effect on Tenant
Payments to Cancel Lease		
By Tenant		
If made to get a renewal or another change in lease	Taxable when received	Amortize cost over life of lease
If not made for above purpose	Taxable when received	Deductible as an expense in year of payment
Purchase of leasehold by tenant	Taxable when received	Amortize the amount paid over the remaining life of the lease

[¶3505]   CHECKLIST FOR LEASE CLOSINGS

Depending on what the lease provides, the appropriate party should have:

Adequate copies of the lease ready for signing.

Bill of sale for personalty.

Title abstracts, certificates, guarantees and affidavits of title.

Appropriate surveys, maps and diagrams.

Insurance policies and assignments.

Mortgage data—terms, status and consents.

Receipts for taxes, assessments and water bills.

Service and maintenance contracts—terms, status and notices.

Certificates of occupancy and inspection from government agencies.

Utility, fuel and other bills to be prorated.

Subordinate leases, tenants' estoppel certificates and data on security deposits.

Consents for alterations and repairs.

Keys to the premises.

Receipts for money and documents delivered to lessor and / or lessee.

All spouses and others whose signatures are essential to the transaction.

Corporate resolutions, powers of attorney or other authorizations.

Notarial service.

Cash or certified check for rent, security and adjustments.

●

For Further Reference . . .

American Jurisprudence, Landlord and Tenant.

Forms of Business Agreements looseleaf Service, Institute for Business Planning, Englewood Cliffs, N.J.

Real Estate Investment Planning (looseleaf service), Institute for Business Planning, Englewood Cliffs, N.J.

LEGAL FEES AND THEIR DEDUCTIBILITY

〔¶3601〕 Legal fees are deductible if they are ordinary and necessary expenses of carrying on a trade or business (§162). In the case of individuals only, a deduction is also allowed for legal expenses paid or incurred for the production or collection of income, for the management, conservation, or maintenance of property held for the production of income, or in connection with the determination, collection, or refund of any tax. These last categories of expenses are generally known as "nonbusiness expenses" (§212).

〔¶3601.1〕 General Rules

Superimposed on these specific statutory rules are certain general rules. Legal expenses incurred in connection with personal, living or family matters are not deductible (§262). Neither are legal fees incurred in connection with capital expenditures (§263), except as they are capitalized as part of the cost and depreciated or applied to reduce gain on a sale. In the case of personal expenditures, the classifications are mutually exclusive; personal expenditures cannot be ordinary and necessary business expenses.

〔¶3601.2〕 Capital Expenses

An expense can be ordinary and necessary, however, and yet still be nondeductible in whole or in part because it is a capital expense. Where a fee is not deductible because it is a capital expense, it is added to cost. Where connected with the purchase of a property, it can be recovered over the life of the property through depreciation or amortization. Where not attributable to a specific item, it generally cannot be recovered until the asset is finally disposed of. In the case of real property, legal fees are usually offset against the purchase price or the proceeds of the sale.

〔¶3601.3〕 Public Policy

Legal expenses are not deductible where the deduction would frustrate sharply defined national or state policies. However, there must be a governmental declaration of the policy (*Lilly,* 343 US 90) and the mere fact that a business is illegal will not bar the deduction (*Sullivan,* 356 US 27). Moreover, where the governmental authority observes its stated policy in the breach, for example, by imposing a black market tax and requiring sales tax permits on a prohibited business, the stated policy is blurred to the point where it will not bar a deduction (*Stacy,* D.C. Miss., TIR 601). No public policy is violated where an attorney is engaged to defend a criminal action. Legal fees in an unsuccessful action are therefore deductible (*Tellier,* 383 US 687).

[¶3601.4]   **Allocation**

Where a fee falls into more than one of the categories described above, it is important to allocate the fee to the various aspects of the transaction on a reasonable basis. The attorney should show the allocation on his bill. This can be done based on the time spent on the respective matters, upon the relative complexity of the problems involved, or some other charge method which will stand up.

Allocation may also be required where services are rendered so as to benefit more than one taxpayer or confer a benefit on another interested party where the fee is charged entirely to one person. Other areas calling for allocation involve the separation of general legal advice from tax advice involving the same transaction, the allocation of a fee between taxable and nontaxable income, and the allocation of a portion of a fee to the interest portion of a recovery.

[¶3601.5]   **Time for Deduction**

Cash basis taxpayers deduct legal fees only in the year when paid. Taxpayers on an accrual basis deduct their legal fees in the year in which the bill is sent and they cannot accrue the expense in the year in which the services are rendered if the bill has not been sent (*Cold Metal Process Company,* 17 TC 916). Where a client wishes a deduction in one year, it is vital for the attorney to send out his bills before the end of that year. This is particularly true with respect to corporations, most of which are on an accrual basis.

[¶3602]   **DEDUCTIBILITY OF SPECIFIC TYPES OF LEGAL FEES**

The deductibility of specific types of legal fees is outlined below in checklist form.

Organizing a Business: The cost of setting up a business is a capital expense and is not deductible currently. This includes the cost of organizing a partnership or forming a corporation. A corporation, however, may elect to amortize organizational expenditures over a period of not less than five years beginning with the month in which the corporation begins business (§248). This would include fees in connection with drafting of the charter and by-laws, and minutes of various organizational meetings. Legal fees in connection with the issuance or sale of stock or the transfer of assets to the corporation are not subject to the amortization election. On dissolution, fees connected with organizational expenditures which have not been amortized may be deducted as a loss (*Malta Temple Association,* 16 BTA 409, acq.).

Corporate Reorganizations: Legal expenses in connection with a corporate reorganization are not deductible regardless of whether the reorganization was accomplished by means of recapitalization, consolidation, merger or bankruptcy reorganization. They are capital expenses and may be deductible on dissolution. Where a new corporation results from the reorganization, the portion of the legal fee attributable to this aspect of the transaction may be subject to the amortization election (Reg. §1.248-1(b)(3)). In the case of a disappearing corporation, legal fees consisting of undeducted organizational expenditures are not yet deductible as a loss until the surviving corporation is also dissolved. At that time, both the undeductible organizational expenditures and perhaps the nondeductible reorganization expenses of both corporations may be deductible.

Abandoned Reorganizations: The legal costs of investigating the possibility of mergers and other forms of reorganizations are deductible where the plans are abandoned and the reorganization does not in fact take place (*Sibley, Lindsay & Curr,* 15 TC 106). Even where a reorganization does take place, if several plans or possibilities have been explored, it should be possible to allocate a portion of the fee to the reorganization which went through and the balance to the deductible abandoned activities.

Liquidations and Dissolutions: The legal expenses incurred in connection with the liquidation of a corporation or the dissolution of a partnership are generally deductible. In addition, where a corporation is completely liquidated into its parent, it may be possible for the disappearing subsidiary to deduct its undeducted organization expenses. However, in this situation, the subsidiary corporation should be prepared to show that the legal fees were incurred on its behalf and not on behalf of the surviving parent (*Standard Linen Service,* 33 TC 1, acq.).

Business Operations: Legal fees incurred by a business in its normal day-to-day operations are generally deductible subject to the general rules above. Among these would fall preparing contracts, collecting debts, general advice, supervising meetings, preparing minutes, and the setting up of pension and profit-sharing trusts and other employee benefit programs.

Licenses and Franchises: Legal fees incurred in connection with a successful application for a license or franchise are nondeductible capital expenditures. They may be amortizable over the term of the franchise. Where the application is unsuccessful, it would seem that the legal fees could be written off as an abandonment. Where an individual rather than a corporation is involved, and the denial of his application prevents him from starting a business, the deduction would seem to be less certain unless he can show that it was a transaction entered into for profit.

Corporate Management and Control: The expenses relative to obtaining control of a corporation are considered capital expenditures and are, therefore, not deductible (*J. Crowley v. Comm.,* 89 F.2d 715). However, the conduct or defense of a lawsuit by a corporate officer for the purpose of keeping his job entails legal fees which are deductible as a business expense (*E. Potter,* 20 BTA 252, *non acq.*). Also deductible are fees paid by a corporate director to defend himself against the charge of malfeasance (*Hochschild,* 161 F.2d 817).

Acquiring Property: Legal fees incurred in connection with the acquisition of property must be capitalized where the property has a useful life of more than one year. They are capital expenditures, treated as part of cost, and recoverable through depreciation or in reduction of the selling price on final disposition.

Perfection and Defense of Title: Under the so-called "defense of title" rule, legal expenses incurred to perfect or defend title or to recover property must be capitalized as additional cost. The rule does not apply and expenses are deductible currently where the right to income is involved as in the case of interest, dividends, rents, royalties, unpaid salaries, or trust income. Also, where the title question is only incidental to a major question the deduction will be allowed where the major issue would permit it. And in the case of a nuisance suit which is without foundation, the current deduction is allowed even though title is involved.

Condemnation and Involuntary Conversions: Attorney's fees incurred in connection with condemnation cases are treated as capital expenditures and are not currently deductible except to the extent allocable to interest on the award. Where the fees are incurred in connection with a claim against an insurer or wrongdoer for the value of property involuntarily converted (i.e., fire), there is a conflict in the cases.

Torts and Damage Suits: Legal fees incurred in defense of an action in tort or contract or for equitable relief are deductible where the claim arose out of the taxpayer's trade or business (for example, malpractice cases or claims arising out of the negligent act of an employee within the scope of his employment). In the case of an individual, they may also be deductible as "nonbusiness expenses." Fees incurred by plaintiffs are generally deductible if the recovery will be business income when collected. In libel cases, legal fees are deductible by the plaintiff if the suit is related to the taxpayer's trade or business reputation rather than his personal reputation. Even where only personal reputation is involved, a portion of the fees attributable to punitive damages which are taxable income may be deductible.

Accountings: Legal expenses incurred by either party to an action for an accounting are deductible business expenses.

Criminal Charges and Statutory Violations: Legal fees incurred in defense of a criminal charge are deductible if the defendant is successful. If the defense is unsuccessful, no deduction is allowed. However, where the charge is not strictly a criminal one, and the business is a legal one, the legal fees incurred in defense of such charges are normally deductible, whether or not the defense is successful (*Heininger,* 320 US 467). IRS still denies the deduction for attorney's fees in connection with an unsuccessful defense of criminal antitrust cases (*Rev. Rul. 62-175,* CB 1962-2, 50). However, fees incurred in connection with an alleged violation of state antitrust laws have been held deductible (*Long-Horn Portland Cement Company,* 148 F.2d 276).

Marital Matters: Generally attorney's fees and other costs paid in connection with a divorce, separation, or support decree are not deductible by the defendant husband (*Patrick Gilmore,* 372 US 39). This is the rule even though the defendant's income-producing property is involved. However, a wife's action for back alimony is considered one for the collection of income, and accordingly legal fees are deductible (*Elliot,* 40 TC 304). And the Tax Court has permitted a deduction to a wife for the legal expenses allocable to obtaining alimony (*Wild,* 42 TC 706). In this case, the attorney's bill divided his fee between the divorce proceeding and the efforts to obtain alimony. However, expenses incurred by a woman in attempting to renegotiate a divorce and property settlement are not deductible (*Neil,* 42 TC 793). No alimony claim was involved.

Fiduciary Expenses: Attorney's fees paid by an executor, administrator or trustee for assistance in the performance of fiduciary duties are generally deductible. Amounts paid in defense of a mismanagement suit are deductible where the trustee is in the business of being a trustee (*Abbott,* 38 BTA 1290) but apparently not by the one-time trustee (*Fayen,* 34 TC 630). There appears to be a liberalizing trend in the Second Circuit (*Ditmars,* 302 F.2d 481) which would apply the same standards to "nonbusiness expenses" as to trade or business expenses (*Bingham's Trust,* 325 US 365). If this trend holds up, the one-time trustee may yet get the deduction.

Investment Expenses: These are the "nonbusiness expenses" described above. They are deductible without regard to current income as long as the property is held for the production of income. Legal fees in connection with advice to a stockholder in that capacity as to his rights or on how to protect his investment are deductible currently. However, many stockholder expenses are nondeductible because capital in nature (i.e., obtaining control or perfecting title).

Estate Planning: Traditional estate planning legal fees, such as for drawing wills and trusts and advice concerning gifts, have been held to be personal in nature and nondeductible. However, where all or a portion of the fee can be allocated to "nonbusiness expenses," it should be possible to deduct a proportionate part of the overall fee. For example, although most trusts would appear not to qualify, a trust created to provide expert management of an income-producing property should qualify under §212. And where part of the fee can be properly allocated to tax advice, it may be possible to deduct that portion (*Davis*, 287 F.2d 168).

Tax Advice: Fees for tax advice in connection with a trade or business are deductible, subject to the general rules. However, one court required a corporation to capitalize a legal expense for tax advice in connection with a particular sale of property where the services were directly related to and only to the sale (*Suckow Borax Mines*, 12 TCM 786). Individuals are permitted to deduct by statute (§212(3)), as a "nonbusiness expense," legal fees in connection with the determination, collection or refund of any tax. Reg. §1.212-1(a) extends the deduction to cover fees for tax counsel or in connection with the preparation of returns. How far this can be carried is uncertain. The Court of Claims (*Davis*, 287 F.2d 168) has permitted a deduction to a husband for a portion of the legal fees in a matrimonial matter which were allocated to the husband's tax advice while denying the deduction to the extent attributable to tax advice to the wife for which the husband was required to pay.

Tax-Exempt Income: Legal fees in connection with the collection of tax-exempt income, such as the proceeds of an insurance policy, are not deductible (*National Engraving Company*, 3 TC 178; §265).

•

For Further Reference . . .
Real Estate Desk Book, Institute for Business Planning, Englewood Cliffs, N.J.
Tax Planning looseleaf Service. Institute for Business Planning, Englewood Cliffs, N.J.

LITERARY AND ARTISTIC PROPERTY

[¶3701] The lawyer will deal with this kind of problem when he represents a writer, an artist, an entertainer, or a publisher, movie producer, radio or television producer, or a packager or broadcaster of programs. Photographers, art dealers, museums, composers, musicians, recording companies may bring him the same kind of problems.

Usually, the problem will be working out the legal arrangements for the most effective exploitation of and the most fully protected rights to a literary or artistic creation, a play, a movie, or a program. He will be dealing with copyright, statutory or common law, the right of privacy, the right to be protected against the unfair appropriation of a title or an identity into which value has been built. He will be grappling with trade and legal practices which have developed in the publishing and entertainment worlds, the past and future services of talent, the opportunity and the right to carve up a literary work and exploit it through book, play, movie, serialization, magazine articles, radio and television dramatization.

To get a clear title to a property of this kind, it is necessary to clear claims of the following character:

1. Copyright — common law or statutory.

2. Right of privacy of any character, actor, or other person involved.

3. The right to compensation for the idea which any person may have.

4. The right to the good will and publicity which someone else may have built into the title or a character which is critical to the presentation.

5. Over and above the rights flowing from a common-law or statutory copyright obtainable in the United States, there are rights under the moral rights clause (MRC) of the Berne Copyright Union which many United States citizens try to get by copyrighting in Canada. This gives an author the right to control publication or presentation of his work, including even whether it shall be published, the right to modify the work and to withdraw it from circulation. He also has the right to have his name on the work, to prevent an alteration and the use of his name, and to prevent the use of his name in connection with the work of others. When he changes his philosophy, he even has the right to require that the work be changed to reflect his new philosophy. These rights cannot be sold or assigned. They may prevent a publisher or producer from changing plays and novels from tragedy to melodrama, inserting scenes which the author thinks harmful to his reputation, etc. One court, for example, held that the publisher of Igor Stravinsky did not have the right to authorize Warner Brothers to insert four minutes of his music in a movie. Stravinsky was upheld in claiming that his music was used as the motif of the movie and that he had the right to stop it under the moral rights clause of the Berne Convention.

[¶3702]   COMMON-LAW COPYRIGHT

Entirely apart from the Federal statutes, the creator of literary material has the exclusive right to make use of it. This common-law copyright is, however, valid only until the material has been published. It exists by mere fact of creation and evaporates by mere act of publication. When the work is offered for public distribution, unless statutory copyright is obtained, it will fall into the public domain and be available for anyone to use. A work may be given some distribution without losing the common-law copyright. A manuscript can be circulated among potential buyers or a limited number of copies may even be printed and circulated to a specific group. A play or a musical composition can be publicly performed. However, as soon as the work is offered to the general public, the common-law copyright is lost.

Common-law copyright is in some respects better than a statutory copyright. It is perpetual. It can be bequeathed to anyone, while surviving spouse or children have a claim on renewal of a statutory copyright.

[¶3703]   STATUTORY COPYRIGHT

Statutory copyright law protects books, periodicals, newspapers, lectures, sermons, addresses (prepared for oral delivery), dramatic or dramatico-musical compositions, musical compositions, maps, or works of art, models or designs for works of art, reproductions of a work of art, drawings or plastic works of a scientific or technical character, photographs, prints and pictorial illustrations including prints or labels used for articles of merchandise, and motion pictures. (See 17 U.S.C.A. §5.) All works to be copyrightable must be original with the author. They don't have to be new to the world or novel. The standard of originality required is not very high, but must rise above mere triviality. A published work is copyrighted by the mere fact of publication and the proper copyright notice.

To get a copyright, these steps must be taken: (1) publication, (2) notice, or mark on the published work to indicate the copyright as required by Sec. 19 of the copyright law, (3) deposit of 2 copies of the work (or photos if copies are impractical), (4) filing of a claim of copyright on forms which the Register of Copyrights in Washington makes available and (5) payment of the nominal fee, usually $4.

A statutory copyright has these advantages:

1. In an action on a statutory copyright, the owner can recover counsel fees from an infringer.

2. The importation of unauthorized copies is prohibited by Federal law.

3. The required filing affords a clear method for an author to prove his claim if anyone alleges an infringement. The owner of a common-law copyright must resort to sending a copy by registered mail and having the envelope unopened

or filing a copy with some kind of registry system such as that set up by the Authors League of America.

[¶3703.1] Renewal of Copyright

The United States copyright is for an original 28-year period with another renewal period of 28 years. A copyright must be renewed within the 28th year after the date of copyright. An application made one day earlier or one day later will result in loss of the protection for the 28-year renewal period. If an author is alive, he may renew it. If he dies before a renewal application is filed, his widow or children may renew it. If he dies without surviving spouse or child, then the copyright can be renewed by the executor of his estate. If an author dies without a will, his next of kin may renew. If the author is alive and has granted all the rights for a renewal term to a publisher, the publisher cannot renew the copyright in his own name, but he is entitled to an assignment of the copyright or the author can be considered to hold the renewal copyright in trust for the publisher. If the author is dead and the copyright is renewed by one of the children, the child who obtained the renewal holds it in trust for the others and can contractually be put in the position where he is holding it in trust for the publisher and getting the proceeds in trust for the author's other children.

[¶3704]   PROTECTION THE COPYRIGHT AFFORDS

A copyright protects only the embodiment of an idea—not the idea itself. To get its protection, the work must be the independent creation of the author. It protects him against anyone else copying his work. It doesn't protect him against someone who might independently produce a similar work or even an identical work. Similarity places upon the author of the second work to be published the burden of establishing originality. This might be an impossible burden for the author of an identical work. The question of originality becomes difficult when two works, as so often happens, stem from a common source which was in the public domain. In this case, anything coming from the common source is not protected but any substantial use of original details found in the first adaptation could be the basis for an infringement suit. To sustain infringement, it is necessary to establish that the second writer developed the unprotected theme in the same way and not independently but by copying from the adaptation which is afforded current copyright protection.

The copyright owner has the exclusive right to print, publish, copy, and sell the work; he has the right to perform dramatizations and compositions publicly for profit.

【¶3704.1】 Fair Use

"Fair use" may be made of copyrighted material by persons other than the copyright owner. This is an exception which the courts have developed to promote scholarship and the diffusion of knowledge. What constitutes fair use has to be determined by a court, measuring the desirability of protecting a copyright owner and the desirability of facilitating research and scholarship. The court looks at the nature of the selections made, the objective in using them, the quantity and value of the materials used, and the degree in which the use of copyrighted material may prejudice the sale, diminish the profits, or supersede the objectives of the original work. Thus a stricter test will be applied to a work prepared for entertainment than for a work of scholarship. The test is frequently whether the use made of another copyrighted work is likely to make the second work a substitute for the original one. There is no quantitative measure. The courts use the language "incidental" or "insubstantial" to describe the use which is permissible and "substantial" to describe the use which is not permissible without explicit permission. Giving the copyright owner credit does not make the use of copyrighted material fair. The only value it may have is that of mitigating the willful character of a taking. An extensive condensation of a work would not be a fair use; but the use of a few lines in the middle of another work by way of reference or authority will probably be found not to impair the sale of the work from which the quotation is taken; and if it had a significant objective in furthering the purpose of the work in which it was used, it would probably be considered to constitute a "fair use." Acknowledgement may also be persuasive — that the use had a legitimate purpose and should therefore be protected by the fair-use doctrine.

【¶3704.2】 Parody and Burlesque

The parody and burlesque of copyrighted material may sometimes be protected by the "fair use" doctrine. The determination of what constitutes "fair use" will be made less strictly where the purpose is to amuse or spoof than in a serious work. Parody and burlesque will usually be safe if it is not repetitive of the entire story which is protected, is confined to an incident or character, or possibly some small amount of dialogue. Parody can safely be made of locale, theme, setting, situation, and even bare basic plots, since only the development and mode of expression are ordinarily protectable.

【¶3705】   INFRINGEMENT ACTION

To maintain an action for an infringement, it is necessary to prove that the alleged offender had access to the work of the copyright owner. Access is frequently presumed from public performance and public distribution. Submission of a manuscript to a publisher has been accepted as the basis for finding a publisher or one of his other authors had access to a work. That's why many publishers, movie and broadcasting producers will not even open unsolicited manuscripts. Compilers and translators frequently insert fictitious names or additional lines or make transpositions in order to nail anyone who takes over their work. The Copyright Act provides minimum damages which the court may award for various types of infringements. Lower damages may be awarded in the case of innocent infringement. Once an infringer, however, is notified of a claim that an infringement exists if he continues to use the material, he will lose the benefit of the limitation on damages provided by copyright law for some classes of innocent infringement. The law provides that damages extend to the harm which the copyright owner may have suffered from the infringement as well as all the profits which the infringer has made. Thus whenever a claim of infringement is made, it is necessary for the person against whom it is made — publisher and author — to decide whether to withdraw the work from circulation or give up his standing as an innocent infringer and stand subject to all the possible damages provided for by the copyright law. Printers and booksellers may be found equally liable for infringement with publishers and authors. As a practical matter, they are rarely named in infringement actions.

[¶3706] PROTECTION OF TITLES AND CHARACTERS

A title, a slogan, an idea, a character cannot be protected by copyright. However, equitable protection is afforded by the law of unfair competition. In using a title it is important to be satisfied that someone else will not be able to make claims against the use. To be protectable under the law of unfair competition, a title must have acquired a secondary meaning. That means that the name or title has acquired new and independent significance as an attribution of the work which it has been used to describe. Secondary meaning is acquired only when the title has become popularized by advertising and publicity so that in the public mind, it has come to mean the work with which it is associated. Once such secondary meaning has been acquired, the owner of the work can protect the name or title against other users. Thus, a title will be safe if no other work having a high degree of popularity is currently carrying it or if it has been used frequently.

To gain protection for a name, a title, or a character, it is necessary to extensively popularize and promote the title or name and to identify it with a particular work by performance, advertising, publicity, and all other means of popularization. In determining whether a title should be protected, the courts will ask these questions:

287

1. Will the use of a title by someone else deceive the public as to the nature or origin of what it is buying?

2. Will it result in the wrongful appropriation of somebody else's work and publicity?

3. Will it dilute the value of the name which someone has or used or a reputation which someone else has built up?

[¶3707]   RIGHT OF PRIVACY

There is the right to prevent the use of one's name and picture without his consent. This right is statutory in New York but applies only to the use of the name or picture for trade or advertising purposes. Utah and Virginia also have similar statutory enactments protecting the right to privacy. Some twenty other states, including California, Illinois, Michigan, New Jersey, Ohio, and Pennsylvania (which with New York account for most of the Amercian market), recognize a common-law right to privacy. This means before a name or picture can be safely used for advertising or entertainment purposes, the person's consent must be obtained. He must waive his right of privacy. But the right to privacy does not extend to the use of one's name in a newspaper story. The right to privacy is limited so that it does not prohibit the dissemination of news and information. It does not require the consent of a person in whom there is public interest before the biography of that person can be written and published. The right to privacy does not exist with respect to the discussion of the life of a person in whom the public has a rightful interest. Anyone who becomes a public person or character gives up his right to privacy with respect to the reporting of his activities. However, he keeps his right of privacy with respect to a dramatized or fictionalized account of his life. But if a person is portrayed in a novel favorably, a court may find that a right of privacy was invaded but that there were no damages. A straight biography of a public figure does not require his consent but a fictionalized or novelized treatment of his life does. Pictures published in a newspaper in connection with advertising constitute an invasion of one's right to privacy while pictures in connection with a news account do not.

[¶3708]   PRACTICAL ASPECT OF LITERARY RIGHTS

The user of literary material will want the supplier to provide warranties with respect to copyright infringement, libel, invasion of privacy. He will want to be sure that he will get the work at some particular time, that it will be satisfactory and that the creator will help him in completing it and making any adaptation which commercial exploitation may indicate as desirable. The creator will want to know that the work will be satisfactorily exploited in all directions and that he will get a specified participation in the fruits of such exploitation. For the purpose of exploitation, a work can be cut up into book rights, magazine rights, newspaper rights, paperback reprint rights, reprint rights, dramatic or musical rights, stock rights, amateur rights, motion picture rights, radio and television rights, mechanical reproduction (records and tapes) rights, condensation and abridgement rights, translation rights, commercial exploitation (the regulations for use of names, characters, titles) rights, etc. Each of these rights may require special handling and can best be exploited by particular types of licensees. This should all be analyzed and discussed in developing any kind of deal for the exploitation of rights to intellectual property. There may be opportunities for developing an equity position in a movie, theatre, or broadcast adaptation of a literary work.

There are generally accepted standards of royalty rates, participation in book club and paperback distributions, in movie and dramatization revenue, in radio and television adaptations. But those with strong bargaining power frequently get a better than the usual split and the amount paid for subsidiary rights is almost always subject to negotiation. For forms, practical considerations, and tax angles in dealing with literary and artistic property, see IBP FORMS OF BUSINESS AGREEMENTS.

●

For Further Reference . . .
Ball, *The Law of Copyright and Literary Property.*
Ernst & Schwartz, *Privacy,* MacMillan.
Forms of Business Agreements looseleaf Service. Institute for Business Planning, Englewood Cliffs, N.J.
Houts, *From Evidence to Proof,* Thomas.
Pilpel and Savin, *Rights and Writers,* Dutton.
Ringer and Gitlin, *Copyrights,* Practising Law Institute, New York, New York.
Rothenberg, *Copyright Law.*
Spring, *Risks and Rights,* Norton.

MATRIMONIAL MATTERS

〔¶3901〕 The lawyer's most common contact with matrimonial matters will be in connection with marriages that are unsuccessful—when divorce or separation is sought. However, he may also be concerned with matters that arise before marriage; e.g., ante-nuptial agreements, as well as with the law governing marriage itself. While much of the lawyer's work in this area will be semi-psychiatric in character and his most constructive work will be in counselling and reconciliation rather than in litigation, he will have to know how to protect property rights before marriage and upon separation and dissolution of marriage, the techniques for providing alimony and dividing property, customary provisions for custody and visitation, the tax treatment of alimony, support payments and property divisions.

〔¶3902〕 **ANTE-NUPTIAL AGREEMENTS**

Although void at common law, ante-nuptial agreements are now recognized, by virtue of the Married Woman's Act, in most states. In many states the courts will not enforce an ante-nuptial agreement if there is no writing sufficient to satisfy the requirements of the Statute of Frauds.

When used, the ante-nuptial agreement generally defines the interest which the parties have in property acquired prior to or during the marriage. The ante-nuptial agreement cannot reduce the obligation arising by law of the husband to support his wife, nor the obligations of the wife to her husband. Absent a statute to the contrary, an ante-nuptial agreement made by an infant during minority will be voidable at the instance of the infant for a reasonable time after reaching majority. Several states have statutes which specifically provide for the enforcement of ante-nuptial agreements by an infant where the parent, guardian or other designated person is joined as a party to the agreement. (See, e.g., *Rieger v. Schaible,* 81 Neb. 33.)

Although an ante-nuptial agreement must be supported by consideration, the marriage itself is generally sufficient consideration (*Prewit v. Wilson,* 103 US 22). The agreement may consist of a release by one spouse of the rights and interest in the estate of the other spouse, an agreement by one spouse to make a will, an agreement by one spouse to advance a sum of money to the other each month. Generally, ante-nuptial agreements will be governed by the same rules as to construction and validity as other contracts.

〔¶3902.1〕 **Tax Effect of Ante-Nuptial Agreement**

In an ante-nuptial agreement special attention should be paid to the tax considerations. The transfer of ante-nuptial property in return for the surrender of the recipient's rights in the transferor's estate and property is not considered a transfer for an adequate and full consideration in money or monies worth, but rather is treated as a gift. The transfer will therefore be subject to the rules applicable to inter vivos gifts (see IRC §2035-2038). If the transfer is characterized as a revocable transfer or a transfer taking effect at death, or a transfer in contemplation of death, it will be included in the transferor's estate for estate tax purposes.

When a claim under an ante-nuptial agreement is unsatisfied at the time of the death of the transferor, the unsatisfied claim cannot be deducted from the decedent's estate as it is not based on adequate and full consideration (*Myers Estate,* 110 F.2d 367; *Adriance v. Higgins,* 113 F.2d 1013).

The transfer of ante-nuptial property constitutes a taxable gift. As noted *supra* the consideration for an ante-nuptial agreement will often be a promise to marry, relinquishment of dower and curtesy rights against the estate—all things which do not constitute adequate and full consideration for the property received (IRC §2512(b)). However, if the gift is timed to occur after the marriage only one-half the gift will be taxable, the other half being exempted by the gift tax marital deduction (IRC §2523). If $6,000 or less a year is transferred, it can be argued that there is no gift tax at all, half being exempt under the marital deduction, with the annual $3,000 exclusion accounting for the remaining sum.

Absent a provision in the agreement which provides for termination of the agreement on the separation or divorce of the parties, the courts will generally not disturb an ante-nuptial agreement upon the occurrence of these events. However, while the concluded transfers will not be set aside, the courts will refuse to enforce the executory portion of the contract in favor of the spouse whose wrongdoing precipitated the marital break.

[¶3903] TERMINATION OF THE MARRIAGE

In most states there are six basic means of terminating or suspending the marital relation:
(a) divorce
(b) annulment
(c) judicial separation
(d) separation agreement
(e) absence — presumption of death
(f) death

The grounds for termination of the marital relation vary extensively from state to state.

【¶3903.1】 Adultery

Adultery is the only ground for divorce which is essentially universal in the United States. Generally it is not necessary to prove the adultery by direct evidence. However, mere proof of bedroom privacy will not be sufficient to establish adultery as other reasons may be present to explain the bedroom privacy.

Adultery need not be continuing to constitute sufficient ground for a divorce decree—proof of a single act of adultery will be sufficient. Where adultery is relied upon as grounds for a judicial separation, it may be necessary to prove that the adultery is so open and notorious as to be cruel and inhuman.

Although there are few prosecutions, adultery is a crime in most states.

【¶3903.2】 Bigamy

Bigamous marriages are not recognized in the United States. Where one spouse has a prior spouse living, the second marriage will be void and not merely voidable. In most states, a bigamy will constitute grounds for annulment. In a few states, it also constitutes grounds for a divorce. In states where bigamy is the basis of both a divorce and annulment action, the party bringing the action will have the option of bringing the action for annulment or for divorce (*Schwartz v. Schwartz,* 173 NE 2nd 393). The availability of an alimony decree will often be important in deciding whether the action should lie for annulment or for a divorce. In some jurisdictions alimony is not available in an annulment action.

Because a bigamous marriage is void and not merely voidable, the parties may treat the marriage as a nullity without bringing formal proceedings. However, in many jurisdictions, the parties will seek an annulment in order to have a decree rendered awarding alimony, child custody and child support.

Bigamy is a crime. Because of the venue and jurisdiction requirements of the criminal law it is generally held that a defendant can be tried for bigamy only in the state where the crime was committed, i.e., where the second marriage was performed. In some states, a spouse may not be convicted of bigamy if the former spouse was absent and not heard from for five years prior to the remarriage and the remarrying spouse believed him or her to be dead (see, e.g., N. Y. Penal Law §341).

【¶3903.3】 Age

As noted, *supra,* each state imposes statutory age requirements for the issuance of marriage licenses. However, a marriage involving a spouse who has not reached the legal age for marriage, either with or without consent, is voidable rather than void in most jurisdictions. An action to have the marriage annulled may be maintained by the spouse who had reached the legal age for marriage, the guardian of the infant or the infant's "next best friend." Annulment for non-age will not be available where the spouse who had not reached the legal age at the time of the marriage freely cohabited after reaching the legal age. The non-age of the one spouse will not be available as grounds for an action of annulment to the spouse who was of legal age at the time of marriage.

[¶3903.4] Crime

In some jurisdictions, a criminal conviction may constitute grounds for divorce or the termination of the marital relationship. The rules vary from state to state but statutory provisions establishing grounds for divorce often include "infamous crimes," "crimes involving moral turpitude," or a felony. In some states, conviction of a crime and an extended sentence will constitute grounds for divorce. Numerous cases say that a person sentenced to life imprisonment is civilly dead.

In New York, although conviction for the crime is not considered grounds for a divorce, the innocent spouse may remarry. The subsequent pardon of the defendant will not revive the marital relation.

[¶3903.5] Cruelty

In many states, cruelty constitutes grounds for a divorce or separation. Cruelty is not limited as a rule to physical violence or effects of physical violence but may include mental cruelty. The following test was applied in one leading English case: "What merely ruins the mental feelings is in few cases, to be admitted, where not accompanied by bodily injury, either actual or menaced. Mere austerity of temper, petulance of manner, rudeness of language, a want of civil attention and accommodation, even occasional sallies of passion, if they do not threaten bodily harm, do not amount to legal cruelty. . . . Under such misconduct of either of the parties . . . the suffering party must bear in some degree, the consequences of an injudicious connection, must subdue by dissent, resistance or prudent conciliation, and if this cannot be done, both must suffer in silence" (*Evans v. Evans,* 161 English Reprint 466).

The following specific acts of cruelty have been held sufficient grounds for divorce.

— Physical violence, even a single act of physical violence if sufficient to endanger life (*Crabtree v. Crabtree,* 154 Ark. 401). However, divorce does not lie for every slight act of violence which a husband may commit against his wife or a wife against her husband (*Morris v. Morris,* 14 Cal. 76; *Hayes v. Hayes,* 86 Fla. 350).

— Habitual intemperance coupled with other acts which make it dangerous for the other spouse to continue in the marital relation (see *Grierson v. Grierson,* 150 Cal. 434).

— Deliberate use of intemperate language with an intent to injure the other spouse (see *Sneed v. Sneed,* 14 Ariz. 17).

— False and unfounded accusations of adultery, especially where made against the wife or a false and unfounded accusation that the wife is a prostitute (see *Cottle v. Cottle,* 40 SE 2d 863).

— Refusal of one spouse to speak to the other for an extended period of time (*Hiecke v. Hiecke,* 163 Wisc. 171).

— Cruel treatment of a child in the presence of the wife (*Poe v. Poe,* 149 Ark. 62).

[¶3903.6] Desertion and Abandonment

In most states, desertion or abandonment for a statutory period of time will be grounds for divorce. The statutory period varies from 6 months to 5 years. To establish desertion or abandonment, it is necessary that the plaintiff establish an intent on the part of the other spouse to abandon or desert. Leaving home to serve the armed forces, to seek employment in a foreign city, to visit a health resort, etc., will not constitute desertion or abandonment. Similarly, separation pursuant to a valid separation agreement will not constitute desertion or abandonment. However, as noted *infra,* where the parties separate pursuant to an agreement, the agreement should be made at or after the time of separation (see ¶3903.14).

Constructive abandonment will be a defense to an action for desertion or abandonment. Thus where the defendant was justified in abandoning the plaintiff, he or she will have a complete defense to the plaintiff's action for abandonment.

Many states have enacted so-called Enoch Arden laws based on the absence of one spouse and the belief on the part of the other spouse that the absent spouse is dead. At the end of the statutory period, the spouse may apply for a dissolution of the marital relation. Generally, it is necessary to show the circumstances under which the missing spouse disappeared and that diligent efforts were made to locate the spouse. If the absent spouse disappeared under circumstances which indicate that it would not be anticipated that he would attempt to contact the other spouse and that efforts to locate would be pointless, the rules will not be applied. If the spouse remarries after a dissolution of the earlier marriage because of the absence of the first spouse and the initial spouse reappears, the validity of the second marriage will not be affected.

[¶3903.7] Drunkenness

Habitual intoxication constitutes statutory grounds for a divorce in most jurisdictions. A single instance of overindulgence or a tendency to overindulge on occasion will not constitute sufficient intoxication to be grounds for divorce where the intoxication is relied upon. The intoxication must be a fixed and almost irresistible habit with considerable frequency. In some states, the statute requires that the habit must have continued for a period of one to two years. The spouse must have developed the habit after marriage.

[¶3903.8] Fraud

Fraud constitutes a ground for annulment in most states although in a few jurisdictions it is also recognized as a ground for divorce. Marriage is essentially a contract and the rules relating to an ordinary contract will be applicable. Fraud which goes to the essence of the contract will constitute grounds for setting aside the contract. In the following situations, fraud has been sufficient to constitute grounds for annulment:

— Misrepresentation as to or concealment of prior marital status.

— Misrepresentation as to intention to subsequently go through a religious ceremony.

— Secret intent not to cohabit or have children.

— Concealment of a venereal disease or other serious health impairment.

— Prior chastity (provided inquiry was made).

— Concealment of a pregnancy at the time of marriage by other than the husband.

— False representations as to citizenship.

[¶3903.9] Insanity

Insanity is a ground for divorce in most states and a ground for annulment in many states. Where the insanity existed at the time of the marriage, if the sane spouse is maintaining an action for annulment, he must establish that he did not know of the condition at the time of the marriage. If an action for annulment because of insanity at the time of the marriage is maintained by the insane spouse after regaining sanity, it is generally necessary to establish that the parties did not cohabit after the insane spouse regained sanity.

Where a spouse has been incurably insane for a statutory period of time (varying from 18 months to 5 years), the statutes of several states specify a procedure whereby the marriage may be annulled. If it is the wife who is insane, the court may require the husband to make provision for her support (see N.Y. Domestic Relations Law §7).

[¶3903.10] Residence Requirements

Courts are generally less liberal in accepting jurisdiction in matrimonial cases than in other civil actions. In most states, there is a statutory requirement that a person maintaining a matrimonial action be a resident of the state for a specified period of time prior to commencing the action. The residence requirement will often vary depending on the public policy of the state for various matrimonial actions, whether the cause of action occurred in the state, the parties were married in the state, the parties are both residents of the state and according to the nature of the action.

The residence requirements spelled out in the various procedural statutes must be strictly adhered to because of the involvement of the state in the marital contract. Because of the interest which the state has in the marital relation, they generally cannot be waived by consent between the parties.

[¶3903.11] Jurisdiction Requirements

In personam jurisdiction is generally not a necessary prerequisite to a valid matrimonial decree, although it will be necessary for a valid support order, alimony decree or order or any other decree or order having the effect of a money decree. Generally, it is held that the court where the marital res is located has sufficient in rem jurisdiction to effect the marital relation. In many cases, the procedural rules spell out different rules for service of a summons in a matrimonial action. In some states, substituted service may not be available. In other states, notation of the nature of the action must be indicated on the summons if a summons is served without the complaint. Stricter rules concerning the process server's proof of service may be applicable. The process server may be required to prove how he identified the defendant.

[¶3903.12] Special Defenses

In addition to the usual defenses to matrimonial actions there are also technical defenses, such as, the plaintiff must have been a resident of the state for a given period of time, and that the wrong, which is the subject of the action, must have been committed before a service of process.

Other defenses relate to rules concerning the obtaining and introduction of evidence. For example, there may be limitations on one spouse testifying against the other and such testimony will get little weight unless fully substantiated. The testimony of a private investigator may be inadmissible without proof that he is licensed or there may be a requirement that his testimony is corroborated.

[¶3903.13] Preparation, Settlement Negotiation and Trial

This is all part of the same process. Factual and unemotional pleadings are the first step. Getting full command of the facts, preparing a comprehensive memorandum of law and getting full information about the financial situation are basic to successful negotiation, settlement and trial. The preparation is in three phases:

1. Establishment of the acts or the facts which constitute the basis for separation and divorce.

2. Development of financial factors which are the basis for alimony and settlement of property.

3. Development of the factors which govern custody and visitation arrangements.

Frequently, the divorce may be considered an ultimate certainty and the questions resolved will be the financial and custody arrangements. In this case it is essential to get all the information about family finances, scale of living, insurance policies, real estate, gifts, how living expenses were met, how support was provided, etc. As to children, the essential picture to pull together is attitude, responsibility and interest taken by each parent, medical and psychiatric histories, persons who might testify as to what will be in the best interest of the children and the relationship of possible witnesses to the parents, etc.

[¶3903.14] Separation Agreement

Generally, a separation agreement will be enforceable where the parties are about to be separated when the agreement is entered into, or the parties have previously separated. The parties should be careful where they are separated without an agreement because absent an agreement, one party may be found to have abandoned or deserted the other. Where they have entered into a separation agreement, the parties should separate immediately thereafter or the agreement may not be enforceable. This is a reflection of the public policy against agreements which tend to break up the marital relation (see *Hill v. Hill,* 74 NH 288; *Galusha v. Galusha* 116 NY 635).

The separation agreement is an agreement between the parties that they will live separate and apart from one another and will not molest one another. The agreement generally will also provide for the disposition of joint property and support rights. Where it appears that the benefits under the contract are conditioned on one party obtaining a divorce or the terms of the agreement encourage divorce, the agreement may be attacked as violative of the public policy against divorce (see *Pryor v. Pryor,* 88 Ark. 302; *Miller v. Miller,* 284 Pa. 414).

By the marital contract, the husband is obligated to support his wife during their joint lives. Notwithstanding the wife's agreement to accept a stipulated amount in lieu of his support, the husband remains liable for his wife's support, at least to the extent of keeping her from becoming a public charge. In many states, a wife cannot contract to relieve the husband from his obligation to support her. In others, she may enter into a separation agreement which provides a regular and substantial payment which will be enforceable to relieve the husband of other support obligations. In a few states, the agreement, if fair and reasonable, will be binding and relieve the husband of any further obligation to support. Generally, the lump-sum settlement should be avoided in a separation agreement because it may be squandered or lost as a result of an unfortunate investment — resulting in obligation on the part of the husband to make further payments for support even though the lump-sum separation payment was fair and reasonable when entered into.

The most delicate portion of the separation agreement often involves the question of child custody. Numerous factors including the age, health, schooling, and sex of the child will be important in determining which parent is to have custody. Similarly, the ability of each parent to care for the child and the availability of help to care for the child in the absence of the parent having custody will be important. As noted *infra,* where the courts are confronted with the question of child custody, the child will be awarded at least partially to the mother absent extenuating circumstances or definite evidence of wrongdoing on the part of the mother (see ¶3907).

The support payments in a separation agreement are based on essentially the same considerations as the alimony except that more flexibility is available in a support agreement than in a court-decreed alimony judgment. (See IBP ESTATE PLANNING, VOL. II, looseleaf Service.

The separation agreement should also deal with the question of insurance. The agreement will often provide that the husband should keep the insurance in effect, and appoint the wife or children as irrevocable beneficiaries.

Tax Considerations of Separation Agreements: Where the following conditions are met, payments pursuant to a separation agreement will be taxed to the wife and deductible by the husband: (1) the husband and wife are separated, (2) the separation agreement was signed after August 16, 1954, (3) the separation agreement is in writing, (4) the payments qualify as periodical, (5) the husband and wife file separate income tax returns. For tax purposes, it is not necessary that the spouses be legally separated nor is it necessary that the agreement be enforceable pursuant to state law. Only payments made after the making of the agreement will be taxable to the wife and deductible to the husband.

[¶3904]   ALIMONY

As an incident to most matrimonial actions the court will grant alimony. In the case of a separation agreement, as noted *supra,* the agreement will generally provide for support payments without necessarily using the term "alimony." However, most of the principles applicable to alimony are also applicable to these support payments.

To render a decree including alimony, the court must have in personam jurisdiction of the defendant against whom the decree is to be entered. Where the court's jurisdiction is limited to in rem jurisdiction over the marital res because of constructive service upon a nonresident defendant, the court will be limited to subjecting the local property of the nonresident defendant to the effect of the alimony decree provided the property was attached prior to the decree.

Alimony will generally take on the form of permanent alimony, or temporary alimony. Temporary alimony will be awarded during the pendency of the action. It is rendered only in the sound discretion of the court after jurisdiction of the parties has been obtained. It is intended to support the wife during the pendency of the action and will be granted on the basis of the reasonable probability of the wife's success in the action, of the needs of the wife and of the ability of the husband to pay — which will be established by affidavit. Temporary alimony should not be confused with counsel fees which are generally awarded separately.

Permanent alimony is generally awarded as part of the divorce decree where all parties are before the court. Where prior to the divorce the parties entered into a separation agreement, the agreement may be merged into the decree. (See ¶3903.14.) Upon being merged into the decree, the agreement will become an integral part of the decree and can be enforced as an alimony decree. The agreement will not be binding upon the court—the court may alter, increase or decrease the provisions of the agreement. Where the court has altered a separation agreement, it is the altered amount and not the original amount which is entitled to the special enforcement procedures of the equity court.

In the absence of an agreement to incorporate a prior separation agreement into the divorce decree, the court will set alimony in its sound discretion. Factors used by courts in setting alimony include:

(a) Conduct of the parties (which party is the guilty party),

(b) Financial condition of the parties,

(c) Anticipated earning capacity,

(d) Social standing of the parties.

In most cases, alimony will continue until the death of either spouse or the remarriage of the recipient. Where a separation agreement is involved, this rule may be modified by the specific agreement of the parties. The cases are in conflict as to whether the remarriage of the recipient will terminate the right to receive alimony where the second marriage is subsequently declared void or voidable.

A decree of permanent alimony may be modified by the court rendering it upon application of either party. Generally, an alimony decree will be modified where there is a showing of need or substantial alteration in financial conditions. The decree will also be modified upon a showing that the husband concealed his assets when the decree was originally entered.

In a few states, the courts have held that they may modify a divorce decree rendered in another state involving a domiciliary where they have jurisdiction over the parties (see *Worthley v. Worthley,* 44 Cal. 2d 465). However, the majority rule is still that a divorce decree must be modified by the court entering it.

[¶3904.1] Tax Aspects of Alimony Decrees

The Internal Revenue Code uses a different classification of payments in matrimonial actions than that utilized by most state courts. From the standpoint of Federal taxes, alimony and separate maintenance payments fall into three classifications: (1) Payments under a decree of divorce or separate maintenance, or under a written instrument incident to divorce or separation; (2) payments under a decree of support; or (3) payments under a written separation agreement. The latter has been considered in ¶3903.14.

Payments under a decree requiring the husband to make payments to the wife for her support and maintenance are taxable to her and deductible by him even though the decree isn't for actual divorce or legal separation provided the following requirements are met:

(1) Husband and wife are separated.

(2) The decree under which the payments are made was entered into after March 1, 1954.

(3) It must be the wife's support or maintenance that is required by the decree.

(4) The payments must qualify as periodic.

(5) The husband and wife must file separate returns.

Payments will be categorized as periodic where they are *not* payments of a principal sum — in lump sum or in installments. Where the payment is a payment of the principal sum in installments which may be or will be paid over a period ending more than 10 years from the effective date of the decree, the installments will qualify as periodic payments only to the extent of 10% of the principal sum per year. The 10% limitation applies to installment payments made in advance, but does not apply to delinquent installments for a prior taxable year of the wife paid during her taxable year.

Where alimony payments are made contingent on death or remarriage, they must be included in income by the recipient even though they may be in payment of a principal amount and the period of payment is not more than 10 years. They are deductible by the spouse making the payment.

Insurance premiums paid by the husband on a life insurance contract assigned absolutely to the wife, with her as the irrevocable beneficiary, are deductible by the husband. But if the policy isn't assigned to her and she is merely a contingent beneficiary, he cannot deduct the premiums (*IT 4001,* CB 1950-1, 27; *Weil,* 22 TC 612). In *Seligmann* (207 F.2d 489), the Seventh Circuit held that life insurance premiums do not qualify as alimony unless the wife's "economic benefit" from the payments of the premiums can be measured in dollars and cents. If her right to the proceeds is contingent, for example, if she is required to survive her husband or remain single in order to benefit, the premiums are not alimony. Premiums which are merely security for alimony payments are not treated as alimony (*Carmichael*, 14 TC 1356).

[¶3904.2] Alimony Trusts

The husband's obligations for support and maintenance of the wife may be met by the establishment of a trust in an appropriate situation. Where an alimony trust is used, the wife will receive the current income and perhaps, ultimately, the principal of the trust. Even if the husband is not able completely to fund the trust at its inception, a trust calling for periodic funding may be utilized.

Where a husband makes a transfer to his spouse or to a trust for her benefit, it is in exchange for a valuable consideration if it is in discharge of his wife's claim for support and maintenance. To that extent it is not a gratuitous transfer and is not subject to a gift tax. However, property settlement transfers made where divorce occurs within two years of agreement are treated as made for full and adequate consideration (see IRC §2516).

A typical alimony trust will provide not only for the wife but for the children as well. Often, the remainder interest will be earmarked for the children. Transfers of capital to the children or in trust for them will be subject to the gift tax except to the extent that these transfers are for the support of the children during minority (Reg. §1.2516-2).

[¶3905] RECOGNITION OF FOREIGN DECREES

The full faith and credit clause of the United States Constitution requires that the courts of one state give full faith and credit to the judgments and decrees of the courts in another state. However, full faith and credit are not afforded a decree where the court rendering the decree did not have jurisdiction over the parties to the action. Similarly, a court need not give any greater credit to a decree of a court rendered in another jurisdiction than the court rendering the decree or another court in that jurisdiction would give the decree. For example, a New York court will look beyond the decree to determine if fraud was committed on an Alabama court in rendering an Alabama divorce where the Alabama court would look beyond the decree for that purpose. However, where a foreign decree has been rendered based on jurisdiction over the parties to the action, the courts in another state, even though it is the domicile of one of the parties to the action, cannot refuse to give the decree full faith and credit.

Foreign divorce decrees are governed by the rules of international comity rather than the stricter rules of full faith and credit dictated by the United States Constitution. However, as a matter of comity, foreign courts will generally recognize a decree of another country, provided it was based on a proper jurisdictional predicate.

[¶3906]   ENFORCEMENT OF ALIMONY DECREES

A decree for permanent alimony may be enforced in the same manner as any debt. However, in most states, the equity court can enforce an alimony decree through contempt proceedings. In most states a husband may be committed for contempt of court after notice and a demand for payment (see *Lipton v. Lipton*, 211 Ga. 442). Alimony does not constitute a debt within the meaning of the constitutional prohibition of imprisonment for debt.

Although bankruptcy does not bar the wife's claims for alimony, the husband will not be required to stay in jail if he establishes a bona fide inability to pay (see *Bradshaw v. Bradshaw*, 133 SW 2d 617).

Sequestration is a means whereby the wife may obtain security for future payments of alimony or a fund from which defaulted payments of alimony may be collected. Where the remedy of sequestration is relied upon, the court may cause the husband's personal property and the rents and profits of his real property to be sequestered and may appoint a receiver for them. In most jurisdictions, enforcement through sequestration will be available for either a domestic or foreign divorce decree.

[¶3907]   CHILD CUSTODY

Where confronted with the question of child custody, the welfare of the child is the paramount consideration before the court. Although a divorce decree may fix the custody of the child, the court, at any time, may alter or amend the custodial provisions. Courts may renew the issue of child custody upon a writ of habeas corpus. Although courts often favor the mother where custody is at issue, they will not hesitate giving custody to the spouse who in the opinion of the court will be best for the child. Where the child is sufficiently mature, the court will generally inquire as to the wish of the child although the child's wishes will be far from conclusive. Ordinarily, an infant of tender years or a girl of more mature years will be given to the mother if she is found to be a fit parent even though the divorce is granted to the father. Where the circumstances of the case require it, the court may grant custody to the grandmother, aunt or other third party to the action. Although they will generally be recognized unless the welfare of the child dictates otherwise, contracts between spouses as to the custody of children will not be controlling on the court (see *Emrich v. McNeill*, 126 F.2d 841, 146 ALR 1146).

Where custody is awarded to one parent, visitation rights will generally be awarded to the other parent (*Scott v. Scott*, 154 Ga. 659). However, the court may limit the right to visit the child to a particular time and place or make the right conditional upon notice, etc.

Upon the death of the spouse having custody of the child, it is generally held that the right to custody will revert to the surviving spouse. However, the surviving spouse will not be entitled to custody if he cannot provide a suitable home.

The court rendering the divorce decree and determining the issue of custody retains jurisdiction to modify or alter the decree as to divorce at any time when it is in the best interests of the child. However, the doctrine of *res judicata* applies to that part of the divorce decree which grants custody, and the court cannot re-examine the facts formerly judicated and make a different order upon them. There must be a substantial change of circumstances to justify a substantial change in the custody order (see *Fortson v. Fortson,* 195 Ga. 750). Where necessary to achieve the purposes of public policy—the best interests of the infant—the custody order may be modified because of facts existing at the time of the original order, although not brought out in court at that time.

Provision should also be made for visitation rights. Where the parties enter into a separation agreement they will generally make some arrangement whereby the children will spend part of their vacations, holidays and weekends with the other parent. Where there is a determination however that one parent is not a fit parent the visitation rights may be highly restricted.

The remarriage of either spouse will not automatically affect the custody of children by the former marriage. However, upon remarriage, the argument is often made that the remarried spouse now has a home for the child to replace the one broken by the divorce.

●

For Further Reference . . .
American Jurisprudence, Divorce and Separation.
Rudick, Harry J., *Federal Tax Consequences of Marriage and Its Termination,* Joint Committee on Continuing Legal Education.
Spellman, H. H., *Successful Management of Matrimonial Cases,* Prentice-Hall, Englewood Cliffs, N.J.

MORTGAGE FINANCING FOR REAL ESTATE

[¶4001] Mortgages are the traditional form of financing real estate. The owner (mortgagor) retains beneficial ownership while offering his property as security for a loan from the lender (mortgagee). In some states, the lender is regarded as holding legal title to the property during the term of the mortgage (title theory of mortgages); in other states, he merely has a lien against the property (lien theory). In both cases, however, it is understood that the lender's interest is solely to protect his loan. In addition, the owner is often personally liable for the loan, which is evidenced by his note or obligation. If a foreclosure of the property leaves a balance still owing the lender, he may proceed to obtain a deficiency judgment which is enforceable against any other assets of the borrower.

Mortgages are classified in terms of *time* or *priority*. In time, mortgages are either short term (usually one year) or long term (over five years). By priority, mortgages are either senior or primary (first mortgages), or junior or secondary (second, third or fourth mortgages). Different lenders specialize in different types, and each type has its particular use.

[¶4002]   CONSTRUCTION FINANCING

The most important use of the short-term (first) mortgage is to provide financing for construction of new buildings or improvement of existing structures. Some lenders are restricted by law from making these loans, and others do not do so from choice. The furthest these lenders will go is to issue a commitment for a "permanent" mortgage when the building is completed (known as a "take-out" commitment). There are two reasons why construction loans involve extra risk. First, possible delays in construction, or unanticipated costs, can result in failure of the project. Second, changes in the real estate or economic picture can make it impossible to obtain a profitable rent roll.

Short-term construction loans are made, however, by commercial banks, some savings institutions, and private mortgage companies and investors who are attracted by the higher return. The loans usually run for 12 to 18 months, although shorter periods can be arranged. The usual procedure for obtaining a construction loan is for the owner to approach the prospective lender with full details about the projected improvements and his own financial position. If the lender agrees to make the loan, it will issue a letter of commitment, which may or may not be legally binding on it, and this will be followed by a formal building loan contract and mortgage. Since it is the intention of both lender and borrower that the building loan will be paid off immediately upon completion of the improvements, there is often an agreement or understanding with the lender who will provide the permanent financing at that time. The result

304

has aptly been termed a financing web in which each party is dependent on the ability and willingness of the others to carry out their commitments. Since the lenders are providing the bulk of the funds for a fixed interest return while the owner keeps the profits, if any, it is understandable enough that the former impose strict requirements for their loans and subject the property to continuous inspections. In the following paragraphs, which discuss the construction financing procedure in detail, emphasis is on the role of the property owner and his attorney and the extent to which they may be able to vary the relatively fixed requirements of the large institutional lenders which do much of the construction financing in this country.

[¶4002.1]   Obtaining the Commitment

The following steps describe the procedure to obtain a construction loan from a large commercial bank in New York City.

1. Application to Lender: The prospective borrower submits all information about the property and preliminary plans and specifications for the improvements. He should include the name of the architect, whose experience can be an important factor, and that of the general contractor (assuming the owner will not act as his own contractor) whose credit will be checked along with that of the owner. The borrower should already have ascertained that the particular lender is interested in the type of loan being sought (e.g., fee or leasehold mortgage, specialty loan, assignment of rents) since lenders vary their loans from time to time in order to keep a balanced portfolio and to seek out areas of highest interest return.

2. Appraisal by Lender: The lender will first obtain a desk opinion (D.O.) from its appraisal division to see if its minimum loan requirements are met. This involves a study of the plans and specifications, a survey or plot plan, zoning requirements, and the economic potential of the proposed building. If this opinion is satisfactory, a physical inspection of the site is made, the title is searched, a formal appraisal (usually using the income capitalization approach) is prepared, and the credit rating of the owner and contractor is checked. The lender will also want to know where the balance of the construction funds will come from and any arrangements which have been made for permanent financing when the building is completed.

3. Out-of-State Loans: If the borrower and the lender are citizens of different states, the lender will normally want to satisfy itself about several important legal matters. One is whether the lender will be "doing business" in the foreign state if it makes the loan or if it later resorts to the foreign court to foreclose its loan. If the lender must qualify to do business in the state, it will want to know what is involved. Sometimes, this problem is avoided by having a local lender participate in the loan and carry on the proceeding in its name. The lender will also inquire about any period of redemption in the event of foreclosure; this may be several years, during which the lender will be unable to dispose of the property. Mechanic's liens vary from state to state, and the lender will want to know if its loan will be subordinate to them. Finally, the lender will want to know about local property taxes and the likelihood of their increase in the future.

4. *Terms of the Loan:* The borrower will normally state in his application the amount of loan requested and the interest rate he is willing to pay. When the lender comes to fixing the amount of loan, it will make it a percentage of the value of the improved property. For example, 70% of the value of an apartment or office building may be loaned, or 50% of the value of a motel or other specialized type of business. In addition, the lender may limit the construction loan to 90% of the "take-out" (the commitment for the permanent mortgage loan). The interest rate will be that prevailing for the type of loan involved. In addition, the lender will charge a "processing fee," which in reality is a discount. The discount varies with the term of the loan and the amount of risk. For example, a $1,000,000 loan may be made at 12% interest plus a $10,000 processing fee. Half the processing fee may be due at the time the letter of commitment is issued and will be non-refundable if the loan does not go through. The other half will be paid at the closing of the loan. The 12% interest will be payable only on funds actually advanced to the owner (although sometimes there is a provision for stand-by interest, payable even though no money is actually loaned). All these factors make the actual interest rate different from the stated rate.

5. *Letter of Commitment:* If the loan negotiations are concluded satisfactorily, the lender will issue a letter of commitment which constitutes an approval of the loan application. The letter sets forth the details of the loan as well as the conditions which must be satisfied before the loan closing (final plans and specifications, bonds, etc.). It is unclear whether the commitment letter is legally binding on the lender. Most jurisdictions do not permit the borrower to sue for specific performance of the commitment, but in some states he may recover special damages if they can be shown.

6. *Closing the Loan:* The final step in the procedure is the loan closing, at which time the mortgage, bond if any, and other documents are executed. The lender then will advance funds to the owner in accordance with their agreement.

[¶4002.2]   Checklist for Building Loan Agreement and Mortgage

The building loan agreement (or the letter of commitment when no more formal agreement is made) substantially sets forth the obligation of the lender to make the loan, and of the owner to construct the improvements described therein. The loan is not made at one time but portions or advances are given when the building reaches each stage of construction specified in the payment schedule. A typical schedule for a large office building might have twelve stages, the final one being upon full completion of the building, including the issuance of a final certificate of occupancy. Other significant provisions of the agreement are as follows:

A. Representations by the Borrower

(1) Corporate Existence: The lender ordinarily will want the borrower to be a corporation so that any question of usurious interest is avoided. In addition, a "one-shot" corporation eliminates the possibility that outside creditors will be able to proceed against the particular property. The borrower will have to represent that the corporation is validly existing and that all necessary resolutions of the directors and shareholders have been passed.

(2) Capital Stock of the Corporation: Since the lender will want to know the true identity of the borrower, the names of all shareholders will have to be submitted. In addition, the corporation and its shareholders may be asked to covenant that no stock will be transferred or issued so that the present shareholders will own less than 51%. The construction lender, more than the permanent lender, looks to the experience and integrity of the building owner since failure to complete the building on time may endanger the loan.

(3) No Violations or Damage: The borrower must represent that no violations exist and the property has suffered no damage at the time of the loan. This too is important because it might affect the completion date.

(4) Building Leases: The construction lender is vitally interested in leases which the builder makes with tenants because the permanent mortgage, the proceeds of which will pay off the construction loan, is conditioned upon satisfactory leases in terms of both quality and amount of rent. The borrower will have to submit copies of any leases already entered into. Sometimes, a "step-up" loan will be made, i.e., the amount of the loan may be increased as new tenants are signed up.

(5) Construction Plans and Specifications: The lender will want to see completed plans for the improvement and the agreement with the general contractor, unless the borrower intends to act as his own contractor. The lender may want to make a separate agreement with the general contractor and the architect that, in the event of a default by the borrower, they will work for the lender under the same agreements they have with the borrower. Where state law makes it possible, the lender may also want the borrower to obtain waivers (in favor of the lender) by the general contractor and major subcontractors of their rights under the lien law.

(6) Performance or Completion Bonds: These may be required to insure completion of the building. They are discussed below under "Building and Construction Agreements."

(7) Permanent Financing: Representations about permanent financing are discussed in the next section.

B. Covenants by the Borrower

(1) Completion of the Improvement: The borrower normally must agree to a definite completion date and agree to proceed with "all reasonable dispatch." Since the failure to comply with either of these usually constitutes a default and accelerates the entire loan, the borrower should make provision for contingencies, such as weather, labor disputes, fire, etc.

(2) Approval of Lender to Change in Plan: The lender wants the right to approve changes because any substantial modifications may terminate the obligation of the permanent lender.

(3) Inspection of Premises; Financial Statements: The lender will want the right to inspect the premises during construction and prior to making any advances. Similarly, it will want the borrower periodically to submit financial statements so that any financial difficulties can be anticipated.

[¶4002.3]   Relationship Between the Construction Loan and the Permanent Mortgage

Construction financing is short-term financing where the source of repayment is clearly understood to be the permanent mortgage which will be placed on the completed building. Construction loans can be classified into four types depending on their relationship to the permanent financing:

(1) Open-End: In an open-end loan, the borrower has no commitment for permanent financing. The construction lender thus assumes a risk that no mortgage can be obtained when the building is finished. This risk normally is assumed only when the real estate market is very strong or where the borrower has an outstanding reputation.

(2) Take-Out: This is the most common type. At the time the construction loan is closed, the borrower already has a commitment for a permanent mortgage. The construction lender thus has an assured source of repayment *provided* the borrower meets the conditions of the permanent loan commitment. See below.

A variation of the "take-out" commitment is the "standby" commitment. This involves an agreement by a lender to make a permanent mortgage loan in a specified amount within a specified period, when called upon by the borrower. The amount of the mortgage loan is substantially below its face amount (that is, the lender will get the mortgage loan at a discount), and the borrower must pay a standby fee, usually 1% or more. The standby commitment is generally used when mortgage money is tight. At such times, interest rates are high and lenders usually demand a discount to make a permanent mortgage loan. In effect, the builder is gambling that the mortgage money picture will change by the time his project is completed, and that he will then be able to get full financing at a lower rate of interest.

For example, a builder may have an FHA commitment to insure a mortgage of $1 million on a proposed apartment house. But no lender will agree to make a permanent mortgage loan in the full amount of the FHA commitment. The best the builder can get is a mortgage loan of 97% of the commitment ($970,000). However, he believes he can get a permanent loan of 100% on completion of the project. So he asks a bank for a standby commitment at 93% ($930,000), expiring in 18 months. The bank agrees, and the builder pays the bank a standby fee of 1% ($10,000). With the standby commitment, the builder can get a construction loan and proceed with the project.

If the builder's estimate of the mortgage market is correct, he will be able to get a permanent mortgage loan for $1,000,000. Of course, he will have paid a standby fee of $10,000. But he will still have a net mortgage loan of $990,000 — or $20,000 more than he could have obtained at first.

The "standby" lender is glad to enter into the arrangement because (1) it receives a fee for lending its credit for a short period of time, and (2) if the builder's estimate of the mortgage market is wrong, then it will get an FHA-insured loan at a substantial discount. (For example, here the lender would pay out $930,000 and receive back an FHA-insured mortgage for $1,000,000.)

Buy-sell agreements are often used in connection with the "take-out" form of construction loan. The agreement essentially provides that the permanent lender will, when the building is finished, buy the construction loan or advance the necessary funds so that the borrower can pay it off. The advantage of the agreement to the construction lender is that he can enforce the agreement against the permanent lender, something he cannot do where there is only a "take-out" commitment in favor of the borrower. The agreement, however, does contain the same conditions as does the commitment, e.g., completion by a given date, satisfactory leases, etc.

In a *two-party* buy-sell agreement, the parties are the construction lender and the permanent lender. Since this doesn't bind the borrower, he might conceivably find a lender willing to make a permanent mortgage under more favorable terms and abandon the original commitment. To prevent this, a *three-party* buy-sell agreement is sometimes used, in which the borrower also is a party and is obliged to accept the permanent loan.

(3) Combination Loan: Sometimes the construction lender will also provide the permanent financing, combining the two loans into one. The advantage of this procedure for the builder is that he makes all his financing arrangements at one place and at one time, and eliminates extra commissions, service charges and fees. The lender benefits in several possible ways: (1) it assures itself of

getting the permanent loan, which is the source of most of its profit; (2) by inspecting the building during construction, it can see that the plans and specifications are properly followed; (3) it can charge a slightly higher overall rate because of the extra risk involved in the construction part of the loan.

The other side of the picture, for the builder, is that by waiting until completion of the building, he may be able to get a 20% larger loan at an interest rate ¼ to ½ point lower. There are several reasons for this. First, many more lenders make permanent loans than construction loans. Second, there is considerably less risk in lending on a completed building. Finally, the builder himself is frequently under less pressure in arranging the permanent financing and so he can shop around more.

There is one situation where the builder may reap a substantial tax benefit by taking out the combined loan. This is when he intends selling the completed property and wants to defer his taxable gain on the sale. This requires that he receive not more than 30% of the sales price in the year of sale. If he takes out only a construction loan, and the buyer arranges for the permanent financing and pays over the mortgage proceeds to the seller, the 30% requirement will not normally be met. But since an existing mortgage assumed by the buyer isn't figured in when computing the 30% payment (except to the extent that it exceeds the seller's basis), the combined building and permanent loan may permit use of the installment method, thus permitting a substantial tax benefit.

(4) Guarantee of Payment: This very unusual type of loan is conditioned upon the borrower's guarantee that the loan will be repaid upon completion of the building. Very few builders are in a position to give such a guarantee, and if they were, there would normally be no need for the loan in the first place. Sometimes, the builder may be able to obtain the guarantee of a third party.

[¶4003] PERMANENT FINANCING

The long-term mortgage loan is the key feature distinguishing real estate from all other forms of investment. In no other area will a lender agree to lend 75% or more of the value of the security for terms of 15 to 30 years. Real estate will support such loans because of its *stability* and *long-term growth potential.* These features in turn derive from the limited and fixed supply of land which must support a constantly growing population.

Actually, the long-term mortgage reflects the same underlying division of interest in real estate as does the long-term lease. Both divide the long-term investor seeking a fixed return from the short- or medium-term operator who seeks a higher but more speculative return. The lender who extends a 20-year mortgage on a building (and who probably will be willing to refinance it at the end of that period assuming it has been well maintained) can be compared to the owner who extends a 20-year net lease with renewal options. Looking at it from the other side, the borrower-owner can be compared to the net lessee. Both may have invested approximately the same amount of "equity" money (the former to buy the building, and the latter to buy the leasehold) and both anticipate an operating income which will represent a high return on their leveraged investment. If the building loses money, each is prepared to abandon his interest to the long-term investor who has provided the major financing. (This assumes, as is usually the case, that neither the operator-owner nor the net lessee is personally liable for his obligations.)

The similarity in interest between the long-term lender and long-term owner is the basis for the sale-leaseback type of arrangement — where a long-term lease is substituted for a mortgage.

The major sources of long-term mortgage money are insurance companies, pension funds, saving and loan associations, mutual savings banks, and commercial banks.

[¶4003.1] Checklist for Long-Term Mortgages

The procedure for obtaining permanent financing is similar to that for construction financing. The borrower applies to the lender, submitting all pertinent data and asking for a loan of stated amount, term and interest. If the lender agrees to make the loan, a letter of commitment will be issued. In the case of an already-existing structure, the closing of the loan will follow shortly thereafter. Where new construction is involved, the formal closing will be postponed until the building is completed and only at that time, and provided the conditions set forth in the commitment are met, will the mortgage be signed and the money paid. Many states have statutory forms of mortgages which may be used if the parties wish; their value is that the meaning of many phrases and clauses is spelled out in the statute. Institutional lenders usually have their own forms which they will require to be used; these, naturally, will tend to favor the lender's position.

The following is a brief description of the important provisions of the long-term mortgage:

(1) Amount: The amount of the loan is most often determined as a percentage of the value of the property at the time of the loan. Thus many institutional lenders are limited to a ratio of 66⅔% or 75%. The lender will make its own careful appraisal of the property to determine its value. Frequently, however, the value of the completed building is substantially higher than the cost of the vacant land plus construction. This is most often true when value is computed by the income capitalization method, i.e., by capitalizing the rental income provided by the existing leases. On occasion, this value may be so much higher than cost that the borrower is able to obtain 100% of his cost — mortgaging out, as it is called.

311

(2) Interest Rate: This is normally determined by market rates for money. Normally, a portion of each repayment by the borrower represents interest to date and the remainder is amortization. If the lender is willing, however, the ratio of interest to principal can be set at any proportion the borrower desires. If the portion allocated to interest is increased (so that part of it is prepaid interest), the borrower gets an additional tax deduction immediately. In the opposite case, interest is accrued and the borrower can postpone part of his interest deduction.

(3) Amortization: Long-term loans may be classified into four groups, depending on the extent that they are repaid prior to maturity.

(a) The standing mortgage—This is extremely rare in long-term loans, since it means that the entire amount remains outstanding until maturity, which can be 15, 20 or 25 years hence. The disadvantage to the borrower is that his interest payments never decline and he must be prepared to raise the necessary cash or to refinance at maturity. The danger to the lender is that the value of the property may decline below the amount of the loan.

(b) The partially amortized mortgage (also called the "balloon mortgage") —This, too, is quite uncommon on long-term loans although it is often used for intermediate-term mortgages. Periodic payments partially reduce the principal, leaving part unpaid at maturity (i.e., the "balloon"). A lender may be willing to make this type of loan where he feels the value of the property is not likely to decline. A borrower may want it because it keeps the amount of amortization within reasonable bounds during the later years of the mortgage and so reduces the possibility that amortization may exceed his depreciation and so require him to use taxable income to meet his mortgage payments.

(c) The fully amortized mortgage—This is by far the most common type and results in complete liquidation of the principal during the term of the loan. It offers the greatest security to both lender and borrower. The lender is most likely to insist on a self-amortizing loan in the case of commercial properties such as motels and shopping centers, where the credit of the borrower as well as the value of the real estate is an important element of security.

(d) The variable-amortization loan—This combines different rates of amortization during the term of the loan (sometimes with periods of no amortization). It is useful where income from the property is expected to vary and the borrower wants to tailor his payments to his expected income. Or the amortization may be tied to depreciation charges which will vary when accelerated methods are used.

(4) Covenant of Repayment: In most long-term loans on real estate, the lender regards the property as his primary security. With respect to the personal obligation of the borrower, three alternatives exist:

(a) Personal liability — The lender may insist that the borrower assume personal liability, either by a covenant to pay included in the mortgage or by

312

a separate instrument. In the latter event, a corporate borrower should seek to use a note instead of a bond, since this eliminates the cost of revenue stamps. This may not be possible where the lender, by law, is limited to loans on *bonds.*

(b) Use of a nominee or dummy — The lender may be willing to waive personal liability but the statute may require it. In that case, a nominee without assets may act for the borrower and later convey the property to him subject to the mortgage. Local law must be checked, however, to see if the assumption of liability by the nominee (who is the borrower's agent) is imputed to his principal.

(c) No personal liability — When the lender agrees to waive any personal liability and the borrower's cash investment in the property is small, the borrower in effect has a long-term option.

(5) Security: The mortgage lien covers all of the real estate described therein; this will include *fixtures,* i.e., personal property affixed to the realty. In addition, the lender often wants the mortgage to include a lien on a personal property. Since the definition of a fixture varies from jurisdiction to jurisdiction, the lender may list all items of personal property in order to eliminate any question about coverage. Sometimes the security clause will apply to after-acquired property as well. Strictly speaking, this is merely a covenant to give a mortgage at the time the property is acquired. Many lenders will require additional mortgage instruments to be executed at that time. The lender must also be sure to record the mortgage both as a *real estate* mortgage and as a *chattel* mortgage in order to preserve his rights.

(6) Prepayment: This is a vital clause for the borrower. In its absence, he may not be able to pay off the mortgage even though the property is condemned or destroyed. More likely, he may want to refinance at a time when interest rates have declined. The lender often will agree to prepayment after a minimum period (e.g., five years) and at a reasonable penalty (e.g., 1%).

(7) Demolition of Improvements: In the usual printed mortgage, any demolition of existing improvements will constitute a default, since it impairs the lender's security. If the borrower is contemplating demolition, appropriate provision should be made. The lender's agreement will be conditioned upon the borrower's obligation to install new improvements.

(8) Insurance Proceeds: The lender, of course, will require the borrower to maintain fire and other insurance on the property for the lender's benefit. If the mortgage is silent, the lender may apply the insurance proceeds to payment of part of the mortgage debt instead of for restoration of the property. In that case, the borrower will have to arrange new financing, and if he can't prepay the outstanding mortgage, this may be impossible. The borrower should seek to require the lender to use the proceeds for restoration or, if that is not possible, obtain the right to prepay the remaining loan.

(9) Condemnation Awards: In the case of a partial condemnation, there is a similar problem as that for insurance proceeds. The lender in this case is much less likely to agree to use the proceeds to restore the property since its security has been reduced by the condemnation.

(10) Prohibition Against Junior Liens: The lender may not want the property encumbered by a second mortgage since this increases the risk of a default followed by a foreclosure by the junior mortgagee, to the possible detriment of the primary mortgagee. A possible compromise is for the borrower to agree that any junior lien will be made subordinate to the existing leases; in this way, a foreclosure cannot terminate the leases, which constitute the real security for the primary lender.

(11) Encumbrances: The lender will normally require that there be no encumbrances on the property ahead of the first mortgage—such as mechanic's liens. In addition, this may be a statutory requirement for institutional lenders. In the case of *leases,* however, the situation may be different. Since, as we noted above, these leases are the true security for the loan, the lender wants to be sure they will not terminate in the event the first mortgage is foreclosed. The mortgage must make provision for this in light of local law. There are two situations:

(a) Foreclosure terminates all subordinate liens—If the jurisdiction requires the mortgagee to join all subordinate liens (and terminate them) in a foreclosure action, the mortgage can make existing leases *superior* to the mortgage lien. If the lender is prohibited from doing this by statute, it may execute a non-disturbance agreement, in which it agrees not to terminate the lease as long as the rent is paid. A non-disturbance agreement may be so broad as to be the equivalent of making the first mortgage a subordinate lien.

(b) Foreclosure terminates subordinate liens at lender's option—Where the lender may join only such tenants as he wishes in the foreclosure action, it need make no provision in the mortgage. However, certain of the *tenants* may be in a position to demand non-disturbance agreements from the lender in order to protect themselves.

(12) Assignment of Leases: The lender may fear that if the borrower is heading toward a default, he may cancel or amend certain leases in favor of the tenants in exchange for cash payments. An "anti-milking" provision may require the borrower to assign all leases to the lender to protect against this contingency. Since this amounts to a future assignment, it may be deemed fraudulent and void in some jurisdictions. As an alternative, the lender may require that no lease be amended or cancelled without its consent.

[¶4004]   LEASEHOLD FINANCING

One type of mortgage which is becoming more important is the leasehold mortgage. Its growth is due to the fact that much of the prime real estate in our metropolitan areas is held by owners (institutional and individual) who never intend to sell it. This means that a builder who wants to improve such real estate must (1) enter into a ground lease with the landowner and (2) obtain mortgage financing to construct the improvement, using the leasehold as security. Such financing, even in the form of a first mortgage, is a secondary lien because the lessor's claim for rent has priority. Put another way, the security for a leasehold mortgage is a *defeasible* estate — the lease — and this is the factor that distinguishes this type of mortgage from the fee mortgage. Many institutional lenders will not make leasehold mortgages and the large loans are generally extended by life insurance companies and mutual savings banks.

Our previous discussion about permanent financing applies as well to leasehold financing. The leasehold mortgagee, however, will be likely to make some changes in the mortgage agreement, and he will scrutinize the ground lease very carefully before deciding to make the loan. We will look at these two aspects of the leasehold mortgage separately.

[¶4004.1]   Leasehold Mortgage Checklist

(1) Amount: The loan will be a percentage of the value of the property as improved. Because of the somewhat greater risk in a leasehold mortgage, the ratio is frequently lower than that in a fee mortgage. The value of the property is computed in the same manner as for the fee mortgage, except that the ground rental is an additional item of expense. Put another way, the value of a leasehold is its economic rent (the rent income received from the sublessees) minus the contract rent (the ground rental). This value is security for the loan.

(2) Term and Interest: Because of the higher risk, interest rates are somewhat higher on leasehold mortgages. The term of the loan will not exceed the term of the lease, and normally must be fully amortized within that period. If renewal terms have been included in measuring the term of the lease, the lender may require the borrower to exercise the renewal option at once or within the first few years of the loan. In the case of an institutional lender, the governing statute may prohibit leasehold mortgages for longer than the initial term (regardless of renewal terms) and may require that the initial term be for at least a certain period of years.

(3) Subordination of the Fee: The lender, as well as the borrower, will benefit if the landowner agrees to join in the leasehold mortgage and make the land additional security for the loan (however, the landowner will not assume personal liability for the loan). The lender benefits because in the event of

315

foreclosure, it may proceed against both land and improvements. This may justify a higher loan than otherwise, benefitting not only the borrower but also the landowner since this will permit a more extensive improvement, creating more income to the lessee and more security for the rent obligation (and perhaps more rent if the lease relates the ground rent to the lessee's income). On the other hand, subordination prevents the landowner from mortgaging the fee and reduces its value, since there is a risk it can be foreclosed. If the borrower contemplates refinancing the leasehold mortgage in the future, he should try to get the subordination agreement to apply to such future financing. The landowner is not likely to agree, however, unless he shares in the refinancing proceeds.

(4) Violation of Lease as Default: Since the mortgagee must be sure it can act for the lessee if he defaults under the lease, the mortgage will provide that a lease default also constitutes a default under the mortgage.

(5) Insurance Proceeds: In a fee mortgage, the lender often refuses to agree to apply insurance proceeds to restoration. In a leasehold situation, however, the lessor will not permit this, since it might mean the property would be left unimproved and no income would be available to pay the ground rent. The lender will want to retain the proceeds and pay them out directly to the contractors working on the property. The application of any excess proceeds is a matter of negotiation. The lender will want to use it to reduce the mortgage while the borrower-lessee will want to keep it.

[¶4004.2] Checklist for Lease Underlying Leasehold Mortgage

The ground lease ordinarily will have been signed at the time the lessee seeks leasehold financing. However, he should be prepared for requests by the lender to modify the lease as a condition to the loan. Whether or not the landowner will agree depends on the relative bargaining positions of the parties.

(1) Term of Lease; Renewal Options: We have already pointed out the relationship between the lease term and the loan term. The greater the time "cushion" is, the greater assurance that the mortgagee will be able to recover its loan in the event financial difficulty requires an extension of the loan or foreclosure. In the event of a takeover, the lender will want the right to exercise any renewal options.

(2) Subordination of Lease: The lease should not be made subject to any existing or future mortgage on the fee since this would place two claims ahead of the leasehold mortgage (the lessor's rent claim and the rights of the fee mortgagee). The lender will want any fee mortgage to be subordinate not only to the lease but the leasehold mortgage as well. The lender will also want to be sure that the lease is not subordinate to any restriction of record on the fee, such as a reverter or possibility of forfeiture.

(3) Assignment: Any restriction on the lessee's right to assign or sublet may make the lease unsaleable by the mortgagee after a foreclosure. The lessor may be willing to extend this right to the mortgagee in the event it takes over the lease after a default on the mortgage.

(4) Default: Here, the leasehold mortgagee is interested in assuring that there is no automatic default provision. He will want the protection of a period of time for the lessee to cure any default. In addition, the mortgagee will want to make sure there is no provision for default on the filing of a petition in bankruptcy or a reorganization. If the lessor won't agree to this, the lender will want an agreement that the lender can have a new lease on the same terms as the old one. Similarly, if the lessee abandons the lease, or any other non-curable default occurs, the lender will want the right to a new lease. The lender must have control over any contingency, curable or otherwise, that might terminate the lease which is its only security for the loan.

(5) Notice of Default: The mortgagee will want any notices to be served on both the lessee and the mortgagee, with ample time to both to cure the default. The mortgagee will want a longer time for itself, since it will be unable to act until the period for action by the lessee (specified in the mortgage) has expired. The mortgagee will also want a right to enter the premises for the purpose of curing a default of the covenant to repair.

(6) Covenant to Rebuild or Restore: If the lease requires the lessee to rebuild the improvements in the event they are damaged or destroyed, the mortgagee will want to insure that the lessee has adequate time to complete the work and that the mortgagee can protect itself if the lessee fails to act.

(7) Insurance Proceeds: The lender will want to see that the lease requires the lessee to carry all necessary insurance. In addition, it will object to a provision giving the insurance proceeds to the lessor instead of requiring its use to restore the premises. If this occurred, it would eliminate the lender's security. From the lender's point of view, the best provision is one assigning the insurance proceeds to it for use in restoring the property.

(8) Condemnation Awards: The mortgagee's primary concern is to see that the mortgage is reduced to the extent that the leasehold's income-producing capacity is reduced. There are three situations:

(a) Full taking— If the entire property is condemned, the lessee's share should at least be equal to the mortgage debt. Since the lessee will normally want his share to be equal to the cost of the improvements, the lender will be protected. Apportioning the award between lessee and lessor on the basis of value may involve a risk to the lender in the event land values rise very rapidly.

(b) Partial taking—If the lease provides that a partial taking will terminate the lease, the lessee's share of the award should be sufficient to pay the

mortgage debt. If a partial taking will abate the rent, the lessor will probably want as much of the award as represents the capitalization of the lost rent. The remainder should go to restoration of the premises and any excess to reducing the mortgage debt. In the absence of any lease provision, a partial taking at common law did not abate the rent; in this event, the lender would probably want the entire condemnation award to reduce the mortgage.

(c) Damage without taking—This might arise through loss of access, etc. The problem is the same as in the case of a partial taking except that restoration of the premises is not a factor.

(9) Mortgagee's Obligations: The mortgagee will want to make sure that if it takes over the property, neither it nor any subsequent owner will be liable under any covenants of the lease except during periods of actual ownership. Certain "title-theory" states make the mortgagee liable on the lessee's covenants even though not in possession. In addition, the lease sometimes seeks to make subsequent lessees liable for the obligations of their predecessors. This may affect marketability of the lease.

(10) Option to Purchase: If the lessee has one, the lender will want the mortgage debt to be an encumbrance on it as well as on the lease.

(11) Transfer of Subleases: The lessor will normally insert a provision in the lease (and in each sublease) that if the lessee defaults and the main lease terminates, the subleases will continue as a direct lease between the owner and the subtenants. The mortgagee, who anticipates taking over the lease if the lessee defaults, will want the owner to agree to assign to it (as the new lessee) its interest in the subleases.

(12) Modification of Lease: To protect itself, the mortgagee will want the lease to provide that it may not be amended or modified without its consent.

(13) Estoppel Certificate: The lease should require the lessor to provide an estoppel certificate, at the time of the mortgage closing, stating the date to which the rent has been paid, that no default exists under the lease, and that the lease has not been modified.

●

For Further Reference . . .
Bagby, *Real Estate Financing Desk Book,* Institute for Business Planning, Englewood Cliffs, N.J.
Conway, Lawrence V., *Mortgage Lending.*
Real Estate Investment Planning looseleaf Service. Institute for Business Planning, Englewood Cliffs, N.J.

PARTNERSHIPS

[¶4101] The partnership and the corporation are the two common methods of bringing together a group of individuals for business purposes. The essential distinction between them is that the corporation becomes an independent legal entity while the partnership does not. As a practical matter, the partnership has several advantages over the corporation. They are:

(1) The retention by each partner of a veto power over the decisions of the partnership.

(2) The avoidance of a second tax which would be imposed on corporate income.

(3) Freedom from the statutory regulations and miscellaneous taxes to which the corporation is subject.

(4) Simplicity in organization operation.

Disadvantages include:

(1) The agency of every partner being able to bind the others.

(2) The joint and several liability of each partner for all the obligations of the business including liability from wrongful acts of another partner, mitigated only slightly by the right of contribution.

(3) The dissolution of the partnership upon contingencies like death of a partner. These rules and the limitations on them are set out in the Uniform Partnership Act, adopted by most of the states. The biggest disadvantage of the partnership, unlimited personal liability, can be avoided for some of the partners by resort to a limited partnership. See Uniform Limited Partnership Act. For a technique of retiring partnership interests, see ¶803.

[¶4102] ## CHECKLIST FOR ORGANIZING A PARTNERSHIP

1. Name: Any name may be used for a partnership unless specifically prohibited by law. Use of a name deceptively similar to that of another business may lead to litigation. Many states have a statutory requirement that partnership names be registered with the Secretary of State, County Clerk, or other appropriate filing officer. Where individuals' names are used in the partnership name, consideration should be given to whether the name will be continued after the death of a partner and whether this is permitted under local law. The use of the name of itself will not make the individual property of the deceased partner liable for any debts contracted by the partnership.

2. Business Activity: A careful statement of the nature of the business is necessary to define the scope of the partnership so that no partner becomes involved in a business against his wishes.

3. Licensing: If the nature of the business is one that might require licensing, etc., state and federal regulatory statutes should be checked. Where a license or permit is required, it is wise to provide that the partnership agreement will not become effective until the license or permit is procured.

4. Term: A definite term of years for the continuation of the partnership business may be agreed upon or the partnership may continue at will. However, any partner may terminate his relations with the partnership even though it be in contravention of the partnership agreement. This may give rise to a suit for damages by the remaining partners, but the partnership nevertheless is dissolved. The partnership agreement may provide for liquidated damages for premature withdrawal which will be enforceable provided that they may not be construed as a penalty rather than damages. Where the agreement specifies a fixed term, the parties may continue the business beyond that term as a partnership at will. However, it is advisable that they either extend the term of the partnership or enter into a new partnership agreement.

5. Partnership Contributions: Careful distinction should be drawn between contributions to the partnership capital and other types of financial relationships (such as loans) between the partners and the partnership. Contributions to partnership capital may consist of cash, property or services. When property is contributed, consideration should be given to the statutory right of the partners to reconcile the tax bases and accounting values of the contributed property. These adjustments may be necessary to prevent distortions in the partnership income shares.

6. Loans and Leases with Partnership: A partner may, in his individual capacity, lend or rent property to the partnership and receive interest or rent. Since the money loaned or the property leased is not part of the partnership capital, they will not be available in the first instance for the satisfaction of partnership debts.

7. Interest on Partnership Capital: Generally, the partnership will not pay interest on its capital. If interest is to be paid, the agreement should so state. In businesses which require a large amount of liquid capital to meet regulatory requirements, the parties may feel that payment of interest should be made, particularly where the capital contributions of various partners differ and the distributions of profits do not reflect each partner's capital contributions. Interest paid by the partnership is deductible for tax purposes.

8. Salary: Ordinarily, a partner is compensated for his services and for his contributions of capital by a share of the profits. Unless provided in the partnership agreement, a partner will not be entitled to salary or other compensation for his services except in the case of a partner winding up the business of a partnership. However, if a partner does receive a salary, this is a deductible expense by the partnership.

9. Sharing Profits and Losses: The essential element in the partnership is the sharing of profits between the partners. While losses are ordinarily shared also, this is not always the case (as when the partner who contributes services only may be relieved from any liability from losses). When both profits and losses are shared, they are usually shared in the same ratio (that is, a partner who is entitled to 10% of the profits is liable for 10% of the losses). However, profits and losses may or may not be shared equally between the partners. (For example, a partner putting up 50% of the capital may be entitled to receive 75% of the profit.) Sometimes, different distribution ratios will apply to different kinds of income (e.g., operating income and capital gains). All of these matters must be spelled out in the partnership agreement. One solution to the problem of unequal financial contributions is to create equal capital accounts and treat additional funds as loans.

10. Tax Treatment of Profits and Losses: The partnership is not a separate entity for income tax purposes. Each partner is taxed on his proportionate share of the profits and is entitled to deduct his proportionate share of the losses. It makes no difference whether or not the partner actually draws or pays any money for the tax period in question. The partnership itself files only an information return.

11. Right to Withdraw Capital: Where the right to withdraw funds from the partnership is limited, this should be spelled out in the partnership agreement. Where a substantial amount of money is to be accumulated in the partnership, the partners should be permitted to take out sufficient money to meet their income tax obligations.

12. Payments to Retired or Deceased Partner: When payments are made to a partner who retires, or to the estate or heir of a deceased partner, the money paid may represent the withdrawing partner's capital interest, his pro rata interest in unrealized receivables and fees, his share of the potential gain or loss on partnership inventory, or mutual insurance among the partners. For tax consequences, see ¶803.

13. Management: In the absence of an agreement to the contrary, all partners have equal rights in the management and conduct of the partnership business. It is, therefore, necessary to have the agreement clearly state each partner's rights and duties. The extent to which the partners are authorized as between themselves to commit and bind the partnership should be clearly spelled out in the agreement. Where a partner assigns his interest in the partnership, the assignee during the continuance of the partnership will not have the right to interfere in the management or administration of the partnership business or affairs unless the agreement provides otherwise.

14. Books and Records: Local law frequently requires that books and records must be kept at the principal place of business of the partnership and every partner shall at all times have access to and may inspect and copy them.

15. Death or Withdrawal of a Partner: Provision can be made in the agreement for the continuation of the business after the death or withdrawal of a partner bearing in mind that such provision may, along with other corporate attributes, give the partnership the tax status of a corporation. In the absence of such a provision, the partnership will be required to wind up its affairs.

16. Partnership Property: Unless a contrary intention appears all property acquired with partnership funds will be partnership property.

17. Accounting by Partners: The agreement should require all partners to account to the partnership full information on matters affecting the partnership.

18. Indemnification of Partner: Without any provision in the agreement the partnership may be required to indemnify each partner for payments made and personal liabilities reasonably incurred in the ordinary and necessary fulfillment of the partnership business, or property.

19. Family Partnerships: Partnership interests can be given to family members and in that way income can be spread over a number of low-bracket taxpayers. But keep in mind that this can be done only where capital is a substantial income-producing factor in the partnership. And the donor-partner must get fair compensation before the balance of the partnership profits are distributed among the remaining partners.

Where a trust is a partner, the trustee should have broad powers and be able to act independently as a partner.

20. Collapsible Partnerships: The partners should be alerted to the "collapsible partnership" rule if it is the intention of one or more of their number to invest in the partnership for a limited period of time. Amounts received by a partner for his partnership interest which are attributable to partnership unrealized receivables or substantially appreciated inventory are treated as ordinary income. (Normally, the sale or liquidation of a partnership interest gives capital gain.)

21. Partnership Treated as a Corporation: In some cases, a partnership will be treated as a corporation despite the wishes of the partners. This will come about when the partnership has more corporate characteristics than non-corporate characteristics under the Federal tax regulations. The four elements that point to a corporation are continuity, centralized management, limited liability, and transferability of interest. If a partnership has three or more of these elements, it may become subject to a double tax on its income (a corporate tax plus a personal tax on each partner).

22. Limited Partnerships: A limited partnership is one step closer to a corporation than is a general partnership because it includes partners who, like shareholders in a corporation, invest capital, have limited liability, and do not share in the management of partnership affairs. The partnership agreement may provide that the limited partner share in profits or may provide that he be paid a specific amount of income whether or not there are partnership profits. In organizing a limited partnership, it is important that the limited partner be given no rights or powers over partnership affairs which may cause him to be treated as a general partner.

For forms of partnership agreement, see IBP FORMS OF BUSINESS AGREEMENTS.

●

For Further Reference . . .

Crane, *Crane on Partnership,* West Publishing Co., St. Paul, Minn.

Forms of Business Agreements looseleaf Service. Institute for Business Planning, Englewood Cliffs, N.J.

Willis, *On Partnership Taxation,* McGraw-Hill Book Co., 1971.

PENSION AND PROFIT-SHARING PLANS

[¶4201] Many of the same general factors require consideration in the design and establishment of either pension, profit-sharing, stock bonus, or thrift plans. To put either type of program into effect requires a written plan which states the requirements for qualification and the manner of determining benefits (or allocation of contributions). If employee contributions are required the amount of employee contributions must be set forth.

If pensions are to be provided by a group annuity or deposit administration plan, the terms of the plan may be contained in a master contract between the insurance company and the employer. Aside from a group annuity a trust agreement is also needed to designate a trustee to hold and invest the funds which are to be accumulated for the future benefit of employees and fix the trustee's duties and obligations. Both the plan and the trust agreement can be combined in a single instrument.

The important difference between profit-sharing and pension plans concerns employer contributions to the plan. In a pension plan the employer has a fixed commitment to contribute enough money to provide a specified amount of pension funds at retirement age except that a money purchase pension plan does not fix benefits but must set forth the method by which the amount of employer contributions is determined, and it may not be dependent on profits.

In a profit-sharing plan the commitment is more flexible as it is contingent upon the profits of the company. This factor makes profit-sharing plans attractive to smaller companies. Furthermore, where pension plans are used the emphasis is on accumulating funds for retirement whereas many profit-sharing plans provide for distribution during employment. This is usually the case with smaller companies. Larger companies generally use deferred compensation plans and combination cash and deferred plans are found predominantly in middle-sized companies.

Another fundamental difference between the plans concerns the allocation of contributed funds. Money contributed to a pension fund can be allocated among the beneficiaries in a manner actuarially calculated to provide the required pension at retirement age. Profit-sharing plans must be allocated according to salary and to a minor extent, length of service may constitute a factor. In short, in a pension fund, a larger portion of the money can be allocated to older employees to fund their pension needs at the expense of the younger employees who have a greater number of years over which to accumulate their pensions. In a profit-sharing plan, age is not a factor in the allocation of funds.

Profit-sharing plans do not run to any particular pattern. They are uniquely designed to the purposes of management, the character of the business and the composition of the work force. This is particularly true with respect to the composition of the work force. This is particularly true with respect to the central provision of how much of company profits will be contributed to the plan. A 10% profit-sharing rate in one line of business may be more generous than a 25% contribution in another type of business. The profit-sharing rate will also vary with the age of the work force, whether they are also covered by a pension plan and other diverse factors. However, virtually all plans seeking to qualify for tax privileges limit the contribution to the 15% of payroll and carryover allowed as a deduction by the Code.

Various forms of pension and profit-sharing plans suitable for both large and small companies will be found in IBP PAY PLANNING (looseleaf service).

[¶4201.1] Tax Advantages of Qualified Plans

The tax advantages of a qualified pension or profit-sharing plan are:

(1) *Employer*—The employer gets a *current deduction* for amounts contributed to the plan, within specified limits, despite the fact that no benefits may have been actually distributed to the participating employees that year. This permits an employer to accumulate a trust fund for his employees with 100-cent pre-tax dollars which, in effect, represent 52-cent after-tax dollars to the employer at present tax rates.

(2) *Employees*—The tax to the employee is *deferred* until the benefits under the plan are actually distributed or made available to him. Moreover, if he receives his entire distribution in one taxable year on account of death, retirement or other termination of employment, he pays only the lower *capital gain tax rate* thereon except that the part equal to employer contributions made after 1973 and forfeitures attributable to employer contributions made after 1973 is taxed as ordinary income under a special 10-year income averaging formula.

(3) *Trust fund*—The income of the trust fund is *exempt from tax* during the entire period of accumulation. Thus, the amount contributed to the trust fund is free from tax at the time of deposit and the entire undiminished fund can earn interest which is also tax exempt. Funds, which are compounded tax free under a qualified plan, will increase at a much greater rate than if such funds were currently distributed to employees and personally invested by them. In the latter case, the amount received by the employees is subject to two tax bites—first, when the employee receives his share of the benefits, and a second time on the investment income earned on what is left after the first tax bite.

[¶4201.2] Choosing Between Pension and Profit-Sharing Plans

Profit-Sharing	*Pension Plans*
(1) Generally, favors younger employees.	(1) Generally, favors older employees.
(2) Need not provide retirement benefits.	(2) Must provide retirement benefits.

Profit-Sharing

(3) Contributions can be made only if profits exist.

(4) Even in profitable years the amount of contribution, if any, can be left to discretion of management.

(5) Deduction for contributed amounts generally cannot exceed 15% of a year's payroll for participants. Deduction for excess contributions may be carried over to future years.

(6) Forfeitures may be allocated in favor of remaining participants.

(7) No more than 49.9% of employer contributions that have accumulated for two years or less may be invested in ordinary life insurance. No limit on amounts accumulated for over two years.

(8) Broad fringe benefits can be included (incidental accident and health insurance).

(9) Employer may never recover any part of contribution or income therefrom.

Pension

(3) Contributions must be made for profitable as well as for loss years.

(4) Amount of contribution is not discretionary; it must be actuarially justifiable and tied to definitely determinable benefits.

(5) No maximum on contributions if they are actuarially justifiable and total compensation is within IRC § 162's limitations. However, there is a limitation on maximum benefit to an individual.

(6) Forfeitures must be used to decrease future cost to employer.

(7) May be invested in life insurance contracts providing death benefits not exceeding 100 times expected monthly retirement benefits. In some cases, up to 50% of employer contributions may be used instead.

(8) Limited fringe benefits can be included (disability pension).

(9) Employer, on termination of plan, may recover excess funds which arose as a result of actuarial error.

【¶4201.3】 Qualifying a Pension, Profit-Sharing or Stock Bonus Plan

A qualified plan is one that meets the standards and requirements prescribed in §401(a) of the 1954 Code, as amended by the Employee Retirement Income Act of 1974. The qualification requirements have been interpreted and supplemented by voluminous Treasury regulations and rulings as well as court decisions. The requirements listed below are applicable to all types of plans (i.e., pension, profit-sharing and stock bonus plans), except requirement (10) which applies only to profit-sharing plans and (12) which applies only to pension plans:

(1) The plan must be primarily a deferred compensation plan.

(2) It must be a permanent program, and not a temporary arrangement.

(3) It must be for the exclusive benefit of the employees and their beneficiaries.

(4) It must cover either a specified percentage of employees or a non-discriminatory class of employees and may not exclude employees for age or service except as permitted in Code §410(a).

(5) It must not discriminate with respect to the benefits and contributions distributable to the participants in the plan.

(6) It must be in writing and communicated to the employees.

(7) The trust instrument must prohibit the diversion of any part of the trust funds to the benefit of persons other than the covered employees.

(8) The trust formed to administer the plan must be organized in the United States.

(9) The plan must be integrated with Social Security benefits if employees earning less than a specified amount a month are excluded from participating in the plan or receive proportionately smaller benefits than those earning over that amount.

(10) In the case of a profit-sharing plan, it is advisable (although not mandatory) that the plan contain a definite formula for computing the profits which the employer is to put into the plan. The plan must have a definite formula for allocating contributions and other benefits among the participants.

(11) Contributions or benefits must be limited to comply with Code §415.

(12) Pension plans must be funded in accordance with Code §412.

(13) The plan must provide for vesting of benefits under one of three minimum standards set forth in Code §411(a)(2).

[¶4201.4] Tax Status of a Non-Qualified Plan

Let's look at the tax treatment of a non-qualified plan, bearing in mind possible tax reform in this area.

(1) *Employer* — The employer gets his deduction *currently* for amounts contributed to the plan, provided that the employees' rights are *nonforfeitable* when the contribution was made. If *forfeitable*, the employer may lose the right of deduction forever but some courts have held that the deduction is available when benefits are paid out.

(2) *Employees*—The employee is taxed *immediately* on the amount contributed to the plan for his account, if his rights are *nonforfeitable*. If *forfeitable*, the employee is taxed when the benefits become nonforfeitable.

(3) *Trust fund*—Most non-qualified plans are of the immediate payment type. Consequently, there is no opportunity to build up a pool of tax-exempt capital and income funds for future distribution to participating employees, as in the case of a qualified plan.

[¶4201.5] Non-Deferred Profit-Sharing Plans

Non-deferred profit-sharing plans do not qualify for the tax benefits under §401. The employee is taxed upon actual or constructive receipt of payments and the employer gets a current deduction.

It is not necessary to establish a trust or any other elaborate device to administer or invest the profit contributions because there are no deferred payments under the plan. For the same reasons, the vesting of employee rights does not present a problem.

The determination of employee eligibility and allocation of contributions is within the discretion of the employer. There is no prohibition against discrimination. However, in determining eligibility, wage-hour problems should be considered. Allocation of contributions is usually based upon the employee's years of service, wage or salary, a merit rating system, or a combination thereof. The objectives of the plan will guide the proper determination of these factors.

The percentage of profits to be contributed is also within the employer's discretion. There is no limitation on the tax deduction as in the case of qualified deferred plans except that the amount must be "reasonable compensation." The desired employee benefits, the financial condition of the company, and the stockholder protection are factors to be considered.

Distributions should be made at specified periodic dates. Frequency of distributions depends upon the employer's convenience and the objectives of the plan. They usually range from monthly payments to annual payments.

A deferred profit-sharing plan and a nondeferred profit-sharing plan may be combined in order to obtain the advantages of both.

[¶4201.6] Self-Employed Retirement Plans (Keogh Plans)

Under Code §401 and 405, self-employed retirement plans may qualify for tax benefits. Under the Code, there are two groups of self-employed individuals: owner-employees with more than 10% interest in the business and those who have less than a 10% interest.

All full-time employees of the company with at least three years' service must be covered by a qualified plan. The contributions for these employees must vest immediately and must not be discriminatory when compared with amounts contributed for the owner-employees. Once money is committed to the plan for owner-employees (over 10% interest), it may not be withdrawn without penalty prior to age 59-1/2.

Contributions on behalf of owner-employees can be made to the plan in the same way as contributions made on behalf of other employees. However, there are special limitations on the amounts that can be contributed on behalf of the self-employed.

For a comparison of corporate and Keogh Plans, see ¶4350.5.

For Further Reference . . .

How to Set Up a Successful Profit-Sharing Plan, Prentice-Hall, Englewood Cliffs, N.J.

Pay Planning looseleaf Service. Institute for Business Planning, Englewood Cliffs, N.J.

PRICES

[¶4301] In general, §2 of the Clayton Act, as amended by the Robin-son-Patman Act (15 USC §13), prohibits price discriminations that result in competitive injury. The related §3 of the Robinson-Patman Act (15 USC §13a) prohibits area price discrimination and sales at "unreasonably low" prices for the purpose of destroying competition or eliminating a competitor.

A client can't practice price discrimination where all of these conditions exist: (1) he is in interstate commerce, (2) he has made at least two sales, (3) these sales are to different customers, (4) the sales cover "commodities of like grade and quality," (5) at least one is in interstate commerce, (6) the commodities are for use, consumption, or resale within the U.S.A. or some place under its jurisdiction.

[¶4302] JUSTIFYING PRICE DIFFERENTIALS

Price differentials can be justified where (1) the difference makes only due allowance for cost savings, (2) it rose in the course of meeting in good faith "an equally low price of a competitor," or (3) it will not result in competitive injury.

The cost saving justification is difficult. First, the cost records kept in the usual course of business frequently do not correlate with the classification involved in a given price comparison. Secondly, much cost saving is based on approximations and allocations that will not satisfy an exacting standard of proof. (See the Federal Trade Commission's decision in *Standard Oil Co.,* 41 FTC 263 (1945).) Thirdly, the reduced price that brings about a differential usually results from competitive conditions, and any coincidence with a cost difference is purely accidental.

The justification of *meeting competition* may be unavailable if all the circum-stances indicate that the seller knew or should have known that the competi-tor's price he met was unlawful (Report of the Attorney General's National Committee to Study the Antitrust Laws, 181-82 (1955)). It will fail if a court decides that the seller was merely emulating an unlawful *system* of pricing used by others (*FTC v. A. E. Staley Mfg. Co.,* 324 US 746 (1945)). It may not be available to meet a competitor's offer in order to gain a new customer, as contrasted with a purely defensive reduction to retain an existing customer (Report of the Attorney General's National Committee to Study the Antitrust Laws, 181, 184 (1955)).

Earl W. Kintner, a former Federal Trade Commission Chairman, set forth the following set of conditions to be met in order to justify *price discounts as being necessary to meet competition:*

(1) The seller does not come within the proviso if he knows or should have known that the competitor's price he met was unlawful. A question exists as to whether the seller has the burden of showing that his competitor's price was lawful. Two circuit courts of appeals have held that he does not.

(2) The lower price posted by the seller must be a price lower than the seller normally could have charged except for the necessity of meeting the particular competitor's price.

(3) The seller's price discrimination must be temporary, not part of a permanent price schedule whereby some customers are systematically charged higher prices than others.

(4) If the seller meets the higher prices as well as the lower prices of a competitor, not attempting to undersell him in markets where the seller has a competitive advantage, the seller does not come within the proviso.

(5) Where a seller's competitor sells to a customer in large quantities at a quantity price, the seller does not come within the §2(b) proviso if he meets that price in selling to the customer in smaller quantities if the competitor's price for such smaller quantities was higher. An equally low price of a competitor means an equally low price for a given quantity.

(6) The seller's discriminatory price must meet a specific individual competitor's price offered to a specific individual customer. The Robinson-Patman Act places emphasis on individual competitive situations rather than on a general system of competition.

(7) The seller must meet, not beat, the competitor's price. That is, the seller must prove the existence of facts "which would lead a reasonable and prudent person to believe that the granting of a lower price would in fact meet the equally low price of a competitor."

(8) A seller may not lower his price to a favored buyer in order to enable the buyer to meet the competition of those competing with the buyer. The seller can only meet his own competition.

To use this defense, advise the client to establish a uniform procedure that requires his salesmen, when recommending a reduced price to meet competition, to submit a copy of the competitor's offer or invoice if they can get one; if not, a letter signed by the customer certifying that a competitor has offered to supply him at a stated price; and if the customer will not sign that, a statement signed by the salesman himself stating all of the facts he can ascertain about the competitor's offer.

[¶4302.1] Functional Discounts

Functional discounts are not expressly permitted but it is generally held that they may be allowed, so long as the amount reasonably reflects the value of the distribution services which the wholesaler performs. However, when the wholesaler also makes some sales at retail, the allowance may be illegal if it is granted on the quantities of the client's product that are thus sold at retail.

Here are some practices to avoid: (1) labeling discriminatory allowances as "cash discounts" to get around the law; (2) allowing customers to "steal" cash discounts after the specified time for payment; (3) giving arbitrary, volume discounts in flat amounts. A graduated scale is safer.

[¶4302.2] Price Discounts via Allowances for Advertising and Services Also Prohibited

Sections 2(d) and 2(c) of the Robinson-Patman Act prohibit price discrimination via payments or allowances for advertising, promotional services furnished by the buyer and services and facilities furnished by the seller.

[¶4303] LEGAL PRICE FIXING

Fixing the resale price of a trade-marked or brand-named product is permitted by state fair trade acts. But these acts are meaningless when they don't also contain a "non-signer clause." This clause gives them teeth. It makes the price-fixing agreement between the manufacturer and the retailer binding upon *all* retailers in the state having notice of it. The term "non-signer" refers to any seller who has not signed a price-fixing contract with the manufacturer of a trade-marked or brand-named product — after one seller *has* signed such a contract with the manufacturer.

At the present time only 21 states are enforcing fair trade acts containing a non-signer clause. They are: Arizona, California, Connecticut, Delaware, Hawaii, Illinois, Maine, Maryland, Massachusetts, Mississippi, Nevada, New Hampshire, North Carolina, North Dakota, Ohio, Pennsylvania, Rhode Island, South Dakota, Tennessee, Virginia, and Wisconsin.

Forms of fair trade agreements and clauses appear in IBP FORMS OF BUSINESS AGREEMENTS looseleaf Service.

[¶4304] RESTRICTIONS ON BELOW COST SALES AND MINIMUM MARKUP REQUIREMENTS

Sales below cost are prohibited in many states if the purpose, intent, or effect of the sale is that of injuring a competitor or destroying competition.

How to figure cost: A manufacturer's cost includes raw material, labor, and *all* overhead. As for wholesalers and retailers, state laws vary. But generally their cost is based upon: (1) invoice or replacement cost—whichever is lower, (2) less all trade discounts except customary cash discounts, (3) plus freight or cartage charges, and (4) the cost of doing business.

Some states set a minimum-markup requirement in the absence of proof of a lesser cost of doing business.

In 29 states, sales-below-cost laws are generally applicable to all commodities. Some states also enforce additional below-cost-sales laws applicable to specific commodities. Merchandise covered ranges from cigarettes to bakery goods.

●

For Further Reference . . .

Alexander, George J., Honesty and Competition: Some Problems in The Pricing of Goods, 31 *Fordham Law Review* 141.

American Jurisprudence, Monopolies §15, 28.

Gardner, William F., The Right to Meet Competition Under the Robinson-Patman Act, 23 *Alabama Lawyer* 255.

Hale, G. E., Practical Robinson-Patman Compliance, 4 *Corporate Practice Commentator* 18.

Kemker, Harry, Price Discrimination Under the Robinson-Patman Act, 14 *University of Florida Law Review* 155.

LaRue, Carl F., Pitfalls for Price Competitors: State and Federal Restrictions on Below Cost or Unreasonably Low Prices, 15 *Western Reserve Law Review* 35.

Legal Aspects of Competitive Business Policies, *California State Bar.*

Rowe, Frederick M., Cost Justification of Price Differentials Under the Robinson-Patman Act, 59 *Columbia Law Review* 584.

Trade Regulation Report, Commerce Clearing House.

PROFESSIONAL CORPORATIONS

[¶4350] Do the tax advantages of incorporating make it worthwhile for professionals? This is the question many professionals are asking themselves these days.

[¶4350.1] **How Professionals Benefit When They Incorporate**

In the checklist which follows, we recapitulate the advantages professionals can get by incorporating. We point out in each instance the contrasting tax treatment for professionals engaged in solo or partnership practice.

1. Profit-Sharing Plan: Working stockholders can participate in a company's qualified plan (§401). Deductible contributions can go up to a maximum of 15% of the working stockholder's compensation. (Partners can only participate in a Keogh plan to the extent of 15% of compensation or $7,500 per year, if less.)

2. Pension Planning: Officer and employee-stockholders can be beneficiaries of a pension trust. A corporation can deduct its payments to the extent allowed by law. Where a regularly taxed corporation has both a pension and a profit-sharing plan, its maximum deductible contributions for both plans may total 25% of the working stockholder's compensation. (Partners may participate only if the pension plan is a Keogh plan. However, the deductible contribution to Keogh plans is limited to $7,500 per partner even if the partnership has both a pension and a profit-sharing plan.)

3. Death Benefits: Benefits up to $5,000 can be received tax free by stockholder-employee's beneficiaries (§101). (No tax exemption for payments to partner's beneficiaries.)

4. Group Term Insurance: Working stockholders of a corporation are eligible for $50,000 of tax-free life insurance protection. (Insurance protection made available to partners is not tax free.)

5. Sick Pay: A corporate employee gets limited tax-free treatment for his accident and sickness pay under §105. (This benefit is not available to a partner.)

6. Corporate Tax Shelter: High tax bracket stockholders get income tax shelter under the corporate setup: The first $25,000 of corporate income is taxed at 22%; excess is taxed at a maximum of 48%. (This may not be as important an advantage as it was prior to the 50% tax ceiling on earned income.)

7. Deferred Compensation: Working stockholders in a corporation may have their compensation deferred and paid out at a time when it can produce the best tax results. (Deferred taxation of compensation to retirement years, when the partner would presumably be in a lower tax bracket, is not available to a partner.)

8. Meals and Lodgings: Working stockholders may exclude from their income the value of any meals or lodging furnished for the convenience of the corporation.

[¶4350.2] Special Corporate Advantages

Income tax saving isn't the whole story. Incorporation will help in the transfer of a practice when the professional retires or something happens to him. It can also produce substantial estate tax savings.

Similarly, when a shareholder leaves, retires, or dies, the corporation or the other shareholders simply buy his stock. It's not like a partnership where the exit of one partner can dissolve the partnership and call for a new partnership agreement.

Preservation of Values Helped: The ease of transfer of corporate stock plus the relative immortality of a corporation can be of immeasurable help in preserving the value of the professional's interest. The corporation survives his leaving.

Tax Savings via Stepped-Up Basis: As the law now stands, when a professional holds stock which has appreciated in value and passes it on to someone else—his son or some other family member—by will, the appreciation escapes capital gain tax. The value of the shares will be included in his estate, but the recipient will never have to pay capital gains on the appreciation that occurred prior to his receipt of the stock. He gets what is called a stepped-up basis figured on the basis of the value when he acquired it, not the professional's basis; that is, the value when the stock was acquired plus any additional contributions to capital that may have been made.

Liability: When professionals incorporate, their business liability is limited to the capital they have invested in the corporation. They can't be held personally liable for corporate debts or judgments based on business activities. The claim or judgment is against the corporation. Professional liability is something else. Each professional remains personally liable for his own malpractice.

Profit-Sharing Bonanza: In some profit-sharing plans, the key participants may be able to pick up more in the way of forfeitures from other employees than they get from the income earned and capital appreciation of the profit-sharing fund. That is to say, a corporate profit-sharing plan, unlike a Keogh plan, may have provisions for delayed vesting of contributions and forfeiture of interests when an employee leaves before his interest becomes vested. The forfeited interests are then divided among the remaining participants.

[¶4350.3] **How the Ceiling on Earned Income Affects the Tax Savings**

A 50% rate ceiling now applies to earned income. For professionals in the over-50% bracket ($52,000 of taxable income is the breakpoint on a joint return), this change could serve to reduce but not eliminate the tax shelter afforded by practicing in the corporate form. But there are situations where the rule would not cut the corporate tax shelter. For example, where a professional has large amounts of "tax-preference income" (e.g., capital gains), the 50% tax ceiling might not be applicable. The rule is that the earned income subject to the 50% ceiling is reduced by each dollar of tax-preference income. Another example is where capital and personal services are a material factor in the earnings of the corporation. Here, only 30% of the earnings would be eligible for the 50% ceiling. For most professional corporations, however, this would not be applicable because capital is not a material income-producing factor.

Assuming that a professional is qualified for the full benefits of the 50% ceiling, here's an example of how incorporation would work out with a one-man operation:

Without the use of a corporation, a professional with $100,000 taxable income taking full advantage of the earned-income ceiling rate would have a tax liability of $42,060. If he incorporated and drew down $60,000 as salary and left $40,000 in the corporation, his personal tax liability, using the tax ceiling, would be $22,060; and the corporate tax would be $15,300—for a total of $37,360. The tax saving is $4,700.

[¶4350.4] **Tax-Preference Tax Shelter**

While the earned-income ceiling may lessen the tax shelter of using the corporate form, there is another aspect to the Code which increases its tax shelter. It relates to the 10% minimum tax on tax-preference income.

There is a 10% minimum tax on preference income for both individuals and corporations. It provides a $30,000 exemption in both categories. Whether a professional operates as an individual or as a partner, he is entitled to only one $30,000 exemption. Where he operates his professional corporate firm, however, he would be entitled to two $30,000 exemptions—a $30,000 exemption at the corporate level and a $30,000 exemption at the individual level. Of course, if there is more than one professional, they, in effect, share the additional $30,000 exemption allowed to the corporation. The total tax savings, assuming that the full exemption is used, comes to about $3,000 per year. Add this to the $4,700 ordinary tax shelter and you're up to tax savings of more than $7,000 per year.

Where the corporation elects Subchapter S treatment, however, there is no tax shelter of preference income because the items of tax preference are apportioned among the shareholders of the corporation; they are not preferences of the corporation.

[¶4350.5] Choosing Between Subchapter S Benefits and Full Retirement Benefits

Another significant provision which has a direct effect on professional corporations is the limitation on pension and profit-sharing plans for shareholders of a Subchapter S corporation. Only 15%, with a maximum of $7,500, of a 5%-stockholder's compensation may be contributed tax free to a profit-sharing or pension plan. The excess contribution is taxable to the stockholder-employee.

How important is the Subchapter S election? Well, in a regular business corporation where personal services and invested capital are a material factor in the earnings of the corporation, the election can be very important because it permits the owners to pass through all the earnings, those attributable to capital as well as those attributable to personal services, without taxation at the corporate level.

Without the election, corporate earnings attributable to capital would be taxed once at the corporate level and again when paid out to the owners in the form of dividends.

Now, in most professional corporations, capital is not apt to be a material factor in the corporate earnings picture. Without a Subchapter S election, it should be possible to pass through substantial amounts of corporate earnings in the form of compensation for personal services and thereby minimize the problems connected with double taxation, e.g., the accumulated earnings tax penalty and personal holding company status. The corporation gets a full deduction for compensation paid so long as it is considered reasonable.

In this connection the ceiling rate of 50% on earned income would help. That particular provision, as we indicated, also covers the situation where capital and personal services are both at work in producing earnings just as a repealed provision of the Keogh law did.

We think, then, that the average incorporated professional isn't apt to lose too much, if anything, by forgoing a Subchapter S election if he's looking to draw as much income as possible.

But, if capital can be considered a material income-producing factor in a professional practice, he might then have a problem with "reasonable" compensation and a Subchapter S election might be a convenient, if not a necessary, solution.

What's more, where he wants to use the corporation as a tax shelter, he will have no interest at all in the Subchapter S election. The election would defeat any tax shelter. Even the shelter relating to the minimum tax and investment interest would be lost.

Of course, the use of the Subchapter S election with a professional corporation does serve a useful purpose by eliminating the problems normally affecting personal service companies; that is, the problems relating to unreasonable compensation, unreasonable accumulations of earnings, and the personal holding company status.

Where the Subchapter S Election Is Considered Necessary: What is the situation if for any reason you conclude that the Subchapter S is necessary or desired?

Here you have the straight question of whether a corporate retirement plan is better than a Keogh plan. That's the real alternative.

First of all, it must be borne in mind that the limitation on the deduction of contributions to corporate plans of Subchapter S corporations is not a limitation on distributions. While the limitation on the deduction of contributions is the same as for Keogh plans, distributions are handled more favorably, and there are other advantages of a corporate plan over a Keogh plan, as we'll see.

Corporate and Keogh Plans Compared: Under a Keogh Plan, an owner-employee is entitled to special favored tax treatment of a lump-sum distribution only upon death, disability, or after age 59-1/2. Under a corporate plan, on the other hand, an employee may receive the special tax treatment for a lump-sum payout made at any age upon his separation from employment. Under either plan, part of the lump sum is treated as capital gain (the part in proportion to the number of pre-1974 years of participation in the plan as compared to total years of participation), and the balance is treated as ordinary income subject to a ten-year averaging provision.

Another important area in which Keogh plans and corporate plans differ significantly is in the matter of voluntary contributions. With a Keogh plan, the owner-employee can make voluntary contributions to the plan only if he has at least one covered employee and then only to the amount of 10% of his compensation or $2,500, whichever is smaller. With a corporate plan, the limitation on voluntary contributions is a straight 10% of compensation without the $2,500 maximum. Thus, with a corporate plan, the professional who earns, say, $100,000 can contribute up to $10,000; whereas with a Keogh plan, he is limited to $2,500. This additional $7,500 can build up tax free within the corporate plan. This in itself can make a big difference in the buildup.

Another advantage of a corporate plan is that it's not subject to the immediate, full vesting requirement of a Keogh plan covering employees. Also, you won't have to wait until age 59½ for a payout as you do with Keogh. And there are also estate and gift tax exemptions available under a corporate plan which are not available under Keogh.

In other words, the real choice is not between diluted retirement benefits (under a corporate plan) and loss of Subchapter S benefits; the real choice is at worst a choice between Keogh and a corporate plan diluted by this provision.

[¶4350.6] Additional Corporate Advantages

Incorporation eases the entry of new members and the transfer of interests. It also helps in the preservation of value, offers tax savings via new tax elections, helps limit liability and may make for better administration.

It also permits a number of fringe benefits not available to self-employed individuals or partners, including group term insurance, $5,000 death benefits payable tax free to a stockholder-employee's beneficiary, deferred compensation contracts and sick pay.

The IRS approval of prototype and master pension and profit-sharing plans may also give a big boost to incorporation. This step makes it possible for the professional corporation to adopt a retirement plan at nominal cost besides expediting the whole process.

But incorporation is not without some problems. Let's consider some.

[¶4350.7] Retirement and Death Benefit Hurdle

One of the more important questions which a professional has to deal with before incorporating is his firm's death and retirement benefits. Accounting firms, for example, have substantial retirement and death benefits for a partner which are many times what his annual share of earnings would be. These amounts are taxed as ordinary income; but at retirement, the partner is in a lower tax bracket. What's more, the remaining partners get a deduction as long as the agreement does not talk about goodwill.

This kind of thing is probably impossible to do with a professional corporation. The corporation can work up some kind of deferred compensation arrangement such as a profit-sharing or pension plan or a nonqualified deferred compensation plan, but the benefits of these arrangements have to bear some relationship to the services performed prior to retirement. They cannot be a subterfuge for a payment for what amounts to goodwill.

With a partnership, on the other hand, you are allowed to make payments for goodwill, as long as they are not so designated in the agreement. The Code recognizes this as a kind of mutual insurance.

[¶4350.8] Tax Evasion

If the principal purpose of a corporation is tax evasion or avoidance, §269 IRC permits IRS to deny a tax deduction or other allowance not otherwise available. But IRS might have difficulty proving such a principal purpose and has said, assuming that it is shown that a corporation was formed principally for the purpose of taking advantage of a qualified plan, "there is some question whether such a purpose would constitute 'evasion or avoidance.'"

Conducting Practice as a Corporation: If the professionals continue to conduct their practices individually instead of through the corporation, there's a good chance that IRS will disregard the corporate entity. Also, under IRC §482, IRS may allocate the income of the corporation to the person(s) who produced it and deny the corporation deductions for contributions to the qualified plan. This approach is supported by the case of *Victor Borge,* 405 F. 2d 673, and more recently *Roubik,* 53 TC 365.

The corporation must look and act like a corporation. The bylaws, for example, should provide for centralized management, including control of such matters as assignment of patients or clients; fixing work deadlines, working hours, fees, salary and bonuses; termination of employment; and selection and rejection of clients. Corporate formalities must be observed in such matters as meetings, record and minute keeping, adopting and using a corporate seal, etc. There should be an employment contract between each professional and the corporation negotiated at arm's length. The corporate name must be used on letterheads, bills, office doors, directories, and the bank account.

[¶4350.9] The PHC Hurdle

Some tax experts predict that IRS will try to tax a professional corporation that has five or fewer stockholders at the last half of the taxable year as a personal holding company (subject to a 70% tax rate on its undistributed "personal holding company income"). Under the Code, "personal holding company income" includes income received under a contract to perform personal services where someone other than the corporation can direct which person shall perform the personal services. If at least 60% of a corporation's ordinary gross income is "personal holding company income," the corporation will be taxed as a personal holding company.

However, this possibility shouldn't be a source of great concern, since the problem can usually be avoided in either of these ways: (1) Have the professional corporation — not the patient or client — designate which of its stockholders or employees will do the work. Thus, the fees will not be personal holding income. (2) If the personal holding income is over 60% of the corporation's gross income, have the corporation pay out its personal holding company income in the form of bonuses to stockholder-employees (to the extent that it is reasonable compensation) and distribute the balance, if any, as dividends. (Profits distributed as dividends are only subject to the regular corporate income tax.)

[¶4350.10] Accumulated Earnings Penalty

Once the corporation has accumulated more than $150,000 of earnings, it may be faced with the penalty tax on accumulated earnings (i.e., 27½% on the first $100,000 of unreasonable accumulation and 38½% on the excess). However, the law says that a corporation may accumulate earnings for purposes of a §303 redemption, i.e., a redemption for purposes of paying estate taxes. It also allows the accumulation of earnings for purposes of redeeming stock from a private foundation under certain circumstances.

Where the professional corporation has earnings that are subject to the penalty, it is forced to distribute earnings to the shareholders. The distribution is taxable as any other dividends, and it would be subject to the $100 exclusion. A Subchapter S election would not seem to help much in this respect. The distributions of earnings through a Subchapter S corporation have been treated as dividends. As such, they apparently would not qualify for the 50% ceiling applicable to earnings. On the other hand, the election would hurt the professionals because of the limitation on contributions to the employee benefit plan.

This does not present a real problem where the corporation distributes most of its earnings to the professionals as compensation because there's only a small amount, if any, left in the corporation to accumulate. However, where the corporation is used as a tax shelter and large amounts are left with it, it does present a problem which the corporation has to cope with effectively.

[¶4350.11] Unreasonable Compensation

Related to the problem of accumulated earnings is the one dealing with unreasonable compensation. The corporation may deduct only "reasonable" compensation, the excess being treated as a dividend to an employee-shareholder. You might say that any compensation paid a professional must be reasonable, since it merely represents amounts paid by clients or patients for personal services, less overhead and operating expenses of the firm; but IRS might say part of the corporation's income is due to goodwill. Also, in some large law firms, senior "partners" tend to earn much of their income through the efforts of juniors, and this may have to be considered.

Here, as with the other hurdles, the watchword is caution. One of the steps the professionals should take to minimize the impact of a disallowance of compensation is to use a reimbursement agreement. They agree to reimburse the corporation for any amounts determined by IRS to be unreasonable. A payment under such an agreement would give the professionals an offsetting deduction and put the money back into the corporation.

[¶4350.12] Problems of the One-Man Operation

When a one-man operation incorporates, the first problem he runs into is the personal holding company question. Another is whether the corporate entity is a sham. With a one-man professional corporation, for example, a professional might find it extremely difficult to operate as a corporation. He has operated as an individual owner and might naturally continue operating that way. Under these circumstances, the corporate entity would be regarded as a sham.

With the exception of accountants and attorneys, some tax experts feel that most self-employed individuals would have this problem unless their professional advisors take the time to teach them how to operate a corporation or otherwise supervise the operation. Many state statutes permit professional corporations to have one shareholder-director. This doesn't assure immunity from attack.

[¶4350.13] Professional Corporation v. Association

Under a very small number of state statutes, the corporate characteristics of a "professional corporation" are so few that the organization may not qualify. In this situation, it may be possible to form an "association" under the same statutes and qualify. These cases will be considered on an individual basis and that the associations organized and operated under most state statutes, however, will clearly qualify.

[¶4350.14] How to Get Out Once He's In

Suppose for some reason a professional changes his mind about using the corporate form. What are some of the problems he has to cope with to get out? You do have a goodwill problem on liquidation. But the corporation may be liquidated without tax. The professional has §333. He can liquidate within one month; and, as long as he doesn't have a fat surplus, the problem of goodwill would be avoided. This would be the case with Subchapter S corporations and where the corporation has distributed its earnings during operations.

A §333 liquidation, of course, would precipitate income to the extent of the recapture under §1245 and 1250 and to the extent of the recapture of investment credit. There may also be income because of the receivables.

With Subchapter S corporations, there would be another problem which should be watched. This is the danger of a double tax on earnings. If the corporation has earnings which have been taxed but have not been distributed, there is a danger that the distribution of these earnings pursuant to a §333 liquidation would be taxable a second time to the shareholders. A Subchapter S corporation can avoid this by making sure that taxed earnings are distributed and are within the safety zone of nontaxability before liquidation.

[¶4350.15] The Alternatives

We've reviewed the benefits and pitfalls of incorporation but we can't make a balanced judgment on whether or not to incorporate until we've considered the alternatives. The main alternative is, of course, to practice as an individual or in partnership with others.

Qualified corporate plans, as we've seen, permit much greater tax shelter than Keogh. Even if for some reason you think it desirable to elect Subchapter S, as discussed above, and so are subjected to the Keogh-type limitations on contributions, a corporate plan will still be better than Keogh for a variety of reasons.

The earned-income ceiling of 50% may serve to reduce the benefits available to high-income practitioners practicing in corporate form, but it will not eliminate the tax shelter. Indeed, in one respect, the corporate form may improve the working of this 50% ceiling by permitting the corporation to carry a tax-preference-generating type of investment and so reduce the earned income eligible for the 50% ceiling by tax-preference income accruing to the individual.

For most professionals, incorporation will be the best route. The way to achieve this is spelled out in *Rev. Rul. 70-101* CB 1970-1, 278, *Rev. Rul. 70-455* CB 1970-2, 297 *and Rev. Rul. 73-596* CB 1973-2, 424.

•

For Further Reference . . .

Pay Planning, looseleaf Service, Institute for Business Planning, Englewood Cliffs, N.J.

Professional Corporations, Associations and Partnerships, looseleaf Service, Institute for Business Planning, Englewood Cliffs, N.J.

REAL ESTATE TRANSACTIONS

[¶4401] The essential elements in the sale and purchase of real estate converge in the contract of sale. Before there is a real deal there must be a meeting of the minds on the essential substantive and dollar and cents elements which have to be reflected in the contract. Here we will checklist the elements which must be negotiated and pinned down to consummate the sale of real estate.

The law requires that a contract for the sale of real estate be in writing. A lot of arrangements are necessary before transfer of the title of real estate can be accomplished with assurance that all parties know what they are doing. The buyer must have time to ascertain if the seller is in fact the owner of the real estate and that there are no defects in his title. Before paying the purchase price the buyer will want to have the seller's title examined and will want to see evidence that the title is good. The contract of sale has to specify the type of title the buyer will get, how he is to be assured that he is getting the kind of title agreed upon and what is to happen if defects in the title are discovered. While all this is being checked and worked out, the contract of sale nails the seller so that he can't turn around and deal with somebody who offers a higher price and it prevents the buyer from changing his mind as long as the seller can deliver the kind of title he promises. In addition, the contract of sale must deal with insurance policies, leases, chattels, mortgages and other items which are related to the real estate. All of this has to be set forth clearly and exactly in the contract of sale. In an installment contract, it is essential to spell out how and when future installment payments are to be paid and what happens if they are not.

The contract must definitely identify the real estate which is being sold and specify what furniture and other personal property go with the real estate. Usually all fixtures automatically go with the real estate while in the absence of specific provision the buyer is not entitled to any personal property associated with the real estate which is not a fixture.

To be enforceable the contract must be complete. All the terms must be settled with none left to be determined by future negotiations. For example, failure to specify when a purchase money mortgage would fall due made a contract unenforceable.

Specify the type of deed to be given. In most states if the contract is silent the seller is required only to give a quit claim deed. In some states where the contract is silent the seller has to give a warranty deed. The buyer should try to commit the seller to give him a warranty deed.

344

〔¶4401.1〕 Marketable Title

Unless the contract makes specific exceptions, the seller is required to convey a marketable title—free from defects, free from doubt, one that will assure the buyer that he can hold and use the real estate free of conflicting claims to possession and free of litigation. The buyer should have reasonable assurance that he will be able to sell the land without encountering any difficulty which would minimize its value. The buyer does not have to take the real estate if it is subject to any mortgages, any liens, any easements, any restrictions, any leases and tenancies, any encroachments unless the contract specifies the existence of these limitations on the title which the buyer will receive. Substantial existing violations of zoning or building ordinances render title unmarketable, but the prudent buyer will have the contract of sale specify that the seller will deliver the property free from all violations of zoning and building ordinances.

The kind of title which a seller must deliver depends on the terms and provisions of the contract of sale. If the contract is silent the seller must deliver marketable title free from encumbrances. If the contract requires the seller to deliver title "free from all defects or encumbrances," the buyer may be able to reject title if there is even a trivial encroachment or a beneficial easement. Usually the seller lists in his contract the encumbrances which exist and the buyer agrees to take title subject to these encumbrances, such as building restrictions, existing mortgages, etc. If the contract says that the contract will be subject to a lot of general language such as "conditions and restrictions of records, easements, existing tenancies, any state of facts which an accurate survey may show" etc., the seller can probably get away with delivering what he has and the buyer is left holding the bag.

One practical way for seller and buyer to make definite the kind of title they are talking about is to check the examination of title made at the time the seller acquired the property, and if the restrictions which then existed are satisfactory to the buyer, have the seller commit to deliver a title subject only to the limitations existing when he acquired the property. Another way is for the contract to require the seller to deliver a marketable title and a policy of title insurance. This permits the buyer to walk out on a contract if a title is not marketable or if the title insurance is not forthcoming. If the contract merely requires the seller to furnish title insurance then the buyer is required to take a title even if it is technically unmarketable as long as a title company will issue insurance, which it will sometimes do on the basis that there is little business risk in a technical defect which may render the title less than fully marketable.

In order to avoid being tied up in delays attendant to clearing a defective title, the buyer may want to fix a time for delivery of the deed and have the contract provide that time is of the essence so that if the seller does not have good title at the time fixed for delivering the deed the buyer can relieve himself of the obligations of the contract.

The buyer should insist that the contract specify the kind of evidence of good title that the seller will be required to produce, i.e., title insurance, abstracts, certificate of title, etc. He should require that the evidence of title show the condition of the title as of the date on which the deed is delivered rather than the date of contract. The contract should give the seller a reasonable time to furnish the buyer with evidence of title, the buyer a reasonable time to examine such evidence and point out any defects and, then, the seller a further reasonable time to eliminate or cure any such defects, and a further time within which the buyer can decide to accept or reject a title still carrying a defect which the seller has been unable to cure.

[¶4401.2] Deposits

When the buyer makes a deposit or a down payment on the contract, that money applies as part payment of the purchase price if he conforms and if he defaults it can be retained by the seller. This should be specifically covered by the contract. The seller should, to protect himself, require a large enough deposit to cover the broker's commission, expense of title search and compensation for his loss of time and loss of opportunity to sell elsewhere if the buyer should default. If the seller can't deliver clear title, then the buyer is entitled to his deposit back.

[¶4401.3] Mortgages

If the buyer is to take the property subject to an existing mortgage, the contract should so state. It should specify whether the buyer is assuming an existing mortgage or merely taking subject to the mortgage. If the buyer is giving a purchase money mortgage as part of the payment, the contract should spell out the interest rates, maturity, amortization payments, the form of mortgage and other details.

[¶4401.4] Contingencies and Loss

The buyer's obligation may be made subject to contingencies such as his ability to get a mortgage, his ability to get a zoning variance, etc. It is important that the contract spell out the kind of mortgage, the kind of variance, who has the responsibility for getting the mortgage or variance, the time within which the contingency is to be satisfied, when the deal is to be terminated if the contingency has not been satisfied by that time. Specify who is to carry the risk of loss and damage to the property, the right of the buyer to cancel out of the deal if there is a substantial loss, his right to insurance money if he does not back out.

[¶4401.5]   **Survey**

If the buyer wants the seller to provide a survey at the seller's cost, the contract should so provide. The time for delivery of the survey should be specified. The contract should require the survey to be satisfactory to the buyer's lawyer and a time should be fixed for the buyer to raise objections based on the survey.

The survey should be verified with local ordinances, private covenants and restrictions, party wall agreements and set back requirements.

Protecting the Buyer Where Survey Not Available: The risk of violations, encumbrances and restrictions can be put on the seller by inserting these provisions in the contract:

1. Subject to local zoning and set back ordinances which are not violated by the present structure.

2. Subject to the state of facts an accurate survey will show, provided they do not render the title unmarketable.

3. Subject to covenants and restrictions of record not rendering title unmarketable or revertible.

A seller will normally refuse to warrant that the property may be used in ways other than that presently used. But a buyer in a strong bargaining position may be able to obtain such a warranty with respect to a use specified in the contract.

[¶4401.6]   **Outstanding Leases and Lease Provisions**

If the purchaser is buying income-producing property as an investment, his attorney will want to examine the leases and check the rentals in those leases against the rental information which the purchaser has been furnished by the seller. The attorney will also want to look for provisions of leases which include many unusual clauses, particularly those which concern the landlord's obligations to make repairs and the tenants' rights to cancel or to renew. Clauses which concern damage or destruction to the premises, either by casualty or fire or taking through eminent domain, will require an intensive scrutiny.

[¶4401.7]   **Limitations as to Use**

The purchaser's attorney will examine the types of restrictions, area restrictions and use restrictions imposed upon the property either by Government regulation or by private covenant. In order to protect his client he may require a provision that the purchaser will not have to buy the property if its intended use is prohibited by such restrictions. The seller of the property will not usually object to this type of a provision unless market conditions are in his favor and he feels that the tying up of the property during the contract period will unfavorably affect the value of the property. A possible compromise for both parties might be the requirement that the purchaser must acquire the necessary knowledge about existing regulations and covenants within a certain amount of time after the contract of sale has been entered into—typically, this type of provision will give an option to the purchaser to terminate the contract (if there is any prohibition on the particular use he intends to put the property to) during the specified period of time.

[¶4401.8] Zoning

The seller will ordinarily provide a warranty that existing structures on the property are not in violation of any zoning regulations and ordinances. If the purchaser plans to change the existing use of the property, this warranty is not enough for him. The same considerations will also apply to a purchaser where he is acquiring vacant land on which he plans to erect a building which he will devote to a particular use. Here the purchaser will insist on a repetition by the seller that the purchaser's contemplated use of the land will not violate zoning regulations and ordinances. The seller, of course, may not be willing to go that far in his assurances. The ultimate disposition of this problem depends on the parties' bargaining position.

[¶4401.9] Performance Time

The seller may want the proceeds of the sale of the property on a particular day since he may intend to either enter into a new venture or to discharge an obligation. In circumstances like that he may want to make time for performance under the contract *of the essence.* Under a "time of the essence" arrangement, seller's obligation to convey the property to the purchaser will be relieved by the purchaser's failure to meet the payments on the specific day. In addition, the seller may have a suit for damages against the purchaser. The purchaser's attorney may insist that if time is of the essence it should be so for both parties. However, the seller has a good argument against that type of arrangement since the purchaser's only requirement generally is to pay cash on the day of title closing but the seller has numerous obligations since he must clear up the property before conveying it to the purchaser. As a possible compromise, the parties may agree that time for performance is of the essence for both parties, but that the purchaser will notify the seller in writing a specified number of days before the date set for the closing of title of all objections to the seller's title. This provision allows the seller to clear up those objections.

348

【¶4401.10】 Purchase Money Mortgage

Sellers often take back a purchase money second mortgage as part of their purchase price for the property. Here, the seller will want to be assured that the purchaser will not milk the property by collecting rents for a certain number of months and then defaulting on the mortgages. The solution is to prepare a timetable which integrates principal and interest payments on the purchase money mortgage with the other obligations of the purchaser (including water charges, taxes, and interest and principal on the first mortgage). Such a timetable assures that the purchaser is obligated to make payments for these different items on different months. This means that the seller can soon find out if the purchaser has defaulted in his obligations.

One other provision that the seller will want is one protecting against a default in the payment of principal or interest on the purchase money mortgage, or on the payment of principal or interest on any other mortgage or on the payment of taxes, water rates or assessment. This provision gives the seller, at his option, the right to accelerate all of the principal amount of the purchase money mortgage on default of any one of the above named obligations by the purchaser.

【¶4401.11】 Personal Property

When a purchaser acquires the building he ordinarily expects to acquire title to the property within that building (as, for example, gas ranges and refrigerators in an apartment house). But gas ranges and refrigerators are usually considered to be personal property and will not be included in the sale of the real estate unless there is an express provision covering them. They may be eligible for investment credit. It is very important, therefore, for the purchaser's attorney to cover all of the personal property included in the sale. The best practice is the requirement of a bill of sale from the seller covering personal property free of all liens and encumbrances.

【¶4402】 CHECKLIST FOR CONTRACTS OF SALE

1. Form of the Contract: This will vary in different parts of the country. The contract may be a straight bilateral agreement between the buyer and the seller, an offer and acceptance form (in which the seller accepts the offer with all its attendant conditions), or a deposit receipt prepared by a broker which contains the conditions of the sale. In some states, the papers and the down payment are held by a third party escrow agent. Regardless of the form of the contract, however, the following considerations should be carefully noted.

2. Date of the Contract.

3. Names and Addresses of the Seller and the Purchaser: (See item #2 under "Purchaser's Considerations." ¶4402.1.)

4. Description of the Property: Usually the description used in the prior deed is satisfactory but use a later survey or title company report if there have been any changes. If the seller has any rights in the street in front of the property, those rights should be included. Same for riparian (water) rights.

5. Purchase Price: The actual purchase price should be stated, including all mortgages. The price should then be broken down into: the down payment and whether it is to be paid in cash or check subject to collection; the amount payable on the closing of title and the form of payment; the amount payable by taking subject to (or by assuming) an existing mortgage; and the amount represented by a purchase money mortgage. If there is an existing mortgage, provision should be made for adjusting the price to reflect any amortization payments made between the contract and the passing of title.

6. Survey: The sale should be subject to a specific survey if there is one, or subject to any state of facts an accurate survey may show.

7. Other Provisions to Which the Sale May be Subject: These include zoning ordinances, easements, restrictive covenants of record, consents to erect structure on, under or above abutting street, party wall agreements, beam rights, encroachments, license agreements, tenancies, other liens.

8. Purchase Money Mortgage: If possible, a copy of the proposed mortgage should be attached to the contract. Otherwise, the contract should indicate the following: the amount and how it will be amortized; the due date; the interest rate and how it is payable; the right to prepay in whole or in part; the type of mortgage form to be used; subordination to any existing or future mortgage; who shall draw the bond and mortgage (ordinarily the seller's attorney at the expense of the purchaser); who shall pay recording fees, mortgage taxes and revenue stamps.

9. Possession of the Premises: Normally, possession will accompany title, but the purchaser may want possession before the closing or the seller may want to remain afterwards. In either case, there may have to be security to vacate (in the purchaser's case, in the event the sale does not go through).

10. Title: The kind of title (e.g., marketable title) should be specified, as well as the evidence which will be satisfactory (e.g., such title as a reputable title company will insure). The kind of deed should be specified, with any warranties which the seller will give. The party paying for revenue stamps should be specified.

11. Risk of Loss: See item #6 in "Purchaser's Considerations," ¶4402.1.

12. Remedies in Case of Default: The seller will normally want a clause permitting cancellation without penalty if he cannot convey title as required by the contract. The buyer may agree to this only if easily remediable defects (such as a lien which can be paid) must be corrected rather than permit cancellation.

13. Personal Property: Fixtures will go with the land but there is much ambiguity about what is included in this term. So all items of personal property which will be included in the sale should be specified. This may impose a sales tax liability on one of the parties.

14. Time and Place of Closing of Title: This is not necessary when an escrow is used, but then a date when the sale must be consummated should be included. A time-of-the-essence clause should be included if either party requires the property on a given date. The seller is ordinarily in a stronger position to insist on this since the purchaser's only responsibility is to appear at the closing with the necessary cash.

15. Real Estate Broker: If one brought about the sale, his name, the amount of his commission, and the one to pay it should be included in the contract or in a separate agreement which is referred to in the contract.

16. Items to be Apportioned: These may include taxes, insurance, assessments, fuel, employees' wages (including fringe and vacation benefits), and unpaid rents. The buyer should normally object to paying the seller immediately the amount of unpaid rents, since the purchaser may never be able to collect them. Payment may be limited to the current month's rent.

17. Taxes and Other Liens: A clause may be included that taxes and other liens will not constitute an objection to title and may be paid out of the purchase price at the closing. The buyer normally will not object provided the seller supplies him with all necessary documents in recordable form so that he is in a position to discharge the liens.

18. "As Is" Clause: Such a clause obligates the purchaser to take the property in the condition it is at the signing of the contract. The seller, however, can't make physical changes to the property before the closing (and he may or may not have an obligation to keep it in repair). Since an "as is" clause indicates the seller makes no warranty about the property's condition, the buyer should not agree to it unless he has made his own inspection.

The basic form of contract is set out in IBP FORMS OF BUSINESS AGREEMENTS.

⟦¶4402.1⟧ Purchaser's Considerations

Since many form contracts are drafted with the interests of the seller primarily in mind, the following items should be especially noted by the purchaser's attorney:

1. Nature of Covenants and Restrictions to Which the Sale Is Subject: If possible, the original documents containing the covenants and restrictions should be examined. If they are not available, add the following: "providing the same are not violated by the existing structure or the present use of the premises, and provided the same may not result in a forfeiture." A purchaser in a strong bargaining position may also be able to add the clause "providing the same are not violated by (specified) future structures or uses."

2. Identity and Marital Status of the Seller: Be sure the named seller is competent and is the sole owner, or if there are co-owners, that he has the authority to enter into the contract and pass good title. If the seller is a corporation, inspect the resolutions authorizing the sale. If the seller has a deceased spouse, check to see if any unpaid estate taxes would be a lien on the real estate (this is true in some states but not with respect to the federal estate tax). If the seller has a living spouse, ascertain if she has any dower or other rights in the property and if so, she must sign the contract. If she does not, the seller in effect has an option since the contract will not be effective until she does sign.

3. Escrow of the Down Payment: In states where a third-party escrow is not used, the seller frequently receives the down payment without any limitation on its use. The purchaser may want to insist that the money be held in escrow (usually by one of the attorneys) if there is any doubt as to whether the seller has good title, is financially responsible, may die or move out of the jurisdiction. When the seller is conveying only his rights under a purchase contract, the purchaser has no vendee's lien against the property and so has no security for his down payment.

4. Any State of Facts Which an Accurate Survey Would Show: If the contract is so subject and an up-to-date survey is not available, the purchaser will want to add: "provided the same does not render title unmarketable."

5. Purchaser's Conditions to Which the Sale Is Subject: Often, the purchaser will want to go through with the sale only on certain conditions. The most common is that he be able to obtain satisfactory financing. The contract should spell out the amount of mortgage, the interest rate and the time limit for obtaining it. The seller may want the right to apply for a mortgage on the purchaser's behalf if the purchaser is unsuccessful. The sale may also be conditioned on the purchaser's being able to obtain a zoning variance for a contemplated use.

6. Risk of Loss: In the absence of a provision in the contract, state law varies as to who assumes the risk of loss between the contract and the passing of title. Even where the seller bears the risk, the purchaser may want the right to cancel in the event that there is substantial damage.

7. Contiguity Clause: If several lots are being conveyed, the purchaser will want a contiguity clause to insure that he will obtain ownership of the entire tract.

8. Existing Leases: If the sale is of income-producing property, the purchaser should carefully examine the actual leases to ascertain if the tenants have future rent concessions, options to purchase or to renew at favorable terms, the right to cancel the lease or other unusual privileges. In addition, the purchaser may want to inspect the premises personally to be sure all the tenants listed by the seller are bona fide.

9. Seller's Obligations Surviving Delivery of the Deed: The usual rule is that obligations set forth in the contract of sale do not continue beyond delivery of the deed unless specified. The purchaser may be able to insist that certain of the representations — such as representations concerning the property's condition — survive the deed.

10. Actual Possession: In some states, the seller is not under a duty to see that the property is unoccupied at the delivery of the deed (this of course assumes the purchaser is not taking subject to existing leases). The purchaser should seek a provision in the contract requiring the property to be available for his actual possession when title is closed.

[¶4402.2] Binders and Deposit Receipts

Because of the common practice of giving binders, deposit receipts or similar memoranda prior to the signing of the actual contract, a word of caution is inserted here. The danger with this type of document is that it's not clear if it is binding on the parties or not, and so if one of them changes his mind, a lawsuit is usually the result. If you are faced with a situation where papers have already been signed by the parties, here are some pointers in determining whether a binding agreement has been entered into.

1. An agreement may be evidenced by letters, telegrams and other memoranda in addition to the binder or receipt itself. So be sure you view all the papers together to determine if a binding obligation has been created. The mere fact that the binder states that a formal contract is to follow is not determinative.

2. The test as to whether a document (or documents) create a binding obligation is whether it contains all of the substantial terms which make up the obligation. Distinguish between details relating to performance and those relating to the essence of the agreement. The former may be omitted, the latter not. Generally, there are four requirements for a contract to sell real estate:

(a) Parties. It must be clear who the buyer and seller are.

(b) Property. The property must be sufficiently described so that it may be identified. But a full legal description is not necessary.

(c) Promises. There must be a promise to buy and one to sell but this may be inferred and need not be stated in so many words.

(d) Price. This is probably the element most frequently open to question. It must be clear what the full price is (i.e., including all mortgages). If a purchase money mortgage is involved, most states require that the amount and interest rate on the mortgage be indicated but some courts will infer it. However, no down payment need be specified or made.

3. An offer to purchase, which states the conditions of the sale and which gives the seller a specified time within which to accept may be binding on the purchaser during that time. The seller thus has an option.

4. A binder or other receipt, which is accompanied by actual possession of the property by the purchaser, is more likely to be considered binding on the parties (and particularly on the purchaser) than when no possession occurs.

[¶4403]   CHECKLIST ON THE TRANSFER OF MORTGAGED PROPERTY

With the average residential mortgage today having a term of 20 years or more, the probability is very great that before it is fully repaid the original mortgagor will have sold his home and moved elsewhere. In most cases, the seller will prepay his mortgage with the proceeds of the sale and the buyer will arrange his own financing. But this may be impossible or undesirable for one of the following reasons: (1) The mortgage contains no prepayment clause and the lender refuses to permit its early discharge; (2) the prepayment clause calls for a heavy penalty; (3) the mortgage carries an interest rate below prevailing money rates or has other desirable features.

In such cases the buyer and seller may wish to transfer the property with the mortgage still outstanding. It is clear that the seller has the right to do this, as a clause in the mortgage prohibiting transfers will be construed as an unreasonable restraint on alienation. (However, a clause permitting the mortgagee to accelerate the maturity of the mortgage in the event of sale is probably legal.)

The following methods of transferring the property subject to the mortgage are normally available to the seller:

(1) Transfer of the Property Without Reference to the Mortgage: While this is an undesirable procedure to follow, a lawyer may occasionally be faced with a situation where this has occurred. The intent of the parties can normally be inferred from the relation of the purchase price to the value of the property. If the price paid to the seller is equal to the market value, in all probability, the parties intended that the seller would apply part of the proceeds to the discharge of the mortgage. On the other hand, if the difference between the price paid to the seller and the market value of the property is approximately equal to the outstanding mortgage, the parties presumably intended that the buyer be liable for the debt.

(2) Transfer of the Property "Subject to" the Mortgage: In a transaction in which the lender plays no part, it is impossible for the seller to transfer the property free of the mortgage lien. Therefore, even where the parties agree that the buyer shall not be personally liable for the mortgage debt, the property remains subject to the mortgage. As long as the buyer continues to make the mortgage payments, there is, of course, no problem. If the buyer defaults, the lender has the option of seeking a personal judgment against the seller (except in the unusual case where the seller is not personally liable for the debt) or of proceeding to foreclose the property. If the lender proceeds against the seller and collects the debt, the buyer remains uninvolved. If the lender forecloses the property, the buyer's loss is limited to the value of the property.

(3) Assumption of the Mortgage by the Buyer Without a Novation: If the buyer is to be liable for the mortgage debt he "assumes" the mortgage. If the lender plays no part in the transaction, only the seller remains liable to the lender. In the event of a default, the lender may foreclose the property and then seek a deficiency payment against the seller. The seller may then recover by an action against the buyer. In addition, under the law of most states, the lender may also proceed against the buyer on the theory that it is the third party beneficiary of the contract between the buyer and seller.

(4) Assumption of Mortgage by the Buyer With a Novation: In unusual cases, the lender may be willing to release the seller and substitute the buyer as the party primarily liable for the mortgage debt. This is a novation. The buyer normally will have no objection to this since as between himself and the seller, he is primarily liable; but the lender, by agreeing to the novation, may be giving up the right to hold both parties personally liable. Consequently, it may demand consideration before selling. For example, it may insist that the mortgage be refinanced at a higher interest rate to reflect prevailing money conditions.

[¶4404]   CLOSING THE TITLE

This is where the deed and final evidence of good title is delivered, the money is paid, the mortgages are executed and charges against the property are prorated.

The buyer should get the deed, a title report or policy or other evidence of good title, a bill of sale of any personal property going with the real estate, a receipt for the purchase price he paid, a survey of the property, insurance policies and assignments thereof, a statement from the mortgagee of the amount due on any existing mortgage, release and satisfaction of any mortgage or other lien paid off but not yet recorded, leases and assignments thereof, letter by seller telling tenants to pay future rents to buyer, letter by seller advising managing agent of the sale and the termination of his authority, statement by seller as to rents paid and due, receipts for taxes, water, gas, electricity, special assessments, assessment of any service contracts and building maintenance guarantees, seller's affidavit of title security deposits and tenants' consent to transfer if required, social security and payroll data on building employees, keys to the building.

The seller receives the balance of the purchase price including any purchase money mortgage and notes. He will want evidence of fire insurance protection if he has a continuous mortgage interest.

[¶4404.1]   After the Closing

The buyer should record his deed and any releases obtained at the closing. The seller should record any purchase money mortgage. The seller should notify managing agent and employees that he is no longer responsible for their compensation. The buyer should arrange for necessary services, get the consent of the insurance company to assignment of policies, get any new insurance necessary, have water, gas, electric and tax bills changed to his name.

[¶4404.2]   Title Closing Checklist

If the preliminary work is done well, the physical act of title closing can be accomplished with dispatch. In order to do this, however, all the documents (deeds, bills of sale, mortgages, bonds, assignments, etc.) must be ready and checked in advance. The actual formal closing then consists of an exchange of documents and checks.

1. Verifying title—the seller's attorney will want to check title and remove any possible objections. The following considerations should be covered:

    (a) Make certain that title evidence has been brought up to date and is in the form agreed upon in the contract. Resolve position as to exceptions and encumbrances (that is, whether or not material; if survey is required by contract, check same). Have building plans and specifications available.

    (b) Is title insurance in the agreed amount and form?

    (c) Does deed conform to contract requirements? (Marital status of seller, acknowledgment, legal description, tax stamps.) The deed should specify that the conveyance is subject to exceptions, liens, encumbrances, restrictions and reservations provided for in the contract. Otherwise, seller will be warranting a better title than he has.

    (d) Title affidavits to cover period between title evidence and the closing.

    (e) Affidavits to clear up objections revealed by abstract and covering mechanics' liens.

    (f) For new construction obtain proper waivers, contractor's statements and architect's certificate.

    (g) Obtain bill of sale covering any personal property included.

2. Amount of unpaid taxes, liens, assessments, water, sewerage charges, etc. on the property should be ascertained.

3. Get statement of amount due on existing mortgages showing unpaid principal and interest, rate of interest and date of maturity.

4. Produce the following:

    (a) Policies of insurance to be transferred.

    (b) Schedule of rents.

    (c) Deed from predecessor-title.

    (d) Vault permits.

    (e) Power of attorney.

5. Deed.

    (a) Include full name and address of seller and purchaser.

    (b) Description of property (same as in contract of sale unless there has been a new survey).

    (c) Covenants and warrants provided for in contract of sale.

    (d) Special clauses in contract of sale.

    (e) Recital of exceptions, restrictions, easements, etc. provided in contract of sale.

　　(f)　Description of mortgages, both the mortgages which the purchaser is taking subject to and which purchaser is assuming. Also recital of purchase money mortgage if there is one.

6.　Additional papers.
　　(a)　Satisfaction, release or discharge of liens.
　　(b)　Purchase money bond and mortgage.
　　(c)　Bill of sale of personal property included in the sale.
　　(d)　Letter of introduction to tenants.
　　(e)　Satisfaction of judgments.
　　(f)　Authorization of sale by corporation if owner is corporation.

7.　Prepare statement showing all apportionment of:
　　(a)　Taxes.
　　(b)　Electric, gas and water charges.
　　(c)　Rents — as adjusted, for prepaid and accrued rent.
　　(d)　Salaries.
　　(e)　Services — exterminator, burglary alarm systems.

8.　Have the deed signed, sealed and executed by the parties necessary to convey good title. Acknowledgments of signatures required. Affix appropriate revenue stamps and prepare proper closing statement and then record purchase money mortgages.

[¶4404.3] Purchaser's Considerations

The purchaser's attorney should consider the following items:

1. Get affidavit of title.

2. Obtain letter of introduction to tenants.

3. Check violations of building regulations, any dwelling laws, health and fire agencies. Determine whether there is a certificate of occupancy outstanding.

4. Look for chattel mortgages or conditional sales contracts on personal property if the latter is included for sale.

5. Examine mortgages and satisfactions of record.

6. Look at existing leases.

7. Check town, city, village and school taxes, water and sewerage rates, assessments.

8. If corporations are involved make sure that state franchise taxes have been paid.

9. Look for assessments and vault permits.

10. See that the premises comply with zoning rules and restrictive covenants.

11. Find out who is in possession, and whether they are entitled to so be.

12. Are there licenses and permits for signs on the street?

13. Have State and Federal transfer and estate taxes been paid?

14. Inspect the premises.
15. Check the age and competency of the seller.
16. Look at insurance policies and assignments of service contracts.
17. Contiguity clause if more than one lot is involved.
18. Final matters — acknowledgment of seller's signature; title company report; power of attorney recorded, if any; revenue stamps on deed and bond.
19. Record deed, have endorsements on transfer of ownership on insurance policies and prepare closing statement.

[¶4404.4] The Closing Statement

The contract of sale should provide for the adjustment of costs and income. Rents up to the time of closing are credited to the seller and costs are charged against him. Any costs paid beyond the closing date are credited to the seller.

Customary items to seller's credit are: (1) unexpired portion of current real estate taxes paid by the seller, (2) unearned insurance premiums, (3) unexpired portion of service contracts paid in advance, (4) unexpired portion of water tax, (5) fuel on hand, (6) supplies, (7) delinquent rents.

Customary items to buyer's credit are: (1) initial deposit or payment, (2) current balance on existing mortgages, (3) unpaid taxes for prior years and pro rata portion of taxes for current year, (4) special assessments due and unpaid, (5) amounts due for electricity, gas and water based on meter readings, (6) accrued wages, (7) prepaid rents, (8) tenant's cash security deposits.

The seller pays for revenue stamps, if any, on the deed and the buyer pays for recording unless the contract provides otherwise.

[¶4405] ESCROW CLOSING

In some areas, sales are closed in escrow. An escrow is "the deposit by the vendor of his deed with a third party to be delivered over to the purchaser upon payment of the purchase price." That third party is the escrowee. Escrows provide a mechanism to insure safety and convenience in carrying out the provisions of previously executed real estate sales contracts. In some cases, however, there is no written contract, the escrow agreement being the sole contract between the parties.

Most of the matters mentioned in the checklist for real estate closings are applicable when the deal is closed through an escrow. The mechanical details of the closing, however, are turned over to the escrowee.

Among the many advantages of escrows are the following: the escrowee assumes the responsibility of the many ministerial tasks involved in a closing; the danger of title defects arising in the gap between the effective date of title evidence and the date of the deed is avoided; the possibility that the deal may fail is decreased.

[¶4405.1]   Contents of Escrow Agreement

1. Documents to be deposited by seller, such as deed, insurance policies, separate assignments of insurance policies, leases, assignments of leases, abstract or other evidence of title, tax bills, cancelled mortgage notes, notice to tenants to pay rent to buyer and service contracts.

2. Deposits to be made by buyer, such as purchase price and purchase money mortgage, if any.

3. When deed is to be recorded, whether immediately or after buyer's check clears, or after seller furnishes evidence of good title at date of contract.

4. Objections to which buyer agrees to take subject.

5. Type of evidence of title to be furnished.

6. Time allowed seller to clear defects in title.

7. How and when purchase price is to be disbursed, with directions as to what items are to be prorated or apportioned, if escrow holder is to do the prorating.

8. Directions to deliver deed, leases, insurance policies, assignments of policy, and service contracts to buyer when title shows clear.

9. Return of deposits to the respective parties where title cannot be cleared.

10. Reconveyance by buyer to seller if deed to buyer has been recorded immediately on signing of escrow agreement and examination of title thereafter discloses seller's title was defective and incurable.

11. Payment of escrow, title and recording charges, broker's commission, and attorney's fees.

●

For Further Reference . . .

Forms of Business Agreements looseleaf Service. Institute for Business Planning, Englewood Cliffs, N.J.

Friedman, Milton R., *Contracts and Conveyances of Real Property,* Practising Law Institute, New York, N. Y.

Kratovil, Robert, *Real Estate Law.*

Real Estate Desk Book, Institute for Business Planning, Englewood Cliffs, N.J.

Real Estate Investment Planning looseleaf Service Institute for Business Planning, Englewood Cliffs, N.J.

REAL PROPERTY TAX REDUCTION

[¶4501] Wherever a taxpayer feels that his real property has been assessed too high, local law affords him an opportunity to petition for a reduction of the assessment. Such a proceeding is usually initiated by making a protest with an application for correction to the taxing authority itself. Only after such an application is denied, either in whole or in part, may a proceeding for judicial review of the assessment be initiated. When tax officials turn down the property owner's protest, this action is usually subject to review by a court in an appeals proceeding. This is a proceeding whereby the tax officials are called upon to produce their records and to certify them to the court so that the court may determine whether the officials have proceeded according to the principles of law which they are required to follow in the performance of their assessing duties.

Local tax authorities usually have forms of application to be used in asking for a review of an assessment. If this application of protest is rejected the next step is to initiate a proceeding in the appropriate court to review the final assessment. The grounds upon which an assessment may be reduced are usually these: (1) overvaluation, (2) inequality and (3) illegality.

Overvaluation: This can be established by showing that the assessment of real property has been set at a sum which is higher than the full and fair market value of the property.

Inequality: This somewhat overlaps with overvaluation and can be established by showing that the assessment was made at a higher proportionate valuation than the assessment of other real estate of a like character in the same area. To obtain relief it is usually necessary to show that the assessment is out of proportion as compared with valuations in the municipality generally. To prove inequality it is necessary to examine a considerable number of parcels of real estate for the purpose of comparing the market values of these properties with their assessed valuation and ascertaining the ratio of assessed value to market value in each instance. You have a case of inequality if such a study shows that the ratio of assessed values to market values generally is substantially lower than the ratio between the assessed value and the market value of your property.

Illegality: This exists when the assessment has been levied in an irregular manner or upon a basis erroneous in law or in fact other than an error in the evaluation itself. An example of an illegal assessment is the inclusion on the tax roles of an assessment of a parcel of real estate which is legally exempt from taxation.

〔¶4501.1〕   Procedures to Follow

To seek a reduction of a real estate assessment take these steps: (1) examine the assessor's report. If this is predicated upon some error of fact such as an incorrect description of the property, an incorrect statement of its actual income or expenses or any other error concerning the property itself, submit proof of the correct facts. (2) Find out what the property cost. Compare the actual cost of the property to the assessment. If the purchase price is substantially below the assessed value which is to be challenged and the date of purchase is not too remote from the tax date, this comparison will be relevant as long as it can be established that the property was purchased in an arm's length transaction. (3) Study the records of income received from the property and the expense of operation over several years prior to the tax date. The earning capacity of income property is the most significant single factor in determining its market value for purposes of seeking reduction of a tax assessment. (4) Make a comparison of sales prices and assessed valuations and of estimates of market value and assessed valuations for other comparable properties in the area. This kind of a comparison will have been made by others and a great deal of the necessary information may be obtained in that way rather than through the laborious, costly method of getting appraisals on a large number of properties. (5) Consult experts. The testimony of expert witnesses is usually the most important proof in court proceedings to seek reduction of real estate taxes. You may want to use the testimony of a building expert as well as a real estate expert. The real estate expert will testify as to sales of comparable property and to the value the property would bring in the market place. The building expert would testify as to the sound structural value or reproduction cost, less depreciation of the building.

〔¶4501.2〕   Review Procedure

The course of a proceeding to review a real property assessment usually runs this way after the attorney is employed. The appraiser is hired to select a number of sample properties anywhere in the assessing jurisdiction whose ratios of assessed valuation he believes to be substantially lower than that of his client. The attorney for the assessing jurisdiction likewise selects his own samples whose assessed valuation ratios will tend to support what he contends to be the prevailing ratio. If the opposing attorneys cannot agree on which of these are to be placed in evidence (and such agreement is hardly likely) they submit both lists to the Court, which proceeds to choose from such lists an agreed-upon number of samples. The appraisers for both sides evaluate and analyze these sample properties before the Court, and are examined and cross-examined as to their respective appraisals of these samples. The Court next makes a finding of the true value of each, compares it with assessed valuation, computes all the ratios, averages them and accepts the result as the prevailing ratio for this particular proceeding. (This finding does not bind any other litigant in any other proceeding, nor may he use it in his own case over objection.)

Finally, the Court listens to both appraisers give their opinions of the full, fair market value of the petitioner's own property, arrives at a decision, applies the "prevailing ratio" just found, and thus determines what the assessed valuation of the subject property should have been.

Of course, this is how the practice works in general. The specific procedure in a particular case will vary depending on whether the state constitution does or does not call for uniformity in real estate taxation, provisions of state real property and tax laws with respect to establishing ratios and providing for equalization rates, and establishing procedural rules for the review of real property tax burdens. For example, in New York, the state establishes equalization rights to be used for the distribution of state aids to localities and for other purposes and by legislative enactment which may be offered in evidence by a party to a certiorari proceeding.

●

For Further Reference . . .

Lee, Harry O., and LeForestier, Wilford A., *Review and Reduction of Real Property Assessments.*

Real Estate Desk Book, Institute for Business Planning, Englewood Cliffs, N.J.

Real Estate Tax Shelter Desk Book, Institute for Business Planning, Englewood Cliffs, N.J.

REHABILITATION AND REORGANIZATION

[¶4601] The financially embarrassed business can get relief under the Bankruptcy Act or by voluntary agreement with creditors.

[¶4602] VOLUNTARY ARRANGEMENTS

We talk here about composition and extensions outside of bankruptcy. In this connection, an arrangement under which the debtor is to pay a percentage of his debts is called a "composition." The main idea of an "extension" is that it gives the debtor more time to pay.

Either a composition or an extension involves two agreements: (1) an agreement between two or more creditors and the debtor; and (2) an agreement between the creditors themselves. Why should the creditors want to approach the matter as a group rather than deal with the debtor on an individual basis? There may be a number of reasons but certainly one of the more important ones is that if a single creditor undertakes to collect the full amount owing him he may precipitate bankruptcy proceedings either by the debtor or the other creditors and in those proceedings he may have to return to the bankrupt's trustee any payment made by the debtor as an unlawful preference and if no payment had been made but he had started legal proceedings which gave him a sort of lien, he would find that his lien was of no value to him, having been dissolved by the bankruptcy proceedings. Hence, a creditor might conclude that it will be better for him to try to work out some arrangement with the debtor and the other creditors rather than to engage in a race to collect his individual debt especially since he could "win" the race in the first instance only to find himself disqualified in the end.

You can't have an effective composition or extension outside of bankruptcy proceedings, however, unless all the creditors go along with it or the great majority of creditors are willing to go along with it and are willing to overlook favored treatment to one or more creditors who won't go along. This is because the dissenting creditors won't be bound by the agreement and can proceed to the recovery of the amount due them by legal process. If you want a composition or extension that will bind the dissenters, the only way to get it is through bankruptcy proceedings or special local proceeding.

There doesn't seem to be any clear line between a composition with creditors and an assignment for the benefit of creditors. However, some authorities have said that the composition requires an agreement between the creditors which an assignment doesn't, and in our discussion of assignments we accept this distinction. Also, a composition discharges the entire claim, which an assignment won't necessarily.

Forms of compositions and assignments for the benefit of creditors appear in IBP Forms of Business Agreements.

Consideration for Composition: The consideration for a composition is usually found in: (1) Immediate payment of part of the amount owing; and (2) mutual surrender of part of their rights and claims by all creditors. Sometimes you may want to offer additional consideration to a particular creditor to induce him to join in the agreement. Don't do it. The private agreement is not only void, but may permit other creditors to invalidate the entire agreement.

Effect of Agreement: A voluntary agreement will generally operate to discharge the debtor only when its terms have been carried out. Thus, a failure to pay notes given under the agreement may operate to revive the original debt even though the agreement doesn't expressly provide for its revival. Local law should be checked on this point.

Care must be exercised to avoid discharging parties secondarily liable with the debtor. An extension of time of payment may, for example, discharge a surety unless he's agreed in advance to permit the extension.

Preferring Creditors: In a composition there's nothing wrong in "preferring" some types of creditors, provided that the preference has some rational or legal basis, as where the creditors "preferred" hold security or are entitled to some type of priority, and provided further all the creditors party to the composition are told about the preference. A secret promise of a preference or other advantage made to one or more creditors will render the agreement fraudulent and void or voidable.

State Insolvency Laws: Before resorting to a composition outside bankruptcy be sure to check the insolvency laws of your own state. They may operate as a limiting factor in the use of these agreements.

[¶4603]   ASSIGNMENT FOR THE BENEFIT
OF CREDITORS

As noted above, the distinction between compositions and assignments for the benefit of creditors isn't always clear. One distinction has been said to be that the former requires the consent of the creditors; the latter does not.[1] However this may be, as a practical matter you can't have an effective assignment for the benefit of creditors unless the creditors at least passively acquiesce. If the creditors don't go along with the idea, they may be able to treat the assignment as an act of bankruptcy and throw the debtor into bankruptcy proceedings.

---

[1] **[Footnote ¶4603]** (1) In Massachusetts consent of the creditors is required.

There's another big difference between a composition and an assignment. In a composition the debtor holds on to his business and works out a readjustment of his debts with his creditors. In an assignment he turns over his business and all his property to an assignee or trustee to be distributed in payment of his debts. Also, a composition contemplates release of the debtor from further liability; not so in the ordinary assignment, although the creditors can, of course, consent to a release or discharge.

In an assignment the debtor has what is called a resulting trust in any assets that may remain after the creditors have been paid but he has no equity of redemption, that is, he can't come in at any stage after he's made the assignment and get his property back by paying off his creditors, unless, of course, all of them consent.

[¶4603.1]　Local Variations in Law

Local variations in the law governing assignments must be checked out. Here are the main areas to be watched:

(1) Assignment of part of property. (In some states a partial assignment is void; in others it's valid if the part not assigned is open to the remedies of all of the creditors.)

(2) What property passes under a general assignment. (Generally, all property, real or personal, tangible or intangible, including good will, trade marks (not personal), patents, interest in insurance policies on assignor's life, and rights under trust, but property held in trust and property fraudulently obtained won't pass.)

(3) Necessity of acknowledging, filing or recording assignment. (Many states have provisions.)

(4) Inventory of property assigned and schedule of creditors who are to participate. (These will be included in assignment usually as a matter of course but statutory requirements should be checked for formal requirements.)

(5) Notice to creditors. (Statutes may prescribe time and form.)

(6) Reservation of control by debtor. (Assignment will be invalidated by reservation of any degree of control. Debtor can't reserve right to revoke or declare future uses or trusts to which assignment is to be subject.)

(7) Reservation of possession. (Some authorities hold that debtor's reservation of possession will invalidate assignment.)

(8) Intent to hinder or delay creditors. (Assignment made with view to debtor's own advantage and to hinder and delay creditors in the just enforcement of their claims is vulnerable to attack as fraudulent.)

(9) Preferential treatment of creditors. (While there's nothing wrong with favoring creditors having recognized priorities, don't include a provision that those creditors will be first paid who will accept their pro rata share on condition that receipt constitutes a full release.)

[¶4604]   REHABILITATION UNDER
                           BANKRUPTCY ACT

An embarrassed business can ask a bankruptcy court to protect it from its creditors while a plan of payment is worked out. Only the financially distressed person or company can initiate a Chapter XI proceeding. Unlike Chapter X which is designated as the corporate reorganization statute, creditors cannot invoke Chapter XI; only the debtor may initiate a Chapter XI proceeding.

The debtor comes into the Bankruptcy Court and says, in effect, that he has been operating a business which is worth saving and that he would like to propose a plan to his creditors. However, he needs the court's help for a period of time in which he can work out such a settlement. The court then, in a sense, places a protective umbrella over this particular business venture, and has the power to issue orders preventing the entire world from proceeding against that person's property while the arrangement proceeding is pending. The Bankruptcy Court has the power to authorize the debtor to operate his business during the time that the proceeding is pending.

In some jurisdictions the court will insist on the appointment of a receiver to operate the business. In other jurisdictions, in accordance with the express mandate of the statute, the Bankruptcy Court will permit the debtor itself to operate the business under proper court supervision.

[¶4604.1]   What Goes into a Plan

A plan must of necessity include provisions for treatment of unsecured debts (§356). They can be whittled down or compromised, or payment may be extended. Usually a plan will do both.

The arrangement must provide for payment in full of claims entitled to priority except as a priority claimant consents in writing to take something less. These claims will have to be paid whether they're included in the plan or not, but nevertheless, it's customary to make express provision in the plan.

Beyond the basic mandatory requirement of §356 that the plan change the rights of unsecured creditors or of some class of them, the plan may include any appropriate provision so long as it's not inconsistent with Chapter XI. Section 357 of the Bankruptcy Act sets forth seven specific types of provision which may be included. We will touch on only those that deserve or require high-lighting.

Classifying Creditors: The plan can treat all unsecured claims on a par or it can divide them into different classes and provide for different treatment for each class. For example, it will often be found desirable to eliminate small creditors, either from the point of view of expediting and facilitating acceptance or reducing bookkeeping and administrative costs. Hence, the plan might provide for payment of 100 cents on the dollar of creditors having claims for $100 or less, instead of carrying them along with the larger creditors in a plan which, let's say, calls for payment of claims at the rate of 1% per month over a period of years.

Continuation of Business: The plan may provide for continuation of the debtor's business with or without supervision or control by a receiver or by a committee of creditors or otherwise (§357(5)). This is a matter likely to generate conflict because the debtor will naturally want to be free of control whereas the creditors will prefer continuous supervision. The debtor will be apt to suggest no control until he's in default. The creditors may come up with any one or more of a wide variety of alternatives, such as provision for audit of the debtor's books at intervals at the debtor's expense and creditors to get control if books show successive monthly operating losses, countersignature of checks by agent of creditors, and provisions designed to allow quick liquidation of debtor on happening of certain events without having to resort to the courts.

[¶4604.2] **How Proceedings Are Handled**

The court refers the matter to a referee. There are provisions for the appointment of receivers and appraisers and for a meeting of creditors on written notice. The referee runs the creditors' meeting, accepts and passes on claims, examines and permits the examination of the debtor and other witnesses and receives acceptances by creditors.

Duly scheduled creditors don't have to file proof of claim to share in a plan, but they can't vote on a plan unless proof is filed and allowed. An important thing to bear in mind is that Chapter XI, unlike the reorganization provisions, permits a debtor to advise his creditors of a proposed plan and solicit their acceptances in advance. In cases where there are few creditors it is not uncommon to find enough creditors have accepted the plan before the first meeting of creditors to put it into effect and the proceedings will then move ahead rapidly to final confirmation.

Acceptance of a plan by a majority in both number and amount of creditors whose claims have been proved and allowed is required. If there are different classes of creditors, the required acceptances must be obtained within each class. Those who want to put through the plan must make sure not only that they get creditors to accept and to send in their acceptances but that they also file proof of their claim, because unless their claim is proved and allowed their acceptance won't count. Contrariwise, if they file proof of claim but don't file an acceptance, they will in effect be counted as voting against the plan. Often a creditors' committee will carry the ball in obtaining acceptances and seeing that acceptors follow through with proof of claim.

The debtor can offer payment in full provided additional time is given, which is frequently designated as an "extension," or he can say that he will pay 25 cents on the dollar in cash, what was once called a "composition." He can also propose a plan which is part extension and part composition.

The confirmation of such a plan, from the point of view of the debtor, has the advantage of being able to give him a new lease on life so far as creditors are concerned. Even the creditors profit by the confirmation of the arrangement if the plan that is negotiated is fair (and the court by statutory mandate has the obligation of finding that the plan is fair), since a fair plan, in most cases, will afford a better return to creditors than an immediate liquidation.

By the express provisions of the statute, the creditors, as a condition for approving a plan, can insist on certain rights to supervise the operation of the debtor's business under the court's jurisdiction after the plan is confirmed.

Among other things, the plan may contain provisions (a violation of which can be made an event of default) to the following effect:

(1) A limitation may be placed on the salaries of officers.

(2) A limitation may be placed on expanding the business into new ventures or on increasing the size of existing ventures.

(3) There may be control of secured borrowings.

(4) Provision may be made obligating the reorganized company to make up operating losses by infusion of some form of new working capital.

(5) There may be a restriction on merger or consolidation.

The effect of a confirmed arrangement is tantamount to the effect of a discharge in bankruptcy, except that the obligations undertaken by the debtor in the arrangement will survive. The debtor is afforded the opportunity of resuming his business, freed of his original debts, except as expressly assumed under the plan.

[¶4604.3] Confirmation

When the required assents have been obtained and filed and the necessary deposit made, the debtor will apply for confirmation of the plan. The plan will be confirmed if the court is satisfied that the provisions of Chapter XI are met; it is for the best interests of the creditors and is feasible; the debtor isn't guilty of any acts barring discharge in bankruptcy; and the proposal and its acceptance are in good faith (§367). The confirmation is binding on all creditors of the debtor and the debtor or any person issuing securities or acquiring property under the plan and the debtor is discharged from all of his unsecured debts provided for in the plan, unless some different provision is made in the plan or in the order of confirmation.

On confirmation costs of administration and other priority claims are paid, and the distribution, if any, called for by the plan will be made to creditors. The case is then dismissed, subject to the jurisdiction which the court is required to retain until final allowance of certain claims, or proof of others as spelled out in §369. Unless jurisdiction is retained to cover performance of the plan, creditors whose claims are covered by the plan can only sue on their claims under the plan and not on their original claims before scaling down.

[¶4605]   CORPORATE REORGANIZATION

The trouble with Chapter XI proceedings is that they'll deal with unsecured creditors only. A reorganization plan, on the other hand, can deal not only with unsecured creditors but with security holders as well; but the plan will be subject to closer control and supervision by the court as well as more stringent statutory requirements; and the chances are good that management will have to yield to a trustee or receiver.

Arrangements rest on voluntary action of the debtor. Proceedings for reorganization may be either voluntary or involuntary. Arrangement proceedings are especially appropriate for businesses in which ownership and management reside in the same individuals. Reorganization proceedings, on the other hand, are apt to be called for where stock and securities are widely held. An arrangement proceeding can be changed into a reorganization proceeding on application of the Securities Exchange Commission or any interested party; the controlling consideration is the public interest.

[¶4605.1]   Who Can Start Reorganization Proceedings

Reorganization proceedings can be instituted by the corporation (voluntary) or against it (involuntary) by three or more creditors whose claims total $5000 or more and are liquidated as to amount and not contingent as to liability, or by an indenture trustee acting on behalf of the bondholders. If the corporation is to take the initiative, it can only do so with proper corporate authorization — usually a resolution of the board of directors.

[¶4605.2]   Plan of Reorganization

The whole idea of a reorganization proceeding is, of course, to develop and carry out a plan of reorganization. The Bankruptcy Act (§216) spells out the mandatory and optional provisions of a plan. Here are the main points:

(1) The plan must alter the rights of at least some class of creditors, secured or unsecured;

(2) It may alter the rights of any class of stockholders;

(3) It must provide for the payment of all administrative costs and expenses and court-approved allowances;

(4) It may provide for the rejection of executory, non-public contracts;

(5) It must specify what claims are to be paid in cash in full;

(6) It must specify the creditors or stockholders not affected by the plan and the provisions, if any, with respect to them;

(7) It must provide for any class of creditors and stockholders affected by the plan which doesn't accept the plan by the required vote, except that no protection need be given stockholders if the debtor is found to be insolvent;

(8) It must provide adequate means for the execution of the plan;

(9) It must provide for the inclusion of the charter of the reorganized corporation prohibiting the issuance of non-voting stock and providing for fair and equitable distribution of voting power among the several classes of security, provisions which are fair and equitable as to the terms, position, rights and privileges of the several classes of securities of the debtor, and, for corporations with liabilities of $250,000 or more, provisions for periodic reports to security holders.

●

For Further Reference . . .

American Jurisprudence, Assignments for Benefit of Creditors; Compositions With Creditors; Corporate Reorganizations.

Collier on Bankruptcy, 11 Volumes.

Hirsch and Krause, *Bankruptcy and Arrangements Under Chapter XI of the Bankruptcy Act,* Practising Law Institute, New York, N. Y.

Mulder, Forman, *Bankruptcy and Arrangement Proceedings,* American Law Institute, Philadelphia, Pa.

Remington on Bankruptcy, 12 Volumes.

REMEDIES AND DEFENSES

[¶4701] When a lawyer is consulted his actual or prospective client will probably want to know what rights he has and how they can be enforced or how they can be protected against the actual or possible assertion by someone else of rights against him. There are multi-volume books setting out forms of pleading for specific rights and remedies and for the assertion of defense against them. When a lawyer has a client with a claim or suffering from some wrong, he has to determine what remedy or remedies may be available. When he does, the other fellow's lawyer has to figure out what defenses can be asserted. There are particular elements of proof needed and defenses appropriate to particular actions.

Here we offer a list of possible remedies and generally available defenses which can be fitted to the needs of clients seeking to assert or to protect themselves against various kinds of claims.

[¶4702]   GENERAL REMEDIES

In the federal courts and the great majority of states the old common law distinctions in form between actions at law and suits in equity have gone by the boards. Instead, there is one form of action and that's known as a civil action. In this single action you can get so-called legal relief, equitable relief or both. Nevertheless, it's still necessary to distinguish between legal and equitable relief because of the constitutional right to a jury trial in "suits at common law" (Amendment 7 of the U.S. Constitution). This test must be made in terms of what relief one could have obtained in the courts of common law at the time the Constitution was adopted. Claims for legal relief fall under four main headings:

(1) Enforcement of money obligations.
(2) Damages for breach of contract.
(3) Damages for tort.
(4) Recovery of property.

Let's now take a closer look at each of these categories so that we will know more precisely the legal relief and conditions of relief available.

[¶4702.1]   Actions for the Enforcement of Money Obligations

Actions for the enforcement of money obligations look to the recovery of a judgment for the amount of money plaintiff is entitled to receive plus interest and fall into these main classes: Actions for: (a) Contract debt; (b) Judgment debt; (c) Unjust enrichment; and (d) Statutory penalties.

Contract Debt: In actions for contract debt plaintiff must show: (a) Promise to pay money (promise may be implied from conduct, as by retention of goods for which defendant has been billed); (b) Consideration for the promise, except where statutory provision eliminates requirement; (c) Performance or happening of conditions, if any, of payment; and (d) Nonpayment.

Judgment Debt: A new judgment for a money debt may be called for when execution of the prior judgment is in jeopardy by reason of the statute of limitations or when property subject to execution is not within the reach of the prior judgment. Plaintiff must show: (a) Judgment; and (b) Nonpayment.

Unjust Enrichment: This is a type of indebtedness not created by contract based on the receipt by the defendant of a benefit he may not in fairness retain. Plaintiff must show: (a) Receipt by defendant from plaintiff of benefits amounting to unjust enrichment; and (b) Nonpayment.

Statutory Penalty: These are actions based on a statutory obligation to pay money. Plaintiff must show: (a) Violation of statute by defendant either by act of commission or omission; (b) Resulting injury; and (c) Nonpayment.

[¶4702.2] Damages for Breach of Contract

In this class are actions based on promises, other than the payment of money, that something will or will not happen. Plaintiff must show: (a) Express promise that something will or will not happen; (b) Consideration for the promise, except where seal or statutory provision eliminates requirement; (c) Performance or happening of conditions, if any, of the promise; (d) Breach of the promise; and (e) Resulting damage.

[¶4702.3] Damages for Tort

This class of actions protects interests in property and person against invasion by an award of damages. In most tort actions the plaintiff must show actual damages, but in some, trespass, for example, plaintiff can get a judgment for nominal damages even though he's suffered no actual damage. Within this class are actions for assault and battery, false imprisonment, fraud and deceit, libel and slander, malicious prosecution, negligence, nuisance, trover and conversion and trespass.

[¶4702.4] Recovery of Property

If you're in possession of real or personal property, the only kind of legal relief you can get for violation of your rights in the property is a judgment for damages. *If you're not in possession* and have an immediate right of possession,

373

you can recover possession, in addition to damages, via one of the following common law actions or their statutory equivalents:

(1) Ejectment: This is the common law action for the recovery of real property. In some states it's still called "ejectment"; in others it may be called an action in the nature of ejectment; and in still others it may be called an action for the recovery of real property. In any case to succeed in these actions it must be shown: (a) That plaintiff has an interest in the property and a right to immediate possession or physical control; (b) Withholding of possession or detention by the plaintiff; and (c) If plaintiff claims damages for loss of use or injury, this must also be shown.

(2) Forcible Entry and Detainer: This is an action for recovery of possession of land taken from plaintiff's possession by defendant. Unlike ejectment, it doesn't involve the right to possession or title to the property and is, consequently, simpler in terms of issues and procedure than ejectment. To recover possession plaintiff must show: (a) That he was in peaceable possession; (b) That defendant dispossessed him by forcible entry; (c) Forcible detention of the property by the defendant.

(3) Replevin: Actions for the recovery of personal property are most commonly called "replevin" actions, but are sometimes referred to as actions for claim and delivery or detinue. If required affidavits and bond are filed, possession may be obtained before trial; otherwise delivery of possession must await the outcome of the trial. To recover possession plaintiff must show: (a) An interest in the property and a right to immediate possession or control; (b) Detention by the defendant; and (c) If plaintiff claims damages for loss of use or injury, this must also be shown.

[¶4703]   KINDS OF EQUITABLE RELIEF

The main types of equitable relief may be listed as falling within one of these classes: (1) Injunctions; (2) Specific performance of contracts; (3) Recovery of property by equitable means; (4) Enforcement of money obligations by equitable means; and (5) Protection against future and multiple claims.

Following is a rundown of what's involved in these separate classes and other equity actions that may be brought.

[¶4703.1]   Injunctions

Here we are mainly concerned with protecting tortious invasions of personal or property rights. An injunction to restrain a breach of contract operates as specific performance of the contract and hence falls under our second heading. Plaintiff must show: (a) An interest entitled to protection (an interest in

374

property, personalty, economic or domestic relations, for example); (b) Threatened invasion of the interest; and (3) Inadequacy of legal remedy (this requires facts showing irreparable injury, insolvency of the defendant, or threatened repetition of violations requiring multiple actions at law). While the threat of future invasion is an essential basis of relief, past torts may be and are commonly used to make out a case, and court may grant damages for past torts or direct specific reparation, as an incident to injunctive relief. Doctrines of comparative injury and balance of conveniences are always applicable and some courts may impose on plaintiff the burden of showing that he will suffer greater harm from being left to his legal remedy than defendant will suffer if equitable relief is granted. In many states plaintiff will be required to furnish bond or other security on the issuance of a temporary injunction.

[¶4703.2] Specific Performance of Contract

Specific performance is a means of judicially compelling a party to do precisely what he agreed to do under the terms of the contract.

Plaintiff must prove (a) Making of a promise; (b) Consideration for the promise (even though the promise is in writing or under seal); (c) Occurrence of act or event, including lapse of time on which promise was conditioned; (d) Performance of all obligations resting on plaintiff, including performance of conditions precedent, or excuse for nonperformance, readiness and tender of performance; (e) Breach of promise or contract by defendant; (f) Facts showing inadequacy or impracticality of legal remedy; i.e., action for damages (money damages are not an adequate substitute for land or, generally, for unique chattels, a work of art, a race horse, etc. Because loss of business profits can't accurately be measured, specific performance of various business deals is quite common).

[¶4703.3] Recovery of Property by Equitable Means

Property may be recovered by equitable means where legal means are inadequate or impractical. Examples of suits involving this type of relief appear in the listing of the elements of common cause of action and include suits to compel specific performance of contracts to convey land, reconveyance of land on rescision of a conveyance because of mistake, fraud, duress or other ground, partition, removal of encroachments, to enforce a trust (express, constructive or resulting) and so-called suits for equitable replevin.

[¶4703.4] Enforcement of Money Obligations by Equitable Means

This may be done in these situations: (1) Plaintiff's interest is one that historically was protected only in equity; i.e., right to trust proceeds, right to alimony or support payments; (2) Where the money obligation is secured and enforcement of the security is sought; (3) Accounting; (4) As incident to suit for other relief which is by itself within jurisdiction of equity. Foreclosure actions and suits in aid of execution are examples of the enforcement of money obligations by equitable means.

[¶4703.5] Protection Against Future and Multiple Claims

Equity may grant relief: (1) To aid in the prosecution or defense of future actions; (2) To prevent future actions; and (3) To prevent multiple actions or suits. Common types of suits seeking relief under this heading are suits: (1) To interpret or declare the meaning of a will, trust, or other instrument; (2) To cancel a written instrument; (3) To reform a written instrument; (4) To quiet title to land; (5) To require numerous claimants having similar claims to make them in one suit; (6) To require persons having claims against a person for the same money or property to set up their claims in one suit; (7) To require a claimant to make his claim in a suit started by the person against whom the claim exists rather than in a later action after defenses may be lost. Other types of suits in this class include suits to require answers to interrogatories, for the taking of a deposition or for discovery but procedural reforms on the law side have made this type of equity suit largely unnecessary.

[¶4703.6] Partition

We can have partition where property is divided among co-owners or co-proprietors or it is sold and the proceeds are divided among the co-owners and co-proprietors. Partition may be either voluntary, i.e., by contract or judicial. As a general rule, property held in joint tenancy or tenancy in common may be the subject of an action in partition *(Shoup v. Cummins,* 334 Ill. 539). It is the co-tenancy which gives the right to a compulsory partition. Generally for an action in partition to lie, it is essential that the party maintaining the action have possession, constructive possession or a right to the possession of the property. An action for partition will not lie where the property is owned severally. The procedure in a partition action is generally regulated by state statute.

[¶4703.7] Reformation

Reformation may be available where the parties were in agreement as to the terms to be embodied in a proposed written agreement but the writing is materially at variance with the intention of the parties. Reformation will also be available where one party at the time the execution of a written instrument

376

knows not only that the writing does not accurately express the intention of the other party but knows what the intention is. See Restatement Contracts §504–505.

[¶4703.8] **Cancellation of Contract or Obligation**

The destruction or cancellation of the document embodying a contract will discharge a contractual duty that arises under a formal unilateral contract where done with the intent to discharge the duty. Surrender of the document to the party subject to the duty or someone on his behalf will have a similar effect (see Restatement §432).

[¶4703.9] **Declaratory Judgment**

In the Federal courts and most state courts the declaratory judgment is recognized by statute. Under the Federal Act there must be an actual controversy (28 USC §400). A declaratory judgment has the force and effect of a final judgment or decree (28 USC §400, Uniform Declaratory Judgment Act §1). A declaratory judgment may be affirmative or negative in form and effect. The Uniform Act provides that a declaratory judgment may declare rights, status and other legal relations (Uniform Declaratory Judgment Act §1).

[¶4703.10] **Mandamus**

Mandamus is used to impel the performance of a ministerial governmental duty or compel action involving judgment and discretion. Mandamus will generally not be available to direct the exercise of judgment or discretion in a particular way. The writ of mandamus is available in the state courts. The Federal rules of civil procedure have abolished writs of mandamus in the Federal courts although the relief formerly available by mandamus may be obtained through other procedures spelled out in the Federal rules of civil procedure (Rule 81(b)).

Mandamus is issued in the sound discretion of the court. It will not issue in doubtful cases. Mandamus will not be available where the required performance is within the letter of the law but not the spirit of the law nor where it would work a public or private mischief *(Duncan Townsite Co. v. Lane,* 245 US 308). It is essential that the complaining party have a clear legal right and no other plain, adequate and complete method of obtaining relief (US Ex. Rel. *Girard Trust Co. v. Helvering,* 301 US 450). Mandamus is available to compel the exercise of discretion but not to direct the method with which the discretion is exercised.

In many states the proceeding in mandamus has been abolished by statute and replaced by other procedural devices. In New York State, for example, a so-called Article 78 proceeding in the nature of mandamus has replaced it.

[¶4703.11]   Quo Warranto

Quo Warranto is generally invoked to test the right or title to office, remedy the usurpation of franchises, remedy the abuse of franchises, test primary nominations and test the right to judicial office. In many states the availability of quo warranto is governed by statutes which have spelled out the cases in which the remedy will lie.

[¶4703.12]   Taxpayers' Actions

Taxpayers' actions are often utilized in proceedings against municipal corporations, counties, towns, etc. The interest of a taxpayer in the Federal Treasury is not sufficient to enable him to maintain a taxpayer's action against the Federal Government. His interest in the monies of the Treasury — partly realized from taxation and partly from other sources—is shared with millions of others; is comparatively minute and indeterminable and the effect upon future taxation of any payment out of the fund so remote, fluctuating, and uncertain that no basis is afforded for an appeal to the preventive powers of a court of equity *(Massachusetts v. Milon,* 262 US 447). The remedies available to the taxpayer may take the form of a bill in equity, quo warranto, mandamus or certiorari.

[¶4703.13]   Civil Arrest

As used in civil litigation, arrest is an extraordinary remedy. It must be distinguished from imprisonment for debt which has been abolished in nearly every jurisdiction. Arrest in a civil proceeding is intended to secure the presence of the defendant until the final judgment. Generally the right of arrest will be limited to a few instances where the defendant's presence will be required for the effective enforcement of the court's judgment or decree and the nature of the action or the nonresidency of the defendant indicates that the defendant may not be available.

Civil arrest statutes generally require that the plaintiff give the sheriff or other official making the arrest security against liabilities which may be incurred and for the defendant posting bail or other security to assure that he will remain within the jurisdiction until the termination of the action or will be available upon the termination of the action.

[¶4703.14]   Attachment

Attachment is a proceeding whereby the plaintiff acquires control over the defendant's property prior to the determination of the issues involved. Where personal jurisdiction over the defendant has not been acquired, attachment may be used as a jurisdictional predicate provided service is made prior to or concurrent with the attachment *(Pennoya v. Neff)*. Where jurisdiction over the property or credits of the defendant is obtained, personal jurisdiction over the defendant is unnecessary unless an in personam judgment is sought *(Harris v. Balk*, 198 US 215).

In the Federal courts the availability of attachment is dependent upon the state's statutes in the jurisdiction wherein the Federal court is sitting. As a general rule an action may not be commenced by attachment in the Federal courts.

Property owned by the defendant in the jurisdiction of the court may be attached. A debt owed to the defendant may be attached provided its situs is within the jurisdiction of the court.

Generally, statutes providing for attachment enumerate certain classes of actions for which the remedy is available or certain conditions which must be met prior to invoking the remedy. Generally, attached property will be released upon the posting of adequate security or a bond.

Where property has been wrongfully attached the owner will generally have a choice of remedies (a) an action for malicious or wrongful attachment, (b) malicious prosecution, or (c) an action upon the attachment bond.

[¶4703.15] Writ of Assistance

The writ of assistance is utilized in carrying out equity decrees much in the same manner as the execution is utilized in carrying out an action at law. The writ of assistance is frequently utilized in many jurisdictions to establish the ownership of property or to put a litigant into possession of property.

[¶4703.16] Certiorari

Certiorari is available in many jurisdictions to review the findings of a lower tribunal or an administrative agency. The availability of certiorari varies from state to state. In some states its availability is governed exclusively by statute. Unless otherwise provided by statute, discretion will be important in determining whether certiorari is available. Essentially, certiorari represents the review of a judicial determination. However, the nature of the action rather than the body taking the action will usually determine whether certiorari is available.

[¶4704] COMMON DEFENSES

Defenses applicable to particular actions are treated in connection with specific actions throughout this book. Here, however, is a checklist of common defenses to actions or suits:

Accord and Satisfaction: An accord and satisfaction is a means of discharging a contract or settling a contract or tort claim by substituting for the contract or claim an agreement for its satisfaction and then performing the agreement. It bars the original claim. To have this effect, however, as a general rule, the agreement must be fully executed. But the parties themselves may by clear language make the agreement itself and not its performance operate as satisfaction of the original claim.

Act of God: May be used as a defense to action on contract or in tort. Defendant must show: (a) Act or event complained of was the result of an act of God; (b) Defendant was not responsible and his negligence did not contribute to it in any way.

Adverse Possession: Defendant must show that his possession was actual and not constructive, under a claim of right, hostile, open and notorious, exclusive and continuous for the period required by law.

Another Action Pending: Defendant must show that there is pending and undisposed of another action in another court by the same plaintiff against the same defendant based on the same cause of action and involving the same parties.

Arbitration and Award: An award made under a valid arbitration agreement ordinarily operates to discharge the claim submitted to arbitration. The party relying on this defense must show: (a) An agreement on the part of plaintiff to submit his claim to arbitration; (b) Submission of the claim to arbitration as agreed; and (c) Making of the award, and notice or publication, if these matters are jurisdictional to proceedings for enforcement.

Assumption of Risk: In negligence cases it is a recognized principle that one who voluntarily assumes the risk of injury from a known danger can't recover. Under some rules of procedure assumption of risk is regarded as an affirmative defense which must be specially pleaded but under others it may be proved under a general denial. While often closely associated with contributory negligence it is distinguishable. Assumption of risk, for example, may bar recovery even though plaintiff may have acted with what might be considered due care. Usually this defense is invoked in cases involving a contractual relationship between plaintiff and defendant (master and servant, or other relationship), but it can be used in other cases as well. Defendant must show: (a) An unreasonable risk in the situation or thing causing the injury; and (b) Knowledge of the risk by the plaintiff at the time.

Breach of Condition Subsequent: Breach of a condition subsequent operates to destroy vested estates and contract rights. Because of their effect they are not favored and will be found to exist only where the language creating them is very clear. In any case, if found to exist, the condition subsequent will be strictly construed.

Capacity or Right of Party to Sue or Be Sued: Examples:

(1) Plaintiff is a foreign corporation doing business within the state without having qualified to do so suing on a business transaction arising within the state;

(2) Plaintiff is not the real party in interest;

(3) Plaintiff is not sui juris;

(4) Other necessary parties are not joined; plaintiff not real party in interest;

(5) Defendant is a foreign corporation, is not qualified to do business within the state and does not do business within the state and the cause of action alleged did not arise within the state;

(6) Defendant is without capacity to be sued as by reason of infancy.

Contributory Negligence: In some states plaintiff in a negligence case must show his freedom from contributory negligence; in others, in some cases, at least, a doctrine of comparative negligence has been adopted under which the plaintiff's contributory negligence won't bar but will only limit recovery; but in most states plaintiff's contributory negligence is a matter of affirmative defense. In the latter states defendant must show: (a) Act or omission on the part of the plaintiff creating an unreasonable risk of harm to his person or property; and (b) Resulting harm contributing to the damage complained of.

Discharge in Bankruptcy: Defendant must show: (a) Details as to filing of petition by or against him, adjudication of bankruptcy and granting of discharge; (b) That plaintiff's claim was due and owing at the time of the bankruptcy proceedings and was included in the schedules filed or was omitted for specified reasons. Unless it appears from the plaintiff's petition that the claim sued on was provable in bankruptcy and was not excepted from discharge by operation of law, the defendant is sometimes also required to show that the claim was provable and not excepted from discharge.

Duress: Defendant must show that execution of the instrument relied on by the plaintiff was induced by fear of violence or imprisonment or the result of other wrongful pressure.

Election of Remedies: Defendant must show that plaintiff had two existing alternative remedial rights, inconsistent and not reconcilable with each other based on the state of facts alleged in the present action and that plaintiff prior to the commencement of the present action elected to pursue the alternative remedy.

Estoppel: The defendant must show conduct or acts, words or silence on the part of the plaintiff amounting to representation or concealment of material facts, with knowledge or imputed knowledge thereof and that such representation, silence or concealment be relied on by the defendant, and defendant's reliance thereon to his damage or detriment.

381

Extension of Time for Payment: Defendant must show written agreement based on valuable consideration extending time of payment until a certain date and that by reason of the extension, the amount claimed is not due and payable.

Failure or Want of Consideration: Whenever consideration is required, want or failure of consideration is a defense. If consideration is required but need not be alleged, want or failure is an affirmative defense. Check state statutes making consideration unnecessary for written promises or creating presumption of consideration when promise is in writing.

Fraud: Some courts distinguish between fraud in the making (person didn't know what he was signing) and fraud in the inducement (knew what he was signing but was induced to sign by fraudulent misrepresentations) and make former negative defense and latter an affirmative defense requiring special plea. Defendant must show false representation by plaintiff with knowledge of falsity made with intent to defraud defendant, and relied on by defendant to his damage.

Laches: Defendant must show claim for equitable relief has been unreasonably delayed and that hardship or injustice to the defendant will result from its enforcement.

License: In actions for damages based on intentional wrong to plaintiff, a showing that plaintiff consented to the wrong will usually bar relief. In actions for assault and battery and false imprisonment, plaintiff must generally show absence of consent, but in actions for intentional damage to property, real or personal, license is an affirmative defense.

Payment: Payment must generally be set up as an affirmative defense.

Privilege: Conduct which under ordinary circumstances will subject the actor to liability may under particular circumstances not subject him to liability, that is, the conduct may be privileged. Examples: (a) Self-defense; (b) Defense of a third person; (c) Public necessity, as where property is destroyed to prevent spread of fire; (d) Protection or defense of property; (e) Parental discipline; (f) Seizure under legal process; and (g) Privilege to abate nuisance.

Release: A release may take the form of a declaration that a particular claim or cause of action has been discharged or the form of an agreement not to sue. In either form, if it is in writing and supported by consideration, or local law dispenses with requirement of consideration, as it may in the case of instruments under seal, it may be pleaded in bar.

Res Judicata: There are three types: (a) Merger (claim is merged in judgment recovered by plaintiff); (b) Bar (in prior action on same claim plaintiff failed to get judgment); and (c) Estoppel (in prior action an issue involved in second action was settled by judgment of court and plaintiff is estopped from relitigating same issue even though cause of action is different and cannot recover in second action unless it's established). If prior judgment is not on the merits, but is based on procedural defect, it will not have effect of res judicata.

Statute of Frauds: Specified transactions are unenforceable unless evidenced by a writing signed by the party to be charged. Transactions within statute: (a) Special promise to answer for debt or default of another (contracts of suretyship and guaranty); (b) Contracts for sale of interests in real property; (c) Contracts for the sale of goods of more than a certain value; (d) Contracts not to be performed within a year; (e) Contract to lease real property for more than a year; (f) Contracts to bequeath property; (g) Contracts to establish a trust; (h) Conveyance or assignment of trust in personal property; (i) Promise to pay debt discharged in bankruptcy; and (j) Contracts made in consideration of marriage.

Statute of Limitations: Generally, failure of the plaintiff to bring an action within the time limited by statute is an affirmative defense. Sometimes plaintiff must show as a condition of relief that action is brought within time limited. There are general and special statutes and defense must make sure it isn't relying on a general statute when a special statute applies.

Ultra Vires: Defendant corporation must show that transaction on which action is based was beyond its express or implied powers.

Usury: Local law must be checked as to legal rates of interest, effect of usury (collection of excessive interest barred, collection of all interest, forfeiture of principal) and whether or not corporation may plead.

Waiver: Defendant must show that prior to action plaintiff voluntarily relinquished interest asserted in action and that defendant relied on the relinquishment.

Want of Jurisdiction: Want of jurisdiction of the person of the defendant must be properly pleaded (almost universally a special appearance is called for) and will be waived by a general appearance. Want of jurisdiction of the subject matter may be raised at any time either by the defendant or by the court on its own motion.

●

For Further Reference . . .
American Jurisprudence, Actions.
Bender's Forms of Pleading, Matthew Bender, New York, N.Y.
Blume, William W., *American Civil Procedure,* Prentice-Hall, Englewood Cliffs, N.J.

SALES AND PURCHASES

[¶4801] The coming of the Uniform Commercial Code to all states but Louisiana calls for a review of selling and buying practices and particularly of sales and purchasing forms. First, the Code provides that an oral contract for the sale of goods for a price in excess of $500 is not enforceable. But the requirements as to the kind of writing necessary to satisfy the statute of frauds have been significantly reduced. Any memorandum of the transaction will do. However, it still must state the quantity of goods involved. If the amount isn't accurately stated, the contract will be enforced but only up to the amount stated, or the amount agreed upon, whichever is less. The writing must be signed by the party against whom enforcement is sought or by his authorized agent or broker.

But there is one exception to this requirement which can impose a binding commitment upon the businessman who does not read his mail or deal with it promptly. Failure to answer a written confirmation of a contract within ten days bars the party ignoring the confirmation from raising the statute of frauds as a defense. The requirements for invoking this clause are: (1) that, within a reasonable time, there be a writing confirming the oral contract; (2) that the writing be sufficient to bind the sender; (3) that it be received; and (4) that no reply thereto be made within 10 days, although the recipient has reason to know of its contents.

Oral statements cannot be used to contradict a written contract, but can be used to explain or supplement those terms by reference to a course of dealing between the parties, trade usage or course of performance, even though the contract is unambiguous. Consistent additional terms can be proven orally unless the court finds the contract was intended as a complete and exclusive statement of the terms agreed upon.

This means that the businessman who wants to change his established method of dealing or depart from trade customs must establish his new practice and negate trade usage in a written provision of the contract.

A written "firm" offer made by a merchant is irrevocable for its specified duration or for a reasonable time not to exceed three months. When an acceptance comes in specifying additional or even different terms from those in the offer, the additional or different terms become part of the contract, unless the offer limits acceptance to the terms of the offer or unless the added or different terms materially alter the offer, or unless the offeror objects to them within a reasonable time after learning of them.

Examples of terms that normally *would* materially alter an offer:

Negation of standard warranties such as that of merchantability or fitness for a particular purpose where either warranty normally attaches.

384

Seller's reservation of power to cancel upon buyer's failure to meet any invoice when due.

Requirement of guaranty of 100% delivery where the usage of the trade allows some quantity leeway.

Here are some additional terms that normally *would not* materially alter an offer:

Fixing a reasonable time for complaints within customary limits.

Provision for inspection by subpurchaser where purchase is for subsale.

Provision for interest on overdue invoices.

Under the UCC, it is easier to allege a subsequent modification of a contract and more important to protect against unwarranted claims that better terms were given after the entry into a sales contract. To do so, have the sales form say something like "This agreement cannot be altered or amended except by a further agreement in writing signed by the parties," and have the buyer separately sign that particular provision.

A sales contract can be enforceable even if the price term is left open *(UCC §2-305)*. If the contract doesn't say anything about the price, the Code sets a reasonable price at the time of delivery. It is also set as the reasonable price at the time of delivery if the price is left to be agreed upon and there's no agreement, or if it's to be fixed in terms of some agreed standard set by a third party and it is not so set or recorded. Under the Code, when the parties intend not to be bound unless the price is fixed or agreed and it is not fixed or agreed, there is no contract.

[¶4802]   PATENT INDEMNITY

In a sales or manufacturing agreement, the buyer should get the seller's indemnification against liability for patent infringement if the buyer uses or resells the product he is getting from the seller. Sometimes sellers try to disclaim such liability. In the absence of a patent indemnification clause, §2-132 of the Uniform Commercial Code provides that a merchant "warrants that the goods shall be delivered free of the rightful claim of any third person by way of infringement or the like." However, it is important to specify the extent and conditions of patent indemnification. A committee of the National Association of Manufacturers has worked with the Patent Committee of the American Bar Association on a survey of indemnity clauses and these conclusions should be helpful in developing a satisfactory clause:

1. Many clauses require the seller to protect the buyer against infringement *by the use* of the goods sold. This provision could readily lead to excessive losses, even though the goods involved in the sale may only be some staple item in common use, such as an ordinary chemical, or machine bolts. It is not generally realized that many goods could be *used* by the buyer in a manner

unforeseen by the seller so as to infringe a patent, particularly a *process* patent.

2. The seller is very often required to indemnify his customer against *all* losses incurred by the latter due to a charge of infringement. Such a broad guarantee leaves the seller wide open for his customer's *consequential* damages resulting from the issuance of an injunction. In the latter case the seller may have to pay all monetary losses such as those due to plant shutdowns. Such consequential damages alone might readily sink a small concern, and stagger a large one.

3. A surprisingly small proportion of clauses make any distinction between goods made to the purchaser's specifications, and those designed or originated by the seller. Liability for infringement should usually be assumed by the party who fixes the specifications or design of the goods.

4. Many clauses fail to provide that the party liable for infringement should be notified promptly of any infringement suit brought against the other party, and should also be given the opportunity to control the defense of any such suit. In most instances, such notice and control should be recognized as a most important safeguard for the party who may be ultimately liable.

〔¶4803〕   DISCLAIMER OF WARRANTIES

Under the UCC, warranty by description and warranty by sample are express warranties and they may not be avoided by any disclaimer which is not consistent with the warranty itself. This means that any disclaimer must be explicit and should immediately follow the language of description.

The implied warranty of "merchantability" and "fitness" can be avoided only by a disclaimer which is written conspicuously and expressed in specific language. All implied warranties are excluded by expressions like "as is," "with all faults," or other language which in common understanding calls the buyer's attention to the exclusion and makes plain that there are no implied warranties.

Note that by making claims on a label or container, the seller undertakes that his goods will conform to the claims.

〔¶4803.1〕 How to Control Obligations in Purchasing and Sales

Written purchase and sales agreements are necessary to:

(1) Control offers, acceptances and confirmations which can inject unwanted conditions into a transaction.

(2) Disclaim warranties.

(3) Control risk of loss.

William Davenport of the Chicago Bar, speaking before the American Bar Association, set down these lists of rules to follow in order to control the impact of the fine print in sales and purchase orders.

(1) If your client is the sender of a sales or purchase order form (or an offeror) and wants no contract except upon his terms, he should include a clause in conspicuous type limiting acceptance to the exact terms of the offer.

(2) If your client is the recipient of a sales or purchase order form (or an offeree) and wants no contract except upon his terms, he need reply only as follows: "I accept your offer (Identifying it) provided you agree to the following additional (or substitute) terms:" Or he may reply "I accept upon the express condition that you agree," or, "I accept if and only if you agree, etc."

(3) If your client may be willing to accept some terms that may be proposed by the other party after he sees what they are, he may use a clause as in (1) above or he may omit it and merely object promptly to the terms that he doesn't want. If he doesn't want a particular term he should always object promptly. He should never assume that the term will not become part of the contract because it will "materially alter" the contract.

(4) In order that your client may be doubly sure that the contract contains all of the terms which he wants included, he should not begin performance or do any act recognizing a contract before all forms have crossed and the terms are settled.

(5) In the case of written confirmations, they should be mailed promptly and preferably by registered mail.

(6) Any legend on the front side of the form incorporating by reference any terms on the reverse side should be in conspicuous type. The terms on the reverse side should be in as large and clear type as possible. In drafting these terms on the reverse side, attention must be paid to other provisions of the Code—for example, §2-316, with respect to the size or color of type and the language used to disclaim or limit warranties (Davenport, 19 *Business Lawyer* 75).

To safeguard against the possible invalidity of a disclaimer of a warranty, it is well to provide for a remedy which is expressly sanctioned by the Code §2-316(2), using some such language as this:

"There are no warranties which extend beyond the description on the face hereof."

Where the warranty of merchantability is excluded there must be a specific reference to merchantability. See UCC §2-316.

There remains a possibility that this kind of a clause might be attacked under the provisions of the Code which authorize the setting aside of all unconscionable provisions.

[¶4804]   LEGAL BASIS OF SALES AND PURCHASES

The legal basis for sales contracts rests in the Uniform Commercial Code.

[¶4804.1] Offer and Acceptance

The UCC has liberalized the rules as to offer and acceptance. Under the Code an offer invites acceptance in any manner and by any medium reasonable in the circumstances *(UCC §2-206)*. However, the rule has not been changed that the person making the offer may limit the manner of acceptance in his offer by clearly indicating a particular manner of acceptance.

Under the UCC, the varying terms of offer and acceptance will not necessarily bar the formation of the agreement. Whether an offer and acceptance has terminated in a contract will depend on the language of the forms. An acceptance which states additional or different terms from the offer may operate as an acceptance except where the acceptance is expressly conditional on the assent to the additional or different terms contained therein.

The offeree will not be able to add terms where the offeror expressly limits acceptance to the terms of the offer. If the offeror receives an acceptance containing variations in his offer which are unacceptable, he should object within a reasonable time after the form containing additional or modified terms is received.

An offer will be revocable unless by its terms it is irrevocable. At common law an irrevocable offer or option had to be supported by consideration. In jurisdictions where the Uniform Commercial Code has been adopted and also which by its terms is irrevocable, will be irrevocable for the stated period of time or a period of time not to exceed 3 months, whichever is less. The irrevocable offer must conform to the Code rules of a writing signed by the person making the offer.

[¶4805] STATUTE OF FRAUDS

The statute of frauds requires a contract for the sale of goods be in writing if the goods are for the *price* of $500 or more. However, part performance would take a contract out of the statute of frauds to the extent of the part performance.

Where goods are to be specially manufactured and are not ordinarily resaleable in the normal course of the seller's business, an oral agreement will be binding where the seller has made a substantial beginning on or a commitment to acquire the goods called for in an agreement.

To meet the requirements of the statute of frauds the agreement generally must be signed by the party against whom it is to be enforced. However, the Uniform Commercial Code provides for the enforcement of a letter of confirmation in transactions between merchants where the person receiving the letter has reason to know of its contents. A person receiving a letter of confirmation may object within 10 days, and avoid its effect.

[¶4806]   **DESCRIPTION**

The subject matter of the sales contract may be described in any form including blueprints, specifications, a sample or model, general language of description, etc. Where there is a conflict between two forms of descriptions, a technical specification will displace inconsistent sample, model or general language description. Also, a sample from an existing bulk will displace an inconsistent general description *(UCC §2-317)*. The description of the goods will generally give rise to express warranty that the goods will conform to the agreement *(UCC §2-313)*. A description of goods in terms of their purpose may create a warranty that the goods will be fit for their purpose if the buyer relied on the seller's skill and judgment in selecting or furnishing the goods and the seller had reason to know, but did not necessarily know as a fact, that the buyer so relied *(UCC §2-315)*. See table at ¶4815.

[¶4806.1] Price

Where the parties have not fixed the price prior to the agreement, the price will be the reasonable price unless the parties have provided machinery whereby the price will be determined.

Here are some of the more popular methods for determining price:

(1) Cost plus overhead and profit. The agreement should spell out the cost to be included in the cost factor. Overhead and profit may be a share of the enterprise's entire overhead or a percentage of cost.

(2) Market price.

(3) Price listed in a trade journal. Unless otherwise agreed between the parties if the publication ceases publication the price will be the reasonable price at the time of delivery *(UCC §2-305(1)(c))*.

(4) Price set by a governmental agency as in the case of price control or regulatory schemes.

(5) Price announced by another. However, you must be careful to avoid violation of antitrust and trade regulations statutes. See ¶4301.

(6) Price to be set by an appraiser. Unless otherwise agreed between the parties, if the appraiser fails to set the price, the price will be the reasonable price at the time of delivery unless it appears that the parties did not intend that there be an agreement in the absence of the appraisal.

(7) Price to be agreed upon. In the event the parties fail to agree upon a price, the Code provides that the price will be the reasonable price unless the agreement indicates that the parties intended a deal only if there was agreement on the price *(UCC §2-305)*.

(8) Price to be set by the seller. The Uniform Commercial Code imposes an obligation of good faith upon the seller setting the price *(UCC §2-305(2))*.

(9) Escalator Clauses. The escalator clause may be geared to one of the standard price indices published by the United States Department of Labor.

[¶4807] DELIVERY

In the absence of a specific agreement between the parties, the place of delivery will be the locale of the goods where they were identified to the agreement at the time the agreement was made. Where the goods were not identified to the agreement at the time the agreement was made, the place of delivery will be the seller's place of business, or if he has no place of business, his home, unless otherwise agreed.

Delivery terms are often spelled out in terms of standard commercial abbreviations. The following checklist of obligations arising from the use of these terms is based upon the definitions contained in the Uniform Commercial Code:

FOB (Place of Shipment): Unless otherwise agreed, the seller must ship the goods and bear the expense of putting the goods in the hands of the shipper. The seller must notify the buyer of the shipment and obtain and deliver necessary documents of title so as to enable the buyer to obtain possession. The buyer must reasonably give the seller proper shipping instructions. *(UCC §2-504, 2-319).*

FOB (Place of Destination): Unless otherwise agreed, the seller must at his own expense transport the goods to the place of destination, give the buyer reasonable notification to enable him to take delivery, tender delivery at a reasonable time, and keep the goods available for a reasonable time to permit the buyer to take possession *(UCC §2-319, 2-503).*

FOB (Car or Other Vehicle): In addition to putting the goods in the possession of the carrier the seller must load them on board the truck, car or other vehicle utilized by the carrier *(UCC §2-319).*

FOB (Vessel): The seller must place the goods on board the vessel designated by the buyer and furnish proper form bill of lading in appropriate case *(UCC §2-319).*

FAS (Vessel): The seller must, at his own expense, deliver the goods alongside the vessel designated by the buyer or on the dock designated in the manner usual in the particular port, and obtain a receipt in exchange for which the carrier is obligated to issue a bill of lading *(UCC §2-319).*

CIF: The price stated includes the cost of goods, insurance and freight to the named destination. The seller is obligated to load the goods, obtain a receipt showing that the freight has been paid or provided for, obtain a negotiable bill of title, insure the goods for the account of the buyer and forward all necessary documents to the buyer with commercial promptness *(UCC §2-320)*.

Where delivery is to be made to the buyer, the buyer must furnish facilities reasonably suited for accepting delivery *(UCC §2-503)*.

Where goods are in a warehouse or otherwise in possession of a bailee and the agreement calls for delivery to the buyer without moving the goods, the seller must render a negotiable document of title or procure acknowledgment by the bailee or warehouseman of the buyer's right to possession of the goods. Unless the buyer objects, a nonnegotiable document of title or a written direction to the warehouseman or bailee to deliver is sufficient tender of delivery. Where the bailee receives notice of the buyer's rights in the goods, those rights are fixed as to the bailee, and all third persons. The risk of loss of the goods will not pass to the buyer until the buyer has had a reasonable time to present the document or direction to the warehouseman or bailee to deliver. Where delivery is tendered in the form of a nonnegotiable document of title, the liability for the failure of the warehouseman to honor the document of title remains upon the seller until the buyer has had reasonable opportunity to present the document. Failure of the bailee to honor the document of title defeats the tender.

[¶4807.1] Inspection

The buyer has the right to inspect goods. The UCC provides that he has the right of inspection upon the tender of delivery or identification to the agreement.

Where the contract requires payment prior to inspection, the non-conformity of the goods does not excuse the buyer unless the non-conformity appears without inspection *(UCC §2-512)*. However, an agreement to pay against documents may be construed as waiving the buyer's right to inspection. Where the parties have agreed to a C.O.D. delivery, the buyer will be presumed to have waived his right of inspection prior to payment *(UCC §2-513)*.

The right of inspection afforded by the Code includes the right to inspect goods in any reasonable manner. Inspection may include testing, where the nature of the goods cannot be adequately determined without testing. If the testing by the buyer is unreasonable, such as where the nature of the goods cannot be adequately determined and the buyer uses an unreasonable quantity of the goods in testing or performs needless tests, his testing may be construed as an acceptance. The cost of testing and inspecting will be borne by the buyer except where the goods fail to conform to the agreement. Where the goods fail to conform to the agreement the UCC provides that the buyer may recover the reasonable cost of inspection and testing from the seller *(UCC §2-513)*.

〔¶4807.2〕 Time of Delivery

Where the agreement is silent as to the time of delivery, the UCC provides that delivery shall be made at a reasonable time. Language calling for delivery immediately, at once, forthwith, directly, promptly, or as soon as possible serves to establish a basis for what is reasonable. A clause stating that time is of the essence indicates that the time of delivery is one of the terms bargained for in the agreement.

Late delivery will be excused where caused by the occurrence of a contingency, nonoccurrence of which was a basic assumption on which the agreement was made, or the seller's compliance in good faith within the applicable governmental regulations whether or not the regulation later proves invalid *(UCC §2-615)*. The Code also provides that the seller's delay in delivery will be excused where caused by his suspension of performance because of the buyer's repudiation or the buyer's failure to cooperate as required in the agreement *(UCC §2-311, 2-611)*.

〔¶4808〕 OPTIONS AS TO PERFORMANCE

Where the agreement leaves particulars of performance to be specified by one of the parties, the Code provides that it will be upheld although specifications must be made in good faith and within limits set by commercial standards of reasonableness so that there is no surprise *(UCC §2-311, Official Comment 1)*. Where the agreement calls for an assortment of goods, the right to determine the assortment will be with the buyer unless otherwise provided between the parties.

〔¶4809〕 RIGHT TO RETURN

The buyer will have the right to return goods where they fail to conform to the agreement. However, the agreement may specifically provide for the right to return goods. Where the buyer has the right to return goods which he is purchasing for his own use, the contract will be characterized as a sale on approval. Where the buyer is purchasing the goods for resale, the contract will be characterized as a sale or return *(UCC §2-326)*. Where the agreement is for sale on approval, the obligation of return and the risk of loss are upon the seller. In a sale or return, the obligation of return is upon the buyer unless otherwise agreed *(UCC §2-326, 2-327)*. A "consignment" or "on memorandum" sale is characterized by the UCC as a sale or return.

[¶4810]   **PASSAGE OF TITLE**

The Uniform Commercial Code has substantially reduced the importance of title in commercial transactions. However, the following rules will be applied in determining where title rests.

1. Seller Controls Performance: Title passes to the buyer when the seller has completed his performance with regard to delivery of the goods to the buyer *(UCC §2-401(2)).*

For example, if the contract calls for delivery FOB cars at the seller's warehouse, title will pass when the goods are placed on the cars at the seller's warehouse.

2. Seller to Ship: Where the agreement requires the seller to send the goods to the buyer but does not require delivery at the place of destination, title to the goods passes to the buyer at the time and place of shipment *(UCC §2-401(2)(a)).*

For example, if the agreement calls for delivery FOB New York and the goods are to be shipped to San Francisco, title will pass to the buyer when the goods are shipped from New York.

3. Seller to Deliver: Where the agreement requires the seller to deliver the goods to the buyer at the place of destination, title to the goods passes to the buyer upon delivery *(UCC §2-401(2)(b)).*

For example, if the agreement calls for delivery by the seller at the buyer's place of business, title will pass when the goods are delivered.

4. Delivery Without Moving Goods — Document of Title: Where delivery is to be made without moving the goods and the seller is required to deliver a document of title, title passes at the time and place where the document of title is delivered *(UCC §2-401(3)(a)).*

For example, if goods in a warehouse are sold with the understanding that delivery will be made by the delivery of a warehouse receipt with which the buyer may take possession of the goods, title will pass upon the delivery of the warehouse receipt by the seller to the buyer.

5. Delivery Without Moving Goods: Where delivery is to be made without moving the goods and the goods have been identified to the agreement at the time of making the agreement, title to the goods passes to the buyer at the time of making the agreement *(UCC §2-401(3)(b)).*

For example, if the buyer agrees to purchase an identified machine located in the seller's yard, the title will pass at the time of making the agreement, if nothing else remains to be done.

393

6. Withdrawal of Acceptance: Where the buyer refuses to accept the goods or withdraws his acceptance of the goods, title revests in the seller by operation of law *(UCC §2-401(4)).*

Sale on Approval: Where the goods are sold primarily for the use of the buyer rather than for resale, with the understanding that they may be returned, and the agreement is characterized as one of sale on approval, title passes to the buyer upon his approval *(UCC §2-326, 2-327).*

For example, if the agreement calls for sale of a machine which the buyer will use in his manufacturing process, he may be given a reasonable time for trial. If after a reasonable trial, he approves it, title will pass when he approves it or decides to keep it. Similarly, if he has not disapproved or rejected the goods before the end of the prescribed trial period, title will pass at the termination of that period.

The parties may not agree that title to the goods will pass to the buyer before the goods are in existence.

[¶4811]   RISK OF LOSS

The Uniform Commercial Code has divorced the question of risk of loss from the question of title.

Following is a set of rules derived from the UCC for determining the risk of loss.

(1) Goods to be Delivered to Carrier: Where the seller is required to deliver the goods to a carrier, the risk of loss shifts to the buyer when the seller duly delivers the goods to the carrier *(UCC §2-509).*

(2) FOB — Place of Shipment: Where the goods are sold FOB place of shipment, the risk of loss shifts to the buyer when the goods are placed in the hands of the shipper *(UCC §2-319).*

(3) FOB—Destination: Where the goods are sold FOB place of destination, the risk of loss shifts to the buyer at the time and place of delivery or the time and place where tender of delivery is made to the buyer *(UCC §2-319).*

(4) Seller to Deliver: Where the seller must deliver the goods to the destination, the risk of loss shifts to the buyer when the delivery is tendered to him so as to enable him to take possession *(UCC §2-319).*

(5) Sale or Return: Where the goods are sold to the buyer for resale, rather than his use, with the understanding that they may be returned, the risk of loss during the return is upon the buyer *(UCC §2-327).*

(6) Sale on Approval: Where the goods are sold to a buyer primarily for his own use, rather than resale, and the agreement calls for a "sale on approval,"

the risk of loss shifts to the buyer when the buyer accepts the goods. If the goods are not accepted, the return is at the seller's risk *(UCC §2-327)*.

(7) Goods Fail to Conform: Where the goods delivered failed to conform to the requirements of the agreement, the risk of loss remains on the seller until the nonconformity is cured or the non-conforming goods are accepted by the buyer *(UCC §2-510)*.

(8) Buyer Revokes Acceptance: Where the buyer initially accepts the goods but subsequently justifiably revokes his acceptance, the buyer may treat the risk of loss as having rested on the seller to the extent of any deficiency in his insurance coverage *(UCC §2-510)*.

(9) Repudiation: Where the buyer repudiates the agreement before title to the goods passes to him, the seller may treat the risk of loss as having rested on the buyer for a commercially reasonable time. The seller is limited in holding the buyer for the risk of loss to any deficiency in his effective insurance coverage *(UCC §2-510)*.

(10) Delivery of Goods at Buyer's Place of Business—Merchant Seller: Where a merchant seller is to deliver the goods at his (the seller's) place of business or the present location of the goods, the risk of loss passes to the buyer upon delivery *(UCC §2-510)*.

(11) Delivery of Goods at Buyer's Place of Business—Non-Merchant Seller: Where a non-merchant seller is to deliver the goods at his (the seller's) place of business or at the present location of the goods to a non-merchant buyer, the risk of loss passes to the buyer upon tender of delivery *(UCC §2-510)*.

(12) Total Protection: Where goods identified to the agreement are destroyed prior to the time the risk of loss would normally have shifted to the buyer without fault of the buyer or seller, the risk of loss is upon the seller. However, he may avoid the agreement if the destruction to the goods is total. If the destruction to the goods is partial, the buyer has the option of accepting the goods with a proper price concession or permitting the seller to void the agreement *(UCC §2-510(3))*.

(13) Nonconforming Goods: Where the goods or their tender fail to conform to the agreement to an extent that the buyer would be entitled to reject the tender of delivery, the risk of loss remains upon the seller until he has cured the defect, or the buyer has accepted *(UCC §2-510(1))*.

(14) Revocation of Acceptance — Insurance Coverage: Where the buyer rightly revokes a prior acceptance, he may, to the extent of any deficiency in his effective insurance coverage, run the risk of loss as having been upon the seller from the beginning *(UCC §2-510(2))*.

(15) Repudiation — Insurance Coverage: Where the buyer repudiates an agreement as to goods which conform to the agreement, the seller may treat the risk of loss as resting upon the buyer to the extent of any deficiency in his effective insurance coverage *(UCC §2-510(3)).*

(16) Loss Caused by Third Party — Prior to Identification: Where a loss is caused by a third party prior to the identification of the goods to the agreement, the seller may maintain an action against the third party *(see UCC §2-501).*

(17) Loss Caused by Third Party — After Identification: Where a loss is caused by a third party after identification of the goods to the agreement, the seller and the buyer both may maintain an action against the third party. Regardless of who sues, any award goes to the one who bore the risk of loss at the time of loss *(UCC §2-722(b)).*

(18) Intent of Parties: Courts will look to the intention of the parties to determine the risk of loss where possible. Where a manufacturer borrowed a gluing machine under circumstances showing that he intended to buy a larger machine, the court found an agreement to return the machine in the same condition and imposed the risk of loss upon the borrower (*Industron Corp. v. Waltham Door and Window Co., Inc.,* 190 NE 2d 211).

[¶4812]   EXCUSED PERFORMANCE

Where goods are destroyed prior to the time the risk of loss shifts from the seller to the buyer, the agreement will be avoided if they were identified to the agreement prior to their destruction and the destruction was without the fault of either party. If goods identified to the agreement when made are so deteriorated as to no longer conform to the requirements of the agreement or have been partially destroyed without the fault of either party, the buyer has the option of treating the contract as avoided or accepting the goods with allowance for the deterioration or destruction *(UCC §2-613).*

The seller will be excused from performance where performance is made commercially impracticable by the occurrence of a contingency, the nonoccurrence of which was a basic assumption on which the agreement was founded *(UCC §2-615).* Similarly, the seller's performance will be excused where his performance is rendered impracticable by compliance in good faith with any foreign or domestic governmental regulations.

Where the inability to perform applies to only part of the seller's productive capacity, the UCC imposes an obligation upon the seller to divide his remaining productive capacity among his customers. He must seasonably notify his customers of their quota of his reduced capacity. Upon receipt of the seller's notification, if the prospective deficiency substantially impairs the value of the contract, the buyer has the option of terminating the agreement or accepting the quantity with which the seller proposes to provide him *(UCC §2-615)*. The seller may include his regular customers in the allocation of production whether or not he has a binding contractual obligation to supply them.

Deposits, Prepayments and Liquidated Damages — the seller is entitled to keep the buyer's deposit if the buyer refuses to accept the goods or otherwise breaches the agreement provided the deposit does not exceed either 20% of the buyer's obligation or $500, unless the buyer has received a benefit or the seller has incurred damages. Where the buyer has received a benefit or the seller has incurred damages, the amount of the deposit which the seller may keep is increased to reflect the benefit or the damages *(UCC §2-317(3)(b))*. The Code recognizes liquidated damages provided they are limited to an amount which is reasonable in the light of the anticipated or actual harm caused by the breach. Where the agreement calls for liquidated damages the seller may keep the deposit if it does not exceed the liquidated damages.

[¶4813]   MODIFICATION

The UCC provides that the modification of an agreement must be in writing if the statute of frauds requires that the agreement as modified be in writing. The parties may, however, agree that any modifications of a written agreement must be in writing even though the statute of frauds does not require the agreement as modified to be in writing *(UCC §2-209)*.

In transactions involving merchants, a provision requiring modifications to be in writing must be separately signed by the party receiving the form where the provision appears in a form supplied by the other party.

[¶4814]   ASSIGNMENT

The Uniform Commercial Code provides that the seller may delegate his obligation to perform unless the buyer has a substantial interest in having the seller perform or control the performance or the right to delegate or assign has been specifically restricted by the terms of the agreement. Delegation will not relieve the seller of the duty to perform or liability for breach of the agreement where the other party fails to perform *(UCC §2-210)*.

All rights of the seller or the buyer arising out of an agreement governed by the Code may be assigned except where the assignment would materially change the duty of the other party or increase materially the burden of risk imposed upon him by his contract or impair materially his chance of obtaining return performance. The right to assign may be restricted by the parties in their agreement. However, the right to recover damages for breach of the entire agreement or a right arising out of the assignor's due performance of his entire obligation may be assigned despite the parties' agreement to the contrary *(UCC §2-210)*.

[¶4815]   **WARRANTY**

The following table summarizes the UCC warranty rules:

Warranties Under the Uniform Commercial Code

	Warranty	Method of Exclusion
Warranty of Title	Seller warrants that good title will be conveyed and that title will be free of any security interest or lien of which the buyer is unaware *(UCC §2-312)*. The warranty of title may be breached by disturbance of quiet possession.	Excluded only by specific language indicating that the seller does not claim title in himself or that he is selling only that title or rights as he has.
Warranty Against Infringement	A merchant warrants that goods which he sells are free of infringement. A buyer, if he has provided detailed specifications agrees to hold the seller harmless against infringement *(UCC §2-312)*.	May be excluded by agreement.
Warranty of Merchantability	A merchant warrants that goods will be merchantable. To be merchantable, goods must: a) Pass without objection in the trade under the contract description. b) Be fit for the ordinary purposes for which such goods are used. c) Run with an even kind of quality and quantity. d) Be adequately packaged and labeled as required by the agreement. e) Conform to promises or statements on the label *(UCC §2-316)*.	Excluded only by language expressly mentioning merchantability. In a written contract, the exclusion must be conspicuous *(UCC §2-316)*.
Course of Dealing Usage of Trade	Course of dealing or usage of trade may give rise to an implied warranty based on that course of dealing or usage of trade *(UCC §2-314)*.	May be excluded or modified by agreement.

398

Warranty	Method of Exclusion

	Warranty	Method of Exclusion
Service of Food	The service of food in a restaurant implies a warranty that goods will be merchantable and fit for consumption.	
Fit for Particular Purpose	Where a merchant has reason to know any particular purpose for which goods are required and the buyer is relying on the seller's judgment or skill, he warrants that the goods are fit for that purpose *(UCC §2-315).*	May be excluded by conspicuous language excluding implied warranties like "There are no warranties which extend beyond the description on the face hereof" *(UCC §2-316).*
Sale by Description	Where goods are sold by a description which becomes part of the basis of the transaction, there is an express warranty that they will conform to the description. The description will not be words but may be technical specifications, blueprints, etc. *(UCC §2-313).*	Language excluding warranties and descriptive language are to be construed as consistent with each other whenever reasonable *(UCC §2-316).* General language of disclaimer will not disclaim the warranties of description and the warranties which arise from a sale by sample where the disclaimer is inconsistent.
Sale by Sample	A sample or model, if part of the basis of the agreement, will create an express warranty that the goods delivered will conform to the sample. Exact or technical specifications displace a sample if there is a conflict. A sample from existing bulk displaces inconsistent general language of description *(UCC §2-317).*	
Express Warranty by Affirmation of Fact or Promise	Any affirmation of fact or promise made by the seller to the buyer which relates to the goods and becomes part of the basis of the bargain becomes an express warranty. Mere statement of opinion as salesman's talk does not *(UCC §2-313).* It is not necessary that specific language of guarantee or warranty be used to create an express warranty.	Express warranties may be excluded or limited by agreement.

Warranty	Method of Exclusion

Warranty to Third Parties of Consumer Goods	The Uniform Commercial Code provides that a seller of consumer goods warrants not only to the buyer but also the buyer's family and guests that the goods conform to the warranty if it is "reasonable to expect that such persons may use, consume or be affected by the goods" *(UCC § 2-318)*.	A seller may not exclude or limit the operation of this section *(UCC § 2-318)*.
When There Is No Warranty	If the agreement uses language "as is" or "with all faults" or other language which calls to the buyer's attention the exclusion of warranties, no warranty arises. If the seller examines the goods or is given an opportunity to examine the goods and refuses, no warranty will arise as to defects which the examination revealed or should have revealed *(UCC § 2-316)*.	

[¶4816]   SELLER'S REMEDIES

Following are the various seller's remedies as spelled out in the UCC.

[¶4816.1]   Buyer's Insolvency

Where the seller learns of the buyer's insolvency, the seller may:

(1) Stop delivery unless the goods have been received by the buyer, acknowledgment has been made by a warehouseman to the buyer, the goods have been reshipped by the carrier (which constitutes an acknowledgment to the buyer that the carrier holds the goods for the buyer) or the carrier has notified the buyer, in which case he was holding the goods as a warehouseman for the buyer rather than as a carrier.

The seller must notify the carrier in time to enable him with reasonable diligence to stop the shipment. Where a negotiable document of title is involved it should be presented to the carrier with the order to stop shipment *(UCC §2-705)*.

(2) Withhold delivery if the goods have not been shipped and wait for the buyer to prepay, even though the contract called for shipment on credit.

(3) Reclaim the goods if they were received while the buyer was insolvent, provided notice is given within ten days. The ten-day limitation does not apply where the buyer has falsely represented his solvency to the seller within three months of delivery *(UCC §2-705)*.

[¶4816.2] Buyer's Repudiation of Agreement

Where the buyer repudiates the agreement, the seller may —

(1) Withhold delivery.

(2) Stop delivery if the goods have not been delivered to the buyer provided the shipment meets the quantity requirements spelled out in the Code, i.e., carload, truckload, ship, etc.

(3) Identify and sell conforming goods as well as recover damages which are the difference between the resale price and the contract price.

(4) Recover damages for repudiation. Where there is an established market price, the damages will be the difference between the market price and the contract price at the time and place for the tentative delivery together with incidental damages but less any expenses saved as a result of the buyer's breach *(UCC §2-708(1))*. Incidental damages include commercially reasonable charges, expenses or commissions incurred in stopping shipment; commercially reasonable charges, expenses of commissions incurred in transportation or care of goods after breach; commercially reasonable charges, expenses or commissions incurred in resale or return of goods; other commercially reasonable charges, expenses or commissions resulting from the breach. Where there is no established market at a place specified for tender, the market price at another locale will be substituted although adjustment should be made for transportation differentials. Where the damages computed by the difference between contract price and market price are inadequate to put the seller in as good a position as he would have been had the buyer not repudiated, the Code permits the seller to recover the profit which he would have made from full performance *(UCC §2-710, 2-708(2))*.

Cancellation after the buyer's repudiation does not extinguish the seller's right to proceed against the buyer for damages *(UCC §2-106, 2-703)*.

Where the contract is repudiated after acceptance by the buyer the seller may maintain an action for the price. An action for the price may also be maintained when the seller has been unable to resell goods identified to the agreement at a reasonable price or the circumstances indicate that efforts to resell would be unavailing. When the seller maintains an action for the price he must remain prepared to deliver the goods. However, if an opportunity arises to sell the goods, he may do so and deduct the resale price from his claim.

(5) Suspend performance and await withdrawal of the repudiation for a commercially reasonable time and demand adequate assurance of performance.

The seller will have an obligation to suspend performance where he has not finished the goods and the completion of the goods or the completion of his performance would result in a material increase in damages.

【¶4816.3】 Buyer's Failure to Cooperate

Where the buyer fails to cooperate as required by the agreement (i.e., specifies assortment, gives needed instruction, etc.), a seller may follow any of these three courses:

(1) Delay his performance without incurring any liability for breach by reason of late delivery.

(2) Proceed to perform in a commercially reasonable manner.

(3) Treat the failure to cooperate as a breach of the agreement.

【¶4816.4】 Buyer's Refusal to Accept Conforming Goods

If the buyer refuses to accept conforming goods or wrongfully withdraws his acceptance of conforming goods, the seller may resell the goods and recover damages. Damages will be the difference between the contract price and the resale price less any expenses saved as a result of the breach, but including any costs incurred in reselling.

【¶4816.5】 Resale

The Code authorizes, as an element of resale costs, reasonable commission charges and transportation charges plus other incidental damages *(UCC §2-701)*.

Where goods are resold, the Code rules for resale must be followed. However, resale need not be by public sale.

A private sale will be justified where indicated by the circumstances except that the buyer must be notified of the sale. The seller must use reasonable efforts to get the highest possible price for the goods.

Where the goods are resold at auction, the sale must be held at the usual place or market for selling such goods if one is available. The goods must also be available for inspection prior to or at the sale.

【¶4817】   DAMAGES

Damages will be measured by the difference between market price and the contract price at the time and place specified for delivery where there is an established market price, provided such damages are adequate to put the seller in as good a position as he would have been if the buyer had accepted the goods instead of wrongfully rejecting conforming goods or wrongfully withdrawing his acceptance of conforming goods. In that case, he is entitled to at least the profits which he would have made if the buyer accepted the goods and fully performed the agreement.

The seller may also bring an action for the price where the goods are not readily resalable or cancel the contract.

[¶4818] BUYER'S REMEDIES

Following are the buyer's remedies based on the UCC:

[¶4818.1] Seller's Insolvency

When the buyer learns that the seller is insolvent he may —

(1) Demand adequate assurance of performance where he has reasonable grounds for insecurity as to the seller's ability to perform.

Where the seller fails to give adequate assurance of performance, the buyer may cancel — cancellation will not relieve the seller of the obligations under the contract.

(2) Recover deposits and prepayments by making provision to obtain the goods elsewhere and recover the difference between the cost of covering and the contract price from the seller.

The buyer also is entitled to recover reasonable expenses from the seller.

[¶4818.2] Seller's Repudiation

Where the seller repudiates the agreement, the buyer may —

(1) Cancel and thereby be relieved of his obligation of continuing to perform. Cancellation will not relieve the seller of his obligation under the agreement.

The buyer may also recover damages in the amount of the difference between the contract price and the market price. He may cover by making other provision to obtain the goods.

The buyer will be entitled to recover from the seller the loss incurred by covering including reasonable commissions and expenses incurred in covering.

(2) Obtain specific performance where the agreement involves unique goods.

(3) Recover the goods where they were identified to the agreement prior to the seller's repudiation if, after reasonable effort, he is unable to effect cover or the circumstances reasonably indicate that an attempt to effect cover would be unavailing.

[¶4818.3] Goods Fail to Conform

Where the goods fail to conform to the agreement, the buyer may —

(1) Reject the Entire Performance. In the case of an installment contract the buyer's right to reject the entire performance will be limited to instances where the nonconformity substantially impairs the value of the installment *(UCC §2-612).*

Where the buyer elects to reject the goods, the rejection must be made within a reasonable time after delivery and the buyer must seasonably notify the seller of his rejection. If the goods are in the buyer's physical possession when he rejects them the buyer has an obligation to hold them with reasonable care at the seller's disposition to permit the seller to recover the goods.

Where the buyer is a merchant, normally dealing in goods of the kind called for in the contract, he may have a duty to follow reasonable instructions from the seller, where the seller has no agent or place of business in the buyer's locale.

(2) Accept the Performance. Acceptance will not extinguish other available remedies unless the buyer fails to notify the seller of the nonconformity within a reasonable time.

If the buyer accepts nonconforming goods he cannot return them because of the nonconformity where he knows of the nonconformity at the time of acceptance or should have known of the nonconformity by reasonable inspection.

(3) Cancel, after refusing to accept nonconforming goods, without extinguishing his rights to cover or recover damages from the seller *(UCC §2-106).* He may also cover by making other provision to obtain the goods. See Repudiation, *supra.*

Where the buyer does not cover, he may be entitled to recover the difference between the market price and the contract price plus incidental and consequential damages.

Incidental damages might include expenses reasonably incurred in inspecting the nonconforming goods, expenses reasonably incurred in the receipt of nonconforming goods, expenses reasonably incurred in transporting the nonconforming goods, loss resulting from general particular requirements and needs of which the seller had reason to know at the time of entering into the agreement and which could not have been prevented by cover *(UCC §2-715).*

●

For Further Reference . . .
Contract Draftsmanship Under Article Two of the Uniform Commercial Code, 112 *University of Pennsylvania Law Review* 564.

Corman, Calvin W., The Law of Sales Under the Uniform Commercial Code, 17 *Rutgers Law Review* 14.

Harris, R. J., A Radical Restatement of the Law of Sellers Damage, 61 *Michigan Law Review* 849.

Hawkland, William, *Sales and Bulk Sales,* American Law Institute.

Peters, Ellen A., Remedies for Breach of Contracts Relating to the Sale of Goods Under the Uniform Commercial Code: A Roadmap for Article Two, 73 *Yale Law Journal* 199.

Vold on Sales (2nd Ed.), West Publishing Co., St. Paul, Minn.

Williston on Sales, Baker, Voorhis.

Witney, *The Law of Modern Commercial Practices,* Baker, Voorhis.

SECURED TRANSACTIONS

[¶4901] Traditional security devices include the pledge, the chattel mortgage, the conditional sales contract, the trust receipt, the assignment of accounts receivable, the factor's lien, the inventory lien. The Uniform Commercial Code uses a single term, "security interest," to cover all techniques for using personal property to secure a money obligation.

A lender or seller wants to be protected against the possibility that other creditors or someone standing in their shoes, such as a trustee in bankruptcy, may be able to claim a superior interest in the collateral, that the debtor may not have title or the right to deal with the collateral, including the possibility that there may be other creditors claiming a prior security interest in the collateral, that buyers from the debtor "in the ordinary course of business" may take free of the creditor's security interest. These risks are augmented when the secured creditor relies on after-acquired property or a "floating lien." Then the acid test is whether the secured creditor's claim will stand up against a federal tax lien. See ¶5501 for a discussion of federal tax liens.

In addition to these legal risks there is, of course, the possible insurable risk that the collateral may be destroyed or disappear, the risk that it may decline in value, the risk that the debtor will not be able to make payments when due and the creditor will have the inconvenience and expense of realizing on the collateral and, possibly, even having to resort to litigation. These non-legal risks have to be minimized by credit investigation, appraisal and similar credit techniques.

From a purely legal standpoint the greatest security will come from the creditor having possession of the collateral, as is the case in a pledge. This eliminates the risk that the debtor will wrongfully deal with the property or that creditors of the debtor will be able to claim an interest by reason of the debtor's apparently unencumbered ownership. But practical business necessities in most instances demand that the security be left in the possession of the debtor and that he be permitted to work on it or try to sell it.

To get a satisfactory security position under the Uniform Commercial Code, the lawyer has to study the application to his transaction of the following complex of rules:

1. The Code's rules as to attaching and perfecting a security interest and making it generally enforceable.

2. The provisions of the Bankruptcy Act, particularly those of §60, 70c and 70e.

3. The Code's rules on priorities between competing security interests.

4. The statutes and cases covering federal tax liens (see ¶5501), and, to a lesser extent, other non-Code statutory lien laws.

[¶4902] HOW TO GET MAXIMUM PROTECTION UNDER THE UNIFORM COMMERCIAL CODE

A lawyer will want to be sure that the security interest of his client:

1. Attaches.
2. Is perfected.
3. Has maximum priority over conflicting interests.

A security interest *attaches* automatically when there is an agreement between the parties that it will attach, value (including the satisfaction of a pre-existing debt) has been given, the debtor has acquired rights in the collateral and the agreement has been put in writing.

The security interest is then *perfected* either by taking possession of the collateral or by giving public notice by filing in the required place. You can file either the security agreement itself or a separate financing statement.

Delay in filing when getting the debtor's signature to the security agreement can destroy a creditor's security position. A purchaser for value, a judgment or other lien by a creditor or someone who subsequently advances money secured by the same collateral and files earlier can step in and take a prior interest in the collateral. Even someone who knew of the unfiled security interest can take priority if the first creditor's security interest is not executed and filed. Worse still, if there is on record a blanket type filing not specifically describing the collateral covered, but merely filed, for example, against "machinery and equipment" owned by the debtor, the creditor holding that kind of a security interest can advance money later on and get priority even though the filing makes no mention of future advances.

To protect against these pitfalls, follow this procedure as closely as possible:

1. Do not make any advance unless all of the other four requirements for creating a perfected and enforceable security interest have previously been met or are thereby met. In addition before the advance is made be satisfied that the debtor's rights in the collateral are adequate in quality and quantity.

2. If the security interest is to be perfected by possession, the collateral is at the time of the advance in the actual possession of the creditor or of a bailee holding in its behalf and that there is at the time no other presently existing security interest therein, including one theretofore perfected through filing.

3. If the security interest is to be perfected by filing, the lender should be satisfied (A) that at the time the advance is made the collateral is not held by or for another secured party; (B) that there is at the time the advance is made no other perfected security interest in existence; and, equally important, (C) that at the time of the secured party's filing there is on record no financing statement with an earlier filing date which mentions any "type" of collateral into which the collateral could fit. If, for example, there was on file an earlier financing statement which mentioned "machinery" or "equipment" or the like, a security interest created later, even under an agreement not now contem-

plated, could be perfected through the earlier filing, and under the Code's "first-to-file" rule would take priority over the earlier perfected interest.

4. Regardless of the method of perfection, the lender must be satisfied that at the time of the advance there is no filing with respect to any federal tax lien on the debtor's property, or other statutory lien, whether for taxes or otherwise, which might come ahead of his security interest.

[¶4902.1] What Should the Security Agreement Contain?

1. That the debtor owns the collateral free from any ownership or security rights of another.

2. That the collateral is in the debtor's possession.

3. That there are no liens obtained by legal proceedings on any assets of the debtor.

4. That no notice of liens for any federal taxes have been filed, nor have additional federal taxes been assessed against the debtor.

5. That the debtor has not signed or filed any other security agreement or financing statement which mentions collateral of the type covered by the present agreement.

6. That all proper corporate steps have been taken to make the agreement effective and enforceable according to its terms.

7. That the making of the agreement does not violate any of the provisions of any other agreement or instrument binding on the debtor.

The agreement would, of course, describe the debt secured; and might or might not include other indebtedness from time to time due to the lender. It certainly should contain a specific promise to pay or a reference to a note which does so. The agreement might also contain a few of the standard covenants as to caring for and insuring the collateral. It would describe the collateral so as to "reasonably identify" it *(UCC §9-110)*. Where specific machinery is involved, this description might well include the manufacturer's name and the machine's serial number. Although the Code covers defaults and remedies generally, the parties will want to specify what is a "default" and might want to fill in some permissive points of Article 9's default provisions. Generally a serious breach of one of the debtor's covenants or representations should be made a default.

Forms of security agreements of various types suitable for use under the Code will be found in IPB FORMS OF BUSINESS AGREEMENTS.

[¶4902.2] How to Make the Search, the Filing, the Advance

Search the Code filing records and any applicable pre-Code chattel security record in order to supplement the debtor's representations on this score. The Code search, of course, may not be limited to present security interests, but must include present filings under which any future security interests could be perfected. Filing of the financing statement may be made contemporaneously. But it does not follow that the date the financing statement is filed will control all priorities if between that date and the date value is given a conflicting lien is obtained by legal proceedings or a federal tax lien is filed. The actual date of perfection of each security interest may control priorities between them. And the debtor might wrongfully create a possessory lien between the time of filing and the time value is given.

Searching the file is not a perfect check; conceivably a filing could have been made in another district or state in which the goods were at the time located. No legal record would disclose that the equipment was stolen goods, or was subject to a possessory security interest or was the property of a lessor. Here the secured party must rely on credit investigation, checking the location of the property, a bill of sale or the like, rather than legal records.

A commitment to make an advance constitutes value just as well as the actual making of the advance. Any commitment obviously should be made subject to the condition that the debtor's claims to the collateral be satisfactory at the time the advance is actually made.

[¶4902.3] How Good a Security Interest Do We Now Have?

First, unless the security interest is being given for an antecedent debt, prompt filing eliminates any question of preference under §60 of the Bankruptcy Act. The transfer and consideration will be contemporaneous in law as they are in fact. Since there was no time interval between the creation of the security interest and its perfection, there could be no intervening lien creditor. There was no trace of actual or constructive fraud which a future lien creditor or a trustee in bankruptcy could use to avoid the security interest. If the debt protected and the collateral covered are sufficiently specific, the danger of having the lien upset as against a federal tax lien under a "choateness" test law is avoided. The debtor need not be given any authority to sell the collateral, so we have no problem of losing the lien by an authorized sale and having to look to the proceeds. If he should wrongfully sell, the secured party can follow the collateral into the hands of the new purchaser and also look to the proceeds. Checking the debtor's possession on the date of the advances gives assurance there could have been no purchaser who took delivery before the filing and no earlier perfected possessory security interest. If a possessory interest is later perfected, the prior filed interest would still be ahead under *UCC §9-312(5)(b)*.

What additional problems do we have if the debtor is going to have unfettered control over the collateral; if we want to give the creditor a "floating lien" which will carry over into the proceeds of a sale of a collateral or into goods subsequently purchased to replace the collateral, and will protect future advances? In other words, how do we deal with *Benedict v. Ratner* problems, the problems of after-acquired property and liens for future advances?

[¶4902.4] How to Make the Security Interest Apply to After-Acquired Property

Here we are dealing with a provision in the agreement between the borrower and lender that property acquired by the borrower subsequent to the loan will also serve as collateral for the loan. And the big question is the effectiveness of this provision against other creditors of the borrower—i.e., can they be kept from claiming against this after-acquired property to satisfy debts owing to them?

The Code supports the general validity of an after-acquired property clause. Of course, if the after-acquired property itself is acquired subject to a purchase-money mortgage or similar interest, that purchase-money interest takes preference over the lender who is depending on the after-acquired-property clause in his agreement with the borrower.

Before the Code, if property subject to an after-acquired-property clause was acquired within four months of bankruptcy of the borrower, the after-acquired property could be deemed to be a preferential transfer for a pre-existing debt and thus voidable. The Code, however, says that the transfer of the after-acquired property under an after-acquired-property clause will be considered to have been for new value rather than for a pre-existing debt and therefore not voidable in a bankruptcy situation, if both of the following conditions are met:

(1) When the original transaction arose under which the secured party got a security interest in the debtor's property, new value was given the debtor. In other words, when the secured party got the security interest in the first place (and a right to include after-acquired property as part of the security), he got it for something other than a debt already existing at that time.

(2) The debtor got his interest in the after-acquired property in the ordinary course of his business or bought it within a reasonable time after new value was given by the secured party *(UCC §9-108)*.

When the After-Acquired Rule Doesn't Apply: The Code's after-acquired-property rules do not apply in two cases: (1) crops coming into existence one year after the agreement (check for possible local variations on this one); and (2) consumer goods (other than accessions) unless the debtor gets rights in them within ten days after the secured party gives value *(UCC §9-204(4))*. "Consumer goods" in this connection are things used primarily for family or household purposes *(UCC §9-109)*.

[¶4902.5] The "Floating Lien"

The Code rules relating to after-acquired property, future advances, dominion and control of the collateral by the debtor, commingling of goods, and transferring the lien on the collateral to the proceeds make possible so-called "floating liens." The concept of a floating lien is that of a lien on a shifting stock of goods or inventory. That is, a lien on collateral in more or less constant flux and undergoing quantitative and qualitative changes. It is a concept that responds to a long-felt need of businessmen for an effective device giving a lender a security interest on goods and materials which the debtor is permitted to retain, process, manufacture or otherwise change and sell, and also covering the proceeds of the sale, and the new goods and materials bought by the debtor with the proceeds in a continuing cycle of business activity. The chattel mortgage has been unable to satisfy this need because of problems in connection with description of the property covered, after-acquired property, and the power of the debtor to sell the collateral and to use the proceeds.

While the concept of a floating lien is not new (it will be found in Factors' Lien Acts and the Uniform Trust Receipts Acts), the Code provides clarification and uniformity and strips the pre-Code concept of some excess fictional baggage. For example, pre-Code practice in many instances both before and after the enactment of Factors' Lien Acts made use of various forms of "possession" of the collateral by the factor which closely bordered on the fictional and the trust receipt concept relied on the near-fiction that the lender had possession via his "trustee." The Code sweeps away the need for resort to this type of fiction, and gives a solid legal basis for a security device which can attach to collateral through all its changing phases.

These changes not only reduce risk and uncertainty for the lender but may also eliminate some direct expenses necessary where the floating lien is not available. For example, it will no longer be legally necessary to resort to the device of field warehousing in connection with inventory financing and this can result in considerable savings — i.e., the cost of setting up the warehouse (partitions, locks, window bars, etc.), maintaining custody and control (custodian's salary, bookkeeping, etc.) and moving the collateral in and out. This is not to say that a lender will not want to police the collateral to some degree for his own protection. He will still want to know about its movement, processing and sale, but this type of policing is apt to be less expensive than that of field warehousing.

The fact that the Code makes legally possible a floating lien does not mean that the secured creditor's interest in collateral covered by the lien will necessarily be entitled to priority over all liens subsequently attaching or perfected in the same collateral. It may be subordinate to subsequent purchase money interests, and there will be problems of priority as against federal tax liens. See ¶5501 for a discussion of federal tax liens and their priorities.

[¶4902.6]   **Future Advances**

The Code makes it clear that you can have a valid security interest in collateral to secure amounts to be advanced in the future, whether or not the advances are to be made pursuant to prior commitment *(UCC §9-204(5))*.

[¶4902.7]   **Getting Preferred Status for Purchase Money Interest**

Purchase money interests have certain advantages over other types of security interests. In some instances (farm equipment costing less than a certain amount and consumer goods) a security interest may be perfected without filing (§9-302(1)(c),(d)); where filing is required a grace period of ten days is allowed against creditors and transferees in bulk (§9-301(2)); and the purchase money interest may take priority over conflicting security interests under an after-acquired property clause (§9-312(3), (4)).

To get the preferred status it is not necessary that the secured party be the seller of the collateral, it is enough that he gives value to enable the debtor to acquire rights in or the use of the collateral if such value is in fact so used (§9-107(b)). To make sure that the value is so used the security agreement should provide that the secured party is to pay the seller of the collateral.

[¶4903]   **PRIORITIES UNDER THE CODE**

The Code has special rules affecting priorities. Here are the most important areas:

(1) Goods Covered by Documents: While goods are in possession of issuer of a negotiable document covering the goods, any security interest in the goods is subject to a security interest in the documents (§9-304(2)).

(2) Proceeds: Secured party has a security interest in identifiable proceeds of collateral. But interest in proceeds becomes unperfected ten days after receipt by debtor unless the filed financing statement also covers proceeds or the secured party gets possession within a ten-day period. In the event of insolvency of the debtor the secured party's interest in the proceeds may extend under some conditions to cash and bank accounts of the debtor without regard to whether or not the funds are identifiable as cash proceeds of the collateral (§9-306(2)-(4)).

(3) Repossessions: Goods which were subject to a security interest and were sold are resubjected to the prior security interest on return of the goods to the seller. And this interest is superior to the security interest of the assignee of the account created by the sale. But a transferee of the chattel paper created by the sale may have a superior security interest (§9-306(5), §9-308).

412

(4) Buyers of Goods Protected: A buyer of inventory in the ordinary course of business other than farm products, takes free of the security interest even if it is filed and he knows about it. In the case of consumer goods and farm equipment costing less than $2,500, a buyer, without knowledge, for value, buying for his own personal, family or household use or his own farming operations takes free of *unfiled* security interest (§9-307).

(5) Purchaser of Chattel Paper or Nonnegotiable Instruments: Purchaser, (including holder of security interest (§1-201(32), (33)), who gives new value and takes possession in the ordinary course of his business and without knowledge has priority over prior security interest perfected by filing or temporary perfection without filing. He also has priority over a security interest in chattel paper which is claimed merely as proceeds of inventory, even though he knows of prior interest (§9-308).

(6) Purchasers of Instruments and Documents: Holder in due course of negotiable instrument, holder to whom a negotiable document of title has been duly negotiated, or bona fide purchaser of a security takes priority over an earlier security interest even though perfected (§9-309).

(7) Liens by Operation of Law: Common law or statutory liens for services or materials take priority unless a statute provides otherwise (§9-310).

(8) Crops: A party who gives new value within three months before planting in order to enable the debtor to produce the crops has priority over an earlier security interest in the crops which secures an obligation which is due more than six months before planting (§9-312(2)).

(9) Purchase-Money Security Interests: A purchase-money security interest has priority over a conflicting security interest in collateral other than inventory if it's perfected within ten days of receipt of the collateral by the debtor. If the collateral is inventory it will have priority over a conflicting security interest if it's filed and notice to other known or filed security interests is given before the debtor receives the collateral (§9-312(3), (4)). Also, §9-301(2) provides that if a purchase-money interest is filed within ten days it takes priority over the rights of a transferee in bulk or of a lien creditor arising between the time the security interest attaches and is filed.

Bear in mind that a purchase-money interest includes cases where a lender advances money to the seller or to the purchaser and the purchaser in fact uses it to buy (§9-107). The best way for a lender to protect himself is to pay the seller directly.

(10) Fixtures: A security interest *attaching to goods before they become fixtures* is superior to all prior claims in the real estate and also to all subsequent claims in the real estate if it is filed before the later claims arise. A security interest in goods *attaching after they become fixtures* is superior only

to subsequent interests in the real estate if filed before the later claims arise, or to prior claimants who have consented in writing to the security interest in the goods as fixtures (§9-313). Both types of security interest, those attaching before and those attaching after the goods become fixtures, are subject to the interest of a prior real estate mortgage of record to the extent of subsequent advances contracted for without knowledge of the security interest and before it is filed (§9-313).

(11) Goods Attached to Other Goods—Accessions: A security interest in goods attaching before the goods become accessions is superior to prior claims in the goods to which they are attached and is also superior to subsequent claims in the whole goods if it is filed before the later claims arise. If the security interest attaches after the goods have become accessions, it is superior only to subsequent interests in the whole if it is filed before the subsequent interests arise. Both types of interest in accessions are subject to subsequent advances contracted for under a prior perfected security interest (§9-314).

(12) Commingled or Processed Goods: A perfected interest in goods which become part of a product or mass continues in the product or mass if (a) the goods lose their identity in processing or (b) the financing statement covers the product. When more than one interest attaches to the mass or product they rank equally in proportion to their contribution to the mass (§9-315).

(13) Unperfected Security Interests vs. Various Third Parties: An unperfected security interest is subordinate to the rights of:

(a) persons entitled to priority under the special rules discussed above or the general rules of priority in §9-312(5);

(b) a person who becomes a lien creditor without knowledge of the security interest;

(c) in the case of goods, instruments, documents and chattel paper, a person who is not a secured party and who is a transferee in bulk or other buyer not in the ordinary course of business to the extent that he gives value and *receives* delivery of the collateral without knowledge of the security interest; and

(d) in the case of accounts, contract rights and general intangibles, a person who is not a secured party and who is a transferee to the extent that he gives value without knowledge of the security interest.

These rules are subject to the rule that if the secured party files with respect to a purchase money interest within ten days after the collateral comes into possession of the debtor, he takes priority over the rights of a transferee in bulk or of a lien creditor arising between the time the purchase money interest attached and was perfected (§9-301).

[¶4904] SPECIAL RULES FOR SPECIAL TYPES OF COLLATERAL

While most of the provisions of Article 9 (Secured Transactions) apply regardless of the type of collateral involved, some sections state special rules for particular types of collateral. The Official Comments following §9-102 set forth a complete index of these special rules for various types of collateral, more specifically, accounts and contract rights, chattel paper, documents and instruments, general intangibles, goods, consumer goods, equipment, farm products and inventory.

[¶4905] INSURANCE FOR CREDITORS

See ¶3101 et seq. and particularly ¶3110.

•

For Further Reference . . .

Coogan, Hogan and Vagts, *Secured Transactions Under the U.C.C.,* Matthew Bender, New York, N. Y.

Denonn, *Secured Transactions Under the Laws of Code and Non-Code States,* Practising Law Institute, New York, N. Y.

Forms of Business Agreements looseleaf Service. Institute for Business Planning, Englewood Cliffs, N. J.

Kripke, Homer, and Felsenfeld, Carl, A Practical Approach to Article 9 of the Uniform Commercial Code, 17 *Rutgers Law Review* 168.

SECURITIES — THEIR OWNERSHIP AND TRANSFER

[¶5101] Stocks and bonds are generally transferable by endorsement by the owner and delivery to the assignee, although occasionally you will find bearer bonds which pass by delivery without endorsement. The endorsement may be on the back of the bond or stock certificate itself or on a separate document, which would be a stock power authorizing an agent to transfer the shares on the books of the corporation.

The endorsement and delivery is sufficient to accomplish the transfer of ownership between the parties. However, as against the corporation for dividend and voting purposes, registration of the transfer on the corporate books will be necessary to complete the transfer.

Any restrictions on transfer should be noted conspicuously on the certificate.

The corporation should keep a record of issuance of certificates on the stubs in the stock book when stock is originally issued. The stub should reflect the name of the holder, the number of shares represented, and the date of issue. Where a new certificate is issued to the transferee of an issued certificate, the stub should be marked with the number of the new certificate and the number of shares represented.

Where a share certificate is presented for transfer, whether by endorsement or by stock power, it should be cancelled and attached to the stub from which it was originally detached. The stock transfer tax stamp must be affixed to the old certficate or to the power and cancelled. Cancellation is accomplished by writing "cancelled" across the face of the certificate or the date and initials on the face of the stamp.

In an accompanying stock ledger, an alphabetical list of share owners should be kept current by registering all transfers of shares.

Protecting Against Corporate Liability: To protect the corporation against liabilities for improper registration of a transfer, or for improper refusal to register, the corporate agent responsible for registering, either corporate employees or a professional transfer agent or registrar, must make sure that each endorsement is genuine and effective. This means:

(1) That the endorsement is real and not forged. This includes getting a satisfactory explanation for variations in spelling of names, use of a mark instead of a signature, etc.

(2) That the endorsement is legally sufficient to effect the transfer in the light of the manner in which the stock is registered and the capacity of the parties making the endorsement; i.e., the requirement of signature by all tenants in common, by all fiduciaries unless there is some controlling instrument, such as a will, authorizing endorsement by less than all.

(3) Authority to sign on the part of an officer of a corporate-registered owner, a partner for a partnership owner, a fiduciary for shares in the name of a decedent.

These assurances are generally obtained by a "guaranteed signature," or documentation, or by both. On listed corporations transfer agents want signatures guaranteed by commercial banks or member organizations of the stock exchange. The guarantee of a signature is accomplished by some authorized person signing his name underneath the text, "signature guaranteed." This warrants to any person taking or dealing with securities or relying on the guarantee that at the time of signing the signature was genuine, the signatory was the appropriate person to endorse the security, and had legal capacity to sign (see UCC §8–312 spelling out the commonly accepted liability). Where transfer agents insist upon additional documentation, it constitutes a double check and may take such forms as a certified corporation resolution to support a corporate transfer, a copy of a power of attorney, a certificate or copies of letters testamentary, letters of administration, letters of guardianship and the like issued to court-appointed fiduciaries. The agent will usually want such additional documentations to be dated within 60 days.

In addition, where securities are registered in the name of a decedent, waivers of inheritance tax claims or affidavits that such waiver is not necessary will be required.

Regardless of the place of incorporation, the transfer agent often requests a waiver from the state of residence if it is listed as the last one. Some states require waivers merely because the corporation is incorporated there and even if the decedent was a nonresident. Some incorporation states do not require waivers for nonresidents but may ask for an affidavit of nonresidents.

[¶5101.1] Completing the Transfer by Delivery

A transfer isn't effective even as between the parties until delivery takes place. When seller and buyer deal with each other directly, fulfilling the requirement of delivery is simple enough—the seller hands the certificate to the buyer, and that's it. It's a little different when you're dealing with a listed stock through a broker on a national or regional exchange. There might be a time lag of several days between the purchase and the purchaser's acquisition of actual possession of the stock. Under the Uniform Stock Transfer Act (and the Negotiable Instruments Law in the case of bonds) transfer of possession of stock to the purchaser was the only method of delivery contemplated. However, the Uniform Commercial Code broadens the concept of delivery to conform to present-day conditions under which most stock transfers take place through brokers on organized exchanges. Code §8–313 provides that delivery

417

to the purchaser occurs when his broker gets possession of a security specially indorsed to or issued in the name of the purchaser, or his broker *sends* him confirmation of the purchase or makes a book entry or otherwise identifies a specific security in his possession as belonging to the purchaser.

[¶5102]   RECORDING TRANSFERS

The stock book, which is usually open to reasonable inspection by shareholders, and sometimes others, shows record ownership. Corporations are authorized by statute to rely on record ownership in determining those to whom notices are to be sent, those who may vote, receive dividends, etc. For these purposes a reasonable record date may be fixed, or the books may be closed to transfers. By-laws may contain provisions regulating the transfer of stock. The recording of transfers, cancellation of the surrender certificates and the issuance of new certificates in the name of the transferee may be carried out by an independent agent, e.g., the transfer agent, or by a department or employee of the corporation.

[¶5102.1]   Liability for Recording Transfers

The parties responsible for recording the transfer, the issuer, the transfer agent, registrar or other agent of the issuer, face two kinds of possible liability:

1. If the party transferring the stock lacks authority, the transfer is void and the issuer or agent can be liable for conversion to the legal owner of the stock whether or not it exercises due care.

2. If the transferor does have authority but is acting in breach of trust, the issuer or agent can be liable to beneficial owners for participation in a breach of trust unless it exercises due care.

This liability has been mitigated by statute:

1. The Uniform Fiduciaries Act limits liability to those situations when the registration of the transfer was made with actual or constructive knowledge that the fiduciary was committing a breach of trust.

2. The Uniform Act for Simplification of Fiduciary Security Transfers provides that a corporation or transfer agent may register a security *in the name of* a fiduciary without inquiring into the existence or extent of the fiduciary relationship. It also relieves them of notice or obligation to examine any court record or document relating to the fiduciary relationship or assignment even though the record or document is in their possession.

3. The Uniform Commercial Code spells out specific requirements in the recordation of stock transfers and the duties and liabilities arising therefrom (See §401–406).

The net effect of these laws is to greatly simplify, limit and clarify the responsibility and the paper work required to make an effective transfer of stock and protect the corporation and transfer agent against liability.

[¶5102.2]   Checklist for Stock Transfer Requirements

In addition to endorsement, delivery and guarantee of signature, the requirements are these:

Registered Owner	Endorsement	Tax Waivers	Special Requirements
Individual(s)	Owner(s)	None	None
Individual	Agent or Attorney	None	Certified copy of power
Joint tenants	Surviving joint tenant	Usually from state of domicile of deceased—sometimes, from state of incorporation. Affidavit of domicile may be called for	Certified copy of death certificate of deceased joint tenant
Decedent	Executor or Administrator	Usually from state of domicile of deceased—sometimes, from state of incorporation. Affidavit of domicile may be called for	Copy of letters testamentary or of administration certified within 60 days
Custodian for Minor	Custodian	None	None
Minor or Ward	Guardian	None	Copy of letters of guardianship certified within 60 days
Trustee, executor, administrator or guardian	Registered owner	None	None
Corporation	Officer acting for corporation	None	Certified copy of resolutions or by-laws creating officer's authority for the transaction

419

Registered Owner	Endorsement	Tax Waivers	Special Requirements
Deceased or Re-signed Trustee	Endorsement by successor trustee	None	Certified copy of trust instrument showing succession

[¶5102.3] Notice of Restrictions on Transfer

If the corporation or the transfer agent is notified that there is an adverse claim to stock affected by a proposed transfer or a restriction on transfer, the immunity from liability afforded by recent statutory enactments is withdrawn. This situation may exist in these circumstances:

1. Corporations frequently file, and are sometimes required by the SEC to file, with the transfer agent a "stop transfer" notice where the shares have not been registered and where the transfer might require such registration — usually shares held by control stockholders. Such a "stop transfer" order usually requires that transfer may be made only with the submission of an opinion, usually by corporate or other designated counsel, that registration would not be required to make a particular transfer legal.

2. Restrictions on transfer may be noted on the certificate, i.e., as is commonly done under an agreement for the restriction of transfers entered into by control stockholders.

3. By formal written communication from a claimant to the shares which identifies him and the registered owner and the issue of which the security is a part and provides an address for communications directed to the claimant (see UCC §8-403(1)(a)).

4. The corporation or the transfer agent has demanded and received, in support of application for registration and for some purpose other than checking the endorsements, copies of the will, trust agreement or other controlling instrument which indicates that the proposed transfer would not be proper.

[¶5102.4] Lost, Stolen or Destroyed Stock Certificates

If the stock certificates are lost, stolen or destroyed and the corporation replaces them with new certificates, it might incur a liability if the original certificate later appears in the hands of a bona fide purchaser. Corporate by-laws frequently provide for replacement conditioned upon the posting of an adequate bond to indemnify the corporation. The Uniform Stock Transfer Act provides for court procedure to compel replacement of a lost or destroyed certificate upon the posting of an adequate bond. Under the Code (§8–405) the issuer is required to replace the lost certificate on posting a bond and complying with other requirements.

[¶5103]   TRANSFER TAXES

New York and Florida have stock transfer taxes. The State interest is limited, being confined to transactions having at least minimal contacts with the State. Definition of minimal State contacts touches intricate questions of conflicts of law which make generalization hazardous. However, generally speaking, a minimal contact exists if either the sale, delivery of certificates, or record transfer is made within the State. That is, the transaction will be subject to State tax even though two of the elements took place outside the State. Hence, there's a risk that the same transfer may be exposed to two separate State transfer taxes, i.e., the sale is made in New York, the delivery of certificates and recording of the transfer on company books take place in Florida. While this factual combination may be remote and border on the purely theoretical, dual state taxation is a likely possibility and calls for conscious tax planning to avoid the tax burden, as by arranging to group the taxable events in one state.

The taxing statutes impose on the transfer agent the duty to assure himself before completing a transfer that the proper transfer taxes have been paid. He must be shown that the taxes have been paid or that the transfer is exempt from tax. The basic rule of exemption is that there is no tax unless there is a distinct change of ownership. There is no change where transfers are from a customer to a broker, from a corporation to a registered nominee of the corporation, from nominees to fiduciaries, and custodians to new custodians.

[¶5103.1] Showing Payment of Taxes

The basic ways of showing payment of the taxes are: (1) with adhesive stamps, and (2) by a notation.

Where stamps are used the stamps are affixed to the certificate together with a bill or memorandum of sale showing the amount of shares, the corporate title of the stock, the price per share and the net amount of the sale. Or a certificate to the effect that "these shares were sold by us at $_____per share,'- signed by the seller and attached.

As an alternative to affixing the stamps, if the transaction is through a national securities exchange, the tax may be paid through the clearing house of the exchange and a member of the exchange may indicate payment, usually by rubber stamp.

[¶5103.2] Tax Rates

State taxes vary both in amount and in the method of computation. The New York tax, for example, is exclusively based on selling price per share as follows: 1.25 cents on shares selling for less than $5; 2.5 cents on shares selling for more than $10 but less than $20; and 5 cents on shares selling for more than $20.

In Florida, the rate for shares with par value is .015 cents per $100 of par value. When shares have no par value, the rate is .015 cents per share.

[¶5104]   PROTECTION AFFORDED ON THE PURCHASE OF STOCK

The law protects the buyer of stock at two levels: (1) vis-a-vis the person transferring the stock; and (2) vis-a-vis the corporation and other persons who may have claims to the stock.

On the first level the law gives a warranty from the transferor to the effect that: (1) his transfer is effective and rightful; (2) the security is genuine and hasn't been materially altered; (3) he knows no fact which might impair the validity of the security *(UCC §8–306)*. The Code makes it clear that these are the only warranties the transferor gives unless it is otherwise agreed between the parties.

The purchaser can't rely on the warranties which are given if at the time of purchase he himself knows of a defect. Under these circumstances estoppel principles apply.

The Uniform Stock Transfer Act imparted negotiability for stock. The Code does it for both stocks and bonds, at least bearer and registered bonds, as discussed in more detail under Negotiability of Bonds at ¶5104.1.

Before a purchaser can get the full benefit of negotiability he has to have a certain status. Under Article 8 of the Code he must be a purchaser for value in good faith without notice of an adverse claim *(UCC §8–302)*. It must be borne in mind, however, that Article 8 of the Code doesn't reach order bonds. As to order bonds, which appear to be within Article 3 of the Code, the status prerequisite to full negotiability is that of a holder in due course. This calls for something more than what it takes to be a bona fide purchaser.

The holder in due course must also have taken the instrument without notice that it's overdue *(UCC §3–302)*, and the instrument must be not so incomplete or irregular as to call in question its validity, terms or ownership or to create an ambiguity as to the party to pay *(UCC §3–304(1)(a))*.

[¶5104.1]   Negotiability of Bonds

Article 8 of the Code, which deals with investment securities, applies to both bearer and registered bonds, but doesn't cover non-registered or non-registerable order bonds. It is clear that the Code via Article 8 imparts negotiability to both bearer and registered bonds, but if you're dealing with a non-registered or non-registerable order bond, you will have to look to the Code on commercial paper to qualify for negotiability. This would be all right if the bond contains an unconditional promise to pay a sum certain in money "and no other promise, order, obligation or power given by the maker * * * except as authorized by * * * Article 3," but the trouble is the bonds may contain other promises, etc., which may not be authorized by Article 3, or §3–112, which sets forth matters not affecting negotiability. This is something that you must be concerned with in dealing with this type of bond. Apart from this area of concern, as a general rule, the Code rules governing bonds are basically the same as those governing stocks. Bearer bonds may be negotiated by delivery; registered bonds may be negotiated by indorsement.

The result is that the bearer or order bond you propose to buy may not be negotiable and you won't get the protection that goes with the status of being a holder in due course of a negotiable instrument.

[¶5105]   TRANSFERS TO AND FROM MINORS

Making gifts of securities to minors may involve many problems and hidden traps. While the law generally allows a direct transfer of securities to a child, few transfer agents will knowingly register securities in a minor's name. This is because of the fear that the minor may disaffirm any sale he may subsequently make. Registration in the name of an adult nominee for the minor has certain drawbacks also. Of course, a transfer can be made to a court-appointed guardian for the child. But this involves a great deal of red tape and expense. A trust is perhaps the most flexible vehicle for receiving a minor's gift property. But unless the amount of the gift is relatively substantial, the costs involved in creating the trust may be a significant drawback. There is a relatively new device—custodianship—which affords many (though not all) of the advantages of a formal trust, yet is both simple and economical to establish and administer.

All of our states, plus the District of Columbia, have custodian statutes. Securities are transferred simply by registration in the name of a custodian for the child in the manner prescribed by the statute of the state whose law is being used. The states have adopted the Uniform Gifts to Minor Act or a variation thereof. The law permits any adult or a trust company to serve as custodian. The custodian may purchase or reinvest in any securities which a prudent man would select for his own funds regardless of any other state laws restricting investments by fiduciaries. In addition, the custodian can use all or a part of the income and principal he holds for the support, maintenance, education and benefit of the child. The custodian delivers the property to the child at the age of majority.

●

For Further Reference . . .

American Jurisprudence, Commercial Code, §15–48.

American Jurisprudence, Corporations, §329–394, 853–863.

Christy, *Transfer of Stock.*

Corporate Planning (looseleaf service), Institute for Business Planning, Englewood Cliffs, N.J.

Thomas, Eliot B., *Federal Securities Act Handbook,* American Law Institute, Philadelphia, Pa.

SETTLEMENTS AND THEIR TAX ASPECTS

[¶5201] The settlement of disputed and unliquidated claims is essentially an art and not an exact science. The taxability and the deductibility of amounts paid in settlement is of great importance. The process involves a series of estimates. To begin with, it involves an estimate of the extent of the damages or injuries in terms of what a court or jury, in the venue where the case is to be tried, is likely to return, assuming they find the defendant liable. You won't be able to come up with a precise figure, of course, but you should be able to fix upper and lower limits of recovery on a realistic basis. When this has been done, you will then have to estimate the risk of establishing liability, and you will then adjust your upper and lower limits of recovery for this liability risk. (In these calculations, you should also take into consideration the tax consequences, if any, flowing from the settlement. That aspect of settlements is covered later in this chapter.)

For example, suppose you estimate the damages in an automobile negligence case to be somewhere between $10,000 and $20,000, but you estimate that the plaintiff has only about a 50-50 chance of establishing liability, either because of the possibility of his own contributory negligence or for other reasons. A realistic evaluation of the claim might be somewhere between $5,000 and $10,000 and a fair settlement might be a split down the middle at $7,500.

A settlement, of course, involves not only your own evaluation of the claim but also your client's evaluation, the adverse party's evaluation, and his attorney's evaluation, and this often means four different figures on what is a "fair settlement." If a settlement is to be worked out, the clients must be prepared by their attorneys to accept a reasonable figure, based on objective evaluation, divorced from emotional bias or unrealistic expectations of getting something for nothing or paying less than the "market price." The character of the clients and who is to pick up the bill has, of course, a direct bearing on the negotiations and settlement. A publicly held corporation or other party not experiencing a personal loss is apt to be more objective than a sole proprietor. But this is only one factor to be considered. Precisely because no personal loss is involved, parties may be less concerned about the legal costs of the action or defense.

There can be no fixed rule as to when settlement negotiations should begin. The stronger your case is in relation to your adversary's the better off you will be. Some attorneys take the view that it isn't advisable to commence negotiations for settlement until you are thoroughly prepared for trial.

When negotiations commence, an evaluation must be made as to whether they are being undertaken in good faith with the idea of reaching a settlement or whether your adversary is merely using them to get as much information as he can about the strengths and weaknesses of your case.

When the negotiations extend down too close to the date of trial, even though you are convinced that a settlement before trial is a certainty, don't bank on it, but go down to the wire on the assumption that you are going to have to try the case so that you won't wind up with your witnesses missing or unprepared if the negotiations fall through.

When the liability sued on is covered by insurance and your claim is substantial, you should undertake to discover the limits of liability under the policy. If your evaluation of the case is in excess of the policy limits, in some states on some policies you can make the carrier liable for the full amount of the jury verdict, regardless of limits of coverage, by offering to accept the maximum coverage in full settlement. Local law must be checked on this point.

Also, it is well to bear in mind, if there is an insurance carrier involved, that they maintain a central index of prior settlements. In consequence the client should be asked if he or members of his family have received prior settlements since this is a factor which may affect negotiations for settlement. Furthermore, it is well to remind and warn the client on this score since otherwise if the matter goes to trial, he may have forgotten about it and so deny prior settlements on cross examination.

What we have considered so far may be viewed as strictly practical considerations for negotiating a settlement. There are also legal considerations. Set out below in checklist form are the major legal considerations:

[¶5201.1]   Checklist for Compromises and Settlements

1. Negotiations for settlement or compromise of a claim should be conducted "without prejudice" with the clear understanding that all written proposals are made subject to withdrawal if agreement is not reached. The danger here is that loosely drawn correspondence and memoranda may be construed as a legal waiver on which the other party can rightfully rely.

2. When clearing up an undisputed liquidated claim (the other party has defaulted, agrees he's liable, but can't meet your terms promptly) get an agreement in writing providing an acknowledgment of the amount due, that there are no defenses, counterclaims or set-off against your claim, and then set forth a schedule of payments in installments over a set number of weeks or months. This clause should specify either that no grace period is given, or if given, the expiration date thereof. There should also be a default clause providing for acceleration (this is not automatic) and sale of collateral, if any. Check the local confession of judgment laws to see what requirements are imposed and whether your claim comes within the statute. Include confession of judgment when possible.

3. Open running accounts should be settled by a simple invoice showing debits and credits and the outstanding balance, and, again, a statement at the

foot of the invoice whereby the customer acknowledges his debt as true and accurate and signs his name thereto.

4. A compromise agreement will be enforceable in many states, if written, even though no technical consideration was given for it. There is no consideration problem when you are settling a disputed, unliquidated claim, since both parties are changing their position under the original agreement, and this sacrifice involves the necessary elements of consideration. But be careful about the settlement of an undisputed claim where no doubt exists as to the amount due. Here, accepting less or extending payment should be done in writing and if the writing itself doesn't eliminate the need, it should be supported by consideration.

5. "Whereas" clauses should be inserted in the beginning of a compromise and settlement agreement, especially if each party has a divergent position honestly in conflict with the other party's position. These recitals perform the vital function of stating each party's basic claim and prove the departures being made to clear up the dispute. They constitute valuable legal evidence, not only of consideration, but of the basic claims which led to the dispute.

6. Where disputed claims are being abandoned in reaching a compromise and settlement, the agreement should contain a release using appropriate language. A rule often applied is that a release will be confined or restricted to the particular claims recited therein (usually in the whereas clauses) unless it can be shown that the parties intended to release all general and unrelated claims. The release clause should not suffer from particularity and yet it should clearly reveal what rights are being surrendered. Both parties should take a hand in drafting this clause, since a release will be construed by the courts adversely to the party who drafted it, and in favor of the party having the inferior bargaining position.

7. Do you want to preserve your original claim position if the other party fails to perform the compromise agreement? If you say nothing about this, your original claim is legally wiped out. The disadvantage of this is that much of the evidence you collected to support your original claim will be technically irrelevant and useless, and you may not be able to make a good case in enforcing the new compromise agreement. Better protection is given by a clause reserving your right to revive original claims in case of default by the other party. If this is done, you must make sure that the release clause is not so broadly worded as to sweep away your right to revive the original claim.

8. Consideration should be given to the effect of a release on the liability of other parties. For example, the release of one responsible for a personal injury may bar an action against the doctor treating the injury based on the doctor's negligence. (See 40 ALR 2d 1075.) To preserve rights against others liable a covenant not to sue may be called for. Check local law.

Various forms of compromises and settlements and clauses are set out in IBP FORMS OF BUSINESS AGREEMENTS.

[¶5202]   TAX ASPECTS OF SETTLEMENTS

In such matters as cancellation of leases, cancellation of distributorships, settlement of taxes, cancellation of debt, and other compromises and adjustments, the method of handling can modify the net cost and the net result to the parties involved. The terms of a complaint, a judgment award or compromise agreement may determine whether money paid over is deductible by the payor or not, and whether it is taxable to the payee or not.

Tax consequences to all parties concerned arise whenever a dispute of any kind is settled or compromised, or the rights and liabilities created by an initial transaction are adjusted by agreement among the parties. Such tax consequences may turn an apparently advantageous solution into a net disadvantage. The tax interests of the different parties may be in conflict. A revision or adjustment favorable to one party from a tax viewpoint may be disadvantageous to the other. To have a complete basis for negotiation, therefore, all participants must be alerted to the tax consequences by their attorneys. In addition, possible tax consequences will be accurately anticipated.

[¶5202.1]   Checklist of Tax Points in Settling Claims

Cancellation of Employment Contract: Since a contract of employment is not a capital asset, any amount received for cancellation constitutes ordinary income to the employee (*W. Morgan Shuster v. Helvering,* 42 BTA 255, aff'd 121 F.2d 643). The same is true for cancellation of a contract with an independent contractor. If a contract of employment is coupled with the sale of stock by the employee to the employer, the amount received in payment for such stock upon settlement will usually be given capital gain treatment. This sometimes requires an allocation where the two elements are involved (*Estate of Severin F. Blain,* 8 TCM 540).

When income is received upon cancellation of a contract, the amount is taxable in the year received even though the taxpayer is on the accrual basis. It cannot be allocated to the years in which it would have accrued had the contract remained in effect. (See *Thos. D. Taylor v. Comm'r,* 51 F.2d 915.)

Conversely, payment made to secure a release from a long-term contract to purchase merchandise should be currently deducted (*Stuart Co.,* 9 TCM 585, aff'd 195 F.2d 176).

Income from Settlement of Business Damage Suits: In the case of a claim involving a business or investment of the claimant, either after litigation or as a result of a settlement between the parties, a recovery for loss of profit is taxable income. Such damages for loss of profits are considered to be merely a substitute for the profit. If the damages are in the nature of a recovery of capital, however, they are not considered to be income. In *Raytheon Production Corp. v. Comm'r,* 144 F.2d 110, cert. den. 323 U.S. 779, the action was for destruction of good will and the recovery was treated as the return of capital taxable only to the extent it exceeded the basis of good will destroyed. Thus, it is essential in a suit or a settlement where both loss of profit and damage to capital are involved, that there be an allocation between the two. Otherwise, the entire recovery will be considered to be income (*W. Walley Inc.,* 7 TCM 137).

Even where it can be shown that the claim is for destruction of capital rather than loss of profit, it is necessary to establish the basis of the capital destroyed or the courts will consider such basis to be zero and the entire damage will be taxable as gain.

Punitive damages received by a complainant in a lawsuit are considered to be income (*Comm'r v. Glenshaw Glass Co.,* 348 U.S. 426). However, even where punitive damages are involved it may be necessary to allocate the recovery between the punitive and other types of damages.

Recovery of Antitrust Damages: Under prior law taxpayers would recover substantial damages due to a patent infringement, a breach of fiduciary duty, or antitrust injury under the Clayton Antitrust Act. Many times these recoveries occur many years after the injury was sustained and are actually included in taxable income at a subsequent time when actually received. As a result in some cases taxpayers were required to include damages in income although the losses which they replaced may not have resulted in a tax benefit.

The Revenue Act of 1969 law provides that in the case of losses resulting from patent infringement, breach of contract, breach of fiduciary duty, or an antitrust injury for which there is a recovery under §4 of the Clayton Act, a special deduction is allowed which has the effect of reducing the amounts required to be included in income to the extent that the losses to which they relate did not give rise to a tax benefit. The amount includable in gross income is the compensatory amount reduced by the amount of the losses which have not been recovered for tax purposes which were sustained as a result of the compensable injury.

The compensatory amount for this purpose means the amount of the award, settlement, or recovery reduced by the amounts paid or incurred in securing it.

The unrecovered losses are the net operating losses for the year to the extent the losses are attributable to the compensable injury, reduced by the net operating losses which are allowed as offsets against income in other years.

This rule applies only to recoveries (which are includable in taxable income) for actual economic injury and not for additional amounts. In the case of treble damage recoveries under §4 of the Clayton Act, for example, the provision applies to that part of the recovery which represents the economic injury and not to the other part which is punitive in nature. (The rule applies to taxable years beginning after December 31, 1968.)

Condemnation Awards: An award in settlement of a claim arising out of condemnation or other involuntary conversion can result in taxable gain or loss.

In a gain situation, the tax can be avoided to the extent that the proceeds are invested in property similar or related in service or use or, except in the case of real property held for business use or investment, a controlling stock interest in a corporation owning such property.

Where only part of your property is taken, a portion of the basis for the whole property must be allocated to the taken part.

Where severance damages to surrounding property are a part of the award, they should be allocated to the surrounding property. Then they are applied in reduction of the basis of the remaining property and are not taxable except to the extent that they exceed its basis.

This also avoids lumping the entire award against the portion of the basis allocated to the taken part and may eliminate gain altogether, thus avoiding the necessity for reinvestment.

Interest on condemnation awards is not part of the award and is taxable as ordinary income (*Kieselbach v. Comm'r,* 317 U.S. 399).

Where the condemning authority takes only an easement, the tax consequences depend on whether its use is limited or total. If limited, the award goes first in reduction of basis and only the excess is taxable.

Where you give up permanently the use of part of the property, retaining only a bare legal title, it is treated as a sale of that part.

Settlement of Personal Damage Suits: Damages received for personal injury claims, alienation of affection, breach of promise to marry, libel or slander, do not constitute taxable income (*Merchant's Loan and Trust Co. v. Smietanka,* 225 U.S. 509; *U.S. v. Safety Car Heating and Lighting Co.,* 297 U.S. 88; *Clark,* 40 BTA 333; *Theodate Pope Riddle,* 27 BTA 1339). The attorney should remember, however, that IRC §104(a)(2) provides that damages received, whether by suit or agreement, as a result of personal injuries or sickness are excluded from the recipient's gross income, *except* to the extent that such items were allowed as deductions for medical expenses for a prior year.

Cancellation of Lease: Any amount received by a *landlord* as the result of a dispute over a lease, whether for cancellation, amendment, or modification results, is taxable as ordinary income. Amounts paid to a tenant for cancellation of a lease are treated as amounts received in exchange for the lease. The character of the lease is, therefore, determinative of the character of the tenant's gain or loss.

Cancellation of Distribution Contracts: Amounts received by a distributor for the cancellation of a distributor's agreement are considered to be received in exchange for the agreement if the distributor has a "substantial capital investment" in the distributorship (§1241). If the distributor's agreement is a capital asset, which it usually is, he would thus have capital gain or loss treatment when he receives the payment for the cancellation of the distributorship. In most cases this would be desirable and therefore particular care should be taken to establish by the records that the distributor owns a significant fraction of the facilities for storing or handling the physical product. The agreement must also relate to "goods" as distinguished from intangible property.

In a case where an agency contract or distributorship is cancelled, and where the agent or distributor has no substantial capital investment, §1241 does not apply and any amounts received would probably be treated as ordinary income.

Damages Received for Injury to Good Will: Damages for injury to good will represent a return of capital, taxable only to the extent that it exceeds the cost or other basis of the good will destroyed. An element of evidence would be the loss of profit, customers or sales. It must be kept in mind that damages awarded on account of such loss of profit would be ordinary income, and therefore documents and pleadings should segregate very carefully capital and income items, showing that evidence as to loss of profits merely bears upon the question of damage to good will where this is true. It is also important in a claim for injury to good will to show the basis of the good will; in the absence of evidence along these lines, it will be assumed that the basis was zero.

Payment in Settlement of Moral Obligation: An obligation arising out of a business transaction is sufficient to support a deduction for a loss — even though the payor could have avoided same by invoking the defenses of the statute of limitations, statute of frauds, or bankruptcy.

Income from Cancellation of Indebtedness: The general rule given in Code §61(a)(12) that a debtor realizes income from the cancellation of his debt has been limited by several exceptions. For example, no income is realized where the cancellation is in proceedings under the Bankruptcy Act, where the taxpayer is insolvent both before and after the cancellation, or where the cancellation is made as a gratuitous gift. In a commercial situation, it is unlikely that a gift will be found. *Comm. v. Jacobson,* 336 U.S. 23, held that a corporation's purchase of its own obligations at a discount constituted income to the debtor-purchaser, and discussed the factors involved.

Where the debtor is insolvent before he discharges his obligation at less than full value, but is solvent afterwards, he realizes income only to the extent that the discharge makes him solvent (*Lakeland Grocery Co.,* 36 BTA 289).

Where a purchase money obligation is reduced to the level of the then fair market value of the property purchased and the debt is cancelled upon payment of the lower figure, no income is realized by the debtor. For instance, in *Hirsch v. Comm.,* 115 F.2d 656, the taxpayer had a purchase money mortgage on his property of $10,000, and, when the property was worth only $8,000, made a settlement with the mortgagee under which the mortgage was cancelled upon the payment of $8,000. The court treated the transaction as a reduction of the purchase price and not as income to the taxpayer.

Where a debt is being litigated, settlement of that claim by the creditor may not result in income because no assets are freed by the compromise. This would result because the liability was denied, and hence there was no liquidated obligation (*N. Sobel, Inc.,* 40 BTA 1263).

Note that income arising on discharge of debt can be avoided by electing to reduce basis of property. You file Form 982 along with your return to make this election. See Code §1017.

Cancellation of Debt Between Stockholder and Corporation: When a stockholder cancels a bona fide debt of a solvent corporation, such cancellation is generally held to be a capital contribution, rather than a bad debt or loss to the stockholder (Reg. §1.61-12(a); *Johnson, Drake & Piper, Inc.,* 27 BTA 585). The same result will usually be reached where a corporate taxpayer cancels a debt of its subsidiary (*Lidgerwood Co.,* 22 TC 1152). Note that while the above regulation apparently restricts the amount of the capital contribution to the extent of the principal of the debt, the Supreme Court approved the rule without this limiting restriction (*Helvering v. American Dental Co.,* 318 U.S. 322).

When a corporation cancels a debt owed to it by a stockholder such cancellation generally constitutes a taxable dividend as of the date of cancellation (*Henry D. Muller,* 16 BTA 1015). Similar treatment may result even where the cancellation was intended as a gift (*Security First Nat. Bank,* 28 BTA 289). Reg. §1.301-1(m) states that "the cancellation of indebtedness of a shareholder by a corporation shall be treated as a distribution of property," thereby indicating that the fair market value of the debt must be considered in determining the amount of dividend income.

Settlement of Subscription Disputes: Payment by a corporation, in settlement of suit brought by one of its shareholders to establish rights to subscribe to stock, is not deductible as a business expense or a loss.

Settlement of Claim Against a Fiduciary: Payments by a fiduciary in compromise of claims against him are deductible as loss or expense if the fiduciary is regularly in the business of acting as such a fiduciary (*Bishop Trust Co. Ltd.*, 47 BTA 737). If the fiduciary is only acting in such capacity as a casual or isolated activity rather than as a business, he will not be allowed to deduct payments which he is required to make because of his improvident or illegal investment (*Abraham G. Reimold*, 2 TCM 334, *aff'd* 144 F.2d 390).

Where a trustee pays legal fees and other expenses in contesting a tax, and in connection with the management of the trust, such items may be deducted as nonbusiness expenses for the management, conservation or maintenance of property held for the production of income (*Bingham's Trust v. Comm.*, 325 U.S. 365; §212; see also *Ditmars*, 302 F.2d 481).

Payments to Protect Business or Property: The courts have laid down two general rules which govern the tax treatment where these payments are made. If it is for the purpose of *establishing* good will for a new business, it normally will be treated as a capital investment, but if it is to *prevent the destruction* of good will which already exists it will be considered as an ordinary and necessary business expense.

Examples of payments held to be for the retention of existing good will, and hence deductible as business expenses, are payments by a corporation to its president to enable him to settle a dispute with a trade association of which he was treasurer—the court said the payment was necessary in view of growing adverse publicity (*Catholic News Publishing Co. v. Comm.*, 10 TC 73); or the payment of legal fees by a corporation in the settlement of a suit brought against a former president for the protection of good will involved in the settlement (*Frank T. Feagans*, 23 TC 208). On the other hand, payment was considered to be a capital expenditure and hence nondeductible in *Carl Reimers Co., Inc. v. Comm.*, 211 F.2d 66, where the taxpayer paid a share of the debts of a bankrupt firm in which taxpayer's chief stockholder had also been a stockholder. The court stated that the payment was to "fulfill a prerequisite to the attainment of something new." In a similar vein, see *Welch v. Helvering*, 290 U.S. 111. Thus, in the settlement of any matter in which the business protection feature is an element, the document should stress that the payment is made to protect or retain the good will already existing.

Settlement of Claims Against Guarantors and Indemnitors: A guarantor who pays upon default by the principal debtor has a bad debt deduction if he cannot collect from the principal; in some instances he may have a loss deduction, instead. An indemnitor usually has a loss deduction. Under Code §166(f) an indemnitor will be able to get an ordinary loss deduction from gross income, as if he had a business bad debt, if the indemnity is based on a debt of a noncorporate borrower who used the proceeds in his own business.

Deduction for Release of Indebtedness: A creditor cannot voluntarily forgive a debt against a solvent debtor and claim a bad debt deduction (*American Felt*

Co. v. Burnet, 58 F.2d 530). But if a business debt is cancelled in whole or in part, on account of the debtor's insolvency, then the creditor should have a full deduction for the bad debt cancelled (*IT 3121,* 1937-2 CB 138). The settlement of the debt must be bona fide if the bad debt deduction is to be allowed. Thus, in a transaction between related corporations where it was not shown that the debt was uncollectible, no bad debt deduction was allowed (*East Coast Equipment Co. v. Comm.,* 222 F.2d 676).

If it can be shown, however, that the forgiveness of a debt owed by a solvent debtor was for the purpose of retaining the debtor's business, such cancellation may give rise to a bad debt deduction (*Cruger Co.,* 11 BTA 306).

A creditor in the business of lending money may claim a loss deduction under §165(a) of the Code when he reduces a debt of an insolvent debtor. Where a note of an insolvent debtor is transferred to a *third party* for less than the face amount, the transaction usually will result in a capital loss since it is a sale rather than a compromise settlement (*A. T. Matthews,* TC Memo, 1955-330). A loss which is so classified is usually only deductible to the limited extent permitted under the capital loss provision.

If the debt which is released or cancelled is a non-business bad debt, the creditor is allowed only a short-term capital loss even though the debtor may be insolvent and the debt actually worthless (IRC §166(d)).

Deductibility of Damages Paid: In order to be deductible as an ordinary and necessary business expense under §162(a) of the Code, payment of damages and expenses attributable to a business dispute does not have to be recurrent in the sense that the same taxpayer must make the payments often. The test is whether the payments are for a purpose common to the general class to which the taxpayer belongs (*Welch v. Helvering,* 290 U.S. 111). The nature of the claim giving rise to the dispute which is settled or compromised generally determines the tax treatment of the payment as damages. The court looks behind the manner of making the settlement to determine the actual purpose and treats the transaction accordingly. See, for example, *Pressed Steel Car Co., Inc.,* 20 TC 198.

Nonbusiness expenses, if made for the production or collection of income, the management, conservation, or maintenance of property held for the production of income, or in connection with the determination, collection or refund of a tax, are deductible under §212 of the Code. Expenses relating to disputes with the Commissioner on such matters would be deductible under §212 as a necessary incident of the determination of the particular item. See *Edward Mallinckrodt, Jr.,* 2 TC 1128.

Statutory Penalties: The deductibility of amounts paid in compromise of statutory penalties of various kinds is denied by the Internal Revenue Service. The rationale is that it would be contrary to public policy to allow a taxpayer to deduct this item as the effect would be to diminish the impact of the penalty. And the Supreme Court has denied the deduction for fines paid by trucking companies for violation of state maximum weight laws. Whether the violation is intentional or not makes no difference. In either case, to allow the deduction would frustrate state policy. The fine paid for the violation of the law is so close to the violation itself, that taking the "sting" out of the fine by allowing the deduction would thwart the state policy (*Tank Truck Rentals, Inc.*, 356 US 30). However, allowing a bookmaker, engaged in activities illegal under state law, to deduct rent and wages paid is not a device to avoid the consequences of law violations (the state could still prosecute him for illegal gambling). There is no question that wages and rent were ordinary and necessary expenses of the gambling business. And the Treasury has recognized gambling enterprises as businesses for federal tax purposes by allowing the excise tax on wagers as a deduction for income tax purposes (*Rev. Rul. 54-219*, 1954-1 CB 51). Consequently, the rent and wages are deductible (*Sullivan*, 356 US 27).

Marital Settlements: Property settlements made in connection with a divorce or separation generally do not give rise either to income to the wife or to a deduction to the husband. Where alimony or separate maintenance is involved, these payments can be income to the wife and deductible by the husband if they meet the periodic payment test (§71).

Appreciated Property: Where appreciated property is transferred in satisfaction of a legal obligation, the transaction is generally treated as a sale and the gain is taxable (*Kenan*, 114 F.2d 217). The amount of the gain is measured by the difference between the basis for the property transferred and the value of what he receives in return. Where this is a dollar obligation, there is no problem. Where the consideration is not expressed in a dollar amount, as in the case of a transfer of property in settlement of marital rights, the Supreme Court has held that the transaction is, nevertheless, a taxable one even though it may be very difficult to place a value on the settlement. In the absence of evidence to the contrary, the value is presumed to be equal to the value of the property transferred (*Davis*, 370 US 65).

Recapture of Depreciation: The lawyer must keep in mind that every time property is transferred in a transaction in which capital gain is realized, all or part of that gain can become ordinary income if the depreciation recapture provisions apply (§1245, 1250). It should also be noted that they override many of the tax-free exchange provisions and can apply even though gain would not otherwise be recognized.

When to Report Receipt of Disputed Income: Where monies in dispute are nevertheless received by the taxpayer, they are includible in gross income for the year received if such receipt is under a "claim of right," even though the taxpayer eventually has to repay or refund such monies (*North American Oil Consolidated v. Burnet*, 286 US 417). It must be noted that the issue of whether a sum is received under a claim of right by the taxpayer is a question of fact. For instance, in *Veenstra & De Haan Coal Co.*, 11 TC 964, a retail coal dealer required his customers to pay advance deposits on contracts to deliver coal to them, which deposits were refundable if the taxpayer could not furnish the coal. The Court held the deposits were not includible in gross income because the transactions were "executory contingent contracts for the sale of unascertained goods. . . . "

Note this, however, about "claim of right" income that is subsequently repaid. If the amount repaid exceeds $3,000, the taxpayer may either: (1) deduct the repayment in the year of repayment; or (2) compute his tax for the year of repayment without the deduction and reduce that tax by the tax paid in the prior year or years attributable to the inclusion of the "claim of right" amount in his income (§1341).

Time When Damages Are Deducted: An accrual basis taxpayer who is compelled to pay damages under judgment or settlement makes the deduction in the year when his obligation becomes definite and final, regardless of actual payment in a later year. A cash-basis taxpayer makes the deduction in the year when payment is made.

Contested Liabilities: Where an asserted liability is contested, such as a tax assessment, and payment is made before the contest is terminated, the payment is deductible in the year it is made. If the liability is thereafter settled for a lesser amount, the difference is included in income in that year (§461(f)). Where an accrual-basis taxpayer does not make payment until after the contest is settled, he can still deduct the amount in the year of settlement.

●

For Further Reference . . .
Tax Planning looseleaf Service. Institute for Business Planning, Englewood Cliffs, N.J.

SHIPPING AND WAREHOUSING

[¶5301] With the rapid increase in specialization and the development of broader markets for the products of industry and our natural resources, articles or commodities produced in one part of the country must often be shipped to another part of the country and sometimes stored and financed until they are to be used. In seasonal industries, goods or commodities produced during one season must usually be warehoused and financed until they are used later in the year. Still other commodities, such as cheese, whiskey and tobacco, require aging in storage.

When goods are shipped, the carrier may warehouse the goods at some stage of the trip or at different stages, and, indeed, even while the goods are in motion, the carrier has possession of the goods and performs functions similar to those exercised by the conventional warehouseman.

It is out of these basic facts of economic life that bills of lading and warehouse receipts assume their economic and legal importance. Both are, of course, receipts for the goods shipped or stored and have come to be accepted as substitutes for the goods themselves in the commercial and financial world.

This chapter spells out the essentials of bills of lading and warehouse receipts and alerts you to the problems they are apt to present in the normal course of business.

[¶5302]   BILLS OF LADING

A Bill of Lading is defined by the Code as a document "evidencing the receipt of goods for shipment issued by a person engaged in the business of transporting or forwarding goods" *(UCC §1–201(6))*. Essentially a bill of lading serves three functions: (1) receipt; (2) contract of shipment; and (3) document of title. Air bills, ocean bills, inland waterway bills, trucking bills, railway bills are all forms of bills of lading adapted to a particular mode of transportation.

For interstate or foreign transactions the Federal Bills of Lading Act, the Carriage of Goods by Sea Act or the Interstate Commerce Act may be applicable. For intrastate transactions the Uniform Commercial Code (Code) will be applicable.

[¶5302.1] What Form Must a Bill of Lading Take?

Neither the Federal Bills of Lading Act nor the Uniform Code spell out the form or contents of a bill of lading. However, the Interstate Commerce Commission has prescribed a form to be used in interstate shipments and this same form has come to be used by intrastate carriers.

[¶5302.2] **"Straight" and "Order" Bills of Lading**

Bills of lading may be negotiable or nonnegotiable. The former are often called "order" bills and the latter "straight" bills. Because of the importance of the distinction between a straight bill and an order bill the ICC regulations require that a straight bill of lading be printed on white paper while an order bill — a negotiable bill — must be printed on yellow paper. See ¶5304 for a discussion of negotiability.

[¶5302.3] **Types of Bills of Lading**

Here are some of the more common types of bills of lading:

Freight Forwarder Bills: Freight Forwarder Bills are bills issued by freight forwarders—forwarders who consolidate shipments of less than a carload into carload shipments. Where recognized (the Code recognizes §1–201(6)), a freight forwarder's bill will be treated as a bill of lading—either negotiable or nonnegotiable. Where not recognized, it cannot be negotiable.

Destination Bills: The Code permits carriers to issue so-called destination bills (§7–305). This legal development flows from the development of modern high speed transportation. It permits the carrier to issue a bill to the consignee at the destination.

Here's how a destination bill would work: A manufacturer in Los Angeles delivers goods to an airline and asks that the airline issue a bill of lading to a bank in New York. The airline gives the shipper a receipt which incorporates the obligation to issue a destination bill and wires its New York freight agent to issue a bill. The manufacturer wires the New York bank a draft on the consignee. The bank will endorse the bill of lading to the buyer when he honors the draft. Through the use of a destination bill you can avoid the delay which would occur if you used an ordinary bill and the goods arrived before the bill.

Through Bills: Through bills are used where more than one carrier is going to have to carry the same shipment. Let's say you're shipping out of New York by rail to Phoenix, Arizona, and the shipment is to be routed to Chicago via the Pennsylvania Railroad and from there to its destination via the Santa Fe Railroad. If the goods were damaged by Santa Fe at the Phoenix end of the trip and you didn't have a through bill of lading, you'd have to make your adjustment with the Sante Fe at its Phoenix office or its main office. And if you couldn't settle the matter amicably and had to sue, you'd have to go after the carrier in its own territory. A through bill of lading extends the liability of the initial carrier to include the breach of the contract of carriage by a connecting carrier.

Through bills are sanctioned by both the UCC §7–302 and the ICC Act. The UCC imposes no obligation to issue through bills. The UCC makes it clear that the connecting carrier holds the goods on the terms defined by the through bill. It also contains a provision giving the initial carrier rights against the carrier directly responsible for the damage.

Bills in a Set: These are original bills issued in two or three parts. Generally, their issuance in domestic trade is prohibited by statute. The UCC expressly prohibits their issuance except where customary in overseas transportation (§7–304) and makes the issuer liable for damages caused by violation of the prohibition. Where bills of lading are lawfully issued in a set in connection with overseas transportation, the provisions of the Hague and Warsaw Conventions and the Carriage of Goods by Sea Act determine their legal effect. Generally, the first holder in due course of the bill will prevail over a subsequent holder; everyone who transfers a part is liable to holders of that part as if it were the whole set; and the bailee is required to deliver against the first presented part of a bill of lading lawfully drawn in a set.

[¶5302.4]   Discrepancies Commonly Found in Bills of Lading

Here's a checklist of discrepancies commonly found by banks dealing with bills of lading:

1. Bill of lading isn't "clean" but has notations qualifying the quality and condition of the goods or its packing.

2. Bill doesn't show "on board" endorsement or endorsement isn't signed by carrier or its agent or initialed by party who signed the bill.

3. Other endorsements or changes in bill aren't properly signed or initialed.

4. "Order" bill is used when order for goods, invoice or other documentation with bill calls for "straight" bill, or vice versa.

5. Bill is not endorsed.

6. Bill is not marked "freight prepaid" when freight charges are included in invoice.

7. Description, marks and numbers of goods are not the same on all documents.

8. Insurance document accompanying bill is not countersigned or endorsed or its date is later than the date on the bill.

9. Insurance coverage doesn't satisfy requirements of other documents accompanying bill either as to risks covered or as to the amount of coverage.

[¶5303]   WAREHOUSE RECEIPTS

A warehouse receipt is similar to a bill of lading except it is given by a warehouseman rather than a carrier. It serves as a receipt, a contract of storage and a document of title. Warehouse receipts are generally governed by state legislation, principally the Uniform Commercial Code.

〔¶5303.1〕 Who Can Issue Warehouse Receipts?

A warehouse receipt may be issued by any warehouseman. A warehouseman is defined as a person engaged in the business of storing goods for hire or profit (see UCC §7–102, 201). The Code does not affect provisions of special licensing or other statutes regulating who may become a warehouseman.

〔¶5303.2〕 The Essential Terms of Warehouse Receipt

Under the UCC, the receipt must contain or show:
(1) Warehouse location.
(2) Date of issue.
(3) Consecutive number of receipts.
(4) Whether the goods will be delivered to bearer, to a specified person, or to a specified person or his order.
(5) The rate of storage and handling charges.
(6) A description of the goods or the packages containing them.
(7) The signature of the warehouseman or his agent.
(8) Disclosure of warehouseman's ownership interest, if any, in the goods.
(9) Statement of advances and liabilities for which warehouseman claims a lien or security interest.

〔¶5303.3〕 Effect of Omitting an Essential Term

The UCC preserves the application of its regulations to receipts omitting "essential" terms and makes the warehouseman liable in damages to persons injured by omission of required terms.

〔¶5304〕   NEGOTIABLE BILLS OF LADING OR WAREHOUSE RECEIPTS

A bill of lading or a warehouse receipt will be negotiable, in the sense that a promissory note or check may be considered negotiable if it calls for delivery of the goods (1) to bearer or (2) to a specified person or to his order. If it runs to a named person only, it's not negotiable.

〔¶5304.1〕 The Value of a Negotiable Bill or Receipt

Negotiable bills of lading and warehouse receipts are generally favored for use in commerce because the bona fide purchaser of a negotiable instrument by *due negotiation* gets maximum protection as against others who may claim interest in the document or the goods it represents. This is not to say that he is absolutely protected. But subject to certain exceptions which we'll mention later, if there's "due negotiation" a bona fide purchaser will get title to the document itself, title to the goods it represents, and the direct obligation of the carrier or warehouseman to hold and deliver the goods. The UCC also gives him "all rights accruing under the law of agency, including rights to goods delivered to the bailee after the document was issued" *(UCC §7–502(1)(c))*.

A bona fide, "due negotiation," purchaser won't lose out because someone up the line orders the goods stopped in transit, or because the goods are surrendered by the bailee (i.e., carrier, freight forwarder, or warehouseman) or because the document was stolen from or lost by a prior owner, or was negotiated by someone in breach of his duty. In other words, he takes free not only of prior equities but also of prior legal interests in the document and goods.

These rights depend on "due negotiation" to him, and we'll spell out in a subsequent paragraph what this means. But it must be borne in mind that even though you stand in the position of a bona fide purchaser after due negotiation, you *can* lose out in some cases, just as the holder in due course of a negotiable note can lose out in some cases.

When Bona Fide Purchaser Is Not Protected: (1) Negotiability can't protect you against the possibility that there is no bailee, or no goods, or if there is a bailee by the name stated in the document, that the document was issued by a forger. Nor can it protect you against the possibility that a bailee who is in default on his obligation to you is insolvent.

(2) You're not protected against the possibility of an unauthorized bailment of the goods in the first instance. If, for example, the goods were shipped or stored by a thief or someone without any power to ship or store, actual or apparent, you'd have no claim against the bailee. The only remedy you'd have would be against the person, if any, who negotiated the document to you or against the wrongdoer, if you could find him.

(3) Where a warehouseman sells fungible goods and he is also in the business of buying and selling the same type of goods, the purchaser of a negotiable document would not have rights superior to the buyer of the fungibles from the warehouseman in the regular course of business.

(4) The holder of the document might also lose out where there's a prior accepted delivery order. An accepted delivery order has the same effect as a bill or receipt issued by the bailee.

(5) Still another case where the holder of a bill of lading might lose out is where it is one originally issued to a freight forwarder who has, as a freight forwarder, issued its own bill for the same goods and the freight forwarder's bill has been duly negotiated to another. In that case the holder of the freight forwarder's bill will win out under the Code §7–502, 503.

[¶5304.2]   What Is Necessary for "Due Negotiation"?

The rights of a purchaser of a negotiable bill of lading or warehouse receipt may be defeated where there's *no negotiation.* Examples of this would be where an indorsement is missing or has been forged. A bearer document or one that has been indorsed in blank or to bearer can be negotiated by delivery alone. A document running to the order of a named person or which has been indorsed to a named person can be negotiated only by indorsement and delivery.

"Due negotiation" both under the Code and its predecessors requires that the purchase be made in good faith, and for value without notice of any defense or claim to the instruments on the part of any person. However, the Code adds an important new concept: if the purchaser is to get greater rights than those held by the person from whom he buys or his predecessors, the purchase must have been made in the "regular course of business or financing" and not in "settlement or payment of a money obligation" *(UCC §7–501).*

[¶5304.3]   How Can You Use Nonnegotiable Bills of Lading and Warehouse Receipts?

Nonnegotiable bills of lading, usually called "straight bills," and nonnegotiable warehouse receipts may both be used as documents of title. But they're not as good for this purpose as negotiable ones. The transferee of a nonnegotiable document will never be in as strong a legal position as the bona fide purchaser of a negotiable document duly negotiated. The issuer of a nonnegotiable document is obligated to deliver the goods to the person named in the document even though he doesn't have possession of the document, unless the issuer has notice of the transfer. Therefore if you are a transferee of a nonnegotiable document, you ought to make sure that the carrier or warehouseman is notified of the transfer to you at the same time that it takes place — especially, if you think there's a chance that your transferor might try to defraud you.

These weaknesses of nonnegotiable documents don't, however, bar their use in business and finance. The weaknesses are in the main weaknesses in the hands of the transferees and not in the hands of the original holder. So that in a financing situation, for example, if the financier, a bank or other lender, is placed in the position of an original holder as the result of advance planning he'll be in as good a position as the transferee of a negotiable document duly negotiated. In some ways he'll be in a better position.

If, for example, he held a negotiable warehouse receipt and his debtor wanted to take part of the goods out of the warehouse to work on, it would be necessary to cancel the receipt. But not so with a nonnegotiable receipt.

[¶5304.4] **Nonnegotiable Documents May be Useful in Financing Situations**

Nonnegotiable or straight bills of lading and nonnegotiable warehouse receipts are also used for financing purposes. Their use in financing may put the financers in a better position than a negotiable document. See ¶5304.3.

[¶5304.5] **Loss of a Negotiable Document**

Where a negotiable bill of lading or warehouse receipt is lost you can obtain delivery on a court order made on satisfactory proof of loss, plus a bond furnished by the claimant and approved by the court. Under the Uniform Commercial Code, a court order may be necessary for either a negotiable or nonnegotiable document. Where a court order is required, the court may direct payment of the bailee's reasonable costs and counsel fees.

[¶5305] **RIGHTS OF THE CARRIER, FREIGHT FORWARDER, OR WAREHOUSEMAN**

The carrier, freight forwarder or warehouseman has a lien on the goods in his possession for his charges for storage or carriage. He has the duty to use care in handling the goods, delivering the goods and to properly describe the goods in the bill of lading or warehouse receipt.

[¶5305.1] **When Can a Warehouseman Remove Goods?**

Where goods are stored for an indefinite term, the warehouseman can require removal within a period fixed by him provided thirty days' notice is given to the depositor and others who may have an interest in the goods. Where storage is arranged for a fixed term, the warehouseman can remove the goods at the end of the period. He should give interested parties notice however.

Where the warehouseman believes that perishable goods are about to decline in value below the amount of his warehouseman's lien (i.e., generally less than the storage charges) he may demand removal within a reasonable time without giving the thirty days' notice generally required. The Uniform Commercial Code provides that the warehouseman can demand removal within a reasonable time where it appears that a price decline jeopardizes his warehouseman's lien.

Hazardous goods may be summarily removed and sold at public or private sale on reasonable notice to interested parties where the warehouseman was unaware of the quality or the condition of the goods at the time of deposit. Hazardous goods would include goods which attract insects, goods prone to leakage, explosives, inflammables and may include goods with offensive odors.

〔¶5305.2〕 How the Bailee's Lien Operates

There are three basic forms of liens running in favor of the carrier or warehouseman: (1) Specific lien; (2) General lien; (3) Security interests based on agreement.

Specific Lien: The specific lien attaches only to the goods stored or shipped. The lien attaches automatically.

General Lien: The general lien attaches not only to the specific goods in relation to which the charges arose but to other goods as well (i.e., other goods stored in the same warehouse). There is no statutory recognition of the general lien for carriers. The warehouseman gets a general lien by stating in the receipt that a lien is claimed for charges and expenses in relation to other goods.

Security Interests Based on Agreement: The warehouseman may have a security interest for money advanced and interest based on a security agreement. Because he has possession of the goods his lien will be perfected without filing. The Uniform Commercial Code, however, requires that the maximum amount of charges for which a security interest is claimed must be stated on the receipt.

〔¶5305.3〕 What the Lien Covers

A warehouseman's specific lien generally covers charges in relation to the goods. The carrier's specific lien covers charges for storage and transportation including demurrage and terminal charges and expenses of preservation necessary and incident to their transportation. It may also include reasonably incurred expenses incident to the sale to satisfy the lien.

Carriers are commonly bound by published charges — therefore, a person dealing with a bill of lading issued by a common carrier will have some gauge of the charges covered.

Warehouse charges are not ordinarily fixed by statute or administration — many factors including weight, size and nature of the goods will go into establishing a rate schedule. Thus, the transferee of the warehouse receipt should check what the charges will be. The warehouseman's lien may also pick up charges which antedate the issue of the receipt.

As against a person to whom a negotiable receipt has been duly negotiated, the lien is limited under the Code to a reasonable charge for storage subsequent to the date of the receipt unless an amount or rate of charges is specified on the receipt.

As against a purchaser for value of a negotiable bill of lading or warehouse receipt the carrier's or warehouseman's lien is limited to a reasonable charge unless the charges are stated in the document or applicable tariff.

Under the Code a warehouseman's lien may extend to charges or expenses in relation to goods other than those covered by the receipt, but this is not true of a carrier's lien.

[¶5305.4] How the Bailee Can Enforce His Lien

The bailee's liens give him the right to withhold delivery of the goods until his charges are paid. Where his charges go unpaid he can enforce his lien by a sale of the goods subject to the lien.

Where goods are stored by a merchant in the course of his business he may sell the goods at a public or private sale. Considerable flexibility is afforded. The sale may be made in bloc or in parcels, at any time and at any place. The terms, however, must be commercially reasonable. Known claimants must be given notice of the amount due, the nature of the sale, and its time and place, if public. Sale in a regular way on an established market or at the current price in such a market will be "commercially reasonable."

Goods may be redeemed until the sale. If there is a sale, proceeds in excess of the amount of the lien are held for the person who had a right to the goods. The Code, unlike its antecedents, protects bona fide purchasers at the sale— even though it may not have been conducted in strict compliance with the statute.

[¶5306] LIABILITIES OF CARRIERS, FREIGHT FORWARDERS, AND WAREHOUSEMEN

A carrier or warehouseman has as a minimum duty that of exercising such care as a reasonable man would exercise under similar circumstances. Generally a warehouseman will not have a greater duty of care unless he agrees to be bound by a higher standard.

A common carrier's liability, however, is more akin to that of an insurer. He may be liable even though he is not negligent. Generally the common carrier will not be liable where the damage is caused by acts of God, or the public enemy, or losses due to the inherent nature of the property or the act of the shipper himself. In a number of states, statutes have been enacted defining the common carrier's liability. The Interstate Commerce Act, applicable to interstate shipments, makes the initial carrier liable for any loss caused by it or by any subsequent carrier under a through bill of lading.

In most jurisdictions, however, a common carrier may limit his insurer's liability by contract provided the limitation is reasonable.

〖¶5306.1〗 How Liability is Limited

Where a warehouseman or common carrier seeks to limit his liability it may be necessary that the limitation appear on the bill of lading or the warehouse receipt which he gives upon receipt of the goods. Generally the limitation of liability will be based on the stated value of the goods. The bailor can increase the stated value of the goods in most cases by paying an increased rate. It is wise to check the bill or receipt to determine whether the warehouseman or carrier has attempted to limit liability. Where liability has been limited the shipper or bailor may want to protect his interests by purchasing insurance.

〖¶5306.2〗 Bailee's Duty to Deliver

Unless he has a recognized excuse or defense, the bailee carrier or warehouseman, on payment of the amount covered by his lien, must deliver the goods to the consignee or bearer as required by the documents of title.

Excuses or Defenses for Non-Delivery Include: (1) Sale of the goods to satisfy the bailee's lien; (2) destruction of the goods without the bailee's fault; and (3) personal defenses of the bailee against the claimant.

If the bailee acts in good faith in delivering the goods and observes reasonable commercial standards, he'll be immune from liability. If he had notice of an adverse claim, the delivery wouldn't be in good faith.

Sometimes a bailee as an accommodation will issue a document without actually having received the goods covered. Generally, if he does so, he can't escape liability to the holder of a negotiable document.

〖¶5306.3〗 Misdescription of Goods

A carrier or a warehouseman can be held liable in damages to persons injured by misdescription of the goods in a bill of lading or a warehouse receipt unless the issuer indicates that it doesn't know whether or not the goods conform to the description. Often the carrier or warehouseman will use language like "said to be or contain," "Shipper's weight, load and count," or "contents, condition and quality unknown," to avoid this liability. The Uniform Commercial Code requires that language indicating a warehouseman's lack of knowledge must be conspicuously indicated on the warehouse receipt *(UCC §7-203).*

〖¶5306.4〗 Effect of Changes in a Bill of Lading or Warehouse Receipt

An unauthorized alteration in a bill of lading or warehouse receipt generally cannot give the holder any greater rights against the issuer than he would have under an unaltered document. The Uniform Commercial Code gives the purchaser of a warehouse receipt the right to treat the unauthorized filling in of a blank as authorized provided he has no notice of the lack of authority.

●

For Further Reference . . .

American Jurisprudence, Carriers §264–314, Bills of Lading and Shipping Receipts.

American Jurisprudence, Warehouses.

Willier and Hart, *Forms and Procedures Under the Uniform Commercial Code,* ¶72.01 et seq.

TAX DISPUTES

[¶5401]   Handling a tax dispute is seldom a simple matter. Familiarity with the terrain is a basic ingredient of success in any contest with IRS. The practitioner who is not familiar with the way IRS operates may find himself using the wrong tactics, with the wrong people at the wrong stage of the dispute—and he will most likely wind up with the wrong result.

[¶5402]   DEALING WITH THE REVENUE AGENT

The Revenue Agent sets the tax dispute in motion. During an audit of your return, he determines that there is a deficiency. If you agree and pay the additional tax, there is no dispute. The agent will then have you sign a formal settlement agreement (Form 870) disposing of the matter. (However, if you later change your mind, you can sue for a refund.) When you disagree with the agent's determination, the tax dispute arises.

Of course, the first opportunity you have to settle the controversy is with the Revenue Agent. In dealing with the Revenue Agent remember that he is trying to discharge his duty to the government and the revenue and still dispose of the matter the best way he can. The most satisfactory results will come from establishing a climate within which you and the agent can engage in a mutual endeavor to determine the proper tax liability.

Limited Authority: The Revenue Agent is the principal fact-finder of the Internal Revenue Service. He has authority to determine what the facts are and apply them to the legal position taken by Internal Revenue Service. A Revenue Agent has no discretion to dispose of an issue where:

(1) IRS has taken a position contrary to the Tax Court. He must follow the position taken by IRS.

(2) Regulations and rulings are available. He must follow these rules.

(3) The law on the subject is not clear.

Since the Revenue Agent has no authority to settle such issues, it's better not to argue these issues with him. No purpose is served. The best course to follow is to inform the Agent that you will not agree on this issue. You should give the agent as much information on the issue as you feel is pertinent.

Advantages of Settling on the Revenue Agent's Level Are: (1) You are required to show less evidence to establish your claim;

(2) You avoid the possibility of having other issues raised by other more experienced IRS agents;

(3) You avoid the expense and anxiety of further proceedings.

448

【¶5403】   INFORMAL CONFERENCE STAGE

After the agent has completed his audit of the tax return, he prepares a written report of the adjustments which he proposes. If you disagree with his findings, you will receive a "ten-day letter," informing you of your right to an informal conference (now known as a "district division conference") with the Conference Section of the District Director's Office. This ten-day letter means that you have ten days within which to make an appointment for an informal conference. However, IRS announced *(Rev. Proc. 64-38)* that field audit cases (i.e., where the agent examines your books on your business premises) will be handled differently.

【¶5403.1】   Field Audit Cases

If the taxpayer disagrees with the adjustment proposed by the revenue agent on a *field audit,* the agent will prepare a complete examination report. Before the report or any conference invitation is sent to the taxpayer, the agent will submit the case file to the district review staff for a thorough review. After such review, the taxpayer will receive a copy of the agent's report, providing him with a detailed explanation of the available appeal procedures and requesting the taxpayer to advise the district, ordinarily within 30 days, of his choice of action.

If the total amount of proposed additional tax, overassessment, or refund claim does not exceed $2,500 for any year, the taxpayer will be granted a "district division conference" (informal conference) on request. But he need not file a written protest unless he so desires.

If the amount involved exceeds $2,500 for any year, the taxpayer, on request, will be granted a "district audit division conference," provided a written protest is filed setting forth the facts, law, and taxpayer's argument.

【¶5403.2】   Hearing Before Conferee

The "informal conference" is held before the examining agent's group supervisor or a conferee. The conferee usually hears all complex cases, all cases where the group supervisor disqualifies himself, and all cases where a taxpayer requests his assignment (usually where the group supervisor has shown that he agrees with his agent's position). Generally, the group supervisor hears relatively simple cases and cases which are in outlying offices which would require incurring travel time and expense.

The purpose of the conference is to provide a means of settling the issues in informal surroundings without the added technical confusion usually associated with affidavits, briefs, and other legalistic documents. Moreover, the taxpayer is afforded an opportunity to reach an early settlement of the disputed issues before the Revenue Agent makes out his final report. Also, taxpayer is given the chance to have an objective review of his case. The conferee does not ordinarily see a case until it's in conference. This is sometimes a sore spot when group supervisors hold the conference.

Second Informal Conference: Where the first informal conference is getting somewhere but the issues are not finally determined, there may be a second informal conference to arrive at a final determination. Also, a second informal conference may be held where the Appellate Division finds that the conferee was in error, and remands the case to the conferee.

Conference Report: This is prepared by the conferee or the group supervisor who holds the conference; the Revenue Agent must follow this report by filing his own written report. Both reports are then reviewed by the Audit Division of the District Director's office.

[¶5403.3] Should You Go to Informal Conference?

Take advantage of the informal conference where it appears that the Revenue Agent has mistakenly interpreted the IRS position or when he has made a clear error as to a finding of fact. If the issues involved do not come within this scope, it would seem better to forgo the informal conference.

Disadvantages of Conference: When you agree to go to a conference, you run the risk of having a new affirmative issue raised by the IRS. The conference stage is still considered to be at an audit level, and the conferee has the power to review the case anew.

When Informal Conference Is Not Available: Where the statute of limitations is about to run on a specific year or issue and you have not signed an agreement extending it, an informal conference will not be offered by the IRS. The reason, obviously, is that the IRS is anxious to stop the running of a statute and to protect its claim.

Waiving the Right to an Informal Conference: If more than $2,500 is involved for any year and if the issues are such that there appears to be little possibility for disposing of them in a "district conference," the taxpayer is encouraged by IRS to bypass such conference in favor of a prompt consideration by the Appellate Division. In such case if the taxpayer does not expressly request an Audit Division conference, the taxpayer's protest and the case file will be forwarded to the Appellate Division. This applies to field audit cases.

You would probably want to waive the right to an informal conference where, for example, your legal position is contrary to the stated IRS position. In this case, it would be useless to go into conference because the conferee is bound by the IRS's legal position. What you do is notify the examining agent that you will not seek an informal conference. A notice then will be issued giving you 30 days to file a formal protest with the Appellate Division.

[¶5403.4] Authority of Conferees and Group Supervisors

They are subject to "post-review" and their authority, like the Revenue Agent's, is principally that of determining facts and applying the IRS position to these facts. They cannot go beyond this authority.

Post-Review: In every district of the Internal Revenue Service there is an office called "post-review." This office reviews all reports on settlements or adjustments of tax liability occurring as a result of an audit or an informal conference. The purpose of the review is to correct any errors in applying the IRS position to the facts. This is an internal IRS procedure; the taxpayer is not given an opportunity to confer on his case in this office.

Requests for Technical Advice: A District Director may request technical advice from the National Office during the Revenue Agent's examination or during the informal conference procedure. This is usually made available where the disputed issue is extremely complex or the disposition of similar issues has not been uniform in other field offices.

The taxpayer has the right to review the facts and issues presented to the National Office. If he disagrees with the District Director's presentation, he can submit his own statement of facts. In addition, he can also submit a memorandum of law.

Requests for Technical Advice by Taxpayer: The taxpayer can himself initiate the request for technical advice. You would usually make such request where you believe that had you requested a ruling on the issue, you would have gotten a favorable result.

Effect of Technical Advice: The District Director is bound by the technical advice given by the National Office. He has to follow it just like any other Internal Revenue Service ruling. A taxpayer, on the other hand, is not bound by this advice; he can appeal. An opinion by the National Office is merely persuasive.

451

Hearing at National Office: The taxpayer can also get a hearing before the National Office. But this can end his administrative appeal. Once he gets a hearing before the National Office, he cannot go to the Appellate Division.

[¶5405]   APPELLATE DIVISION STAGE

After no agreement at the informal conference level or if the taxpayer waives an informal conference, he then receives a so-called "30-day letter." This tells the taxpayer of his right to file a "protest" with the Appellate Division. With the 30-day letter, he will receive instructions on how to file a protest with the District Director.

Your protest should be a simple statement of the basic facts and your legal position as to the proposed adjustments.

Alternatives After Receiving 30-Day Letter:
1. Pay the tax and end the case.
2. Pay the tax and then file a suit for a refund.
3. File a "protest" within the 30 days.
4. Allow the 30 days to elapse and then sue in the Tax Court after getting the "90-day letter" (notice of deficiency).
5. Request a "90-day letter."

Conference With Appellate Division: The Appellate Division is a type of appellate tribunal within the IRS's administrative department. It is not a division of the District Director's office; the District Director has no jurisdiction over this department. The Appellate Division settlement authority is derived from the Regional Commissioners.

The Appellate Division conference is also informal. A formal transcript of the proceedings is not made. New evidence may be submitted and considered. In that case, however, the Appellate Division may send the case back to the District Director (informal conference level) to determine the case in light of this new evidence. It is advisable to submit any new evidence in advance of the informal conference.

Authority of Appellate Division: The Appellate Division has broad authority to settle cases. It can evaluate and settle cases on the basis of the Government's and the taxpayer's respective strength and weakness and the risk of litigation. Issues of law and mixed issues of law and fact can be settled at this level. A settlement by the Appellate Division (by signing Form 870AD) is considered by the IRS to be a final disposition of the case.

[¶5404.1]   Advantages and Disadvantages of Going to
Appellate Division

Advantages:

1. If the case is settled by the Appellate Division, publicity is avoided. Normally, the facts of a particular case are not made known until a petition is filed in the Tax Court.

2. The possibility that a satisfactory settlement may be reached, and, therefore, the expense and anxiety of litigation avoided.

3. If there is more than one issue, the possibility of eliminating one of these issues. If the taxpayer intends to use the District Court or the Court of Claims to litigate his case, he first has to pay *all* of the tax due. By eliminating one of the issues, he minimizes this burden.

4. Settlement will stop the running of interest on the proposed deficiency. (Of course, interest also stops running if the tax dispute is settled at the agent or the informal conference level.)

5. Keeps open the choice as to the court in which he will litigate the issue.

Disadvantages:

1. The biggest disadvantage is the possibility of the Appellate Division raising new issues. The Appellate Division is made up of the ablest tax technicians that IRS has. They are well trained in the interpretation and application of the tax law and it's not unusual for them to see issues in a case which were not seen by the Revenue Agent or the conferee at the informal conference level.

2. Increasing taxpayer's burden of proof by raising new issues at this level. When a new issue is raised after a notice of deficiency is issued and a petition filed in the Tax Court, the affirmative burden of proof is on IRS; when the issue is raised at the Appellate Division level, the affirmative burden of proof is on the taxpayer.

3. Weaknesses in the Revenue Agent's case may be detected and plugged.

[¶5405]   CHOICE OF FORUM

If settlement is not reached in the Appellate Division, or the conference before the Appellate Division is waived, IRS then issues a statutory notice of deficiency wherein it sets forth its claim for additional tax. This notice is called the "90-day letter."

Alternatives After Receiving "90-Day Letter":

1. Pay the tax and close the matter.

2. Try a further settlement through a conference in the Appellate Division.

3. Pay the tax demanded and file a suit for refund in the District Court or in the United States Court of Claims.

4. File a petition for redetermination in the Tax Court.

[¶5405.1] "Refund Route"

The taxpayer who takes this route has two courts in which to bring his suit: The United States District Court in the district where the tax was paid or the United States Court of Claims which sits in Washington, D.C. Before a taxpayer will be allowed to bring suit in one of these courts he will have to pay the *entire* tax which is due (including interest and penalties). He cannot pay a part of the tax and have the entire deficiency determined by these courts. In these courts he can only sue for refund of taxes paid.

The way to proceed is to first pay the tax and then file a claim for refund (Form 843) with the IRS. Upon its rejection by IRS or the expiration of six months, file your suit for refund.

The taxpayer who takes this route cannot later change his mind and bring suit in the Tax Court. In the first place, the 90-day period in all likelihood would have expired. Secondly, since he has paid the tax due there is no deficiency over which the Tax Court could take jurisdiction.

On the other hand, taxpayer may not file his petition in the Tax Court and then pay the tax and sue for refund. Once the Tax Court has acquired jurisdiction it will not let go — even upon stipulation of counsel.

District Court: Suit in this court is brought against the District Director (personally) who collected the tax, or the United States Government. In either event, a jury trial is available. The availability of a jury is the major advantage of bringing the suit in the District Court. Decisions in this court are appealable to the United States Circuit Court of Appeals.

Court of Claims: This is a five-judge court which sits in Washington. Although there is no jury trial, this court has been known to listen to the "equities" of a taxpayer. A decision by this court is final, except for a reversal by the U.S. Supreme Court. Decisions are appealable only to the Supreme Court by grant of certiorari.

A taxpayer who elects to use this court has to be mindful that he is giving up a valuable right to an appellate review of his case. But, this may work to a taxpayer's benefit as well as to his detriment.

Where the issue in dispute has been decided by this court in your favor, you can virtually assure yourself of victory by paying the tax, and then suing for refund in this court. Since the choice of forum is yours, you have a decided advantage.

In Either Court: The burden of proof is on the taxpayer to establish that he is entitled to the refund. But this is the same as in the Tax Court, except that there you have to prove that the deficiency is wrong, which is in effect the same issue.

[¶5405.2] "Tax Court Route"

The Tax Court's jurisdiction is invoked only after IRS has issued its "90-day letter," and the taxpayer has filed a *timely* petition to have its case heard. This petition must be filed within 90 days or the Tax Court will not get jurisdiction. There can be no extensions of time to file a petition.

One of the major advantages in filing a petition in the Tax Court is that you can have the deficiency determined without paying any part of the tax which is due. Some taxpayers, after filing a petition, do pay the tax, but this is only to stop the running of interest. It is not necessary. In fact, if the tax is paid before the mailing of a statutory notice of deficiency, the Tax Court would not have jurisdiction over the dispute.

Decisions by the Tax Court are appealable to the United States Circuit Courts of Appeal. The circuit where taxpayer filed his return is normally the place where an appeal will be taken. The Circuit Courts of Appeal have exclusive jurisdiction over decisions by the Tax Court and the District Courts.

Small Claims Procedure: The Tax Court has a small claims division which handles cases involving tax deficiencies or overpayments which do not exceed $1,500. Both income and estate tax deficiencies are handled here. The decisions in these cases are based upon a brief summary opinion instead of formal findings of fact and are not precedent for future cases. The procedure is optional with the taxpayer.

[¶5406] ODDS IN TAX COURT AND DISTRICT COURT

Do appeals from determinations made by the lower echelons of IRS to higher echelons within IRS pay off? A report by the Commissioner reveals that during 1973 taxpayers did well in settling cases at the highest level of IRS. Of 18,974 disputes that weren't appealed to the Tax Court, IRS settled deficiencies and penalties for a little over 40% of the amount claimed (up from 30% in 1972). With cases docketed in the Court, IRS settled about 33% (compared with 30.4% in 1972).

Taxpayers who paid taxes assessed and filed suit in the Court of Claims or district courts recovered 58% of the amount claimed in the Court of Claims and 44% in the district courts. Once the dispute went beyond the Tax Court and district court level, the odds against taxpayers were substantial. Only 22% of the cases were won by taxpayers on appeal.

For Further Reference . . .

Arent, Albert E., and Hall, James Fay, How to Settle a Tax Controversy, ¶25,064, *Corporation Report,* Prentice-Hall, Englewood Cliffs, N.J.

Federal Tax Desk Book, Institute for Business Planning, Englewood Cliffs, N.J.

Hariton, Gannet, Friedman, Rosenzweig and Mednick, *New York University Institute on Federal Taxation,* 1964, p. 59 et seq.

Tax Planning looseleaf Service. Institute for Business Planning, Englewood Cliffs, N.J.

TAX LIENS

[¶5501] Anyone giving or selling a security interest is probably a Federal taxpayer, and this means that the Federal tax lien may creep in to get priority over money advanced by a private party. If the government has made a demand on the taxpayer for payment, IRC §6321 gives the government a lien on any and all property belonging to him. IRC §6324 imposes a special lien for nonpayment of estate and gift taxes.

A Federal tax lien which was *not filed* is not valid as against a mortgagee, pledgee, purchaser, or judgment creditor *until notice has been filed* in the office designated by the law of the state in which the property subject to the lien was situated. Therefore, if you are a purchaser, or get a valid mortgage or pledge of specific property from a taxpayer before notice of a tax lien against him is filed, you ordinarily have nothing to worry about. Under IRC §6323 (as amended by the Tax Lien Act of 1966), the same protection is extended to "mechanic's lienors," and "holders of security interests."

The phrase "holders of security interests" is to conform the IRC to Uniform Commercial Code terminology (see below). Also, §6323 now protects judgment *lien* creditors, rather than simply judgment creditors. This makes statutory the rule of a number of judicial decisions (see *United States v. Security Trust & Savings Bank of San Digeo,* 340 U.S. 47 (1950)).

IRC §6323(h) defines a "purchaser" as one who, "for adequate and full consideration" in money or money's worth, acquires an interest (other than a lien or security interest) in property which is valid under local law as against subsequent purchasers without notice. A bona fide bargain purchaser for value who hasn't completed performance on his obligation will be protected.

"Security interest" is given the same definition as it has under the Uniform Commercial Code, i.e., a person who acquires an interest in property by contract for the purpose of securing payment or performance of an obligation or as indemnification against loss or liability. A security holder is protected to the extent that he has parted with money or money's worth. See UCC, §9-107.

Under IRC §6323(b) the following categories of interests are protected even where notice has been filed (called "superpriorities"):

(1) Attorneys' liens based upon a local law lien on a judgment or other amount settling a claim, cause of action, or contract enforceable against the judgment or settlement. IRC §6323(b)(8).

(2) Repairmen's similar possessory liens if the holder has been continuously in possession of the property from the time the liens arose. IRC §6323(b)(5).

(3) Mechanics' liens on residential property if the contract price of the job is $1,000 or less. IRC §6323(b)(7).

(4) Real estate taxes and special assessment liens. IRC §6323(b)(6).

(5) Insurance company policy loans. IRC §6323(b)(9).

(6) Passbook loans, provided the bank keeps the passbook in its possession until the loan is paid. IRC §6323(b)(10).

(7) Tangible personal property bought at retail in the ordinary course of business. IRC §6323(b)(3).

(8) Casual purchases of household goods, personal effects or other tangible personal property exempt from levy for collection of taxes if the sales price is $250 or less. IRC §6323(b)(4).

IRC §6323(c)(1) establishes priority for security interests arising out of certain common types of financing agreements entered into after the notice of the tax lien is filed. This pertains to: (1) commercial transactions financing agreements, (2) real property construction or improvement financing agreements, or (3) obligatory disbursement agreements. IRC §6323(c)(2), (3), and (4).

A "commercial transaction financing agreement" is defined as an agreement entered into by a taxpayer in the ordinary course of his trade or business to either (1) make loans to the taxpayer to be secured by commercial financing security acquired by the taxpayer in the ordinary course of his trade or business, or (2) purchase commercial financing security, but not inventory, also acquired by taxpayer in the ordinary course of his trade or business.

"Commercial financing security" is defined as accounts receivable, mortgages on real property, inventory, and paper of a kind ordinarily arising in commercial transactions.

Protection for commercial transaction financing agreements is afforded only where the loan or purchase is made not later than 45 days after the tax lien filing (unless actual notice or knowledge of the filing is obtained sooner) and only where the inventory, accounts receivable, etc., are acquired before the 45 days have elapsed. IRC §6323(c)(1).

"Real property construction or improvement agreements" are those that generally involve disbursements to an owner of property for the construction or improvement of real property, or to a builder for a contract to construct or improve real property, as well as disbursements for the raising or harvesting of farm crops or the raising of livestock or other animals. Protection is limited to interests arising from cash disbursements by the lender except in the case of the financing of a farm crop, livestock, or other animals, where the disbursement may also be in the form of supplying goods or services. IRC §6323(c)(2).

"Obligatory disbursement agreements" are agreements entered into by a person under which he is obliged to make disbursements because someone other than the taxpayer has relied on his obligation. An example would be an irrevocable letter of credit where a bank issuing the letter must honor a demand for payment by a third party who advances credit in reliance upon the letter.

This also covers cases where a surety agrees to finance the completion of a contract entered into by the taxpayer.

No limitation is placed in these obligatory disbursement agreements on the time during which a disbursement may be made as long as the person is obligated to do so at the time of the tax lien filing by a written agreement. IRC §6323(c)(4).

Mortgagees, pledgees and other holders of security interests which come into existence as a result of payments made before the 46th day after notice of the tax lien is filed are protected, but only as to property in existence when the tax lien is filed and which is covered by a written agreement entered into before filing. IRC §6323(d).

IRC §6323(e) extends the priority of the basic lien to payments for interest and other expenses if they are also given the same priority under local law. The types of items referred to here are:

(1) Interest or carrying charges (including finance and service charges) on the obligation secured by a lien or security interest;

(2) Reasonable expenses of an indenture trustee (such as a trustee under a deed of trust) or agent holding a security interest;

(3) Reasonable expenses incurred in collecting and enforcing a secured obligation (including reasonable attorneys' fees);

(4) Reasonable costs of insuring, preserving, or repairing the property subject to the lien or security interest;

(5) Reasonable costs of insuring payment of the obligation secured (such as mortgage insurance); and

(6) Amounts paid by the holder of a lien or security interest to satisfy another lien on the property where this other lien has priority over the Federal tax lien.

See Bankruptcy ¶601 et seq., and Secured Transactions ¶4901, for a discussion of related material.

[¶5501.1] How to Analyze and Protect Against Tax and Other Competing Liens

In analyzing a case involving the relative priority of competing liens (including a Federal tax lien) or in analyzing the applicable precedent, the practitioner will find his task greatly simplified if he utilizes the following technique:

1. Make a chronological list of all events related to the liens.

2. With respect to those interests arising before the Federal tax lien, ask the following question: Did the interest operate under state law to negate a finding of property in the taxpayer to which the subsequent Federal tax lien could attach?

3. With respect to interest arising after the Federal tax lien, ask the following question: Did the interest operate under state law to negate a finding of

property in the taxpayer to which even a prior Federal tax lien could have attached?

If your lien arose before the Federal tax lien, an attempt should first be made to prove that under state law the taxpayer had no property to the extent of that interest to which the tax lien could attach.

•

For Further Reference . . .

Coogan, Peter F., and Mansfield, Harry K., *Secured Transactions Under U.C.C., Coogan, Hogan and Vagts,* Chapter 12, Matthew Bender, New York, N.Y.

Plumb, W. T., Federal Tax Collection and Lien Problems, 13 *Tax Law Review,* 459.

Status of Liens for Taxes and Debts Owing the United States in Bankruptcy Proceedings, *American Jurisprudence,* §993-995.

TAX PLANNING

[¶5601] Many of the matters with which the lawyer is called upon to deal have income tax implications and often present special opportunities for tax planning for the client. The areas in which tax planning situations may be found cover the waterfront—they can range from the manner in which a new business is set up and the form it takes, through the operation of the business, the withdrawing of profits from the business, to the ultimate winding up of the business. They can be involved in the areas of investment in which a client may be involved—real estate, securities, the setting up of transactions so as to give tax-favored capital gains instead of highly taxed ordinary income. And they can involve the personal relationships within the family and the desire to reduce the overall family tax bill (and preserve more capital for the family unit) by shifting income from high-bracket taxpayers to those in lower tax brackets. And here the attorney may be involved with trusts, family partnerships, and even alimony and other marital settlements.

The following checklists highlight the objectives in tax planning in the various areas with which the lawyer has contact and point out the techniques available and the pitfalls to avoid in accomplishing successful tax planning. Greater detail is available in IBP Tax Planning.

[¶5602] OBJECTIVES IN TAX PLANNING FOR THE BUSINESSMAN

In tax planning we usually have some combination of the following objectives:

(1) Reduce unnecessary costs and increase net profit.

(2) Increase the amount of cash at work in the business.

(3) Secure business and competitive advantages through the desire of customers, suppliers, investors, and employees to minimize their own tax liability.

The main routes by which taxes can be saved may be listed this way:

(1) Stabilizing income to keep out of peak brackets.

(2) Spreading income over a long period of time to avoid peak rates and defer tax. The use of income averaging can reduce the tax on income bunched into one year.

(3) Accelerating or postponing income and expenses as indicated by the tax rates prospectively applicable including the added tax on tax preference income.

(4) Dividing income among a number of taxpayers; for example, spreading income among the members of a family partnership or the beneficiaries of a family trust.

461

(5) Converting ordinary income into capital gain.

(6) Building capital values by deductible expenditures; for example, promotion, research and development, and the accelerated charge-off of plant and equipment. Also, by using the 7% investment credit.

(7) Utilizing the exemptions and deductions allowed under the law; for example, the depletion allowance or tax-exempt bonds.

(8) Selecting a form of business appropriate to your plans with respect to drawing down income; for example, using a limited partnership, a proprietorship or Subchapter S corporation to carry a venture through the period when anticipated losses can be charged against highly taxed personal income, then throwing the business income into a corporation to be taxed at the fixed corporate rate, instead of the graduated individual rates. Income thus brought under a corporate umbrella may subsequently be converted into capital gain by liquidation or by sale of the corporate stock.

(9) Utilizing specific elections in the law, i.e., accounting elections, choices as to method of depreciation, class life election, etc.

(10) Creating business relationships between taxable entities which will make the most effective total use of applicable tax rates, earning power, actual and potential losses, depreciable assets (e.g., mergers, sale-leasebacks, other arm's length contractual relationships).

[¶5603]   TAX CONSIDERATIONS IN SETTING UP A BUSINESS

The Form of Business—whether or not to incorporate—if we incorporate, shall we elect to avoid the corporate tax under Subchapter S? Note limitation on contributions to qualified retirement plans.

How Many Entities Do We Want—multiple corporations—a combination of incorporated and unincorporated entities? Consider loss of multiple surtax exemptions and accumulated earnings credit.

What Shall We Put in the Business—what will we hold out? Real estate or equipment may be leased, patents or know-how may be licensed.

How Should Assets Be Transferred to the Business—by sale, by taxable exchange, by tax-free incorporation?

What Kind of Capital Structure Do We Want—how much equity, how much debt—what kind of equity, what kind of debt?

Loss Risk—how can we best cushion this risk?

Tax Risk—how can we set up the best leverage, the best capital gain potential while minimizing the risk that receipt of stock or exercise of warrants will be taxed as ordinary income?

The tax considerations affecting the decision whether or not to incorporate and, if the corporate route is chosen, the type of capital structure and the number of entities to be used is discussed in ¶1704.

[¶5603.1] How to Cushion Loss

(1) Operating losses can be deducted against the investor's outside income by using a partnership or a Supchapter S corporation.

(2) Investment loss on stock can be deducted against ordinary income by issuing the stock under IRC §1244.

(3) An investor can buy and own real estate or machinery and lend or lease to a corporate business. If there's a loss, he shoots for a §1231 deduction. Also, he may trade current depreciation against ordinary income for capital gain by later sale to a corporation. This won't work as to premature disposition of investment credit property or depreciation on personal property (§1245) nor as to part or all of accelerated portion of depreciation of real property on dispositions (§1250). Capital gain treatment will be denied if he, his spouse, and his minor children and grandchildren own more than 80% of the outstanding stock (§1239).

(4) Take debenture or preferred stock and give it to a foundation while it has original value. This gives cash back now as tax deduction to extent of tax rate. For example, an investor in the 70% bracket donates preferred stock worth $5,000 directly to a foundation. In effect, this is an exchange of preferred stock for $3,500 cash.

(5) Where an individual has a note that is a potential bad debt, he may find that by transferring it into a new corporation a greater tax saving can be obtained. The note will be picked up by the corporation at its value at the time of purchase or transfer to the corporation.

Thus, the deduction allowed will only be to the extent that the value of the debt at the time of purchase exceeds the amount received. *J. H. Hillman & Sons Co.,* 2 TCM 91. However, this deduction will be offset against ordinary income as a business bad debt deduction.

(6) Make an investment in a corporation, which has earning power sufficient to provide assurance against permanent loss, by putting money in this corporation for stock or debt, and then have the corporation make the loan to the new venture, provided the corporation has the power under its charter to make the loan in question.

(7) Risk advances as individual guarantor to individual to get full loss allowed in §166(f). Full bad debt deduction depends on the borrowed funds being used in the business of the borrower and the borrower's obligation being worthless at the time the guarantor pays off. But this requires inability to collect from individual; so it may not be practical.

**[¶5604]   ACCOUNTING METHODS AND TAXABLE
                              YEARS**

Having set up the business, we now have to be concerned (from a tax viewpoint) with its accounting year and methods. While much of the accounting aspects of the business will naturally be the concern of the accountant, the lawyer has to be aware of the tax consequences of the selection of an accounting period and method so he can help his client with proper preparation.

Tax accounting in many respects differs from conventional business accounting. In other cases, it is the same, but elections as to available choices have to be made.

A good deal of tax planning may go into the choice of an accounting year, for example. And as for accounting method, in addition to the usual choices as between a cash and accrual method (when that choice is available), special methods must be considered for special situations — deferring income on installment sales, treatment of long-term construction contracts.

Choices of methods also crop up when we come to valuing inventories — the major choice being between the First-In-First-Out (FIFO) and the Last-In-First-Out (LIFO) methods.

[¶5605]   PLANT AND EQUIPMENT

Once the business is ready to operate, a major expenditure will involve its plant and equipment. And here tax considerations can have a decided influence on the methods of acquisition and maintenance of the property. Many of these factors will, of course, be taken into account by the lawyer in planning with the client the setting up of the business (in projecting capital needs, for example, the availability of tax credits and deductions can play a major role).

We have many choices as to how necessary plant and equipment is acquired, maintained and charged off. First, we can either lease or purchase plant and equipment, and if we own it, we can convert it into working cash by a sale-leaseback.

In purchasing plant and equipment we have these tax opportunities:

(1) The 7% investment credit.

(2) The 20% first year writeoff of equipment.

(3) The selection of a method of depreciation—200 or 150% (fastest rate on commercial real estate) declining balance, sum-of-digits or straight line.

(4) Selecting the class life system or establishing a useful life on the old "facts and circumstances" basis.

(5) Whether to sell all the equipment or trade it in.

(6) Whether to build plant on leased or owned land.

By a proper maintenance policy, the value of plant and equipment can be kept up by deductible expenditures. You need to know what expenses can be expensed and what must be capitalized and how the automatic percentage allowance under the class life system works.

[¶5606] TAKING MONEY OUT OF THE CORPORATION

As early as the time when we are setting up a new corporation, we must consider the tax cost of taking profits out of the business and getting them into the hands of the stockholders. Projecting ahead is an important tax planning requirement in determining the pros and cons of different business forms for a particular client.

Once the corporation is in operation, the owners can take money out as compensation subject to the maximum tax on earned income to the extent of the reasonable value of the services they render to a corporation. Then, they can declare dividends which are usually fully taxable. They may be charged with the receipt of dividends if they have the corporation carry their expenses or assume other obligations or even if they borrow from the corporation.

The owners may come out better in the long run if they accumulate earnings in the corporation and cash in by selling or redeeming stock or by selling or liquidating the entire business. But there are restrictions and penalties for accumulating earnings and failing to distribute the earnings of a personal holding company.

When money has been accumulated in the corporation, it may be taken down at capital gain rates by sale of stock, by liquidation, partial or complete, or be redemption of stock. But we must watch the collapsible corporation rules and stay within one of the several available methods of redeeming or liquidating our investment on a capital gains basis. See ¶5608.3.

[¶5607] PLANNING FOR CAPITAL TRANSACTIONS

Special tax breaks are available for gains arising from capital transactions —deals involving sales other than in the ordinary course of business or income earned by investment property.

However, it is often possible, by casting a proposed course of action in a different mold, to convert what would otherwise be ordinary income into tax-favored capital gain. To do this, and to get the advantages of capital gain treatment in any event, it is necessary to know and follow the specific requirements written into the tax law.

[¶5607.1] Advantages of Capital Gain Treatment

The advantage of capital gain treatment is the preferential tax rate. Basically, if you qualify for capital gain treatment, only half your gain is taxable if you're an individual. And if your gain falls in the more-than-50% bracket (so that the effective rate—taking into account that only half the gain is taxed—exceeds 25%), the 25% ceiling applies on the first $50,000. This is achieved by electing to use the alternative tax. Half of the excess, after 1972, is taxable at regular rates.

Corporations get a somewhat similar treatment. Here, you can have your capital gains taxable at ordinary rates. Or you can elect an alternative tax of 30%.

Since the lowest corporate rate on the first $25,000 of ordinary income is 22%, you'll elect to use the alternative tax only when the ordinary income exceeds $25,000.

To get capital gain treatment, you need two things: (1) property that qualifies for capital gains treatment—capital assets, trade or business assets; (2) a sale or exchange—an actual sale or exchange or a transaction which by law is treated as if it were a sale or exchange. Otherwise, your gain will give you ordinary income, not capital gain.

Not all capital gains qualify for the preferred tax treatment. Only long-term gains get that treatment. To have a long-term gain, you need a holding period for your property of more than six months. The normal rule is that the holding period begins the day after you buy and ends on the day you sell. Also, you figure in terms of months, not in terms of days. For individuals, one-half of capital gains to the extent that they exceed the net short-term capital loss and, for corporations, the ratio of the difference between the tax rate for capital gains and the general corporate tax rate is considered tax-preference income subject to the minimum tax (IRC §56-58).

[¶5608] HOW TO CONVERT POTENTIAL ORDINARY INCOME TO CAPITAL GAIN

Proper planning can often convert what would otherwise have been ordinary income into tax-favored, long-term capital gain. The various techniques that may be applied are discussed below.

[¶5608.1] Compensation and Professional Fees into Capital Gain

Salary or other compensation from the job can be turned into capital gain by:

(1) Stock Options—If he has the option to buy stock of his employer for 100% of the fair market value at the time the option is granted and other technical requirements of §422 are met, the employee has this tax saving: The

dollar difference between the option price at the time of grant and at the time of exercise is not taxed to the employee as compensation income when he exercises the option (but is considered a tax preference subject to the minimum tax). This increase in value is taxed at the capital gain rate only when the stock is finally sold.

(2) Stock Warrants—When you buy a warrant from your employer you pay the ordinary income rate on any excess in value of the warrant at the time received over the purchase price; increase in value of the stock will be reflected in the value of the warrant which can be sold after six months at the capital gain rate.

(3) Stock Purchase—The employer finances or helps you finance the purchase of stock. If you are firmly committed you realize capital gain on sale; no tax if the company redeems the stock when you die.

(4) Profit-Sharing or Pension Plan—Up to 15% of your compensation can be paid tax free in the form of a contribution to a profit-sharing trust. If paid to you in a lump sum upon retirement, employer contributions are taxable under favorable special rates.

(5) Restricted Property—Restricted stock or other property given in compensation for services is taxable to the employee as though it were unrestricted. But if his right to the property is subject to a substantial risk of forfeiture, then it is not taxable to him until it becomes nonforfeitable unless he elects to have it taxed to him on receipt. See IRC §83.

(6) Stock With Low Value—There is little or no tax upon the receipt of stock with low or only nominal value when received; if it has growth possibilities, the stock can be sold later, with the growth taxed as capital gain. Corporations sometimes organize new subsidiaries to undertake new projects. Selling stock at the beginning, when the value is low, to employees gives them the opportunity of cashing in at capital gain rates if the subsidiary is very successful.

(7) Incorporating Your Talent—This is done by actors and other professionals. The corporation should have some outside stockholders and engage in producing and other activities rather than merely representing the star. The star, in fact, might have no contract with his own corporation. Subsequent sale of the stock can give capital gain.

(8) Sale of Properties in Related Fields—Taking advantage of your talent to pick up properties in related fields can set up capital gain opportunities. For example, a motion picture producer was able to pick up some stories with movie possibilities and realize capital gain on selling them. This was not ordinary income because his business was producing pictures, not buying and selling stories.

(9) Combine Salesmanship With a Distributorship—Your salesmanship can build up the value of your business. If the distributorship involves a capital investment in inventory, subsequent sale or cancellation of the distributorship will then give you capital gain.

(10) Professional Fee in Stock of Company About to Go Public—If you are willing to take your chances on the company's future, look for an opportunity to buy the stock before it is offered to the public. At that time, the stock's future value is still uncertain (contingencies usually still have to be met before the public offering can be made). So you can pay a price based on what the company has at that time (i.e., its book value)—even if shortly after that the public is willing to pay more. Then later when you sell, you have capital gain for the increase over the price you paid. Two cases have approved capital gains in this type of arrangement: *Berckmans,* TC Memo 1961-100; *McNatt,* 321 F.2d 143.

[¶5608.2]   Dividends into Capital Gain

Here are some ways you can turn dividends into capital gains:

(1) Sale Before Stock Goes Ex-Dividend—If you sell after a big dividend has been declared but before the record date determining eligibility, the dividend, reflected in the sales price, will be taxable as capital gain instead of as ordinary income.

(2) Sale After Stock Goes Ex-Dividend—If a corporation buys stock before the date of dividend, and sells the stock immediately after it goes ex-dividend, low capital gain rate is changed to even lower ordinary income rate. Dividend is reflected as a capital loss, to be offset against other capital gain. 85% dividend deduction reduces tax rate on dividend to maximum of 7.2%. But this method is now severely limited; corporation must hold the stock at least 16 days.

(3) Sell Short Before Stock Goes Ex-Dividend—Cover the sale after it goes ex-dividend. Assuming the stock drops by an amount equal to the dividend, this allows you to convert a capital loss into an ordinary deduction by creating a capital gain. Assuming you have a capital loss (not otherwise useful) before the deal, you can use that loss to offset the gain you'll realize on covering the short sale. But since the stock paid a dividend while you were short, you have to pay out that amount. And that is an ordinary deduction. *Note:* If you buy a call to assure that you'll be able to buy the stock at pre-dividend date price less the dividend, the Tax Court says you can't deduct your short dividend (*Main Line Distributors,* CA-6, 321 F.2d 562, *aff'g* 37 TC 1090). So you have to take your chances that the price will fall by about the amount of the dividend.

468

(4) Mutual Funds—Dividends are taxed as capital gains to the extent they arise from corporate capital gains.

(5) Low-Dividend Stock—If you're in a high bracket, buy into corporations with policy of plowing back earnings rather than distributing them; increase in value will be capital gain when you sell the stock.

(6) Preferred Stock—Unpaid preferred dividends included in the redemption price pay tax at the capital gain rate instead of at the ordinary income rate.

(7) Run Dividends Through Your Corporation—A corporation gets an 85% credit for dividends received from another corporation; this isn't a capital gain angle, but you can cut your taxable dividends 85% by having your corporation hold your stock — a better tax break than capital gains.

(8) Dividends in Kind—If property has appreciated in value, the corporate tax on the appreciation is avoided by distributing the property itself, rather than selling it and distributing the proceeds. But if property is depreciable, the corporation may realize gain under §1245 or §1250.

(9) Return of Capital Dividends Is Available—Some corporations—including closed-end regulated investment companies—have large paper losses (on securities they've held since before the depression of the 1930s). Each year they sell enough of those loss securities to create a loss sufficient to wipe out their current earnings—for tax purposes. So any dividends they pay are tax free until basis is recovered; after that those dividends are taxed as capital gains.

[¶5608.3] Corporate Profits into Stockholders' Capital Gains

Here are tested and approved methods of cashing in on your corporation's increased value via the capital gain route.

(1) Sale to Outsiders—This is the safest way to turn stock appreciation reflecting accumulated corporate profits into capital gain. Preferred stock can be sold without sacrificing voting control, provided it was original stock or stock issued for new capital.

(2) Disproportionate Redemptions—You can get capital gain by having your corporation redeem part of your stock. But, you have to end up with less than 80% of the common stock interest you had in the corporation before your stock was redeemed, as well as less than 50% of the corporation's voting stock.

(3) Complete Redemption of One Stockholder's Interest—You can get capital gain if your entire interest is redeemed and you are not deemed still to be a stockholder because of others' holdings. But you can continue on as a creditor.

(4) Complete Liquidation of the Corporation—This lets the stockholders pull out the corporation's accumulated earnings at capital gain rates. And if they

want to sell off the corporation's assets, that can be done via a 12-month liquidation without a double tax.

(5) Partial Liquidation — Where there is a contraction of the business, stockholders can pull out part of the corporation's profits at capital gain rates via a partial liquidation.

(6) Spin-offs, Split-offs, and Split-ups—Dividing the corporate property into one or more additional corporations, with the original stockholders becoming stockholders in the new companies tax free, sets up opportunities in the future to sell off some of the new companies at capital gains.

(7) Selling the Operating Assets — Continuing as an investment company after selling off the operating assets lets you avoid capital gain on liquidation of the non-operating (investment) assets.

[¶5608.4] Interest into Capital Gain

Opportunities to turn interest income into capital gains are very often overlooked. Here are some of them.

(1) Redemption of Original Issue Discount Obligations Before Maturity— Part of the discount can be converted into capital gain. But you must be prepared to show there was no collusion between you and the issuing corporation to get early redemption. Original issue discount is required to be included in the holder's income on a ratable basis over the life of the bond (IRC §1232). As he includes the discount in income, his basis is correspondingly increased. When the bond is redeemed before maturity, he has capital gain based on his adjusted basis in the absence of collusion.

(2) Mortgages, etc., Nearing Maturity — By selling before maturity date, anything that would be taxable as ordinary income will become capital gain.

[¶5608.5] Rents and Royalties into Capital Gain

Here's another area where good opportunities are often overlooked. Here are some of them.

(1) Sublet Lease— Rent from sub-lease of a leasehold is ordinary income. Sell the leasehold, and try for capital gain.

(2) Sale Back of Lease— Business profits may be attributable in part to a low rent for a favorable location. If the landlord will pay to recover the property, gain on the sale back will be capital gain.

(3) Sale v. License of Patent— Transfer of the right to make, use and sell is a sale, taxed as capital gain. Transfer of anything less is a license, taxed as ordinary income.

(4) Copyright—Royalties from a copyrighted book, painting, composition, etc., are ordinary income. If transferred to a corporation, the profits can be turned into capital gain by liquidation of the corporation. But beware of the "collapsible" and personal holding company rules.

(5) Improvements to Rented Property—Landlord can turn ordinary income into capital gain by accepting lower rental in return for tenant's agreeing to make improvements. Value of latter becomes capital gain when the property is sold. Make sure that tenant's improvements are not required as a substitute for additional rent; otherwise their value will be taxable as rent.

(6) Inventions—Professional or amateur inventors, or investors who finance inventions, can get capital gain treatment by transferring the rights to make, use and sell. Same applies to transfer of an undivided interest in an invention.

【¶5608.6】 Business Operations Get Capital Gain

Capital gain opportunity isn't limited to salary and investment assets. Here are six ways business operations can be used to produce capital gain.

(1) Gain on the sale of operating equipment.

(2) Gain on the sale of equipment used by salesmen, demonstrators, etc.

(3) Gain on the sale of assets leased to customers.

(4) Gain on the sale of favorable contracts.

(5) Gain on the sale of franchises, patents, trademarks, good will.

(6) Gain on the sale of partnership interests.

【¶5609】 INVESTMENT PLANNING

Many investments are of particular appeal because of the "tax shelter" or other tax advantage they may offer, subject to the possible effect of the added tax on tax preferences (IRC §56-58).

The factors which give tax shelter to an investment are:

(1) The yield of tax-free income — e.g., tax exempt bonds.

(2) A deduction from income which has no relationship to actual costs — e.g., the percentage depletion deduction allowed against income from oil, gas and minerals.

(3) A return of capital tax free while investment yield is maintained and money value of the property may be maintained — e.g., income buildings, where the cost is returned tax free via depreciation allowance, while inflation and deductible repairs may maintain — and even enhance — the value of the property.

(4) An assured buildup in value which can be realized tax free — e.g., life insurance proceeds.

(5) An assured buildup in value which can either be realized at capital gains rates or be used to produce income based on matured values — e.g., a citrus grove, a timber tract, in which natural growth enhances value in such a way that higher values cannot be taxed until the property is sold.

(6) Definite buildup in value which cannot be taxed until realized and on which a substantial part of the realization can be indefinitely postponed—e.g., building up a cattle herd in which value is enhanced by both growth and propagation.

(7) Capital value which can be acquired with substantially deductible expenses—e.g., oil drilling, where intangible drilling expenses and dry holes can be charged off against other income, while oil strikes constitute capital largely purchased with tax money.

(8) Investments with a high degree of security against loss and also a potential of sizable capital gain — e.g., convertible bonds.

(9) Investment in which capital loss can be deducted against ordinary income over as many years as necessary at the rate of $1,000 a year, and in which the prospect of capital gain is high in relation to the impact of possible loss — e.g., common stock warrants.

(10) Investment yields having special protection — e.g., dividends received by a corporation.

(11) Income received at capital gain rates—e.g., sale of timber, mutual fund dividends.

(12) Income which can be taken or reported currently or postponed—e.g., interest on E bonds, forfeitable restricted property as compensation for services.

[¶5610] INVESTMENTS IN REAL ESTATE

From the tax and financial standpoint, real estate is a highly flexible and versatile type of asset. Here are 19 tax features which can be used to bring about profitable real estate deals.

(1) Real estate can be purchased or rented, sold or leased, with different tax results. A piece of real estate can be divided into different types of fees, leasehold and mortgage investments, each tailored to the tax position of its owner.

(2) When sold at a loss, the loss may be fully deductible.

(3) When sold at a profit all or part of the gain may be qualified for a favorable capital gains treatment.

(4) When leased, the cost of occupancy can be charged off fully.

(5) A properly arranged security deposit isn't taxed until the end of the lease.

(6) When owned, much of the cost of the investment can be recovered tax free by depreciation deductions. This reduces the size of the investment, and steps up the yield which a real estate investment can show.

(7) Ownership can be financed in a way that gives the owner depreciation charges on the mortgagee's investment, increasing his equity with tax-free funds.

(8) The cost of land can be made tax deductible by a sale, followed by leaseback for a long period. The investment in the building is recovered tax free through depreciation charges.

(9) The owner of real estate may be able to get his property improved tax free by having his tenant make the improvements.

(10) The owner can elect to deduct or capitalize interest and taxes paid to carry unimproved property.

(11) The owner of real estate can sometimes build up the value of his holdings by tax-deductible repair expenditures.

(12) The ownership of real estate can be held in whatever entity—partnership, corporation, trust or personal ownership—will best protect the income from tax. When held in corporate ownership, income can accumulate at lower tax rates than might apply if personally owned. The tax savings can be applied to build up equity and future capital gain by improving the property and paying off mortgages.

(13) Tax on the sale of real estate may be postponed by electing the installment method of sale, a deferred payment sale, or by using option agreements, executory contracts, conditional contracts, leases with purchase options, escrow arrangements and contingent price arrangements.

(14) Even after an installment sale, we may be able to change our minds to have the gain taxed earlier, if that should prove to be desirable, by disposing of the installment obligations.

(15) On the sale of real estate, there are methods of getting cash in advance, yet deferring the taxability of gain.

(16) Real estate held for investment can be built up in value and traded tax free for other real estate to be held for investment.

(17) Leases can be cancelled for money which is taxed at capital gain.

(18) Condemnation awards can be received without tax if reinvested in real estate.

(19) A residence can be sold without capital gain tax if the proceeds are used to buy or build a new residence—or without reinvestment when sold by an over-65 individual.

[¶5611] **SHIFTING INCOME IN THE FAMILY**

Part of the answer to the problem of accumulating funds for education, retirement, etc. lies in getting income into lower brackets. Here's a list of some methods that might be used:

(1) *Getting Income to Relatives*—for example, to a child who has no income. Transferring $500 of annual income to a child so that it is taxable to him instead of to you can save $250 a year if you are in the 50% tax bracket. And the savings can be multiplied by the number of children involved. It doesn't matter how much income we shift if the child is under 19 or if he is at school. We can still claim the personal exemption for the child on our return as long as we are supplying his chief support. On the other hand, a man who is supporting a parent out of current income might save a good deal in income taxes if he could transfer income so that it will be taxable to the parent. Each parent who is over 65 gets a double exemption. Besides, the Code gives a retired person over 65 a retirement income credit on up to $1,524 ($2,286 on a joint return, both 65 or over) a year of investment income. Thus a man who shifts $3,600 of his income to parents can save about $1,800 if he is in the 50% bracket.

The combination of the personal exemptions of $750 each plus the $100 dividend exclusion permits the tax-free transfer of $850 of investment income to a child or other member of the family who has no other income. Where the child is under 19 or a full-time student even though he files a separate return and has income in excess of the amount of the personal exemption the parent still may claim his child as a dependent provided he furnishes 50% or more of his support. The child may claim a $1,300 low-income allowance, but only to offset his or her own earned income.

(2) *Passing up the income-splitting device normally used by the husband and wife*—letting each make a separate return—and letting each pay his or her own medical expenses or charitable contributions. The law limits the deduction for those items to percentage computations. Sometimes it is possible to gain considerably by having the husband and wife pay their own costs, or those of their direct dependents.

(3) *Moving property and its income into lower bracket members of the family* —There you figure the graduated tax of a child, or a parent, against your own. Then you try to find the gift tax cost of what you can give them in income-producing property. That may involve paying a gift tax. In the end, you may find much lower tax in the assignments.

(4) *Managing investments—shifting income within the family so one member fairly charges the other for the right to use the property*—There you begin to get into deductions charged the heavy bracket taxpayer—and income assumed by the lower bracket child, father, or dependent.

474

(5) *Incorporating family-owned property*—or family-owned business in order to get the advantages of stepped-up costs for assets (paying capital gains tax) and lots of other advantages that come with the incorporation of the family business. The corporation can be a tax shelter but we must see that business policy and the character of investments afford protection from the penalty tax aimed at a tight dividend policy and the use of incorporated pocketbooks.

(6) *Splitting a family business into a partnership*—or subdividing existing partnerships to get further income splitting can keep family business income in lower brackets. Limited partnerships can also be useful planning instruments. Great care must be exercised in drawing partnership agreements because they have so serious an impact on the tax result.

(7) *Planning new ventures, new investments, new undertakings—so that the members of the family ratably take their share of income and losses that come out of the deal*—For example, you may (without any gift tax) take a couple of members in the family into a new business, a limited partnership, a fling at anything else. And they or you might gain—without tax cost to you.

(8) *Buying property through estates by entirety, or joint tenancies or tenancies in common*—Each of these set-ups has its distinct tax pros and cons you may want to consider with members of the family.

(9) *Setting up family insurance in the most advantageous manner*—the net protection available may vary widely as ownership and premium paying responsibility falls on the insured, members of his family, a trust, a corporation.

(10) *Setting up interfamily annuities — in which one member of a family transfers something for income from another*—These might produce considerable savings without gift taxes—and no other types of taxes at the time of the transfer — or for a long period after that.

(11) *Setting up family foundations* in which family income and capital can be conserved for educational, charitable, scientific and religious work.

(12) *Careful nursing of interfamily deals for interest, pay, rent or anything else they may have between them*— penalty for sloppiness is usually loss of the deduction for the loss. There's a lot of ritual to watch here if you want the tax saving.

(13) *Making sure that alimony or separation payments allot the tax between the couple fairly*— there's a lot to be studied by the lawyer making these arrangements if he seeks the full deduction for the paying spouse.

•

For Further Reference . . .

Caldwell, Bernard L., Tax Factors Which Affect Real Estate Values, *Appraisal Journal,* October 1964.

Tax Planning (2 vol. looseleaf service), Institute for Business Planning, Englewood Cliffs, N.J.

TECHNOLOGICAL PROPERTY

[¶5701] Millions of dollars are spent annually to create and enhance the value of this kind of property. It includes inventions, designs, plans and drawings, models, tooling, test data, etc. It may be patented, in which case it includes the patent. It may be held as a trade secret (See ¶3001 et seq.).

The practicing lawyer will come into contact with this kind of property in many transactions—employment; sale of a business; manufacturing, research, and distribution contracts; licensing arrangements; international investments; etc. When he does, he will be well advised to seek the cooperation of an experienced patent lawyer who is a specialist in the protection of intellectual property—namely, patents, inventions, designs, know-how, trade secrets and the like and related problems of unfair competition.

Certainly the prosecution of a patent application before the Patent Office to secure the issuance of a patent should be handled by a patent specialist. Beyond that, the drafting of license agreements and other conveyances respecting patents is highly technical and is best performed by, or after consultation with, a patent man.

Provisions relating to "hold harmless," "most favored nation," "validity," "policing of infringement," are not frequently encountered outside the realm of patent licenses. Licensing and cross-licensing provisions may involve serious antitrust aspects. An assignment of an undivided interest in a patent creates rights that are not paralleled in any other branch of the law.

Finally, the value of patents and the course to be pursued in exploiting them frequently hinge on technical knowledge and conceptions which are likely to be beyond most business lawyers. But to work effectively with a patent lawyer and to bring his knowledge to bear on the objectives of your business clients, it is important to know the broad procedures and alternatives in this area. These comments are intended to help the general lawyer and the patent specialist to work more fruitfully together.

In drafting a license, the advice of general counsel as to business organization, financing, tax aspects, etc., is essential. Similarly, advice of general counsel is essential to mapping out a patent exploitation program within the broad framework of a corporate venture; and in litigation, consultation as to broad tactics, goals, settlement, etc., is essential. Patent bar associations disapprove of fee-splitting with a referring attorney for services rendered exclusively by the patent attorney. However, this rule does not prevent the apportioning of fees on a *quantum meruit* basis when general and patent counsels work together.

The practicing lawyer will probably approach a problem involving technological property as an invention, a new idea which has great potential merit, a research program for which his client has great hopes, etc. He will be expected to advise on ownership, protection, exploitation, minimization of tax

476

impact, etc. There are so many facets to this kind of problem that we will here content ourselves with laying them out in checklist form:

1. Ownership: Generally, he who pays, owns or should own, but it will usually be desirable to put into effect an agreement making ownership clear and defining the extent and the obligations of ownership. If the development is being worked out in the client's own plant, the necessary agreements will be with employee. If it is being done on a research and development contract with another company, a research and development contract will be necessary. If somebody else already owns the invention which the client is to exploit, an assignment or license agreement will be called for.

2. Employee Agreements: If there is no agreement with an employee, the employer may be entitled to a "shop-right" in the employee's invention and may be entitled to claim ownership under an implied agreement to assign. If the employee has been hired to invent or in a capacity which gave rise to the expectation that he would assign his invention to the employer, the courts will usually recognize an obligation to assign the invention to the employer. No matter what capacity an employee works in, if he patents an invention he conceived and developed on the job, the employer has a "shop-right" to use the invention in his own business, but only if the invention was developed during working hours, on the company's time, and with its materials. To avoid the uncertainty of proof of an implied obligation to assign and the non-exclusivity and other limitations of the shop-right, it is important to get a written agreement with an employee who is likely to contribute to an invention, obligating him to assign it to the employer. Moreover, full protection for the employer requires more than creating an obligation to assign patent rights. It may be just as important to place him under obligation not to disclose secret or confidential information or knowledge obtained during his employment for a period of time after he leaves that employment. It may be desirable to restrict him from engaging in any activity in a specified field of industry or research and development for a period of time after termination. An employee can be obligated to assign improvements to an invention made after employment, provided they relate to an invention made during employment. See also ¶2311 of this volume, and IBP FORMS OF BUSINESS AGREEMENTS.

3. Research and Development Contracts: Here the problem of specifying your client's right to patents and placing restrictions on the other party's use of confidential information is somewhat akin to that encountered in the employment agreement. The other party's trading power may be greater than an employee's, so that it may be necessary to cross-license improvements or give the other party rights outside your client's line of business. This agreement should specify ownership of drawings, plans, models, tools, etc. It should define the basis of compensation, specify reporting obligations, and establish other appropriate controls over the progress of the work, its direction, and the amount of time consumed in it. However, such arrangements should be checked under the anti-trust laws. For an appropriate agreement see IBP FORMS OF BUSINESS AGREEMENTS looseleaf Service.

4. To Patent or Not: Patenting involves ultimate public disclosure. A new development may conceivably get more protection if it is kept as a trade secret. Or, the probable patent protection may be so meager that it is not worth the expense, or it is considered better to rely on trade name, nondisclosure of techniques, accumulation of know-how, etc. Or, the business prospect may be worthwhile but not sufficient to justify the cost of patenting. As a general rule, if the invention is to be commercialized, patenting is warranted.

5. What Kinds of Patent Protection Are Available? A patent can be obtained for any "new and useful process, machine, manufacture or composition of matter, or any new and useful improvement thereof." New methods, new combinations, and new designs have been patented. On the other hand, you won't get a patent for a new or better idea for doing business. The advice of a patent lawyer is essential on the prospective patentability of a new development.

6. Patent Searches: In a preliminary patent search, sometimes called a patentability search, the object is to see whether there are any patents outstanding which would indicate that the proposed development is not novel and that it would therefore be a waste of money to file an application. It is also designed to turn up matters which are related and which may be of help to the patent attorney in preparing the patent application. There are other types of patent searches:

(a) Validity Search — designed to find earlier patents which would throw doubt upon the validity of a patent which has been interfering or threatens to interfere with the client's business. This is an extensive search which is usually made as a basis for a patent lawsuit contesting the validity of a patent.

(b) Infringement Search — to determine if a proposed product or improvement will infringe on the claims of an unexpired patent.

(c) Assignment Search — to determine who is the present recorded owner of a particular patent.

(d) Index Search — to determine what patents have been issued to a particular inventor or patent holder.

7. When to Apply: There are several considerations here, most of which involve meeting statutory requirements:

(a) If the invention is described in a publication, used publicly, or placed on sale by the inventor, it is necessary for the inventor to apply for the patent within one year from the time of publication, use, or sale.

478

(b) It is necessary to file before the first patenting abroad on an application filed more than a year before the U.S. filing date.

(c) Where two or more parties are competing for a patent on the same invention, the first to file prevails in the great majority of cases. The other party has the very heavy burden of proof that he is the first inventor.

8. Who Should Apply: Only the inventor should apply. Patents issued in the name of anyone other than the true inventor or inventors are invalid if the facts are proven except where it can be shown that a wrong party was included through error and without any deceptive intent. The employer has no right to designate an applicant who is not the true inventor. The inventor is the one who takes the inventive step. If there is more than one person, they should join in the application.

9. Establishing the Date of Invention: This is important if two or more applicants claim the invention or where validity is challenged on the basis that the invention was known before the date of the applicant's discovery. There is a practice among inventors of writing a description of the invention, executing it before a notary public, mailing it to themselves by registered mail, and locking it up to provide proof of date of invention should that ever become necessary. This is of doubtful value since at best it shows only conception. An early date of conception is of little value unless it can be shown that it was followed by diligence in adapting and perfecting the invention. The acts which help in establishing priority of invention are these: reduction to practice, diligence in adapting and perfecting the invention, disclosure to others, making the first written description and the first drawing, and then only, early conception. The date of reduction to practice is the most decisive factor bearing on the date of invention. Filing an application is constructive reduction to practice, and early filing avoids expensive proof that otherwise would be required. But if an adverse claim is based on invention before filing, it requires corroboration to establish date of invention, and disclosure of all essential details of the invention to others is important in proving not only conception but also diligence and reduction to practice. Diaries and laboratory notes are recommended as a means of recording the progress of an invention, its conception, due diligence in reducing it to practice, etc.

10. Foreign Patents: The decision whether or not to seek foreign patents involves a business judgment on the potential for the product in foreign markets, the value of the protection afforded there, the best place for the manufacture and distribution of the product in foreign markets, the pattern of exploitation, etc. Foreign patent applications involve translations, other heavy expenses, time limitations. Once the decision to seek foreign patent protection is made, its execution has to be left to patent counsel.

11. Assignment Versus Licensing of Patent: This question comes up in acquiring rights under a patent or in disposing of patent rights. A patent is assigned when all the rights under it are granted to another party. It's a license when something less than full rights are granted; i.e., the right to use, to make, or to sell is limited. A territorial grant, full rights of the patent confined to a particular geographic area, is an assignment. In deciding whether to make an instrument an assignment or merely a license, the considerations are these:

(a) Assignments should be recorded; licenses need not be.

(b) All owners of title must join in suit against an infringer but a licensee need not be joined (except in limited cases).

(c) Receipts from an assignment, although a percentage royalty, may be treated as capital gains, whereas receipts from a license are fully taxable as ordinary income. License payments may be deducted; the price paid for an assignment may be depreciated. Even when the price is on a percentage basis, under the *Associated Patentee* case (4 TC 979) — these percentage payments may be deducted as depreciation of the patent.

For forms of assignment and licensing agreements see IBP FORMS OF BUSINESS AGREEMENTS.

12. Negotiating and Drafting a Patent: This is an intricate art. The extent of the license and limitations placed upon it must be defined. These may be geographic, confined to fields of industry or application, etc. Many technical phases, familiar only to patent lawyers, must be covered — improvements, estoppel against challenging validity, the right and duty to sue for infringement, whether the license is exclusive or nonexclusive. If it is exclusive, royalties should be guaranteed or the continued exclusivity should be contingent upon the maintenance of minimum royalties. The determination of guaranteed and minimum royalties is something of an art. The negotiation of the royalty rate, the price to which the royalty will attach, the definition of sales — these are of the utmost importance. For guidance in drafting a licensing agreements, see IBP FORMS OF BUSINESS AGREEMENT; Ellis on PATENT LICENSES; PATENT LICENSING, Practising Law Institute.

13. Infringement: Sometimes a client will have a question as to whether to license or infringe a patent. Damages for infringement may be collectible for a period of six years preceding the date of instituting the suit for infringement. In the event of a wilful infringement, there may be triple damages. The big risk in infringing is the danger of being forced to discontinue a business in which heavy investment has been made. Preliminary injunctions are seldom obtained in patent suits because, among other reasons, if the suit fails, the party enjoined would have a case for heavy damages against the party claiming infringement. To get a preliminary injunction, it has to be shown that irreparable harm would be done if the infringement continued, that the validity of the patent is clear, and that the infringement is beyond any reasonable doubt. Injunctions are almost always granted when infringement has been adjudicated, but there have been cases where injunction was denied the victor in an infringement suit on the basis that the injury to the infringer would be greater than the benefit to the owner of the patent. Of course, the owner of the patent gets an accounting of profits. In patent infringement suits, agreements with others executed in good faith before the beginning of the suit have been held to set a standard for reasonable royalty.

14. Misuse of Patent: This can render a patent unenforceable in an infringement suit. A violation of the antitrust laws will be a misuse. A patent gives its owner the right to exclude others from making, using, or selling the thing patented; and this right may be exercised by infringement suits or by granting a license to make, use or sell. However, when the owner seeks to control unpatented things or otherwise unlawfully restricts the licensee by contract, he is misusing his patent. The owner of a patent on a motion picture projector could not enforce his patent in an infringement and contributory infringement action where he sought to compel the purchase from him of a patented film used in the projector (*Motion Picture Patent Company v. Universal Film Manufacturing Company,* 243 US 502). See also *Mercoid Corp. v. Midcontinent Company,* 320 US 661. A patentee may fix the price at which a manufacturing licensee may sell a patented article (*U.S. v. General Electric Company,* 272 US 476) but may not fix a resale price of a patented product once sold (*U.S. v. Univis Lens Company,* 360 US 241). The owner of a license may not combine with another patentee under a cross-license agreement to fix prices under their respective patents. It is a misuse for a patent owner to compel a prospective licensee to take a license on patents he does not want in order to obtain a license under the patent he does want.

15. Contributory Infringement: Selling a component of a patented machine, manufacture combination or composition, or a material or apparatus for use in practicing a patented process, constituting a material part of the invention, *knowing the thing sold to be specially made or specially adapted for use in an infringement of the patent and not a stable article or commodity of commerce suitable for substantial noninfringing use,* constitutes contributory infringement. The contributory infringer can be held liable for damages. However, the purchaser of a patentable device may acquire repair or replacement parts from any source and neither the supplier nor the customer is guilty of contributory patent infringement (*Convertible Top Replacement Co. v. Aro Manufacturing Co.,* 365 US 336). However, supplying replacement parts to an infringing device is contributory infringement.

16. Know-How and Technical Services: Technological property accumulated from research and experience may not be patentable and still be developed into an asset which can be sold or licensed. The thing is to make these intangibles as tangible as possible. This frequently has to be accomplished by careful and sometimes exhaustive definition. An idea must be reduced to concrete form. It must be spelled out. The elements of know-how must be detailed—including such things as these: plans, calculations, design sheets, design data, manuals, drawings, processes and materials, and performance and purchasing specifications, test data, operating instructions, assistance in selecting factory sites, supplying of engineers and technicians for installing machinery, assistance in purchase of machinery, technical service bulletins, special assistance by engineers and other technicians, architectural assistance, including factory layouts, provision and training of key personnel.

Spell out secrecy agreements on know-how, and require that the specified limitations are to be imposed on employees. Specify that all information is to be returned on termination of the agreement.

Cover obligation to meet expenses of providing personnel and transmitting information. Specify clearly the number of personnel to be provided, and the time limits within which information is to be made available. If sublicensing is permitted, require the licensor to be responsible for the sublicensee's performance in every respect.

In know-how licenses, duration is an important factor. The average life of know-how is 5 years and dissipates rapidly as the product or service becomes better known. Once know-how becomes worthless, the license arrangement is weakened and is subject to abuse by the licensee. The license should be geared to the lifetime of the know-how or process, or to a lesser time period if given on an experimental basis.

Although difficult to protect, know-how can be safeguarded by restrictive covenants whereby the licensee agrees not to divulge trade secrets to others or to use it himself after the license expires. This restrictive covenant should also prohibit disclosure to other than key personnel in the licensee's organization and provide for the prompt return of materials and processes on the expiration date of the license.

Know-how involves, in part, trade secrets, formulae, processes, designs, accumulated technical experience, skills, and other elements. The courts have not brought down a clear decision on the status of know-how as a capital asset, and the question must be considered undecided. However, there is a strong professional opinion that know-how is property, and thus, qualifies as a capital asset. In light of this undecided state of the law with respect to know-how, it is well to shape know-how transactions to emphasize secret formulae, unpatented inventions or secret processes evidenced by tangibles, drawings or writings. These would seem most likely to be deemed a capital asset available for capital gain treatment if sold. Of course, patents and trademarks provide an even stronger assurance of capital gain treatment.

For forms dealing with sales and licenses of know-how, see IBP FORMS OF BUSINESS AGREEMENTS looseleaf Service.

●

For Further Reference . . .
American Jurisprudence, Patents.
Calvert, *Patent Practice and Management,* Reinhold.
Costas, Peter L., and Harris, Daniel E., Patents, Trademarks and Copyrights — The Legal Monopolies, *Connecticut Bar Journal,* December 1962.
Davis, et al., *Patent Licensing,* Practising Law Institute, New York, N.Y.
Ellis, *Patent Licenses, Patent Assignments.*
Ellis, *Trade Secrets.*
Forms of Business Agreements looseleaf Service. Institute for Business Planning, Englewood Cliffs, N.J.
Lindsey, *Plagiarism and Originality,* Harper and Row.
Mulder, John E., Voltz, Marlin M., and McDonald, Donald, *The Drafting of Partnership Agreements,* Joint Committee on Continuing Legal Education.
Navin, *Patents,* Practising Law Institute, New York, N.Y.
Seidel, Arthur H., *What the General Practitioner Should Know About Patent Law and Practice,* Joint Committee on Continuing Legal Education.
Woodling, *Inventions and Their Protection,* Clark Boardman.

TRADEMARKS AND TRADE NAMES

[¶5801]   Trademarks indicate origin, serve to assure the quality of goods or services with which they are associated and, through advertising, operate to create and maintain a demand for the goods or services. The practitioner with business clients should, therefore, have a basic familiarity with trademark law. The name which a corporation uses to market its goods or services, be it the corporate name or a trade name assumed for use in connection with a portion of the corporate business, may also have great value.

Trademarks, unlike patents and copyrights, are not exclusively with the federal domain. Federal power to regulate trademarks is based on the commerce clause and in the past a narrower view of "interstate commerce" has been adopted than in other branches of the law. For example, Federal registration of trademarks has been denied hotels, restaurants, service stations, etc., even though their customers may come from across state lines and are solicited by interstate advertising. However, a recent registration of a service mark used in only one state may possibly reflect a new trend.

Because of the narrow view of interstate commerce taken and because most state acts make no provision for the registration of service marks, as distinguished from so-called true trademarks, that is, those used to distinguish goods, there is a big gap in the trademark system.

This gap is not, however, a complete void but is in part filled by common law rules and principles antedating and surviving the statutory systems, state and federal. The true owner of a trademark used for goods and services may at common law prevent the unauthorized use of his mark or of a similar mark on the same or similar goods or services by another to the confusion of the public and his own detriment. Thus, while the owner of a trademark operating in a common law, "no-registration" area is not completely without legal protection for his mark, it must be recognized that the absence of registration makes the establishment of ownership difficult and encourages unscrupulous competitors to try to get away with appropriating the mark. At the same time, the absence of registration makes it difficult for even well-intentioned competitors to discover the prior mark. In any case conflicts which might have been avoided by registration are apt to flourish.

State Trademark Laws: The great diversity which exists in the terms of the various state trademark statutes rules out detailed consideration of them in this work. However, some indication of their scope and limitations will be apparent from the following comparison with the federal law:

(1) Federal provisions are broader in terms of marks registrable than any state act;

(2) Federal law gives better relief than state law, except as to penalties;

(3) Federal registration is notice to entire country (state to state);

(4) Federal registration, but not state, gives right of registration in large number of foreign countries;

(5) Federal registration, but not state, gives right to prevent importation of goods bearing infringing marks; and

(6) Federal registration by itself gives right to sue in federal courts (state registration requires other elements of federal jurisdiction).

[¶5802] FEDERAL TRADEMARK ACT

The Trademark Act of 1946, popularly known as the Lanham Act, forming Chapter 22 of Title 15 of the U.S. Code is the basic law on the subject, and is supplemented by the Trademark Rules of Practice. Section 45 of the Act defines a trademark as including "any word, name, symbol, or device, or any combination thereof adopted and used by a manufacturer or merchant to identify his goods and distinguish them from those manufactured or sold by others." These are the so-called true trademarks. But the Act also provides for the registration of service, certification, and collective marks.

"Service marks" are those used in the sale or advertising of services to distinguish those of one person from another.

"Certification marks" are those used on or in connection with the products or services of persons other than the owner of the mark to certify the origin or other characteristics of the goods or services. The Good Housekeeping "Seal of Approval" would be an example.

"Collective marks" are those used by a group to indicate membership in an organization.

In order to be eligible for registration a mark must be used in interstate commerce and not: (1) Be immoral, deceptive, or scandalous; (2) Use or simulate any kind of governmental insignia, domestic or foreign; (3) Use the name, signature or portrait of a living person, or of a deceased President of the United States, without proper consents; and (4) Not resemble a registered mark or a mark or trade name previously used in the United States by another and not abandoned.

[¶5802.1] Federal Registration

The Act sets up two registers: (1) Principal; and (2) Supplemental. The first takes so-called "true" or "technical" marks, that is, coined, arbitrary, fanciful or suggestive marks, if otherwise qualified. Marks not qualified for registration on the principal register may nevertheless be registered on the supplemental register if they are capable of distinguishing the applicant's goods and have been used in commerce for at least a year.

A mark, if otherwise eligible, may be registered on the principal register unless it consists of a mark which (1) when applied to the goods of the applicant is merely descriptive of them, or (2) when applied to the goods of the applicant is primarily geographically descriptive or deceptively misdescriptive of them, except as indications of regional origin, or (3) is primarily merely a surname, except as it is shown that such marks have become distinctive as applied to the applicant's goods in commerce. (Proof of continuous use for five years makes out a prima facie case.)

Registration in the Principal Register: Registration here gives:
(1) Constructive notice of claim of ownership;
(2) Prima facie evidence of the validity of the registration, the registrant's ownership of the mark, and the registrant's exclusive right to the use of the mark, subject to any conditions and limitations which may be stated in the registration; and
(3) The right to prevent importation of goods bearing an infringing mark.

Registration in the Supplemental Register: Registration here gives none of this protection but it does give the registrant:
(1) The right to sue in the federal courts and statutory remedies;
(2) Possible right of registration in foreign country whose laws require prior registration in home country; and
(3) Protection against registration by another of the same or a confusingly similar mark in either register.

[¶5802.2] Applications for Registration

An application for registration must be filed in the name of the owner of the mark, include a request for registration, and must give details as to a variety of matters including the date of the applicant's first use of the mark as a trademark on or in connection with goods specified in the application, the date of the first use of the mark in interstate commerce, specifying the nature of the commerce, the manner in which the mark is used in connection with the goods, the class of merchandise according to the official classification if known to the applicant. It must also contain various averments as to ownership and right to use the mark. Further, it must be signed and verified and must include a drawing of the mark, five specimens or facsimiles, and the required filing fee. There are special rules for foreign applicants. The Patent Office will supply printed forms of applications for (1) individuals, (2) firms or (3) corporations or associations.

The drawing must be a substantially exact representation of the mark as actually used. (If the mark is incapable of representation by drawing then application must describe.) Regulations cover such matters as the type of paper and ink, the size of the sheets and margins, the heading, the character of the lines, the use of linings for showing color, and how the drawings are to be shipped. The Patent Office will make drawings when possible, at applicant's request and expense.

The five specimens should be duplicates of actually used labels, tags, containers, or displays or portions thereof if flat and not larger than the size of the drawing. If due to the mode of applying the mark or using it or the nature of the mark, specimens can't be furnished, then a photograph or other acceptable reproduction not larger than the size of the drawing may be used. If a disc recording is to be registered special regulations apply.

If on examination of the application and the accompanying papers it appears that the applicant is entitled to have his mark registered in the Principal Register it will be published in the Official Gazette and will be subject to opposition by any person who believes he'll be damaged, a period of 30 days after publication being provided for filing opposition. If the Patent Office finds a conflict between two copending applications, an interference will be instituted to determine which applicant is entitled to register. If there's no notice of opposition and no interference a certificate of registration will issue in due course.

Forms of assignment of a trademark registration and of an application for registration are set out in IBP FORMS OF BUSINESS AGREEMENTS.

[¶5802.3] Trademark Searches

To minimize the possibility of opposition or conflict a search may be run before making application for registration. While there are one or two outstanding private collections which cover state and federal registrations, and unregistered common law marks, most searches are run in the Patent Office. Word marks are classified on an alphabetical basis. Non-word marks are classified according to a system of symbol classification. There are two main locations or collections. The first comprises subsisting and expired registrations and the second published and pending registrations. The search system is not without serious deficiencies: (1) Doesn't cover prior unregistered marks; (2) Classification system is alphabetical and not phonetic and doesn't take into account synonyms and foreign equivalents; (3) Doesn't cover applications abandoned before publication; and (4) Doesn't show current use or status of mark.

Because of the weaknesses or deficiencies in the classification system an effective search requires skill and imagination on the part of the searcher, takes time, and is apt to be fairly expensive and neither attorney nor client should be taken in by those advertising "searches" at "low, low" prices.

The Patent Office also has records of assignments of registered marks and pending applications by which ownership of marks or of applications may be searched.

If an owner is to effectively protect his mark against dilution and be in a position to oppose published applications for marks, he must maintain a continuous search of the Official Gazette.

Searches such as those above discussed are best done by trademark specialists. There is one type of search that the general practitioner can make and that is via the trademark section of *Shepard's Federal Reporter Citations* which will contain a reference to every trademark litigated or mentioned in any state or federal case.

How to Preserve Exclusive Rights in a Trademark: Rights in a trademark are first acquired through *use,* that is, by selling the product with the mark affixed either to the product or its container. If the mark is to be registered, ship it to a customer in another state.

Keep a Record of Your First Use of the Mark: The following will make a good record:

(1) A copy of the invoice. The invoice must show the trademark followed by the generic description of the product.

(2) The bill of lading signed by the carrier.

(3) A letter from the buyer stating he received the product and mentioning the trademark.

This first use doesn't mean that exclusive rights have been acquired to the mark. Someone else may have been using it before—no search you make can leave you absolutely sure that your client is the first user. So don't allow the client to start extensive selling and advertising campaigns until initial test sales leave you reasonably sure there's no infringement and, as a result, the mark won't have to be abandoned.

After the first use, continued and proper use of the mark is necessary to establish your exclusive rights. What is "proper" use?

Use the trademark as an adjective only to modify the *generic name* of the product, and at least once on every page. Don't separate the trademark and the generic name with another word or any punctuation.

Use the mark in a distinctive way, that is, different type face, italics, capitals, within quotation marks, or in some way to make it more conspicuous than the other words preceding and following it.

The use of the mark must be consistent. Once adopted, the mark must be stuck to.

The client should encourage his employees, especially the sales and marketing staff and executives, to report any suspected infringement of his trademark.

[¶5803]   **PRACTICAL CONSIDERATIONS IN**
TRADEMARK MATTERS

In any approach to trademark matters, whether under the aegis of federal or state law, the general practitioner will do well to bear in mind at the outset that he is dealing with something other than a purely legal question. He is, indeed, dealing with a mixed question of business and law and many legal specialists in the trademark field have adopted the general philosophy that the business aspect predominates in importance. They will not inject themselves into the matter of selecting a mark but will recommend that the choice be left to specialists in advertising, marketing and the like; and they will go along with the idea that a mark which is good from an advertising and sales angle but legally weak is better for the client than one which is legally strong but practically weak.

Select a Mark That Is Registrable: Although registration is not obligatory, when selecting a trademark it may be well to anticipate that you will register it. So avoid adopting a mark that will be refused registration like these:

1) Name, portrait or signature of a living person without his consent.

2) Name, portrait or signature of a deceased U.S. President during the life of his widow, without her consent.

3) Flag or coat of arms of the United States, any state, municipality, or foreign nation.

4) A mark that is merely descriptive of the goods, or deceptively misdescriptive, or

5) When applied to the goods is primarily geographically descriptive or deceptively misdescriptive of the goods, or is

6) Primarily merely a surname, or

7) Resembles a trademark previously registered or used by another and not abandoned, if its use is likely to cause confusion or mistake or to deceive purchasers, or

8) Disparages or falsely suggests a connection with persons, living or dead, institutions, beliefs, or national symbols, or brings them into disrepute, or contempt, or is

9) Immoral, deceptive or scandalous.

A mark can be registered even though it is merely descriptive, or geographically descriptive, or is primarily a surname, if it has become distinctive of the registrant's goods in commerce. Five years of exclusive and continuous use prior to filing application may be accepted by the Commissioner as prima facie evidence that the mark has become distinctive. Marks that are unregistrable because of the other prohibitions noted above can never become registrable as distinctive.

[¶5804]　　　　**PROTECTING TRADE NAMES**

Trade name value may inhere in a corporate name or the name of a product. A corporate name may be protected by the creation of inactive corporations in the states in the market area. The name of a product may be protected by incorporating it in a trademark which is used and registered.

Corporate-name statutes grant only a limited protection. They merely insure that the name will be protected against subsequent adoption as a corporate name by another entity within the state and against granting of permission to a foreign corporation to do business in that state under that corporate name. The usual corporate-name section grants no protection against use of the same name as a trade name or mark; rather, the corporation must seek its relief under the non-statutory precedents available to it in the state law of unfair competition. Further, such statutes do not purport to protect a corporate trade name against names used by unincorporated businesses.

Apart from these procedures judicial protection of business names has developed as a part of the overall law of unfair competition. Suppose, however, that a first user without regard to area, desiring to expand to another city or state, encounters another user subsequent in time generally but prior in time in the expansion territory. Or, suppose that a first user generally, while not expanding to the second area, wants to prevent the use of the name in other cities or states. In many such cases the first user has successfully established its right to exclusive use; in many others, it has not. The distinguishing factor between these results seems to be the extent of public awareness in the second area of the name of the prior user in the first area at the time the subsequent user begins operation. This potential-customer knowledge is usually shown by presenting evidence of extensive advertising in the second area, although actual marketing there commenced later or not at all. The requisite consciousness of a name or mark on the part of the public in the second area may be brought about not only by commercial advertising, but also by the spread of a reputation resulting when residents of the second area visit the first and are impressed by the products or services offered by the party seeking protection. Or, a strong reputation in non-market areas may result from the peculiar circumstances of the origination and early history of a business.

Forms of agreements permitting the use of names and likenesses are set out in IBP FORMS OF BUSINESS AGREEMENTS.

[¶5804.1]　　Fictitious-Name Statutes

All but a handful of the American states have enacted a fictitious-name statute in one form or another. Generally, they provide that one doing business under an assumed or fictitious name must file certain information in affidavit form in each county where business is transacted, and, in addition, may require other acts on the part of the user calculated to inform the public of the actual ownership of the business. Some of these statutes apply by their terms to corporate trade names; some which do not have been construed to apply to corporations when transacting business under names other than their corporate names.

The purpose of these acts is universally recognized to be the prevention of fraud by providing potential customers and more especially potential creditors with information about those with whom they are dealing. Whether or not sanctions are enforced to a degree sufficient to compel compliance with a particular statute, it is apparent that no substantive protection is sought to be given to a name registered or certified under its terms.

[¶5804.2] Trade Name Statutes and Comprehensive "Trade Symbol" Statutes

Certain states have adopted statutes directed to the problem of the business name which is neither a corporate name nor amenable to registration under a mark statute. The simplest of these is a provision of the California Business and Professional Code which appears to be merely a restatement of the non-statutory principles of protection as developed in California; there are no registration provisions in this Act.

Several states have adopted specific "trade name" statutes. A Nebraska act provides that trade names may be registered with the Secretary of State, following which the certificate issued by the Secretary of State must be published in a local newspaper and proof of this publication filed with the County Clerk. "Any such trade name registered shall be of such a nature as to distinguish it from that of any other trade name registered in the office of the Secretary of State."

•

For Further Reference . . .
American Jurisprudence, Trademarks.
Forms of Business Agreements looseleaf Service. Institute for Business Planning, Englewood Cliffs, N.J.
Seidel, *What The General Practitioner Should Know About Trademarks and Copyrights,* Joint Committee on Continuing Legal Education.
Trademarks in the Market Place; Today's Problems in Their Creation, Development and Use, 53 *Trademark Reporter* 688, 1963.
Yarbrough, Fletcher L., Protection of Territorial Rights in Corporate Names and Trade Names, *The Business Lawyer,* July 1964.

TRUSTS

[¶5901]   There are three broad reasons for the creation of a trust during life:

(1) To transfer the property beyond the control of the grantor, to save estate taxes, to shift investment income produced by the trust property to the tax return of the trust or that of the trust beneficiaries. These purposes require an irrevocable trust.

(2) To shift income while retaining the privilege of using the trust property at a specified time in the future. This purpose requires a reversionary trust and its term must be at least ten years in order to shift income for tax purposes.

(3) To transfer property to a trust for management during the life of the grantor and, if he doesn't revoke the trust before he dies, have the trustee either continue to manage the property or make the testamentary distribution spelled out in the trust instrument. This is a revocable trust.

Apart from the tax savings, the practical purposes of a trust are:

(1) Place the property beyond the reach of an inexperienced and possibly improvident member of the family or one who might be able to exercise an unfavorable influence over the beneficiary if the property were given to the beneficiary outright.

(2) Place the management of the trust property in the hands of an experienced and reliable trustee who can be given broad powers to manage the property to the best advantage, or whose investment activities can be restricted, controlled and directed by the trust instrument.

(3) Create the authority and the capacity to apply the income and corpus of the trust to the problems of the beneficiaries as they develop in the future. This can be done through discretionary powers to distribute, giving the beneficiary limited rights to a withdrawal, creating powers of appointment over the corpus of the trust in persons who will be in a position to watch and understand the needs and problems of the family in the future.

(4) Obtain privacy and save probate expense at the death of the grantor, who would, in the absence of creating the trust, own the property, and through whose estate it would have to pass.

[¶5902]   THE TAX PLANNING OF TRUSTS

The creation of a trust by lifetime transfer can save income taxes and accelerate the accumulation of capital in three basic ways, which can be combined with each other.

(1) Annual income tax savings can be achieved by the transfer of income-producing property to a trust in which the income is taxed either to the trust or to the trust beneficiary. This step will transfer income from the top

brackets of the settlor to the lower bracket of a trust or beneficiary. But check IRC §677 which will tax income to grantor if he retains any interest or power specified there and §668 and 669 dealing with the taxation of distributions of accumulated income.

(2) A trust arrangement may utilize the additional exemptions of the trust and the beneficiary to provide tax-free income.

(3) Income tax savings can be achieved by the so-called sprinkling trust, which gives the trustee discretion to distribute trust income among beneficiaries in varying proportions from year to year, depending on their needs. Trust income can be kept out of the higher income tax brackets by giving it to the beneficiaries in lower income brackets, who presumably need it more.

Estate tax savings can be achieved if the trust is set up so that the corpus is not includible in the estate of the grantor or the beneficiary. Trust property will be taxed in the grantor's (settlor's) estate if the grantor alone, or in conjunction with another, retains the power to alter, amend, or revoke the trust, or to designate who is to enjoy the trust income or corpus (IRC §2038). Retention of even the right to the income is sufficient to tax the grantor's estate. The grantor's estate is taxed also if the transfer to the trust isn't intended to take effect until his death (§2037).

The trust property will be includible in the estate of the beneficiary if the beneficiary has too broad a power to withdraw or appoint corpus as specified in IRC §2041.

[¶5903]   INVASION OF TRUST PRINCIPAL

Here are some special arrangements which we can set up for the beneficiary's lifetime use of trust principal, together with their effect on the includibility for subsequent death tax purposes in the beneficiary's gross estate.

(1) *Beneficiary has an unlimited right to withdraw all or any part of the trust corpus*—The entire trust corpus would be included in the beneficiary's gross estate (IRC §2041(a)(2)).

(2) *Beneficiary has a non-cumulative right to withdraw up to 5% of the trust corpus or $5,000 annually, whichever is greater*—This right will cause the inclusion in the beneficiary's estate of only the amount of the unexercised withdrawal privilege in the year of the beneficiary's death (IRC §2041(b)(2)).

(3) *Beneficiary has a right to withdraw such sums from trust corpus in own discretion for health, support and maintenance*—No part of the trust corpus would be included in the beneficiary's gross estate solely on account of this provision (IRC §2041(b)(1)(A)).

(4) *Beneficiary is to receive a fixed amount of principal each year, these payments to cease upon the beneficiary's death*—No part of the trust corpus

would be included in the beneficiary's gross estate solely on account of this provision.

(5) *Beneficiary has no right of withdrawal, but trustee has the power to make payments of principal to the beneficiary for the beneficiary's support and maintenance, or for any reason* — No part of the trust corpus should be included in the beneficiary's gross estate solely on account of this provision. (NOTE: Where a provision is made authorizing the trustee to invade principal for the income beneficiary's support and maintenance, sometimes the question comes up as to whether the trustee should take the beneficiary's independent income and / or capital into account. It is wise to make a clear-cut provision covering this in the governing instrument so as to avoid a costly construction suit later on.)

[¶5904] WHO GETS TRUST PRINCIPAL AFTER THE DEATH OF THE BENEFICIARY?

This can be specified in the trust instrument, or another way is to give the income beneficiary (or anybody else, for that matter) the power to appoint trust principal either during his or her lifetime or by will. Another way is to have the governing instrument itself specify when and to whom trust principal is to be distributed following the death of the income beneficiary.

A *power of appointment* can be created so as to put off this ultimate decision until the death of the holder of the power, as where a power is created which is exercisable by will only. The beneficial effect of this is that a final decision is being postponed until a time when more facts are at hand on which to base such decision.

If the power given is a *general power of appointment* so that the trust principal may be appointed to anybody at all including the holder, such principal will be included in the holder's gross estate whether or not the power is in fact exercised. (A beneficiary's absolute power to invade trust corpus for himself is the equivalent of a general power of appointment exercisable during lifetime.) A general power can be limited so that it can only be exercised by will.

If the right to appoint principal is limited to a certain class of beneficiaries, i.e., children, etc., then we have a *limited* or a *special power of appointment*. Thus, if a power is given to a wife as beneficiary to dispose of the trust corpus at her death only among her and her husband's issue, the trust corpus will not be included in her gross estate on account of this special power.

For Further Reference . . .

Curtis, *The Modern Prudent Investor—What the General Practitioner Should Know About Investments,* Joint Committee on Continuing Legal Education.

Estate Planning (looseleaf service), Institute for Business Planning, Englewood Cliffs, N.J.

Estate Practice and Procedure (looseleaf service), Institute for Business Planning, Englewood Cliffs, N.J.

Michaelson, *Income Taxation of Estates and Trusts,* Practising Law Institute, New York, N.Y.

Nossman, *Trust Administration and Taxation,* Matthew Bender, New York, N.Y.

Scott, *Scott on Trusts,* Little, Brown, Boston, Mass.

Stephenson, *Drafting Wills and Trusts,* Little, Brown, Boston, Mass.

TRUTH-IN-LENDING

[¶5950] The Federal Consumer Credit Protection Act of 1968 (15 U.S.C. 1601), the so-called "Truth-in-Lending Act," gives the federal government jurisdiction over virtually every type of consumer credit extended to individuals. Its detailed full disclosure rules took effect on July 1, 1969, and its restrictions on garnishment became effective July 1, 1970.

The law applies to everyone who regularly extends or arranges for the extension of consumer credit. It covers the extension of credit primarily for personal, family, household or agricultural purposes. Under the law, every detail of transactions within its purview must be spelled out, so that the prospective buyer or borrower does not have to make any computations of his own to translate percentages into dollar amounts, or vice versa. This characterizes it as a "meaningful" disclosure.

The Act provides a standardized language and mode of making diclosures. Regulation Z promulgated by the Federal Reserve Board spells out specific methods of making the statutory disclosures and prescribes the precise language to be used. Although the Federal Reserve is authorized to promulgate regulations to implement truth-in-lending it is only one of nine federal agencies which have jurisdiction over enforcement of the Act.

Attorneys for those who extend credit will have to make sure that their clients' credit transactions fully comply with the truth-in-lending law. There are both civil and criminal penalties for noncompliance, so that the lawyer's vigilance is essential to his client's well-being.

Similarly, lawyers for those to whom credit is extended will want to review all agreements under which their clients have either received consumer credit, or are about to receive such credit. In some instances, noncompliance with federal disclosure requirements will give rise to suits for damages against the noncomplying extender of the credit.

[¶5950.1] Exemption of Certain States

The federal truth-in-lending law does not apply in any state that has a substantially similar law with "adequate provisions for enforcement." The job of deciding which states have such laws is left to the Federal Reserve, which will issue regulations that will keep the disclosure and recission parts of the federal law (the parts on advertising, loan-sharking or garnishment) from operating in those states.

There are now a number of states with "truth-in-lending" laws of their own and many others have consumer credit laws requiring disclosure of varying types of information. Some of these state laws go further than the federal law in many respects. Check your own jurisdiction to see whether state consumer credit laws exempt your state from the federal law and Regulation Z. Also watch for specific Federal Reserve regulations identifying such states.

Where state laws are substantially similar to truth-in-lending disclosure and recission provisions, state law will prevail. However, with regard to the loan-sharking, garnishment, and advertising sections of the Act, the federal law preempts the field.

Check your own jurisdiction for consumer credit laws. If, by some chance, your local law is even more stringent than federal truth-in-lending, you must comply with those added requirements.

[¶5950.2] Coverage of the Act

The types of consumer credit covered by truth-in-lending are: (1) credit extended to individuals for personal, family, agricultural or household purposes not exceeding $25,000; (2) all real estate credit extended to individuals for the same purposes as in (1), regardless of amount, and (3) all advertising of credit covered by (1) and (2).

Truth-in-lending imposes neither uniform interest rates nor finance charges. Rather, it addresses itself to the mode and language of disclosure. It is thus primarily procedural, except insofar as it creates a new three-day right of rescission of credit sales involving liens on homes and restricts garnishment of wages. The Consumer Credit Protection Act of 1968 also makes loan-sharking a federal offense.

Lenders Covered: Lenders who fall within any of the following three categories are covered:

(1) Those who regularly extend credit to consumers, or
(2) Charge a finance charge, or
(3) Allow a customer to repay in more than four installments.

[¶5950.3] Transactions Exempt From the Federal Truth-in-Lending Act

The following transactions are exempt from the Act's provisions:
(1) Extensions of credit to:
    (a) Corporations
    (b) Trusts
    (c) Estates
    (d) Partnerships
    (e) Co-operatives
    (f) Associations
    (g) Government subdivisions or agencies.
(2) Extensions of credit for business or commercial purposes, other than agricultural.

(3) Transactions in securities or commodities accounts with a broker-dealer registered with the SEC.

(4) Nonreal property credit transactions in which the amount financed exceeds $25,000 or the express written commitment by the creditor to extend credit exceeds $25,000.

(5) Transactions involving services under public utility tariffs which are regulated by any governmental agency.

[¶5950.4] Who Is Required to Make Disclosures?

Anyone who extends credit must comply but the Federal Reserve Board has expanded the list to include the following categories: savings and loan institutions, retailers, credit card agencies, credit unions, automobile dealers, plumbers, dentists, small loan companies, mortgage bankers, electricians, doctors and hospitals, and many others when they extend credit in the conventional sense or make special arrangement for payment of bills.

Doctors and Other Professionals: Regulation Z governs all professionals when they impose a finance charge or, by agreement, allow patients or clients to pay their bills in more than four installments (even without a finance charge being imposed).

Four-Payments Rule: To discourage the practice of burying a finance charge in a cash price, if there is no finance charge and no agreement between the professional and his client to pay in more than four installments, then Regulation Z would not apply. Therefore, the most prudent way of handling these bills is to have a patient decide unilaterally to pay in installments. The doctor can then accept the payments and not have to comply with Regulation Z and its attendant paper work.

[¶5950.5] Specific Areas in Which Disclosure Is Required

Specific areas covered by Federal Reserve Board "Public Position Letters" include:

(1) Commitment Fees or Standby Fees From Real Estate Developer to Lender: Such fees are to be included in the finance charge as *prepaid finance charges.*

(2) Compensating Balances: Disclosure must be made in credit transactions which require 20% deposit balances that will be taken out of the proceeds of a separate but simultaneous loan from the identical creditor. The 20% compensating balance could be provided from either a cash fund of the debtor, proceeds of a separate loan, or withholding from the proceeds of the loan being consummated.

For disclosure purposes in the first loan, the compensating balance must be deducted and disclosures made accordingly. But there is an exception for prior compensating balances that existed prior to the extension of credit and for those in which a bank has a security interest.

Observation: In order to provide the required compensating balance, sometimes a separate loan which would be subject to all the disclosure requirements of Regulation Z is granted. However, there is an exclusion provision concerning required deposit balances. The exception covers "a deposit balance or investment which was acquired or established from the proceeds of an extension of credit made for that purpose upon written request of the customer."

(3) Note Renewals: When the original note is made, certain disclosures are required, but the original disclosures do not cover renewals. Renewals must be accompanied by full disclosure even though the interest remains unchanged and no "new" money is actually advanced.

(4) Home Improvements: Real estate brokers who arrange financing for home improvements or remodeling as part of the sale of a house are also subject to the disclosure requirements.

(5) Mortgage Transactions: Both those who extend credit and those who arrange for the extension of credit must make disclosures.

Arranging Credit: If a builder assists in preparing the loan application or initiates a credit report but received no fee for doing this, he is not an "arranger." If the builder prepares the note and mortgage or other contract documents, he is an "arranger."

Mortgage Assumptions: If a purchaser of real estate assumes an existing mortgage, disclosures must be made by the lender. Under Regulation Z, a mortgage is assumed if a purchaser of real estate is personally liable for the debts and there is a written agreement between the lender and the assuming party. Note that local law may differ.

If there is an "assumption" in which the mortgage lender does not participate, there is no assumption with respect to the lender and no disclosure is required.

Mortgage Refinancing: Any material change in the terms of the mortgage constitutes a new transaction, and disclosure must be made. However, the right of rescission does not apply to new money if the amount of the new transaction does not exceed the amount of the unpaid balance plus any accrued and unpaid finance charge.

Second Mortgages: Although first mortgages for the purchase of a home are exempted from disclosing total dollar amount of interest, full disclosure is required for second mortgages. The rationale behind this requirement is the stress under which home owners often seek to raise money fast and may unwittingly overlook material omissions in the mortgage contract.

⟦¶5950.6⟧   Definitions

Credit: "The right granted by a creditor to a customer to defer payment of debt. . ." The Act contemplates a voluntary agreement between a debtor and creditor that gives rise to a debt.

Consumer Credit: Credit offered or extended to a natural person for personal, family, household or agricultural purposes and for which either a finance charge is (or may be) imposed or which, by agreement, is or may be payable in more than four installments.

Creditor: Any person or business entity that in the ordinary course of business regularly extends or arranges for the extension of credit is a "creditor."

If a builder takes back a purchase-money second mortgage, that makes him a person who extends credit, and he must make disclosures. But a private party selling his own home who takes back a purchase-money mortgage is not one who extends credit under the law.

⟦¶5950.7⟧   General Disclosure Procedures

The statutory disclosures required must be made clearly, conspicuously and in logical order. Except for advertising credit terms, all amounts and percentages must be stated in figures and printed boldly.

The terms "finance charge" and "annual percentage rate" must be printed more conspicuously than other required terms.

If there are two or more debtors, only one need be given a copy of the completed disclosures. However, if one of these multiple debtors is not primarily but secondarily liable; e.g., as guarantor or endorser, disclosures must be made to both parties.

⟦¶5950.8⟧   Checklists of Specific Disclosure Requirements

The truth-in-lending law, as implemented by Regulation Z, lays down detailed requirements of terminology and content of disclosures. They are summarized here according to the general area of consumer credit to which they pertain.

(I) Extension of Credit Not in Connection With the Sale of Goods: These are primarily small loan transactions which are "closed end" in nature. The following disclosures are mandated:

(1) Date on which the finance charge begins to accrue if different from date of transaction.

(2) The finance charge expressed as an annual percentage rate, using the term "annual percentage rate."

Exception: Disclosure of the finance charge as an annual percentage rate is not required where (1) the finance charge does not exceed $5 and applies to an amount financed not exceeding $75, or (2) the finance charge does not exceed $7.50 and applies to an amount financed exceeding $75.

Note: The law specifically prohibits the seller from dividing a transaction into two separate loans so as to bring both within the $75 or $7.50 exception.

(3) Number, amount, and due dates or periods of scheduled payments and, with certain exceptions, the sum of such payments, using the term "total of payments." This does not apply to a loan secured by a first lien or equivalent security interest on a dwelling and made to finance the purchase of that dwelling or in the case of a sale of that house.

(4) Identification of any "balloon" payment.

(5) Amount or method of computing amount of any default, delinquency, or similar charges payable in event of late payments.

(6) Description or identification of type of security interest held or to be retained or acquired by creditor, including statements concerning after-acquired property subject to the security interest or other or future indebtedness secured by any after-acquired property where appropriate.

(7) Identification of the property to which security interest relates.

(8) Description of any prepayment penalty that may be imposed by creditor or his assignee, with an explanation of the method of computation.

(9) Provisions concerning refund of unearned finance charges in the event of prepayment.

Note: The penalty is separate and distinct from finance charges.

(10) Amount of credit, excluding prepaid finance charges and required deposit balances, to be paid to customer or for his account or to another person on his behalf, including all charges, individually itemized, which are included in the amount of credit extended but which are not part of the finance charge, using the term "amount financed."

(11) Amount of any prepaid finance charge, using the term "prepaid finance charge."

(12) Amount of any required deposit balance, using the term "required deposit balance."

(13) Sum of prepaid finance charges and required deposit balances, using the term "total prepaid finance charge and required deposit balance."

(14) Total amount of finance charge, with description of each amount included therein, using the term "finance charge." This requirement does not apply to a loan secured by a first lien or equivalent security interest on a dwelling and made to finance the purchase of that dwelling.

(15) Notice of customer's right of recission, if applicable.

(II) Non-Open-End Credit Sales: The first nine disclosures required in non-sale extensions of credit are also required in credit sales which are closed-end transactions, such as automobile sales, rather than revolving accounts.

(III) Credit Sales in General: The following disclosures are mandatory for all credit sales:

(1) Date on which the finance charge begins to accrue if different from date of transaction.

(2) The finance charge expressed as an annual percentage rate, using the term "annual percentage rate."

Exception: Disclosure of finance charge as an annual percentage rate is not required where (1) the finance charge does not exceed $5 and applies to an amount financed not exceeding $75, or (2) the finance charge does not exceed $7.50 and applies to an amount financed exceeding $75.

(3) Number, amount, and due dates or periods of scheduled payments and, with certain exceptions, the sum of such payments, using the term "total of payments." This does not apply to a loan secured by a first lien or equivalent security interest on a dwelling and made to finance the purchase of that dwelling, or in the case of a sale of that house.

(4) Identification of any "balloon" payment.

(5) Amount or method of computing amount of any default, delinquency, or similar charges payable in event of late payments.

(6) Description or identification of type of security interest held or to be retained or acquired by creditor, including statements concerning after-acquired property subject to the security interest or other or future indebtedness secured by any after-acquired property where appropriate.

(7) Identification of the property to which security interest relates.

(8) Description of any prepayment penalty that may be imposed by creditor or his assignee, with an explanation of the method of computation.

(9) Provisions concerning refund of unearned finance charges in the event of prepayment.

(10) Cash price of property or service purchased, using the term "cash price."

(11) Amount of buyer's down payment, itemized as applicable, using the term "cash down payment" for property traded in, using the term "trade-in"; and the term "total down payment" for the sum of these.

(12) Difference between cash price and total down payment, using the term "unpaid balance of cash price."

(13) All charges, other than cash price, individually itemized, which are included in amount financed but which are not part of finance charge.

(14) The sum of unpaid balance of cash price and all other charges which are included in amount financed but which are not part of finance charge, using the term "unpaid balance."

502

(15) Amounts to be deducted for prepaid finance charge or required deposit balance. "Prepaid finance charge," "required deposit balance," and "total prepaid finance charge and required deposit balance" must be used where applicable.

(16) Difference between unpaid balance and prepaid finance charge or required deposit balance or total prepaid finance charge and required deposit balance, using the term "amount financed."

(17) Total amount of finance charge, with description of each amount included, using the term "finance charge."

Note: This is not required in most sales of dwellings, nor is (18).

(18) Sum of the cash price, all other charges included in amount financed but which are not part of finance charge, and the finance charge, using the term "deferred payment price."

(19) Notice of customer's right of rescission, if applicable.

[¶5950.9] Open-End Credit Transactions

Open-end credit transactions are agreements under which a customer may, if he desires, keep on making new purchases under the original extension of credit and add the amount of these purchases to the outstanding balance, up to an agreed ceiling. The customer usually has the option of prepaying or of paying in stated installments. The creditor may impose a finance charge on the balance, and it is this total finance charge which is the subject of truth-in-lending's main thrust.

New Accounts: Before a customer opens a revolving credit account or obtains a credit card, the seller must disclose to him:

(1) *Conditions* under which a finance charge may be imposed, including an explanation of the time period, if any, within which any credit extended may be paid without incurring a finance charge.

(2) *Method of determining the balance* on which a finance charge may be imposed.

(3) *Method of determining the amount of the finance charge,* including the method of determining any minimum, fixed, check service, transaction, activity, or similar charge, which may be imposed as a finance charge.

(4) Where *one or more periodic rates* may be used to compute the finance charge, each such rate, the range of balances to which applicable, and the corresponding annual percentage rate determined by multiplying the periodic rate by the number of periods in a year.

(5) If the creditor so elects, the *Comparative Index of Credit Cost* in accordance with 12 Code Fed Reg §226.11.

(6) *Conditions under which any other charges* may be imposed and method by which they will be determined.

503

(7) *Conditions under which creditor may retain or acquire any security*interest in any property to secure payment of any credit extended on the account, and description or identification of the type of interest or interests which may be so retained or acquired.

(8) *The minimum periodic payment required.*

Periodic Billing: Once the revolving credit account has been contracted for, the seller is required to include all the following disclosures on each statement:

(1) *Outstanding balance* in the account at the beginning of the billing cycle, using the term "previous balance."

(2) *Amount and date of each extension of credit* or date such extension of credit is debited to the account during the billing cycle and, unless previously furnished, a brief identification of any goods or services purchased, or other extension of credit.

(3) *Amounts credited* to the account during the billing cycle for payments, using the term "payments," and for other credits including returns, rebates of finance charges, and adjustments, using the term "credits," and unless previously furnished, a brief identification of each item included in such other credits. Separate itemizations are permitted if they do not appear on the face of the statement. They must, however, accompany the statement and identify each charge and/or credit.

(4) *Amount of any finance charge,* using the term "finance charge," debited to the account during the billing cycle, itemized and identified to show amounts, if any, due to the application of periodic rates and the amount of any other charge included in the finance charge, such as a minimum, fixed, check service, transaction, activity, or similar charge, using appropriate descriptive terminology.

Note, however, that this does *not* require the seller to state the portions of the finance charge due to application of two or more periodic rates separately. The periodic rates that apply to the account and the applicable range of the balances must be disclosed, but no further detailed breakdown is required.

Example: If the finance charge is 1½% per month for the first $500 of the balance and 1% per month for amounts exceeding $500, the total monthly charge on an outstanding balance of $600 would be $8.50, which must be stated. But the $7.50 and $1 components need not be spelled out.

(5) *Each periodic rate,* using the term "periodic rate" (or "rates"), that may be used to compute the finance charge, whether or not applied during the billing cycle, and the range of balances to which applicable.

(6) *Annual percentage rate or rates,* using term "annual percentage rate" (or "rates"), and, where more than one rate, the amount of the balance to which each rate is applicable.

(7) If the creditor so elects, the *Comparative Index of Credit Cost* in accordance with 12 Code Fed Reg §226.11.

(8) *Balance* on which the finance charge was computed, and a statement of how that balance was determined. If the balance is determined without first deducting all credits during the billing cycle, that fact and the amount of such credits must also be disclosed.

(9) *Closing date* of billing cycle and the outstanding balance in the account on that date, using the term "new balance," accompanied by the statement of the date by which, or the period, if any, within which, payment must be made to avoid additional finance charges.

Finance Charges: Any charge which is imposed on the customer either directly or indirectly in order to obtain credit must be disclosed fully as a "finance charge." This classification includes, among others, (1) loan fees, (2) credit investigation fees, (3) finder's fees, (4) time-price differentials, (5) points in mortgages, (6) premiums for credit life insurance where required by the lender and (7) interest.

The following incidental charges are not deemed finance charges: (1) taxes, (2) license fees, (3) registration fees, (4) certain title fees, (5) fees fixed by law and payable to public officials, and (6) real estate appraisal fees.

Discounts for prompt payment are deemed finance charges but do not have to be disclosed on the original contract. Inclusion on the face of the regular statement rendered is sufficient for compliance.

Finance charges must be spelled out, both in total percentages and dollars and cents, to the closest quarter of 1%.

[¶5950.10] Credit Other Than Open-End

All required disclosures for transactions other than open-end credit agreements must be made together either (1) on the same side of the note or other instrument evidencing the obligation on the page and near the place for the customer's signature, or (2) on one side of a separate statement which identifies the transaction. The required disclosures must be made before the contractual relationship between the creditor and the customer is created, irrespective of the time of performance by either party, except in the cases of orders by mail or telephone or a series of sales.

[¶5950.11] Open-End Credit

Required disclosures for open-end credit accounts for which a billing cycle has been established must be made on the face of the periodic statement or on its reverse side or on an attached supplementary statement. A notice must direct the buyer to see the reverse side or accompanying statement(s) for important information.

The disclosures must not be separated in any manner which might confuse or mislead the customer or obscure or detract attention from the requisite information.

[¶5950.12] Annual Percentage Rate

The annual percentage rate which the law insists must be printed in bold type is familiarly known as the APR in banking parlance.

This actual dollars-and-cents cost to the customer is derived by consulting actuarial tables or using the unpaid balance method. The disclosure is designed to reflect the "true" cost of credit to the prospective customer. Applicable tables may be obtained from regional Federal Reserve Banks or from the FRB in Washington.

Computation: Under the actuarial method, the annual percentage rate is the same where equal payments are made at equal intervals.

Example of Actuarial Method: Suppose a bank grants a small loan for $100 repayable in monthly installments over one year at a 6% add-on finance charge. The borrower would repay $106 over the year, but he has the use of the full $100 only until he makes the first payment on the loan. When he begins to repay the principal, he has less money left from the loan at his disposal.

However, if the 6% were discounted in advance, he would receive only $94 from the bank. He still has to repay the full $100 and has use of the $94 only until he makes the first payment on the loan. In effect, he is paying 11½% interest. It is this type of disclosure which is mandated by truth-in-lending so that small loans will not be a trap for the unwary who do not realize the actual amount of cash they have to work with on a discounted loan.

APR for Revolving Charge Accounts: In this form of open-end credit, the finance charge is divided by the unpaid balance to get the rate for the time period used. Multiply this rate by the number of time periods used by the creditor during the year. Thus, on a typical department store "easy payment account" where bills are rendered monthly, a 1½% charge on the unpaid balance cumulates to an annual 18% rate. It is this total rate which is a revelation to some consumers.

Discount Exception to APR Requirement: Where the seller offers a discount of less than 5% for the prompt payment of installments, it is not necessary to spell out single payment discount transactions in terms of annual percentage rates.

APR and Usury: Statement of the "real" annual percentage rate which, on its face, might appear to violate local usury laws, does not prejudice the vendor because transactions covered by the truth-in-lending law are deemed sales rather than loans.

[¶5950.13]   Exceptions to Disclosure Requirements

(1) Home Owner: A seller who is not a "creditor" is not required to comply with Regulation Z when he sells his home and takes back a second mortgage as part of the purchase price.

If a home owner is, in the ordinary course of his business, involved with the extension of consumer credit, the credit he is extending on his private home does not emanate from his business and does not require compliance with Regulation Z.

(2) Farm Loans: As noted above, loans for agricultural purposes are included in the extension of credit. However, the Federal Reserve Board has made it easier for lenders to comply with the law when making loans to farmers because these loans are often seasonal. It is often difficult to estimate the annual percentage rate, repayment schedule, or finance charge.

If the amounts or dates of advances and repayments are unknown on a farm loan, the lender can simply state those details that are known instead of estimating a finance charge and annual percentage rate.

This is not a blanket exemption for all farm loans from the requirements of Regulation Z. If you do know all the terms when the papers are signed, you must disclose the finance charge, annual percentage rate, and other required information which you have in hand.

(3) Periodic Statements by Mortgage Lenders: Since mortgage loans are classed as "closed-end transactions," no periodic statements are required by lenders. But if a lender elects to send statements, he must then disclose the annual percentage rate and date by which payment must be made in order to avoid late charges.

(4) Insurance Premiums: It is the opinion of the Federal Reserve Board that direct financing of premiums by insurance companies is an exempt transaction even though insurance companies levy service charges upon monthly installment payments by its insureds. The opinion specifically includes the situation where failure to make payments results in the cancellation of insurance. However, it must not be forgotten that the financing of insurance premiums by third parties or subsidiaries of the company might create a legally collectible debt.

Insurance Premiums Paid by Creditors to Protect Collateral: Even though the premiums are added to the existing obligation, the payment of these premiums by the debtor does not constitute a new credit transaction and no disclosures are required. It is not considered a new transaction even though an additional finance charge is imposed on the debtor.

(5) Telephone or Mail Orders: These orders are exempt where there has been no personal solicitation and where the catalog sets forth deferred payment and finance charge schedules.

(6) Add-on Sales: These are sales which are part of a series of sales to the same buyer and the deferred payment cost of the current purchase in that series is to be added to the buyer's outstanding balance. In these cases, the customer must have approved all terms in writing. These add-on sales are excluded from prior disclosure only if the vendor takes no security interest in any property for which he has been paid an amount that is equal to the sale price plus finance charges. In other words, this provision cannot be circumvented by using it to refinance a mortgage and thereby avoid statutory disclosure provisions.

(7) Student Loans: Disclosure need not be made until final papers are prepared. Disclosure is not required on making the loan agreement but must be made before the repayment schedule begins.

(8) Purchase-Money Mortgages: First mortgages for the purchase of a home are exempt from the requirement of disclosing the total dollar amount of interest, but the percentage rate must be clearly stated. The mortgage fraternity has always made it a practice to disclose rates, and so this is not a radical departure from past practice.

【¶5950.14】 Disclosures Which Are Inconsistent With Local Law

State law is regarded as inconsistent with federal truth-in-lending requirements if it requires the creditor to make disclosures which differ regarding form, content, terminology or time of delivery, or requires disclosure of the finance charge or annual percentage rate of the charge determined in a manner other than that prescribed by Regulation Z. Creditors may elect to make disclosures which differ from the federal law if they make them separately or in conjunction with the required federal disclosures but identify them separately as being inconsistent with federal law.

【¶5950.15】 New Right of Rescission

Although the truth-in-lending law is primarily concerned with disclosures, it does confer an important substantive right on prospective borrowers: the right to rescind a contract within three days if the collateral is a "security interest" in the borrower's home. This does not include first mortgages or purchase-money mortgages but is aimed at situations in which an artisan's lien or mechanic's lien is retained as security. The right of recission operates as follows:

A borrower has three days to rescind certain mortgage loans following the "date of consummation of the transaction." Under Regulation Z, that date occurs when a "contractual relationship" arises between the creditor and debtor.

A "security interest" is any interest in property which secures payment or performance of any obligation, including security interests under the Uniform Commercial Code, real property mortgages, deeds of trust, other liens whether or not recorded, mechanics', materialmen's, and artisans' liens; vendors' liens in both real and personal property; the interest of a seller in a contract for the sale of real property; any lien on property arising by operation of law; and any interest in a lease when used to secure payment or performance of an obligation.

A "residence" is any real property in which the customer resides or expects to reside and includes land on which the customer resides or expects to reside.

Creditor must furnish the customer with two copies of the required notice, printed in bold-face type on one side of a separate statement which identifies the transaction to which it relates.

Unless the right of recission does not apply or the customer has waived or modified his right to rescind until the three-day period has expired, the lender may not:

(a) Disburse any money other than in escrow,

(b) Make any physical changes in customer's property,

(c) Perform any work or service for customer, or

(d) Make any deliveries to the customer's residence.

Timely Exercise: The right of rescission must be exercised by midnight of the third business day following consummation of the transaction or delivery of the required disclosures, whichever occurs later. Notice of rescission can be given by mail, telegram, or other writing. The creditor's notice of right to rescind can be used, if dated and signed by the customer, to rescind the transaction.

Multiple Parties: The right of recission may be exercised by any one of the joint owners who is a party to the transaction, and the effect of rescission will apply to all the owners.

Handling Rescission From Lender's Viewpoint: Local law should be examined to ascertain whether confessions of judgment or cognovit clauses are permitted in transactions of the type governed by truth-in-lending. If they are still permitted in your jurisdiction, there is a strong possibility that their very inclusion in an agreement for a second mortgage or other lien on realty would trigger the borrower's exercise of the right of rescission. This would occur if the existence of such a clause results in a lien on the debtor's home without notice. The right of rescission may be sidestepped by setting up a commitment procedure with the object of creating a contract at the very outset.

Waiver of Right of Rescission: The customer may waive his right to rescind if an extension of credit is needed to meet a bona fide, immediate personal

509

financial emergency of the customer or if delaying the creditor's performance three business days will jeopardize the customer's health or property and the customer furnishes the creditor with a separate hardship statement describing the situation and modifying or waiving his right of rescission.

The use of a printed form to modify or waive the right of rescission is prohibited. A waiver of right of rescission is invalid unless signed by all joint owners who are parties to the transaction.

Transactions to Which Right of Rescission Does Not Apply: Inasmuch as the creation of the right of rescission was prompted primarily by the policy of avoiding foreclosure on personal residences for liens not directly connected with homes, the law specifically exempts the following transactions from the exercise of customer's right to rescind:

(a) Creation, retention, or assumption of a first lien or an equivalent security interest to finance acquisition of a dwelling in which customer resides or expects to reside.

(b) A first lien retained or acquired by a creditor in connection with financing the initial construction of the customer's residence, or a loan committed prior to the completion of construction of the customer's residence to satisfy that construction loan and provide permanent financing.

(c) Any subordinated lien exempt from the right of rescission when originally created.

(d) Any advance for agricultural purposes made under an open-end real estate mortgage or similar lien provided the disclosure of the right to rescind was made when the security interest was acquired by the creditor or prior to the first advance made.

[¶5950.16] Other Prohibited Practices

Creditors are advised to avoid the practice of leading their customers to believe that truth-in-lending now legally requires increased credit charges. The following misleading statements should also be avoided in any guise:

(1) Finance charges may now be imposed where formerly there were none.

(2) Finance charges may be computed before payments are credited to open-end accounts.

(3) Discounts for prompt payment are to be discontinued under the law.

(4) Noninterest bearing 30-, 60-, and 90-day accounts must now be discontinued.

(5) Customers with long-standing open accounts must be summoned to appear before the store's credit manager.

In other words, the lender must not make any representations which lead the borrower to believe that the Act sanctions any increase in interest rates or any irregular treatment of finance charges. Furthermore, disclosures beyond the statutory minimum must not contradict the required disclosures nor may they be placed or worded in such a manner as to confuse the customer.

The use of sales contracts containing any blank spaces is absolutely forbidden by the truth-in-lending law.

[¶5950.17] Sanctions Imposed by the Truth-in-Lending Act

Civil damages for failure to make proper disclosures are pegged to the finance charges in the contract and may not exceed $1,000. In some instances, damages may be doubled. Erroneous disclosure may be corrected within 15 days of discovery to avoid these sanctions.

On the criminal side, however, fines of up to $5,000 and/or jail terms up to one year may be imposed for willful failure to comply with the law.

There is a one-year statute of limitations on civil suits. Creditors must keep records of compliance open for inspection for two years from the date on which disclosures were required to be made.

Even if a debtor recovers damages against a creditor who has violated the disclosure rules, he is still liable on the principal debt. Noncompliance by the lender does not operate as forgiveness of the debt.

Creditor's Defenses to Civil Suit: The creditor has the burden of proof of nonwillful violation of disclosure rules. This means that he must show, by a preponderance of the evidence, that his violation was unintentional and that it was the result of an "honest" error.

[¶5950.18] Advertising of Credit

The federal truth-in-lending law also applies to advertising of consumer credit. "Advertising" includes all types of publications, billboards, and radio and television commercials. It prohibits stating that the advertiser will extend certain terms to buyers unless the advertiser usually and customarily arranges such terms for its customers.

In the advertising of open-end credit, if one single credit term is advertised, all other credit terms must be included. It is not legal to advertise just one of the aspects of the credit arrangement. For instance, the retailer cannot advertise "$20 down" for a dinette set and omit the rest of the terms, which might include details such as "balance to be paid in twelve monthly instalments of $20 with carrying charges of ..."

Moreover, for other than open-end credit transactions, the total sum due after adding down payment, installments, and all service charges must be stated, inasmuch as it is definitely ascertainable beforehand.

Ads which contain no specific terms are still permissible. Thus, you can make one blanket statement, "Easy credit terms," without any further amplification. However, if you do state any credit term, then you must include all terms — all or nothing at all.

Advertising of residential real estate mortgages must comply, but advertising of purchase-money first mortgages does not have to disclose either the deferred payment price or the sum of the payments.

Exceptions: As with the other sections of the truth-in-lending law, the advertising requirements do not apply to commercial or business credit, securities transactions, transactions over $25,000, credit advanced to governmental units or organizations, or certain transactions involving public utility tariffs. Remember, however, that transactions with securities salesmen who are not registered with the SEC *do* come within the purview of truth-in-lending.

The law specifically exempts media in which credit advertising appears from any liability for circulating false or misleading credit information contained in such advertisements.

[¶5950.19] Restrictions on Garnishment

The truth-in-lending law contains the first federal restriction on garnishment of wages (Title III). The amount that can be garnisheed in any single workweek is limited to the lesser of 25% of an employee's disposable income (gross pay minus all deductions required by law) or his disposable income less 30 times the federal minimum hourly wage. The law applies to any business directly or indirectly involved in interstate commerce and thus has broad coverage which will affect virtually every employer. The new law also prevents employers from firing employees merely because their wages have been garnisheed.

Where there is a conflict with existing state law, the more stringent of the two will prevail. Thus, in a jurisdiction where garnishment is kept to an even lower percentage of wages, that statute will control.

Creditors' Alternatives: For those creditors who fear an upsurge of uncollectible debt as a result of limitations on garnishment, utilization of confessions of judgment or conventional wage assignments may be a more prudent course. Naturally, the credit rating of the debtor will determine the manner of assuring eventual repayment. An assignment of wages or salary is not the prudent way to deal with sales to highly paid executives or buyers who have substantial liquid or fixed assets.

[¶5950.20] Anti-Loan-Sharking Provisions

The Act makes it a federal crime to make "extortionate" loans (Title II). A loan transaction is deemed "extortionate" on its face if:

(1) It would be unenforceable at law; and

(2) The rate of interest is more than 45%; and

(3) The debtor knew, or had good reason to believe, at the time the credit was extended that force or violence might be employed in collecting; and

(4) The debtor owes the creditor a total of more than $100.

Penalties for conviction are fines up to $10,000 and/or imprisonment for up to 20 years.

[¶5950.21] Uniform Consumer Credit Code and National Consumer Act

The federal act is apparently having a "multiplier" effect, because increased pressure for the various states to enact the Uniform Consumer Credit Code or National Consumer Act is now being exerted. Uniformity would eliminate the discrepancies between the federal law and the state laws and might lead to procedural simplification of the conflicting "disclosure" terminology and forms.

The UCCC and NCA have already been enacted by several states.

[¶5950.22] Significance for the Practitioner

As counsel for banks, retail merchants, small loan companies, medical groups, and artisans, you will have to review all installment agreements and scrutinize all advertising copy to insure full compliance. The paper work may seem astronomical at first, but there are many standard forms available which you may utilize in drafting contracts suited to your client's requirements. At the end of this chapter, appropriate references may be found.

As counsel on the other side of the fence—consumer advocate—you will naturally find more clients coming to you with questions about dubious practices and outright violations by lenders and sellers. Remember that only the structure of the contract is covered by the federal law. Interest rates suspect as usury still are the province of local or state law. You should be cognizant of consumers' civil remedies.

Other Statutory Considerations: When considering the total interest rate and all other finance charges, be certain to check local laws to guard against possible usury which would invalidate your transaction.

Also check to make sure your jurisdiction has not enacted its own version of the Uniform Consumer Credit Code or National Consumer Act which might affect the mode of making required disclosures under the federal act.

•

For Further Reference . . .

Bratter, Herbert, "Some Pointers for Directors on Truth-in-Lending," *Banking,* June, 1969.

Clontz, Ralph C., Jr., *"Truth-In-Lending Manual,"* Revised Edition, *The Banking Law Journal.*

"Federal Truth in Lending Act," 5 *American Jurisprudence Legal Forms Anno.* §1285, Lawyers Co-operative Publishing Company, Rochester, New York.

Kass, Benny L., *Understanding Truth-in-Lending,* Small Business Administration, Washington, D.C. 20416.

"New Lending Law: What You Must Tell Your Customers," *Nation's Business,* June, 1969.

Schober, Milton W., "Highlights of the Federal Truth in Lending Act," 39 *New York Certified Public Accountant* 8.

Truth in Lending, Regulation Z: Annual Percentage Rate Tables. Vol. 1, 1969, Board of Governors of the Federal Reserve System, Washington, D.C. 20551.

What You Ought to Know about Federal Reserve Regulation Z, Board of Governors of the Federal Reserve System, Washington, D.C. 20551.

What You Ought to Know About Truth in Lending, International Consumer Credit Association, 375 Jackson Ave., St. Louis, Mo. 63130.

WILLS

[¶6001]   Before actually preparing a will, it is essential to take the client through the estate planning process described in ¶2501 et seq. Here we offer some guides to the procedure and mechanical steps in completing a will. See ¶2504.1 on the important marital deduction provisions.

[¶6002]   **CHECKLIST OF INFORMATION NEEDED FOR WILL DRAFTING AND ESTATE PLANNING**

1. Get names and addresses of client and all relatives who might be distributees (and thus be required to be cited on the probate).

2. Get details concerning testator and immediate family including:

(a) ages

(b) financial status and potential

(c) personal facts that may bear on estate plan

3. Obtain complete list of all assets owned by testator and his spouse including:

(a) personal effects and household furnishings

(b) real property

(c) investments and bank accounts, including marketable securities, mortgages, oil or gas property, patents, copyrights, etc.

(d) miscellaneous property such as yachts, automobiles, planes, art, libraries, collections, etc.

(e) employee benefits such as pension, profit-sharing, death benefits, stock options, Social Security, etc.

(f) personal life insurance, annuities, and related policies

(g) business interests—corporate, partnership, proprietorship with complete details including operative documents, stock certificates, etc.

(h) interests in trusts or estates of others including financial statements, tax returns, power to appoint property

4. Examine all documents related to property owned including: stock certificates, deeds, contracts, letters patent, insurance policies, wills and trust agreements.

5. Obtain complete list of all debts and obligations, both personal and those relating to business interests owned. Again, all pertinent documents should be examined to assure the accuracy of the testator's understanding of them.

6. Examine any other documents directly or indirectly bearing on the status or transfer of testator's property such as marital agreements, records of any gifts made, inter vivos trust agreements, prior wills, etc.

7. In connection with bequests find out exact corporate name and tax exempt status of charities the testator desires to name. Also find out names, addresses and legal status (age, competence to take gift, etc.) of individual beneficiaries.

8. Check income, gift and possibly estate tax returns (where a spouse has recently died), both Federal and state. Get projection of client's income and taxes.

9. Obtain names and addresses of testator's advisors such as attorney, tax advisor, accountant, trust officer, life underwriter, stock broker, etc.

10. Obtain detailed account of testator's stated objectives at the time of the first interview. It will be your duty to advise how these objectives can be best accomplished from both the standpoint of the law and the tax consequences. It may also be proper to make suggestions where trusts or charitable gifts seem appropriate to the stated plan. In other words, after finding out *whom* the testator wishes to benefit with his property, it is the lawyer's duty to advise as to *how* these wishes can best be carried out.

[¶6003]   WILL CHECKLIST

There is an infinite variety of detail which should be considered and dis-cussed preliminary to the preparation of a will. Much of this detail comes out of the testator's own experience, his appraisal of his property and his heirs, and his aspirations for them. There are some technical matters on which he should think and develop his own ideas, so that he can discuss them properly with whoever is planning his estate for him.

The following series of questions provides a useful check for the estate owner to stimulate his thinking prior to the preliminary conversation with his estate planner, and to the planner to make sure he has obtained all necessary informa-tion.

Any Special Instructions for Funeral Arrangements, Upkeep of Cemetery Plot, etc.?—Instructions can be spelled out in your will. Burial instructions in a will are useless where the provisions of the will remain secret until some date after death and after burial has already taken place. The matter can be left to the discretion of your family. Or you may leave a special letter addressed to your executor or to your family to acquaint them with your wishes.

Who should Get Your Personal Belongings?—If you do not provide for the disposition of clothing, jewelry, furniture, etc., such articles, unless state law provides otherwise, will go into the residue of your estate and possibly impose upon your executor the obligation to sell them. Tangible personal property should always be disposed of by separate will provisions. This is because under IRC §662 all amounts distributed to a beneficiary for the taxable year shall be included in the gross income of the beneficiary to the extent of the distributable net income of the estate. Under §663, any amount which, under the terms of the will, is distributed as a gift of specific property all at once or in not more than three installments is excluded from the operation of §662. Thus, if the tangible personal property is separately disposed of in the will and is distributed to the legatee all at once, its distribution will have no income tax consequences. However, if disposed of as part of the residue, its distribution might be taxable as income to the legatee. It may be wise to specify the individuals who are to receive the most valuable of your personal possessions and leave the balance to someone in whom you have confidence, with instructions to divide them at his discretion among those close to you.

Do You Want to Make Any Cash Bequests?—When you leave a specific amount of money to an individual or to a charity, your executor is required to pay that amount in full before he makes any distribution to the beneficiaries who are to share the balance of your estate. If your estate should be smaller than you expect, such a cash bequest could result in your unintentionally having made inadequate provision for other beneficiaries. You can guard against this by providing that cash bequests shall be paid only if the total estate exceeds a specified minimum. Or bequests to individuals and charities can be made in fractions or percentages of the estate, rather than in fixed dollar amounts.

What Do You Want to Do With Your Real Estate?—Do you want to leave your solely owned real estate outright, place it in trust (possibly a residence trust in which your wife has the rights to the house), have it sold and the proceeds distributed, give one beneficiary—for example, your wife—the right to use it for life with ownership going to your children on her death? Under the law of some states, your spouse may have dower or curtesy rights in your real estate.

Do You Want to Leave an Income For Anybody?—You may want to assure a regular income for your parents, dependent relatives, or others. You may do this through a trust established by will or by directing your executors to buy annuities for named beneficiaries. In the event that you establish the trust, you can specify the individual to whom the trust property will go after it has produced the required income for a specified period of time.

Whom Do You Want to Have the Remainder of Your Estate?—Decide who is to share in the bulk of your estate. Then divide the balance, after specific bequests, in fractions or percentages. By being overly exact in allocating particular assets to certain beneficiaries, or in specifying interest in dollar amounts, you can frustrate your own objectives in the event of important changes in the size or value of your estate. If you divide the bulk of the estate by fractions of a share, you won't be in the position of having to revise your will repeatedly because of changes in asset values. Be sure your will names alternate or contingent beneficiaries who are to receive the share of any beneficiary who fails to survive you.

What Can You Do to Protect the Interests of Minor Beneficiaries? —It is usually necessary to have a guardian appointed by the court to manage the child's property until he or she attains majority. The guardian must furnish bond, make periodic accountings and secure court approval on many of the actions he will have to take. Guardianship is both burdensome and expensive. Your will can simplify this matter by directing the property be turned over to a trust to be held for the benefit of minors until majority. The trustee can be authorized to use the trust property to provide maintenance, support and education for the minor.

What Can You Do to Protect the Interest of Adult Beneficiaries? —Adult beneficiaries can dissipate outright gifts quickly. You should decide whether you want to leave your property outright, turn it over to beneficiaries in installments, or have it held and managed for their benefit by an experienced trustee.

How Do You Want Trust Property Handled? —Subject to local law, you can determine whether the income of trust property is to be distributed or accumulated in order to build up future value. You can determine how much of the income is to be distributed and how much of it is to go to each beneficiary. You can authorize the trustee to distribute some of the trust principal to your beneficiaries if income is insufficient to maintain living standards or meet emergencies. Again subject to local law, you can decide when the trust is to terminate—for example, whether it should be distributed to your children or held for your grandchildren. You should decide at what age your beneficiaries should be capable of handling the property themselves. You may wish to have them receive trust principal gradually in installments.

Whom Do You Want as Executor and Trustee? —An executor and possibly a trustee must be designated to handle the settlement and management of your estate. This responsibility must be accepted. The details of settling an estate must be handled. Your property must be managed until it is turned over to your beneficiaries. These are tasks which call for a high degree of skill and experience. The choice of an executor and trustee may determine whether your plans for your family and your property shall succeed or fail.

Other Points to Consider —Whether or not you have a will, changes in the law and new developments in your own affairs may have made your post-mortem plans obsolete. Here are points you should discuss with your lawyer, unless you have reviewed them very recently—

(1) Does your will take full advantage of the marital deduction, which can exempt as much as half of your estate from tax?

(2) Are your insurance arrangements integrated with your will?

(3) Are inheritance taxes to be paid by each beneficiary or by the estate?

(4) Should your executor have authority to carry on your business or should he be directed to dispose of it?

(5) Have safeguards been established to minimize the possibility that your property will be taxed twice—once when you die and again when your wife dies?

(6) Has provision been made for the possibility that you and your wife may die under such circumstances that it is impossible to determine which of you died first?

(7) Does your executor have the right to borrow money, to pledge estate assets and to renew existing obligations?

(8) Should your executor have the power to retain real estate or to sell, mortgage or lease it?

(9) Should your executor have the right to retain assets owned by you at the time of your death, whether or not they constitute a legal investment for trust and estate funds?

(10) Does your trustee have broad discretion in the investment and reinvestment of trust funds? Do you want to give him any specific instructions?

(11) Have income provisions for trust beneficiaries been protected against inflation?

(12) Does the trustee have the right to make special provision for beneficiaries in the event of emergencies?

(13) Will there be enough liquid funds to meet estate tax obligations and other cash requirements which will confront your executor and trustee?

(14) Has the future distribution of your property been studied with a view to minimizing the tax drain on the income it will produce?

(15) Have you given your executor the right to file a joint income tax return with your surviving spouse?

[¶6004]   EXECUTION AND MAINTENANCE OF A WILL

Here are some of the things that can be done to insure that the will is kept intact and no pages or provisions are substituted.

(1) When a will is being typed, make it an invariable practice to use the same typewriter throughout. This will facilitate detection of forgery by typewriter.

(2) Avoid erasures (never allow corrections of figures or names). Use uniform margins at top, bottom and sides of each page leaving as little room as

possible for additional words to be filled in. Some draftsmen make it a practice to rule out all blank spaces at the end of sentences, etc.

(3) Tie the pages together with a ribbon and seal the ribbon on the last page, next to the testator's signature. Staples, brass fasteners and the like may be removed and replaced without detection, so don't give much protection.

(4) Have the testator sign or initial each page in the margin and refer to this fact in the attestation clause. A signature is harder to imitate than initials, so gives better protection.

[¶6004.1]   Executing the Will

The execution of the will should take place preferably under the supervision of the draftsman. When this is not possible, an attorney who is fully familiar with the requirements for execution of wills should supervise. Only in exceptional cases should a will be executed without the presence of an attorney.

Strict observance of the statutory formalities governing the execution of wills is a must. Every attorney should establish the exact procedure to be followed in executing a will, and stick to it. Then if he is ever called on to testify as to what happened when a particular will was executed he can truthfully testify that he always observes the statutory requirements for execution and must have in this case. Or an attorney can make a memorandum at the time of execution setting forth exactly what took place and file it with the office copy of the will. Such memorandum may be admissible in evidence as a record made in the regular course of business of the attorney, should it be needed.

[¶6004.2]   Witnesses

Although most states require only two witnesses, it is good practice to have three whenever possible. The will is then qualified for probate (at least as to the number of witnesses) in every state. Even though only two witnesses prove necessary, having a choice makes it easier to obtain two witnesses at probate.

Since the witnesses may be considered the most qualified persons to testify as to the testamentary capacity of the testator, if there are apt to be any questions on this score, they should be persons who know him well, can give favorable testimony and are likely to be available when needed. The draftsman should be a witness unless he is named as a beneficiary, since he is perhaps the best qualified to testify as to the testamentary capacity of the testator.

Where the testator wishes a beneficiary to be a witness, he should be informed that should such beneficiary be necessary as a witness to probate the will, he may lose his bequest (at least to the extent it exceeds his intestate share).

Where the testator wishes to leave a legacy to his attorney, the question of undue influence may be raised on the probate of the will. In such circumstances, the best course is to have another lawyer draw the will.

[¶6004.3] Checklist for Executing a Will

The following checklist of procedures for execution of wills can be useful as a guide to assure that the statutory requirements are observed. It also contains a number of suggestions designed to eliminate problems frequently associated with will contests. It should not be used until after you have first carefully checked it against the statutory requirements of the state whose law will govern the execution of the will.

(1) The will should be declared in an instrument in writing.

(2) The testator should sign it; if he can't do so, another person should sign for him in his presence and at his request.

(3) This signature of either the testator or the person who signs for him must follow the text of the will immediately and without leaving any intervening space.

(4) At least three witnesses should attest the testator's signature.

(5) None of the witnesses should be a beneficiary or person with a financial interest in the estate.

(6) The testator should expressly:

(a) Declare the instrument to be his will; and

(b) Ask the attesting witnesses to witness "the execution of his will."

(7) All the witnesses to the testator's signature should either:

(a) See him sign; or

(b) Hear him say that he acknowledges as his own a signature that is already on the instrument and which is pointed out to them and actually seen by all of them. If he can't write his signature, all of the witnesses should observe that:

(a) The testator expressly requests the person who signs for him to sign; and

(b) the person requested does sign in the presence of the testator.

(8) Each witness should sign his name and write his address in the testator's presence.

(9) All of the witnesses, the testator, and (if that is the case) the one who signs for the testator, should be present simultaneously throughout the entire process of execution. Even if not required as in some states, it is good practice to have witnesses and testator present throughout and see each other sign the will.

(10) The will should be dated by fully and correctly stating the place; and the day, month and year it was executed.

(11) The typical attestation clause recites the formalities of execution in some detail. Where none of the witnesses are available at the time of probate, it can

be used to show that that the statutory requirements were observed. It is not required by most states, but is used by most draftsmen.

The procedure of execution should follow precisely the statements that appear in the attestation clause. So, where the clause recites ". . .this attestation clause having first been read aloud," the clause should be read out loud so all those present can hear what has been said. Such a reading seems more effective than merely having the witnesses sign below the attestation clause, since there is a good likelihood they may not read the clause under such circumstances.

(12) Only the original of the will should be subscribed by the testator and the witnesses. Where more than one copy of a will has been executed — all copies must be produced at the probate or their absence satisfactorily explained. For example, in most states, where an executed will or copy was known to be in the possession of the testator and cannot be found at the time of probate there is a presumption that the will was revoked by destruction by the testator.

To avoid the possibility that the testator might inadvertently sign a copy of his will at a later date, it may be a good idea to conform all copies at the time of execution.

(13) The original will should be placed in a safe place as soon as possible after execution. For convenience, the safe deposit box of either the draftsman or the named executor would be suitable. If the testator's box is used, a court order to open the box must be obtained after the testator's death in most states before the will can be obtained. Also, if the original is in the possession of the testator, failure to produce it at the time of probate will bring into play the presumption of revocation by destruction by the testator. Some states provide for filing wills with the probate courts for safekeeping, but not much use is made of such provisions.

(14) Prior wills are, normally, revoked by later ones by specific language to that effect. But, where nothing is said about prior wills, a will of prior date would be effective to dispose of property not covered by the later will. Also where the testator has property in a number of states and foreign countries it is not at all uncommon for him to have an "American Will," "French Will," etc. each disposing of property within the stated countries or places. In these instances, all pertinent wills would be probatable and should be treated as if they were the original and kept in the same place.

In other cases, a later will may be invalid for a number of reasons such as lack of testamentary capacity. In such cases, a prior last will, executed during a time when the testator did have testamentary capacity, may well be probatable.

The draftsman would be the proper person to keep any prior wills since he is the best judge of how they should be used.

522

USEFUL PLANNING TOOLS

TABLE OF CONTENTS

Administration of Trusts and Estates

TAX RATES AND LEVIES

The tables set out in this section are designed as tax planning aids in various phases of business and estate planning.

FEDERAL INCOME TAX RATES

INDIVIDUALS

Taxable Income (in thousands of dollars)	Tax Percentages[1] (Actual Tax Rate/Marginal Tax Rate)			
	Single Taxpayers	Married Taxpayers		Head of Household
		Joint Return	Separate Return[2]	
0-0.5	14/14	14/14	14/14	14/14
0.5-1	14/15	14/14	14/15	14/14
1-1.5	15/16	14/15	15/16	14/16
1.5-2	15/17	14/15	15/17	14/16
2-3	16/19	15/16	16/19	15/18
3-4	17/19	15/17	17/19	16/18
4-6	17/21	16/19	17/22	17/19
6-8	19/24	17/19	19/25	17/22
8-10	20/25	17/22	20/28	19/23
10-12	21/27	18/22	22/32	19/25
12-14	22/29	19/25	24/36	20/27
14-16	23/31	20/25	25/39	21/28
16-18	24/34	20/28	27/42	22/31
18-20	25/36	21/28	29/45	23/32
20-22	26/38	22/32	30/48	24/35
22-24	27/40	23/32	32/50	25/36
24-26	28/40	24/36	34/50	26/38
26-28	29/45	25/36	35/53[3]	27/41
28-30	30/45	25/39	36/53	28/42
30-32	31/45	26/39	37/53	29/42
32-34	32/50	27/42	38/55	30/45
34-36	33/50	28/42	39/55	31/45
36-38	34/50	29/45	40/55	31/48
38-40	35/55[3]	30/45	41/58	32/51[3]
40-42	36/55	30/48	42/58	33/52
42-44	37/55	31/48	42/58	34/52
44-46	38/60	32/50	43/60	35/55
46-48	39/60	33/50	44/60	36/55

[1]There is also a 10% minimum tax on tax-preference income.
[2]Estates and trusts pay at this rate.
[3]The top marginal rate for earned income is 50%. Where applicable, this will lower the actual tax rate also.

FEDERAL INCOME TAX RATES

INDIVIDUALS (continued)

Taxable Income (in thousands of dollars)	Tax Percentages[1] (Actual Tax Rate/Marginal Tax Rate)			Head of Household
	Single Taxpayers	Married Taxpayers		
		Joint Return	Separate Return[2]	
48-50	40/60	33/50	45/60	37/55
50-52	40/62	34/50	45/62	37/56
52-56	41/62	35/53[3]	46/62	38/58
56-60	43/62	36/53	47/62	39/58
60-64	44/64	37/53	48/64	41/58
64-68	45/64	38/55	49/64	42/59
68-70	46/64	39/55	50/64	43/59
70-74	47/66	40/55	50/66	43/61
74-76	48/66	40/55	51/66	44/61
76-80	48/66	41/58	52/66	45/62
80-84	49/68	42/58	52/68	46/63
84-88	50/68	42/58	53/68	46/63
88-90	51/68	43/60	54/68	47/64
90-100	51/69	44/60	54/69	48/64
100-110	53/70	45/62	55/70	49/66
110-120	55/70	47/62	57/70	51/66
120-130	56/70	48/64	58/70	52/67
130-140	57/70	49/64	59/70	53/67
140-150	58/70	50/66	60/70	54/68
150-160	59/70	51/66	60/70	55/68
160-170	59/70	52/68	61/70	56/69
170-180	60/70	53/68	61/70	57/69
180-190	61/70	54/69	62/70	57/70
190-200	61/70	55/69	62/70	58/70
200-250	62/70	56/70	63/70	59/70
250-300	63/70	58/70	64/70	61/70
300-350	64/70	60/70	65/70	62/70
350-400	65/70	62/70	66/70	63/70
over 400	66/70	63/70	66/70	64/70

[1] There is also a 10% minimum tax on tax-preference income.
[2] Estates and trusts pay at this rate.
[3] The top marginal rate for earned income is 50%. Where applicable, this will lower the actual tax rate also.

STATE CORPORATE INCOME TAX RATES

Alabama:	5% (14)	Massachusetts (Continued):	values or net worth plus 8.55% of net income; $114 Min. Direct: 4.56%
Alaska:	18% of Fed tax (13, 19)		
Arizona:	2% 1st $1000; 3% 2d $1000; 4% 3d $1000; 5% 4th $1000; 6% 5th $1000; 7% 6th $1000; 8% bal.	Michigan:	7.8% (16, 19)
		Minnesota:	12% (6, 18). Min. $10
		Mississippi:	3% 1st $5000; 4% bal.
		Missouri:	5% (19)
Arkansas:	1% 1st $3000; 2% 2d $3000; 3% next $5000; 4% next $14,000; 6% bal. (19)	Montana:	6-3/4%. Min. $50 (19)
		Nebraska:	3% (19)
		New Hampshire:	7% (2)
California:	9%. Min. $100 (1)	New Jersey:	5-1/2% (8)
Colorado:	5% (19)	New Mexico:	5% (19)
Connecticut:	8%. Min. $45 (12, 15)	New York:	9%. Min. $125 (10, 13, 20)
Delaware:	7.2% (13) plus 20% surcharge	North Carolina:	6%
		North Dakota:	3% 1st $3000; 4% next $5000; 5% next $7000; 6% bal. (5, 19)
District of Columbia:	8%. Min. $25		
Florida:	5% (23)	Ohio:	4% 1st $25,000; 8% over $25,000
Georgia:	6%		
Hawaii:	5.85% 1st $25,000; 6.435% bal. (19)	Oklahoma:	4% (15)
		Oregon:	6%. Min. $10 (3, 19)
Idaho:	6.5% plus $10 excise (19)	Pennsylvania:	12% (13)
Illinois:	4% (19, 22)	Rhode Island:	8% (11)
Indiana:	3% (13, 19)	South Carolina:	6%
Iowa:	6% 1st $25,000; 8% next $75,000; over $100,000, 10%	Tennessee:	6%
		Utah:	6%. Min. $25 (9, 19)
Kansas:	4-1/2% (4, 19)	Vermont:	6%. Min. $25
Kentucky:	5% 1st $25,000; 7% bal.	Virginia:	6%
Louisiana:	4%	West Virginia:	6% (17)
Maine:	4%; alternate tax 1% of local sales (21)	Wisconsin:	2.3% 1st $1000; 2.8% 2d $1000; 3.4% 3d $1000; 4.5% 4th $1000; 5.6% 5th $1000; 6.8% 6th $1000; 7.9% bal.
Maryland:	7% (7)		
Massachusetts:	Excise: $5.76 per $1000 on tangible		

NOTES: See following page (A6).

STATE CORPORATE INCOME TAX RATES

NOTES

(1) For franchise tax; no min. for income 7% tax.

(2) Business profits tax on corporations, partnerships, individuals, organizations for profits (for profits earned starting 1-1-70).

(3) Credits: personalty tax paid (limited; pollution control facility cost).

(4) Plus 2-1/2% surtax over $25,000.

(5) Starting 1-1-70, added 1% net income tax on privilege of doing business in ND (min. $20). Credit for new industry: 1% on in-state salaries and wages; 1/2% for 4th and 5th year (for 1st ND incorporation or certification after 1-1-69).

(6) Includes 1.8% added tax, plus surtax of 10% of rate. Basic rate, 8-1/2%.

(7) Domestic corporation gets credit for franchise tax in excess of $40. Also, for state personalty taxes.

(8) Also tax on higher of allocated net worth, total assets or capital stock.

(9) No minimum for direct tax.

(10) Other minimums: 9% of apportioned income plus compensation, or 1.6 mills on value of apportioned business and investment capital. Added tax: 0.8 mill per $1 subsidiary capital.

(11) Alternative tax, if larger, 40¢ per $100 of corporate excess.

(12) Or 4 mills per $1 of corporate excess, if greater.

(13) Credit against tax allowed for investment in ghetto areas and/or training hard core unemployed. In Alaska, also for industrial incentive.

(14) Domestic corporation gets credit for income tax paid out of state.

(15) Credit allowed for pollution control facilities.

(16) Credit for Mich. city income and limited property tax; also limited credit for contributions to "educational institutions."

(17) Credit for Business & Occupation tax paid and investment for business expansion.

(18) Credit for occupation tax on copper-nickel mining and pollution control equipment.

(19) Multistate Tax Compact member. Compact requires optional tax for small taxpayer. Rules: Colo., 1/2%; Me., 1%; Mich., 2/5%; N.M., 3/4%; N.D., to $20,000—6/10%, $20,000 to $55,000—8/10%, over $55,000—1%; Ore. 1/4%; Utah, 1/2%. Rates are applicable if local sales not over $100,000 annually, sales only instate activity and no instate property owned or rented.

(20) 1% investment credit.

(21) Alternate tax applicable if local sales not over $100,000 annually, sales only in-state activity and no in-state property owned or rented. This is same as provisions of the multistate tax compact constitutional amendment OK'd at 11-70 election.

(22) $1,000 standard exemption allowed.

(23) $5,000 standard exemption allowed.

STATE SALES AND USE TAXES

Alabama:	4%	Missouri:	3%
Arizona:	3%	Nebraska:	2-1/2%
Arkansas:	3%	Nevada:	3%
California:	5%	New Jersey:	5%
Colorado:	3%	New Mexico:	4%
Connecticut:	6-1/2%	New York:	4%
District of Columbia:	5%	North Carolina:	3%
Florida:	4%	North Dakota:	4%
Georgia:	3%	Ohio:	4%
Hawaii:	4%	Oklahoma:	2%
Idaho:	3%	Pennsylvania:	6%
Illinois:	4%	Rhode Island:	5%
Indiana:	4%	South Carolina:	4%
Iowa:	3%	South Dakota:	4%
Kansas:	3%	Tennessee:	3-1/2%
Kentucky:	5%	Texas:	4%
Louisiana:	3%	Utah:	4%
Maine:	5%	Vermont:	3%
Maryland:	4%	Virginia	4%
Massachusetts:	3%	Washington:	4-1/2%
Michigan:	4%	West Virginia:	3%
Minnesota:	4%	Wisconsin:	4%
Mississippi:	5%	Wyoming:	3%

NOTE: These figures are for the state rates, additional local (county, city, town, school district, etc.) taxes ranging from 1/8% to 4% are imposed in many states including: Ala., Alaska, Ariz., Ark., Calif., Colo., Ill., Kan., La., Minn., Mo., Neb., Nev., N.M., N.Y., N.C., Ohio, Okla, S.D., Tenn., Tex., Utah, Va., Wash., and Wis.

FEDERAL ESTATE TAX

Note: The federal tax both with and without the maximum credit for state tax is given. In general, state tax will at least equal the amount of credit To the extent that your state inheritance tax exceeds the maximum credit the total of state and federal tax will exceed the maximum federal tax.

Taxable Estate Before Exemption		Federal Tax Without Marital Deduction*		Maximum Credit for State Death Tax		Federal Tax with Maximum Credit for State Tax	
		Tax on lowest amount in first column	Plus this % of excess	Credit on lowest amount in first column	Plus this % of excess	Tax on lowest amount in first column	Plus this % of excess
$ 0	$ 60.000	0				0	
60,000	65,000		3%				3%
65,000	70,000	$ 150	7			$ 150	7
70,000	80,000	500	11			500	11
80,000	90,000	1,600	14			1,600	14
90,000	100,000	3,000	18			3,000	18
100,000	110,000	4,800	22		.8%	4,800	21.2
110,000	120,000	7,000	25	$ 80	.8	6,920	24.2
120,000	150,000	9,500	28	160	.8	9,340	27.2
150,000	160,000	17,900	28	400	1.6	17,500	26.4
160,000	200,000	20,700	30	560	1.6	20,140	28.4
200,000	300,000	32,700	30	1,200	2.4	31,500	27.6
300,000	310,000	62,700	30	3,600	3.2	59,100	26.8
310,000	500,000	65,700	32	3,920	3.2	61,780	28.8
500,000	560,000	126,500	32	10,000	4.0	116,500	28.0
560,000	700,000	145,700	35	12,400	4.0	133,300	31.0
700,000	810,000	194,700	35	18,000	4.8	176,700	30.2
810,000	900,000	233,200	37	23,280	4.8	209,920	32.2
900,000	1,060,000	266,500	37	27,600	5.6	238,900	31.4
1,060,000	1,100,000	325,700	39	36,560	5.6	289,140	33.4
1,100,000	1,310,000	341,300	39	38,800	6.4	302,500	32.6
1,310,000	1,560,000	423,200	42	52,240	6.4	370,960	35.6
1,560,000	1,600,000	528,200	45	68,240	6.4	459,960	38.6
1,600,000	2,060,000	546,200	45	70,800	7.2	475,400	37.8
2,060,000	2,100,000	753,200	49	103,920	7.2	649,280	41.8
2,100,000	2,560,000	772,800	49	106,800	8.0	666,000	41.0
2,560,000	2,600,000	998,200	53	143,600	8.0	854,600	45.0
2,600,000	3,060,000	1,019,400	53	146,800	8.8	872,600	44.2
3,060,000	3,100,000	1,263,200	56	187,280	8.8	1,075,920	47.2
3,100,000	3,560,000	1,285,600	56	190,800	9.6	1,094,800	46.4
3,560,000	3,600,000	1,543,200	59	234,960	9.6	1,308,240	49.4
3,600,000	4,060,000	1,566,800	59	238,800	10.4	1,328,000	48.6
4,060,000	4,100,000	1,838,200	63	286,640	10.4	1,551,560	52.6
4,100,000	5,060,000	1,863,400	63	290,800	11.2	1,572,600	51.8
5,060,000	5,100,000	2,468,200	67	398,320	11.2	2,069,880	55.8
5,100,000	6,060,000	2,495,000	67	402,800	12.0	2,092,200	55.0
6,060,000	6,100,000	3,138,200	70	518,000	12.0	2,620,200	58.0
6,100,000	7,060,000	3,166,200	70	522,800	12.8	2,643,400	57.2
7,060,000	7,100,000	3,283,200	73	645,680	12.8	3,192,520	60.2
7,100,000	8,060,000	3,867,400	73	650,800	13.6	3,216,600	59.4
8,060,000	8,100,000	4,568,200	76	781,360	13.6	3,786,840	62.4
8,100,000	9,100,000		76	786,800	14.4	3,811,800	61.6
9,100,000	10,060,000	5,358,600	76	930,800	15.2	4,427,800	60.8
10,060,000	10,100,000	6,068,200	77	1,076,720	15.2	5,011,480	61.8
10,100,000		6,119,000	77	1,082,890	16.0	5,036,200	61.0

*To obtain the estate tax where the full marital deduction is used subtract one-half of the adjusted gross estate from the net taxable estate and use this table to calculate the tax on the remaining sum.

FEDERAL GIFT TAX

The table below sets forth the gift tax rates as they appear in the Code. These rates apply to the net taxable gift, after exclusions, after exemptions and after splitting the gift with the donor's spouse or the marital deduction if the gift is made to the donor's spouse.

Note that the tax rates are for the total gifts made in prior years and the current year. The current year's taxable gifts are added to the total of the prior years' taxable gifts and the gift tax for the grand total is determined. Then, from this grand total, the total gift taxes paid in prior years is subtracted. The remaining amount is the gift tax liability for the current year.

Gift	Tax
Not over $5,000.	2 1/4% of the taxable gifts.
Over $5,000 but not over $10,000.	$112.50, plus 5 1/4% of excess over $5,000.
Over $10,000 but not over $20,000.	$375, plus 8 1/4% of excess over $10,000.
Over $20,000 but not over $30,000.	$1,200, plus 10 1/2% of excess over $20,000.
Over $30,000 but not over $40,000.	$2,250, plus 13 1/2% of excess over $30,000.
Over $40,000 but not over $50,000.	$3,600, plus 16 1/2% of excess over $40,000.
Over $50,000 but not over $60,000.	$5,250, plus 18 3/4% of excess over $50,000.
Over $60,000 but not over $100,000.	$7,125, plus 21% of excess over $60,000.
Over $100,000 but not over $250,000.	$15,525, plus 22 1/2% of excess over $100,000.
Over $250,000 but not over $500,000.	$49,275, plus 24% of excess over $250,000.
Over $500,000 but not over $750,000.	$109,275, plus 26 1/4% of excess over $500,000.
Over $750,000 but not over $1,000,000.	$174,900, plus 27 3/4% of excess over $750,000.
Over $1,000,000 but not over $1,250,000.	$244,275, plus 29 1/4% of excess over $1,000,000.
Over $1,250,000 but not over $1,500,000.	$317,400, plus 31 1/2% of excess over $1,250,000.
Over $1,500,000 but not over $2,000,000.	$396,150, plus 33 3/4% of excess over $1,500,000.
Over $2,000,000 but not over $2,500,000.	$564,900, plus 36 3/4% of excess over $2,000,000.
Over $2,500,000 but not over $3,000,000.	$748,650, plus 39 3/4% of excess over $2,500,000.
Over $3,000,000 but not over $3,500,000.	$944,400, plus 42% of excess over $3,000,000.
Over $3,500,000 but not over $4,000,000.	$1,157,400, plus 44 1/4% of excess over $3,500,000.
Over $4,000,000 but not over $5,000,000.	$1,378,650, plus 47 1/4% of excess over $4,000,000.
Over $5,000,000 but not over $6,000,000.	$1,851,150, plus 50 1/4% of excess over $5,000,000.
Over $6,000,000 but not over $7,000,000.	$2,353,650, plus 52 1/2% of excess over $6,000,000.
Over $7,000,000 but not over $8,000,000.	$2,878,650, plus 54 3/4% of excess over $7,000,000.
Over $8,000,000 but not over $10,000,000.	$3,426,150, plus 57% of excess over $8,000,000.
Over $10,000,000.	$4,566,150, plus 57 3/4% of excess over $10,000,000.

CORPORATE COSTS AND FEES

Corporate costs and fees, including initial organizational costs, annual maintenance and the costs of corporate qualification outside the home state, may play a vital part in corporate planning and operation. The tables in this section are designed as planning aids in this area.

INCORPORATING FEES (Principal Incorporating States)

The tables below are designed as a quick and ready reference for counsel to determine the costs incident to organizing corporations in the principal states used for incorporating outside the home state.

CALIFORNIA

Filing Fee—based on authorized capital stock—nonpar valued at $10.00 per sh.

To $25,000	$ 15.00	$200,001 - 500,000	$ 75.00
$25,001 - 75,000	25.00	500,001 - 1,000,000	100.00
75,001 - 200,000	50.00	Over $1,000,000	$100 + 50.00 per
			$500,000 or part

Recording, certifying, etc., $20.00

Minimum franchise tax prepayment. . . $100.00

CONNECTICUT

Organization Tax, based on authorized capital stock as follows: Under 10,000—1 cent; 10,000 to 100,000—1/2 cent; 100,000 to 1,000,000—1/4 cent; over 1,000,000—1/5 cent; (minimum $50)
Filing Fee - $20.00
Incidental Fees - $15.00

DELAWARE

Tax Based on Authorized Capital Stock ($10.00 minimum)

Par Value Stock – per $100		No-Par Value Stock – per share	
To $2,000,000	1¢	To 20,000 shares	1/2¢
Next $18,000,000	$200 + 1/2¢	Next 1,980,000 shares	$100 + 1/4¢
Over $20,000,000	$1,100 + 1/5¢	Over 2,000,000 shares	$5,050 + 1/5¢

Other Fees - About $50.00

ILLINOIS

License tax based on value, expressed in dollars, of entire consideration received for issued shares, at rate of 1/20 of 1%.

Franchise tax on that proportion of total stated capital and paid-in surplus which sum of value property instate and gross business transacted in or from Illinois bears to sum of value of all property and gross amount of business; rate is 1/10% of proportion. Pay tax in advance: initially on qualification and on the anniversary thereafter. Min. $25; max. $1 million.

Filing fee - $20.00

Recording - $8.00 (approx.)

MASSACHUSETTS

Filing fee based on total authorized capital stock at rate of 1/20 of 1% on par value stock (minimum par value allowed for filing fee purposes is $1.00 per share even if actual par value is lower than $1.00 per share) and 1¢ per share on nonpar stock with a $75.00 minimum.

NEW JERSEY

Tax based on authorized capital stock at rate of 1¢ per share up to 10,000 shares of par value stock and 1/10 of a cent per share over 10,000 shares with a minimum fee of $25.00; maximum fee $1,000.

NEW YORK

Tax based on authorized capital stock at rate of 50¢ per $1,000 (1/20%) on par value stock and 5¢ per share on no-par shares with a $10.00 minimum.

Filing fee - $50.00

PENNSYLVANIA

Excise tax based on authorized capital stock at rate of 1/5 of 1% on the total stated capital and authorized capital stock.

Filing - $40.00

Publications costs - $40.00 (approx.)

ANNUAL CORPORATE TAXES AND FEES
(Principal Incorporating States)

The tables below show the annual costs, taxes and fees, incident to operation of a corporation in the principal states used for incorporating.

CALIFORNIA

Franchise - Income Tax - 7% of net income allocated to the state based on income for the preceding calendar or fiscal year with a minimum of $100 on the franchise tax.

CONNECTICUT

Annual Report Filing Fee - $16.

Business Income Tax - 8% of net income from instate business plus added tax equal to amount by which 4 mills per $1 corporate excise allocable to Connecticut exceeds 8% tax on net income. Minimum $45.

DELAWARE

Annual Report Filing Fee - $10.

Franchise Tax lesser of (1) or (2) with minimum of $20.00 and maximum of $110,000.

(1) Based on number of authorized shares, par or nonpar:

To 1,000 shares	$20,000	3,001 to 5,000 shares	$30.25
1,000 to 3,000 shares	$24.50	5,001 to 10,000 shares	$60.25
		Each added 10,000 shares or fraction	$30.25

(2) $121 for $1,000,000 of assumed par value capital. If the assumed par value is less than $1,000,000 the tax is proportionately reduced.

Income Tax - 6% of taxable income from business carried on and property located in Delaware plus 20% surcharge. Corporations merely maintaining statutory corporate office in Delaware are exempt.

ILLINOIS

Franchise Tax - Based on that proportion of total stated capital and paid-in surplus which sum of value property instate and gross business transacted in or from Illinois bears to sum of value of all property and gross amount of business; rate is 1/10% of proportion. Min. $25; max. $1 million.

Corporation Income Tax - 4% on the taxable income received in Illinois.

MASSACHUSETTS

Excise Tax - Tax is total of:

    (a) 8.55% of allocated net income; and

534

    (b) $7.98 per $1,000 of the corporation's taxable tangible property, if a tangible property corporation, or, of the corporation's taxable net worth if an intangible property corporation.
    (c)   Minimum tax is $114.

Income Tax - 4.56%.

Filing Certificate of Condition - $25.00.

NEW JERSEY

Filing Fee for Annual Report - $10.

Franchise Tax - the greatest of following:

    (a)   Tax on proportion of entire net worth allocable to State, at rates of 2 mills per dollar on first $100,000,000; 4/10ths mill on second; 3/10ths mill on third; and 2/10ths mill on excess.
    (b)   Tax on 5/10ths mill per dollar on first $100,000,000 of total assets allocated to State; 2/10ths mill per dollar thereafter.
    (c)   Tax which is least of (a) amount based on authorized capital stock if not over 5000 shares; $25, 5001 to 10,000; $55, over 10,000 shares; $55 plus $27.50 per added 10,000 shares or (b) 11/100 mill per $1 on total assets or (c) $100,000.
    (d)   Minimum tax of $25.

In lieu of all the foregoing, corporations having total assets everywhere (less reasonable reserves for depreciation) of less than $150,000, may elect to pay tax based upon total assets, according to a special tax table.

Income Tax - 4-1/4% of net income allocable to the State.

NEW YORK

Franchise Tax - the greatest one of the following:

1.   (a)   9% of the entire net income or the portion thereof allocated to New York, or
    (b)   16 mills per dollar of the total business and investment capital or portion thereof allocated to New York, or
    (c)   9% of the following or the proportion thereof allocated to New York: 30% of the entire net income plus salaries and other compensation paid to elected or appointed officers and to every stockholder owning more than 5% of the issued capital stock, less an exemption of $15,000 and any net loss for the reported year—or
    (d) $125

And in addition:

2.   A tax of 8/10 mill for each dollar of the portion of the subsidiary capital allocated to New York.

PENNSYLVANIA

Capital Stock Tax - 10 mills per dollar of taxable portion of the actual value of the whole capital stock at the end of the tax year. Exemption is allowed for capital which is invested in manufacturing, research or development, the distillation or other production of alcoholic liquors and processing.

Income Tax - 12% of net income allocated to Pennsylvania.

Corporate Loans Tax - Tax of 4 mills per dollar on corporate loans held by Pennsylvania residents, if interest is paid thereon. Tax is on the holders of corporate loans but must be withheld by the corporation from the interest when paid, and remitted to the Commonwealth.

535

The lawyer called upon to counsel or plan interstate business transactions must be familiar with the laws of all jurisdictions touching the transaction.

The tables in this section are designed to alert the practitioner to legal variations within the states in many topics which might concern him.

RETAIL INSTALLMENT SALES ACTS
OR TIME SALES ACTS

More than 80% of our states have some form of retail installment sales or time sales acts. Their precise scope and operation varies considerably from state to state. Some cover all goods; others only motor vehicles. Most exempt goods to be resold or used for business; some aren't completely clear. Some exempt sales involving more than a certain amount. Some in terms apply only to conditional sales contracts, others take in unsecured transactions.

Most acts go into great detail as to what the contract must say (or can't say) and how it must be said, specifying in many cases the kind and size of type. They will usually call for the cash price, down payment, insurance charges, finance charges, other charges, installment sale price, balance, number, date and amount of payments. Sometimes other details are called for.

Most acts give the buyer a right to a copy of the contract and a right to prepay and get a rebate. Some give buyers the right to redeem repossessed property; the right to a receipt for payments made in cash; the right to an acknowledgment of payment in full; or the right to notice of sale on repossession. Others deal with the buyer's rights on assignment of the contract.

Some of these statutes in addition to everything else require licensing of sellers and financers engaged in retail installment sales financing.

Because of the wide variations in the statutory provisions only a check of your particular state's law will give you a safe guide to action. The table which follows lists the states which have adopted one form or another of retail installment sales acts, and those which require licensing. It is taken from Installment Sales, Prentice-Hall, Inc. (looseleaf service current to May 7, 1974) and reproduced by permission of the publisher.

TIME SALES ACT

State	Goods Covered	Finance Charge Limit?	License?	Effective Date
Alaska	All Goods	Yes	No	1/ 1/63
Arizona	Vehicles	Yes	Yes	7/ 1/61
California	All Goods	Yes	No	1/ 1/60
	Vehicles	Yes	No	1/ 1/62
Colorado.	All Goods	Yes	No	5/11/59
	Vehicles	Yes	Yes	1951
Connecticut	All Goods	Yes	Yes	1947
Delaware	All Goods	Yes	No	11/ 6/60
	Vehicles	Yes	Yes	10/ 7/60
Dist. of Columbia.	Vehicles	Yes	Yes	5/22/60
Florida.	All Goods	Yes	Yes	1/ 1/60
	Vehicles	Yes	Yes	10/ 1/57
Georgia	All Goods	Yes	No	10/ 1/67
	Vehicles	Yes	No	10/ 1/67
Hawaii	All Goods	Yes	No	1941
Illinois	All Goods	Yes	No	1/ 1/68
	Vehicles	Yes	No	1/ 1/68
Indiana	All Goods	Yes	Yes	7/ 1/35
Iowa.	Vehicles	Yes	No	7/ 4/57
Kansas	All Goods	Yes	Yes	5/14/58
Kentucky.	Vehicles	Yes	No	1956
	All Goods	No	No	1/ 1/63
Louisiana	Vehicles	Yes	Yes	1/ 1/59
Maine.	All Goods	No	No	1/ 1/68
	Vehicles	Yes	Yes	1/ 1/58
Maryland	All Goods	Yes	No	6/ 1/41
Massachusetts	All Goods	Yes	Yes	11/ 1/66
	Vehicles	Yes	Yes	1/19/59
Michigan.	All Goods	Yes	No	3/10/67
	Vehicles	Yes	Yes	1951
Minnesota	Vehicles	Yes	Yes	7/ 1/57
Mississippi	Vehicles	Yes	Yes	7/21/58
Missouri.	Vehicles	Yes	Yes	10/11/63
	All Goods	Yes	No	7/ 1/59

• In addition, North Carolina has a statute that requires disclosure of contract terms but not much else.

537

TIME SALES ACT (Continued)

State	Goods Covered	Finance Charge Limit?	License?	Effective Date
Montana	All Goods	Yes	Yes	5/25/65
Nebraska	All Goods	Yes	Yes	7/ 1/65
Nevada	All Goods	Yes	No	7/ 1/65
New Hampshire	Vehicles	Yes	Yes	10/ 1/61
New Jersey	All Goods	Yes	Yes	9/ 7/60
New Mexico.	Vehicles	Yes	No	6/19/65
	All Goods	Yes	Yes	6/15/59
New York	Vehicles	Yes	Yes	1956
	All Goods	Yes	Yes	7/ 1/57
North Dakota	All Goods	Yes	No	1949
Ohio.	All Goods	Yes	No	1/ 1/58
Oklahoma	All Goods	Yes	No	9/ 1/67
Oregon	All Goods	No	No	10/ 1/63
	Vehicles	Yes	No	6/28/47
Pennsylvania	All Goods	Yes	No	4/ 1/67
	Vehicles	Yes	Yes	7/ 1/57
Rhode Island	All Goods	Yes	No	7/ 1/69
South Carolina	Vehicles	Yes	No	7/31/68
South Dakota	Vehicles	Yes	Yes	3/15/61
Tennessee.	All Goods	Yes	No	1953
Texas.	All Goods	Yes	No	1/ 1/68
	Vehicles	Yes	No	1/ 1/68
Utah.	All Goods	Yes	Yes	1/ 1/64
Vermont	Vehicles	Yes	Yes	1/ 1/62
	All Goods	Yes	Yes	1/ 1/64
Virginia	All Goods	No	No	1/ 1/69
Washington	All Goods	Yes	No	1/ 1/68
Wisconsin	Vehicles	Yes	Yes	1938

● In addition, North Carolina has a statute that requires disclosure of contract terms but not much else.

538

STATE GUIDE TO INTEREST RATES*

State	Maxi-mum Legal Rate	Maximum Contract Rate	Maximum Judgment Rate	Penalty for Usury	Corporation's Defense of Usury
ALABAMA	6%	8%	6%	Forfeit all interest.	No defense on loan over $100,000
ALASKA	6%	4% above FRB discount rate of 12th Dist.	8%, but in no event over 10%.	Borrower recovers double interest paid; lender forfeits all interest.	No defense.
ARIZONA	6%	10%	As set out in contract.	Forfeit all interest; borrower recovers interest payments or applies them against principal.	No defense on loan over $5,000 at up to 1-1/2% a month.
ARKANSAS	6%	10%	6%	Contract void.	No provision.
CALIFORNIA	7%	10%	7%	Forfeit all interest; borrower recovers triple interest paid over 10%; violation is misdemeanor.	Can defend.
COLORADO	6%	As set out in contract.	6%	No provision.	No defense.
CONNECTI-CUT	6%	12%	6%	Fine up to $1,000 or imprisonment up to 6 months or both; loan void.	No provision.
DELAWARE	6%	9%	6%	Borrower recovers excess paid; greater of $500 or three times excess paid after maturity.	No defense.
DISTRICT OF COLUMBIA	6%	8%	6%, but can set rate to 8%.	Forfeit all interest. Borrower recovers interest or applies it against principal.	No defense.

539

			STATE GUIDE TO INTEREST RATES*		
State	Maxi-mum Legal Rate	Maximum Contract Rate	Maximum Judgment Rate	Penalty for Usury	Corporation's Defense of Usury
FLORIDA	6%	10%	Lesser of 6% or rate agreed agreed on.	Forfeit all interest. When rate 25% or more, forfeit principal and interest.	Usury, if rate over 15%.
GEORGIA	7%	8%. 9% secured by real estate. Over 9% VA and FHA loans.	7%	Forfeit all interest; borrower may set-off excess interest paid against principal.	No defense on loan over $2,500. No limit on loans of $100,000 or more.
HAWAII	6%	12%	6%	Recover only principal less interest paid.	No defense on loan over $750,000.
IDAHO	6%	10%	6%	Borrower recovers triple interest paid.	12% over $10,000; no defense.
ILLINOIS	5%	8%	5%	Forfeit all interest; borrower recovers double interest.	No defense.
INDIANA	8%	8%	6%, but may contract up to 8%.	Forfeit excess over 6%.	No defense.
IOWA	5%	9%	5%, but may contract up to 7%.	Forfeit all interest, plus 8% of principal unpaid at time of judgment; additional 8% to school fund.	No defense.
KANSAS	6%	10%	8%, but may contract up to 10%.	Forfeit double interest over 10%; excess over 10% applied against principal and interest.	No defense.

540

State	Maximum Legal Rate	Maximum Contract Rate	Maximum Judgment Rate	Penalty for Usury	Corporation's Defense of Usury
KENTUCKY	6%	7%, but may contract to 8-1/2% to buy or repair 1 family home.	6%	Forfeit interest; debtor can recover twice interest paid, plus reasonable attorney's fees.	No defense unless principal asset is one- or two-family house.
LOUISIANA	7%	8%; 10% immovables.	7%	Forfeit all interest.	No defense, including limited and in commendam partnerships, endorsers, guarantors and co-makers.
MAINE	6%	No maximum, if in writing; 16% a year simple interest on personal loans over $2,000.	10%	Personal loans over $2,000, lender forfeits all principal, interest and charges, plus reasonable attorney's fees.	No provision.
MARYLAND	6%	8%; unsecured loans 12%; no limit on business loans over $5,000. Interest must be stated as a simple annual rate.	6%	Forfeit greater of 3 times excess interest and charges or $500.	No defense.
MASSACHU-SETTS	6%	No maximum stated.	No provision.	Criminal penalties	No provision.
MICHIGAN	$5 upon $100 a year.	7%	5%	Forfeit all interest and charges, plus attorney's fee and court cost. It's criminal usury to charge interest over 25% a year.	No defense. Can agree in writing to any rate of interest.

STATE GUIDE TO INTEREST RATES*					
State	Maxi-mum Legal Rate	Maximum Contract Rate	Maximum Judgment Rate	Penalty for Usury	Corporation's Defense of Usury
MINNESOTA	6%	8%	6%	Contract void; borrower gets back all interest paid but one-half goes to school fund.	No defense.
MISSISSIPPI	6%	8%	6%, but may con-tract to 8%.	Forfeit all in-terest; both in-terest and prin-cipal if rate is over 20%.	No defense if loan over $2,500.
MISSOURI	6%	8%	6%, but may contract to 8%.	Forfeit excess and pay costs of action.	No defense.
MONTANA	6%	10%	6%	Double interest charged.	No provision.
NEBRASKA	$6 a year for each $100.	$9 a year for each $100.	6%, but may contract to 9%.	Forfeit all in-terest.	No defense.
NEVADA	7%	12%	7%, but may contract to 12%.	Forfeit excess over 12%.	No provision.
NEW HAMP-SHIRE	6%	8%	6%	No provision.	No provision.
NEW JERSEY	6%	Between 6% and 8%, as prescribed by Commis-sioner of Banking and Insurance.	No provi-sion.	Forfeit all interest. Fine up to $500.	No defense.
NEW MEXICO	6%	10%; 12% if no col-lateral.	6%, but may contract to 12%.	Forfeit all inter-est; borrower recovers double interest paid.	No defense.

542

STATE GUIDE TO INTEREST RATES*

State	Maximum Legal Rate	Maximum Contract Rate	Maximum Judgment Rate	Penalty for Usury	Corporation's Defense of Usury
NEW YORK	$7\frac{1}{2}\%$	8% effective 8/15/73. No limit on notes over $5,000.	6% except where otherwise prescribed by statute.	Contract void. Exception: savings banks and savings and loan assns. forfeit all interest.	No defense unless (1) interest exceeds 25%, or (2) corporation's principal asset is 1- or 2-family house and corporation was formed or control of it acquired within 6 months before loan and mortgage.
NORTH CAROLINA	6%	No limit over $300,000; 12% over $100,000 to $300,000; 9% $100,000 or less provided non-business and non-real estate loan; 10% over $50,000 to $100,000 for business property; 8% $50,000 or less secured by realty; 10% $50,000 or less nonresidential realty payable 2 to 10 years; 10% on $7,500 or less secured by realty payable 1 to 10 years.	6%	Forfeit all interest; borrower recovers double interest.	Can defend.
NORTH DAKOTA	4%	Greater of 3% above maximum interest payable on deposits authorized by state banking.	4%	Forfeit all interest plus 25% of principal; borrower recovers double interest paid plus 25% of principal or set off double interest against.	No defense. No limit on business loans over $25,000.

543

State	Maxi-mum Legal Rate	Maximum Contract Rate	Maximum Judgment Rate	Penalty for Usury	Corporation's Defense of Usury
NORTH DAKOTA (continued)		board, or 7%.		principal debt; violation is misdemeanor.	
OHIO	6%	8%. No limit on loans over $100,000.	6%, but may contract to 8%.	Apply excess interest paid against principal.	No defense.
OKLAHOMA	6%	As stated in the con-tract.	10%	Forfeit double interest charged; bor-rower can re-cover double in-terest paid plus costs.	No defense.
OREGON	6%	10%	6%, but may contract to 10%.	Forfeit entire interest.	No defense on contract not over 12%.
PENNSYL-VANIA	6%	6% on loans under $50,000.	6%	Forfeit excess over 6%; bor-rower recovers excess paid over 6%.	No defense.
RHODE ISLAND	6%	21%	6%	Contract void; borrower re-covers all payments.	No provision.
SOUTH CAROLINA	6%	8%	6%	Forfeit all in-terest; borrow-er recovers double interest paid.	No defense capital stock of $40,000 or more has been issued. No de-fense on loans $50,000 or more. 10% limit on loans over $50,000 and up to $100,000; 12% limit on loans over $100,000 and up to $500,000.

	Maximum Legal Rate	Maximum Contract Rate	Maximum Judgment Rate	Penalty for Usury	Corporation's Defense of Usury
STATE GUIDE TO INTEREST RATES*					
SOUTH DAKOTA	6%	10%	6%, but may contract to 8%.	Forfeit all interest.	No defense.
TENNESSEE	6%	10%	6%	Forfeit excess interest.	Can plead.
TEXAS	6%	10%	6%, but may contract to 10%.	Forfeit twice amount of interest charged; forfeit both principal and interest if rate is double allowed.	1-1/2% a month $5,000 or more; no defense.
UTAH	6%	No limit if not subject to Uniform Consumer Credit Code	8%, but may contract to 10%.	Forfeit all interest; borrower recovers triple interest paid and attorney's fees. Violation is misdemeanor.	No defense. Domestic and foreign corporations can borrow any amount under the installment loan law, provided the interest or discount rate isn't more than 14% per annum.
VERMONT	7-1/2%	7-1/2%. Interest must be stated as an effective annual percentage rate.	No provision.	Borrower recovers excess interest paid, plus interest from payment date plus costs and reasonable attorney's fees. Willful violation $500 fine, 6 mos. jail or both.	Up to 12%. No provision.
VIRGINIA	6%	8%. No limit on first mortgage realty loans, if nonagricultural.	No provision.	Borrower can recover twice interest paid if suit brought within two years.	No defense for corporations, partnerships under Title 50, c. 3, professional assn., or real estate investment trusts.

545

STATE GUIDE TO INTEREST RATES*				
State	Maxi-mum Legal Rate	Maximum Contract Rate	Maximum Judgment Rate	Penalty for Usury	Corporation's Defense of Usury
WASHING-TON	6%	12%, plus "set up charge" of lesser of 4% or $15 on loans from $100 to $500; minimum of $4 on loans under $100.	8%, but in no case to exceed 10%.	Forfeit all interest; borrower may apply double interest paid against principal; debtor can collect costs and reasonable attorney's fees. Usury laws apply to out-of-state loans made to residents, same as if loan made in state.	No defense for corporations, Massachusetts trusts, associations, limited partnerships, and persons in money lending business or real estate improvement, if transactions over $100,000.
WEST VIRGINIA	6%	8%	No provision.	Forfeit all interest; borrower can recover greater of $100 or 4 times interest charged.	No defense.
WISCONSIN	5%	12%	5%	Forfeit all interest and principal under $2000; borrower recovers interest paid and $2000 of principal.	No defense.
WYOMING	7%		7%, but may contract to 10%.	Forfeit all interest.	No defense.

---

* Prentice-Hall loose-leaf book "Installment Sales" as of last revision dated 5/7/74. Most states have special laws governing interest rates on small loans, consumer credit, time sales, bank installment loans and credit unions. A special check for these laws should be made if the transaction appears to be within possible range.

546

WHEN INFANTS ARE COMPETENT TO CONTRACT

The following table shows the age at which infants attain majority in the various states. The table also indicates those instances in which females reach majority before males. The effects of marriage upon a minor's disability to contract are shown where such a disability may be removed by appropriate court proceedings.

State	Age		State	Age	
Alabama	21	(1)	Montana	18	
Alaska	19	(3)	Nebraska	19	(2)
Arizona	18		Nevada	18	
Arkansas	*21		New Hampshire	18	
California	18		New Jersey	18	
Colorado	18		New Mexico	18	(2)
Connecticut	18		New York	21	
Delaware	18		North Carolina	18	(4)
District of Columbia	21		North Dakota	18	
Florida	18	(2)	Ohio	18	
Georgia	18		Oklahoma	18	
Hawaii	18		Oregon	18	
Idaho	18	(3)	Pennsylvania	18	
Illinois	18		Rhode Island	18	
Indiana	18		South Carolina	21	
Iowa	18	(2)	South Dakota	18	
Kansas	18		Tennessee	18	
Kentucky	18		Texas	18	
Louisiana	18		Utah	*21	(2)
Maine	18		Vermont	18	
Maryland	18		Virginia	18	
Massachusetts	18		Washington	18	(4)
Michigan	18		West Virginia	18	
Minnesota	18		Wisconsin	18	
Mississippi	21		Wyoming	19	
Missouri	21				

*   Female attains majority at age 18.
(1)   Married person attains majority at age 18.
(2)   Married person attains majority upon marriage, regardless of age.
(3)   Married male attains majority at age 18, married female upon marriage.
(4)   Married person has limited rights, if spouse is over age 21.

REAL ESTATE PLANNING AIDS

Planning or evaluating a real estate transaction often calls for planning depreciation and mortgage payments. The tables set out below offer a quick guide in this area.

COMPARATIVE DEPRECIATION TABLES

Year	Straight Line		200% Declining Balance		150% Declining Balance		125% Declining Balance		Sum of Digits	
	Annual %	Cum. %	Annual %	Cum. %	Annual %	Cum. %	Annual %	Cum. %	Annual %	Cum. %
					25-YEAR LIFE					
1	4.00	4.00	8.00	8.00	6.00	6.00	5.00	5.00	7.69	7.69
2	4.00	8.00	7.36	15.36	5.64	11.64	4.75	9.75	7.39	15.08
3	4.00	12.00	6.77	22.13	5.30	16.94	4.51	14.26	7.07	22.15
4	4.00	16.00	6.23	28.36	4.98	21.92	4.29	18.55	6.77	28.92
5	4.00	20.00	5.73	34.09	4.68	26.60	4.07	22.62	6.47	35.39
6	4.00	24.00	5.27	39.36	4.40	31.00	3.87	26.49	6.15	41.54
7	4.00	28.00	4.86	44.22	4.14	35.14	3.68	30.17	5.85	47.39
8	4.00	32.00	4.46	48.68	3.89	39.03	3.49	33.66	5.53	52.92
9	4.00	36.00	4.10	52.78	3.66	42.69	3.32	36.98	5.23	58.15
10	4.00	40.00	3.78	56.56	3.43	46.12	3.15	40.13	4.93	63.08
11	4.00	44.00	3.48	60.04	3.23	49.35	2.99	43.12	4.61	67.69
12	4.00	48.00	3.19	63.23	3.03	52.38	2.84	45.96	4.31	72.00
13	4.00	52.00	2.94	66.17	2.86	55.24	2.70	48.97	4.00	76.00
14	4.00	56.00	2.71	68.88	2.68	57.92	2.57	51.23	3.69	79.69
15	4.00	60.00	2.49	71.37	2.52	60.44	2.44	53.67	3.39	83.08
16	4.00	64.00	2.29	73.66	2.37	62.81	2.32	55.99	3.07	86.15
17	4.00	68.00	2.11	75.77	2.23	65.04	2.20	58.19	2.77	88.92
18	4.00	72.00	1.94	77.71	2.10	67.14	2.09	60.28	2.47	91.39
19	4.00	76.00	1.78	79.49	1.97	69.11	1.99	62.26	2.15	93.54
20	4.00	80.00	1.64	81.13	1.85	70.96	1.89	64.15	1.85	95.39
21	4.00	84.00	1.51	82.64	1.74	72.70	1.79	65.94	1.53	96.92
22	4.00	88.00	1.39	84.03	1.64	74.34	1.70	67.65	1.23	98.15
23	4.00	92.00	1.28	85.31	1.54	75.88	1.62	69.26	.93	99.08
24	4.00	96.00	1.17	86.48	1.45	77.33	1.54	70.80	.61	99.69
25	4.00	100.00	1.08	87.56	1.36	78.69	1.46	72.26	.31	100.00

COMPARATIVE DEPRECIATION TABLES (Continued)

Year	Straight Line Annual %	Straight Line Cum. %	200% Declining Balance Annual %	200% Declining Balance Cum. %	150% Declining Balance Annual %	150% Declining Balance Cum. %	125% Declining Balance Annual %	125% Declining Balance Cum. %	Sum of Digits Annual %	Sum of Digits Cum. %
					30-YEAR LIFE					
1	3.33	3.33	6.67	6.67	5.00	5.00	4.16	4.16	6.45	6.45
2	3.34	6.67	6.22	12.89	4.75	9.75	3.99	8.16	6.24	12.69
3	3.33	10.00	5.81	18.70	4.51	14.26	3.83	11.99	6.02	18.71
4	3.33	13.33	5.42	24.12	4.29	18.55	3.67	15.65	5.81	24.52
5	3.34	16.67	5.06	29.18	4.07	22.62	3.51	19.17	5.59	30.11
6	3.33	20.00	4.72	33.90	3.87	26.49	3.37	22.54	5.37	35.48
7	3.33	23.33	4.40	38.30	3.68	30.17	3.23	25.76	5.17	40.65
8	3.34	26.67	4.12	42.42	3.49	33.66	3.09	28.86	4.94	45.59
9	3.33	30.00	3.84	46.26	3.32	36.98	2.96	31.82	4.73	50.32
10	3.33	33.33	3.58	49.84	3.15	40.13	2.84	34.66	4.52	54.84
11	3.34	36.67	3.34	53.18	2.99	43.12	2.72	37.38	4.30	59.14
12	3.33	40.00	3.12	56.30	2.84	45.96	2.61	39.99	4.09	63.23
13	3.33	43.33	2.92	59.22	2.70	48.66	2.50	42.49	3.87	67.10
14	3.34	46.67	2.72	61.94	2.57	51.23	2.40	44.89	3.65	70.75
15	3.33	50.00	2.53	64.47	2.44	53.67	2.30	47.19	3.44	74.19
16	3.33	53.33	2.37	66.84	2.32	55.99	2.20	49.39	3.23	77.42
17	3.34	56.67	2.21	69.05	2.20	58.19	2.11	51.50	3.01	80.43
18	3.33	60.00	2.07	71.12	2.09	60.28	2.02	53.52	2.80	83.23
19	3.33	63.33	1.92	73.04	1.99	62.27	1.94	55.45	2.58	85.81
20	3.34	66.67	1.80	74.84	1.89	64.16	1.86	57.31	2.36	88.17
21	3.33	70.00	1.68	76.52	1.80	65.96	1.78	59.09	2.15	90.32
22	3.33	73.33	1.56	78.08	1.70	67.66	1.70	60.79	1.94	92.26
23	3.34	76.67	1.46	79.54	1.62	69.28	1.63	62.43	1.72	93.98
24	3.33	80.00	1.37	80.91	1.54	70.82	1.57	63.99	1.61	95.49
25	3.33	83.33	1.27	82.18	1.46	72.28	1.50	65.49	1.29	96.78
26	3.34	86.67	1.19	83.37	1.39	73.67	1.44	66.93	1.07	97.85
27	3.33	90.00	1.11	84.48	1.32	74.99	1.38	68.31	.86	98.71
28	3.33	93.33	1.03	85.51	1.25	76.24	1.32	69.63	.65	99.36
29	3.34	96.67	.97	86.48	1.19	77.43	1.27	70.89	.43	99.79
30	3.33	100.00	.90	87.38	1.13	78.56	1.21	72.11	.21	100.00

COMPARATIVE DEPRECIATION TABLES (Continued)

Year	Straight Line		200% Declining Balance		150% Declining Balance		125% Declining Balance		Sum of Digits	
	Annual %	Cum. %	Annual %	Cum. %	Annual %	Cum. %	Annual %	Cum. %	Annual %	Cum. %
					35-YEAR LIFE					
1	2.86	2.86	5.71	5.71	4.29	4.29	3.57	3.57	5.56	5.56
2	2.86	5.72	5.38	11.09	4.10	8.39	3.44	7.02	5.40	10.96
3	2.85	8.57	5.07	16.16	3.93	12.32	3.32	10.34	5.24	16.20
4	2.86	11.43	4.78	20.94	3.76	16.08	3.20	13.54	5.08	21.28
5	2.86	14.29	4.51	25.45	3.60	19.68	3.09	16.63	4.92	26.20
6	2.85	17.14	4.25	29.70	3.44	23.12	2.98	19.60	4.76	30.96
7	2.86	20.00	4.01	33.71	3.29	26.41	2.87	22.48	4.60	35.56
8	2.86	22.86	3.78	37.49	3.15	29.56	2.77	25.24	4.44	40.00
9	2.85	25.71	3.56	41.05	3.02	32.58	2.67	27.91	4.29	44.29
10	2.86	28.57	3.36	44.41	2.89	35.47	2.57	30.49	4.13	48.42
11	2.86	31.43	3.17	47.58	2.77	38.24	2.48	32.97	3.97	52.39
12	2.85	34.28	2.99	50.57	2.65	40.89	2.39	35.36	3.81	56.20
13	2.86	37.14	2.82	53.39	2.53	43.42	2.31	37.67	3.65	59.85
14	2.86	40.00	2.66	56.05	2.42	45.84	2.23	39.90	3.49	63.34
15	2.85	42.85	2.51	58.56	2.32	48.16	2.15	42.05	3.33	66.67
16	2.86	45.71	2.37	60.93	2.22	50.38	2.07	44.12	3.18	69.85
17	2.86	48.57	2.23	63.16	2.13	52.51	2.00	46.11	3.02	72.87
18	2.85	51.42	2.10	65.26	2.03	54.54	1.92	48.04	2.86	75.73
19	2.86	54.28	1.98	67.24	1.95	56.49	1.86	49.89	2.70	78.43
20	2.86	57.14	1.87	69.11	1.86	58.35	1.79	51.68	2.54	80.97
21	2.86	60.00	1.76	70.87	1.79	60.14	1.73	53.41	2.38	83.35
22	2.86	62.86	1.66	72.53	1.71	61.85	1.66	55.07	2.22	85.57
23	2.86	65.72	1.57	74.10	1.64	63.49	1.60	56.68	2.06	87.63
24	2.85	68.57	1.48	75.58	1.56	65.05	1.55	58.22	1.90	89.53
25	2.86	71.43	1.40	76.98	1.50	66.55	1.49	59.72	1.75	91.28
26	2.86	74.29	1.32	78.30	1.43	67.98	1.44	61.15	1.59	92.87
27	2.85	77.14	1.24	79.54	1.37	69.35	1.39	62.54	1.43	94.30
28	2.86	80.00	1.17	80.71	1.31	70.66	1.34	63.88	1.27	95.57
29	2.86	82.86	1.10	81.81	1.26	71.92	1.29	65.17	1.11	96.68
30	2.85	85.71	1.04	82.85	1.20	73.12	1.24	66.41	.95	97.63
31	2.86	88.57	.98	83.83	1.15	74.27	1.20	67.61	.79	98.42
32	2.86	91.43	.92	84.75	1.10	75.37	1.16	68.77	.63	99.05
33	2.85	94.28	.87	85.62	1.06	76.43	1.12	69.88	.47	99.52
34	2.86	97.14	.82	86.44	1.01	77.44	1.08	70.96	.32	99.84
35	2.86	100.00	.77	87.21	.97	78.41	1.04	72.00	.16	100.00

SELF-LIQUIDATING MORTGAGE PAYMENTS - ANNUAL INTEREST

The following tables are planning tools to enable you to determine quickly the constant payments, the annual interest, the annual amortization payment, and the remaining balance of a $1,000 loan on self-liquidating mortgages at interest rates of 6, 8 and 10% for 10, 20 and 30 years. A close estimate of the same figures for other interest rates may be extrapolated. For example, the figures at 7% interest will be midway between those for 6 and 8%.

10-YEAR TERM

	6% interest - $133.32 constant payment			8% interest - $145.68 constant payment			10% interest - $158.64 constant payment		
Year	Int.	Amort.	Bal.	Int.	Amort.	Bal.	Int.	Amort.	Bal.
1	57.96	75.36	924.64	77.54	68.14	931.86	97.23	61.41	938.59
2	53.31	80.01	844.63	71.87	73.81	858.05	90.81	67.83	870.76
3	48.35	84.97	759.66	65.74	79.94	778.11	83.72	74.92	795.84
4	43.13	90.19	669.47	59.12	86.56	691.55	75.86	82.78	713.06
5	37.56	95.76	573.71	51.94	93.74	597.81	67.19	91.45	621.61
6	31.67	101.65	472.06	44.17	101.51	496.30	57.62	101.02	520.59
7	25.38	107.94	364.11	35.73	109.95	386.35	47.03	111.61	408.98
8	18.73	114.59	249.52	26.61	119.07	267.28	35.35	123.29	285.69
9	11.68	121.64	127.88	16.72	128.96	138.32	22.44	136.20	149.49
10	4.14	127.88	0*	6.02	138.32	0*	8.17	149.49	0*

20-YEAR TERM

	6% interest - $86.04 constant payment			8% interest - $100.44 constant payment			10% interest - $115.92 constant payment		
Year	Int.	Amort.	Bal.	Int.	Amort.	Bal.	Int.	Amort.	Bal.
1	59.28	26.76	973.24	79.24	21.20	978.80	99.25	16.67	983.33
2	57.62	28.42	944.82	77.47	22.97	955.83	97.49	18.43	964.90
3	55.86	30.18	914.64	75.58	24.86	930.97	95.59	20.33	944.57
4	54.01	32.03	882.61	73.49	26.95	904.02	93.44	22.48	922.09
5	52.03	34.01	848.60	71.29	29.15	874.87	91.09	24.83	897.26
6	49.92	36.12	812.48	68.85	31.59	843.28	88.51	27.41	869.85
7	47.72	38.32	774.16	66.21	34.23	809.05	85.62	30.30	839.55
8	45.32	40.72	733.44	63.37	37.07	771.98	82.45	33.47	806.08
9	42.83	43.21	690.23	60.32	40.12	731.86	78.94	36.98	769.10
10	40.16	45.88	644.35	56.99	43.45	688.41	75.08	40.84	728.26
11	37.33	48.71	595.64	53.36	47.08	641.33	70.81	45.11	683.15
12	34.34	51.70	543.94	49.46	50.98	590.35	66.07	49.85	633.30
13	31.14	54.90	489.04	45.26	55.18	535.17	60.86	55.06	578.24
14	27.77	58.27	430.77	40.67	59.77	475.40	55.11	60.81	517.43
15	24.16	61.88	368.89	35.67	64.77	410.63	48.71	67.21	450.22
16	20.35	65.69	303.20	30.31	70.13	340.50	41.68	74.24	375.98
17	16.30	69.74	233.46	24.51	75.93	264.57	33.90	82.02	293.96
18	12.01	74.03	159.43	18.20	82.24	182.33	25.32	90.60	203.36
19	7.44	78.60	80.83	11.33	89.11	93.22	15.83	100.09	103.27
20	2.54	80.83	0*	3.97	93.22	0*	5.35	103.27	0*

* The final payment is often different from the regular payment.

30-YEAR TERM

	6% interest - $72.01 constant payment			8% interest - $88.09 constant payment			10% interest - $105.37 constant payment		
Year	Int.	Amort.	Bal.	Int.	Amort.	Bal.	Int.	Amort.	Bal.
1	59.67	12.34	987.67	79.70	8.39	991.62	99.75	5.62	994.39
2	58.91	13.10	974.57	79.01	9.08	982.54	99.16	6.21	988.19
3	58.10	13.91	960.67	78.25	9.84	972.71	98.52	6.85	981.34
4	57.24	14.77	945.91	77.44	10.65	962.06	97.80	7.57	973.78
5	56.33	15.68	930.23	76.55	11.54	950.53	97.01	8.36	965.42
6	55.37	16.64	913.60	75.60	12.49	938.04	96.13	9.24	956.18
7	54.34	17.67	895.93	74.56	13.53	924.52	95.16	10.21	945.98
8	53.25	18.76	877.18	73.44	14.65	909.87	94.10	11.27	934.71
9	52.09	19.92	857.27	72.22	15.87	894.00	92.92	12.45	922.26
10	50.87	21.14	836.13	70.90	17.19	876.82	91.61	13.76	908.51
11	49.56	22.45	813.68	69.48	18.61	858.21	90.17	15.20	893.31
12	48.18	23.83	789.85	67.93	20.16	838.06	88.58	16.79	876.53
13	46.71	25.30	764.56	66.26	21.83	816.24	86.82	18.55	857.99
14	45.15	26.86	737.70	64.45	23.64	792.60	84.88	20.49	837.50
15	43.49	28.52	709.19	62.49	25.60	767.01	82.74	22.63	814.87
16	41.73	30.28	678.91	60.36	27.73	739.28	80.37	25.00	789.88
17	39.87	32.14	646.77	58.06	30.03	709.26	77.75	27.62	762.26
18	37.88	34.13	612.65	55.57	32.52	676.75	74.86	30.51	731.75
19	35.78	36.23	576.43	52.87	35.22	641.53	71.66	33.71	698.05
20	33.54	38.47	537.96	49.95	38.14	603.40	68.13	37.24	660.82
21	31.17	40.84	497.13	46.78	41.31	562.10	64.24	41.13	619.69
22	28.65	43.36	453.78	43.36	44.73	517.37	59.93	45.44	574.25
23	25.98	46.03	407.75	39.64	48.45	468.93	55.17	50.20	524.06
24	23.14	48.87	358.89	35.62	52.47	416.46	49.91	55.46	468.61
25	20.13	51.88	307.01	31.27	56.82	359.65	44.11	61.26	407.35
26	16.93	55.08	251.93	26.55	61.54	298.11	37.69	67.68	339.68
27	13.53	58.48	193.46	21.45	66.64	231.48	30.61	74.76	264.92
28	9.92	62.09	131.38	15.91	72.18	159.30	22.78	82.59	182.34
29	6.09	65.92	65.47	9.92	78.17	81.14	14.13	91.24	91.11
30	2.03	69.98	4.51*	3.44	84.65	3.50*	4.58	100.79	9.68*

* The final payment is often different from the regular payment.

SELF-LIQUIDATING MORTGAGE PAYMENTS - MONTHLY PAYMENTS

The following table shows the constant monthly payment required to liquidate a mortgage loan of $1,000 running for any number of whole years between 5 and 30 years inclusive and at interest rates from 6% to 12%.

Yrs. of Loan	6%	6-1/2%	7%	7-1/2%	8%	8-1/2%	9%	9-1/2%	10%	10-1/2%	11%	11-1/2%	12%
5	$19.33	$19.57	$19.80	$20.04	$20.28	$20.52	$20.76	$21.00	$21.25	$21.49	$21.74	$21.99	$22.24
6	16.57	16.81	17.05	17.29	17.53	17.78	18.03	18.27	18.53	18.78	19.03	19.29	19.55
7	14.61	14.85	15.09	15.34	15.59	15.84	16.09	16.34	16.60	16.86	17.12	17.39	17.65
8	13.14	13.39	13.63	13.88	14.14	14.39	14.65	14.91	15.17	15.44	15.71	15.98	16.25
9	12.01	12.25	12.51	12.76	13.02	13.28	13.54	13.81	14.08	14.35	14.63	14.90	15.18
10	11.10	11.35	11.61	11.87	12.13	12.40	12.67	12.94	13.21	13.49	13.78	14.06	14.35
11	10.37	10.62	10.88	11.15	11.42	11.69	11.96	12.24	12.52	12.80	13.09	13.38	13.68
12	9.76	10.02	10.28	10.55	10.82	11.10	11.38	11.66	11.95	12.24	12.54	12.83	13.13
13	9.25	9.51	9.78	10.05	10.33	10.61	10.90	11.19	11.48	11.78	12.08	12.38	12.69
14	8.81	9.08	9.35	9.63	9.91	10.20	10.49	10.78	11.08	11.38	11.69	12.00	12.31
15	8.44	8.71	8.99	9.27	9.56	9.85	10.14	10.44	10.75	11.05	11.37	11.68	12.00
16	8.11	8.39	8.67	8.96	9.25	9.54	9.84	10.15	10.46	10.77	11.09	11.41	11.74
17	7.83	8.11	8.40	8.69	8.98	9.28	9.59	9.90	10.21	10.53	10.85	11.18	11.51
18	7.58	7.87	8.15	8.45	8.75	9.05	9.36	9.68	10.00	10.32	10.65	10.98	11.32
19	7.36	7.65	7.94	8.24	8.54	8.85	9.17	9.49	9.81	10.14	10.47	10.81	11.15
20	7.16	7.46	7.75	8.06	8.36	8.68	9.00	9.32	9.65	9.98	10.32	10.66	11.01
21	6.99	7.28	7.58	7.89	8.20	8.52	8.85	9.17	9.51	9.85	10.19	10.54	10.89
22	6.83	7.13	7.43	7.74	8.06	8.38	8.71	9.04	9.38	9.73	10.07	10.42	10.78
23	6.69	6.99	7.30	7.61	7.93	8.26	8.59	8.93	9.27	9.62	9.97	10.33	10.69
24	6.56	6.86	7.18	7.50	7.82	8.15	8.49	8.83	9.17	9.52	9.88	10.24	10.60
25	6.44	6.75	7.07	7.39	7.72	8.05	8.39	8.74	9.09	9.44	9.80	10.16	10.53
26	6.34	6.65	6.97	7.29	7.63	7.96	8.31	8.66	9.01	9.37	9.73	10.10	10.47
27	6.24	6.55	6.88	7.21	7.54	7.88	8.23	8.58	8.94	9.30	9.67	10.04	10.41
28	6.15	6.47	6.80	7.13	7.47	7.81	8.16	8.52	8.88	9.25	9.61	9.99	10.37
29	6.07	6.39	6.72	7.06	7.40	7.75	8.10	8.46	8.82	9.19	9.57	9.94	10.32
30	5.99	6.32	6.65	6.99	7.34	7.69	8.05	8.41	8.78	9.15	9.52	9.90	10.29

CREDITORS' REMEDIES

The tables set out in this section are designed to give the practitioner quick familiarity with the basic remedies available to the creditor in all jurisdictions, and to
alert him to possible pitfalls.

STATE GUIDE TO ATTACHMENTS*		
STATE	Can Attachment Be Made Prior To Judgment?	Amount Of Bond Required
ALABAMA	Yes	Twice amount claimed.
ALASKA	Yes	Amount claimed.
ARIZONA	In specific instances. See statute.	Amount claimed.
ARKANSAS	Yes	Bond that plaintiff shall pay defendant all damages sustained by reason of the attachment.
CALIFORNIA	Yes, when claim is $50 or more.	1/2 amount claimed, but not under $50.
COLORADO	Fraud only.	Twice amount claimed.
CONNECTICUT	No	None - except cost bond by non-resident plaintiff.
DELAWARE	No	Yes, for costs and damages.
DISTRICT OF COLUMBIA	Yes	Twice amount claimed.
FLORIDA	Yes. See statute.	Twice amount claimed.
GEORGIA	Yes	Twice amount claimed.
HAWAII	Yes. See statute.	Twice amount claimed. If over $50,000, not less than 1 1/2 times amount claimed.
IDAHO	No	Amount claimed.
ILLINOIS	No	Twice amount claimed.
INDIANA	Fraud only.	Yes, for costs and damages.
IOWA	Yes, fraud and other conditions.	Twice amount claimed.
KANSAS	If court permits.	Twice amount claimed.

*Reproduced from PROFITABLE USE OF CREDIT IN SELLING & COLLECTING by Allyn M. Schiffer, published by Fair-
child Publications, Inc., New York; price $12 per copy.

554

STATE GUIDE TO ATTACHMENTS*		
STATE	Can Attachment Be Made Prior To Judgment?	Amount Of Bond Required
KENTUCKY	Yes	Limited to twice amount claimed.
LOUISIANA	Yes	Amount claimed.
MAINE	No	Twice amount claimed if personal property.
MARYLAND	Fraud only.	Twice amount claimed.
MASSACHUSETTS	No	Not provided.
MICHIGAN	If court permits.	Tort actions only.
MINNESOTA	Not usually.	At least $250.
MISSISSIPPI	Yes. See statute.	Twice amount claimed.
MISSOURI	Yes	Twice amount claimed.
MONTANA	Fraud only.	Twice amount claimed.
NEBRASKA	Yes	Twice amount claimed.
NEVADA	Fraud only.	Not less than $200, nor less than 1/4 of claim.
NEW HAMPSHIRE	No	None
NEW JERSEY	If court permits.	Discretion of court.
NEW MEXICO	Yes	Twice amount claimed.
NEW YORK	Fraud only.	For costs. Minimum: $250.
NORTH CAROLINA	No	Not less than $200, at court's discretion.
NORTH DAKOTA	Yes	Not less than $250. $50 in justice court.
OHIO	Fraud only.	Twice amount claimed.
OKLAHOMA	Yes	Twice amount claimed.

*Reproduced from PROFITABLE USE OF CREDIT IN SELLING & COLLECTING by Allyn M. Schiffer, published by Fairchild Publications, Inc., New York; price $12 per copy.

STATE GUIDE TO ATTACHMENTS*		
STATE	Can Attachment Be Made Prior To Judgment?	Amount Of Bond Required
OREGON	No	Amount claimed. Minimum bond $100.
PENNSYLVANIA	Not usually.	Twice amount claimed.
RHODE ISLAND	No	None
SOUTH CAROLINA	Fraud only.	Not less than $250.
SOUTH DAKOTA	Yes	Twice amount claimed. If claim exceeds $1,000, bond is amount claimed, not exceeding $10,000.
TENNESSEE	Yes	Twice amount claimed.
TEXAS	Yes	Twice amount claimed.
UTAH	Fraud only.	Twice amount claimed.
VERMONT	Permitted on partly due running accounts.	Cost bond.
VIRGINIA	Yes	Twice value of property claimed.
WASHINGTON	Yes	Twice amount claimed.
WEST VIRGINIA	Yes	Twice amount claimed.
WISCONSIN	Yes	On unmatured claim, triple amount of claim.
WYOMING	Yes	Twice amount claimed.

*Reproduced from PROFITABLE USE OF CREDIT IN SELLING & COLLECTING by Allyn M. Schiffer, published by Fairchild Publications, Inc., New York; price $12 per copy.

GARNISHMENT GUIDE

The chart below is from Prentice-Hall, Inc. - Installment Sales (looseleaf service current to May 7, 1974) and is reproduced by permission of the publisher. It summarizes state laws on garnishment. It shows the limit each state imposes on the amount of wages that can be garnisheed for specific kinds of wage earners (for example, heads of families), and gives the order in which garnishments must be paid (if the state specifies). The penalties employers face for failure to follow garnishment procedure are listed at the end of the chart; the figures in brackets after the name of each state show which penalty applies in that state.

Federal restrictions: Federal law exempts an employee's earnings during a workweek equal to 30 times federal minimum wage or 75% of employee's "disposable earnings," whichever is greater. "Disposable earnings" means earnings minus all deductions required by law. Exemption won't apply, however, to any court order for support of any person; court order of bankruptcy (under Ch. XIII, Bankruptcy Act); or any debt due for any state or federal tax. Union dues, initiation fees, employees' share of health and welfare premiums and repayment of credit union loans aren't considered deductions required by law in determining "disposable income", but amounts withheld for unemployment and workmen's compensation insurance pursuant to state law, are considered such deductions.

Law also prohibits employer from firing an employee by reason of the fact his wages have been garnisheed for any one indebtedness (i.e., a single debt regardless of number of garnishment proceedings brought to collect it.) Penalty for wilful violation: up to $1,000 fine or one year's imprisonment, or both.

If federal and state laws don't agree, law that provides for lesser garnishment or greater restriction on firing will control.

Secretary of Labor, acting through Wage-Hour Division, will enforce federal garnishment provisions.

Alabama: [2][5] Laborers and resident employees: 75% of wages is exempt.

Alaska: [3] Head of family: $350 of worker's income due him or received by him from any source within 30 days preceding levy of execution, if necessary for his use or use of his family which he supports. Other exemptions are automatic payroll deductions for care of children not in his custody and child support payments ordered paid to court trustee. Single person: $200 is exempt.

Arizona: [2][5][8] 50% of earnings for personal services performed within 30 days before service of garnishment papers is exempt, if necessary for the support of the employee's family.

The earnings of a minor child aren't subject to garnishment for parent's debt if the debt wasn't for the special benefit of the child.

Arkansas: [2] Laborers and mechanics: Wages for 60 days are exempt provided employee files affidavit with court stating that 60 days' wages together with other personal property he owns doesn't exceed state constitutional limitation ($200 for single resident not head of a family, $500 for married resident or head of a family). First $25 of net wages of all mechanics and laborers absolutely exempt without need for filing schedule of exemptions. "Net wages" means gross wages less following deductions actually withheld: Ark. income tax, fed. income tax, social security, group retirement, group hospitalization insurance premiums and group life insurance premiums.

Employees of railroads have an exemption of $200 before judgment against them by the creditor.

California: [8] 100% of earnings is exempt if they are necessary for the support of the employee's family residing within the State. This exemption doesn't apply if the debt is for (1) necessaries or (2) services rendered by an employee of the worker. 50% of the earnings for personal services performed within 30 days before service of garnishment papers is exempt.

Employer may be required to attend court and be examined.

Discharge: Employee can't be discharged for garnishment for one indebtedness prior to final order or judgment of court.

Colorado: [2][5] Head of family: 70% of earnings, proceeds of health, accident or disability insurance, and pension or retirement benefits is exempt. Single persons: 35% of such earnings and proceeds is exempt.

The employer can withhold claims that he would have had if he hadn't been garnisheed.

Connecticut: [2][5] Greater of (a) 75% of disposable earnings for workweek or (b) $65 or 40 times federal minimum hourly wage in effect when earnings are payable is exempt. Tax collector can garnishee wages for local taxes due.

Priorities: Only one execution at a time can be satisfied. They're satisfied in the order they're presented to the employer. Execution of wages for support of wife or minor child (children) takes priority over other executions and two or more can be levied at same time provided total levy doesn't exceed maximum permitted.

Employer can't discipline, suspend or discharge employee because his wages have been garnisheed, unless more than 7 garnishments in any calendar year.

Delaware: [5] New Castle County residents: 90% of wages is exempt if debt is for necessaries of life or State taxes. If debt is for board and lodging, and claim doesn't exceed $50, all wages may be attached.

Kent and Sussex County residents: 60% of wages is exempt except that if debt is for board and lodging, and claim doesn't exceed $50, all wages may be attached.

In all counties: In child support cases, 25% of net salary can be attached by court order plus another 5% for each child. Attachment prevails over other exemptions. Employer liable for fine or jail for dismissal of employee due to attachment.

Priorities: Only one attachment may be made per month.

Discharge: It's unlawful for employer to discharge employee for garnishment.

District of Columbia: [2] Following wages can be garnisheed in a calendar month: 10% of gross wages up to $200; plus 20% of gross wages over $200 and up to $500; plus 50% of gross wages over $500. However, these percentages don't apply to judgments for support of wife, former wife or children; instead, 50% of the employee's gross wages is exempt.

$200 of earnings (other than wages), insurance, annuities or pension or retirement payments are exempt for each of two months if person is a resident or earns major portion of his livelihood in D.C. and is principal support of a family before service of garnishment papers. If husband and wife live together, their total earnings determine the exemption; $60 of earnings (other than wages), insurance, etc., are exempt for each of 2 months before service of garnishment papers, if person doesn't support a family.

Priorities: Only one attachment is satisfied at one time. Attachments are satisfied in order of priority. However, judgment for support takes priority (in discretion of court).

Florida: [4] Head of family residing in Florida: All wages are exempt.

Earnings of any person or public officer, state or county, (whether the head of a family or not residing in Florida) are subject to garnishment to enforce Florida court order for alimony, suit money or support. Court, in its discretion, determines the amount to be garnisheed.

Georgia: [4][5] Greater of 75% of disposable earnings or 30 times federal minimum wage, is exempt. $1,000 of wages due deceased employee of railroad company or other corporation is exempt. Salaries of officers of corporations (except municipal corporations) are subject to garnishment if more than $500 a year.

Claim of exemption from garnishment is ineffective against decree for alimony [Huling v. Huling, 194 Ga. 819, 22 S.E. (2d) 882, (1942)].

Default judgment against employer for failure to answer can be modified on motion to 125% of amount due employees, less exemption, from time of service to last day on which timely answer could be made but not less than 15% of amount of employee's judgment.

Garnishment for debt for state tax is governed by state law [O.A.G., 9-12-60].

Discharge: Employee can't be discharged for garnishment for any one indebtedness, whether or not debt is for state taxes [O.A.G., 9-12-69].

Hawaii: [5] The following wages are exempt from garnishment: 95% of the first $100 per month, 90% of the next $100 and 80% of all sums over $200.

The employer can withhold (liquidated) claims that he would have had if he hadn't been garnisheed.

Priorities: Garnishments are paid in order of service of process on employer. If 2 or more are served at the same time, order of issuance from court determines priority.

559

Employer can't suspend or discharge employee because he was summoned as garnishee in action where employee is debtor or because employee filed petition to pay his debts under wage earners plan of Bankruptcy Act.

Idaho: [4][5] Greater of 75% of disposable earnings or 30 times federal minimum wage is exempt. Doesn't apply to support orders, debt for state or federal tax.

Illinois: [2] $65 a week if employee is head of family and $50 a week if he isn't, or 85% of gross wages, salary, commissions, bonuses and periodic payments under retirement or pension plan, whichever is greater, but no more than $200 a week is exempt.

The employer can withhold claims that he would have had if he hadn't been garnisheed.

Employer can deduct greater of $2 or 2% of amount paid because of deduction order on same debt.

Indiana: [4] Resident householder: $15 a week and 90% of the excess wages is exempt.

Single person not a resident householder: 90% of total wages is exempt.

Wages cannot be garnisheed if the employee and creditor are nonresidents and the employer is a resident of Indiana.

Iowa: [2] Greater of 75% of disposable earnings or 30 times federal minimum wages is exempt; $250 plus costs is maximum amount of wages that can be garnisheed by one creditor.

Exemptions don't apply if judgment against employee is for (1) alimony and he hasn't remarried or (2) support of minor child.

Kansas: [2][5] Greater of 75% of disposable earnings or 30 times federal minimum wage, is exempt. Doesn't apply to court order for child support, order of bankruptcy court or debt for state or federal tax.

No one creditor can issue more than one garnishment during month.

No prejudgment garnishments orders can be issued against wages.

Discharge: Employee can't be discharged for garnishment for any one indebtedness.

Kentucky: [3][5] Greater of 75% of disposable earnings or 30 times federal minimum wage, is exempt. Doesn't apply to support orders, bankruptcy orders, debt for state or federal tax. Garnishment is lien on wages during pay period in which served; if less than 2 weeks, or employee paid in advance, during succeeding pay period.

Prejudgment garnishments can be obtained by making demand on defendant in writing, advising him of grounds of suit and his right to hearing.

Priorities: Orders have priority in date of service.

Discharge: Employee can't be discharged for garnishment for any one indebtedness.

Louisiana: [2][10] 75% of disposable earnings or excess over 30 times federal minimum wage is exempt,but exemptions can't be less than $70 a week of disposable earnings.

Priorities: A debt between employer and employee is treated as a prior garnishment. However, garnishment of father's wages for child's support always takes priority over all garnishment orders.

Maine: [2] Greater of 75% of disposable earnings or 30 times federal minimum hourly wage is exempt; $10 is exempt in all cases. Wages of minor children and wife aren't subject to garnishment for parent's or husband's debt.

The employer can withhold claims (except unliquidated damages) that he would have had if he hadn't been garnisheed. Employer isn't trustee of money due employee until after judgment.

Maryland: [2] Greater of $100 times number of weeks wages due at date of attachment were earned, or 75% of such wages due, is exempt.

Caroline, Worcester, Kent and Queen Anne's Counties: Greater of 75% of wages due or 30 times federal minimum wage is exempt.

Exemption doesn't apply to garnishment for state income tax.

Court can order lien on earnings of defendant in paternity suit. Nonsupport court orders will be lien on notification by Probation Dept.

Discharge: Employee can't be discharged for garnishment on any one occasion in calendar year.

Massachusetts: [4] $125 a week of wages due is exempt; $100 a week of pensions payable to an employee is exempt.

Wages due for personal services of defendant's (employee's) wife or minor child are exempt.

The employer can withhold (liquidated) claims that he would have had if he hadn't been garnisheed.

Michigan: [3][5][12] If first garnishment —Householder head of family: 60% of wages is exempt. If wages are for one week's labor (or less), the most that is exempt is $50 and the least is $30. If wages are for more than one week's labor maximum exemption is $90, minimum $60.

Others: 40% of wages is exempt. Most that is exempt is $50 and least is $20.

In all other cases — Householder head of family — 60% of wages is exempt. If wages are for one week or less, the most that is exempt is $30 and the least is $12. If wages are for more than one week but no more than 16 days, the most that is exempt is $60 and the least is $24. If wages are for more than 16 days, maximum exemption is $60 and minimum $30.

Others: 30% of wages is exempt. The most that can be exempt is $20 and the least is $10.

Employer can offset claims he has against his employee.

Wages earned by an employee at the time the garnishment papers are served on the employer, but not payable on the next regular payday, are not subject to garnishment.

The amount paid under a judgment for alimony or child support is exempt.

Minnesota: [2][5]   Greater of 75% of disposable earnings or an amount of such wages equal to 8 times number of business days and paid holidays (not exceeding 5 per week) times federal minimum wage, is exempt.   All earnings for preceding 30 days, if needed for use of family supported wholly or partly by his labor are exempt.   If the employee was on relief, all his wages for six months after his return to work are exempt.   This exemption can be claimed only once every three years.

The earnings of a minor child cannot be garnisheed for the debt of his parent unless the debt was for the special benefit of the minor.

Priorities: Garnishments are paid in the order of service of the garnishee papers on the employer.   More than one garnishment can be paid at a time subject to total nonexempt disposable earnings.

If amount garnisheed is less than $10, garnishment is ineffective and employer is relieved of liability.

Discharge: Employee can't be discharged for garnishment unless more than 3 garnishments served within 90 days on more than one debt.

Mississippi: [2][5]   75% of wages, salary or other compensation due resident employees or laborers is exempt.

The proceeds of any trust created by an employer as part of a pension plan, disability of death benefit plan or any trust created under a retirement plan which are exempt from Federal income tax aren't subject to garnishment.

Court orders or judgments for payment of alimony, separate maintenance or child support are exempt from garnishment.

Missouri: [4]   Resident head of family: 90% of wages for last 30 days' service is exempt.   Greater of 75% of disposable earnings or 30 times federal minimum wage is exempt.

Exemption doesn't apply if garnishment is for (1) alimony; (2) support or maintenance of a child; or (3) maintenance by a married woman.

Montana: [5]   Head of family: All earnings for personal services performed within 45 days before service of garnishment papers are exempt, if necessary for support of employee's family.

If the employee's debts are for the necessaries of life or gasoline, then only 50% of his earnings are exempt.

An unmarried employee, over 60, is entitled to the same exemption as the head of a family.

All earnings for preceding 30 days are exempt in actions for $10 or less.

Discharge: Employee can't be discharged or laid off for garnishment.

<u>Nebraska:</u> [2][5] Head of family: 85% of wages is exempt. Exemption doesn't apply to wages of employee who has left (or is about to leave) the state.

Priorities: Where several garnishments are issued, the justice who issued the first determines the priorities.

<u>Nevada:</u> [1][5][8] Lesser of 25% of disposable earnings or excess over 30 times federal minimum wage is exempt. Exemption doesn't apply to any court orders in bankruptcy for support or debt due for state or federal taxes.

<u>New Hampshire:</u> [2][5] All wages earned by the employee after the service of garnishment papers on the employer are exempt.

All wages earned before service of garnishment papers are exempt, unless judgment on debt is issued by state court. In such cases, exemption for each week is 50 times federal minimum wage.

Earnings of the wife and minor children of the employee are exempt.

$50 a week of wages earned by the employee before service of garnishment papers is exempt if the main action is based on a small loan contract.

All the wages of a married woman are exempt if the action is based on a small loan contract to which her husband is an obligor.

Exemptions don't apply in an action for taxes by Tax Collector.

<u>New Jersey:</u> [1] If the employee earns at least $48 a week, 10% of his wages may be garnisheed. If the employee earns more than $7,500 a year, a court may increase the percentage to be garnisheed.

Priorities: Only one execution can be satisfied at a time in order in which they are served on employer; except support orders for child or wife have priority over other executions served on same day.

<u>New Mexico:</u> [2] Either 75% of disposable earnings each pay period or 40 times federal minimum hourly wage each week, whichever is greater, is exempt.

Priorities: Liens will be satisfied in order in which they are served.

<u>New York:</u> [1][5][7] Income execution: 10% of income is subject to income execution in court of record where judgment debtor (employee) is receiving or will receive more than $85 a week.

Earnings of recipients of public assistance are exempt.

Garnishment proceeding, court not of record: 10% of earnings can be garnisheed by court order if judgment has been recovered in a court not of record against an employee whose income is (1) $30 or more a week if he resides or works in a city of 250,000 or more, or (2) $25 a week in any other case. Only one garnishment can be satisfied at a time. If two or more are issued simultaneously, they are satisfied in the order they are served on the employer [Justice Court Act § 300].

Priorities: Assignment or court order for support of minor child and/or spouse takes priority over other assignment or garnishment of wages, etc., except as to deductions made mandatory by law.

No employee may be laid off or discharged because garnishee order has been served against his wages.

North Carolina: [2] Head of family: All earnings for 60 days before the service of the garnishment papers are exempt if necessary for the support of the employee's family.

Garnishment for collection of taxes is limited to 10% of monthly salary or wages. Wages due officials or employees of the state, its agencies, instrumentalities and political subdivisions are subject to garnishment for delinquent taxes.

North Dakota: [2][8] Resident head of family: $50 a week is exempt, also $5 a week for each dependent up to maximum of $25. Resident not head of family: $35 a week wages is exempt.

Ohio: [2][3] Greater of 175 times federal minimum wage or 82-1/2% of disposable earnings is exempt for services performed within 30 days before issuing garnishment (when exemption claimed in bankruptcy 82-1/2% of gross earnings for 30-day period ending on 10th day prior to filing bankruptcy petition). Garnishment may be granted after judgment. There must be at least 30 days between garnishments. Support orders have priority over all other garnishments and no part of wages is exempt from them. They are paid in order received. Employer may deduct up to 1% as service charge.

Priorities: Priorities may be determined by court order.

Discharge: Employee can't be discharged solely for attachment for no more than one action in garnishment in any 12-month period.

Oklahoma: [2][3][5] Resident head of family: 75% of all wages for services performed within last 90 days is exempt.

All wages for services performed within 90 days before issuing of garnishment papers are exempt if they are necessary for the support of the employee's family, but not if judgment is for child support or maintenance.

Resident not head of family: 75% of all wages for services is exempt.

Judgments on consumer credit sale, lease or loan: Lesser of 25% of disposable earnings or excess over 30 times federal minimum wage is maximum subject to garnishment. Employee can't be discharged unless employer garnisheed for 1 or more judgments on more than 2 occasions in 1 year.

Priorities: Priorities may be determined by court order.

Oregon: [3][4][5] Greater of 75% of disposable earnings or 30 times federal minimum wage in effect 4-30-69 is exempt. Doesn't apply to support orders, bankruptcy orders, debt for state or federal tax. Protection of law can't be waived.

Pennsylvania: [5] All wages are exempt.

Exceptions: Wages are subject to garnishment for 4 weeks' board and lodging.

A husband's wages can be garnisheed to pay support for wife and children. Likewise, wages can be garnisheed for alimony.

564

Taxes: On tax collector's written notice and demand, employer must deduct from employee's wages, commissions or earnings then owing (or that become due within 60 days thereafter), or from any unpaid commissions or earnings in his possession (or that come into his possession within 60 days thereafter), a sum sufficient to pay employee's, or his wife's, delinquent per capita, poll or occupation tax and costs, and must pay this sum to tax collector within 60 days after receipt of notice. Employer may keep up to 2% of money collected for extra bookkeeping expenses.

Rhode Island: [2] $50 a week of earnings is exempt; all earnings of wife and minor child of employee are exempt; all wages of seamen are exempt. If employee was on relief, all his wages for one year are exempt.

South Carolina: [3] Head of family: All earnings for personal services performed within 60 days before the garnishment order are exempt, if necessary for a family supported by the employee.

15% of an employee's earnings (but not more than $100) can be garnisheed to pay a judgment for food, fuel or medicine.

South Dakota: [2][5] Head of family: All earnings for personal services performed within 60 days before the garnishment order are exempt, if necessary for family's support.

Tennessee: [2][5] Resident head of family: Greater of 50% of net weekly salary, wages or income or $20 a week is exempt, subject to a maximum of $50 a week. An additional $2.50 a week for each dependent child under 16 is exempt.

Resident not head of family: Greater of 40% of net weekly salary, wages or income or $17.50 a week is exempt, subject to a maximum of $40 a week.

Only salary, wages or income earned at time of service of garnishment papers are affected. Net amount of earnings or income is gross amount earned during pay period to time of service of garnishment papers less social security and withholding taxes.

Exemptions don't apply if judgment against employee is for alimony or child support.

Employee's salary, wages or income not subject to garnishment by same creditor more than once every other pay period.

Priorities: Priorities are determined by time of service of papers; if served at same time, according to time of filing. If creditor with priority doesn't claim entire amount allowed over exempt amount, next creditor may claim excess; but service of more than one garnishment in a pay period won't reduce exempt amount.

Texas: All current wages for personal services are exempt.

Utah: [2][5] Head of family or married man: 50% of earnings for personal services performed within 30 days before service of garnishment papers is exempt if necessary for support of family. Minimum exemption, $50.

The earnings of a minor child aren't subject to garnishment for parent's debt if the debt wasn't for the special benefit of the child.

The employer can withhold claims that he would have had if he hadn't been garnisheed.

Judgments on consumer credit sale, lease or loan: Greater of 75% of disposable earnings or 40 times federal minimum wage is exempt. No prejudgment garnishment is permitted. Employee can't be discharged for any one indebtedness.

Vermont: [2][5] $30 of wages, plus 50% of wages above $60, for each week (or part of week) owed for work performed before service of garnishment papers, is exempt.

Wages due minor child can't be garnisheed in action against parent; wages due married woman can't be garnisheed in action against husband.

Employer can withhold claims (based on express or implied contract) that he would have had if he hadn't been garnisheed.

Wages over $25 are subject to a lien for delinquent poll tax or old age assistance tax at rate of $4 a week.

Discharge: It is unlawful for employer to discharge employee because employee's compensation has been garnisheed unless employer has been previously garnisheed for that employee on 5 or more separate occasions arising from separate actions, or unless employer establishes there were other substantial causes contributing to the discharge.

Virginia: [1][5][6] Greater of 75% of disposable earnings or 30 times federal minimum wage is exempt. Doesn't apply to court-ordered support bankruptcy order or debt for state or federal taxes. Earnings include wages, commissions, bonuses and payments under pension or retirement programs.

Wages of minors are exempt from garnishment for debts of parents.

Discharge: Employee can't be discharged for garnishment for any indebtedness.

Washington: [2][5] Greater of 40 times state minimum wage or 75% of disposable earnings is exempt. Deductions as contributions toward pension or retirement plan established pursuant to collective bargaining agreement are not part of disposable earnings.

Exemption doesn't apply to garnishment for child support if (a) based on judgment or court order; (b) amount doesn't exceed 2 months support payments and writ contains such statement. Continuing lien on wages can be obtained.

Priorities: Liens have priority as served. Only 1 garnishment can be satisfied at a time.

Discharge: Employee can't be discharged for garnishment unless employer is garnisheed on 3 or more separate indebtednesses served within 12 consecutive months.

West Virginia: [1][5] 80% of earnings in a week is exempt; wages payable to the employee cannot be less than $20 a week.

Priorities: Only one garnishment is satisfied at a time. However, where two or more have been served and the first garnishment has been satisfied, nonexempt wages remaining are applied toward the satisfaction of junior garnishments in the order of their priority.

Wisconsin: [2][5][8] Worker with no dependents: Basic exemption–
60% of the income of the employee for each 30-day period before service of process
in proceeding to collect a debt. The exemption cannot be less than $75 nor more
than $100. The employee can elect to have the exemption computed on a 90-day basis.

Worker with dependents: Basic exemption–On the income of the employee
for each 30-day period before service of process in proceeding to collect a debt,
$120 plus $20 for each dependent. However, the total exemption cannot exceed 75%
of total income. The employee can elect to have the exemption computed on a 90-
day basis.

"Income" means gross receipts less federal and state withholding and social
security taxes.

Subsistence allowance: When earnings are subjected to garnishment, employer
pays (on date earnings are payable) subsistence allowance to employee of greater of
75% of disposable earnings or 30 times federal minimum wage. Doesn't apply to
support orders, bankruptcy orders, debt for state or federal tax or orders in voluntary proceedings by wage earners. Garnishment action against earnings can't be
started before judgment.

Discharge: Employer can't discharge employee because his earnings have
been garnisheed for any one indebtedness. Willful violation punishable by fine up to
$1,000, jail; or both.

Wyoming: [1][5] Head of resident family: 50% of earnings for personal
services performed within 60 days before service of garnishment papers is exempt,
if necessary for support of family.

[1]   If employer doesn't follow garnishment procedure, he may be subject
to civil action by his employee's creditor.
[2]   If employer doesn't follow garnishment procedure, he may be liable
for all or part of the claim that the creditor has against his employee.
[3]   If employer doesn't follow in garnishment procedure, he may be subject to contempt proceedings; in Mich., he may be liable to arrest.
[4]   If employer doesn't follow garnishment procedure, judgment may be
taken against him.
[5]   Salaries of employees of the State and/or its subdivisions may be subject to garnishment.
[6]   Employer is governed by return date of summons but after service or
knowledge of issuance of summons employer can only pay employee exempt wages
[OAG, 6-16-70].
[7] $85 a week floor on garnishment earnings applies to all income execu-
tions in effect on or after 9-1-70 even if previously filed [OAG (Informal) 7-13-70]
(N.Y.).
[8]   Based on decision in Sniadach v. Family Finance Corp. of Bay View
(US S.Ct., 1969) 395 US 337; 89 S.Ct. 1820, laws in following states allowing prejudgment garnishments are invalid: Ariz. [Termplan,Inc. v. Superior Ct. of Mari-
copa Cty., Ariz. Sup.Ct., 12-29-69]; Calif. [McCallop v. Carberry, Cal. Sup.Ct.
1-30-70]; Nev. [O.A.G., 4-1-70]; N.Dak. [O.A.G., 7-8-69]. (After Sniadach
decision, Wisc. amended its law to provide for no prejudgment garnishments.)
[10]   For effect of new garnishment exemptions on existing court ordered
garnishments, Dept. of Justice advises that employer should "continue to follow the
judgment of the court under the garnishment proceedings, until such time as the
judgment is amended by the court upon application of an interested party."

MECHANIC'S LIEN LAWS

The statutory requirements for mechanic's liens differ widely from state to state in many details. Many states have statutory forms of notice of lien. Here are the main areas to be checked under the law of the particular state you are concerned with:

(1) Who Is Entitled to the Lien? Generally, any one furnishing labor or materials adding to the value of realty but the mere sale of material without reference to the building in which it is to be used won't give rise to a lien. The labor or material furnished must be on the credit of the building. Some statutes require a written contract describing the building or improvement and fixing the amount.

(2) Right of Subcontractors - Some states give the subcontractor a direct lien on the realty regardless of whether there is a debt due the principal contractor; but in other states the subcontractor cannot recover more than is due the contractor.

(3) Material Furnished Subcontractor - Some states grant, others deny, liens for materials furnished subcontractors.

(4) Contractual Provision Against Liens - In some states a contractual provison against mechanic's liens bars the contractor from claiming a lien; in others it does not bar the contractor but only subcontractors, laborers and materialmen; but in others, subcontractors, laborers and materialmen are not barred. Where the contract between the contractor and the subcontractor provides that no lien is to be filed by the subcontractor, or where the subcontract adopts the principal contract containing such a provision, the subcontractor will be barred.

(5) Time of Filing - May vary from 30 days to 120 days from completion of work or furnishing materials.

(6) Contents of Notice of Lien - Usually must describe claim and property.

(7) Duration of Lien - There is usually a short statute of limitations for the commencement of a foreclosure action. Some statutes make provision for renewal of lien.

JUDGMENT NOTES—ATTORNEYS' FEES

The chart below is from Prentice-Hall, Inc. Installment Sales (loose-leaf service current to October 27, 1970) and is reproduced by permission of the publisher. It contains state by state information showing: whether there is any statutory provision governing judgment notes; whether confessions of judgment are recognized (and any conditions limiting such recognition) as well as indicating conditions and limitations on collection of attorneys' fees for those jurisdictions which permit inclusion of this provision in a contract or note.

Alabama: Judgment notes: No statutory provision. Confessions of judgment: Invalid, if made before suit. In Jefferson County, small loan licensee may not use judgment note. Attorneys' fees: No statutory provision.

Alaska: Judgment notes: No statutory provision. Confessions of judgment: Valid, if made by debtor in person, or by debtor's attorney-in-fact under power of attorney. Attorneys' fees: Retail installment contract may provide for reasonable attorneys' fees.

Arizona: Judgment notes: No statutory provision. Confessions of judgment: Valid only if executed after note matures; cannot be made in connection with small loan. Attorneys' fees: Motor vehicle time sales contract may provide for reasonable fees.

Arkansas: Judgment notes: No statutory provision. Confessions of judgment: Valid if personally made by debtor in court. Attorneys' fees: Enforceable, if doesn't exceed 10% of principal and accrued interest.

California: Judgment notes: No statutory provision. Confessions of judgment: Valid, if taken for money due or to become due, or to secure contingent liability. But prohibited in time sales contract; also, in contracts of industrial loan company or property broker or small loan licensee. Attorneys' fees: May be awarded to prevailing party in any action on time sales contract or installment contract, or on motor vehicle time sales contract.

Colorado: Judgment notes: No statutory provision. Confessions of judgment: Invalid in motor vehicle time sales contracts. Attorneys' fees: Valid in time sales contracts, including motor vehicle time sales contract, if not more than 15% of balance due.

Connecticut: Judgment notes: No statutory provision. Confessions of judgment: May be offered before trial in pending action. Not permitted in time sales contract or installment loan contract, or in small loan contracts. Attorneys' fees: Valid in note or other evidence of indebtedness, but court may modify amount. Also valid in installment contract or installment loan contract, if not more than 15% of balance due.

Delaware: Judgment notes: Valid. Confessions of judgment: Permitted, if made by warrant of attorney. Attorneys' fees: In action on note, contract or other written instrument, court may award reasonable fees (up to 5% of amount awarded for principal and interest), if instrument provides for payment of such fees.

Florida: Judgment notes: No statutory provision. Confessions of judgment: Void if executed before or without an action; not permitted in small loan contracts. Attorneys' fees: Valid in time sales contracts of motor vehicles, or of other goods.

Georgia: Judgment notes: No statutory provision. Confessions of judgment: Permitted only in suit; invalid in small loan contracts. Attorneys' fees: Void, unless debtor given 10 days' notice before suit and fails to pay.

Hawaii: Judgment notes: No statutory provision. Confessions of judgment: Enforceable, up to $1,000, if taken for money due or to become due. Enforceable in time sales contract, but only on buyer's default. Not permitted in small loan contracts. Attorneys' fees: Court will award in actions on notes or contracts, if fee specified therein or in separate agreement; but not more than 25%.

Idaho: Judgment notes: No statutory provision. Confessions of judgment: Valid, if for money due or to become due, or to secure against contingent liability. Not permitted in small loan contracts. Attorneys' fees: No statutory provision.

Illinois: Judgment notes: Valid. Confessions of judgment: Enforceable in time sales contracts after buyer's default; valid in small loan contracts. Attorneys' fees: Enforceable in time sales contracts, if fee reasonable.

Indiana: Judgment notes: Void. Confessions of judgment: Void. Use of same or judgment note is misdemeanor. Prohibited in small loan contracts. Attorneys' fees: Void, if payment depends on any condition. Time sales contract may include provision for payment of delinquency charges, including attorneys' fees.

Iowa: Judgment notes: No statutory provision. Confessions of judgment: Valid, if for money due or to become due, or to secure against contingent liability. Not permitted in small loan contracts. Attorneys' fees: If note or contract provides for payment of fees, court will allow 10% of first $200, 5% on excess through $500, 3% on excess through $1,000 and 1% on amounts over $1,000.

Kansas: Judgment notes: No statutory provision. Confessions of judgment: Debtor may offer to confess judgment at any time before trial. Attorneys' fees: No statutory provision.

Kentucky: Judgment notes: No statutory provision. Confessions of judgment: Void. May not be included in motor vehicle time sales contracts, or in small loan contracts. Attorneys' fees: Permitted in motor vehicle time sales contracts, but can't exceed 15% of balance due.

Louisiana: Judgment notes: No statutory provision. Confessions of judgment: May not be made before obligation matures, except for purpose of executory process. Not permitted in small loan contracts. Attorneys' fees: Permitted in motor vehicle time sales contract, if not more than 25% of balance due, with $15 minimum.

Maine: Judgment notes: No statutory provision. Confessions of judgment: Prohibited in home repair agreement, and in small loan contracts. Attorneys' fees: Permitted in home repair agreement and motor vehicle time sales contracts, if reasonable fee.

Maryland: Judgment notes: No statutory provision. Confessions of judgment: Prohibited in all time sales contracts, with a cash sales price of $5,000 or less, if seller takes back security interest; also, in small loan contracts. Attorneys' fees: Permitted in time sales contracts, up to 15% of balance due.

Massachusetts: (General Laws). Judgment notes: Prohibited. Confessions of judgment: Inclusion in note or contract void. Prohibited in time sales contracts of goods and motor vehicles. Attorneys' fees: No statutory provision.

Michigan: Judgment note: No statutory provision. Confessions of judgment: Valid, if made in separate instrument. Prohibited in time sales contracts or retail charge agreements; also, in small loan contracts. Attorneys' fees: Permitted in home repair installment contract, but not to exceed 20% of balance due. Also permitted in retail charge agreement, if fee reasonable.

Minnesota: Judgment notes: No statutory provision. Confessions of judgment: Valid, if made in separate verified statement. Prohibited in motor vehicle time sales contracts, and small loan contracts. Attorneys' fees: Enforceable in motor vehicle time sales contracts up to 15% of balance due.

Mississippi: Judgment notes: Void. Confessions of judgment: Void, including small loan contracts. Attorneys' fees: Enforceable in motor vehicle time sales contracts, up to 15% of balance due.

Missouri: Judgment notes: No statutory provision. Confessions of judgment: Valid, if taken for money due or to become due, or as security against contingent liability, and made in separate verified statements. Attorneys' fees: Enforceable in time sales contracts of goods, up to 15% of balance due; also, on same conditions, in motor vehicle time sales contracts.

Montana: Judgment notes: Void. Confessions of judgment: Valid, if made by separate verified statement. Attorneys' fees: Enforceable in time sales contracts up to 15% of balance due.

Nebraska: Judgment notes: No statutory provision. Confessions of judgment: May be made by debtor in person, with creditor's consent. Not valid in small loan contracts. Attorneys' fees: Court may grant reasonable fees in action for balance due on purchase of necessaries, up to $1,000, and debtor failed to pay after 90-days' notice.

Nevada: Judgment notes: No statutory provision. Confessions of judgment: Valid, if for sums due or to become due, or to secure contingent liability. Invalid in small loan contracts. Attorneys' fees: Provision for reasonable fee in time sales contract valid. Also valid in small loan contracts, if provide fee to be fixed by court in event suit necessary to collect.

New Hampshire: Judgment notes: No statutory provision. Confessions of judgment: Prohibited in motor vehicle time sales contracts; also prohibited in small loan contracts. Attorneys' fees: Provision for reasonable fee in motor vehicle time sales contracts valid; not recognized as permissible delinquency charge under small loan laws.

New Jersey: Judgment notes: Not permitted. Confessions of judgment: Invalid in time sales contracts, or in separate instrument relating thereto; also, invalid in home repair contracts, and small loan contracts. Attorneys' fees: Enforceable in time sales contracts, if not more than 20% of first $500 and 10% of excess; also, in home repair contracts, if "reasonable". If credit union reduces loan to judgment or gives to attorney for collection after default, it may collect attorneys' fees up to 15% on first $500 and 12-1/2% on excess.

New Mexico: Judgment notes: Void. Confessions of judgment: Void, if made before cause of action accrues on negotiable instrument or contract to pay money. Not permitted in time sales contracts or retail charge agreements. Attorneys' fees: Provision for reasonable fees permitted in time sales contracts, retail charge agreements or small loan agreements.

New York: Judgment notes: No statutory provision. Confessions of judgment: May be made on debtor's affidavit; but judgment void if entered on affidavit made before debtor's default on installment purchases up to $1,500 of goods for non-business or non-commercial use. Prohibited in time sales contracts, including motor vehicles; revolving credit agreements; small loan contracts. Attorneys' fees: Valid up to 20% of balance due on revolving credit agreements; up to 15% of balance due on motor vehicle time sales contracts; void on retail installment contracts. Credit unions may collect reasonable fees actually spent for necessary court process after debtor's default.

North Carolina: Judgment notes: Not recognized. Confessions of judgment: Enforceable, if made by signed, verified statement for money due or to become due, or to secure against a contingent liability. Prohibited in small loan contracts. Attorneys' fees: Provision not enforceable, but does not affect negotiability of instrument.

North Dakota: Judgment notes: No statutory provision. Confessions of judgment: Enforceable, if entered on debtor's signed, verified statement for a specific sum. Invalid in time sales contracts; also, small loan contracts. Attorneys' fees: Void as against public policy in notes and other evidences of debt.

Ohio: Judgment notes: Recognized. Confessions of judgment: May be made by debtor personally in court, with creditor's consent. Attorneys' fees: Not permitted in time sales contracts.

Oklahoma: Judgment notes: No statutory provision. Confessions of judgment: Enforceable, if entered under warrant of attorney acknowledged by debtor, and if debtor first files affidavit as to the facts. Attorneys' fees: Small loan contracts may provide for reasonable fees to be assessed by court.

Oregon: Judgment notes: No statutory provision. Confessions of judgment: Valid, if for money due or to become due or to secure contingent liability; may be entered, with creditor's consent, if acknowledged by debtor. Unenforceable in motor vehicle time sales contracts; invalid as to small loan contracts. Attorneys' fees: May provide for reasonable fees in time sales contracts of goods and revolving charge accounts; also, in motor vehicle time sales contracts.

Pennsylvania: Judgment notes: Recognized. Confessions of judgment: Invalid in small loan contracts. Attorneys' fees: Fees up to 20% of balance due permitted in home improvement contracts. Credit unions may collect fees to public officials and reasonable fees of attorneys and outside collection agencies; but total of such fees can't exceed 20% of outstanding loan balance.

Rhode Island: Judgment notes: No statutory provision. Confessions of judgment: Prohibited in small loan contracts. Attorneys' fees: Reasonable attorney's fees allowed if suit is brought to realize on collateral used to secure loan.

South Carolina: Judgment notes: No statutory provision. Confessions of judgment: Enforceable, if made by verified statement. Prohibited in small loan contracts. Attorneys' fees: May provide in small loan contracts for reasonable fee to be fixed by court.

South Dakota: Judgment notes: No statutory provision. Confessions of judgment: Valid, if made by verified statement. Attorneys' fees: Void as against public policy.

Tennessee: Judgment notes: Invalid. Confessions of judgment: Invalid, if made before action started. Attorneys' fees: No statutory provision.

Texas: Judgment notes: Invalid. Confessions of judgment: Invalid, if made before action started. Prohibited in small loan contracts. Attorneys' fees: No statutory provision.

Utah: Judgment notes: No statutory provision. Confessions of judgment: Valid, if made on debtor's verified statement for money due or to become due or to secure contingent liability. Prohibited in small loan contracts. Attorneys' fees: May provide for reasonable fees in revolving charge agreement.

Vermont: Judgment notes: No statutory provision. Confessions of judgment: Valid, if made by debtor in writing, with creditor's consent. Prohibited in small loan contracts. Attorneys' fees: Enforceable as to time sales contracts of goods, revolving charge accounts, and motor vehicle time sales contracts.

573

Virginia: Judgment notes: Valid; but warrant of attorney in note must name attorney and court in which judgment may be confessed. Confessions of judgment: May be entered in clerk's office at any time, but debtor has 21 days after notice of entry in which to move to have judgment set aside. Prohibited in small loan contracts. Attorneys' fees: No statutory provision.

Washington: Judgment notes: No statutory provision. Confessions of judgment: May be made on debtor's verified statement. Prohibited in small loan contracts. Attorneys' fees: May provide for reasonable fee in time sales contracts or revolving charge accounts.

West Virginia: Judgment notes: No statutory provision. Confessions of judgment: May be made in action. Prohibited in small loan contracts. Attorneys' fees: Provision for same does not make note non-negotiable.

Wisconsin: Judgment notes: Valid, but judgment is invalidated if judgment debtor isn't notified by certified mail within 30 days of entry of judgment. Confessions of judgment: Prohibited in small loan contracts. Attorneys' fees: No statutory provision.

Wyoming: Judgment notes: Valid. Confessions of judgment: May be made by debtor in open court, with creditor's consent; but attorney confessing judgment must show warrant of attorney. Attorneys' fees: No statutory provision.

ESTATE AND TRUST MATTERS

The estate planner must frequently be familiar with not only the law of his own jurisdiction but with the law of other jurisdictions that may affect his client's interests under the plan. The tables in this section offer planning aids in many areas of general concern to the estate planner.

AGE OF TESTAMENTARY CAPACITY

| | Generally | | | Exceptions | | |
	Full Age or 21	18	Other Age	Personal Property 18	Certain Armed Forces Members Waived Entirely	Other
Alabama	x			x		
Alaska		x				
Arizona		x				x^d
Arkansas		x				
California		x				
Colorado		x				
Connecticut		x				
Delaware		x				
D. of C.	x					x^a
Florida		x				
Georgia			14			
Hawaii		x				
Idaho		x				
Illinois		x				
Indiana	x				x^e	
Iowa		x				
Kansas	x					
Kentucky		x				x^b
Louisiana		x				x^f
Maine		x				x^d
Maryland		x				x^c
Massachusetts		x				
Michigan		x				
Minnesota	x					
Mississippi		x				
Missouri		x				
Montana		x				
Nebraska			19			
Nevada		x				

| | Generally | | | Exceptions | | | |
| | | | | Personal Property | Certain Armed Forces Members | | Other |
	Full Age or 21	18	Other Age	18	18	Waived Entirely	
Ohio	x						
Oklahoma		x					
Oregon	x						x^d
Pennsylvania	x				x		
Rhode Island	x			x			
South Carolina	x						x^h
South Dakota		x					
Tennessee		x					
Texas			19			x	x^d
Utah		x					
Vermont	x						
Virginia	x			x			
Washington	x				x		x^i
West Virginia		x					
Wisconsin	x					x	x^j
Wyoming	x^k						

[a] Minimum 18 for females.

[b] No person under 18 may make will except in pursuance of special power, and except a father may appoint guardian for his child.

[c] For property other than "lands, tenements, and incorporeal hereditaments", common law rule of 14 for males and 12 for females apparently applies.

[d] Married person or one who has been married (widow or widower).

[e] Applies to member of armed forces or merchant marine of United States or its Allies.

[f] Statute must be checked for exceptions in favor of emancipated married minor, unemancipated minor with consent of relatives and gifts by minor over 16 in prospect of death.

[g] Person under 21 may appoint testamentary guardian.

[h] Married and over 18.

[i] Married and over 18, and all females married to a person of full age (21) are deemed to be of full age.

[j] Married woman over 18.

[k] No definite provision, but 21 seems to be the age by statutory construction.

ELECTION OR RIGHT OF WIDOW OR SURVIVING SPOUSE TO TAKE AGAINST WILL

	No Election or Right	Right in Surviving Spouse	Right in Widow Only	Amount or Rule		No Election or Right	Right in Surviving Spouse	Right in Widow Only	Amount or Rule
Ala.			x	1	Mont.			x	18
Alaska		x			Neb.		x		2
Ariz.	x				Nev.	x			
Ark.		x[a]		2	N. H.		x		19
Calif.		x		3	N. J.		x		20
Colo.		x		4	N. M.	x			
Conn.		x		5	N. Y.		x		21
Dela.			x[b]	6b	N. C.		x		21
D. of C.		x		7	N. D.	x			
Fla.			x	6	Ohio		x		23
Ga.			x	6c	Okla.		x		24
Hawaii			x	6	Ore.		x		25
Idaho	x				Pa.		x[d]		26
Ill.		x		8	R. I.			x	6
Ind.		x		9	S. C.	x			6
Iowa		x[e]		34	S. D.	x			
Kans.		x		2	Tenn.		x		27
Ky.		x		10	Tex.	x			
La.	x				Utah			x	28
Maine		x		11	Vt.		x		29
Md.		x		12	Va.		x		30
Mass.		x		13	Wash.	x			
Mich.			x	14	W. Va.		x		31
Minn.		x		15	Wisc.			x	32
Miss.		x		16	Wyo.		x		33
Mo.		x		17					

[a] Surviving husband can elect only as against will executed prior to marriage.

[b] Either surviving spouse may elect intestate share against will executed prior to marriage.

[c] Election of dower will be in lieu of interest in any lands devised to widow but does not deprive her of interest in personalty bequeathed unless expressed to be in lieu of dower.

[d] Election must also be against conveyances within scope of certain provisions of Estates Act of 1947, as amended.

[e] The statutes provide for an election. It is provided, however, that where the surviving spouse is named as a devisee in a will, it shall be presumed, unless such intention is clear and explicit to the contrary, that such devise is in lieu of such distributive share, homestead and exemptions.

Amount or Rule

[1] Dower interest in lands and intestate share of personalty limited to $50,000.00 if no children or descendants. (Intestate share: No children -- all; one child -- one-half; two to four -- child's share; more than four -- one-fifth.)

[2] Intestate share of estate.

[3] One half of separate property of decedent which would have been community property if domiciled in state at time of acquisition.

[4] One-half of estate.

5 Life use of one-third in value of all property, less debts and charges.

6 Dower.

7 Intestate share of all property, subject to right to elect dower in realty in lieu of legal share, but not to exceed one-half of net estate, or if dower elected, not to exceed dower plus one-half of net personalty.

8 One-third of property if descendants; one-half if no descendants.

9 One-third of net estate, subject to limitation if survivor is childless, second or subsequent spouse.

10 Life estate in one-third of realty at death or held during coverture and one-half of personalty absolutely.

11 Intestate share not to exceed share of spouse where "kindred" also survive.

12 Dower in lands and intestate share of personalty or intestate share of real and personal estate.

13 One-third if issue; one-half if kindred but no issue, except that excess over $25,000.00 for life only. If no issue or kindred, survivor takes $25,000.00 and one-half of remaining property absolutely.

14 Homestead rights and dower or intestate share not to exceed one-half of personalty over $5,000.00 and one-half of realty.

15 One-third of personalty and one-third of realty of which decedent was seized at any time during marriage, subject to qualifications, but if only one child or issue of deceased child survive share of personalty and realty is one-half.

16 Intestate share not to exceed one-half, subject to limitation depending on value of survivor's separate property.

17 If descendants one-third, if no descendants one-half, "of estate subject to the payment of claims."

18 Dower in lands and intestate share in personalty not in excess of two-thirds of husband's net estate, real and personal.

19 One-third of personal estate if issue; but if no issue and testate, $7,500.00, plus one-half of remainder of personal estate in excess of $7,500.00; and similar but not identical provision as to an intestate deceased.

20 If valid devise of realty made to spouse, the spouse may refuse to accept in bar of dower or curtesy in other realty.

21 Intestate share subject to statutory limitations, conditions and exceptions which include limitation to one-half of net estate, and limitation of right to elect where will makes gift in trust of an amount equal to or greater than intestate share with income payable to surviving spouse for life (see statute).

22 Intestate share not to exceed one-half, subject to limitation where there are lineal descendants by prior and none by second or successive marriage.

23 Intestate share not to exceed one-half of net estate.

24 Intestate share except as to property not acquired by joint industry; testator is not required to give more than one-half in value to surviving spouse.

25 One-fourth interest in personalty and dower or curtesy.

26 One-third if survived by more than one child or one child and issue of deceased child or children; otherwise one-half.

27 One-third of personalty, and dower or curtesy in realty if 2 or less children survive; but if more than two children, then the surviving spouse shall share equally with children except that the husband shall still have his curtesy in realty.

28 One-third of realty possessed by husband at any time during the marriage.

29 One-third in value of realty or one-half if only one heir who is issue of both or adopted heir of both.

30 One-third of personal estate if descendants, or one-half if no descendants, and dower or curtesy in realty.

31 Share survivor would have taken if decedent died intestate leaving children.

32 Intestate share of personal estate and same right of dower and homestead as if husband had died intestate leaving lawful issue.

33 One-half except where decedent leaves child or descendants of child of previous marriage and no child or descendant of child of subsequent marriage, then share is limited to one-fourth.

34 One-third of realty. All personalty exempt from execution and in decedent's hands at the time of death as head of family. One-third of all other personalty less charges.

RULES AGAINST PERPETUITIES

Whenever a trust (or a legal life estate) is set up, whether during lifetime or by will, the draftsman must always be careful that the interest being created does not violate the rule against perpetuities. This rule, sometimes called the rule against remoteness in vesting, stems from the general public policy against the withdrawal of property from commerce. The idea is to invalidate future interests which vest (become absolute) at a time too far in the future.

According to the common law rule against perpetuities no interest is good unless it must vest not later than 21 years after some life or lives in being at the creation of the interest. Most states preserve this rule, whether by specific reference to it in their own statutes, by incorporating its provision in their own statutes, or by case law or implication. Some have made statutory modifications, either by providing for shorter or longer measuring methods, by measuring the period by a specific number of lives in being, or by basing their statutes, not upon vesting of interests, but upon the suspension of the absolute power of alienation (i.e., the duration of a trust). The checklist which follows is of a general nature only; to fully understand the perpetuities rule of a particular state, it is still necessary to read that state's statute and related interpretive materials. Here, listed for each state, is the period for measuring the rule against perpetuities:

21 years after some life or lives in being at the creation of the interest:

Alabama	Kansas	North Carolina
Alaska	Kentucky	North Dakota
Arizona	Maine	Ohio
Arkansas	Maryland	Oregon
California	Massachusetts	Pennsylvania
Colorado	Michigan	Rhode Island
Connecticut	Mississippi	South Carolina
Delaware	Missouri	Tennessee
District of	Montana	Texas
Columbia	Nebraska	Utah
Florida	Nevada	Vermont
Georgia	New Hampshire	Virginia
Illinois	New Jersey	Washington
Indiana	New Mexico	West Virginia
Iowa	New York	Wyoming

As to real property, 25 years after lives in being at the creation of the limitation; as to personal property, no limitation:

Idaho

15 years after the death of the creator or after the death of the beneficiary, whichever occurs later:

Louisiana

As to real property, 21 years after 2 lives in being at the creation of the interest; as to personal property, 21 years after lives in being at the creation of the interest:

Minnesota [1]

Lives in being at the creation of the interest:

Oklahoma [1]   South Dakota [1]

As to real property, 30 years after lives in being at the creation of the interest; as to personal property, no limitation:

Wisconsin

As to real property, 55 years from the creation of any interest:

Hawaii

[1] There is an exception in favor of certain unborn contingent remaindermen.

RULES AGAINST ACCUMULATIONS

Concurrent with the rule against perpetuities, and in most cases, as an adjunct of that rule, as a matter of public policy almost all states either by statute, by case law, or by the common law, place some kind of a limit on the time during which such income shall be permitted to accumulate. Following is a rundown of the rules of the various states:

Accumulations permitted for lives in being plus 21 years:

Alaska [1]	Iowa [1]	North Carolina [1]
Arizona [1]	Kansas [1]	North Dakota [1]
Arkansas [1]	Kentucky [2]	Ohio [1]
California	Maine [2]	Oklahoma [1]
Colorado [1]	Maryland [1]	Oregon [1]
Connecticut [2]	Massachusetts [1]	Pennsylvania [4]
Delaware [1]	Mississippi [1]	Rhode Island [1]
District of	Missouri [1]	South Carolina [1]
Columbia [1]	Montana	Texas [1]
Florida [1]	Nebraska [1]	Utah [1]
Georgia [1]	Nevada [3]	Vermont [1]
Hawaii [1]	New Hampshire [1]	Virginia [1]
Idaho [1]	New Jersey [1]	Washington [1]
Illinois	New Mexico [1]	West Virginia [1]
Indiana	New York	Wyoming [1]

[1] No statutory provision, but application of common law would appear to permit accumulations for lives in being plus 21 years.
[2] No statutory provision, but case law permits accumulations for lives in being plus 21 years.
[3] Accumulations of income in spendthrift trust permitted for lives in being plus 21 years; no statutory provisions covering other situations, but application of common law would appear to permit accumulations for lives in being plus 21 years.
[4] The period of lives in being plus 21 years does not begin until the expiration of the period when someone alive at the creation of the interest can alienate the entire legal and beneficial interest.

Accumulations of income from real property permitted only during minority; for personal property-lives in being plus twenty-one years:

Minnesota   South Dakota

Accumulations permitted only during minority; but in no event longer than 33 years from the date of the death of the maker of any will:

Michigan

Accumulations permitted for 10 years, or until minor beneficiary attains age 21:

Alabama

Accumulations for 15 years after the death of the creator or after the death of the beneficiary, whichever occurs later:

—————   Louisiana [5]

[5] While there's no statutory provision, rule indicated appears to be the law.

Accumulations of income permitted as directed by creator:

Wisconsin

VALIDITY OF POUR OVER TRUSTS

	Trust Valid	Basis of Validity			Application of Statute to Prior Wills				Extent or Conditions of Validity				
	Trust Valid	Uniform Testamentary Additions to Trust Act *	Other Statutory Provisions	Decision or Opinion	Effective Date	Only Wills Executed After Effective Date	Wills Prior to Act	No Express Provision	Valid Even If Trust Amended After Will	Valid If Trust Not Amended After Will	Other Conditions	Trust Invalid	No Statute, Decision, or Opinion Available
Ala.	x		x		9/9/61		x		x				
Alaska													x
Ariz.	x	x			3/22/61	x			x				
Ark.	x	x		x	6/13/63	x			x				
Calif.	x			x							x		
Colo.	x		x		5/18/59	x[1]							
Conn.	x	x			10/1/61		x		x		x[8]		
Dela.	x		x		6/5/57			x					
D. of C.	x			x	12/5/63				x		x[8]		
Fla.	x		x		6/22/61			x					
Ga.	x			x							x		
Hawaii													x
Idaho	x	x			5/18/63	x			x				x
Ill.	x		x		1955			x	x				
Ind.	x		x		1953			x	x				
Iowa	x			x							x		
Kans.	x			x							x		
Ky.	x			x							x		
La.	x		x	x								x	
Maine	x	x		x	1963			x	x				
Md.			x						x				
Mass.	x	x		x	12/1/63				x		x[8]		
Mich.	x	x			4/24/62	x			x				
Minn.	x	x			2/20/63	x			x	x			
Miss.	x		x		5/6/58		x		x				

583

	Trust Valid	Uniform Testamentary Additions to Trust Act *	Other Statutory Provisions	Decision or Opinion	Effective Date	Other Wills Executed After Effective Date	Wills Prior to Act	No Express Provision	Valid Even If Trust Amended After Will	Valid If Trust Not Amended After Will	Other Conditions	Trust Invalid	No Statute, Decision, or Opinion Available
Mo.	x			x					x				
Mont.	x		x		3/7/59			x	x				
Neb.	x		x		5/19/57			x	x		x²		
Nev.	x			x					x				
N. H.	x	x			3/30/61		x		x				
N. J.	x	x		x	2/20/63	x			x				
N. M.													x
N. Y.	x			x					x				
N. C.	x		x		7/1/55			x³	x				
N. D.	x	x			7/1/61	x			x				
Ohio	x		x		10/6/61		x		x				
Okla.	x	x			3/7/61	x			x				
Ore.	x		x		5/24/57			x		x⁴			
Pa.	x		x		7/11/57			x	x		x⁵		
R. I.	x		x		5/12/59	x			x				
S. C.	x	x			3/17/61	x			x				
S. D.	x	x			1963	x			x	x			
Tenn.	x	x			3/17/61	x			x				
Tex.	x		x		8/28/61			x	x				
Utah	x		x		2/23/61			x	x				
Vt.	x	x⁶			7/11/61	x			x				
Va.	x		x		3/31/62	x			x		x⁷		
Wash.	x		x		3/16/59			x	x				
W. Va.	x	x			6/1/61	x			x				
Wisc.	x		x		8/22/63			x	x				
Wyo.	x		x		8/22/63				x				

VALIDITY OF POUR OVER TRUSTS (Continued)

* UNIFORM TESTAMENTARY ADDITIONS TO TRUSTS ACT
(Statute adopted in any jurisdiction must be checked for variations from "Uniform Act")

Section 1 (Testamentary Additions to Trusts):   A devise or bequest, the validity of which is determinable by the law of this state, may be made by a will to the trustee or trustees of a trust established or to be established by the testator or by the testator and some other person or persons or by some other person or persons (including a funded or unfunded life insurance trust, although the trustor has reserved any or all rights of ownership of the insurance contracts) if the trust is identified in the testator's will and its terms are set forth in a written instrument (other than a will) executed before or concurrently with the execution of the testator's will or in the valid last will of a person who has predeceased the testator (regardless of the existence, size, or character of the corpus of the trust).   The devise or bequest shall not be invalid because the trust is amendable or revocable, or both, or because the trust was amended after the execution of the will or after the death of the testator.   Unless the testator's will provides otherwise, the property so devised or bequeathed (a) shall not be deemed to be held under a testamentary trust of the testator but shall become a part of the trust to which it is given and (b) shall be administered and disposed of in accordance with the provisions of the instrument or will setting forth the terms of the trust, including any amendments thereto made before the death of the testator (regardless of whether made before or after the execution of the testator's will) and, if the testator's will so provides, including any amendments to the trust made after the death of the testator.   A revocation or termination of the trust before the death of the testator shall cause the devise or bequest to lapse.

Section 2 (Effect on Prior Wills):   This Act shall have no effect upon any devise or bequest made by a will executed prior to the effective date of this Act.

1   Does not invalidate devise or bequest to trustee by will executed prior to effective date.

2   Unless the will provides otherwise, the property will not be deemed to be held under a testamentary trust if the designated trustee is a corporate trustee authorized by law to act as an executor or administrator.

3   Statute does "not apply to actions pending as of the effective date hereof."

4   If amended after its execution, the statute seems to require execution of a codicil.

5   Statute also applies to "trust to be established in writing at a future date."

6   Adds, following word "lapse" at end of § 1 of Uniform Act, this sentence: "However, when the testator's will specifically sets forth the terms of the trust, whether or not such trust is subsequently amended, revoked or terminated, the property devised or bequeathed under the will shall be deemed to be held under a testamentary trust of the testator and shall be administered and disposed of in accordance with the provisions of the testator's will."

7   Statute contains proviso to the effect that at least one trustee must be an individual resident of Virginia or a corporation or association authorized to do a trust business in the state and that if corporation or association is a trustee, it must be one authorized to do business in Virginia.

8   Revocation of trust prior to death revokes devise to trust in will.

585

Both in the planning stage as well as in the administration phase of trusts and estates with interstate connections it will be important to know various state laws affecting the process. The tables below cover some of the basic areas of concern.

INVESTMENT RULES FOR TRUSTEES*

	Unrestricted Prudent Man Rule	Restrictions on Prudent Man Rule	Investment in Equities Prohibited	Percentage Limitation on Investment in Equities	Common Trust Funds Authorized	Investment Company Shares Expressly Permitted
Ala.		x	x		x	
Alaska¹					x	
Ariz.¹					x	
Ark.	x				x	
Calif.	x				x	
Colo.	x				x	x
Conn.	x				x	x
Dela.	x				x	
D. of C.		x		40%	x	
Fla.	x				x	
Ga.		x	x		x	
Hawaii	x²				x	
Idaho	x				x	
Ill.	x				x	
Ind.	x				x	
Iowa		x	x		x	
Kans.	x				x	x
Ky.		x			x	
La.		x	x		x	
Maine	x				x	x
Md.	x				x	
Mass.	x				x	
Mich.	x				x	x³
Minn.	x					
Miss.	x				x	x
Mo.	x				x	
Mont.		x	x			
Neb.		x		40%	x	x
Nev.	x				x	
N. H.		x		Varied	x	x
N. J.		x		40%	x	x
N. M.	x				x	x
N. Y.		x		35%	x	
N. C.		x			x	
N. D.		x		2		x
Ohio		x		35%	x	x

*Where the instrument is silent.

586

	Unrestricted Prudent Man Rule	Restrictions on Prudent Man Rule	Investment in Equities Prohibited	Percentage Limitation on Investment in Equities	Common Trust Funds Authorized	Investment Company Shares Expressly Permitted
Okla.	x				x	x
Ore.	x				x	
Pa.		x			x	x
R.I.	x					
S.C.		x		30%	x	x
S.D.	x				x	
Tenn.	x				x	x
Tex.	x				x	
Utah	x				x	
Vt.	x				x	
Va.		x			x	
Wash.	x				x	x
W.Va.		x		35%	x	
Wisc.		x			x	
Wyo.		x	x			

[1] No statute or decision found.

[2] At least 15% must be invested in U.S. Bonds.

[3] By Probate Letter.

STATUTORY RULES FOR ALLOCATION OF PRINCIPAL AND INCOME*

	Uniform Principal and Income Act in Force	Only Parts of Uniform Principal and Income Act	Broad Statute Differing from Uniform Act	Limited Apportionment Provisions	No Statutory Provisions		Uniform Principal and Income Act in Force	Only Parts of Uniform Principal and Income Act	Broad Statute Differing from Uniform Act	Limited Apportionment Provisions	No Statutory Provisions
Ala.	x					Mont.	x				
Alaska					x	Neb.					x
Ariz.	x					Nev.					x
Ark.				x^4		N. H.					x
Calif.	x^2					N. J.			x		
Colo.	x					N. M.	x				
Conn.	x					N. Y.			x		
Del.				x^5		N. C.	x				
D. of C.					x	N. D.					x
Fla.	x					Ohio				x^5	
Ga.				x		Okla.	x				
Hawaii					x	Ore.	x				
Idaho	x^7					Pa.	x				
Ill.	x					R. I.				x^4	
Ind.				x^4		S. C.	x^7			x^4	
Iowa				x^4		S. D.					x
Kans.	x					Tenn.	x				
Ky.	x					Tex.	x				
La.	x^1					Utah	x				
Maine		x^6				Vt.	x				
Md.	x					Va.			x		
Mass.			x			Wash.			x^3		
Mich.					x	W. Va.	x				
Minn.		x^3				Wisc.	x				
Miss.				x^4		Wyo.	x^7				x
Mo.				x^4							

*Where governing instrument is silent.

[1] Textual variations will often be found.

[2] Known as Principal and Income, Civ. Code §§ 730-730.15.

[3] Similar to §§ 2 and 5 of Uniform Act.

[4] Rents on death of life tenant.

[5] Bond premium or discount.

[6] Section 6 of Uniform Act adopted.

[7] Revised Act adopted by Commissioners in 1962.

EXECUTORS' COMMISSIONS

Most states have a statutory schedule of fees for executors. Some merely call for reasonable fees, the reasonableness to be determined by the courts. In a number of states, fees for testamentary trustees are the same as those allowed to executors. Some states provide for a distinct statutory fee for trustees, but most provide for reasonable fees to be determined by the court, more often than not based in large measure upon trust receipts -- with 5% annually being a fairly reasonable national average. In the case of both executors and testamentary trustees, additional reasonable fees may usually be charged for extraordinary services.

Note that the general rule is that there is nothing to prevent the testator from specifying the executor's commission right in the will (or even directing that there shall be no commissions). Then it's up to the executor to accept or refuse appointment under those terms.

The table that follows relates exclusively to compensation of executors and administrators, and is based both upon statutory fee allowances and the usual fees which are charged by corporate executors where a statutory rate does not apply. As to the latter, there are sometimes variations in different areas of the same state. *

Alabama
Not more than 2-1/2% of receipts and disbursements.

Alaska
First $1,000 -- 7%
Next $1,000 -- 5%
Next $2,000 -- 4%
All above $4,000 -- 2%

Arizona
First $1,000 -- 7%
Next $9,000 -- 5%
All above $10,000 -- 4%

Arkansas
First $1,000 -- Not more than 10%
Next $4,000 -- 5%
All above $5,000 -- 3%

California
First $1,000 -- 7%
Next $9,000 -- 4%
Next $40,000 -- 3%
Next $100,000 -- 2%
Next $350,000 -- 1-1/2%
All above $500,000 -- 1%

Colorado
First $25,000 -- 6%
Next $75,000 -- 4%
All above $100,000 -- 3%

Connecticut
No statutory fee schedule or minimums. The following schedule has been suggested as reasonable:
First $10,000 -- 5%
Next $40,000 -- 3%
Next $200,000 -- 2-1/2%
Next $750,000 -- 2%
Next $1,000,000 -- 1-1/2%
All above $2,000,000 -- 1%
Minimum fee -- $200.

Delaware
No statutory fee schedule or minimums. Fees are determined by the Register of Wills. Some typical percentage fees allowed on total gross estates are as follows:
Less than $1,000 -- $100
$10,000 - 20,000 -- $800 + 5% over $10,000
$40,000 - 60,000 -- $2,150 + 3-1/2% over $40,000
$100,000 - 125,000 -- 4.0% gross estate
$200,000 - 250,000 -- 3.2% gross estate
$350,000 - 400,000 -- 2.8% gross estate
$500,000 or over -- 2.5% gross estate

District of Columbia
Not under 1% nor more than 10% of inventory.

Florida
First $1,000 -- 6%
Next $4,000 -- 4%
All above $5,000 -- 2-1/2%

---

* - March 1969 figures.

For latest information write to: American College of Probate Counsel,
10964 West Pico Blvd., Los Angeles, Calif.

Georgia

2-1/2% of receipts and disbursements.

Hawaii

On receipts, 7% of first $5,000 -- all above $5,000, 5%.
On principal:
  First $1,000 -- 5%
  Next $9,000 -- 4%
  Next $10,000 -- 3%
  All above $20,000 -- 2%

Idaho

First $1,000 -- 5%
Next $9,000 -- 4%
All above $10,000 -- 3%

Illinois

No statutory fee schedule or minimums. The following is an example of customary rates:
  First $25,000 -- 5%
  Next $25,000 -- 3-1/2% - 4%
  Next $50,000 -- 3% - 3-1/2%
  Next $150,000 -- 2-1/2% - 3%
  Next $750,000 -- 2% - 2-1/2%
  All above $1,000,000 -- 1-1/2% - 2%

Indiana

No statutory fee schedule or minimums. The following is an example of customary rates for a corporate fiduciary:
  First $25,000 -- 5%
  Next $25,000 -- 4%
  Next $50,000 -- 3%
  Next $650,000 -- 2%

Iowa

First $1,000 -- not more than 6%
Next $4,000 -- 4%
All above $5,000 -- 2%

Kansas

No statutory fee schedule or minimums. The following is an example of customary rates:
  First $10,000 -- 5%
  Next $15,000 -- 4%
  Next $25,000 -- 3%
  Next $50,000 -- 2%
  All above $100,000 -- 1%

Kentucky

Not more than 5% of income and 5% of personal estate.

Louisiana

Fee is 2-1/2% of the inventory of the estate -- it may be increased by the court upon showing that usual commission is inadequate.

Maine

Not more than 5% of personal estate with rate being reduced as a matter of practice in larger estates.

Maryland

First $20,000 -- Not less than 2% or more than 10%.
All above $20,000 -- Not more than 4%.

Massachusetts

No statutory fee schedule or minimums. The following is an example of customary rates:
  3% of gross personal estate, plus 3% on any real estate that is sold, with rate being reduced as a matter of practice as the size of the estate increases.

Michigan

First $1,000 -- 5%
Next $4,000 -- 2-1/2%
All above $5,000 -- 2%

Minnesota

No statutory fee schedule or minimums. The following is an example of customary rates for a corporate fiduciary:
  First $50,000 -- 4%
  Next $50,000 -- 3%
  Next $100,000 -- 2-1/2%

Mississippi

Not less than 1% nor more than 7% on amount of estate administered.

Missouri

First $5,000 -- 5%
Next $20,000 -- 4%
Next $75,000 -- 3%
Next $300,000 -- 2-3/4%
Next $600,000 -- 2-1/2%
All above $1,000,000 -- 2%

Montana

First $1,000 -- 7%
Next $9,000 -- 5%
Next $10,000 -- 4%
All above $20,000 - 2%

Nebraska

First $1,000 -- 5%
Next $4,000 -- 2-1/2%
All above $5,000 -- 2%

Nevada

First $1,000 -- 6%
Next $4,000 -- 4%
All above $5,000 -- 2%

New Hampshire

Up to $10,000 -- reasonable compensation
$10,000 - 100,000 -- 5%
Excess over $100,000 - 500,000 -- 4%

New Jersey

On income, 6%. On corpus not exceeding
$100,000 -- 5%.
On excess over $100,000, the percentage, not
in excess of 5%, in discretion of the Court.
Usual rates -- 5% of first $100,000 and 5% of
excess.

New Mexico

First $3,000 -- 10%
All above $3,000 -- 5%
For cash, U.S. Savings Bonds, or life insurance
proceeds, the compensation is 5% on the first
$5,000 and 1% on everything above that figure.

New York

First $25,000 -- 4%
Next $125,000 -- 3-1/2%
Next $150,000 -- 3%
All above $300,000 -- 2%

North Carolina

Not more than 5% of receipts and disbursements.

North Dakota

First $1,000 -- 5%
Next $5,000 -- 3%
Next $44,000 -- 2%
All above $50,000, within the discretion of the
Court, but not above 2%.

Ohio

First $1,000 -- 6%
Next $4,000 -- 4%
All above $5,000 -- 2%

Oklahoma

First $1,000 -- 5%
Next $5,000 -- 4%
All above $6,000 -- 2-1/2%

Oregon

First $1,000 -- 7%
Next $9,000 -- 4%
Next $40,000 -- 3%
All above $50,000 -- 2%

Pennsylvania

No statutory fee schedule or minimums. The
following is an example of suggested fees:
On principal:
  First $100,000 -- 5%
  Next $100,000 -- 4%

Pennsylvania (contd.)

Next $550,000 -- 3%
Above $750,000 -- a matter of court discre-
tion on work done.
Many corporate fiduciaries have established
their own fee schedules by agreement with
testator.

Rhode Island

Statute provides for just compensation. An
example of customary charges follows:
3% to 3-1/2% of principal value, depending
on complexity of estate.

South Carolina

Not more than 2-1/2% or receipts and disbursements.

South Dakota

First $1,000 -- 5%
Next $4,000 -- 4%
All above $5,000 -- 2-1/2%

Tennessee

No statutory fee schedule or minimums. The
following is an example of suggested reasona-
ble rates:
  First $20,000 -- 5%
  Next $80,000 -- 4%
  Next $200,000 -- 3%
  All above $200,000 -- 2%

Texas

Not more than 5% of the value of the administered estate. If compensation unreasonably
low, court may allow reasonable compensation.

Utah

First $1,000 -- 5%
Next $4,000 -- 4%
Next $5,000 -- 3%
Next $40,000 -- 2%
Next $50,000 -- 1-1/2%
All above $100,000 -- 1%

Vermont

Statute provides $4 for each day's attendance
on business. Customary charges, in addition,
are 4% of probate estate on the first $100,000,
with declining rates on sums over $100,000.

Virginia

No statutory fee schedule or minimums. The
following is an example of suggested reasona-
ble fees:
On principal:
  First $50,000 -- 5%
  Next $50,000 -- 4%

Virginia (contd.)

Next $900,000 -- 3%
All above $1,000,000 -- 2%
On income:
5% on all receipts

Washington

Statute provides for reasonable compensation minimum.
The following is an example of reasonable fees:
First $5,000 -- 5%
Next $5,000 -- 4%
Next $10,000 -- 3-1/2%
Next $180,000 -- 3%

West Virginia

Statute provides for reasonable compensation "in the form of a commission on receipts or otherwise." Example of customary rate is 5% on receipts.

Wisconsin

Fee is based on the actual time required and consumed -- $10 per day, plus --
First $1,000 -- 5%
Next $19,000 -- 1%
All above $20,000 -- 2%

Wyoming

First $1,000 -- 10%
Next $4,000 -- 5%
Next $15,000 -- 3%
All above $20,000 -- 2%

INDEX

References are to Paragraph [¶] Numbers